MW01055677

Reading the Classics
with C. S. Lewis

Reading the Classics
with C. S. Lewis

Thomas L. Martin, editor

Baker Academic
A Division of Baker Book House Co
Grand Rapids, Michigan 49516

paternoster

Published by Baker Academic
a division of Baker Book House Company
P.O. Box 6287, Grand Rapids, MI 49516-6287

and

Paternoster Press
P.O. Box 300
Carlisle, Cumbria CA3 0QS
United Kingdom

Second printing, September 2001

Printed in the United States of America

Library of Congress Cataloging-in-Publication Data

Reading the classics with C. S. Lewis / Thomas L. Martin, editor.
      p.   cm.
    "List of Lewis's major critical works": p.
    Includes bibliographical references and index.
    ISBN 0-8010-2234-7 (pbk.)
    1. Lewis, C. S. (Clive Staples), 1898–1963—Knowledge—Literature. 2. English
literature—History and criticism—Theory, etc. 3. Criticism—England—History—20th century. I. Martin, Thomas L. , 1960–

PR6023.E926 Z85 2000
823′.912—dc21   00-058680

British Library Cataloguing-in-Publication Data
A catalogue record for this book is available from the British Library.
ISBN 1-84227-073-7

For information about academic books, resources for Christian leaders, and all new releases
available from Baker Book House, visit our web site:
                http://www.bakerbooks.com

For My Parents

Contents

Preface

An underlying conviction of this book is that while many continue to read Lewis for his fictional, apologetical, and theological writings, they underappreciate this fact: Lewis's mind was nurtured on the study of literature. Those of us in English departments—those who have exchanged the wardrobe door for the university door—have always understood this. Studying literature has for us served a means of going farther up, deeper in.

Over the years, I have found many English teachers and students who value Lewis as a guide to literature. Whether providing a crystalline comment on fundamental literary principles and figures or a subtle insight appropriate to advanced inquiry, Lewis has been for them an important touchstone. Indeed, not until I was immersed in the present project did I realize the breadth of his insight, insight that spans not merely a single author or period, but the entire scope of literary history. Few modern critics have commented so broadly that a guide like this could be written from their work, with chapters devoted to several genres and all the major periods in English literary history. Lewis's criticism not only remains compelling—even half a century after its original publication, a remarkable feat given the brief shelf life of contemporary criticism—it also, like fine wine, has seasoned with age. It retains both its substance and freshness and sounds better and better—becoming more rich, full, and robust—the more we return to it and gradually realize, with a dawning sense of recognition, how right he was. The following pages explore some of the reasons why.

While we have strived to make the book accessible to a variety of readers, we particularly have in mind two audiences: teachers and students of literature as well as readers of Lewis's own works. Lewis's merits as a teacher are well known. Besides his learning, Lewis returns a charm to literary studies—the sense of wonder and awe that attracts many of us to literature in the first place but easily gets lost in the mundane aspects of the pursuit. Readers will find here both the learning and the charm. They will also find an assessment of Lewis's criticism by other critics representing a wide range of expertise on literature and on Lewis himself. As for the other audience—the readers of

Lewis—they will find in these pages a unique guide—a literary guide—to his thought. Our aim is that both audiences will gain new insight into Lewis's life and outlook as well as the literature he cherished.

But first a word about the organization of this book. In "*De Descriptione Temporum*" Lewis expresses his reservations about making grand historical and cultural distinctions because they inevitably falsify the material they seek to elucidate. Nevertheless, no historian or critic can completely avoid them. With those limitations duly noted, we follow in this book what has become the traditional breakdown of literary studies into separate periods. The same provisional understanding applied to historical distinctions should also be extended to the disciplinary boundaries between literature, philosophy, theology, and ethics. While the focus and approach here is first of all literary, the chapters draw not only from Lewis's critical works, but also from his essays, theological writings, correspondence, and even his poetry and fiction.

As we look to Lewis as a guide for reading literature, we are aware that the art and discipline of reading has fallen on hard times. Many, as Lewis laments, read "inattentively." Engaged and sensitive reading is simply not the passion it once was. Following Lewis, the reader develops an appreciation of what it means to read broadly and deeply. Perhaps the success of this book, then, should be determined by how many books readers will add to their own reading lists. The value of that, in turn, can only be seen in how many doors open up before them.

Many people worked on this book, too many to thank each one individually. I would, however, like to mention the debt of gratitude I owe to Leland Ryken and Wayne Martindale for their guidance through all stages of the project. I am also grateful to Wade Center curators Christopher Mitchell and Marjorie Mead for their valuable input and support. Greg Solem extended many encouragements along the way. Rosemary Stelz regularly achieved near miracles on the administrative end. My research assistants, Bob Gormley and Tyler Thornberg, contributed their bright talents. Baker Academic's Brian Bolger and Amy Nemecek worked hard and long to bring the book to print. Last, and certainly not least, I am grateful to my wife, Delena, and my children, Hannah and Ben, for their loving patience and undying support.

Contributors

David Barratt was for many years Senior Lecturer in English at University College, Chester, England. He has also taught in Pakistan, California, and North Carolina. His own interest in children's literature developed over a number of years while teaching courses for B.Ed. students and in-service teachers. He has written *C. S. Lewis and His World* (1987) and co-edited *The Discerning Reader: Christian Perspectives on Literature and Theory* (1995).

Joe R. Christopher wrote his Ph.D. dissertation on Lewis, "The Romances of Clive Staples Lewis" (1969), turning its bibliography into part of his book, *C. S. Lewis: An Annotated Checklist of Writings about Him and His Works*, co-authored with Joan K. Ostling (1974). Since then, he has written a volume, *C. S. Lewis*, in Twayne's English Author Series (1987). He has published forty-seven essays in whole or part on Lewis, mainly (in recent years) on Lewis's poems. Besides his own verse, short stories, and a drama, Christopher also has published essays on the Pearl Poet, Shakespeare, Coleridge, Poe, Tennyson, Mark Twain, and many others.

Kath Filmer-Davies is Senior Lecturer in English at the University of Queensland, Australia. A two-time winner of the Mythopoeic Society's Scholarship Awards in Myth and Fantasy Studies, she is author of *The Fiction of C. S. Lewis: Mask and Mirror* (1993), *Scepticism and Hope in Twentieth-Century Fantasy Literature* (1992), and *Fantasy Fiction and Welsh Myth: Tales of Belonging* (1996). She is also author of more than two hundred academic articles, poems, short stories, newspaper features, and other works.

David C. Downing is Associate Professor of English at Elizabethtown College, Associate Editor of *The Canadian C. S. Lewis Journal*, and author of *Planets in Peril: A Critical Study of C. S. Lewis's Ransom Trilogy* (1992), which was named an Outstanding Book by Choice and received the Scholarly Book of the Year Award from the Mythopoeic Society. His essays and reviews on Lewis have appeared in a wide range of publications.

Kate Durie was formerly Lecturer in English Literature at the University of Aberdeen, but has since taught part-time for a series of other higher educational institutions, including the Open University, the Universities of Glasgow and Stirling, plus summer schools at Denver Seminary. Her research interests have included Charlotte Yonge, Dorothy Sayers, and George MacDonald. Her published work includes an evaluation of Lewis and MacDonald in *The Gold Thread: Essays on George MacDonald* (1990).

Colin Duriez is General Books Editor for Inter-Varsity Press, United Kingdom. He is author of *The C. S. Lewis Handbook* (1990), *The J. R. R. Tolkien Handbook* (1992), and *The C. S. Lewis Encyclopedia* (2000). A handbook on the Inklings is in preparation as well as an anthology of biblical poetry, "The Poetic Bible." He served as a consulting editor for the *Dictionary of Biblical Imagery* (1998).

Bruce L. Edwards is Associate Dean of the College of Arts and Sciences and Professor of English at Bowling Green State University. He teaches and speaks on Lewis regularly and maintains a Lewis web page. Among his many publications on rhetoric and literature are *The Taste of the Pineapple: Essays on C. S. Lewis as Critic, Reader, and Imaginitive Writer* (1988) and *Searching for Great Ideas* (1997; co-authored with Thomas Klein and Thomas Wymer).

Charles A. Huttar, Professor Emeritus of English, Hope College, edited *Imagination and the Spirit* (1971), co-edited *Word and Story in C. S. Lewis* (1991) and *The Rhetoric of Vision: Essays on Charles Williams* (1996), and has published numerous essays on Milton and other sixteenth- and seventeenth-century authors as well as on Lewis and other members of the Inklings. He is currently working on a history of the Conference on Christianity and Literature, of which he was a founding member in 1956, and a book on angels in the modern imagination.

David Lyle Jeffrey is Professor Emeritus of English Literature at the University of Ottawa and Honorary Professor of Peking University (Beijing). Jeffrey is general editor and co-author of *A Dictionary of Biblical Tradition in English Literature* (1992). Among his other books are *English Spirituality in the Age of Wesley* (1987; 1994); *The Law of Love: English Spirituality in the Age of Wyclif* (1988); *Toward a Perfect Love: The Spiritual Counsel of Walter Hilton* (1986); *Chaucer and Scriptural Tradition* (1984); *By Things Seen: Reference and Recognition in Medieval Thought* (1979); *Modern Fiction and the Rebirth of Theology* (1973); *People of the Book: Christian Identity and Literary Culture* (1996).

Carolyn Keefe is Professor Emerita of Communication Studies, West Chester University. She is editor of *C. S. Lewis: Speaker and Teacher* (1974). She has written and spoken widely on Lewis, religious communication, and forensic education. For outstanding teaching, scholarship, and service, Keefe was named by CASE the Pennsylvania Professor of 1990.

Maria Kuteeva was born in St. Petersburg, Russia, where she received degrees in children's literature and English. In 1994 she was awarded a scholarship at the University of Manchester, where she wrote her M.Phil. and Ph.D.

theses on the ideas of language and myth in the works of Barfield, Lewis, and Tolkein. She is currently Assistant Professor in the Department of Communication Sciences at Fernando Pessoa University in Oporto, Portugal.

P. Andrew Montgomery earned his M.A. in classics from the University of Washington and is currently completing his Ph.D. in classics at the University of Iowa. His special interests include archaic Greek literature, the epic, and Latin historiography. He is currently working on a book devoted to classical literacy for modern readers based on readings from ancient historians. He and his wife, Ellyne, share their love for Lewis with their children, five young, eager readers.

Colin Manlove was reader in English literature at the University of Edinburgh, Scotland, until his retirement in 1993. Since then he has continued his critical writing, publishing *The Chronicles of Narnia: The Patterning of a Fantastic World* in Twayne's Masterwork Series in 1993, as well as two books on Scottish fantasy and one on English fantasy. His eight earlier books include the classic *Modern Fantasy* (1975), *C. S. Lewis: His Literary Achievement* (1987), and *Christian Fantasy: From 1200 to the Present* (1992).

Thomas L. Martin taught English at Wheaton College for four years before becoming Assistant Professor of English at Florida Atlantic University, where he teaches literary theory and the history of criticism. He is the author of several articles on Renaissance literature and on possible-worlds semantics and literary theory.

Wayne Martindale is Associate Professor of English Literature at Wheaton College, where he teaches, among other subjects, the literature of the Romantics and a course on C. S. Lewis. He is co-editor of *The Quotable Lewis* (1989), editor of *Journey to the Celestial City: Glimpses of Heaven from Great Literary Classics* (1995), and a contributor on Lewis to many books and journals.

Doris T. Myers is the author of *C. S. Lewis in Context* (1994), which won the Mythopoeic Scholarship Award in Inklings Studies; an elementary textbook in general linguistics, *Understanding Language* (1984); and numerous articles on C. S. Lewis, science fiction, rhetoric, and linguistics. She is Professor Emeritus of English at the University of Northern Colorado.

Michael W. Price has published articles on Donne, Shakespeare, Milton, Sir William Cornwallis, and Willa Cather. He is currently developing a book manuscript on Donne's *Paradoxes and Problems*. He, his wife, Tambi, and his son, Andrew, live in Grove City, Pennsylvania, where he is assistant professor of English at Grove City College. His favorite Lewis work is "Learning in War-Time."

Leland Ryken is Professor of English at Wheaton College, where he has taught since 1968. He has authored and edited a total of twenty books, including *A Dictionary of Biblical Imagery* (1998), *Realms of Gold: The Classics in*

13

Christian Perspective (1991), *The Liberated Imagination* (1989), and *Words of Delight: A Literary Introduction to the Bible* (1992).

Peter J. Schakel is Peter C. and Emajean Cook Professor of English at Hope College. He is editor of *The Longing for a Form: Essays on the Fiction of C. S. Lewis* (1977), co-editor of *Word and Story in C. S. Lewis* (1991), and author of *Reading with the Heart: The Way into Narnia* (1988), *Reason and Imagination in C. S. Lewis* (1984), *The Poetry of Jonathan Swift: Allusion and the Development of a Poetic Style* (1978), and many articles and papers on verse satire in eighteenth-century England.

Gene Edward Veith is Professor of English at Concordia University-Wisconsin. He is the author of nine books—including *Postmodern Times* (1994), *Reading between the Lines: A Christian Guide to Literature* (1995), and *Reformation Spirituality: The Religion of George Herbert* (1985)—and numerous essays on Christianity, culture, and the arts.

List of Titles

To enhance readability, works are given by their full names the first time they appear in a chapter; thereafter, by their short titles. Citations conform to the *MLA Style Manual* and appear parenthetically in the text by short title only.

Short Title	Full Title
Abolition	*The Abolition of Man*
Allegory	*The Allegory of Love*
American	*Letters to an American Lady*
Battle	*The Last Battle*
Chair	*The Silver Chair*
Children	*Letters to Children*
Collected Poems	*Collected Poems*
Concerns	*Present Concerns*
Discarded	*The Discarded Image*
Divorce	*The Great Divorce*
Dock	*God in the Dock*
Experiment	*An Experiment in Criticism*
Faces	*Till We Have Faces*
Glory	*The Weight of Glory*
Grief	*A Grief Observed*
Heresy	*The Personal Heresy*
Hideous	*That Hideous Strength*
Horse	*The Horse and His Boy*
Letters	*Letters of C. S. Lewis*
Lion	*The Lion, the Witch and the Wardrobe*
Literary	*Selected Literary Essays*
Loves	*The Four Loves*
Malcolm	*Letters to Malcolm*
Medieval	*Studies in Medieval and Renaissance Literature*

Mere	*Mere Christianity*
Miracles	*Miracles*
Narrative	*Narrative Poems*
Nephew	*The Magician's Nephew*
Night	*The World's Last Night*
Of Other Worlds	*Of Other Worlds*
Of This and Other Worlds	*Of This and Other Worlds*
Pain	*The Problem of Pain*
Paper	*They Asked for a Paper*
Perelandra	*Perelandra*
Planet	*Out of the Silent Planet*
Poems	*Poems*
Preface	*A Preface to "Paradise Lost"*
Psalms	*Reflections on the Psalms*
Reflections	*Christian Reflections*
Regress	*The Pilgrim's Regress*
Rehabilitations	*Rehabilitations*
Road	*All My Road Before Me*
Screwtape	*The Screwtape Letters*
Sixteenth	*English Literature in the Sixteenth Century Excluding Drama*
Spenser's	*Spenser's Images of Life*
Spirits	*Spirits in Bondage*
Stand	*They Stand Together*
Stories	*"On Stories" and Other Essays on Literature*
Surprised	*Surprised by Joy*
Tower	*The Dark Tower*
Transposition	*Transposition*
Voyage	*The Voyage of the Dawn Treader*
Words	*Studies in Words*

1

Reading Literature with C. S. Lewis

Leland Ryken

It was only after compiling the indexes for several of my own books that it dawned on me that C. S. Lewis is the critic from whom I quote more often in my literary criticism than any other, without consciously having set out to do so. That I do the same in my classroom teaching is evident when I preface a quotation with the question, "As *who* said?" only to have students usually guess C. S. Lewis. What follows is not a scholarly inquiry into the literary criticism of C. S. Lewis (that will come in the essays to follow), but instead an informal reflection on exactly what it is that makes Lewis so appealing and useful as a reading companion. Why do so many people want to read literature with C. S. Lewis? That is the question I shall address.

Virtually all of my exposure to Lewis's criticism came after I began to teach college literature, not in my experiences as an undergraduate English major or graduate student in literature. Lewis was therefore in no sense something imposed on me. On the contrary, his criticism was something that I discovered on my own and that won its way with me simply on the basis of its usefulness.

The formative influence of Lewis's criticism on me came as I was mastering material or preparing to teach it for the first time. Some (though not all) of the qualities for which I will praise Lewis's criticism are ones that are particularly useful as introductions to various authors, works, and literary periods. While the usefulness of the insights is perennial, I doubt that they would have produced the same impact if I had encountered them after I had taught Spenser or Milton for a decade or two. I think it fair to say, therefore, that C. S. Lewis is preeminently the critic for the initiate, the student, the common reader, or the literary professional getting started on a given body of material. This is not to deny the refreshment I receive from rereading a Lewis book or essay on material that I have taught for a long time.

I also need to acknowledge at the outset a frank paradox regarding the criticism of Lewis. The appeal of that criticism is stronger among readers with Christian sympathies than it is in the world at large. Yet while Lewis's literary views have nearly always been useful to me in my integration of literature with Christianity, Lewis himself was apparently little interested in such integration. I certainly would not regard him as a model for "Christian criticism," nor do I have a compelling explanation for why his appeal has been primarily to Christian readers (though I will venture a possible explanation later).

The Gift for Organization

One of the most obvious gifts of Lewis as critic is his penchant for organization. The result is a plethora of "lay-of-the-land" generalizations that provide overviews for vast stretches of literature. For me, these organizing schemes have been equally useful as prospective signposts telling me what to look for as I have embarked on a body of literature for the first time, or as a retrospective vantage point from which to make sense of data I have already encountered.

In a single packed sentence in *The Allegory of Love*, Lewis organizes a lot of ancient classical literature with the observation that "in ancient literature love seldom rises above the levels of merry sensuality or domestic comfort, except to be treated as a tragic madness . . . which plunges otherwise sane people (usually women) into crime and disgrace" (4). Who can doubt it? Now the downside of such organizing generalizations is that they represent a streamlined version of the data that actually exists. We all know that. This stricture does not, however, cancel the usefulness of the overview, and it is the latter that was a specialty of Lewis.

Often the insights that I have found most useful in Lewis's criticism have been "asides" that were subordinate to the main argument. Early in *Allegory*, for example, as Lewis is preparing to make the case for the novelty of courtly love as a way of thinking about the relation between the sexes, he notes in passing, "It seems to us natural that love should be the commonest theme of serious imaginative literature" (3). Well, yes, now that Lewis mentions it, it is obvious how dominant a motif romantic love has been in Western literature.

The implications of the statement extend throughout literary history to the latest slate of movies.

In the weeks preceding teaching my first class at Wheaton College, as I was giving thought to an opening day theoretical lecture on reading literature within a Christian context, my sister just happened to give me the newly released book containing the essay "Christianity and Culture." To this day I marvel at how much theoretic mileage I got out of this essay alone. As Lewis pursues the idea that although the *virtues* espoused by Western literature have generally been Christian, the *values* have not been, he provides the following overview of the value structure of Western literature: "Some of the principal values actually implicit in European literature were . . . (a) honour, (b) sexual love, (c) material prosperity, (d) pantheistic contemplation of nature, (e) *Sehnsucht* awakened by the past, the remote, or the (imagined) supernatural, (f) liberation of impulses" ("Culture" 21–22). Yes, this is a simplification, but it accounts for a large proportion of the literature that I teach from classical antiquity to the modern age.

Some of Lewis's general comments are observations not on a body of literature but on literary theory. In *Reflections on the Psalms*, as Lewis prepares to explain Hebrew parallelism, he observes, "The principle of art has been defined by someone as 'the same in the other'. Thus in a country dance you take three steps and then three steps again. That is the same. But the first three are to the right and the second three to the left. . . . Rhyme consists in putting together two syllables that have the same sound except for their initial consonants, which are other" (*Psalms* 4). In a similar vein, Lewis identifies the rhetorical structure of Shakespeare's sonnets as "that of theme and variations" (*Sixteenth* 506). As aesthetic principles go, probably none is more universal than *idem in alio*, and Lewis rendered me a great service in laying this principle out before me. Also in *Psalms*, Lewis clarifies a key principle of lyric poetry when he speaks of "all the licenses and all the formalities, the hyperboles, the emotional rather than logical connections, which are proper to lyric poetry" (3).

Undergirding Lewis's organizing penchant is an analytic bent of mind that is always ready to break a topic into constituent parts, which he often enumerates. Here are specimens of a formula that Lewis used dozens of times: Sidney's "defence of poetry will not be rightly understood unless we keep two facts carefully in mind" (*Sixteenth* 318); "two ways in pastoral lay open before Spenser" (360); "the prose fiction of this period may be divided into three classes" (418); "at least five different forms in which evil appears in *The Faerie Queene* may be distinguished" (*Spenser's* 67); the grandeur of Milton's style "is produced mainly by three things" (*Preface* 40); "Dante's similes may be divided . . . into four classes" ("Similes" 66); the golden lyric of the sixteenth century "differs from the old kind in three ways" (*Sixteenth* 482); the subject matter of Shakespeare's sonnets cannot be readily categorized, "and this, for two reasons, makes singularly little difference" (504). As an organizing strategy, the technique works wonders (deconstructive theory notwithstanding), and it is a major ingredient of Lewis's helpfulness to readers who want to get a handle on an author or work.

Aphorism and Humor

One of the things that makes Lewis so quotable, whether in the classroom or in print, is his aphoristic ability. Several qualities converge here—quickness of mind and wit, an analytic impulse that wants matters sharply defined, the organizing mentality that wants to see big tracts of data made manageable, and dislike of prolixity. Some of Lewis's greatest discussions wind their way to a climactic formula that makes the whole work under discussion fall into place: "I am defending Milton's style as a ritual style" (*Preface* 61); what Chaucer did in *Troilus and Criseyde* was "a process of *medievalization*" ("*Il Filostrato*" 27); the medieval view of the cosmos, though untrue, is to be understood as "a work of art" ("Imagination" 62).

Some of Lewis's aphorisms relate to a whole body of literature. One of the most useful sentences that Lewis ever penned is this one: "The Romantic poet wishes to be absorbed into Nature, the Elizabethan, to absorb her" (*Sixteenth* 341). I myself substitute the word "Classical" for "Elizabethan" in getting mileage out of these contrasting aesthetic ideals of nature that organize so much of Western poetry. In a similar way, what vast tracts of the romance tradition are encapsulated by Lewis's formula "interlocked stories of chivalrous adventure in a world of marvels" (*Allegory* 308). In talking about the bookishness of the medieval mind, Lewis describes the *literati* of the Middle Ages as "literate people who had lost most of their books. And what survived was . . . a chance collection" ("Imagination" 44).

Other aphorisms apply to specific authors. Thomas More's English prose style "is stodgy and dough-like," while "poor Wyatt seems to be always in love with women he dislikes" (*Sixteenth* 180, 229). On Surrey's translation of Virgil's *Aeneid*, the first blank verse in the English language, Lewis writes, "We should stand by the first English blank verse as reverently as we stand by the springs of the Thames" (234). Again, regarding Milton's emphasis on hierarchy in *Paradise Lost*, "We shall be in constant danger of supposing that the poet was inculcating a rule when in fact he was enamoured of a perfection" (*Preface* 81). The tendency of utopias to circumscribe life with rules is rendered memorable in Lewis's sardonic understatement that "it is not love of liberty that makes men write Utopias" (*Sixteenth* 168).

Some vintage Lewis aphorisms bring aspects of literary theory into focus. "There is hope for a man who has never read Malory or Boswell or *Tristram Shandy* or Shakespeare's *Sonnets*," writes Lewis, "but what can you do with a man who says he 'has read' them?" ("On Stories" 17). Entertainment, as a function of literature, "is like a qualifying examination. If a fiction can't provide even that, we may be excused from inquiry into its higher qualities" (*Experiment* 92). One of Lewis's classic one-liners is on the importance of form in literature: "It is easy to forget that the man who writes a good love sonnet needs not only to be enamoured of a woman, but also to be enamoured of the Sonnet" (*Preface* 3). Another is his comment on metaphor: "Every metaphor is an allegory in little" (*Allegory* 60). In one of the few passages in which Lewis speaks self-consciously as a Christian critic, he comments thus about the relative unimportance of literature compared to the ultimate spiritual issues: "The Christian knows from the outset that the salvation of a single soul is more important than the production or preservation of all the epics and tragedies in the world" ("Literature" 10). Lewis's essay "The Literary Impact of the Authorised Version," a classic to this day, has rendered permanently memorable the difference between a literary source and an influence in this aphorism: "A Source gives us things to write about; an Influence prompts us to write in a certain way" (133).

Finally, some of Lewis's choicest aphorisms extend beyond literature to life, and these, too, endear him to the person who has developed a taste for reading literature with him. Examples abound: "the magician asserts human omnipotence; the astrologer, human impotence" (*Sixteenth* 6); "great subjects do not make great poems; usually, indeed, the reverse" (377); "must Noah *always* figure in our minds drunk and naked, never building the Ark?" (*Preface* 92); "it is not the remembered but the forgotten past that enslaves us" ("*Temporum*" 12); "no man would find an abiding strangeness on the Moon unless he were the sort of man who could find it in his own back garden" ("On Stories" 13).

Aphorisms of the type I have noted are a close relative to humor, and this, too, is a quality that makes Lewis an inviting companion on one's literary sojourns. Some of the most delicious humorous aphorisms of Lewis come in his denigration of bad writing. Much of this sardonic humor is at the expense of some acknowledged "losers" of literary history. Writes Lewis, "When medieval literature is bad, it is bad by honest, downright incompetence: dull, prolix, or incoherent," whereas the badness of some neo-Latin work of the Renaissance is something new—"the badness which no man could incur by sheer defect of talent but only by 'endless labour to be wrong'" (*Sixteenth* 24). William Webb "is in a class by himself, uniquely bad" (429), while George Chapman's *Shadow of Night* possesses some of the characteristics that "we expect in the poem of a *coterie*. There are degrees of silliness which the individual can hardly reach in isolation" (*Sixteenth* 510).

Lewis does not spare the masters from his withering satire. Consider, for example, his verdict that "of the *Shepherd's Calendar* as poetry we must confess that it commits the one sin for which, in literature, no merits can compensate; it is rather dull. . . . I have never in my life met anyone who spoke of it in tones that betray real enjoyment" (*Sixteenth* 363). Of one of his favorite Renaissance authors Lewis writes, "There is so much careless writing in *Astrophel and Stella* that malicious quotation could easily make it appear a failure. Sidney can hiss like a serpent ('Sweet swelling lips well maist thou swell'), gobble like a turkey ('Moddels such be wood globes'), and quack like a duck ('But God wot, wot not what they mean')" (*Sixteenth* 329). One of the *tour de forces* of Lewis's criticism is his attempt (I think unconvincing) to discredit the claims for the superiority of the rhythms of the King James Bible. As a rhythmic equivalent for "after the earthquake, a fire; but the Lord was not in the fire: and after the fire a still small voice," Lewis gives us, "After the cocktail, a soup—but the soup was not very nice—and after the soup a small, cold pie" (214).

Because he was a person with a temperamental taste for humor, the note of humor finds unobtrusive expression at many turns in Lewis's criticism. It is in Lewis's nature to pass on the anecdote of G. K. Chesterton about "a boy who was more afraid of the Albert Memorial than anything else in the world" ("On Three Ways" 31), and Samuel Johnson's view that "the Irish, sir, are an honest people. They never speak well of one another" ("Literary Impact" 126). Regarding a book by Kipling, Lewis quipped that "I know I am not alone in finding that one actually laughed less than one would have thought possible in the reading of it" (*Paper* 74).

Entering Imagined Worlds

The helpfulness of Lewis's commentary on authors and texts resides partly in the theory of literature that undergirds the commentary. The most important ingredient in that theory is the notion of literature as world making. World making is the most obvious feature of Lewis's fiction; likewise Lewis's criticism is predicated on the premise that to read literature is to enter a distinct world that has identifiable characteristics that remove it from waking, empirical reality.

When Lewis finally wrote his only major work of literary theory, the argument wound its way in the famous last chapter to a theory that literature is an alternate world. The "good" of literature, Lewis concludes, is that "we want to be more than ourselves. . . . We want to see with other eyes, to imagine with other imaginations, to feel with other hearts, as well as with our own" (*Experiment* 137). To clinch the point, Lewis writes, "We demand windows. Literature as Logos is a series of windows, even of doors" (138); it "admits us to experiences other than our own" (139). We should note in passing the comprehensiveness inherent in the human faculties that Lewis lists as being awakened in the process of reading: the perception (surely metaphoric as well as visual), the imagination, and the affections or emotions.

Despite the regularity with which Lewis talks about the ideas of literature, he never limits his attention to the ideational level. The premise that literature is more than ideas underlies the statement that "in reading imaginative work" we are concerned primarily with "entering fully into the opinions, and therefore also the attitudes, feelings and total experience" of other people (*Experiment* 85). To read a play "as primarily a vehicle for . . . philosophy" is "an outrage to the thing the poet has made for us," because a poem "is not merely *logos* (something said) but *poeima* (something made)" (82).

A good index to Lewis's theory of reading literature as a process of entering an alternate world of the imagination is his classic essay "On Stories." After cataloging the qualities of the imagined world in Kenneth Grahame's story *The Wind in the Willows*, Lewis concludes that "the book is a specimen of the most scandalous escapism" that might be expected to "unfit us for the harshness of reality and send us back to our daily lives unsettled and discontented" (14). The reverse, however, is actually true: "the whole story, paradoxically enough, strengthens our relish for real life. This excursion into the preposterous sends us back with renewed pleasure to the actual" (15). Underlying this account of a specific book is the conviction that "all reading whatever is an escape. It involves a temporary transference of the mind from our actual surroundings to things merely imagined or conceived" (*Experiment* 68).

Here, in microcosm, is Lewis's theory of reading as a process of entering an alternate world that is merely imagined yet intimately related to the empirical world in which we live. One of Lewis's greatest virtues as a critic springs directly from this theory: he consistently steps forward as the reader's travel guide, helping provide an entrée into a new world, pointing out highlights of the landscape, sharing the delights and insights of the journey. Lewis is at his best in the role of writing general introductions—to an author (his introductory essay on Spenser), a work (*A Preface to "Paradise Lost"*), an era (his survey of sixteenth-century English literature), a book (*Reflections on the Psalms*), a tradition (*The Allegory of Love*). Writing at a time when it would have been easy to reduce these to a history-of-ideas format, Lewis instead maintains an allegiance to them as worlds of the imagination. Lewis's real interest in his historical criticism is "the history of imagination" (*Allegory* 82).

Lewis's special gift is to highlight what a reader would most benefit from knowing at the beginning of an acquaintance with an author or work. Even the minor authors whom Lewis treats briefly in his book on sixteenth-century English literature emerge from his account as creators of an imagined world that we enter with both pleasure and instruction. Indeed, one of Lewis's great gifts is to convey a sense of the momentousness of the imagined worlds of literature, as when he calls pastoral literature "a region in the mind which does exist and which should be visited often" (*Allegory* 352). Everywhere we turn in Lewis's literary criticism we find ourselves in the presence of someone who simply assumes that the world of literature is a self-rewarding world of overwhelming importance. I think, for example, of the glimpse Lewis gives us of his experiences with Shakespeare's *Hamlet*: "From our first childish reading of the ghost scenes down to those golden minutes which we stole from marking examination papers on *Hamlet* to read a few pages of *Hamlet* itself, have we ever known the day or the hour when its enchantment failed?" ("Hamlet" 92). Lewis later calls *Hamlet* "something of inestimable importance" in which "the real and lasting mystery of our human situation has been greatly depicted" (104).

Lewis also held specific ideas about the general traits of the imaginative world we enter when we read. It is a world that is "simplified and heightened" (*Sixteenth* 341). It is, moreover, a world of concrete human experience: in an extended comparison between ordinary, scientific language and poetic language, Lewis comes to the conclusion that "the most remarkable of the powers of poetic language" is the ability "to convey to us the quality of experiences" ("Language" 133). In elaboration of that thesis, Lewis notes that poetry, when compared to straight prose, "contains a great many more adjectives. . . . From Homer, who never omits to tell us that the ships were black and the sea salt, or even wet, . . . poets are always telling us that grass is green, or thunder loud, or lips red" (131).

A large part of the world of the imagination consists, moreover, of recurrent images and motifs that Lewis variously calls "Stock themes" (*Preface* 57), the products of "the primitive or instinctive mind" (*Allegory* 312), "very basic images in the human mind (*Preface* 57), and (despite his skepticism about Jungian theory) "archetype[s]" (58) or "archetypal patterns" (48, 52, 59). The older literature, claims Lewis, is adept at showing us that "love is sweet, death bitter, virtue lovely, and children or gardens delightful" (57). Primeval images such as "giants, dragons, paradises, gods, and the like are themselves the expression of certain basic elements in man's spiritual experience." Lewis's book *Spenser's Images of Life* is a masterful example of what some critics would call archetypal criticism, exploring the master images and motifs of the poem.

As for the value of entering imagined worlds, Lewis assumes at least four things, as his actual commentary on works of literature demonstrates. One is that it is simply pleasurable to enter such worlds. He hints at this in his apology for culture: "when I ask what culture has done to me personally, the most obviously true answer is that it has given me quite an enormous amount of pleasure" ("Culture" 21). The most obvious attractiveness of reading with C. S. Lewis is that he makes the experience a pleasurable one. A second value of entering imagined worlds is that it "strengthens our relish for real life" ("On Stories" 15), so that, for example, reading about enchanted woods, far from making us despise real woods, "makes all real woods a little enchanted" ("On Three Ways" 30). A third value is intellectual. Entering imagined worlds allows a reader to clarify values and world views; in Lewis's words, "To judge between one *ethos* and another, it is necessary to have got inside both, and if literary history does not help us to do so it is a great waste of labour" (*Sixteenth* 331). And there is finally the "enlargement of our being" that we derive from entering alternate worlds where we "see with other eyes, . . . imagine with other imaginations, . . . feel with other hearts" (*Experiment* 137).

In his book on Spenser's *Faerie Queene*, Lewis speaks at one point of becoming "an inhabitant of its world" (*Spenser's* 140). Lewis had a knack for delineating the features of an author's world. Regarding the world of *The Wind in the Willows* Lewis writes, "The happiness which it presents to us is in fact full of the simplest and most attainable things—food, sleep, exercise, friendship, the face of nature, even (in a sense) religion" ("On Stories" 14). Again, "I have already mentioned youthfulness as a characteristic of Froissart's world. We misread all medieval romance and chronicle if we miss this quality. Whatever age the knights and ladies may actually be, they all behave as if . . . 'they should never be old'" (*Sixteenth* 155). In his headnote to the opening of *The Faerie Queene*, Lewis writes that the selection to follow "at once creates the atmosphere of Spenser's 'faerie lond,' remote (yet somehow familiar), beautiful, voluptuous, and troubled with the sense of hidden dangers" (Headnote 110). Spenser's *Faerie Queene* presents us with a world of "quests and wanderings and inextinguishable desires" ("Spenser" 126), while the "Epithalamion" is a poem that harmonizes "all the diverse associations of marriage, actual and poetic, pagan and Christian: summer, landscape, neighbors, pageantry, religions, riotous eating and drinking, sensuality, moonlight" (130).

Governing Lewis's attention to the properties of the world of literary works is the premise that to read well we need first of all "to respond to the central, obvious appeal of a great work" (*Sixteenth* 26). Lewis is accordingly critical of the Renaissance humanists who "could not really bring themselves to believe that the poet cared about the shepherds, lovers, warriors, voyages, and battles. They must be only a disguise for something more 'adult'" (28). Lewis the travel guide is the friend of the general reader. In his essay on *Hamlet* (a small classic, but, then, so are many of Lewis's essays), Lewis sets out "to recall attention from the things an intellectual adult notices to the things a child or a peasant notices—night, ghosts, a castle, a lobby where a man can walk four hours together, . . . a graveyard and a terrible cliff above the sea, and amidst all these a . . . dishevelled man whose words make us at once think of loneliness and doubt and dread, of waste and dust and emptiness" ("Hamlet" 104). Lewis's brief sketches of works in his big book on sixteenth-century English literature are filled with outlines of the imagined world that we enter in the work, like this one on Skelton's *Bouge of Court*: "Things overheard, things misunderstood, a general and steadily growing sense of being out of one's depth, fill the poem with a Kafka-like uneasiness" (*Sixteenth* 135). Not surprisingly, Lewis values "atmosphere" as a literary quality ("On Stories" 7).

As a footnote to my picture of Lewis as the friend of the general reader, let me note in passing that as a travel guide Lewis never loses his instincts as a teacher. In particular, he is always ready to toss in a bit of helpful theory about how to read (indeed, as his lone book of literary theory shows, his essential stance was to pay attention to how people read). "A narrative style," Lewis notes, "is not to be judged by snippets. You must read for at least half a day and read with your mind on the story" (*Sixteenth* 277). "The first thing to grasp about the sonnet sequence," Lewis wants us to know, "is that it is not a way of telling a story. It is a form which exists for the sake of prolonged lyrical meditation" (327). The term "lifelike," Lewis tells us helpfully, can mean two very different things in the literary realm: it can be not only "like life as we know it in the real world," but also "seeming to have a life of its own," by which criterion Captain Ahab, old Karamazov, Caliban, Br'er Rabbit, and the giant who says "fee-fi-fo-fum" in *Jack the Giant-Killer* are all lifelike ("Spenser" 135).

The most salient quality that I experience when Lewis introduces me to authors and works is a desire to read them. After reading his introductory essay on Spenser as an undergraduate, I knew at once that I wanted to be a serious student of Spenser and *The Faerie Queene*. Reading *A Preface to "Paradise Lost"* on my own during the weeks preceding my first term in graduate school made me want to master Milton, who became the subject of my dissertation. In rereading *The Allegory of Love* recently, I found myself wanting to dip into Jean de Meun simply because I was intrigued by Lewis's account of his quirks as a writer—the fact that he had the misfortune "to have read and remembered everything: and nothing that he remembered could be kept out of his poem" (151), as well as his ability to produce inspired moments without unifying them: "To-morrow he will be thinking differently, feeling differently, making a different kind of poetry" (154).

If Lewis can thus entice readers into individual works and authors, he does something similar for the entire world of imaginative literature. The key to it is Lewis's immense range of reading. I know of no twentieth-century critic who refers to so many works and writers (he seems to surpass even Northrop Frye). In the single essay "On Stories" (which doubtless ranks as one of Lewis's lighter, more popular essays), he refers to no fewer than two dozen authors and an equal number of specific works. One by-product of all this reading is that it conveys a sense of the momentousness of literature, along the lines of Lewis's observation that "those of us who have been true readers all our life seldom fully realise the enormous extension of our being which we owe to authors" (*Experiment* 140).

Making the Older Literature Accessible

By a logical extension, Lewis's ability to provide entry into the imagined worlds of specific authors and works also expresses itself in his skill at making the whole world of the older literature accessible to modern readers for whom the past seems foreign. In his inaugural lecture given when he assumed the chair of Medieval and Renaissance Literature at Cambridge University, Lewis stepped forward aggressively as "the spokesman of Old Western Culture" ("*Temporum*" 12). On the same occasion Lewis confided, "I myself belong far more to that Old Western order than to yours" (13).

Lewis claimed, moreover, to possess the ability to read "as a native" texts that most moderns "read as foreigners" ("*Temporum*" 13). And he expressed finally his "settled conviction that in order to read Old Western literature aright you must suspend most of the responses and unlearn most of the habits you have acquired in reading modern literature." The claim was no doubt exaggerated, yet it explains much of what Lewis does in his criticism. In *A Preface to "Paradise Lost,"* Lewis challenges the theory that we should read the older literature only for what is universal in it and offers instead the following view: "Instead of stripping the knight of his armour you can try to put his armour on yourself. To enjoy our full humanity we ought, so far as is possible, to contain within us potentially at all times, and on occasion to actualize, all the modes of feeling and thinking through which man has passed" (64). Speaking autobiographically, Lewis credits Barfield with delivering him from "chronological snobbery," defined as "the uncritical acceptance of the . . . assumption that whatever has gone out of date is on that account discredited" (*Surprised* 207).

In addition to telling us why we should read the older literature, Lewis drops hints as to how the study should be undertaken. One principle is that "the literary historian . . . is concerned not with those ideas in his period which have since proved fruitful, but with those which seemed important at the time. He must even try to forget his knowledge of what comes after" (*Sixteenth* 4–5). A second bit of methodology is to study "things outside the poem" and to steep oneself "in the vanished period," thereby re-entering the poem "with eyes more like those of the natives; now perhaps seeing that . . . what you thought strange was then ordinary and that what seemed to you ordinary was then strange" ("*Audiendis*" 3).

It would be misleading, though, to picture Lewis as valuing only what the original audience saw in the literature of the remote past. Lewis is equally adept at bridging the gap from the ancient world to the modern. He writes, for example, that "we are tempted to treat 'courtly love' as a mere episode in literary history," whereas "an unmistakable continuity connects the (French) love song with the love poetry . . . of the present day" (*Allegory* 3). Despite the apparent remoteness of the world of Spenser's *The Faerie Queene*, its "houses and bowers and gardens . . . are always at hand" (*Sixteenth* 391). One of the most creative of all Lewis's critical excursions is the essay in which he shows the realistic human psychology at work in the demons who speak in Milton's imagined council in hell (*Preface* 104–07).

To return to an earlier point, Lewis the tour guide to the older literature is at the same time Lewis the writer of introductions to works and eras. His *Preface to "Paradise Lost"* remains the best introduction to epic as a genre and to Milton's poem. His epoch-making book *The Allegory of Love* opened the way for modern readers to enjoy courtly love literature, while his essay on Chaucer's *Troilus and Criseyde* ("*Il Filostrato*" 27–44) is one of the best doorways to understanding that great medieval work. In similar manner, Lewis's book *The Discarded Image* is essentially an introduction to the medieval and Renaissance world view, with emphasis on the "otherness" of that world compared to the modern one.

As a footnote to Lewis as the "salvager" of what might otherwise be lost to a reader, I would note in passing that we are indebted to his sharing of critical viewpoints gleaned from out-of-the-way places. Lewis is the one who popularized Charles Williams's quip "Hell is inaccurate" to indicate that Satan lies about every subject he mentions in *Paradise Lost* (*Preface* 97). Lewis is likewise the one who calls attention to how Crabbe notes, "in a passage not often enough quoted," that "a grim and distressful tale may offer a complete escape from the reader's actual distresses" (*Experiment* 69).

28

The Personal Touch

To read literature with C. S. Lewis is to get to know Lewis himself, and this is part of the appeal of his criticism. Criticism as an impersonal scholarly inquiry did not occur as an option to Lewis. His own tastes and personality come through at nearly every turn.

Sometimes this takes the form of incidental insights into life that Lewis tosses in gratuitously. About Thomas More's *Apology*, writes Lewis, "we see More being drawn, as all controversialists are drawn, away from the main issue into self-defence" (*Sixteenth* 173). More's *Dialogue of Comfort*, "written under the shadow of the scaffold," is "full of comfort, courage, and humour.... Thus some men's religion fails at the pinch: that of others does not appear to pluck up heart until the pinch comes" (176). Spenser chose Truth rather than Grace as the guide to Holiness because he was writing in an age of religious doubt when the discovery of truth was a prerequisite to the conquest of sin, "a fact which would have rendered his story uninteresting in some centuries, but which should recommend it to us" (*Allegory* 334). Regarding Machiavelli's unorginality, Lewis comments, "Not to be, but to seem, virtuous—it is a formula whose utility we all discovered in the nursery" (*Sixteenth* 51).

To read literature with C. S. Lewis is to share anecdotes that stick in our memories with a certain British quaintness. "Beyond all doubt," writes Lewis, "it is best to have made one's acquaintance with Spenser in a very large—and, preferably, illustrated—edition of *The Faerie Queene*, on a wet day, between the ages of twelve and sixteen" ("On Reading" 146). Having sketched the ideal, Lewis then softens the requirements a bit: "It is not, perhaps, absolutely necessary to have a large edition *in fact*; but it is imperative that you should think of *The Faerie Queene* as a book suitable for reading in a heavy volume, at a table ... for devout, prolonged, and leisurely perusal" ("On Reading" 146–47). Lewis's ideal happiness "would be to read the Italian epic—to be always convalescent from some small illness and always seated in a window that overlooked the sea, there to read these poems eight hours of each happy day" (*Allegory* 304).

Some of Lewis's anecdotes are real-life ones. We can all verify his observation that children "ask for the same story over and over again, and in the same words. They want to have again the 'surprise' of discovering that what seemed Little-Red-Riding-Hood's grandmother is really the wolf. It is better when you know it is coming" ("On Stories" 18). We are at Lewis's side in a secondhand bookstore as he looks at editions of narrative poems with underlining on the first two pages only, with the rest of the books virginal, proof that the readers set out looking for "good lines" and were soon frustrated in their quest (*Preface* 1–2). We sit with Lewis at dinner as he remarks to someone that he "was reading Grimm in German of an evening but never bothered to look up a word I didn't know," adding, "So that it is often great fun guessing what it was that the old woman gave to the prince which he afterwards lost in the wood" ("On Stories" 13). We overhear a fellow examiner repulse Lewis's attempt to discuss a writer on whom several students had written with the put-down, "Good God, man, do you want to go on *after hours*? Didn't you hear the hooter blow?" (*Experiment* 7). I note in passing that for an American, one of the charms of reading Lewis is the continuous flavor of Britishness that permeates the discussion.

29

Lewis as Travel Guide

Lewis the critic is primarily a travel guide. His knowledge of the territory far surpasses that of his readers, though he never flaunts his superiority. Lewis is the most companionable of travel guides. The reader comes to relish him as someone with whom to share literary experiences.

While this is the strength of Lewis's criticism, some of his deficiencies as a critic are also those of a travel guide. He knows too much, with the result that one often has to endure vast stretches of specialized scholarship before arriving at useful material. While the journey through the byways of Lewis's interests can make for an interesting holiday amble, these same byways sometimes betray a failure to define the focus and keep to the subject at hand. Then, too, Lewis is so intent on traversing the territory that he neglects choice opportunities for leisurely stays at individual sites. His analysis of the approach to Paradise in *Paradise Lost* (*Preface* 48–51) and his delineation of the rhetorical structure of some of Shakespeare's sonnets (*Sixteenth* 506–07) show that Lewis could have left a legacy of brilliant explications of texts, but in fact he left virtually none.

Another stricture that one might make is that Lewis is too unsystematic in his treatment of authors and texts. It is true that one can discern a loose Horatian framework of the pleasures of literature and its intellectual or moral usefulness. But traveling with Lewis in the realms of gold is a trip through the miscellaneous. One never knows what aspect of an author or work Lewis will discuss.

There is, however, a positive side to this tendency that may partly account for Lewis's popularity with Christian readers. In allowing each work and author he discusses to set forth their own concerns, Lewis signals his commitment to do what he recommends in *An Experiment in Criticism*—to "receive" a work instead of "using" it. Lewis thereby shows a respect for the literature he discusses that is akin to Christians' respect for the Word that they regard as authoritative, whether it comes as Scripture or creed. In a day of ideological criticism in which critics use literature chiefly to advance their own political agenda, Lewis instead *listens* to authors and works. The model he provides in this regard may, indeed, be his greatest legacy as a literary critic.

Works Cited

Lewis, C. S. *The Allegory of Love: A Study in Medieval Tradition.* New York: Oxford UP, 1936.
———. "Christianity and Culture." *Reflections* 12–36.

———. "Christianity and Literature." *Reflections* 1–11.

———. *Christian Reflections.* Ed. Walter Hooper. Grand Rapids: Eerdmans, 1967.

———. "Dante's Similes." *Medieval* 64–77.

———. "*De Audiendis Poetis.*" *Medieval* 1–17.

———. "*De Descriptione Temporum.*" *Literary* 1–14.

———. *The Discarded Image: An Introduction to Medieval and Renaissance Literature.* Cambridge: Cambridge UP, 1964.

———. "Edmund Spenser, 1552–99." *Medieval* 121–45.

———. *English Literature in the Sixteenth Century Excluding Drama.* Oxford: Oxford UP, 1954.

———. *An Experiment in Criticism.* Cambridge: Cambridge UP, 1961.

———. "Hamlet: The Prince or the Poem?" *Literary* 88–105.

———. Headnote to *The Faerie Queen.* Selection 1. *Major British Writers.* Ed. G. B. Harrison. Vol. 1. New York: Harcourt, 1954.

———. "Imagination and Thought in the Middle Ages." *Medieval* 41–63.

———. "The Language of Religion." *Reflections* 129–41.

———. *Letters of C. S. Lewis.* Ed. W. H. Lewis. New York: Harcourt, 1966.

———. "The Literary Impact of the Authorised Version." *Literary* 126–45.

———. *Of Other Worlds: Essays and Stories.* Ed. Walter Hooper. New York: Harcourt, 1966.

———. "On Reading *The Faerie Queene.*" *Medieval* 146–48.

———. "On Stories." *Of Other Worlds* 3–21.

———. "On Three Ways of Writing for Children." *Of Other Worlds* 22–34.

———. *A Preface to "Paradise Lost."* New York: Oxford UP, 1942.

———. *Reflections on the Psalms.* New York: Harcourt, 1958.

———. *Selected Literary Essays.* Ed. Walter Hooper. Cambridge: Cambridge UP, 1969.

———. *Spenser's Images of Life.* Ed. Alastair Fowler. Cambridge: Cambridge UP, 1967.

———. *Studies in Medieval and Renaissance Literature.* Ed. Walter Hooper. Cambridge: Cambridge UP, 1966.

———. *Surprised by Joy: The Shape of My Early Life.* New York: Harcourt, 1955.

———. *They Asked for a Paper: Papers and Addresses.* London: Geoffrey Bles, 1962.

———. "What Chaucer Really Did to *Il Filostrato.*" *Literary* 27–44.

2

In the Tutorial
and Lecture Hall

Carolyn Keefe

Places have a way of getting inside us—of shaping our memories of sights, sounds, and smells. Once they have entered our experience, they stay, making their presence known at unbidden times and in circumstances far removed from the original location. A May breeze can transport us back to the time when lavender wisteria clung to quadrangle walls, and dormitory windows were open to spring sounds, new learning, new love.

The Town-Gown Setting

Among the sharpest, most cherished memories of many people are those shaped during college and university days. In fact, some higher education settings have such evocative power that students, and even travelers, are drawn there partly to absorb the ambience. A case in point is Oxford University,[1] which stands its ground within the modern commercial cityscape like a dragon fighting for its medieval lifestyle. Located within a town of 116,400 inhabitants and on the popular tourist route from London to Stratford-upon-Avon, the university, which dates back to the twelfth century, has grown to thirty-six small colleges. Each has its own architectural grandeur, but none has more natural beauty than Magdalen (pronounced "Maudlen") College, where C. S. Lewis taught for many years. Throughout its colorful history, the university has attracted men ennobled by birth or brains or both—the likes of Anthony Ashley Cooper, 1st Earl of Shaftesbury (1621–83), Henry Spencer Churchill, Lord Randolph (1849–95), and the three impoverished eighteenth-century Wesley brothers, Samuel, John, and Charles. Since 1919–20 the Oxford men have had to share the magnificent buildings, the ancient libraries, and the Oxford path to opportunity with women seeking a degree, and even earlier (the 1870s) with women who could only attain a diploma. It is reasonable to assume that each Oxonian has left the university with a sense of place permanently welded to impressions of his or her teachers. As one alumnus writes, "For me, to recall Lewis is to recall Magdalen, those large rooms in the New Buildings, on sunny days or winter evenings, with the Cher [Cherwell River] and the Deer Park nearby and the lawn leading to the Cloisters" (Moynihan 11).

Now, three decades after C. S. Lewis's death, we are attempting to understand what it was like to study with Lewis. Toward that end nothing can equal the face-to-face contact with Lewis that time and space have eluded all except a few readers. Therefore, most of us must look to other ways of knowing him. Within the extensive material about Lewis are firsthand accounts of his students, particularly from his Oxford years. Then, too, we have his own writings and those of people connected with him in various capacities. From these sources we can construct a composite view that will be recognizable to those who knew him and instructive to those who never had that privilege. When that portrayal emerges, it will be enhanced by all the rest of the chapters in this volume as *how* he taught connects with *what* he taught.

Lewis's University Appointments

Lewis's teaching career spanned thirty-nine academic years (1924–63). Getting a start in the profession, however, was very trying for him. In spite of his brilliant undergraduate record at Oxford's University College—earning three First Class ratings, as well as winning the Chancellor's Prize for an English essay—he was virtually unemployed his first year out of college. University positions were scarce, and Lewis's preference for the colleges of Oxford limited his job search. After several dashed hopes, in 1924 he secured a one-year, fill-in appointment in philosophy at his alma mater, University College. This temporary job launched "the most 'bookish' man" (Bailey 91) into the career for which his pre-Oxford tutor, William T. Kirkpatrick, had thought him best suited. The next year he successfully competed for an opening in English and gained the title Fellow of Magdalen College, one he carried until 1954 when Cambridge University appointed him to the new chair of Medieval and Renaissance English at its Magdalene College. The chair had been created especially for him. He thereby attained the rank of professor, a distinction that Oxford had withheld from him.[2]

The Tutorial System

As an Oxford fellow or don, Lewis was responsible for giving lectures open to all the colleges and for tutoring undergraduates. As a Cambridge professor, Lewis no longer held tutorials (called "supervisions" at Cambridge), but he still lectured. Being a tutor did not mean that he was affiliated with a tutoring center such as those now found in American colleges and universities to provide students with extra help in English, math, and other subjects. In the role of tutor he was part of the most characteristic feature of the Oxford and Cambridge educational system. He met weekly with his students, usually singly but sometimes in pairs. For an average time of about twenty minutes (depending, apparently, on student inclination rather than a fixed time limit) the student read his original essay to Lewis; and the remainder of the hour was devoted to discussion of the essay and related matters. Then Lewis dispatched the undergraduate to engage in further study and essay writing until seven more days had lapsed and the routine was repeated. There were no classes for the tutee to attend, and the lectures were not compulsory.

None of the students, however, could avoid the examinations that determined their academic standing. If they passed the First Public Examination, they could prepare for the Second Public Examination or Final Honour School. Usually, about two years lapsed between the two exams. For these mental marathons, the students dressed in the Oxford regalia of a black academic gown, mortarboard, and suit, set off by a white shirt and bow tie. Over a five-day period, the students sat writing their responses in the huge Examination Schools where the high-arching vestibule was as dwarfing as their task. Failure meant being "sent down" from the university without a degree, but success brought them Third-, Second-, or First-Class honors.

Lewis's Career Constants

What did students affiliated with Lewis, usually for several years, get from him? Like all students they got what each teacher brings to the educational endeavor—himself or herself with all the accompanying resources, quirks, and limitations. In the material about Lewis as a tutor, three of his characteristics seem predominant and can be rightly called constants.

First, Lewis had extraordinary intelligence. A precocious storywriter in childhood; a brilliant translator of Greek plays and a mature, original literary critic in his youth; a top-notch English scholar in his college years—all these abilities point to an uncommon mind. In describing his mental powers, his students seize upon superlatives: "I found Lewis the most impressive mind I had ever seen in action" (Tynan 4), and he had "perhaps the most powerful and best trained intellect in the world" (Bailey 79).

The second constant was his dedication to a lifetime of learning. Among his most worthwhile and pleasurable times were those spent in the study or library. Once he started to read, he never stopped. "I am a product . . . of end-less books," he has told us (*Surprised* 10). In his boyhood home, Little Lea, books were everywhere, and he took full advantage of the resources. His lengthy correspondence (1914–63) with his friend Arthur Greeves shows that, wherever he happened to be, he immersed himself in books, not just to cover academic requirements, but out of sheer love for reading, analyzing, critiquing, and expounding.

"Born with the literary temperament" (Green and Hooper 45), Lewis was as compulsive about writing as he was about reading, and his mastery over both gave him an "aura of learning" (Edmonds 47). One of his few female students describes him as "a man of formidable learning" who "also possessed a Johnsonian power of turning knowledge into wisdom" (Berry 68). The words of a male student also show the basis of Lewis's reputation: "He was super-human in the range of his knowledge and in the height of his intellectual vision . . ." (Fryer 29). Apparently, the mere sight of him inspired awe. "There goes the great dragon," this same student quotes another; "There goes the great leviathan" (34).

Behind Lewis's astounding productivity was the third constant, his disci-plined work habits. He harnessed his talents and will to a daily schedule. His comfort with a regimen that would bore and frustrate most schoolboys was already in evidence when he studied with Kirkpatrick (19 September 1914–20 March 1917). Lewis told Greeves that it ran like this: 8:00–9:15 a.m., break-fast and an airing; 9:15–11:00 a.m., reading the *Iliad*; 11:00–11:15 a.m., a break; 11:15 a.m.–1:00 p.m., Latin study; 1:00–5:00 p.m., lunch and free time for read-ing, writing, and meandering around the environs; 5:00–7:00 p.m., further study; 7:30–bedtime, dinner and reading a course in English literature (*Stand* 53). Lewis thrived on the life at Great Bookham and wanted it forever. His youthful hopes became an adult reality. As an Oxford don his round of work continued much in the former vein but with the additional demands of tutor-ing, lecturing, and various other professional duties. After his conversion to Christianity, he started his weekdays with matins and Sundays with the Eucharist service.[3]

35

The industrious Lewis, who regarded his free-choice reading as recreational, seldom took time off from his academic and domestic posts. His best-loved getaways were walking tours through rambling countrysides with his friends, especially the literary Owen Barfield and D. C. Harwood, and his military historian brother, Warren. But extended vacations were a rarity. In June 1949, while lying in an Acland Nursing Home bed where he was recovering from exhaustion and a strep infection, he agreed to a month's vacation in Ireland. "Poor man," Warren entered in his diary, "it will be the first holiday he has had for at least fifteen years" (W. H. Lewis 227). As things turned out, it was Warren who took the trip, and Lewis stayed at home. Then in 1960 he went on the longest trip of his life. A bachelor for all but three of his nearly sixty-five years, Lewis acceded to his ailing wife's desire to visit Greece. In some ways he was never closer to home.

Lewis's vacation-deficient schedule would have been less productive had he not learned how to cope with interruptions. And he had plenty of them. After observing that "no man was better equipped for silent industry, hour upon hour," John Lawlor adds that "few men had more calls upon their time" (71). Students, societies, clubs, other scholars, radio and television audiences, letter-writing fans, and his readers all wanted to hear what he had to say. Also, he had domestic duties imposed by Mrs. Janie Moore, his adopted "mother" and resident housekeeper. As errand boy, scullery maid, and cleaning man, he lost valuable time but not his concentration. Warren Lewis reports that his brother, having completed his chores, could return to his writing without losing his train of thought (Green and Hooper 66). Dame Helen Gardner, a colleague who had observed him at work in the Duke Humphrey Library of the Bodleian, depicts Lewis as "an object lesson in what concentration meant" (qtd. in Hooper 55). Quite simply, he did not waste time. He focused intently on what he had to do, did it, though often interrupted, and then moved on to the next task.

The Tutorial Setting

As a benefit of employment at Magdalen College, Lewis was provided a three-room suite (two sitting rooms and a bedroom) in the New Buildings. He had the option of living there, but inasmuch as he already had set up a household with Mrs. Moore and her daughter, Maureen, he put the rooms primarily to professional use. Probably designed by Dr. George Clarke, in consultation with James Gibbs, and built by William Townesend in 1733, the structure has a relatively plain design. An architectural source describes it in this way: "No intricacy here, no variety, no elaborate decoration, none of the tradition of collegiate quads" (Sherwood and Pevsner 154). Twenty-seven bays wide and with a ground-level arcade across twenty-one of them, the unadorned but impressive three-story building housed Lewis on the second floor.[4] One set of windows overlooked a wide expanse of lawn, the Cloisters beyond, and the famed Magdalen Tower with its paired bell openings and eight pinnacles. Another view provided a pastoral scene, nothing to suggest the metropolis, only the grass, trees, and animals for which the area is known as Deer Park, the Grove. It was to this building in this setting that Lewis's students arrived week after week to read with him.

Once up the wooden stairs and through an oak door, they found a suite that had, as realtors are wont to say, "great possibilities." But Lewis was blind to them. Caring nothing about how his quarters looked or the message it communicated, he, who needed only a table and a chair for his prolific pen to do its work, lived among shabby furnishings. In the larger sitting room two battered armchairs stood astride the marble fireplace, effecting a dissonance between the unkempt and the elegant. For tutorials Lewis sat in one, the student in the other. Tobacco smoke swirled in the air and permeated every fiber of the place.

The Tutor's Appearance

Not all the visual effects in Lewis's suite were jarring. His attire was the perfect complement to the furnishings. "He dressed in tweeds and flannels (jacket and trousers, respectively) verging on the shabby," recalls Luke Rigby, "and I have a strangely detailed memory of a tattered pair of carpet slippers" (39). The antithesis of a clothes horse, he rarely bought a new sports jacket. When Lewis did, Derek Brewer says, he always took notice of it (54). Anne Scott, who heard Lewis lecture during World War II, thinks she knows where he purchased his wardrobe: "His clothes looked as if he'd picked them out of . . . what you call a thrift shop . . . like he'd put them on at random in the dark" (6). If ever he had paid any attention to his grooming—and some photos from his pre-tutoring days indicate that he had—by the time he settled into his career he must have given his wardrobe the lowest priority. His brother's account of Lewis's "complete indifference" to clothes (*Letters* 15) and the reminiscences of students support this conclusion.

When a tutee sat opposite C. S. Lewis, what else did he (or the rare she) see? The answer partly depends upon when in Lewis's life the person encountered him. He, like everyone else, changed over the passing of time. On the short side and softer rather than muscular, he became increasingly "tubby" (Rook 15; Brewer 54), a true endomorphic body build.[5] At forty he still had a rather young

37

appearance, but already his hair had thinned, and his hairline had receded. Until sickness stole his vigor, he had an alive, ruddy face that at times appeared jolly.[6] Upon hearing a good joke in an essay, he would laugh heartily. How he demonstrated the expression "with tongue in cheek" still amuses at least one reminiscer (Brewer 47). A characteristic way he regarded a student was to peer over his glasses with his brown eyes. In bodily movement he was clumsy, not fit for sports or brain surgery, but only for pushing a writing instrument across a page. His tread was heavy and noisy, and if his sitting down resembled his kneeling in chapel (Fryer 34), then he dropped with a loud thud. Fond of smoking, he was seldom without a cigarette or pipe and during tutorials made a ritual of selecting and filling his pipe (Edmonds 40). He listened intently to the student's essay, and, depending on its interest value, he would make notations or doodle.

The Tutor's Voice

The voice that boomed, "Come in!" when black-robed students knocked on his door for their tutorials was Lewis's best physical feature. It could be hearty and loud, appropriate for a jocular encounter. It also could be well modulated, ideal for his lectures and radio talks and, as Kenneth Tynan discovered, for English essays. Tynan had a stammer that grew worse during early contacts with his famous tutor. To ease the situation, Lewis offered to read the essays. Tynan admits that "it became quite a test to write essays that could survive being read in that wonderfully resonant voice of his. I found I was writing better because I knew he was going to be reading them to me" (3–4). Baritone in pitch (Keefe, "Notes" 133), pleasingly mellow in quality, his voice reminded one audience member of cuisine: "It's what I would call a port wine and plum pudding voice" (Scott 6). Another who heard him lecture reports that she "can still recall the lilt of his rich voice, with its hint of an Irish accent . . . " (Hart 2). His voice, whether live or recorded, lingers in the memory like the fabled bells of Oxford.

Lewis's Approach to the Educational Process

Although Lewis's quarters, appearance, and voice contributed to the tutorial atmosphere, they *per se* did not advance undergraduate education. These and other nonverbal elements, however, functioned in combination with verbal exchanges to produce the learning experience of reading literature with Lewis. Our next task, then, is to distill what has been disclosed about the specific ways Lewis carried out his work as educator. The material will be presented under seven categories.[7]

Lewis Shared Information

Although Lewis was lackadaisical about his furnishings and attire, he relentlessly groomed the mental world he inhabited, the life of learning. Through reading, writing, experience, discussion, and debate, he formulated his belief system, including his ideas about education.

From what he wrote on the life of the mind within the university setting, we know the sort of student he hoped would walk into his suite and what his own role should be. The student would be curious, thirsty for knowledge, and passionate for literature, one who was conversant with classical languages and literature and eager and ready to debate ideas with an older scholar. Lewis was single-minded about his obligation toward such a student. It was to challenge his mind by provoking him to reexamine old assumptions and gain new insights. He refused to be a drill sergeant, a policeman, or even, as he told his tutees, a schoolmaster (Bradshaw 25; Lawlor 70). He only wanted to be an energizing, provocative traveling companion, the older with the younger, going wider and deeper into the territories that captivated them both. With his ideas and duties firmly in place, he conducted his tutorials with whatever degree of scholar sat in the chair.

Obviously, Lewis had no intention of spoon-feeding his students by dispensing the information they needed to know. That was not his major tutorial job. He was there to listen and react to what they had discovered through study that week. If they wanted a block of information and analysis, they could attend his lectures.

Still, the tutor seized whatever opportunity he had to present facts, opinions, examples, and insights. Lewis also amplified the topics introduced in the essay[8] and pointed out matters that without an experienced guide would have been overlooked. Additionally, he commented on the student's use of structure, rhythm, clarity, and precision (Brewer 47). From the student accounts we can infer that Lewis at some time or another must have explained the importance of reading the texts themselves (not abridgments), knowing the classical languages and literature, studying Anglo-Saxon,[9] and paying attention to etymology, spelling, and source citation. Also, George Bailey mentions Lewis's attempts to teach thinking by referring to the "squiggles" that successively form in the mind and are rejected until a valid one finds its place (84). To get across his ideas, he avoided the jargon of academia and employed his brand of vivid metaphors. "He could make you see the world through the eyes of a medieval poet as no other teacher could do," extols Tynan. "You felt that you had been inside Chaucer's mind after talking to him." Tynan also wants to make sure that his old tutor is remembered as "a very witty and funny man, deeply humorous . . ." (7).

From the above summary no implication should be drawn that all these ways of sharing information occurred weekly. The tutorial with its unpredictable essay lengths, flow of topics, and clash of arguments is not an efficient way to present information orally. The lecture method better serves that function.[10]

If students wanted to learn specific details that would expand their understanding while helping them prepare for the examinations, the place to go was wherever Lewis lectured. John Wain claims that Lewis's lectures, unlike those of Charles Williams and J. R. R. Tolkien, "were, above all, *teaching* lectures; he set out to impart information, and many parts of his discourse, heavily loaded with precise references, had to be taken more or less at dictation speed" ("C. S. Lewis" 80). In 1955 Dabney A. Hart, a Fulbright scholar at King's College, went from London to Oxford where Lewis, then a Cambridge professor, gave a series of four guest lectures. She writes:

> Within a few moments, his audience had become enthralled with his witty remarks about works few of us had read, Milton's Latin poems. Of the fifth elegy he said that its technique made it more fun to write than to read. That was typical of Lewis's technique of lacing his erudition with insights about the reader's enjoyment. (2)

Alan Rook also affirms the informative nature of Lewis's lectures: "Many students wanted the facts distinctly presented, in the way Lewis did" (13). They viewed his lectures as helpful in preparing for examinations.

In 1947 when *Time* ran its cover story on Lewis, he was hailed as the most popular lecturer at Oxford ("Don v. Devil" 65). The anecdotal evidence supports that claim. We learn, for example, that Lewis's lectures, unlike those of some colleagues, were always crowded (Hart 1; Brewer 54). "While I was at Oxford," attests Bailey, "he was by far the most popular lecturer at the university. His lecture series 'Prolegomena to Renaissance Poetry' always attracted overflow crowds" (82). Brewer estimates the undergraduate attendance at about four hundred when the lectures were held in the Examination Schools. "The same lectures in Cambridge attracted a mere handful," he reports without comment (54). Scott observes that students flocked from many disciplines, not just English, to hear Lewis: "[A]ll sorts of students would just turn up and you would never see them at any other lecture" (5). Norman Bradshaw's term *packed* (24) seems to be the definitive word.

The usual location for his lectures was a large hall in the Examination Schools, but during World War II when student enrollments were down and a hospital occupied the High Street facility, Lewis lectured in the college Hall, the refectory.[11] Scott recalls that he stood on the slightly elevated section where the faculty dined at High Table. Lewis spoke from a desk that had been situated there. All around him, sitting on the chairs, tables, benches, and floor, was his audience. For Scott the pleasure of hearing him was so great she could barely take notes (6). But no matter where he spoke, the audience heard the same "musical voice . . . full and rich" (Moynihan and Moynihan 13) deliver a carefully prepared lecture that always had some humorous twists. The halls of Oxford well knew the ripple of laughter from his audiences.

+ Comments on other aspects of Lewis's delivery can help us "see" and "hear" him at the lectern. Did he use a manuscript, notes, or only his memory? If he carried out his original intention of extemporaneous delivery, then he spoke from notes (*Letters* 99). On the other hand, he, like other writers who also are speakers, might have realized the publication potential of his oral language and voted in favor of the manuscript. The fact that volumes of what Lewis said in lectures are in print gives weight to that speculation. Gervase Mathew, a colleague who worked closely with Lewis, can state authoritatively that Lewis used various methods of delivery—written text, skeleton notes, and improvisation (96), by which he seems to mean impromptu speaking. From an audience's standpoint the question was moot: whatever mode of delivery he employed, it was unobtrusive. As to his manner of delivery, opinions vary slightly. "He had a superbly unaffected delivery" (Routley 34) nudges against "He was a bit of an actor" (Bradshaw 24). Actually, both statements seem to fit because although Lewis avoided dramatic delivery vocally and bodily, his exceptionally fine voice, which still can be heard on audio cassette,[12] shows an emotionally restrained quality that, if it had been released, could have transformed him into a James Mason or Winston Churchill. Be that as it may, there is scant evidence[13] that his audience members thought him other than "marvelous" (Cowan 62). Then, when the time allotted for the lecture had lapsed, Lewis "would abruptly snatch up his papers and run out of the room . . ." (Wain, "C. S. Lewis" 80). Scott pictures the movement of this round-faced, round figure in his billowing academic gown as a study in rich curves (6).

Turning back to his tutorials, we find that frequently his students mention two topics that, if Lewis discussed at all in their tutorials, received only minimal treatment. The first is Christianity. "Of the 'devil-dodging,' razor-sharp Christian apologist, I saw little. . . ," says E. L. Edmonds (48). When Christianity had some bearing on the literature under discussion, "he would take up the point and develop it," recollects John Lawlor. "But never would he intrude his beliefs" (72). It took George Sayer over two years to discover that Lewis was a Christian. He ventures the opinion that his tutor did not bring up the matter because he considered it "wrong and improper for him to have influenced his pupils in that sort of way" (Interview 10).

The second subject about which students learned virtually nothing was Lewis's life. Even those who found Lewis friendly and jovial saw his stay-at-arm's-length signals (Bayley 80; Bradshaw 19; Wain, "Clerke" 70–71). He had no interest in giving students a glimpse into his life nor did he pry into theirs. Yet when students disclosed the need for his advice or aid, he gave it (Brewer 53–54; Tynan 7). Apparently, he drew his teaching examples from situations and sources other than himself. Thus he kept his sessions from the autobiographical chitchat into which one-on-one teaching can degenerate, but his impersonality gave those who saw nothing to the contrary the impression that he was cold and standoffish (Bailey 86; Bradshaw 25; Rook 11, 12).

Lewis Recited Literature

Even if Lewis's students had said nothing about his having recited poetry and prose to them, we could have guessed that he had, for who of us has not heard an English literature teacher read from authors we should and had better know? By so doing an educator can explicate and defend a point, and, if the material and delivery are vivid, can stamp the setting, plot, imagery, and characters on the hearers' minds. What set Lewis apart from most teachers is that he did not need a book to accomplish these ends: the lines flowed in orderly succession from his mental storehouse.

That Lewis recited literature for pedagogical purposes can be seen in these excerpts: "He had an astonishing verbatim memory and could repeat whole passages of prose to illustrate a point arising in discussion. Given any line in *Paradise Lost*, he could continue with the following lines" (Brewer 47). In another place a listener reflects with obvious pleasure: "No pupil of his will ever forget the way he quoted the poetry he enjoyed. The voice was rich, the delivery rhythmical with full attention to the meter of the lines. There would be a light in his eyes and a look of intense joy on his face. His delight was infectious" (Sayer, *Jack* 204). Through orally demonstrating the sense and sound of literature, Lewis helped increase his students' understanding of and appreciation for the literary pasturelands where he bade them roam.

Lewis Asked Questions

During the formative years when Lewis lived in the Kirkpatrick household, he not only studied languages and literature, but the dialectical use of communication. His every conversation with Kirkpatrick was subject to confrontation. Young Lewis discovered that fact immediately upon his arrival. "Stop!" was his tutor's response to Lewis's casual remark that Surrey was much "wilder" than he had anticipated. "What do you mean by wildness and what grounds had you for not expecting it?" (*Surprised* 134). That question incorporates the two thrusts of Lewis's subsequent training in the verbal art of offense and defense. His teacher insisted that all terms be defined and conclusions be supported with evidence. One way to determine whether these requirements have been met is through cross-examination. Kirkpatrick constantly put his pupil on the stand. Lewis enjoyed being there, saying that for him the experience was "red beef and strong beer" (*Surprised* 136).

Armed with the questioning skills he learned from his sparring with Kirkpatrick and his reading of Plato, Lewis the tutor was well prepared to use them on his students. The examples that have come out of his tutorials show strategic intent behind his queries. By asking Sayer what he meant by "sentimental," Lewis was trying to clarify information. His follow-up question shows he wanted to elicit an admission that would damage the student's position: "Well, Mr. Sayer, if you are not sure what the word means or what you mean by it, wouldn't it be very much better if you ceased to use it at all?" (*Jack* 198). As Bailey observes, "Lewis was always either forming or guarding the definition" (81). Lewis bombarded Lawlor with questions such as, "How could a materialist like [you] have anything on which to base the notion of value?" He thereby exposed his tutee's weaknesses in evidence and reasoning and helped Lawlor develop his dialectical abilities (74–75).

The most general purpose of Lewis's questioning was to provoke students into defending their essays. Lawlor reports that even some of the ablest scholars wilted under the hot light of inquiry. The effect was an "unhappy silence on the part of the pupil, while Lewis would boom away in unavailing efforts to draw a response, or eventually fall silent in turn" (72). For others—and here, too, the mental ability levels were mixed—the verbal exchanges between tutor and tutee were so energizing that students survived, but as underdogs. The student arsenal had few weapons. The reporter claims that his own defense was a peashooter. Lewis held a howitzer (74).

Lewis Showed Disagreement

During the defense segment of a tutorial, two major types of verbal exchange occur: debate and discussion. In debate the participants confront each other in disagreement, and the contest of wits results in a winner and a loser. In discussion, however, the tutor and student look for areas of agreement and sort out actual disagreements from those made for the sake of argument. Tutorial debate is informal with no official judge or codified rules, and it commingles with discussion, much in the nature of Socratic dialogues. In any given tutorial, the time breakdown between the direct challenge of debate and the consensus building of discussion varies with situational factors, including student knowledge, student ability, essay quality, time availability, tutor knowledge, tutor ability, and even the health of the participants.[14] As we have seen, sometimes in the Lewis tutorials the whole process caved in on itself and silence took over.

Strong evidence points to the conclusion that Lewis debated more than he discussed. Students report that he "loved to throw out challenges and see if a student would pick them up" (Edmonds 47), "liked to demolish an opponent's argument" (Bradshaw 21), and "liked to win or to score" (Bayley 80). Lewis himself told Rook, "I'm a butcher—a rough and brutal man." The remark prompted the student later to write: "What he meant, I think, was that even in casual conversation . . . he would suddenly demolish an argument like a butcher bringing down a meat cleaver—almost to the point of rudeness" (13). The essay format gave Lewis certain areas for attack: basic assumptions, sources, definitions, premises, evidence, reasoning, conclusions, omissions, critical theory, and composition. The student reminiscences, however, provide only fragmentary information on how Lewis mounted his offense. If, for example, a student failed to build a strong argument, Lewis would say, "Too much straw and not enough bricks" (Bailey 81). On one occasion Lewis chided, "Ho, ho, ho, so you think Milton was ascetic, do you? Ho, ho! You are quite wrong there!" (80). He also disagreed with Brewer's opinion about the late romances by Shakespeare and a metaphor in a poem by Lady Winchelsea (48, 49). When Bradshaw praised a line from Eliot's "The Wasteland," Lewis showed that it had been lifted from Dante (19). Unfortunately, these and the other few specific instances of Lewis's refutation are too limited and disconnected for us to reconstruct the attack and defense of an actual tutorial with Lewis.[15] This is true even when we include (as we should) the cross-examination questions as part of Lewis's strategy.[16]

Less a puzzle is how students reacted to the verbal jousting that for at least one student became a get-him-before-he-gets-you contest (Wain, "C. S. Lewis" 80). The widest range of response in a single individual started with dislike and hostility and moved to stubborn affection and finally to gratitude (Lawlor 72). Undergoing a long series of operations is the way Bradshaw describes his tutorials. Eventually the surgery improved his reasoning (18) but not without causing a temporary disinterest in literature (25). Subjecting his essay to Lewis's criticism brought initial terror to George Bailey (79), and Alan Rook reveals that "to be continually up against his ineluctable logic was distinctly chilling" (11). Peter Bayley, a student who became a colleague, admits that he "always remained a little frightened of him" (80).

The fear of these able men is understandable. By its very nature, debate is a threatening experience and immeasurably more scary against an opponent with the argumentation skills, photographic memory, language facility, and literary background of Lewis. Scared or not, the tutees who survived the intellectual warfare remember long afterward that they also felt challenged, exhilarated, and fortunate to have squared off with him.

The women who tell their tutorial story show no battle scars, although one confesses to having had slight transitory fright. "It was a joy to study with Lewis," she enthuses. "He treated us [the tutorial pair] like queens" (Cowan 62). This can only mean that Lewis did not attack their essays with the dialectical intensity he used on the men. The time when these tutees were in Oxford was the early forties, and women still expected and generally received male courtesy. More often than not, the trade-off for regal treatment was intellectual undervaluation. In the chauvinistic environment of Oxford at that time, Lewis might have toned down his booming voice and discussed more than debated with his women students. Without realizing his condescension and intending no discredit, he might have altered his communication behavior in these or other ways and thus reduced his power of intimidation.

† Lewis Showed Acceptance

In this context *acceptance* means that the tutor agrees with the student's ideas, feelings, and behavior. The term does not denote praise, but, as we know, the affirmation given by a teacher, especially one of Lewis's stature, which arouses an internal state that feels almost as satisfying as praise.

Given Lewis's role of interrogator and that of the student as defender, we cannot expect to find frequent references to agreement. From one such instance Martin Moynihan still seems to take pleasure. He tells how, after he had read his essay and a general discussion had ensued, he managed to extract a concurrence:

> I remember he once said to me, "Well, you couldn't have a duty to yourself, could you?" He was attacking my then Idealism, in the philosophical sense.

> And I said, "Well, I think you could. I think if probably you were—[sic] learning to swim you might feel you had a duty to yourself to learn to dive."

> And, to my surprise Lewis laughed at that, and said, "Well you know, that's just the point I've reached in swimming. And I agree with you. You could have a duty to yourself." (Moynihan and Moynihan 7)

In another case Lewis gave words of reinforcement to Sayer who "rather casually" told him that he had become a Roman Catholic: "Good. I'm glad you've become a Christian of some sort" (Interview 10).

The students who *seem* to have received the most acceptance from Lewis are those who shared with him a deep regard for certain authors or works. G. K. Chesterton and George MacDonald were cherished meeting grounds (Blamires 11; Sayer, *Jack* 205). When a friendship developed from a tutorial—

45

and it happened infrequently, as might be expected—the stimulus was a common interest, a process described by Lewis in his treatment of *philia* or friendship in *The Four Loves* (87–127).

Lewis Gave Mild Praise

Unlike many current educators, Lewis did not involve his students in activities to increase their self-concept and engender pleasant feelings, nor did he design his tutorials to promote their career readiness. Instead, every aspect of his teaching shows that he aimed at quite a different goal, one he described for an undergraduate audience: "We are not going to try to improve you; we have fulfilled our whole function if we help you to *see* some given tract of reality" ("Syllabus" 87). Literary study is what he was all about, keeping his students focused on the English syllabus tract of land to see what they could see.

Week by week the essays revealed what, if anything, the students had seen in their sequential study of texts from Anglo-Saxon times to 1830. When praise was warranted, Lewis gave it but often obliquely. For an average essay a student would hear, "There is something in what you say"; for a good one, "There is a good deal in what you say"; and for a still better one, "Much of that was very well said" (Bailey 81). Sometimes he buried praise and criticism in an epitaph: "Here lies Nolly Goldsmith, for shortness called Noll, / Who wrote like an angel, and talked like poor Poll" (Blamires 10).[17]

But Lewis also commended students more directly. Bailey basked for five minutes in praise over his usage of a single word in reference to Dryden's poetry: "bracing" (81). Edmonds remembers that Lewis was generous in recognizing the knowledge he brought with him to Oxford (41). Plaudits from Lewis also came in other forms and times—a critical but encouraging letter about a student's published poetry (Rook 14) and a kind word of recall: "You know, I'll always remember a very good essay you wrote on Mallory" (Blamires 10). The most charming remark went to a woman: "He told me I reminded him of a Shakespearean heroine—a compliment I've always cherished" (Cowan 62).

Now that we have seen Lewis in a noncombative mode, it should be clear that any attempt to abstract Lewis's traits from only his attack dog stance is bound to result in an incomplete and, worse yet, inaccurate viewpoint. Fortunately, his students, as a whole, have not made that mistake. They have discovered in him qualities other than verbal pugnaciousness and therefore can describe him as magnanimous, cheerful, genial, witty, interesting, kind, courteous, friendly, encouraging, super hospitable, gentle, even tender, jovial, and shy.

46

Lewis Gave Directions

On a spectrum numbered from one to ten and labeled "Directions to Students," Lewis would fall close to the low end. That he did not hand out a syllabus is understandable because until the copy machine became standard office equipment, syllabi were uncommon. But he did not even distribute a general reading list, much less one of recommended books. He was adamant in his opposition to educators who had the temerity to think they could and should choose "the best books" for English school students. Lewis believed in turning them loose:

> In the great rough countryside which we throw open to you, you can choose your own path. Here's your gun, your spade, your fishing tackle; go and get yourself a dinner. Do not tell me that you would sooner have a nice composite *menu* of dishes from half the world drawn up for you. You are too old for that. It is time you learned to wrestle with nature for yourself. ("Syllabus" 93)

Just how well Lewis carried out this philosophy in making weekly assignments can be seen in a student's reenactment. As Harry Blamires and Lewis are wrapping up a tutorial on the Romantic period, Lewis asks:

> "What about Sir Walter Scott? Would you like to tackle Scott?"
> "Yes."
> "Have you read any Scott?"
> "Well, I read *The Talisman* at school."
> "Yes, well, that's much. Let me recommend *Waverley, Old Mortality, Guy Mannering, The Heart of Midlothian, The Bride of Lammermoor*, don't miss that. *Rob Roy* is good, if you've time. *Redgauntlet* and perhaps *The Chronicles of Canongate*. Lockhart, of course, you must have a look at the biography. And bring me an essay next week." (8)

Before students left on vacation, Lewis pointed them toward the pleasures of leisure. For two who were meeting in tandem, he rattled off (from memory) the titles of twenty or thirty Elizabethan and Jacobean plays that they might read during one rather brief Christmas break. Noting that the men rolled their eyes, Lewis laughed heartily. The titles were only "suggestions" (Brewer 50).

How Lewis gave directions reveals the most pointed application of his educational philosophy. Weekly, he opened the huge iron gates to over ten centuries of great and not-so-great English literature. Inasmuch as Lewis regarded his tutorial students as adults, who no longer needed the shaping of a schoolmaster, he saw no reason to impose order on their research nor even to prepare them specifically for the comprehensives. As students rambled around the past, eventually they would come to an understanding of the people living there and gain a feeling for the times. He believed that by studying the past, not by speculating about the future, students could make some sense of the present. For those who had decided to pursue a career in learning, their literary explorations would become habitual. Lewis rather grudgingly acknowledged that not every student yearned for the scholar's life. For those who had other ambitions, their literary study would still be worthwhile because it would have lifted them out of their provincialism and enabled them to discover "what varieties there are in Man" ("English Doomed?" 29).

Some Benefits of Studying with Lewis

For however long they studied with Lewis, what do his students say they gained? Even when they do not address this matter directly—after all, their accounts are reminiscences rather than answers to the same questions—the students give the impression that they value their time with him. "Lewis was undoubtedly the most powerful and informative influence of my whole life up to that point," assesses Tynan (4). Giving a more specific reply, Bailey credits Lewis with teaching him to write for the ear, not the eye (82). Lawlor, who battled with Lewis week after week for three years, looks back: "I count it the greatest good fortune to have sorted out my intellectual equipment . . . under his vigilant and genial eye" (77). Then there is Bradshaw who says that Lewis "taught me little that directly increased my appreciation of literature . . ." (25). Yet Lewis "prepared me excellently to see that Christianity was not only a reasonable system of belief but probably the *only* reasonable one" (23–24). It was Lewis, says Edmonds, who gave him a deep love for Anglo-Saxon literature, "a 'romantic passion' for Arthurian legend . . . ; a great love of Spenser and Milton; an even greater love of Wordsworth" (48). Claiming that for her Lewis was a good and great man, Berry adds that "to have been taught by him has been one of the greatest privileges of my life" (70). Lewis would have accepted negative comments with courtesy and the positive ones with gratitude (he even thanked children for saying they liked his stories), but no doubt he would have found greatest satisfaction in knowing that students, while exploring the literary terrain, had fallen in love with it.

48

Conclusion

To some extent this chapter has attempted to discover "what varieties there are" in C. S. Lewis the tutor and lecturer. Mainly, we have relied on firsthand accounts from his students. They relate how their brilliant, disciplined, hard-working tutor, who was housed in an impressive building and a clumsy body, used his argumentation skills to challenge his students into clearing their heads and perfecting their expression. Still remembering the impact of his public address, they help us picture the throngs in the Examination Schools where Lewis's lectures on literature attracted more than literature lovers. We have heard from those who survived his high expectations, adroit questioning, and overpowering logic. The survivors who looked deeply into his persona found the contrasts that are a part of their depiction and should be of ours. As one describes him, he was "courteous yet harsh; gentle, yet a 'butcher'; arrogant, obsessive about his own pride, yet humble; sensuous yet puritanical; learned yet ordinary; magnanimous yet limited; sympathetic yet intolerant; wise yet blind; simple but complicated . . ." (Bradshaw 26).

It has been rightly said, "To teach is to touch a life forever." For most teachers, however, that influence is diminished by their retirement and certainly by their death. C. S. Lewis is a notable exception. Through his voluminous writings and those about him, as well as the enthusiasm of his fans and professional publicists, new students are constantly being added to his tutorial roster. More remarkably, Lewis is teaching across several disciplines, the generations, and the world.

Notes

1. A delightful, instructive anthology showing the attractions—and distractions—of Oxford from 1200–1945 is that of Jan Morris. See Morris, *The Oxford Book of Oxford*.

2. Stephen Schofield offers his explanation of why Lewis was never granted a professorship at Oxford. See "Oxford Loses a Genius."

3. For Lewis's account of his Oxford schedule in 1931, see *Letters* 144–45.

4. Warren Lewis says his brother's suite was on the first floor (*Letters* 15). What the British call the first floor, Americans regard as the second. For an excellent, wide-lens view of New Buildings, see Coren 33.

5. For a discussion on stereotypical responses to body types, see Richmond, McCroskey, and Payne 29–31. Rigby 38–39 describes how Lewis's body type and appearance gave both true and false clues about him.

6. For Lewis at 40, see Coren 2; for him at 60, see Gilbert and Kilby 64.

7. These categories are adapted from a descriptive study of forensic coaching. Justification for using the study in this chapter rests on the similarities between Lewis's tutorials and forensic coaching. Both require the student to find sources, read widely, compile notes, write an original composition, and present the work orally for the educator's criticism. See Keefe, "Verbal Interactions."

8. Brewer, who kept a diary, presents some of Lewis's specific topics and remarks. See 48–50.

9. To help students understand Old English, which they would need to unlock *Beowulf*, Lewis held Beer and Beowulf Evenings. See Hooper 749 and Edmonds 44–45.

10. McKeachie et al. 53–70 summarize the research findings on the lecture method of teaching and suggest applications thereof.

11. A photograph of the college Hall, with its sixteenth-century paneling, can be seen in Brooke, Highfield, and Swaan 87.

12. Hooper 779–80 provides information about extant recordings of Lewis.

13. For negative opinion about his lecturing, see Rook 13 and Lawlor's remarks in Futch 4.

14. Brewer recorded in his diary that on 1 March 1946 the tutorial had been dull and less than an hour long. Both conditions were unusual. He draws a causal link to Lewis's cold (48).

15. For a hypothetical Socratic dialogue between C. S. Lewis, John F. Kennedy, and Aldous Huxley (all three died on 22 November 1963), see Kreeft.

16. See *Letters* 90 for a humorous account of how Lewis, by asking a series of questions, pinned down a student vying for a classical scholarship.

17. The transcription is printed here with corrections by Professor Blamires to accurately reflect his own statement as well as the sally originally found in Boswell's *Life of Johnson*.

Works Cited

Bailey, George. "In the University." Keefe, *Speaker* 79–92.

Bayley, Peter. "From Master to Colleague." Como 77–86.

Berry, Patricia (Thomson). "Part B: With Women at College." Schofield, *Search* 67–70.

Blamires, Harry. Interview with Lyle W. Dorsett. Wheaton, IL. 23 Oct. 1983. Tapescript Marion E. Wade Collection. Wheaton College, Wheaton, IL.

Bradshaw, Norman. "Impressions of a Pupil." Schofield, *Search* 17–27.

Brewer, Derek. "The Tutor: A Portrait." Como 41–67.

Brooke, Christopher, Roger Highfield, and Wim Swaan. *Oxford and Cambridge*. Cambridge: Cambridge UP, 1988.

Como, James T., ed. *C. S. Lewis at the Breakfast Table and Other Reminiscenses.* New ed. San Diego: Harcourt Brace Jovanovich, 1992.

Coren, Michael. *The Man Who Created Narnia: The Story of C. S. Lewis*. Grand Rapids: Eerdmans, 1994.

Cowan, Rosamund. "Part A: With Women at College." Schofield, *Search* 61–66.

"Don v. Devil." *Time* 8 Sept. 1947: 65+.

Edmonds, E. L. "C. S. Lewis, the Teacher." Schofield, *Search* 37–51.

Fryer, W. R. "Disappointment at Cambridge?" Schofield, *Search* 29–35.

Futch, Ken. "Notes from Oxford." *The Lamp-Post of the Southern California C. S. Lewis Society* 2.3 (1978): 4–5.

Gilbert, Douglas, and Clyde S. Kilby. *C. S. Lewis: Images of His World*. Grand Rapids: Eerdmans, 1973.

Green, Roger Lancelyn, and Walter Hooper. *C. S. Lewis: A Biography*. New York: Harcourt, 1974.

Hart, Dabney A. Letter to Thomas L. Martin. 30 Sept. 1996. Marion E. Wade Collection. Wheaton College, Wheaton, IL.

Hooper, Walter. *C. S. Lewis: A Companion and Guide*. San Francisco: Harper San Francisco, 1996.

Keefe, Carolyn. "Notes on Lewis's Voice." Keefe, *Speaker* 131–36.

——. "Verbal Interactions in Coaching the Oral Interpretation of Poetry." *National Forensic Association Journal* 3.1 (1985): 55–69.

——, ed. *C. S. Lewis: Speaker and Teacher*. Grand Rapids: Zondervan, 1971.

Kreeft, Peter. *Between Heaven and Hell: A Dialogue Somewhere beyond Death with John F. Kennedy, C. S. Lewis and Aldous Huxley*. Downers Grove: InterVarsity, 1982.

Lawlor, John. "The Tutor and the Scholar." *Light on C. S. Lewis*. Ed. Jocelyn Gibb. New York: Harcourt, 1965. 67–85.

Lewis, C. S. "Is English Doomed?" *Present Concerns*. Ed. Walter Hooper. New York: Harcourt Brace Jovanovich, 1986. 27–31.

——. *The Four Loves*. New York: Harcourt, 1960.

——. *Letters of C. S. Lewis*. Ed. W. H. Lewis. New York: Harcourt, 1966.

——. "Our English Syllabus." *Rehabilitations and Other Essays*. 1939. Freeport, NY: Books for Libraries, 1972. 81–93.

——. *Surprised by Joy: The Shape of My Early Life*. New York: Harcourt, 1955.

——. *They Stand Together: The Letters of C. S. Lewis to Arthur Greeves (1914–1963)*. Ed. Walter Hooper. New York: Macmillan, 1979.

Lewis, W. H., *Brothers and Friends: The Diaries of Major Warren Hamilton Lewis*. Ed. Clyde S. Kilby and Marjorie Lamp Mead. San Francisco: Harper, 1982.

Mathew, Gervase. "Orator." Como 96–97.

McKeachie, Wilbert, J., et al. *Teaching Tips: Strategies, Research, and Theory for College and University Teachers*. 9th ed. Lexington, MA: Heath, 1994.

Morris, Jan, ed. *The Oxford Book of Oxford*. Oxford: Oxford UP, 1978.

Moynihan, Martin. "C. S. Lewis." *The Canadian C. S. Lewis Journal* 90 (Autumn 1996): 8–11.

——, and Monica Moynihan. Interview with Lyle W. Dorsett. Wimbledon, Eng. 24 July 1984. Tapescript Marion E. Wade Collection. Wheaton College, Wheaton, IL.

Richmond, Virginia P., James C. McCroskey, and Steven K. Payne. *Nonverbal Behavior in Interpersonal Relations*. 2nd ed. Englewood Cliffs, NJ: Prentice Hall, 1991.

Rigby, Luke. "A Solid Man." Como 38–40.

Rook, Alan. "The Butcher." Schofield, *Search* 11–15.

Routley, Erik. "A Prophet." Como 33–37.

Sayer, George. Interview with Lyle W. Dorsett. Wheaton, IL. 10 and 12 Oct. 1989. Tapescript Marion E. Wade Collection. Wheaton College, Wheaton, IL.

——. *Jack: A Life of C. S. Lewis*. 2nd ed. Wheaton, IL: Crossway, 1994.

Schofield, Stephen, ed. *In Search of C. S. Lewis*. South Plainfield, NJ: Bridge, 1983.

——. "Oxford Loses a Genius." Schofield, *Search* 147–55.

Scott, Anne. Interview with Jerry Root. Oxford, Eng. 8 June 1988. Tapescript Marion E. Wade Collection. Wheaton College, Wheaton, IL.

Sherwood, Jennifer, and Nikolaus Pevsner. *The Buildings of England: Oxfordshire*. 1974. Baltimore: Penguin, 1975.

Tynan, Kenneth. "Part B: Exhilaration." Schofield, *Search* 3–9.

Wain, John. "A Great Clerke." Como 68–76.

——. "C. S. Lewis." *The American Scholar* 50 (Winter 1980–81): 73–80.

51

3
Classical Literature

P. Andrew Montgomery

ogne parte ad ogne parte splende
[each part shines on every other part]

Dante, *Inferno* 7.75

Whether writing toward a scholarly, imaginative, didactic, or personal end, C. S. Lewis consistently displays a vast comprehension of Western literature and thought. But he is rarely, *if ever*, considered a classical scholar. Is it appropriate to place another burden on him and demand that he now, as *caducifer*, lead us on a downward journey, like Hermes, to explore the rich literary deposits of the Greek and Roman worlds? Indeed, I believe that Lewis offers the reader many valuable insights into what is the foundation of Western literature, the classics. However, in order to answer this question we must first determine the extent to which the classical world has shaped Lewis's own thinking, for a guide must know the terrain. His own great love of the literature and his methodologies as a scholar and writer can then perhaps inspire us to read the classics and model reading protocols for us as we embark upon that journey.

An Ancient Alphabet: The Classics and Lewis's Literary Education

Lewis initially had some difficulty finding an academic position. In 1922 he unsuccessfully interviewed for a temporary position as a classical lecturer at University College, Reading. In July of that year, after learning he had not been offered the position, he wrote to his father:

> For geographical reasons I had hoped this would combine—by means of a season ticket—the diplomatic or "advertisement" advantages of keeping in touch with Oxford with the advantages of a salary. This however turned out to be impossible. As well pure classics is not my line. I told them quite frankly, and they gave the job to some one else. (*Letters* 79)

Two observations emerge from his remarks. First, although Lewis's scholarly interests overlapped the classics, those interests were broader than, or perhaps derivative from, the realm of "pure classics." A vast area of study, the classics encompasses two great Mediterranean cultures, Greece and Rome, and spans the millennium beginning with the rise of Greek literacy in the eighth century B.C. and continuing to the third or fourth century A.D. when the literary genius of pagan Rome began to wane and Christian literary efforts exerted an increasing influence upon the Mediterranean world. (Certainly, to catalogue the significant classical authors would exceed the scope of this essay, though we will meet several in these pages.) As vast as classical studies are, Lewis chafed at the boundaries imposed upon a *pure* classicist. Second, his nomination for the position at Reading suggests that his academic training would have enabled him to devote himself to a career in classics had he been inclined to do so. We do not know for certain why Lewis did not get this position, but we do have his comments to his father that he likely biased the process by indicating that he did not see himself as a classicist.[1]

What training in classics did Lewis receive? Even prior to being sent off for his formal education, he learned French and Latin from his mother. This education was continued at a succession of schools. *Surprised by Joy* offers glimpses of what a classical education in Edwardian England was like. At Malvern, Mr. Smewgy, one of two teachers whom Lewis looked back upon with appreciation from his boyhood days, first inspired him to love classical literature as literature:

> In those days a boy on the classical side officially did almost nothing but classics. I think this was wise; the greatest service we can do to education today is to teach fewer subjects. No one has time to do more than a very few things well before he is twenty, and when we force a boy to be a mediocrity in a dozen subjects we destroy his standards, perhaps for life. Smewgy taught us Latin and Greek, but everything else came in incidentally. The books I liked best under his teaching were Horace's Odes, Aeneid IV, and Euripides *Bacchae*. I had always in one sense "liked" my classical work, but hitherto this had only been the pleasure that everyone feels in mastering a craft. Now I tasted the classics as poetry. (112–13)[2]

53

By the time he reached the most formative period of his education at Bookham, he had already learned to read both Latin and Greek.

At Bookham, under the private tutelage of William T. Kirkpatrick, the "Great Knock," Lewis's classical education intensified. His first day of instruction began with Homer, a name which "struck awe into [his] soul" (140). Kirk's pedagogical method might best be described as language acquisition through reading. Providing very little instruction in the grammar, he would recite a passage of Homer in Greek, translate the passage, offer a few explanations, and then set Lewis to work reading the passage on his own. Lewis records that the curious method of instruction worked. Though it was difficult at first, Lewis progressed in the language. Soon he was reading beyond the assigned passage and even began to process the Greek without mentally translating the passage into English, crossing "the great Rubicon" in his classical education (140–41).

Homer was the beginning, and this is fitting because Homer himself stands at the beginning of Greek, indeed of European, literature: "Day after day and month after month we drove gloriously onward, tearing out the whole *Achilleid* out of the *Iliad* and tossing the rest on one side, and then reading the *Odyssey* entire, till the music of the thing and the clear, bitter brightness that lives in almost every formula had become a part of me" (145). In addition to Homer, Kirkpatrick directed Lewis through oratory (Demosthenes and Cicero), philosophy (Lucretius), history (Tacitus and Herodotus), Roman poetry (Catullus and Virgil), tragedy (Euripides, Sophocles, and Aeschylus), and composition lessons in both Greek and Latin (144).[3]

Strongly grounded in the classics by Kirkpatrick, he continued in his studies at Oxford taking up "Mods," a curriculum focusing on Greek and Latin texts. His diary and correspondence during this time are sprinkled with the authors, titles, and subject matter related to classics on which he was working. In a letter to Arthur Greeves, his lifelong friend from Ireland, he wrote that in his university studies, "I am reading as fast [as] I can & am more than half way through the Iliad. I have to read all Homer, all Virgil, all Demosthenes & all Cicero, besides four Greek plays[4] and a special subject instead of verse. I think in my case it will be Logic, but I am not quite sure" (*Stand* 246–47).[5]

We can observe both the influence this reading had on the development of his own thoughts and the way his personal experiences related to the literary territories he explored. Although names like Euripides and Lucretius mean very little to the modern reader (and perhaps the same thing could be said even for the average reader of Lewis's day), at critical points in the development of his own thought and beliefs, the influence of such authors is demonstrable. On the one hand, Lucretius was an influential literary companion to Lewis as he left Christianity behind for the atheism of his adolescence. And it is no wonder that Lucretius appealed to Lewis then. *De Rerum Natura* is a didactic work championing Epicurean philosophy and Democritean atom-ism to a Roman audience using dactylic hexameter. Its sophisticated subject matter, often concerned with correcting the lies of religion with the philoso-phy of Epicurus, is matched by the beauty of masterful poetry.[6] In looking back at this time of his life, Lewis notes that the faith he had experienced as a younger boy was one borne out of fear. He reports being "egged on by Shaw and Voltaire and Lucretius with his *Tantum religio*" to exaggerate the role that fear played in his life of faith. Lucretius's "meaningless dance of atoms" held out the hope that there would be no continuation of the pain and fear of pun-ishment in an afterlife. Human life itself, being composed of nothing more than atoms, would be dissolved. The Lucretian model of the universe had what the Christian model did not: a door with an exit sign, a way out (*Surprised* 171–73).

Just as Lewis found a classical author to identify with as he embraced athe-ism, so another classical author played an important role in Lewis's life as he renounced atheism for theism. When he returned as a student to Oxford after the First World War, he began to adopt a "New Look," an intellectual position that rejected pessimism, yet which found no recourse in supernaturalism or romanticism (201). However, a number of important factors combined at that time to undermine this New Look, especially the conversion of his friend Owen Barfield. An "Adversary" was stalking him. As the underpinnings of the New Look began to disintegrate, he reread the *Hippolytus* of Euripides. Faced with the argument in one chorus, he was unable to ward off the conviction that the New Look was but an intellectual desert; his posture had merely been "a long inhibition." As he recalls it, the voice of his "Adversary" spoke through Euripi-des. "I had simply been ordered—or, rather compelled—to 'take that look off my face.' And never to resume it either" (217). Though this does not record his conversion to theism or subsequently to Christianity, it marks a watershed in his intellectual and spiritual development. It illustrates the important role that literature, in particular classical literature, played in shaping not only his academic life, but the whole of his outlook and character.

Although Lewis had the training to become a classicist, his broader inter-ests prevented the classics, strictly speaking, from becoming the primary focus of his scholarly pursuits. The classics were, for Lewis and many young people of his day, the foundation of a liberal arts education. It became for Lewis a kind of alphabet by which he learned to read the rest of literature. From an early age he read both broadly and extensively, permitting no artificial bound-aries between one epoch or another, or between one genre and another, to confine him. His years as a student at Oxford attest to this fact. He read three separate curricula, Mods, Greats, and English, receiving a First Class in each. Between his own personal reading and his academic training, he canvassed

55

almost the entirety of Western literature. This breadth enabled him to appreciate fully both the development and coherence of European literature.

An Ancient Heritage: The Classics and Lewis's Understanding of Western Literature

Although it is possible to concentrate upon an individual work, author, or even generation, Lewis would consider it merely one strand in a great tapestry. Beautiful in its own right, the individual strand is also part of something greater. Hence, if you take it out and isolate it from the whole, something is lost; both the whole and the part suffer. To fully appreciate the strand is to see it as part of a larger pattern, properly recontextualized.[7] Lewis stresses this point on the occasion of accepting the chair of Medieval and Renaissance studies at Cambridge:

> The field "Medieval and Renaissance" is already far too wide for my powers. But you see how to me the appointed area must primarily appear as a specimen of something far larger, something which had already begun with the *Iliad* and was still almost unimpaired when Waterloo was fought. Of course within that immense period there are all sorts of differences. There are lots of convenient differences between the area I am to deal with and other areas; there are important differences within the chosen area. And yet—despite all this—the whole thing, from its Greek or pre-Greek beginnings down to the day before yesterday, seen from a vast distance at which we stand today, reveals a homogeneity that is certainly important and perhaps more important than its interior diversities. That is why I shall be unable to talk to you about my particular region without constantly treating things which neither began with the Middle Ages nor ended with the end of the Renaissance. ("*Temporum*" 11–12)

Considering Lewis's understanding of the nature of Western literature itself (as much as his particular training in classical languages and literature), we can determine whether Lewis is a fit guide for our own reading. For Lewis would insist that it is impossible to read a writer such as Dante, Spenser, or Milton without a consideration of his literary forebears. Similarly, he would position Homer or Virgil within a continuum which perseveres long after them. Their themes and craft, informing shared human experience, endure, affecting and being affected by their successors. In *Surprised*, he rephrases the point: "Plainly it does not matter at what point you first break into the system of European poetry. Only keep your ears open and your mouth shut and everything will lead to you to everything else in the end—*ogni parte ad ogni parte splende*" (53).

Thus, when Lewis remarks that he will be unable to confine himself to the strict boundaries of the medieval and Renaissance periods, he simply verbalizes a methodology already implicit throughout his writings. This methodology—this crossing from one period to another and to another—so pervades his writing that it becomes part of the rhythm of his thought. The rhythm, however, does not distract from his purpose at hand, but rather augments it. For example, in a lecture on the meaning of "membership" within the body of Christ, the church, he begins by disputing the notion that people can relegate the Christian religion to their private lives. Paradoxically, Lewis observes, social pressures confine religious expression to private life while they minimize the solitude which nourishes spirituality and individuality. He illustrates his point, drawing from the resources of Western literature: "If a really good home, such as the home of Alcinous and Arete in the *Odyssey* or the Rostovs in *War and Peace* or any of Charlotte M. Yonge's families, existed today, it would be denounced as *bourgeois* and every engine of destruction would be leveled against it" (*Glory* 31). Here within a single sentence he gathers together both ends of Western literature (from Homer at the remote beginnings to the nineteenth century) and three separate cultures (Greek, Russian, and English). Despite the many differences among these works, the shared values make it appropriate to unite them. Such grouped allusions are commonplace in Lewis and encapsulate both the comprehensiveness of his literary knowledge and the knack he possessed for appreciating its unity amidst its diversity. I could enumerate many other examples of this sort (indeed, any study along those lines would illuminate the breadth and rich allusiveness of his mind). I include this particular allusion, though, to show that Lewis almost instinctively crossed boundaries of time, place, and culture to illustrate the deeper, more fundamental unity that underlies literary history. After reading Lewis, one puzzles at how certain critical theorists can remain so insistent about the inscrutability of the literary past.[8] Lewis characteristically oversteps these boundaries not only in something as simple as tying allusions together, as illustrated above, but also in his scholarly studies of texts and authors, as will be discussed below.

Lewis, as guide to the literature of ancient Greece and Rome, would not view that distant age as something foreign and discrete from our own experience. He believes the past lives, its voice resounding through each generation, even to the dawn of our own age. Since each generation joins its voice to the chorus, examining any particular voice offers one ample opportunity to hear the voice of the others. By considering other authors and their relationship to the past, Lewis invites us into the world of classical literature. Thus it should come as no surprise that we must meet him, for example, in Milton's seventeenth-century England in order to follow him deep into the first millennium before Christ.

Time-Honored Forms: The Classics and Lewis's Scholarly Methodology

His *Preface to "Paradise Lost"* begins with the premise that to understand the reasons Milton chose the epic literary form as opposed to lyric or tragedy is to understand the poem aright. In order to elucidate the nature of the epic for modern readers, Lewis offers a "biography of the literary kind" (8), beginning with Homer,[9] and provides a vivid picture of culture in ancient Greece.[10]

He first notes that all ancient poetry is meant to be recited orally[11] to an audience rather than read silently by a reader (18). Until we grasp this concept, which is foreign to the contemporary reader, the wonder and beauty of ancient epic cannot be fully appreciated. It is this orality which shapes the diction, as well as the structure, of the entire work. The repetition of stock words, phrases, and similar scenes may at first seem to be a curiosity, perhaps even quaint, to the modern reader. It makes sense, however, within the context of oral composition and performance.

Lewis counters a potential objection—that the stock formulae of epic are somehow crutches "on which the poets fall back when inspiration fails them" (20)—by directing us to consider what it is like to hear epic poetry performed. The audience of epic poetry must literally *hear* the work to appreciate it. The modern literary audience approaches the epic with different expectations:

> A line which gives the listener pause is a disaster in oral poetry because it makes him lose the next line. And even if he does not lose the next, the rare and ebullient line is not worth making. In the sweep of recitation *no* individual line is going to count for very much. The pleasure which moderns chiefly desire from printed poetry is ruled out anyway. You cannot ponder over single lines and let them dissolve on the mind like lozenges. That is the wrong way of using this sort of poetry. It is not built up of isolated effects; the poetry is in the paragraph, or the whole episode. To look for single, "good" lines is like looking for single "good" stones in a cathedral. (21)

Lewis explains that rather than cheapen the artistic effect of the poetry, the stock formulae enhance it in three ways. First they provide the bard a structure upon which to develop his story. Second, by using the ready-made, the bard releases the formulae's store of human experience. In fact, when the bard invokes the muse to sing through him, he taps precisely this potential stored within the poetic devices. Finally, the poetic formulae aid the audience by introducing the familiarity of ritual, which is distinct from day-to-day existence. It uses "a language which is familiar because it is used in every part of every poem, but unfamiliar because it is not used outside poetry" (21–22). But what does the Homeric audience hear? How does this language shape the

Homeric world? Indeed, what is the Homeric world that Lewis invites us to experience?

Lewis's answer to the last question is simply that the reader of Homer reads about the world as it really is with no hint of romanticism. The poetic diction with its panoply of stock phrases, epithets, and other structural formulae creates this effect. Over and over the reader hears the voice of the muse in the repetition of such formulae as *wine-dark sea, rosy-fingered dawn, Poseidon shaker of earth.* The rhythm of the repetition creeps into the heart and mind of the audience, underscoring the reality we all experience. "The sonorous syllables in which he has stereotyped the sea, the gods, the morning, or the mountains make it appear that we are dealing not with poetry about the things, but almost with the things themselves" (25).

An unchanging world indifferent to mortal affairs, a world devoid of ultimate meaning, a world unmoved by human tragedy or triumph backlights Homer's stories. The story of the *Iliad*, as Lewis sees it, "is a purely personal story—that of Achilles' wrath, suffering, repentance, and killing of Hector. About the fall of Troy, Homer has nothing to say, save incidentally" (29). Indeed, the poet emphasizes his theme by making "wrath" the first word of the Greek text. This wrath of Achilles confines the Greek army under the walls of Troy; and the plot of the story turns on the questions of when and whether his wrath will be assuaged and ultimately how it metamorphoses into the raging wrath which destroys not only Hector, but also himself. Lewis concludes that the greatness of the Homeric epic lies "in the human and personal tragedy built up against this background of meaningless flux" (31). There is no meaning to be gleaned from the human suffering. There is merely suffering. "Only the style—the unwearying, unmoved, angelic speech of Homer—makes it endurable. Without that the *Iliad* would be a poem beside which the grimmest modern realism is child's play."[12]

In *Preface*, Lewis has directed us to Milton's generic precursors. Although Lewis ostensibly seeks to illuminate Milton, he does precisely with Homer what he wants us to do with Milton by reaching beyond the limitations imposed by our experience into another culture. Lewis seeks to enhance our experience of the poetry by helping us to hear Homer as an ancient Greek audience would have heard and experienced him.[13] We are to do likewise with Milton. Of the many available readings of the *Iliad*, modern students of Homer would have to go a long way to find a better entrée into the story.[14]

As Lewis makes a transition from Primary Epic to Secondary Epic[15] in *Preface*, we must prepare ourselves to step from the Homeric world to the Roman world—that is, the Roman world envisioned by Virgil's great and revolutionary epic, the *Aeneid*. Many Roman authors before Virgil attempted to write a Roman epic. Homer was, to varying degrees, their model; in fact, Ennius claimed to be the reincarnation of Homer in his *Annales*, and Ennius's innovation—using the Greek epic meter, the dactylic hexameter, in place of the Roman Saturnian verse—is an important step in the development of Roman literature. Lewis describes the pre-Virgilian Roman epics as "metrical chronicles" to indicate that their subject matter records vast sweeps of Roman history (33). Their focus on the big picture reveals an important difference between the Roman and Greek minds: the Romans were obsessed with the greatness of Rome, which did not arise in the flash of a brilliant generation or one noteworthy leader. Rome emerged over a long period of time, and that slow process demands a view very different from the timeless and apathetic Nature of the Homeric poems. If Rome is a nation of destiny, Time and Cosmos are agents to actualize this destiny. The Roman authors vested history itself with meaning. The literary failings of the early Roman epic writers, inasmuch as we can surmise based on the fragmentary remains, is that their canvas is too broad. While Homer had told the story of an individual, the Roman authors tell the story of a nation.[16]

Consequently, Virgil faced the same problem as he prepared to write the Roman epic; he achieved greatness by transforming the literary art of epic—a genre in decline for many generations—into something much different from what it was in Homer's time. Lewis explains:

> His solution . . . was to take one single national legend and treat it in such a way that we feel the vaster theme to be somehow implicit in it. He has to tell a comparatively short story and give us the illusion of having lived through a great space of time. He has to deal with a limited number of personages and make us feel as if national, or almost cosmic issues are involved. He must locate his action in a legendary past and yet make us feel the present, and the intervening centuries, already foreshadowed. After Virgil and Milton, this procedure seems obvious enough. But it is obvious only because a great poet, faced with all but an insoluble problem, discovered this answer and with it discovered new possibilities for poetry itself. (34)

Virgil chose to tell the story of Rome through the story of Aeneas, "Arms and the man I sing. . . ." But how, Lewis asks, will Virgil evoke the present in the past, the national and cosmic interests wrapped up in the remnant fugitive band from Troy? Lewis identifies three techniques. In the first place, Virgil elicits feelings of the expanse of time: the significance of the past and the inevitability of the future in the lives of Aeneas and his men. Second, and related to this, Virgil sensitizes the audience to the transition from one world order to another, events so momentous they permit no retreat into the past while simultaneously molding the future. And finally, Virgil unites these in a hero who has a sense of vocation and duty. From the very opening verses of the *Aeneid*, Virgil unfolds his story over both time and space. Beginning *in medias res*, Virgil intimates the significant past, the remnant fleeing Troy, while before them gapes the future. They hover between the two. The opening verses, Lewis notes, contain many of Virgil's techniques for bringing future and past into the *now* of the story. For example, the narrator invokes Troy, Italy, and Carthage within a few verses. The mention of Troy recalls a seemingly distant past from which the survivors flee not only the destruction of Troy, but also the wrath of Juno, which bears down on them, imperiling their call to found Rome. The coasts of Italy shimmer in the distant future, yet Aeneas and his men must, by destiny, fulfill their vocation. And Carthage intervenes, a future enemy and a present obstacle. This technique, established at the beginning, structures the Virgilian poem much as the continual repetition of formulae underlies the Homeric poems.

Though prevalent and forceful, this technique does not stand alone. Lewis considers a mark of Virgil's genius that he combines the technique with a sense of progress found in those "moments at which we realize that we have just turned some great corner, and that everything, for better or worse, will always henceforth be different" (36). In order for Aeneas to become the founder of Rome, he must leave Troy behind and overcome all obstacles. Throughout the poem Virgil stresses that a great transition is underway: Aeneas, the ghost of Troy, becomes the father of Rome. Lewis comments that the reader is made to feel this change in many ways, sometimes even imperceptibly: "the old Aegean hatreds have slipped far enough behind for *crafty Ulysses* to become *unfortunate Ulysses*." Scenes abound in which the past blurs, fades, and disappears, until, finally, the great shift from East to West concludes.

Were Aeneas a character similar to Homer's Achilles, Lewis observes, this great transition could never occur. Achilles may have been a character of great passion and bravery, but in comparison with Aeneas he is "little more than a passionate boy" (37). No character of Achilles's type could rise to the occasion required by the *Aeneid*. A man, rather than boy, Aeneas possesses a keen sense of calling laid on him by the decree of Jove. Unlike Greek heroes, he sees beyond the timeless present and apathetic Nature and hears the voice calling him to a distant shore; indeed, he obeys, driven by a sense of duty, a servant of something greater and nobler. Aeneas exemplifies what it means to be a Roman. Lewis's *Preface* continues from this point, leaving the classical precedents behind; but it first notes that in Virgil the epic genre matures much like the central character of his epic matures. It is no longer what it once was in Homer, nor can it ever return to that. As Lewis observes, "Any return to the *merely* heroic, any lay, however good, that tells merely of brave men fighting to save their lives or to get home or to avenge their kinsmen, will now be an anachronism. You cannot be young twice" (39).

Thus, Lewis's biography of epic leads to the threshold of a discussion of the Miltonic epic, but that door must remain shut to this essay. The aim here has not been specifically to follow the winding of that argument to its conclusion,

61

but rather to see in one small way how Lewis, the scholar who was early trained in the classics, but whose interests directed his career away from "pure" classics, nevertheless *considered the classics as integral to his work as a literary scholar.* The aim has also been to show how in the *Preface* his use of this era might help us, in turn, to appreciate both the classics as well as the whole of Western literature. A standard feature of his reading is to examine the classical precedents of the work in question. Examples are readily apparent from his other works as well. In chapter 3 of *The Discarded Image* Lewis traces classical sources of the medieval model of the cosmos in The Dream of Scipio, in Lucan, Statius, and Apuleius. In "Dante's Similes" and "Dante's Statius" (contained in *Studies in Medieval and Renaissance Literature*), Lewis works with classical models found in Dante. However, Lewis's scholarly methodology does not exhaust the ways in which he draws upon the classical heritage of Western literature. Quite the contrary, the echoes of its allusions reverberate throughout his writings, not only providing material to the scholar, but also giving shape and substance to his creative mind. The perceptive reader of Lewis's imaginary fiction will not fail to recognize those echoes, sometimes heard as an allusive melody working its way into Lewis's song, other times as the symphony of an ancient myth told in full.

Echoes of the Past: The Classics in Lewis's Imaginative Writing

At the close of Book Ten of Homer's *Odyssey*, the wandering hero Odysseus learns of a terrible fate awaiting him. In order to continue his homeward journey toward Ithaca, he and his men must sail into the underworld to ask directions from the dead prophet Teiresias. Thus, Homer introduces the *catabasis* to Western literature. Many a hero or heroine makes that solemn journey into the underworld in ancient myth. And as dangerous as the journey is, the return is more dangerous still. As Virgil says, *"Facilis descensus Averni . . . / Sed revocare gradum superasque evadere ad auras, / Hoc opus, hic labor est"* ("The descent to Avernus is easy. . . . But to recall your steps and escape to the upper air—this is the toil, this the labor") (*Aeneid* VI.126). Heracles makes the journey in order to bring the three-headed hound, Cerberus, back to the upper world. Demeter goes to win the release of her daughter Persephone from the underworld, but not before her abductor, Hades, tricks Persephone into eating pomegranate seeds, thereby requiring her to return to the underworld for a portion of each year.[17] Orpheus, whose bride is killed by a venomous snake, journeys to the underworld in a nearly successful attempt to lead her back to the land of the living.[18] Aeneas, retracing Odysseus's footsteps, journeys to Hades and hears his dead father, Anchises, prophesy Rome's future greatness.

Even the comic playwright Aristophanes sends the god Dionysus into the underworld to bring back Euripides to revitalize the Athenian stage. The journey to the underworld is one of the most enduring *topoi* of Western literature: it manifests itself not only as a journey to the land of the dead, but as an attempt to understand the meaning of the present life by discovering what lies beyond it. The journey also may suggest, metaphorically, any dangerous excursion into darkness and uncertainty. In the Middle Ages and Renaissance, the catabasis is assimilated by the Christian tradition. Christ the Victor descends into hell, bursts the bars of death, and leads prisoners from the infernal world. With him they are raised to new life and ascend, not merely to the terrestrial world whence they came, but to heaven.

Thus, Lewis, drawing on the fullness of this heritage in *The Silver Chair*,[19] sends his heroes, two children and a Narnian marshwiggle, into the cavernous underworld of Narnia in search of the abducted Prince Rilian. To be sure, Lewis does not simply replicate the underworld story of his ancient and medieval models; rather he suggests to our memory the aspirations, perils, and failures associated with them. Rilian, like Persephone, is abducted by an underworld potentate and held against his will. Jill, like Orpheus, is inattentive to the instructions given to aid the quest, nearly bringing an Orphic-like disaster upon the rescue mission. Finally, when the queen of the underworld assumes her true shape—that of a serpent—the heroes slay her and reascend to Narnia. In this and what follows, Lewis underscores the Christian undercurrents of the catabasis tradition. Upon returning to Narnia, Prince Rilian witnesses the death of his elderly father, King Caspian. We see that death is a catabasis for all. Then as Eustace and Jill walk together with Aslan, they come upon the dead king lying submerged in a stream. Aslan commands Eustace to draw blood from his paw with a thorn; the drops of his blood falling into the stream transform the elderly king's body into the youthful king, bringing him back to life.

At times, Lewis's classical allusions and motifs work their way into his fantasy and science fiction, occasionally structuring an entire tale. If Homer's *Iliad* is the story of one man's wrath, the *Odyssey* is the story of one man's quest for home, wandering across unfriendly seas, encountering adventures fraught with danger and seduction, yearning for a home awaiting its master to reestablish justice. In a sense, all subsequent stories of sea voyages, wanderings, and homecomings owe a debt to the *Odyssey*. The experience imbedded within the *Odyssey* resonates deeply within the human experience, finding concord with the soul's yearning for a place of rest. So, too, the voyage of King Caspian and his crew in *The Voyage of the Dawn Treader* is a quest for home. For in addition to Caspian's own hope of finding his father's seven loyal companions (whom the usurper Miraz had exiled from Narnia), the valorous Reepicheep has vowed never to return to Narnia, but to continue sailing eastward until he reaches Aslan's country. Like Odysseus, the crew visits strange islands, encountering many adventures and perils along the way. Caspian himself faces his own sirens, almost causing the crew to bind him to the mast when he threatens to abdicate his throne to join Reepicheep in his eastward journey. At the end of the tale, the children return home and Reepicheep takes his final journey across a watery horizon—reminiscent of the Norse hero buried in his ship and sailing his last journey, the classical soul arrived in the underworld and shuttling across the Styx, and the Christian believer wearied of this world and yearning to be transported to the next. In what is surely one of the most poignant scenes of the Chronicles, the stouthearted mouse prepares his coracle for sailing, flings his sword into the sea, and says good-bye to the children, "trying to be sad for their sakes; but he was quivering with happiness" (244).

Sometimes, the introduction of the classical element seems incidental, appearing unexpectedly. Bacchus—with his maenads and old Silenus in tow—bursts onto the scene in *Prince Caspian*, providing revelry, refreshment, and creative energy. The reader uninformed of Bacchus's place in literature will enjoy the lighthearted scene, but the reader mindful of his portrayal in Euripides's *Bacchae* will doubtless give some pause. Lewis's Bacchus is wild, but the darker nature of Euripides's Bacchus is merely hinted at when Susan comments, "I wouldn't have felt safe with Bacchus and all his wild girls if we'd met them without Aslan." Lucy's reply, "I should think not." And perhaps this is the point. Bacchus has been transformed, no longer the same character we find in Euripides, wild and destructive, demanding his rightful worship, but one of Earth's lords called into Aslan's service. The festivities and sensual pleasures associated with Bacchus are not in principle opposed to Aslan, but rightly come under his dominion. Lewis gives us neither a Manichaean universe where evil is eternally set against good nor a Gnostic universe where body forever wars with spirit. His world embodies the Christian ideal that whatever is true, good, noble, and virtuous is sacred and, as such, has its rightful place in God's kingdom.

At other times, the ability to understand the classical allusion is essential to the meaning of the tale. "Forms of Things Unknown" is a short story of four moon missions, three of which have taken place prior to the action of the story. Each of the three previous missions met with a mysterious end. Communication between earth and the lunar explorers was inexplicably cut off shortly after the astronauts began to describe the moonscape. As the sole astronaut of the fourth mission explores the moon's surface, he comes upon several stone statues which he recognizes as perfect replicas of astronauts. He wrongly surmises that the stone images before him are the workmanship of unknown lunar life forms. As he prepares to transmit the astonishing discovery back to earth, he sees the shadow of a human head with hair blowing in the wind.

("And what a head of hair. It was all rising, writing—swaying in the wind perhaps. Very thick the hairs looked.") Then, as he realizes that the moon has no wind, he turns. The story ends with the words, "His eyes met hers." Without a knowledge of Medusa, the Gorgo, whose gaze turns mortals to stone, the reader is left without the key to unlock the door at the end of the story.

The Past Reborn: A Classical Myth Retold

The crown of Lewis's productive literary career, *Till We Have Faces*, goes beyond the well-wrought allusion to antiquity. As the subtitle informs, the story is an extended retelling of the myth of Apuleius's Cupid and Psyche.[20] The myth captivated Lewis's imagination as early as 1917 while preparing for his entrance examinations to Oxford.[21] It is tempting to imagine its potentiality wrapping itself in a cocoon within the recesses of Lewis's soul while he was still in his youth, being transformed ever so slowly, first by his conversion and then later by the blossoming relationship to his soon-to-be wife, Joy Davidman,[22] finally emerging reborn in Lewis's retelling. Although we can only introduce the subject here, a study of the similarities and differences between Lewis's story and that of Apuleius provide insight into how mythic image—the "real though unfocused gleam of divine truth" (*Miracles* 134n)[23]—may be reenvisioned by a literary artist to illumine truths unseen in the original.
From one perspective, the mythic image of Cupid and Psyche evokes the struggle of the human soul to become divine. Love—as personified in Cupid—has the power to draw the soul from its baser tendencies toward a nobler and purer existence. From another perspective, the same image suggests the soul's *inability* to transcend its mortal existence. Apuleius's story suggests that the soul, struggling between the larger forces at work within and without, wars between sensual desire and divine love. Apuleius's story contains both.[24] One approach scholars have used to interpret *Faces* is to focus on how Lewis has transformed the Apuleian myth.[25] Indeed, this has been a productive angle and one that Lewis himself has perhaps encouraged when in a note he mentions a "central alteration" in his version, namely that he has made Psyche's palace invisible. He further claims that he has not intended to reproduce "the peculiar quality of the *Metamorphoses*," describing Apuleius as a "source" for the myth rather than a "model" (*Faces* 313). We must understand that Lewis is operating here well within the practices and expectations of even an ancient author. We should also remember that in choosing the story of Cupid and Psyche, Lewis has adopted a certain set of mythic "facts" which act as boundaries for the Cupid and Psyche story. The author retains a certain amount of freedom within these boundaries to introduce novel material and make alter-

65

ations suitable to his own end. He may at times even transgress the boundaries and "contaminate" the story. But if he wishes to tell the Cupid and Psyche story, he must generally adhere to the overall mythic scheme. It is the story which gives birth to the meaning. Thus, in Lewis's telling of the myth, we can see that he has preserved many of the basic story elements.

Where *Faces* departs from the Apuleian version is not so much in character or plot as it is in perspective, so that the plot changes are those demanded by the change in perspective. The omniscient narrator is substituted with the first-person narrator, Orual, the older sister of Psyche. The advantage Lewis gains from such a shift is his ability to focus on the nature of love and how love is transformed in the seeking soul. In Apuleius, the sisters of Psyche serve little purpose other than to persuade Psyche to look at her husband, Cupid, while he is sleeping—an act he specifically forbade. Once Psyche, acting upon the advice of her sisters, is estranged from him, the sisters are irrelevant to the story, and they pay for their jealousy with their lives. Such could not be possible in *Faces*. It is Orual's love that is of primary concern, first its tyranny and then its metamorphosis. Like Psyche in Apuleius, Orual must undergo trials. In *Faces*, however, these trials are the means by which the pretentions of her persona and her own misconceptions of love are successively stripped away, revealing to her the consuming and destructive nature of her love.

Interestingly, Lewis uses the Apuleian formulation of the myth to provide Orual with the motive for writing her story, thereby initiating her ultimate transformation. In her golden years as queen of Glome, Orual "resolved to go on a progress and travel in other lands" (237). Upon this journey she inadvertently discovers a shrine erected to her sister who has now become a minor deity, though unbeknownst to Orual. Inquiring about the identity of the deity, she hears the Apuleian account of Psyche's story from the priest. "It was as if the gods themselves had first laughed, and then spat, in my face," she writes. "So this was the shape the story had taken. You might say, the shape the gods had given it" (243). Because of the distortions of the tale—preserved for us by Apuleius—and the direct affront to her pride, Orual determines to write her complaint against the gods. Indeed, the book *is* her complaint, from its inception to resolution.

Orual's initial complaint is to accuse the gods of injustice against her. The tale, as she had heard it, promoted lies about her. Thus, by her accusation she seems intent to render the "Apuleian" myth null and void. In the end, however, this earlier myth, with its veiled references to the sisters' jealousy, tells more of the truth than lies.[26] Orual's love for Psyche had been a base and self-serving love. Slowly and painfully she realizes that her love for the Fox and Bardia had also been self-serving. *She* is Ungit—"that all-devouring, womb-like, yet barren, thing" (*Faces* 276)—a barbaric manifestation of Venus. Her complaint is at once the vehicle by which this realization is possible and the means by which her self-serving love becomes self-sacrificing love. The seeds of *Faces* lie buried within the former, awaiting a new imagination to bring them to full form.

Faces illustrates Lewis's lifelong love for classical literature in a unique way. As noted above, Lewis read the story for the first time on the eve of his entrance into Oxford while still a young man of eighteen. He wrote this, his "best book" (*Children* 73), near the end of his literary career. His own life is wrapped up with the myth: his odyssey from childhood bliss and the joys of fraternal companionship, his tutelage under a master of logic, the loss of faith, the first stirrings of his conversion, and his mature faith stripped bare of pretension. The potentiality of the myth resonated with his own experiences, enabling his literary imagination to transform the mythic image into the substance of a story. Yet even though one might (correctly) point to certain "autobiographical" elements within *Faces*—parallels between his life and Orual's—it would be wrong to minimize it with the label "autobiographical" as if he means merely to tell his own story. Quite the contrary. The tale is not one man's journey. For Lewis, it is everyman's journey. He chooses the myth precisely because it resonates in our lives as well as his own. He understands that myth often brings the deepest truths about humanity into view.

Framing a Life: The Classics a Lifelong Avocation

In the closing days of Lewis's life, classical literature remained a staple of his literary diet and even graced his conversation with friends. In a letter to D. H. Banner dated 1 November 1963—just three weeks before his death—Lewis wrote, "I am rereading the *Iliad* and enjoying it more than I have ever done" (qtd. in *Sayer* 408). What could have been his motive for reading Homer when so ill? Could it not be, as this quote suggests, for the mere pleasure that Lewis had first discovered when reading Homer under "The Great Knock"? Sayer also includes another appropriate anecdote in his biography. In the autumn prior to Lewis's death he accompanied Sayer on an afternoon's automobile tour. Enraptured by the autumnal beauty of the landscape, Lewis commingled his conversation with prayers and praise to God as well as at least one quotation, in Greek, from Plato's epitaphs (408–09). Classical literature, like his faith, formed an essential part of his being. It not only informed his work as a scholar, nor did it merely provide source material for his fiction—it lived within him. What he ingested as reader and scholar, he passed on to new generations of readers in many ways. And while he left us no body of critical writing on the "pure classics"—upon which we might make our own critical assessments—he engenders in his readers a genuine appreciation of the classics and provides valuable instruction on how to approach them. More than anything else, he would have us learn the language and history to hear the ancient voice as its audience would have heard it. And careful readers will see that his own writings capture some of that ancient quality, reverberating with thoughts and images of antiquity. Like good writers of all time, Lewis transforms the stories of the past into stories for ages to come.

Notes

1. In his biography, A. N. Wilson suggests that Lewis was indeed offered the position but turned it down (74). No evidence from the Lewis papers and other published accounts of Lewis's life corroborates this claim.

2. Through this budding appreciation for the classics, he notices that Greek mythology has a very different quality to it than the Northern mythologies. It expanded his imagination to include "something Mediterranean and volcanic, the orgiastic drum beat. Orgiastic, but not, or not strongly, erotic" (*Surprised* 113). It is another side to beauty heretofore unseen by him, and it is one which will come to play an important role in the development of his thought.

3. See also *Stand* (84–85), where Lewis outlines a typical day at this time. He says Thucydides, Homer, and Tacitus filled his morning, Plato and Horace the late afternoon between tea and supper.

4. Lewis's personal library held in the Marion E. Wade Collection, Wheaton College, Wheaton, IL, contains R. Jebb's text and commentaries of *Oedipus Tyrannus, Electra, Antigone, Ajax*. Perhaps these are the texts of tragedy he alludes to here. The publication dates of these commentary editions certainly allow for that possibility.

5. As a further example of Lewis's reading, a quick survey of his diary (published as *Road*) in April and May 1922 shows numerous references to working on Greek and Roman history, reading Aristotle, the *Republic*, Herodotus, and Thucydides.

6. Even though the Greek philosopher Epicurus had disapproved of poetry as an appropriate medium for philosophic discourse, Lucretius justifies it in order to teach the Epicurean doctrines to those unaccustomed to philosophy. He compares himself to a physician who uses honey on the rim of a cup full of bitter medicine to trick a child into taking the medicine. His object, he says, is to engage the mind with the poetry so that the reader can learn the nature of the universe. See *De Rerum Natura* I.921–50 and IV.6–25.

7. This analogy is not meant to diminish the importance of the individual work. Seen from another perspective, the individual work may be a microcosm of the larger literary universe.

8. I am thinking particularly of the new historicists, who problematize the literary past as something radically other. See, for example, Montrose and its bibliography. By way of critique, one might see Stewart and Thomas.

9. Lewis divides his discussion of Epic into Primary and Secondary Epic (*Preface to "Paradise Lost"* 13). Homer along with *Beowulf* are his illustrations of Primary Epic. The purpose of this discussion, however, is not to give a detailed analysis of *Preface*, but to extract some of his insights into classical literature. Consequently, I overlook his discussions of *Beowulf* and other topics which are found side by side with the classical epics.

10. I use the term "literary" here with some reservation as it is not, strictly speaking, appropriate. The Homeric poems are perhaps the pinnacle of a very rich and long culture of oral perform-

ance. Though they came to be written down in the eighth century B.C., they represent the genius of a preliterate society. Scholarship has only recently begun to understand, appreciate, and explore this. See following note.

11. Lewis's discussion of the orality of the Homeric poems largely overlooks the question of oral composition. However, many of Lewis's distinctions of Primary Epic anticipated some of the questions currently driving scholarship forward, namely the nature and context of performative poetry. For a thorough overview of the issues related to Homer and the oral tradition, see Foley. For a more detailed investigation into the subject, see Lord, Parry, and, more recently, Nagy. The works of Parry and Lord, based on studies of twentieth-century bards in Yugoslavia, were instrumental in proving that epic bards use many oral techniques (such as the application of stock formulaic phrases) to compose while they sing. Nagy's recent work contains an extensive and up-to-date bibliography.

12. I find it interesting to juxtapose this conclusion on Homer with an anecdote from Lewis's experiences in the first world war: "One imaginative moment seems now to matter more than the realities that followed. It was the first bullet I heard—so far from me that it 'whined' like a journalist's or peacetime poet's bullet. At that moment there was something not exactly like fear, much less like indifference: a little quavering signal that said, 'This is War. This is what Homer wrote about' " (*Surprised* 196).

13. Compare this sentiment to Lewis's statement in "*De Descriptione Temporum*": "I would give a great deal to hear any ancient Athenian, even a stupid one, talking about Greek tragedy. He would know in his bones so much that we seek in vain. At any moment some chance phrase might, unknown to him, show us where modern scholarship has been on the wrong track for years" (13).

14. A survey of readings can be found, for example, in Schein; Myrsiades; and Bremer, de Jong, and Kalff.

15. The designations of "Primary" and "Secondary" Epic are Lewis's own invention to distinguish the earlier poems from the later poems, which evolve out of the earlier. He explicitly denies any value judgments that may imply that Secondary means "second rate" (*Preface* 13).

16. In his *Poetics*, Aristotle defines epic as whole and complete action which has its own beginning, middle, and ending. Homer's story of the "Wrath of Achiles" told against the backdrop of the Trojan War fits these criteria. History, according to Aristole, differs from epic in that it treats of time rather than a single action. Thus, Lewis's designation of 'metrical chronicles' conforms to the Aristotelean definitions and underscores the problem facing the Roman writer.

17. *Hymn to Demeter* in the so-called *Homeric Hymns*.

18. See Virgil's *Georgic* 4.453 ff. and Ovid's *Metamorphoses* 10.1–11.

19. The most obvious catabasis in Lewis's fiction is, of course, *The Great Divorce*. An adequate exploration and analysis of that subject, however, are far beyond the limits of this essay. Such a study would merit a careful look not only at the catabasis tradition, but also the tradition surrounding The Dream of Scipio, certainly Dante's *Inferno*, as well as a number of more modern works.

20. For an excellent commentary of Apuleius with Latin text and English translation see Kenney. It should be noted that *Faces* is one of two mythological retellings attempted by Lewis. The other is the unfinished story, "After Ten Years," telling the story of the reunion of Menelaus and Helen. The story, following the tradition found in Stesichorus and Euripides's *Helen*, develops the idea that the real Helen did not go to Troy at all, but was whisked away to Egypt. The gods fashioned an image of Helen, the image which Paris stole to Troy and which had been the cause of the Trojan War. Lewis's story breaks off in mid-sentence right where Menelaus would have first cast his eyes upon the real Helen in Egypt.

21. See *Stand*, 158, 183–84.

22. George Sayer says that Joy played an important and intimate role in the writing of *Faces*. She helped him develop the original idea and read and critiqued it as it was written (*Jack* 361).

23. See chapter on Lewis and myth in this volume.

69

24. It is not entirely clear what his source material may have been. We have no other full treatments of the myth. The iconographic evidence for Cupid and Psyche stories suggest that there are numerous myths in which the two are in different types of relationships: harmonious, discordant, adversarial, etc. (see Kenney, 20–21). Apuleius borrows from this tradition as suits his purposes and infuses a Platonic psychology into the myth and suggests that the human soul—bound to a corporeal existence—yearns for divine love and is transformed by that love when finally united to it.

Apuleius tells the Cupid and Psyche story within the context of the much larger *Metamorphoses* (also known as *The Golden Ass*). A story within a story, it is meant to illustrate the themes of the main story in which the main character, Lucius, a young man interested in learning magic, is transformed into an ass. He undergoes a number of adventures before finally being transformed back into a man by the goddess Isis (who is identified with Venus). Psyche and Lucius share many common characteristics in this story, including their disastrous curiosity and their ultimate transformation at the hands of a god.

25. See, for example, Van Der Wheele.

26. The poet Hesiod—writing within a generation or so from Homer—reminds the reader to be savvy. The muses, he writes, tell many lies resembling the truth, but they know how to sing the truth as well.

Works Cited

Bremer, J. M., J. F. de Jong, and J. Kalff, eds. *Homer: Beyond Oral Poetry. Recent Trends in Homeric Interpretation*. Amsterdam: B. R. Grüner, 1987.

Foley, John Miles. "Oral Tradition and Its Implications." *A New Companion to Homer*. Ed. Barry B. Powell and Ian Morris. Leiden: Brill, 146–73.

Kenney, E. J., ed. and trans. *Cupid and Psyche*. Cambridge: Cambridge UP, 1990.

Lewis, C. S. "After Ten Years." *Of Other Worlds* 127–48.

———. *All My Road Before Me: The Diary of C. S. Lewis 1922–1927*. Ed. Walter Hooper. London: HarperCollins, 1991.

———. "*De Descriptione Temporum*." *Selected Literary Essays*. Ed. Walter Hooper. Cambridge: Cambridge UP, 1969. 1–14.

———. *The Discarded Image: An Introduction to Medieval and Renaissance Literature*. Canto Edition. Cambridge: Cambridge UP, 1994.

———. "Forms of Things Unknown." *Of Other Worlds* 119–26.

———. *Letters of C. S. Lewis*. Ed. W. H. Lewis. New York: Harcourt, 1966.

———. *Letters to Children*. Ed. Lyle W. Dorsett and Marjorie L. Mead. New York: Macmillan, 1985.

———. *Miracles: A Preliminary Study*. New York: Macmillan, 1947.

———. *Of Other Worlds: Essays and Stories*. Ed. Walter Hooper. London: Geoffrey Bles, 1966.

———. *A Preface to "Paradise Lost."* London: Oxford UP, 1942.

———. *Studies in Medieval and Renaissance Literature*. Ed. Walter Hooper. Cambridge: Cambridge UP, 1966.

———. *Surprised by Joy: The Shape of My Early Life*. London: Geoffrey Bles, 1955.

———. *They Stand Together: The Letters of C. S. Lewis to Arthur Greeves (1914–1963)*. Ed. Walter Hooper. New York: Macmillan, 1979.

————. *Till We Have Faces: A Myth Retold*. Grand Rapids: Eerdmans, 1956.

————. *The Weight of Glory and Other Addresses*. Grand Rapids: Eerdmans, 1965.

Lord, A. B. *The Singer of Tales*. Cambridge, MA: Harvard UP, 1960.

Montrose, Louis. "New Historicisms." *Redrawing the Boundaries: The Transformation of English and American Literary Studies*. Ed. Stephen Greenblatt and Giles Gunn. New York: MLA, 1992. 392–418.

Myrsiades, Kostas, ed. *Approaches to Teaching Homer's* Iliad *and* Odyssey. New York: MLA, 1987.

Nagy, G. *Homeric Questions*. Austin: U of Texas P, 1996.

Parry, M. *The Making of Homeric Verse: The Collected Papers of Milman Parry*. Ed. A. Parry. Oxford: Oxford UP, 1971.

Sayer, George. *Jack: A Life of C. S. Lewis*. Wheaton: Crossway, 1988.

Schein, S. L. *The Mortal Hero: An Introduction to Homer's Iliad*. Berkeley: U of California P, 1984.

Stewart, Stanley. "Pure Situating." *New Literary History* 35 (1994): 1–19.

Thomas, Brook. *The New Historicism: And Other Old-Fashioned Topics*. Princeton: Princeton UP, 1991.

Van Der Wheele, Steve J. "From Mt. Olympus to Glome: C. S. Lewis's Dislocation of Apuleius's 'Cupid and Psyche' in *Till We Have Faces*." *The Longing for a Form: Essays on the Fiction of C. S. Lewis*. Ed. Peter J. Schakel. Kent, OH: Kent State UP, 1977. 182–92.

Wilson, A. N. *C. S. Lewis*. New York: Norton, 1990.

4
Medieval Literature

David Lyle Jeffrey

Rare is the reader who entirely overcomes the youthful remembrance of a few favored tomes through whose pages he or she has tumbled, smitten, into a lifelong literary garden. C. S. Lewis, for all the fullness of his later reading and critical intelligence, was not in this respect rare: his early passions formed his future loves and prejudices. Even in his professional criticism of English literature, at least until fairly late in life, he seems to have preferred that literature which most clearly resembled the romantic poetry with which he had first fallen in love. With respect to medieval texts in particular, there is therefore no better predictor of his affections or even of his manner of reading than his schoolboy response to nineteenth-century romantic medievalism.

Early Reading

At thirteen years of age Lewis met joyously with *Siegfried and the Twilight of the Gods.* He read it in the popularization of Margaret Armour, illustrated by Arthur Rackham (*The Bookman*, Christmas, 1911).[1] From Wagner's adaptations of the Nibelung saga he passed on quickly through some anthropological works on the Teutons to the *Prose Edda* and *Elder Edda* (in translation); by the summer of 1914, at the age of sixteen, he was deeply immersed in an earnest poetic imitation of his own, *Loki Bound* (*Surprised* 78).

The following term he discovered William Morris, and entirely lost himself in the still more aureate fantasies of Morris's neo-medieval poems and romances. These took him back to earlier imaginative evocations of the medieval and pagan past: Malory's *Morte D'Arthur* and Spenser's *The Faerie Queene* were read over the next year. On 4 March 1916, he added to the "circle," as he called it, George MacDonald's "faerie Romance," *Phantastes.* From that point on, MacDonald would become Lewis's mentor and a bridge to the luxuries of romantic medievalism.[2] But for understanding Lewis's affection for things medieval, there really is no more useful point of reference than the William Morris he read as a sixteen-year-old.

He had begun to read Morris at Wyvern (in 1914). As readers of *Surprised by Joy* will remember, by the next year he had found in the bookcase of his friend Arthur Greeves Morris's *The Well at the World's End*, a prose romance whose first chapter is entitled "The Road to Love" and whose monarch is King Peter. Lewis, hooked by a browse and by chapter headings in Greeve's copy, quickly purchased his own and read it. Then, enchanted, he quickly moved on to *The Earthly Paradise*, of which he wrote: "The growth of the new delight is masked by my sudden realization, almost with a sense of disloyalty, that the letters WILLIAM MORRIS were coming to have at least as potent a magic in them as WAGNER" (*Surprised* 164). *The Earthly Paradise* (1868–70) is a long poem modeled structurally on Chaucer's *Canterbury Tales* and Boccaccio's *Decameron*. Metrically the model is Chaucer; like them both it is a cycle of tales (twenty-four in all). A general prologue establishes the frame as a flight from pestilence, much as in Boccaccio, except that the tellers are neither Florentines nor English folk, but a company of Norsemen. They set sail in search of the Earthly Paradise, said to lie "across the western sea where none grow old." Their journey fails of its hope, and old and weary they come at last to an island, a "nameless city in a distant sea" where the ancient Greek gods are still worshipped. There they live out their lives, meeting with their courteous hosts twice a month for feasting and the telling of a tale. The narration, shared equally by guest and hosts, alternates accordingly between northern and classical Greek legends. Much more than Chaucer, if not than Boccaccio, Morris charged many of his tales with an erotic appeal, typical of a very unmedieval but markedly Victorian (and especially pre-Raphaelite) taste, a mystical eroticism. Lewis liked it.

Later in life, even as he was approaching his conversion, he was to overcome some evident guilt over his taste for the erotic element in Morris through reading the same author's *Love Is Enough*, a poem whose sublimation of eroticism to religious sentiment he was apparently relieved to approve (*Stand* 365–67).[3] Thus, the romantic medievalism of Morris which had been so formative of his early taste in literature was to be affirmed again at the most pivotal moment in his mature spiritual life, a point by which he was well embarked upon his professional university career. By this time, indeed, *The Allegory of Love* was not only fully formed in his mind (it had been so since 1925), but partially written. The first two chapters were complete, and lecture material leading to the rest of the book was already being deployed, especially, one can see retrospectively, concerning the book's crowning subject, Spenser's *The Faerie Queene.*

Sentimental Journey

All of this to say that Lewis came to medieval literature by way of a sentimental journey. The front door to this magic wardrobe, if you will, was the belated romanticism of the nineteenth-century "medieval revival." The rear panel was an idealism of the imagined past as he found it in the archaisms of Malory and Spenser. What opened on the other side, as a consequence, was a canonical hierarchization of medieval literature favoring above all the "romance." It also seems to have led in Lewis to an impatience for much of what was not romance, or could not be construed by him as romance. Thus, though he taught medieval literature, especially Old and Middle English literature, throughout much of his life, the reader will look in vain for any substantial criticism on such major works as Chaucer's *Canterbury Tales* and *House of Fame, The Pearl, Piers Plowman,* the Caedmonian biblical poems, the great Corpus Christi biblical plays, spiritual writings such as those of Rolle, Hilton, Julian of Norwich, or even on the celebrated medieval lyrics, many of which we know he had a powerful experience reading in 1930. Jacob Boehme's *Signatura Rerum,* he said, "has been about the biggest shaking up I've got from a book since I first read *Phantastes,*" but he never wrote about it (Green and Hooper 105).

Lewis goes so far as to insist, astonishingly, that *The Canterbury Tales* "have always been sterile," indeed that "none of our early poets has so little claim to be called the father of English poetry as the Chaucer of *The Canterbury Tales.*" (He allows that *The Canterbury Tales* have had some influence on English prose.) One feels forcefully his deep disappointment that "William Morris's discipleship to Chaucer was an illusion" (*Allegory* 163). The most cursory early comparison of *The Earthly Paradise* with *The Canterbury Tales* must have revealed to him not only how radically unsentimental and even perhaps antiromantic Chaucer could be, but also how determined upon repentance and self-examination. Chaucer's pilgrims make their Lenten pilgrimage not in search of an earthly paradise but rather the completion of an act of penance and communal reconciliation at Canterbury Cathedral, the national shrine of Thomas à Becket. Chaucer makes it clear that it is this process of repentance that will enable them, through grace, to re-enter the ordinary world, forgiven.

Of course, there is more: in the Parson's prologue to his concluding sermon on repentance he prays:

> And Jhesu for his grace wit me sende
> To shew you the wey in this viage
> Of thilke parfit glorious pilgrymage
> That highte Jerusalem celestial. (*Canterbury Tales*
> 10.48–51)

This "celestial Jerusalem" is not for Chaucer or his parson an earthly paradise or some wished-for utopian Arthurian kingdom in the here and now, nor is it Valhalla.

Lewis's copy of *Troilus and Criseyde* is heavily annotated, mostly with philological teaching notes. His surviving copies of *The Canterbury Tales*, as far as I know, are not.[4] The minor poems of Chaucer in the courtly style fare little better: underlinings occur in "Anelida and Arcite" and, as might be expected, he approves Chaucer's adage in the *Parliament of Fowls* that

> . . . out of olde feldes, as men seyth,
> Cometh al this newe corn fro yer to yere.
> And out of olde bokes, in good feyth,
> Cometh al this newe science that men lere. (lines 21–25)

Lewis's other early preparation—and it was a magnificent apprenticeship—was as an avid reader of classical Greek and Roman verse in the original, a training (and disposition) he turned to excellent advantage in *The Discarded Image* (1962), a much later product of his scholarship. But it didn't help him in his formative years to affirm more of Chaucer, not even Chaucer's classical and most Dantesque poem on the need for authority in interpretation, *The House of Fame*. Of it he wrote in 1922 that it was "a work I do not much care for" (*Stand* 122).[5] In the same year he found *The Legend of Good Women* "pretty, but hopelessly medieval" (123). In his *Allegory* he regrets the style of Chaucer's *Book of the Duchess*, in which he finds traces of "courtly love" as he imagines it, but no allegory (167).[6] Indeed, a persistent problem for Lewis reading Chaucer is this "resistance" to his own model of love-allegory: he laments that "nowhere do we find in Chaucer what can be called a radically allegorical poem" (166).

The resistance Lewis himself feels would seem to have to do with more than simply the apparent absence of allegory. In his copy of R. L. Greene's *Selection of English Carols*, annotated late in his life, Lewis shows himself to be most interested in the question of pagan origins of the genre, in dancing carols, and the association of the carol with witchcraft, as well as with feasting and merry-making. The religious carols receive no attention. In his older annotations (probably 1927–28) of E. K. Chambers and F. Sidgwick's *Early English Lyrics*, he shows himself most interested in metrics and in affinities of medieval to Renaissance verse: "Sodenly afraid / Halfe waking half sleping," is compared, for example, to Skelton's "Wonderfully Amazed." But it is clear that he sees the medieval lyrics as, on the whole, inferior; on No. 26, to the lines "She is right true, I do it see; / My heart to have she doth me bind . . . " he writes, "true drab age."

His most annotated Dante is the *Vulgaria Eloquentia*, and early in his life at least there is little sense of the *Commedia* being as important for him as Dante's poem about what Lewis regarded as the spiritualization of love, the *Vita Nuova*. This latter poem he read not as an adequation of Provençal courtly love tradition to an essentially Augustinian poetic or as a celebration of the progress of love from carnal appetite to friendship to the love of God, but as a literal valorization of the code of courtly love.[7] That is, he did not see the allegory. To the *Commedia* he came, for his own purposes, much later. When he did he wrote magisterial essays on "Dante's Similes" (1940), Dante's use of classical Latin poetry ("Dante's Use of Statius," 1957), and "Imagery in the Last Eleven Cantos of Dante's Comedy" (1948). Of these, only in the last, on the *Paradiso*, does Lewis engage Dante's great Christian theme directly, and that within the most reserved decorum. Nowhere, perhaps, except in *The Great Divorce* (1945) do we see the Christian theology of Dante really fire the imagination of Lewis in fulsome fashion.[8]

Much might be made, I suspect, of the consonance among these avoided works of a Christian (and particularly Catholic) spirituality far more explicit than anything medieval Lewis wrote about. Lewis was raised a Belfast Protestant, after all, and despite the growing catholicity of his taste in later years, his early would-be atheism and affection for the secular romance would be consistent with an aversion to the overt Christianity of much mainstream medieval literature. I do not wish to push such a hypothesis too far; nevertheless, apropos his preferences and manner of reading as a medievalist the neglected titles are nearly as suggestive as his avowed passions.

76

Chaucer

Let us take up the most notable instance of neglect. Chaucer, by a long-standing consensus among readers of medieval literature of the most various persuasions, is the signal poet of the English Middle Ages. Among his works, *The Canterbury Tales* has always been regarded as his *magnum opus* and as the most "English" of his poems. Even during the middle years of the twentieth century, when in England (though not North America) *Troilus and Criseyde* was the usual "set" text, *The Canterbury Tales* has universally been regarded as a work of astonishing variety, richness of narrative strategy, and of readerly interest generally—so much so that it almost completely dominated the critical commentary on Chaucer for the whole of the century.

But it does not fit Lewis's own model for medieval literary greatness as outlined in *The Allegory of Love*. That is, it does not well conform to his ideal of "courtly love"; indeed, many of Chaucer's tales are parodic or mocking of courtly love, whether as a literary convention or as an idealized social ambiance (e.g., Knight's Tale, Miller's Tale, Wife of Bath's Tale, Clerk's Tale, Merchant's Tale, Franklin's Tale, Nun's Priest's Tale, etc.).[9] Accordingly, Lewis discards the great work—with much ado by way of qualification—saying in effect that since Chaucer was not truly "a poet of courtly love" except in *Troilus and Criseyde*, he "ceases to be relevant" to his study. *Troilus and Criseyde*, however, fits. It needs no historical contextualizing, Lewis says, and "goes straight to the heart of every reader" (*Allegory* 176). The widow Criseyde's behavior is excused because "love has nothing to do with marriage" (183). Lewis finds her betrayal of Troilus in liaison with Diomede discomfiting but defends her vanity and opportunism by an appeal to Coventry Patmore (!) and praises Pandarus (the panderer) as "a man of sentiment" (191). Book 3 of the poem stands out for him "as some of the greatest erotic poetry in the world" (196).

Lewis writes notably of Chaucer in only one other place (the subject again being *Troilus and Criseyde*)—in his essay "What Chaucer Really Did to *Il Filostrato*" (1932). Here he is concerned to analyze Chaucer's departures and innovations while "retelling" the Boccaccio poem in *Troilus and Criseyde*; it is an attempt to prove, somewhat awkwardly, that "the majority of his [Chaucer's] modifications are corrections of errors which Boccaccio had committed against the code of courtly love" ("*Il Filostrato*" 29–30). While Lewis allows (correctly, I think) that the most significant changes are Chaucer's incorporations from Boethius's *Consolation of Philosophy*, he does not in any way see that Chaucer's changes remake the story into a deeply philosophical as well as political poem, and that they thus underscore Chaucer's constraint of the very sentiment Lewis hopes to find unfettered and rampant.

Courtly Love

Courtly love, though Lewis represents it in his beautifully written *Allegory* as historical reality, is itself a literary fiction. Lewis thought it so lovely a fantasy it must be true. By the "code" or conventions—thought in the early part of the century by Gorra (1912), Jeanroy (1934), Wechsler (1909), and others to have derived from the heretical poets of Provence—an adulterous, self-abasing, courteous love of a knight for another man's wife was taken to be the highest, most "religious" sort of love. A tale of passion constrained by an elaborate "noble" code—and then of course secretly indulged whenever possible—had a special appeal for certain nineteenth-century European readers. That appeal has much to do with the success of Victorian medievalism, its misty retellings of Malory's account of Lancelot and Guinevere's deceptions of King Arthur, or Tristan and Isolde's adultery and betrayal of her husband King Mark. Here the term "courtly" refers to a lofty mannerism and Ovidian style (often parodic); "love" signifies "romance" in the modern rather than medieval sense of the word (the medieval genre *romans*, variant on the classical Roman epic narrative: OF *romans* = "of the Romans"). "Courtly love" was dubbed by some medievalists a "doctrine," perhaps, they thought, originally a heretical doctrine to flaunt the asceticism of the Catholic Church.

It is now apparent that this "doctrine of courtly love" was a social construction of post-Enlightenment rather than medieval minds (Robertson, "Book of the Dutchess"; Benton, "Collaborative Approaches"). But for the pre-World War II generation nourished on Victorian romantic medievalism and Wagner, the lack of empirical warrant for the literary fantasy had not yet become apparent. Lewis's summary (*Allegory* 2) is not original, but it is an accurate representation of that "worship" of the *femme fatale* so much heralded by European contemporaries of William Morris. Lewis sees that stylistically it owes to Ovid, especially the ironic *Ars Amatoria*, but like his modernist continental predecessors, he assumes that any Ovidian satiric element must be by this point absent, especially from Provençal poetry (11). The "theory" of courtly love he takes to have been provided by *De Arte Honeste Amendi* of Andreas Capellanus, a thirteenth-century Latin prose satire written for a courtly audience, probably that of Marie de Champagne (*Allegory* 32–35). Since then it has become more plausible that at least some of the relevant Provençal poetry is likely to have been inspired by a gnostic pursuit of sexual knowledge as a means to salvation, particularly among radical groups such as the Cathari. Misunderstanding of this eccentric context, coupled with a somewhat skewed appreciation that for the Catholic Church "passionate love" (the more accurate adjective would have been "lecherous" or "lustful") "was wicked and did not cease to be wicked if the object were your wife" (14), led Lewis to think that "medieval marriages had nothing to do with love," and that therefore "any idealization of sexual love, in a society where marriage is purely utilitarian, must begin by being an idealization of adultery" (13). On this reading, the adulterous love of Lancelot for Guinevere is held to be a much nobler passion than the married love of Arthur and Guinevere, even if it destroys the Round Table (i.e., the symbolic edifice of social stability) and becomes the means of undoing for many more. This predilection makes for good Tennyson, but not for an accurate reading of Lazamon.[10] Lewis is preoccupied in the first chapter of his *Allegory* with the conjugal act; he finds that the medieval Church had a distressingly pragmatic view of it and that "all such passionate and exalted devotion as a courtly poet thought worthy of the name—was more or less wicked" (17). The "love religion of the god Amor" (18) in consequence becomes a kind of passionate proto-Protestant revolt in the name of love, exalted in an idealization of individual sexual passion.

Here, then, is the point at which Lewis most misunderstands the Middle Ages. His projection of nineteenth-century medieval revivalism back onto the literature of the Middle Ages caused his *Allegory*, for all its eloquence and fine insight (especially in regard to Spenser), to come to be regarded by most medievalists as fanciful. His former pupil Derek Brewer remembers being shown by Lewis the Everyman Library (unreliable) translation of Chrétien which he had used "for that remarkable and splendid, though misleading book *The Allegory of Love*" (Brewer 47). Lewis's friend and colleague, the historian Gervase Mathew, fails to cite Lewis in his magisterial work *The Court of Richard II* (of which several chapters are devoted to literature, one to chivalry, another to marriage, and one to Chaucer specifically), but one knows who he has principally in mind when he writes: "It has sometimes been asserted that romantic love was conceived as essentially adulterous, but it is difficult to maintain this in view of any close analysis of medieval texts" (133–34). Mathew goes on to show that the highly stylized literary conventions of love poetry Lewis and others associated with *amour courtois* were used by Chaucer among others, in fact, to describe married love (134–36). And D. W. Robertson, Jr., the distinguished American medievalist, while similarly forbearing to cite Lewis, devotes more than one hundred pages to a systematic critical rejection of "courtly love." Robertson finds even the term itself an anachronism; there is no historical evidence for actual "practice" of courtly love, the only textual basis for it being merely Ovidian-styled satire, especially the *De amore* of Andreas Capellanus, royal chaplain to Marie de Champagne (*A Preface to Chaucer* 393–503; also Benton, "Court of Champagne"; cf. Cantor, Kelly; Astell).

It is one of the thought-provoking ironies of twentieth-century literary scholarship that Robertson, a professed agnostic, did more than anyone to root the understanding of medieval poetry (and Chaucer's *Canterbury Tales* in particular) in Christian textual tradition, especially patristic and medieval biblical exegesis. Lewis, though a celebrated believer, had little interest in these matters, preferring a neo-romantic and pagan literary context for his reading of more secularizable "romance" texts. Malory's prose *Morte D'Arthur*, in which even residual Christian doctrine is almost entirely elided in favor of a nostalgic idealization of chivalry, remained far more important to Lewis than the overtly Christian poetry of the eighth to fourteenth centuries. If the Chaucer of *The Canterbury Tales* is not for him the "father of English poetry," Lewis offers as his own candidate Malory's romance, "for it is no specialist's book; it is Milton's book, Tennyson's book, Morris's book, a sacred and central possession of all who speak the English tongue" ("*The Morte D'Arthur*" 104). That was in 1947, in an unsigned review of Eugene Vinaver's *Works of Sir Thomas Malory*. Four years earlier he had in the same vein reviewed J. J. Parry's translation of Andreas Capellanus, *The Art of Courtly Love*.[11] In these matters, so germinal to his imagination and indeed his own works of fiction, the influence of his early reading continued to predominate, despite what must have been occasional moments of embarrassment. In one such moment he wrote in his diary for 4 July 1926:

> I spent the afternoon and evening between spells of working on "Sigfrid" (which I did with incredible difficulty, but finally pleased myself) and beginning to re-read *The Well at the World's End*. I was anxious to see whether the old spell still worked. It does—rather too well. This going back to books read at that age is humiliating: one keeps on tracing what are now quite big things in one's mental outfit to curious small sources. I wondered how much even of my feeling for external nature comes out of the brief, convincing little descriptions of mountains and woods in this book. (*Road* 141)

He was then twenty-eight. At fifty, it appears, he hadn't much changed his mind. The medieval elements of his novel *That Hideous Strength* (1945)—Merlin, the Pendragon, Logres, Bracton Wood with its wall and "Merlin's well," Edgestow, even Filostrato (the mad Italian scientist who thinks that there will "never be peace and order and discipline as long as there is sex"), and the concluding carnival of Venus—all follow naturally from Malory, Morris, and the aura of courtly love (cf. Hannay, Branson).

80 ✝ Reader of Old Western Culture

Happily, there is more to Lewis as a reader of medieval literature than this essentially modernist obsession with romantic love. In fact, in many other respects he was so emphatically anti-modernist, suspicious of twentieth-century attempts to project backward onto medieval texts the presuppositions and linguistic naiveté of our age, that he was able to style himself quite plausibly a critical dinosaur, "a spokesman of Old Western Culture" ("*Temporum*" 12).[12] Bearing thence into academic battle the scaly plates of his antique languages and learning, Lewis was on these grounds far more formidable—almost, one wants to say, a holy terror. Not that holiness as such much entered into his critical purview even here: he says that there are "two possible approaches to medieval literature" which he will not adopt, "the theological and the anthropological" (8). The anthropological, represented chiefly by scholars like Loomis and Weston, is one he has clearly been attracted to for its recollection of pagan elements, and he takes some time to explain his final rejection of it. The theological approach he dismisses in a mere paragraph, partly because "it leads critics to equate the edificatory value of a work with its value as literature" (a worthy point) and partly because he anticipates "that most modern readers will be in no danger of excessive leniency to it" (a point perhaps debatable as to its sufficiency). That said, his eloquent and reasoned defense of a rigorously historical approach to ancient and medieval texts is bracing, and salutary from a theological as well as a literary perspective.

Here are his principles. First, if the reader is not sufficiently fluent in the language of a poet's composition, be it Latin, Italian, French, German, Norse, or Middle English, his interpretation will be so amateurish as to be nugatory, no matter how clever the reader:

> If we read an old poem with insufficient regard for change in the overtones, and even the dictionary meanings, of words since its date—if, in fact, we are content with whatever effect the words accidentally produce in our modern minds—then of course we do not read the poem the old writer intended. What we get may still be, in our opinion, a poem; but it will be our poem, not his. If we call this *tout court* "reading" the old poet, we are deceiving ourselves. (*Words* 3)

T. S. Eliot notwithstanding, if one is to avoid this self-deception, "knowledge is necessary. Intelligence and sensibility by themselves are not enough" (4). Putting it still more bluntly (and nowadays unfashionably), he insists that "it is not enough to make sense. We want to find the sense that the author intended" (5).

Second, in his own words, "in order to read Old Western literature aright you must suspend most of the responses and unlearn most of the habits you have acquired in reading modern literature" ("*Temporum*" 13). For Lewis this is a little like the difference between an authentic cultural traveler and a vulgar tourist:

> There are two ways of enjoying the past, as there are two ways of enjoying a foreign country. One man carries his Englishry abroad with him and brings it home unchanged. Wherever he goes he consorts with other English tourists. By a good hotel he means one that is like an English hotel. He complains of the bad tea where he might have had excellent coffee. He finds the "natives" quaint and enjoys their quaintness. In his own way he may have a pleasant time; he likes his winter-sports in Switzerland and his flutter at Monte Carlo. In the same way there

81

is a man who carries his modernity with him through all his reading of past literatures and preserves it intact. ("*Audiendis*" 2)

It is not that Lewis could not imagine another set of values, or even that he failed to foresee our own very different contemporary principles. In a note to his inaugural Cambridge lecture he observes, "In music we have pieces which demand more talent in the performer than in the composer. Why should there not come a period when the art of writing poetry stands lower than the art of reading it? Of course rival readings would then cease to be 'right' or 'wrong' and become more and less brilliant 'performances' " ("*Temporum*" 9n). But, in a gesture at once apparently conciliatory to such impulses and yet crushing as the teeth of the dinosaur for the ambition that they become a well-paid practice, he adds another note:

> As my examples show, such misinterpretations may themselves produce results which have imaginative value. If there had been no Romantic distortion of the Middle Ages, we should have no *Eve of St. Agnes*. There is room both for an appreciation of the imagined past and an awareness of its difference from the real past; but if we want only the former, why come to a university? (12–13n)

That Lewis himself qualified on the first of his own principles there can be no doubt; that he qualified under the second is, as I have shown, more doubtful. But that he made a more valiant effort than most among his peers in this regard is evident enough, and that his general defense of historical method is more vigorous than that of any other leading English medievalist of this century, with the exception of Robertson, will I think be obvious to those familiar with the field. It is a matter of note that Robertson's principles were essentially the same as those of Lewis, with the notable exception that he thought the surest way to counter modern literary habits was a thorough acquaintance with medieval Christian tradition in its most rigorous patristic and exegetical expression. An agnostic, Robertson apparently had less to fear from the "theological approach."

Lewis is never better, it seems to me, than when he is reading the Latin texts of late antiquity and the early Middle Ages such as we find him doing in *The Discarded Image*. His discussions of Chalcidius on the *Timaeus* of Plato, the taxonomies of Macrobius on dream theory, Pseudo-Dionysius on angels, and Boethius in his *Consolation* are exemplary, an invaluable guide for the serious student (*Discarded* 52–91). Here he fears no *odium theologicam* from aestheticist peers. His papers on "Dante's Similes" and "Dante's Statius" show to beautiful advantage the superior stylistic analysis that can only result from a combination of excellent philological skills and a superbly trained eye and ear for medieval poetry. Few have equaled him in these respects.

Lewis did turn to medieval spiritual literature toward the end of his life, and without setting aside his critical perspective. He read volume one of Sanford Brown Meech and Hope Emily Allen's edition of *The Book of Margery Kempe* shortly after it appeared in 1961, annotating especially those passages in which Dame Margery is preoccupied with the notion that her "felyngs shuld be wretyn" (30, 34, 55), and with her notion that by the priest's transcription of her dictation in the form of a book she would have "preuyd hir felyngys trewe" (74, 83). Less critically and more personally, he had reread Walter Hilton's *The Scale of Perfection* for the "2nd time, June 1, 1950," as his note at the end of his copy informs us, underlining especially heavily passages having to do with the barrier placed between the self and God by self-preoccupation. In the introduction of Dom M. Noetinger he had on first reading (c. 1930) underlined the passage: "It is not so much a question of finding ourselves as finding our Lord; we have to go forth from our egoism and turn wholeheartedly towards God" (Hilton xxix). In the 1950 ink he marks another passage which reads:

> Pride cometh by night to assail a soul when it is despised and reproved of other men, that it should, by that, fall into heaviness and sorrow. It cometh also as an arrow flying in the day, when a man is worshipped and praised of all men, whether it be for worldly doing or for ghostly, that he should have vain joy in himself restingly, and false gladness in a passing thing. (338)

This underscored passage in Hilton is strikingly evocative of a confession by Lewis two years previously in his letter of 27 March 1948 to the Italian priest Don Giovanni Calabria of his recurrent temptation as an academic: "*desiderio di essere stimato . . . timore di essere rifiutato*"—longing to be thought well of, fear of being rejected (Moynihan 47). These persistent tensions and apprehensions of a cloistered life are the means by which many a vice comes, as they did also to Criseyde, which may be why so many academic readers of *Troilus and Criseyde* identify with her. Lewis fought not more successfully than many of us with these conflictual desires and fears, and it is evident that his losses on this front naturally enough offset somewhat his talent and training as a reader of medieval literature. But he also rose above his limitations to gain a purpose that was little short of a high desire to recover the truth of his author's intent in writing. In his sincere valuation for the integrity of the other who writes, and his willingness faithfully to submit to a patient hearing before composing a critical reply, he models a decorum of obligation worthy of any reader's thanks and praise.

Notes

1. See *Surprised by Joy* (72). In *C. S. Lewis: A Biography*, Green and Hooper argue that this moment in Lewis's literary life was prepared for by a childhood reading of Longfellow's poem on "Balder the Beautiful," but confirm it as the real inception of his "craze for all things 'Northern'" (32; cf. 35).

2. Lewis's own account in *Surprised* places the reading of *Phantastes* in August 1915; Green and Hooper correct this, on other grounds, to 4 March 1916.

3. Green and Hooper record that "shortly after reading *The Angel in the House*, Lewis exchanged his Bombay edition of Kipling for the complete works of Morris" (107). In his letter to Greeves he revises his earlier opinion that Morris was "the most essentially pagan of poets," and comes to believe "for the first (and last) time the light of *holiness* shines through Morris's romanticism, not destroying it but perfecting it" (Green and Hooper 107–08).

4. I am indebted to Marjorie Mead and Christopher Mitchell of the Marion E. Wade Collection at Wheaton College for the opportunity to examine the medieval texts in the C. S. Lewis library. Among these Lewis owned A. W. Pollard, *The Works of Chaucer* (London: Macmillan, 1928), which seems to have been a teaching copy. While there are no notes on *The Canterbury Tales*, there are many on *Troilus and Criseyde*, though most are philological and textual rather than reflecting matters of literary commentary. The text has been annotated by Lewis at various times, both in pencil and in ink. Derek Brewer, whose tutor he was, found Lewis a "romance critic," and "oddly enough . . . least stimulating (at least to me) on medieval literature." Brewer, himself later to become an accomplished medievalist, found that Lewis had "little to say on medieval drama," and records that in later years Lewis himself admitted "he had little to say about Chaucer, although he greatly enjoyed him, and especially *Troilus and Criseyde*, which he had first discovered while convalescing from his war wound . . ." (Brewer 48).

5. This seems a pity, because precisely the sort of skills possessed in yet greater abundance by Lewis enabled Koonce to show the richness of the poem as a brilliant harvesting of the tradition Lewis championed in *The Discarded Image*. See also Jeffrey 207–28. For an interesting discussion of the fourth section of *The Allegory of Love* in relation to Lewis's feelings about Chaucer, see Morris.

6. Today, after the work of many to show the contrary, this judgment of Lewis might seem especially perplexing. See Wimsatt, Cherniss, Tisdale, and Robertson's "The Book of the Duchess." Curiously, Lewis, in his copy of W. W. Skeat, ed., *Chaucer: the Minor Poems* (1896), annotated the *Book of the Duchess* mostly with philological and textual corrections, but noted his then belief (probably early) that Octavien (lines 368ff.) "represents Edward III"!

7. Cf. Goldin, esp. 207ff.; also Freccero.

8. A. N. Wilson, in his *C. S. Lewis: A Biography*, believes so, except that he also thinks "none of Lewis's portraits is more cruel than that of the figure of Dante himself, who appears at the end [i.e., of *The Great Divorce*] as a figure so besottedly in love with his own unhappiness, and with what he calls his love for his lady, that he cannot let go" (201). Charles Williams, on the other hand, wrote to Lewis that the whole of *The Allegory of Love* was "practically the only one that I have ever come across, since Dante, that shows the slightest understanding of what this very particular identity of love and religion means" (Letter, 12 March 1936, qtd. in Green and Hooper 134). A 1984 dissertation by Marsha-Ann Daigle, "Dante's Divine Comedy and the Fiction of C. S. Lewis," examines his use of Dante's greatest poem more closely, while an essay by Dominic Manganiello may help to explain something of the "romantic" version of Dante which emerges in *The Great Divorce*. It is entitled "*The Great Divorce*: C. S. Lewis's Reply to Blake's Dante," *Christian Scholar's Review* 27.4 (1998): 475–89. I am indebted to Professor Manganiello for allowing me to read his excellent essay in manuscript.

9. According to Walter Hooper, toward the end of his life Lewis renewed his interest in Laȝamon's *Brut*, contemplating at Hooper's suggestion a translation (*Medieval* x).

10. See Lewis's review of Parry's translation of *The Art of Courtly Love*. His review copy is annotated, and makes it clear that he accepted Parry's "vivid picture of life in a medieval court" and his historically unfounded opinion that *amour courtois* was "probably also practiced," a fusion of "sensual" and "spiritual" tradition. One tangential comment of Lewis in the margin reaches forward, however, to his more substantial lectures on the classical foundations of medieval thought. On p. 9 of Parry, Lewis writes, "The fact that when Platonism came in later [Renaissance] it harmonized so well with CL [courtly love] suggests that the silence of med. writers about all this proves they never knew it. If they had they would have used it."

11. See Sims, who says that "Lewis's objective as a critic was not to be creative, or to add his interpretation, but to read a text as a native" (223).

12. Lewis could be curt with what he took to be slovenly, unnecessarily subjective work. In his copy of Bruno S. James's *St. Bernard of Clairvaux* (London: Hodder and Stoughton, 1957), he has written on the front flap: "As sawdusty a book as ever I tried to read, and sometimes a touch of fatuity." Glynne Wickham's discussion of loose biblical translation in medieval drama (in *Early English Stages: 1300–1600* [London: Routledge, Kegan Paul, 1959], 1.145) he finds "silly." On many a book margin he wrote "Bosh," "No!" or simply "?!" But it seems evident that he refrained from publishing negative criticism wherever possible.

Works Cited

Astell, Ann W. *The Song of Songs in the Middle Ages*. Ithaca: Cornell UP, 1990.

Benton, John F. "Collaborative Approaches to Fantasy and Reality in the Literature of Champagne." *Court and Poet: Selected Proceedings of the Third Congress of the International Courtly Literature Society*. Ed. Glyn S. Burgess. Liverpool: Francis Cairns, 1981.

———. "The Court of Champagne as a Literary Center." *Speculum* 36 (1961): 551–91.

The Book of Margery Kempe. Ed. Sanford Brown Meech and Hope Emily Allen. EETS O.S. 212. London: Oxford UP, 1940; 1961.

Branson, David A. "Arthurian Elements in *That Hideous Strength*." *Mythlore* 19.4 (1993): 20–21.

Brewer, Derek. "The Tutor: A Portrait." *C. S. Lewis at the Breakfast Table and Other Reminiscences*. Ed. James T. Como. 1979. San Diego: Harcourt Brace Jovanovich, 1992. 41–67.

Cantor, Norman F. *Inventing the Middle Ages: The Lives, Works, and Ideas of the Great Medievalists of the Twentieth Century*. New York: William Morrow, 1991.

Chambers, E. K., and F. Sidgwick. *Early English Lyrics, Amorous and Divine, Moral and Trivial*. London: Sidgwick and Jackson, 1926.

Chaucer, Geoffrey. *The Complete Poetry and Prose of Geoffrey Chaucer*. Ed. John H. Fisher. New York: Holt, Rinehart and Winston, 1977.

———. *Minor Poems*. Ed. W. W. Skeat. 2nd ed. London: Chaucer Society 1896. (Lewis's annotated copy).

Cherniss, Michael D. "The Boethian Dialogue in Chaucer's Book of the Duchess." *JEGP* 68 (1969): 655–65.

Daigle, Marsha-Ann. "Dante's Divine Comedy and the Fiction of C. S. Lewis." Diss. U of Michigan, 1984.

Freccero, John. *Dante: The Poetics of Conversion*. Ed. Rachel Jacoffn. Cambridge, MA: Harvard UP, 1986.

Goldin, Fredrick. *The Mirror of Narcissus in the Courtly Love Lyric*. Ithaca: Cornell UP, 1967.

Green, Roger Lancelyn, and Walter Hooper. *C. S. Lewis: A Biography*. 1974. Glasgow: Collins, 1979.

Greene, Richard Leighton, ed. *A Selection of English Carols*. Oxford: Clarendon Press, 1962.

Hannay, Margaret. "Arthurian and Cosmic Myth in *That Hideous Strength*." *Mythlore* 2.2 (1970): 7–9.

Hilton, Walter. *The Scale of Perfection*. Ed. Dom M. Noetinger. London: Burns, Oates and Washbourne, 1927.

Jeffrey, D. L. *Chaucer and Scriptural Tradition*. Ottawa: U of Ottawa P, 1984.

Kelly, H. A. *Love and Marriage in the Age of Chaucer*. Ithaca: Cornell UP, 1975.

Koonce, Benjamin G. *Chaucer and the Tradition of Fame*. Princeton: Princeton UP, 1966.

Lewis, C. S. *The Allegory of Love: A Study in Medieval Tradition*. 1936. London: Oxford UP, 1958.

———. *All My Road Before Me: The Diary of C. S. Lewis 1922–1927*. Ed. Walter Hooper. New York: Harcourt Brace Jovanovich, 1991.

———. "*De Audiendis Poetis*." *Medieval* 1–17.

———. "*De Descriptione Temporum*." *Literary* 1–14.

———. *The Discarded Image: An Introduction to Medieval and Renaissance Literature*. Cambridge: Cambridge UP, 1964.

———. "*The Morte D'Arthur*." *Medieval* 103–10.

———. Review of *The Art of Courtly Love*, trans. John J. Parry. *Review of English Studies* 19 (Jan. 1943): 77–79.

———. *Selected Literary Essays*. Ed. Walter Hooper. Cambridge: Cambridge UP, 1969.

———. *Studies in Medieval and Renaissance Literature*. Ed. Walter Hooper. Cambridge: Cambridge UP, 1966.

———. *Studies in Words*. Cambridge: Cambridge UP, 1960.

———. *Surprised by Joy: The Shape of my Early Life*. 1955. Harcourt, Brace and World, 1984.

———. *They Stand Together: The Letters of C. S. Lewis to Arthur Greeves (1914–1963)*. Ed. Walter Hooper. New York: Macmillan, 1979.

———. "What Chaucer Really Did to *Il Filostrato*." *Literary* 27–44.

Loomis, Roger Sherman. *Celtic Myth and Arthurian Romance*. New York: Columbia UP, 1927

Mathew, Gervase. *The Court of Richard II*. London: John Murray, 1968.

Morris, Francis-Joseph. "Metaphor and Myth: Shaping Forces in C. S. Lewis' Critical Assessment of Medieval and Renaissance Literature." Diss. U of Pennsylvania, 1977.

Moynihan, Martin, trans. and ed. *Letters: C. S. Lewis and Don Giovanni Calabria*. Ann Arbor: Servant Books, 1988.

Robertson, D. W., Jr. "The Book of the Duchess." *A Companion to Chaucer Studies*. Ed. Beryl Rowland. Toronto: Oxford UP, 1968. 332–40.

———. *A Preface to Chaucer: Studies in Medieval Perspectives*. Princeton: Princeton UP, 1963.

Sims, John A. "In Defense of Permanent Truths and Value." *Permanent Things*. Ed. Andrew A. Tadie and Michael H. MacDonald. Grand Rapids: Eerdmans, 1995. 222–39.

Tisdale, Charles P. "Boethian 'Hert-Hunting': The Elegiac Pattern of the Book of the Duchess." *American Benedictine Review* 24 (1973): 365–80.

Weston, Jessie L. *From Ritual to Romance*. Cambridge, Cambridge UP, 1920.

Wilson, A. N. *C. S. Lewis: A Biography*. London: Collins, 1990.

Wimsatt, James. *Chaucer and the French Love Poets*. Chapel Hill: U of North Carolina P, 1968.

5
Spenser

Doris T. Myers

Edmund Spenser is best known today as the answer to the trivia question, "Who wrote the longest poem in the English language?" Although only half finished, Spenser's *Faerie Queene* weighs in at 34,695 lines—not mingy, anorexic haiku lines either, but robust iambic pentameters and hexameters. Its epitaph might be, "No man ever wished it longer," but C. S. Lewis almost did. After reading it on weekends for about six months, he wrote to Arthur Greeves, "I have at last come to the end of the Faerie Queene: and though I say 'at last', I almost wish he had lived to write six books more as he hoped to do—so much have I enjoyed it" (*Stand* 93).

Few people today would share Lewis's enthusiasm. Although Spenser (1552–99) was an Elizabethan, roughly contemporary with William Shakespeare (1564–1616), Shakespeare seems much less remote than he. It was not always so. As Lewis noted, for many years Spenser was the one from whom schoolboys first discovered that they liked poetry ("Spenser" 132). He has been called "the poets' poet" because so many of them learned to write by imitating him: Milton, Dryden, Pope, Thomson, Collins, Gray, Coleridge, Wordsworth, Keats, Shelley, and Tennyson. David Radcliffe begins his reception history with the words, "If English poetry does not begin with Edmund Spenser, a case could be made that English *literature* does" (vii).

The Trouble with Spenser

If Spenser is "easy," why does *The Faerie Queene* seem so much less accessible than *A Midsummer Night's Dream*, since the two are roughly contemporaneous?[1] One reason is the language. Shakespeare's language, especially the spelling, has been silently modernized for all but the most scholarly editions; Spenser's language, deliberately archaic even in his own time, has seldom been modernized because his quaint spellings, old grammatical constructions, and dated vocabulary are considered essential to his poetic creation.[2] First, the variant spellings are part of Spenser's versifying technique. The complex stanzaic pattern of *The Faerie Queene* lends itself to the use of many inexact rhymes, and Spenser carefully varied spellings to smooth the rhyming and suggest subtle shades of pronunciation, thus exploiting the Elizabethan flexibility of both.[3] Also, the artistically antiqued grammar and vocabulary usages were supposed to suggest the language of Chaucer, whom Spenser called his master.[4]

Besides the language difficulty, there is the general resistance to long narrative poems. Even literature majors often read only the first two books of *Paradise Lost*, only the *Inferno* of Dante's *Commedia*, while Elizabethan drama is fairly accessible to them because the plays of today maintain many of the same structures and conventions as Shakespeare's. In contrast, Spenser's epic form has largely been displaced by the novel. Moreover, drama is always much more compact than narrative, and the excessive length of *The Faerie Queene* compares unfavorably with even a five-act play, which in practice is shortened for production. But the biggest obstacle, perhaps, is unfamiliarity with how allegory works and the kind of attention it demands from the reader.

With so many strikes against it and so many alternative sources of entertainment, what can *The Faerie Queene* offer the contemporary reader? On the simplest level, it offers adventure. Its premise is that before Prince Arthur became king he made an extended journey to Fairyland, a parallel world having its own history and ruled by Gloriana, the fairy queen. In *The Faerie Queene* Arthur was supposed to accomplish great deeds for Gloriana, deeds somehow related to those of twelve other knights.[5] This was a training for kingship, just as Merlin sends Prince Arthur to live among the ants and other creatures in T. H. White's *The Once and Future King*.

On a slightly more complex level, *The Faerie Queene* offers principles of human behavior made visible as personages, journeys, and battles. As allegory, its premise is that each knight's adventures set forth one of the twelve virtues necessary to "a gentleman or noble person," and the fairy queen represents fame or glory, the goal of great-spirited princes and nobles. Arthur represents magnificence, the sum of all the virtues. His quest is to win Gloriana and aid the other knights.[6] Adventure and allegory are unified by the lush, sometimes vivid pictorial quality of Fairyland as the place where such things happen.

Once the reader becomes accustomed to the language of allegory, the poem offers a complex, sophisticated exploration of human personality—the interactions of virtuous aspirations, motivations, and internal resistances to virtue; the choices and behaviors that lead to fulfillment or disaster; and the individual in society and his duties toward his fellows. The allegory thus places the poem within a whole group of medieval-Renaissance literary productions dealing with the education of heads of state,[7] and Spenser considered his primary audience to be the queen and her courtiers. Just as his master Chaucer told stories to instruct the court of Richard II in noble behavior, so Spenser hoped his work would instruct the court of Elizabeth I.[8] To enhance their interest, the poet made some of his characters recognizable in the real world, so that there is a level of political—i.e., historical—as well as moral allegory.

Strategies for Reading The Faerie Queene

In his charming introduction to Spenser for the anthology *Fifteen Poets*, Lewis describes three ways to begin one's acquaintance with *The Faerie Queene*. As a very young child one could have been read to from some book called "Stories from Spenser" ("On Reading" 146).[9] Later, one's first contact with the actual text should be made, Lewis says, "in a very large—and preferably, illustrated—edition of *The Faerie Queene*, on a wet day, between the ages of twelve and sixteen...."[10] He goes on to suggest that the mature reader who has missed acquaintance with Spenser in childhood and adolescence must begin by reading for the action while simultaneously paying attention to the moral allegory. He says, "It is of course much more than a fairy-tale, but unless we can enjoy it as a fairy-tale first of all, we shall not really care for it" ("Spenser" 133). But for full enjoyment, says Lewis, we need "a haunting memory" that we have met all of Spenser's questers before ("On Reading" 148); the mature reader will find this feeling in the moral allegory—that is, the portrayal of psychological laws and the struggles of men and women to become truly human. In following the travels of Spenser's knights, the reader meets archetypal characters and themes which the mature beginner has previously met in his own psychology, so that he reads the allegory with the shock of recognition that Lewis's ideal adolescent gets from having heard "Stories from Spenser" in his childhood.

There is another strategy for the contemporary reader that Lewis could not have adduced: applying to Spenser the skills and habits learned from reading

Tolkien's *The Lord of the Rings*. Like Spenser, Tolkien uses archaic forms of English; he even creates a language for his elsewhere land. Nor do contemporary fantasy readers find the great length of Tolkien's work and its use of narrative rather than dramatic conventions daunting.[11] As Lewis once said, *The Faerie Queene* is for people who enjoy such stories, no matter what kind of fiction happens to be popular at the time ("Spenser" 133). The common denominator is the taste for adventure and strangeness combined with indifference toward the individualized, introspective, self-aware characters found in the realistic novel. Like the characters in all literature of wonder (which includes modern science fiction as well as Tolkien's secondary world), Spenser's protagonists derive their characterization from their traditional forms, and these forms determine what they do. They fight evil by killing dragons, not by introspecting about their childhoods or analyzing their personal temptations to adultery or fraud.

Although Tolkien professed to dislike allegory, in a sense all fantasy is allegorical, because the fantastic scenes, characters, and conflicts suggest internal psychological struggles and societal states; thus readers of Tolkien often experience "a haunting memory" of having experienced the sufferings of Frodo and Sam in their own lives and times.[12] Nevertheless, the allegorical habit of thought is foreign to present-day consumers of novels and films, and Lewis's claim that "[t]he allegory that really matters is usually unmistakable" (*Sixteenth* 388) rather overstates the case.

He is right to this extent: in one's first reading one need not puzzle over what people and places mean, because Spenser tells us what they mean. For example, in book 2, The Book of Temperance, Mortdant is captured and then enchanted by Acrasia, mistress of the Bower of Bliss and dispenser of "drugs of fowle intemperaunce." When Mortdant's wife Amavia comes to free him, Acrasia gives him an enchanted drink of pleasure which will make water deadly to him. As the two travel they come upon a bubbling well; Mortdant drinks, and when he dies, his wife Amavia stabs herself. Guyon, the knight of temperance—that is, moderation—comments, "The strong through pleasure soonest falles, the weake through smart [pain]" (2.1.57). This terse observation gains subtlety through Acrasia's original charm over the cup, which explains the names of the knight and his wife:

> Sad verse, give death to him that death does give,
> And losse of love to her that loves to live. (2.1.55)

Mort-dant, then, means "death-giving" and Ama-via means "life-loving."[13] Acrasia's name is not specifically explained,[14] but she is obviously the opposite of Guyon, the knight of temperance. Without moderation the masculine fierceness of Mortdant and the feminine compliance of Amavia are both destructive.

A person who knows something about the faculty psychology of Spenser's time might associate Mortdant with the irascible and Amavia with the concupiscible passions—or, in Freudian terms, the *morbido* and the *libido*; indeed the whole episode teases its readers by hinting that it means even more than we can verbalize. But as Lewis wisely says, reading allegory is like going to sleep: the harder we try, the worse we fare. If we "surrender ourselves with childlike attention" ("Spenser" 137), we grasp holistically the unforgettable family picture of the dead knight, his dying lady with the knife in her breast, and their innocent baby with her blood on his hands. And this picture conveys the tragedy of immoderate pleasure-seeking, not as an intellectual conclusion, but as a visceral revulsion.

In other words, understanding the moral allegory is not merely the intellectual action of discovering that *x* equals *y*, but also an emotional, sometimes physical perception of what the moral quality feels like.[15] The title of book 3 tells us that Britomart is the knight of chastity; the surprise comes when we learn that chastity is not the colorless "abstinence" of modern jargon, but a robust girl who dresses in armor, fights six knights at once, falls in love with the image of the noble knight Artegall, and searches persistently for him (object: matrimony). The foes to chastity that she encounters are superficial passion, boorish sexuality, wimpish fear of femininity, manipulative flirtation, and the underlying cruelty of the mannered, sophisticated upperclass dalliance that literary historians call "courtly love." Spenser's allegory is not a preachment, but the portrayal of sexual virtue as an adventure.

Because the images, events, and personages have many overlapping meanings, the allegorical mode is admirably fitted to deal with the complexities of humanity and its spiritual aspirations. As Lewis put it,

> We are too apt to say of allegory "A is B" (and therefore not C, D, or E). But the allegorist was really saying "A is like B"; therefore quite possibly like C, D, and E as well. Thus B, C, D, and E can change and melt into one another, now this predominant, now that, in the fluidity of the poem. Waves at sea are not less beautiful because you cannot represent them in a contour map. ("Neoplatonism" 160–61)

The complexity and polysemy of *The Faerie Queene* allow it to appeal to readers on many different levels, as Lewis found in his repeated readings of it.

Lewis's Encounters with The Faerie Queene

Lewis himself encountered *The Faerie Queene* first as a fairy tale and then as a moral allegory. Later he gained a deeper, more universal understanding of its wisdom, and especially the way the shape of allegorical language fits the shape of spiritual life. His interest in the work was never purely academic; he read it for pleasure and spiritual growth. For him, reading *The Faerie Queene* was a continuing, lifelong process. Above all, his comments on Spenser show how his own life experiences deepened his literary response to *The Faerie Queene* over the years. The increased subtlety of his changed response contradicts, at least in the realm of literary criticism, the portrait of him as an emotionally immature person who feared modern psychology, hated women, and never changed his mind about anything.[16]

Lewis first began to read *The Faerie Queene* at age sixteen, when he was studying the classics with Kirkpatrick. His first impressions, after reading book 1 and half of book 2, are recorded in a letter to Arthur Greeves, conjecturally dated 5 October 1915: "Of course it has dull and even childish passages, but on the whole I am charmed . . ." (*Stand* 83). On 7 March 1916, he reports finishing it.[17] Since he was at this time alienated from Christianity,[18] and the first book deals with the quest for Holiness, we can infer that Lewis did not begin with a consuming interest in the moral allegory. What did he find in the poem?

First, despite its lack of surface realism, the adolescent Lewis found in *The Faerie Queene* a useful portrayal of sexual passion. Thus he argues that he is qualified to discuss love even though he has had no personal experience, because he has seen love through "the great love-literature," and he includes Spenser along with Sappho, Shakespeare, Austen, and Charlotte Brontë (*Stand* 85). Second, the poem, like the Surrey landscape where Lewis was living, delighted him because of its "intricacy" and "unpredictable variety." As he remembers in *Surprised by Joy*, "To walk [there] gave one the same sort of pleasure that there is in the labyrinthine complexity of Malory or the *Faerie Queene*" (146). He also found a romantic shagginess in it and remarked to Arthur: "I do wish Dürer had illustrated 'The Faerie Queene'." Dürer's "shaggy and tusked" boars reminded him of the "fantastic strength of the dwarfs in Rackham" (*Stand* 246), and both boars and dwarfs might well have been found in Spenser's trackless forest.

More importantly, *The Faerie Queene* fed the hunger for fantasy, the "love for myth and marvel" that Lewis shared with Arthur. After finishing the first three books, he turned to a rereading of Morris's *The Well at the World's End* (*Stand* 87). Later he mentions plans to read "another of Morris' romances, or his translation of one of the sagas" when he finishes *The Faerie Queene* (90). In the March letter reporting his completion of Spenser's epic, Lewis also first mentions having found "by hazard" George MacDonald's *Phantastes* (92–93), which was to be another great influence in his life. Both Morris and MacDonald had been influenced by Spenser; in fact, Spenser is quoted in the epigraph of chapter 20 of *Phantastes*.[19] All these fantasies fed Lewis's "feeling of something strange and wonderful that ought to happen";

he speculates that "the chance of a change into some world of Terreauty (a word I've coined to mean terror and beauty) is in reality in some allegorical way daily offered to us if we had the courage to take it" (97). His consciousness of "Terreauty" awakened by fantasy was to be the basis of all his subsequent work as a writer—his literary criticism and apologetics as well as his fiction.

Lewis's appreciation of fantasy in Spenser also led to an enthusiastic reading of Milton—not the neoclassicist Milton of *Paradise Lost*, but the earlier, more Spenserian bard. Thus Lewis describes *Comus* as "a play written on an episode from the Faerie Queene, all magic and distressed ladies and haunted woods" (*Stand* 131). But the taste for fantasy also led Lewis to praise Algernon Blackwood's *The Education of Uncle Paul*, which recounts a trip to "a primaeval forest at dawn" (88), and to judge Charles Doughty's epic *Mansoul, or the Riddle of the World*, with its "fine well-at-the-worlds-end kind of scenery in the first book" as "one of the *really* great things that will stand out like Dante or Milton . . ." (266–67). Although these fantasies were literary dead-ends, they are part of the experience that shaped Lewis's policy of approaching every book with "a preliminary act of good will" because "[w]e can find a book bad only by reading it as if it might, after all, be very good" (*Experiment* 116).

As Lewis changed, his experience of Spenser changed. The qualities he first found in the poet during his teens and early twenties—fantasy, adventures in shaggy, trackless forests, and the taste of experience—he continued to enjoy, but he became increasingly interested in the moral allegory. Nevill Coghill remembers how Lewis as a postwar Oxford undergraduate enthusiastically "championed [Spenser's] ethical attitudes as well as their fairy-tale terms." While keeping his adolescent zest for "the ugliness of the giants and . . . the beauty of the ladies," he also "rejoiced," Coghill says, "in their spiritual significances."[20] It was with this love for both allegory and fantasy that Lewis began writing *The Allegory of Love* in 1928 (*Letters* 256), finishing it in 1935 (*Stand* 474). Between 1928 and 1935 came his return to Christianity,[21] including the famous conversation with Tolkien and Dyson in 1931, and also the writing of his own allegory, *The Pilgrim's Regress*, published in 1933. That these experiences affected his understanding of Spenser is supported by a letter to Arthur Greeves in December 1935. In it Lewis announces that the Clarendon Press has accepted *Allegory* for publication and also reports rereading *The Faerie Queene* "with enormous enjoyment." He adds, "It must be a really great book because one can read it as a boy in one way, and then re-read it in middle life and get something very different out of it—and that to my mind is one of the best tests" (*Stand* 475). (I have not found it recorded that Lewis reread *The Education of Uncle Paul*

93

or *Mansoul* in this way, but his own Chronicles of Narnia surely pass the test.)

In the concluding chapter of *Allegory* we learn that the adult, Christian Lewis reads Spenser as a sage and serious teacher of the Christian life. Having been brought to his Christian commitment at least partly through the good offices of English literature, Lewis praises Spenser for "the rustic and humble piety of his temper—that fine flower of Anglican sanctity which meets us again in Herbert or Walton" (*Allegory* 328; see *Surprised* 213–14). He says Spenser's poetry is wise but not intellectual, for it is the wisdom most often found in "inarticulate people" (*Allegory* 359). Lewis also explains more fully the experience of life he found in *The Faerie Queene* as a teenager: the scenes and incidents are not realistic, "but the experience of reading is like living," for "[Spenser] makes imaginable inner realities so vast and simple that they ordinarily escape us as the largely printed names of continents escape us on the map . . ." (*Allegory* 358–59).

Lewis repeated this idea in *English Literature of the Sixteenth Century*, describing Spenser as "the poet of ordinary life, of the thing that goes on" (391). His continued admiration of this quality in *The Faerie Queene* may have contributed to his increasing awareness, originally set forth in *The Abolition of Man*, of just how complex is the socialization of a human being, and how easily modern education distorts the process. About the same time that he was working on the Clark Lectures[22] (delivered at Cambridge in 1944), the core of *Sixteenth*, he was also working on the Riddell Lectures (delivered in 1943), which became *Abolition*. In the latter he argued the importance of teaching young people to make the proper emotional responses, and in the former he praised Spenser for providing such training. He says,

> [Spenser] is not the poet of passions but of moods, . . . those prolonged states of the "inner weather" which may colour our world for a week or even a month. . . . In reading him we are reminded not of falling in love but of being in love; not of the moment which brought despair but of the despair which followed it; not of our sudden surrenders to temptation but of our habitual vices; not of religious conversion but of the religious life. (*Sixteenth* 391)

It is not surprising, then, that the training of the emotions began to be a more intentional element in Lewis's own fiction, particularly *That Hideous Strength*, the companion piece to *Abolition*, and the Chronicles of Narnia, which he began to publish in 1950. (See "Lewis's Spenserian Fiction" below.)

As the emotional training Lewis received from Spenser interacted with his writing and experience of life, his reading became deeper. In a 1954 essay he expands Britomart's experience in the House of Busirane to apply not only to the rejection of an obsessive courtly love relationship, but also to apply to any psychological self-imprisonment ("Spenser" 140). In a 1961 book review, published after his own experience with love and marriage, he describes Spenser's attitude to the sexes as characterized by "fruitful tensions and sensitive ambiguities" ("Neoplatonism" 157). Lewis is now aware of the subtlety with which Spenser, while accepting the conventional doctrines concerning feminine submission, portrays women who are strong as well as gentle. Una is "[as] superior to St George as Grace is to sinful man (1.8.1)," and Britomart both "defeats Arthegall" her lover and also "rescues him from slavery (5.7.37 seq.)"; nevertheless, both behave "humbly, like [women] in love, paradisially unaware of [their] high destiny" ("Neoplatonism" 157). Lewis's personal involvement with *The Faerie Queene* was one of his strengths as a critic. There were also weaknesses.

Lewis's Criticism of Spenser   ✝

As a Spenser critic, Lewis belonged to no school and was frequently at odds with his contemporaries—or sometimes, apparently, with his own principles. Despite his controversy with E. M. W. Tillyard on the "Personal Heresy," he explains the discrepancy between the letter to Raleigh and the actual contents of *The Faerie Queene* by describing his own intuitive perception of Spenser's personality and motivations.[23] Although he heartily approved of Spenser's didactic purpose, he insisted that pleasure, not self-improvement, was primary. As one who read for pleasure both *The Faerie Queene* and *The Education of Uncle Paul*, both E. Nesbit and Homer (in Greek), he was out of sympathy with F. R. Leavis's efforts to establish a ranking of works within the "Great Tradition."[24] Lewis dismissed those who seek to improve their minds, who want to read only "the best," as "status seekers" and "literary Puritans" (*Experiment* 9, 8, 10). Nevertheless, he more than once remarked that I. A. Richards's "conception of a poem as a health-giving adjustment of impulses ... certainly covers the *Faerie Queene*" (*Sixteenth* 393).

Lewis's forte in criticism, as in other nonfiction writing, was to epitomize or describe the contents of old books in a simple, fresh style.[25] He did just this, admirably, in his two introductions to Spenser for general readers: "Edmund Spenser, 1552–99" for *Major British Writers* (1954) and "On Reading *The Faerie Queene*" for *Fifteen Poets* (1941). These appear, along with three essays for specialists, in *Studies in Medieval and Renaissance Literature* (see Veith, chapter 6 in this volume).

Lewis's reputation in Spenser studies depends chiefly on *Allegory*, in which he describes the romantic love celebrated by French poets in the eleventh

95

century (conveniently, if inaccurately, called "courtly love"), arguing that it was one of (Western) history's three or four "real changes in human sentiment" (*Allegory* 11).[26] The last chapter treats *The Faerie Queene* as "the final defeat of courtly love by the romantic conception of marriage" (298).

Allegory was an exciting, fresh synthesis of widely divergent lines of thought. Helen Gardner, in her obituary for Lewis, called it "a masterpiece of literary history, the work of a truly original mind" that forever changed the reader's "imaginative map of the past."[27] In 1965 John Lawlor classified *Allegory* as one of "a very small class of [scholarly and critical] books . . . [for which] a future can be predicted." Such books, says Lawlor, share three qualities: they handle a large subject; they pioneer a new way of looking at the literature; and they are themselves literature—a readable account of "the adventures of the soul among masterpieces" (Lawlor 77). For many years *Allegory* was the respected, essential starting point for Spenser criticism. Graham Hough calls it "my first real guide to the reading of the poem" (6), and Roche praises it as "still the best introduction to the poem and by far the most sensitive reading" (210). In 1986, fifty years after its publication, Hannay noted that it has continued "to delight and to infuriate scholars," even though Lewis's "sweeping generalizations" are "intrinsically vulnerable to counterexample" (41, 47). In 1996 Radcliffe, though describing Lewis as "somewhat marginal[ized]" by "his opposition to modernism," says, "Lewis's chapter makes more original observations about the *Faerie Queene*—sources, prosody, philosophy, and design—than all of nineteenth-century criticism laid end to end" (169, 168).

The most important fault of the book is an overly narrow definition of the term "allegory," which Lewis applies only to the invention of persons and other "*visibilia*" to express "immaterial fact[s]." He distinguishes allegory from what he calls "symbolism or sacramentalism" (*Allegory* 44–45).[28] Thus he is forced to begin the chapter on *The Faerie Queene* by admitting that Spenser seldom uses "medieval allegory" (in his sense) and then to call Spenser's strongest uses of the allegorical mode "imagery."

However, in the introduction to Spenser for *Major British Writers* (1954), Lewis explicitly retracts his previous "nineteenth century" formulation, instead calling allegory a "picture-language . . . ultimately derived . . . from the unconscious" ("Spenser" 141). It is "the natural speech of the soul, a language older and more universal than words." He says Freud and Jung "and the practice of many modern poets and prose writers" have taught us this (137).[29] In addition to psychiatrists and writers, he had also learned from the iconographic researches of Erwin Panofsky, Jean Seznec, and Edgar Wind. Unavailable when Lewis was writing *Allegory* in the thirties, these researchers explain many of the visual images found in Spenser's pageants and masques.[30] Unfortunately, this later, more considered understanding of allegory continues to be less known than the facile, overly intellectual definition in the earlier book.[31]

Spenser's Images of Life represents Lewis's later understanding of allegory and the pictorial qualities of *The Faerie Queene*. Renaissance scholar Alastair Fowler has expanded on Lewis's Cambridge lecture notes, supplementing them with his memories of the lectures and his own knowledge of the field. In his preface Fowler says, "Most of the ideas and some of the words in this book are [those of Lewis]," adding that he has "freely and tacitly interpolated developments of [his] own . . ." (*Spenser's* vii, viii).[32] Although it is impossible to determine that any one passage represents Lewis's *ipse dixit* without examining the original lecture notes, the influence of the iconographers on his understanding of Spenser is unmistakable. For example, in the introductory lecture he urges his hearers to "see Seznec," and declares, "You haven't *seen* the *Primavera* till you read Wind" (Marion E. Wade Collection, Wheaton College, Wheaton, IL., ms. 4; cf. *Spenser's* 10). His changed approach is also seen in a 1960 review of a scholarly work on Spenser. In it Lewis praised the author for her treatment of Spenser's "images of good and evil" but wished she had said more about the "iconography of pageant and emblem." Concerning her logical analyses of certain passages, he emphasized that "When logic suggests anything contrary to the actual *quality* of Spenser's images—their immediate impact on the eye and the emotion—logic is, I believe, misleading us" ("Review" 643, 645). If Lewis had lived to write *Spenser's Images of Life* himself, in his clear but passionate style, the present evaluation of his Spenser criticism would be very different.

.There is, however, another weakness: Lewis's relative lack of interest in medieval-Renaissance theories of government.[33] Unconcerned with that period's ideal of "common profit," he misses the subtle relationship between Chaucer and Spenser, saying, "his discipleship to Chaucer exists only in profession, not in practice" (*Allegory* 305). Lewis's recommendation to ignore the historical allegory is sensible for beginning readers; however, the political ideal of Troynovant becomes more poignant when juxtaposed with the veiled references to actual historical events. That Lewis did understand this element of Spenser on some deeper level is shown in his own fiction, for in *Hideous* he juxtaposes the societies of Belbury and St. Anne's, and Narnia with Calormene in the Chronicles.

97

Lewis's Spenserian Fiction

In describing Lewis's criticism of Spenser, Katherine Gardiner says, "It has become an independent creation." She concludes her essay: "We can learn most from his discussion of the *Faerie Queene* if we permit him . . . to make Spenser's stories his own by making his own stories from master-pieces" (9–10). Although she referred to Lewis's criticism, these words are even more applicable to his fiction. Whether his awareness came primarily from Spenser or not, Lewis became deeply cognizant of the need for Spenser-like reading materials in the modern world. In *Abolition* he argues that emotional responses to literature, art, and beauty in nature are not just a matter of personal taste, but of making the proper response to the shape of reality, the Way the World Is (25–28).[34] In other words, there are objective truths other than verifiable physical facts. It is the duty of parents, poets, artists, and educators to train young people in making the proper emotional responses, for without trained emotions people do not have the motivation to behave morally. Such training is directed to the heart, and young people who do not have it grow up to be what Lewis calls "Men Without Chests" (*Abolition* 34).

According to his own account in the preface, Lewis wrote *Hideous* as a fictional counterpart to *Abolition*. In writing this novel Lewis uses images from *The Faerie Queene* to guide the reader into making the proper emotional responses—specifically, in finding the sterility of the N.I.C.E. revolting, and the friendship, humility, and ceremony of St. Anne's attractive.[35] The contrast between sterility and vitality echoes the contrast between Acrasia's Bower of Bliss and the Garden of Adonis.[36] The male protagonist, Mark, is a man without a chest, unable to resist corruption because his heart has never been trained. By resisting the falseness of "the Objective Room" as Guyon resists that of the Bower of Bliss and Britomart resists that of the House of Busirane, Mark breaks the power of Belbury over him. The female protagonist, Mark's wife Jane, has the same problem of adjusting to marriage as Spenser's Amoret, even though Jane is a three-dimensional character in a novel while Amoret is an allegorical personage (*Hideous* 334–37, 13–14, 379–80).[37]

Lewis followed Spenser even further in writing the Chronicles of Narnia. Having lived for so many years with Spenser's Fairyland, he created a parallel universe of his own, filled with images of life. Although the Chronicles have been called "a sort of Bible for a Bibleless age" (Huttar 123), the series can also be understood as a miniature *Faerie Queene*. Like Spenser's six finished books, each of the Chronicles has a central theme, and several of these are expressed as a place, i.e., an allegorical core. In *The Magician's Nephew* it is the creation scene, and secondarily, the Wood Between the Worlds, the place of pure materiality without form (31–43, 112–17).[38] These places function as allegorical cores, since a major theme of this sixth book is the relationship between the scientific or magical manipulation of Nature and the moral law. In *The Last Battle*, the allegorical core is the stable which is also a stage—the locus of illusion and deceit by Shift the Ape and the Calormenes, but also the gateway to death and a new life (114, 194–95).[39] In the last part of the book, the good characters leave the stage setting and enter the real Narnia.

Like Spenser, Lewis uses different degrees of allegory, ranging from thoroughly externalized characters like Bacchus and Father Christmas to well-individualized persons like Eustace and Jill. Like Spenser, Lewis is a synthesizer, melding symbols from the Bible, classical and Germanic mythology, English and European literature, and Irish old wives' tales. In some cases one cannot say whether Lewis draws an image from Spenser or whether both are drawing from a common source such as *The Aeneid*. And because Lewis was writing his own miniature *Faerie Queene* instead of directly imitating Spenser, one cannot expect to find an allegorical core in each book. But both, in their own way, image forth the virtues of the Western tradition—faith, moderation, love and friendship, justice and mercy, courtesy, and especially courage.

The qualities Lewis praises in *The Faerie Queene* apply equally well to the Chronicles: "They [speak] immediately to what [is] most universal and child-like in gentle and simple alike" (*Allegory* 311); they combine "the sublime and the ridiculous" to figure forth "the harmonious complexity of the world" (357). Lewis's statement that "Spenser's work is one, like a growing thing, a tree" (359) also applies to the Chronicles, for the child named Peter in the first book, *The Lion, the Witch and the Wardrobe*, is, like St. Peter, the doorkeeper of the Narnian heaven at the end of the series. And this description of *The Faerie Queene* also describes the Chronicles: "Spenser, with his conscious mind, knew only the least part of what he was doing, and we are never sure that we have got to the end of his significance. The water is very clear, but we cannot see to the bottom" ("Spenser" 143).

People try to get close to a beloved author by finding out the facts of his life. A better way is to follow him through the books he read. Learning about Spenser leads us into Lewis's inner life. In many ways Spenser was a model for Lewis, and the qualities he perceived in Spenser can be found in his own writing. Whether he was engaged in apologetics, literary criticism, or children's fantasy, he manifested honesty, humility, the avoidance of trendiness, "ordered exuberance," and "robust tranquillity" (*Sixteenth* 393). Then let us read Spenser's *Faerie Queene*, sharing Lewis's adolescent delight in trackless forests and shagginess, his young adult approval of the poem's moral teaching, his mature appreciation of Spenser's emotional health and wisdom. To read Spenser is to learn something important about Lewis's mind; it may even lead to sharing his delight in *The Faerie Queene* and his deeply spiritual participation in Spenser's images of life.

Notes

1. In *Shakespeare A to Z* Boyce lists the commonly accepted tentative date of *A Midsummer Night's Dream* as 1595 or early 1596 (436); the first three books of *The Faerie Queene* were published in 1590 and all six in 1596.

2. In *Edmund Spenser's Poetry*, MacLean and Prescott introduce "only those elements of modernization that seem required to render the text easily accessible to modern readers" (xi). Like the old Riverside edition of R. E. Neil Dodge, it modernizes the usage of *u/v* and *i/j*. It contains only books 1 and 3 and the Mutability cantos complete, with selections from the other books. Douglas Brooks-Davies's Everyman edition is a thorough modernization of both spelling and punctuation. It contains book 1 complete, most of books 2 and 3, and one or two cantos from books 4 and 7, completely omitting book 5. The most easily available paperback edition of the complete *Faerie Queene* is Roche and O'Donnell's Penguin Edition; it is also the most conservative in spelling.

3. Spenser's concern with spelling can perhaps be traced to his early education under Richard Mulcaster.

4. The relationship between Chaucer and Spenser is discussed later in this chapter.

5. Lewis called this premise Spenser's "second of the subordinate structural ideas" (*Sixteenth* 381–84).

6. Much critical argument has been devoted to the identification of *the* twelve virtues "according to Aristotle and the rest." Lewis remarks that "the Aristotelian influence on Spenser is fitful and superficial. The [*Nichomachean*] *Ethics* was not at all his kind of book" (*Sixteenth* 384). But perhaps the operative words are "and the rest," so that Spenser was referring globally to the whole tradition of Western ethics. According to Horton, a better understanding of his design may be found in Alexander Barclay's *Mirror of Good Manners* and Lodowyck Bryskett's *A Discourse of Civil Life* than in Aristotle's *Ethics* (15–16, 45).

7. That it was so taken by Spenser's contemporaries is shown in *A Discourse of Civil Life*, in which Bryskett's Spenser declines an invitation to discourse on the "Ethicke part of Morall Philosophie" on the ground that he is already working on this subject. Cited by Roche in *The Kindly Flame* (39).

8. Paul A. Olson in *The "Canterbury Tales" and the Good Society* discusses Chaucer "as a poet who addressed the immediate intellectual and social discussion of his age and his court . . ." (xvii).

9. Retellings of Spenser for children are now difficult to find. See "The Faerie Queene, children's versions," in *The Spenser Encyclopedia*. We can only hope that some talented film cartoonist will translate the golden plots of *The Faerie Queene* into videos.

10. In 1917, while taking military training before being sent to the front, Lewis actually had the experience of reading Spenser in a big folio edition (*Stand* 192).

11. Ironically, Tolkien said he found *The Faerie Queene* impossible to read because its archaic language was so philologically implausible; he also professed a hatred for allegory. See his "On Fairy-Stories."

12. In denying that his work was allegorical, Tolkien was denying that it presents an intellectual puzzle or explicit moral teaching.

13. Without Acrasia's explanation one would interpret "via" as the Latin "way," but it is closer to the French "vie."

14. *Acracy* is defined in the *OED* as "without self-rule, intemperate, incontinent." The earliest citation is from *The Faerie Queen*; the last is dated 1818.

15. Perhaps this sort of response is what was lost when T. S. Eliot's "dissociation of sensibility" occurred in the seventeenth century ("The Metaphysical Poets"). Concerning the physical basis of metaphor see Lakoff and Johnson, 56–60. For the unity of the "psychic" and the "physical," see the example, "I have no stomach to the business" in Barfield's *Poetic Diction*, 80n.

16. On misogyny and inability to change, see Filmer, 2, 54–56, 103, 104–05, 137–38, *et passim*; on immaturity, see *Owen Barfield on C. S. Lewis*, 25, and Holbrook, throughout.

17. Sayer's statement that Lewis read *The Faerie Queene* at one sitting (58) must refer to something else.

18. In *Surprised by Joy* Lewis says, "I allowed myself to be prepared for confirmation, and confirmed, and to make my first Communion, in total disbelief . . ." (161).

19. The epigraph to the Spenser chapter of *The Allegory of Love* is from MacDonald: "The quiet fulness of ordinary nature" (297). It expresses one reason Lewis admired both MacDonald and Spenser.

20. Quoted by Hannay *Taste*, 75 n. 3.

21. Lewis's dramatic account of his conversion in *Surprised*, 228–38, has so impressed many readers that they forget his earlier religious experiences, also recorded there. As a child, he notes, "I was taught the usual things and made to say my prayers and in due time taken to church. I naturally accepted what I was told . . ." (7). At "Belsen," he says, "the most important thing that befell me" was that "there first I became an effective believer" (33). Later he analyzes the factors turning him against Christianity: interest in the occult, lack of proper spiritual direction, doubt that Christianity was more valid than pagan mythology, and ingrained pessimism (58–66).

22. Lewis was asked to write volume 3 of *The Oxford History of English Literature* as early as 1935. In *C. S. Lewis: A Companion and Guide* Hooper says a large portion of it had been written at the time of the Clark Lectures in 1944. Magdalen College gave him a year off to finish it from October 1951 to October 1952, and it was finished in May 1952 (474, 478, 480).

23. Lewis's introduction to Spenser in *Fifteen Poets* describes how Spenser's friends at Cambridge wanted him to be "fashionable," i.e., "an extreme Puritan and a servile classicist," but Spenser ignored them to write about "the Middle Ages as he imagined them to have been" ("On Reading" 147, 148). The passage in *English Literature in the Sixteenth Century Excluding Drama* dealing with the poet's education, friends, and reading begins with a statement that his mind was simple and quiet, "more ordinary" and "less clever" than Sidney's, and a biographical tracing of the causes. However, Lewis does call these personal remarks "supposals" (357). A more dramatic, perhaps overstated, excursus into Spenser's psychology is found in *Spenser's Images of Life*, 139.

24. Other modernist critics who denigrated Spenser included D. A. Traversi, René Wellek, Allen Tate, Cleanth Brooks, Yvor Winters, and poet-critic T. S. Eliot. Even Charles Williams, writing in *Reason and Beauty in the Poetic Mind* (1933), trivialized Spenser's moral allegory (Radcliffe 172–74).

25. For instance, Lewis describes Martianus Capella's *The Marriage of Philology and Mercury* as the poet's "curiosity shop of his mind" (*Allegory* 79) and builds his summary of the book on this metaphor. Similarly, the "Christian Behaviour" section of *Mere Christianity* is an exposition of standard medieval instructional material on the cardinal and theological virtues. To notice this lack of originality is not a denigration of Lewis, who never sought to be original.

26. In *The Pilgrim's Regress* Lewis depicts courtly love as a message from the Landlord (157–58) similar to pagan myths and the Romantic love of Nature.

27. Quoted by Hannay (*Pineapple* 59). Hannay's evenhanded account of critical reaction to *Allegory* with respect to the Bower of Bliss and the Art-Nature polarity demonstrates both the genius of Lewis's accomplishment and its weaknesses.

28. Lewis actually used this distinction in the structure of *Regress*. See Myers, 11–15. Piehler attributes it to "the Coleridgean polarity of allegory and symbolism," but says Lewis's appreciation of allegorical literature transcended his definition of allegory (88–89). Also see Morris, 187–89.

29. This statement implies a knowledge of Freud, Jung, and modern writers that refutes the stereotype of Lewis as one completely out of touch with modern thought. See Bishop (7) for a list of books on psychoanalysis in Lewis's library.

It is also noteworthy that his appreciative remarks about allegory are remarkably similar to the more ironically expressed ones of his feminist and modernist contemporary, Virginia Woolf

(1882–1941). See "The Faery Queen" in *The Moment and Other Essays* (1948), usefully anthologized in Maclean and Prescott.

30. These works are cited in *Spenser's*: Erwin Panofsky, *Studies in Iconology*, 1939 (New York: Harper Torchbooks, 1962); Jean Seznec, *La Survivance des dieus antiques*, 1940 (Pub. as *The Survival of the Pagan Gods* in 1953) (Rpt. New York: Harper Torchbooks, 1961); and Edgar Wind, *Pagan Mysteries in the Renaissance* (1958).

31. In a 1956 letter to Peter Milward, Lewis seems to return to the old definition in *The Allegory of Love* but in context he is defining "allegory" in contrast with "myth," not distinguishing between allegory and symbol (*Letters* 458).

32. In "Provocative Generalizations" 44–45 Hannay cites Lewis's original notes; cf. *Spenser's* 45–46. A photocopy of these notes is now available in the Marion E. Wade Collection, Wheaton College, Wheaton, IL. I regret that I was not able to make extensive use of it in preparing this essay.

33. Still another source of critical controversy has been Lewis's interpretation of Spenser's Bower of Bliss, exhaustively traced by Hannay.

34. The title of John Polkinghorne's book reconciling particle physics with Christian doctrine. Lewis himself uses the term "Tao," which for contemporary readers has misleading connotations. See Myers, 73–84, for a detailed comparison of Alec King and Martin Ketley's *The Control of Language*, called "The Green Book" by Lewis, and *The Abolition of Man*.

35. See McClatchey, 166–93, for a sensitive treatment of the novel's contrasts of images and emotional states.

36. The resemblance is in the mood of the two places and such details as the metallic-looking foliage. The N.I.C.E. does not allegorically represent intemperance, nor St. Anne's the fecundity of nature.

37. Both Jane and Amoret are recently married, and both are reluctant to move from the virgin's proper reticence to the joyful acceptance of physical surrender to the male. See Roche's discussion of Amoret in the House of Busirane, 77–87.

38. That the Wood Between the Worlds represents sheer materiality may be inferred from the fact that the Greek *hylē* means both "wood" and "material," while the Latin *silva* means "wood" and "forest." In the *Cosmographia* of Bernardus Silvestris, the allegorical personification of chaos is called "Silva." See Myers 171–72.

39. Myers 169, 171–72, 175. The Spenserian qualities of the Chronicles, including the allegorical cores, are discussed in some detail in "The Context of Christian Humanism" (Myers 112–81).

---

102   Works Cited

Barfield, Owen. *Owen Barfield on C. S. Lewis*. Ed. G. B. Tennyson. Middletown, CT: Wesleyan UP, 1989.

———. *Poetic Diction*. 3rd ed. Middletown, CT: Wesleyan UP, 1973.

Bishop, Leigh C. "C. S. Lewis on Psychoanalysis: Through Darkest Zeitgeistheim." Marion E. Wade Collection. Wheaton College, Wheaton, IL. n.d.

Boyce, Charles. *Shakespeare A to Z*. New York: Roundtable Press, 1990.

Edwards, Bruce L., ed. *The Taste of the Pineapple*. Bowling Green, OH: Bowling Green State UP, 1988.

Eliot, T. S. "The Metaphysical Poets." *Modern British Literature*. Ed. Frank Kermode and John Hollander. New York: Oxford UP, 1973, 512–19.

Filmer, Kath. *The Fiction of C. S. Lewis: Mask and Mirror*. New York: St. Martin's, 1993.

Gardiner, Katherine. "C. S. Lewis as a Reader of Edmund Spenser." *The Bulletin of the New York C. S. Lewis Society* 16 (Sept. 1985): 1–10.

Hamilton, A. C., ed. *The Spenser Encyclopedia*. Toronto: U Toronto P, 1990.

Hannay, Margaret P. "Provocative Generalizations: *The Allegory of Love* in Retrospect." *Seven* VII (1986): 40–60. Rpt. in *The Taste of the Pineapple* 58–78.

Holbrook, David. *The Skeleton in the Wardrobe. C. S. Lewis's Fantasies: A Phenomenological Study.* London: Associated UP and Lewisburg: Bucknell UP, 1991.

Hooper, Walter. *C. S. Lewis: A Companion and Guide*. San Francisco: Harper San Francisco, 1996.

Horton, Ronald Arthur. *The Unity of "The Faerie Queene."* Athens: U Georgia P, 1978.

Hough, Graham. *A Preface to the Faerie Queene*. New York: Norton, 1964.

Huttar, Charles A. "C. S. Lewis's Narnia and the 'Grand Design.' " *The Longing for a Form: Essays on the Fiction of C. S. Lewis*. Ed. Peter J. Schakel. Kent, OH: Kent State UP, 1977. 119–35.

Lakoff, George, and Mark Johnson. *Metaphors We Live By*. Chicago: U of Chicago P, 1980.

Lawlor, John. "The Tutor and the Scholar." *Light on C. S. Lewis*. Ed. Jocelyn Gibb. New York: Harcourt, Brace and World, 1956. 68–82.

Lewis, C. S. *The Abolition of Man*. 1943. New York: Macmillan, 1947.

———. *The Allegory of Love: A Study in Medieval Tradition*. 1936. London: Oxford UP, 1958.

———. *The Chronicles of Narnia*. 1950–56. New York: HarperCollins, 1994.

———. "Edmund Spenser, 1552–99." *Medieval* 121–45.

———. *English Literature in the Sixteenth Century Excluding Drama*. Oxford: Oxford UP, 1954.

———. *An Experiment in Criticism*. Cambridge: Cambridge UP, 1961.

———. *Letters of C. S. Lewis*. Ed. W. H. Lewis. 1966. Rev. ed. Ed. Walter Hooper. London: HarperCollins, 1988.

———. "Neoplatonism in the Poetry of Spenser." *Medieval* 149–63.

———. "On Reading *The Faerie Queene*." *Medieval* 146–48.

———. *The Pilgrim's Regress: An Allegorical Apology for Christianity, Reason and Romanticism.* 1933. London: Geoffrey Bles, 1950.

———. "Review of *The Allegory of The Faerie Queen* by M. Pauline Parker, I.B.V.M. Oxford: Clarendon [1960]." *The Cambridge Review* 81 (11 June 1960): 643, 645.

———. *Spenser's Images of Life*. Ed. Alastair Fowler. Cambridge: Cambridge UP, 1967.

———. *Studies in Medieval and Renaissance Literature*. Ed. Walter Hooper. 1966. Cambridge: Cambridge UP, 1980.

———. *Surprised by Joy: The Shape of My Early Life*. New York: Harcourt, 1955.

———. *That Hideous Strength: A Modern Fairy-Tale for Grown-Ups*. 1945. New York: Macmillan, 1965.

———. *They Stand Together: The Letters of C. S. Lewis to Arthur Greeves (1914–1963)*. Ed. Walter Hooper. New York: Macmillan, 1979.

MacDonald, George. *Phantastes* and *Lilith*. 1964. Grand Rapids: Eerdmans, 1976.

McClatchey, Joe. "The Affair of Jane's Dreams: Reading *That Hideous Strength* as Iconographic Art." Edwards 166–69.

Morris, Francis Joseph. "Metaphor and Myth: Shaping Forces in C. S. Lewis' Critical Assessment of Medieval and Renaissance Literature." Diss. U of Pennsylvania, 1977.

Myers, Doris T. *C. S. Lewis in Context*. Kent, OH: Kent State UP, 1994.

Olson, Paul A. *The "Canterbury Tales" and the Good Society*. Princeton: Princeton UP, 1986.

Piehler, Paul. "Visions and Revisions: C. S. Lewis's Contributions to the Theory of Allegory." Edwards 79–91.

Radcliffe, David Hill. *Edmund Spenser: A Reception History*. Columbia, SC: Camden House, 1996.

Roche, Thomas, Jr. *The Kindly Flame: A Study of the Third and Fourth Books of Spenser's "Faerie Queene."* Princeton: Princeton UP, 1964.

Sayer, George. *Jack: C. S. Lewis and His Times*. San Francisco: Harper and Row, 1988.

Spenser, Edmund. *The Complete Poetical Works of Spenser*. Ed. R. E. Neil Dodge. Boston: Houghton Mifflin, 1908.

———. *Edmund Spenser's Poetry*. Ed. Hugh MacLean and Anne Lake Prescott. 3rd ed. New York: Norton, 1993.

———. *The Faerie Queene*. Ed. Thomas P. Roche, Jr., and C. Patrick O'Donnell, Jr. New York: Penguin Books, 1978, rpt. 1987.

———. *The Fairy Queen*. Modernized and ed. by Douglas Brooks-Davies. London: Everyman, 1996.

Tolkien, J. R. R. "On Fairy Stories." *Essays Presented to Charles Williams*. Ed. C. S. Lewis. Grand Rapids: Eerdmans, 1966. 38–89.

Woolf, Virginia. "The Faery Queen." Spenser, *Edmund Spenser's Poetry* 672–75.

6

Renaissance

Gene Edward Veith

"I *believe* I have proved that the Renaissance never happened in England," remarked C. S. Lewis to his fellow Oxford don Nevill Coghill. "*Alternatively . . .* that if it did, *it had no importance!*" (Coghill 61). Such a sweeping generalization—breathtaking in its audacity and iconoclasm—exemplifies Lewis's way with literary history. The statement, in fact, sums up his contributions to Renaissance scholarship throughout his career, culminating in his appointment to the professorship Cambridge University designed especially for him, a chair in Medieval *and* Renaissance literature.

Lewis's point was that the Renaissance of the sixteenth century, with its blossoming of literature and the arts, was no discrete, new phenomenon, but was actually a continuation of the Middle Ages. The conventional wisdom had been that the sixteenth century, with its neoclassical learning and the advent of humanism, was a time of "rebirth" from the barbarism of medieval darkness, marking the beginning of modern culture. Lewis argued instead that the Middle Ages and the Renaissance shared a common world view and that the aesthetic monuments of the Renaissance rest on medieval foundations. If there are "modern" elements in the Renaissance, they are mostly to be found in the more sterile strains of the sixteenth century, in what he labeled the "drab" poetry and the pedantic, unimaginative narrowness of humanistic learning, traditions that continue in literary modernism. The high points of the age, however, are found in the "golden" verse of poets such as Sidney and, especially, Spenser, whose rich, evocative language and luminous symbolic imagery have their roots in medieval allegory.

As a critic of Renaissance literature, Lewis combines a breadth of scholarship—he seems to have read everything,[1] and not just the canonical texts of the current critical fashion—with incisive aesthetic judgments. He is the sort of critic who, in the course of overturning stereotypes, recreates the sensibilities of other times, and in so doing helps his readers not only understand but also enjoy old books. Lewis had another agenda, though, as a literary critic. In the course of his scholarship as a literary historian, Lewis was also developing a critique of literary and critical modernism, as well as developing aesthetic principles that he would employ in his own imaginative fiction.

Getting Inside

Lewis made his reputation as a literary scholar with *The Allegory of Love* (1936). Just as his friend J. R. R. Tolkien taught readers how to enjoy *Beowulf* as a work of literary art, rather than as a mere archeological curiosity,[2] Lewis took obscure and (for moderns) practically unreadable medieval allegories such as *The Romance of the Rose* and, in effect, showed us how to read them, revealing them to be profound explorations of the psychology of love and brilliantly imagined works of art. For Lewis, literature is a way to enter other points of view, to see through other eyes (*Experiment* 137–41). Literary history helps make this possible by ushering readers into another time and another sensibility. "To judge between one *ethos* and another," he observed, "it is necessary to have got inside both, and if literary history does not help us to do so it is a great waste of labour" (*Sixteenth* 331).

The point is not to read a work in terms of the concerns and interests of our own times but to "get inside" alien ways of thinking and feeling. To use contemporary critical jargon, Lewis was most interested in the "otherness" of the past. But this "otherness" can be accessed, he believed, through literature and with the help of literary scholarship. In the tapestry of the intellectual history, the analysis of the psychology of love conventions, and the close readings of poetry that constitute *Allegory*, Lewis's aim was to get inside the medieval imagination—and that of the Renaissance, since the medieval allegorical and romantic traditions not only continued but came to their fruition in the Renaissance romances of Ariosto, Tasso, and especially Spenser. To enter into this by now quite alien sensibility by way of romantic allegory, Lewis shows, is to enter a universe charged with meaning and mystery, where every fact of existence carries multi-leveled symbolic depths.

Much later, a course of lectures Lewis gave several times at Oxford was published as *The Discarded Image: An Introduction to Medieval and Renaissance Literature* (1964). Here Lewis further explores the richness of the medieval

and Renaissance world view, explicating the Ptolemaic universe in its attendant learning and imaginative power. Describing the medieval sense of the
"heavens," of crystalline spheres within spheres animated by the light of God,
Lewis is not satisfied with mere academic description but places the reader
in a medieval night sky:

> Whatever else a modern feels when he looks at the night sky, he certainly feels
> that he is looking *out*—like one looking out from the saloon entrance on to the
> dark Atlantic or from the lighted porch upon dark and lonely moors. But if you
> accepted the Medieval model you would feel like one looking *in*. The Earth is
> 'outside the city wall.' When the sun is up he dazzles us and we cannot see inside.
> Darkness, our own darkness, draws the veil and we catch a glimpse of the high
> pomps within; the vast, lighted concavity filled with music and life. And, look-
> ing in, we do not see, like Meredith's Lucifer, 'the army of unalterable law', but
> rather the revelry of insatiable love. (*Discarded* 118–19)

This is a far cry from the meaningless, absurd universe of existentialism and
the modernists. Lewis offers an exposition of the medieval and Renaissance
cosmology, but he also helps the modern reader *feel* what it would be like to
live in a universe ruled by "the revelry of insatiable love." Furthermore, his
evocation of an eminently *meaningful* universe offered an implicit alternative to the much narrower, bleaker world view of his contemporaries.

In his remarkable epilogue to the book, Lewis makes a confession:

> I have made no serious effort to hide the fact that the old Model delights me as
> I believe it delighted our ancestors. Few constructions of the imagination seem
> to me to have combined splendour, sobriety, and coherence in the same degree.
> It is possible that some readers have long been itching to remind me that it had
> a serious defect; it was not true. (*Discarded* 216)

He goes on to agree that it was not true, but then—in a startling anticipation
of postmodernism—argues for the provisional nature of all models:

107

> We can no longer dismiss the change of Models as a simple progress from error
> to truth. No Model is a catalogue of ultimate realities, and none is a mere fan-
> tasy. Each is a serious attempt to get in all the phenomena known at a given
> period, and each succeeds in getting in a great many. But also, no less surely,
> each reflects the prevalent psychology of an age almost as much as it reflects the
> state of that age's knowledge. (222)

Our own materialistic, evolutionary model will also pass away, he argues, not
only when new evidence emerges but when "far-reaching changes in the mental temper of our descendants demand that it should. The new Model will not

be set up without evidence, but the evidence will turn up when the inner need for it becomes sufficiently great."

Lewis's fondness for allegories, symbolic cosmologies, and imaginative sub-creations is evident also in his own fiction, from the Chronicles of Narnia to the space trilogy. His critique of modernist materialism for its claustrophobic constrictions and imaginative impoverishment is a major theme of his works in Christian apologetics. Although Lewis seemed to have three different careers—as literary scholar, fantasy author, and Christian apologist—they were mutually reinforcing and, ultimately, of one piece.

The Period That Never Happened

Lewis's major work in Renaissance studies is his flatly titled *English Literature in the Sixteenth Century Excluding Drama* (1954), the third of twelve volumes in the Oxford History of English Literature. In 1944 Lewis had been invited to deliver the Clark Lectures at Trinity College in Cambridge, and his topic was sixteenth-century English literature. To turn his lectures into an exhaustive, comprehensive literary history of the period, as Oxford University Press required for their series, took Lewis ten years of tedious academic labor.

A thorough literary history of a particular time period must be a study of what was actually written and read at the time, he maintained, not merely the masterpieces that are still read today. Furthermore, Lewis believed that a critic should not comment on a work without having first read it. Lewis spent a decade—while he was also writing the Narnia books—poring over polemical tracts, political chronicles, and bad popular poetry, as well as, of course, works by great poets such as Sidney and Spenser. With the added burden of researching each writer and attending to the bibliographical minutiae, Lewis complained bitterly about the demands of "OHEL," which he pronounced, "Oh Hell."[3]

The finished product, however, reflects none of this misery. It is a *tour de force* of learning, wit, and critical acumen, proof that even ostensibly uninteresting material can come alive at the hands of a good writer. It was also a *tour de force* of Renaissance scholarship, shattering conventional assumptions, turning established judgments upside down, and offering new ways of understanding and appreciating works of literature. Furthermore, as Dame Helen Gardner—one of the greatest Renaissance scholars of the day—pointed out, it is astonishingly enjoyable to read. "Who else," she asked, "could have written a literary history that continually arouses delighted laughter!" (qtd. in Green and Hooper 283).

Lewis begins by turning topsy-turvy the conventional wisdom of generations of scholars and teachers. In his notorious opening chapter, "The New
Learning and the New Ignorance," Lewis argues that the humanists were not
humane and that the Puritans were not puritanical.

The common assumption has been that the humanists' rediscovery of
classical civilization caused an awakening of intellectual and literary vitality
after the obscurantism of medieval scholasticism. Actually, however, "The
war between the humanists and the schoolmen was not a war between ideas:
it was, on the humanists' side, a war against ideas. It is a manifestation of the
humanistic tendency to make eloquence the sole test of learning" (*Sixteenth*
30). The humanist exaltation of style, of rhetoric at the expense of logic, was
in fact an anti-intellectual movement. "In the field of philosophy humanism
must be regarded, quite frankly, as a Philistine movement: even an obscurantist movement. In that sense the New Learning created the New Ignorance" (31).

After excoriating the classical humanists, Lewis acknowledges their contributions: "Despite the immense harm they did, despite their narrowness,
their boasting, and their ferocity—for it is a strange delusion that represents
them as gentle, amiable, and (in that sense) 'humane'—our debt to them can
never be cancelled" (31). Their scholarship did make available again the Greek
and Latin classics (though many had been known and used throughout the
Middle Ages). But, for all of their criticisms of medieval romance, romances
continued to be written. Their actual influence on the literature of the day, at
least in England, was minimal. "The more we look into the question, the harder
we shall find it to believe that humanism had any power of encouraging, or
any wish to encourage, the literature that actually arose" (2).

As for the Puritans, "nearly every association which now clings to the word
puritan has to be eliminated when we are thinking of the early Protestants.
Whatever they were, they were not sour, gloomy, or severe" (34). On the contrary, their enemies accused them of being too libertine. Lewis offers a fair-
minded description of what it meant for those early Calvinists to believe that
salvation is by grace alone. In many ways, Puritans were the liberals of their
day, the ones who called for personal freedom and institutional, political, and
cultural change. "Unless we can imagine the freshness, the audacity, and
(soon) the fashionableness of Calvinism, we shall get our whole picture wrong.
It was the creed of progressives, even of revolutionaries. It appealed strongly
to those tempers that would have been Marxist in the nineteen-thirties" (43).
To be sure, Lewis is not entirely sympathetic, inasmuch as the Puritans also
tended to be allied with the humanists.

The sixteenth century was a religious age, not merely in its fondness for
theological controversy but in its unspoken assumptions about everyday life,
what Lewis calls its "ubiquitous piety."

> It is, indeed, best seen in the writers who are not dealing with religion; in Tusser, the chroniclers, Shakespeare, or Hakluyt's voyagers. In all these we find the assumption, unemphasized because it is unquestioned, that every event, every natural fact, and every institution, is rooted in the supernatural. Every change of wind at sea, every change of dynasty at home, all prosperity and all adversity, is unhesitatingly referred to God. The writers do not argue about it; they know. (38)

In other words, Christianity was more than a set of theological maxims; it was (and, for Lewis, is) an all-encompassing world view, one which needs explaining in the modern world, whose own world view is far less interesting.

The Drab and the Golden

Amidst all of the book's encyclopedic detail and its judicious assessments of the literary merit of historians, tract writers, and Latin poets—some of whom were dull but some of whom, Lewis convinces us, were stylists worth reading despite their obscure subject matter—Lewis develops a paradigm that accounts for nearly the whole range of sixteenth-century literature: "the drab" and "the golden."

Lewis, despite his loaded terminology, was ostensibly trying to be descriptive, not pejorative, in discussing the drab writers. These were the poets and prose stylists who tried to be realistic, down to earth, and colloquial. They sometimes affect a certain cynicism, and they scorn the lush, ornamented language and idealized subject matter of other writers. Sir Thomas Wyatt and Henry Howard, Earl of Surrey, are drab, as is John Donne.

Golden poets, on the contrary, are in the tradition of the medieval romance writers, romantics who anticipate and would influence the later romantics such as Shelley and Keats. Contrary to that of the drabs, their language is rich, beautiful, and evocative. They are idealistic, exalted, aiming at transcendence. Golden poets include Sir Philip Sidney, Sir Edmund Spenser, and William Shakespeare. (In the next century, Milton would be a golden poet.)

To illustrate the distinction, Lewis offers some comparisons. Sackville is drab:

> O Sorrow, alas, sith Sorrow is thy name,
> And that to thee this drere doth well pertaine,
> In vayne it were to seeke to cease the same. . . .

Sidney is golden:

> You Gote-heard Gods that love the grassie mountaines,
> You Nimphes that haunt the springs in pleasant vallies,
> You Satyrs joyde with free and quiet forrests. . . .

To prevent the accusation that he is stacking the deck, Lewis gives examples in which the drab poetry is superior to the golden. In a translation of a sonnet by Petrarch, Wyatt is lucid, psychologically realistic, and *drab*:

> The pillar perish'd is whereto I leante
> The strongest stay of mine unquiet minde;
> The like of it no man agayne can finde,
> From east to weste still seekynge though he wente.

A dirge from Sidney's *Arcadia* is equally morose and rather more vapid, but its language glows:

> Farewell O Sunn, *Arcadias* clearest light;
> Farewell O pearl, the poore mans plenteous treasure:
> Farewell O golden staffe, the weake mans might:
> Farewell O Joy, the joyfulls onely pleasure.
> Wisdom farewell, the skillesse mans direction:
> Farewell with thee, farewell all our affection.[4]

The difference is not simply a matter of ornamentation, degrees of colloquialism, or realism as opposed to idealism. Rather, a different aesthetic and a different sensibility are at work. Lewis's paradigm of "the drab" and "the golden" brings to mind Northrop Frye's "high mimetic"—literature that is exalted and exalting, aiming at transcendence—as opposed to the "low mimetic," the realm of subversion, sordid truths, and irony.[5]

Lewis applies the two categories with such justice—even to prose writers such as the drab humanist Sir Thomas Elyot and the golden theologian Richard Hooker, with his luminous theological language—that the reader cannot help but apply it also to non-Renaissance writing. All literature, perhaps, aspires either to drabness or goldenness. Lewis clearly favored the latter. His own evocative style, in both his prose and his fiction, is certainly, by his own definition, golden. He was writing, however, in an age that celebrated the drab.

The 1940s, when Lewis was writing *Sixteenth*, was the high point of literary and critical modernism. John Donne and the metaphysical poets had been rediscovered and were being exalted, Lewis felt, beyond all measure. Donne's tortured intellectualism, his down-to-earth and somewhat shocking imagery, and his multi-leveled ironies fit well with the sensibilities of twentieth-century modernism. The verse of T. S. Eliot, one of Donne's first champions, had many of the same qualities. Donne's poetry also had appeal not only for modernist poetry but for modernist criticism. His verse, with its convoluted imagery and multivalent meanings, was tailor-made for the New

Criticism, with its penchant for untangling and explicating the literary text as puzzle.

Thus in Lewis's scholarly assessment of the drab poets of the English Renaissance and his defense of the golden aesthetic, he was directly challenging the literary establishment of his own day. For Lewis, Donne and Eliot and modernism were insufferably drab. Donne, Lewis would tell his friends, was a "minor poet."[6] Lewis the Christian apologist did not care for the poetry of these fellow Christians, much preferring the golden verse of the atheist Shelley.[7] At the beginning of his career, Lewis's ambition was to be a poet, but the shift in fashion toward the wasteland style dashed his hopes.[8] He craved the literature of romance, of high fantasy, of the transcendent yearning that he defined as Joy.

✝ Our Sage and Serious Poet

One of Lewis's favorite writers—and perhaps the one most influential to his own imaginative fiction—was Spenser. In the pantheon of English literature, Spenser ranks with Chaucer and Milton in the tier just under Shakespeare. It is odd that a writer of his stature is so little read. Perhaps the greatest writer that hardly anyone ever reads, Spenser had a champion, an elucidator, and a disciple in Lewis.

Lewis may have written more about Spenser than he did any other individual author. His contributions to Spenser scholarship are the subject of another chapter. Spenser was, however, the prime focus of Lewis's Renaissance criticism. As such, a few words on what Lewis saw in Spenser—and what he took from him—may be in order, as exemplifying Lewis's appropriation of the Renaissance.

What Lewis found in Spenser was the imaginative author, as it were, of his dreams. Here was golden language, allegory, and romance. Here too was the appeal of fairy tales and a self-contained fantasy world, all bound together in an imaginatively realized Christianity. Milton considered Spenser to be the model Christian poet, and so he was for Lewis.

Milton's "sage and serious poet," celebrated in *Areopagitica* as a better moral teacher than Scotus or Aquinas, is credited by Lewis—in one of his characteristically stunning generalizations—for a monumental conceptual shift in Western civilization. In the literary and cultural tradition, courtly love and marriage were actually portrayed as being in conflict. One nearly always fell in romantic love with someone who was already married, giving the experience either its poignant hopelessness or its dramatic and tragic conflict (as in the triangle of King Arthur, Guinevere, and Lancelot).

According to Lewis, it was Spenser—in his sonnets to the woman who would become his bride, in his sublime marriage poem "Epithalamion," and in his allegory of love in *The Fairie Queene*—who channeled the passions and devotions of romantic love into the institution of marriage (*Allegory* 298, 360).

Now it doubtless overstates the case to credit Spenser for the present-day practice of marrying for love. It is also an oversimplification to say that the Middle Ages never integrated romantic love with marriage (see chapter 4 of this volume). Chaucer did, particularly in "The Franklin's Tale," which is precisely about a marriage built on romantic love, setting forth a new standard of mutuality, in which the man is "Servant in love and lord in marriage" (line 121). And yet, Lewis is on to something here, recognizing cultural structures and seismic shifts that literature both reflects and shapes. Although no one ever accused Lewis of being a feminist, in zeroing in on the relationships between men and women and what can only be described as the cultural construction of love, he was anticipating feminist scholarship by half a century.

But it was allegory that Lewis did most to rehabilitate in his criticism and in his own writing. As Lewis explains it, allegory, properly speaking, is not simply a point-by-point narrative puzzle to be solved with a key; nor is it merely a way to convey preset ideas with the help of a picture story. Rather, in his treatment, allegory is essentially symbolic fantasy.

Lewis appreciated Spenser's "golden" imagery and language, but he valued him above all as a storyteller (*Sixteenth* 389). In *The Faerie Queene*, Spenser creates a fully realized, variegated imaginary world—anticipating Tolkien by nearly four centuries. Peopled with all the denizens of medieval romance—knights, maidens, shape-shifting wizards, giants, dragons, assorted monsters, and even the Questing Beast—Faerie Land is also a symbolic exploration of theological, moral, and even psychological truths. Book 1 is a symbolic exploration of holiness, understood in the Reformation sense of the futility of human merit and dramatizing the rescue of God's Grace. Book 2 dramatizes temperance, the virtue of self-control, in the face of sensuously rendered temptations. Book 3, with its formidable female warrior Britomart, is about the power of chastity and the sanctity of marriage. The other books—on friendship, justice, courtesy, and a brief fragment of a seventh book on mutability—make up half of Spenser's unfinished vision of a twelve-part epic on the Twelve Moral Virtues.[9]

Lewis not only explicated this combination of high fantasy and religious symbolism in his work on Spenser, but he imitated it in his own fiction. Not only the Chronicles of Narnia, which Lewis was writing while he was working on *Sixteenth*, but *Pilgrim's Regress*, the space trilogy, *The Great Divorce*, and *Till We Have Faces* all employ allegory in the specifically Spenserian mode.

Except for *Regress*, which is more of the conventional Bunyanesque type of allegory, his fiction is allegorical in the somewhat expanded sense developed in his criticism of medieval and Renaissance literature. When Lewis in *Allegory* interprets the allegorical significance of *The Romance of the Rose* or a scene in Spenser, he does not stick mechanically to the four levels of medieval typology or some other hermeneutical scheme. Sometimes a scene represents one kind of meaning, he shows, sometimes another. Nor does Lewis assume that once he has gotten the interpretation, the passage is thereby fixed and formulated, so that we can go on, as if the only significance of the literature were its intellectual code. More important to Lewis is the imaginative and the aesthetic impact of the symbol, its goldenness.

What Spenser does with Faerie Land, Lewis does with Narnia.[10] Lewis likewise creates a magical, medieval-style universe, both beautiful and terrifying. This realm, like Faerie Land, becomes the site for adventures that are exciting and imaginatively stimulating in their own right. These adventures also sometimes lapse into allegory, symbolizing and exploring the depths of theological truth. The allegory, however, is not a point-by-point theological tableau as in Bunyan; rather, it emerges naturally, as needed, from the fantasy world.

It may be stretching the similarities to observe that both *The Faerie Queene* and the Chronicles of Narnia consist of seven books (Spenser having completed only a few cantos of number seven, while Lewis completed his whole unified saga), but there can be little doubt that the two are intimately related. Spenser's Prince Arthur is an earthling who unknowingly crosses into Faerie Land after having a vision of the Faerie Queene Gloriana one day in the woods. Falling in love, he pursues her until he finds himself in another world, peopled by elves and rustics, satyrs and beautiful witches, beings who are not always what they appear. Lewis's children likewise find themselves moving from twentieth-century England into a fairy-tale world. For all of their charms and marvelous populations, the two realms are also landscapes of spiritual testing.

What Lewis says about the structure of Spenser's allegories also seems to apply to his own. In his explication of *The Faerie Queene*, Lewis shows how each book contains its own key, an allegory-within-an-allegory that sets forth the book's central theme: "Thus in each book Spenser decided that there should be what I have called an 'allegorical core' (or shrine, or inner stage) where the theme of that book would appear disentangled from the complex adventures and reveal its unity" (*Allegory* 381). The allegorical core of book 1 is Redcrosse Knight's sojourn in the House of Holiness; book 2 has the House of Alma; book 3 has the Garden of Adonis, and so forth. Around this core,

Spenser arranges incidents that are allegorical to various degrees—and some, significantly, that are not allegorical at all.

Similarly, Lewis builds the narrative of at least several of his Narnia books around a pivotal symbolic scene, an "allegorical core." In *The Lion, the Witch and the Wardrobe*, this is the passion, the sacrifice, and the resurrection of Aslan. In *The Voyage of the Dawn Treader*, the whole saga of Eustace's transformation is crystalized in the scene where the evil child is turned into a dragon and made human again by Aslan. In *The Silver Chair*, the allegorical core would be the witch's temptation underground in which she almost persuades the children that the upper world does not exist. These symbolic tableaux—which are perhaps the most memorable scenes in the books (much of the stories not being allegorical at all)—define the theme explored throughout each story (for example, in these three books the respective themes of redemption, sanctification, and faith).

While the humanist scholars of his day, including many of his own friends and colleagues, were ridiculing medieval romances, fairy tales, and ideas, Spenser was re-imagining them for his own age. "He devoted his whole poetical career to a revival, or prolongation, of those medieval motifs which humanism wished to abolish" ("Spenser" 122). The same could be said of C. S. Lewis.

Unsound but Brilliantly Written

What was the influence of Lewis's Renaissance scholarship? Did he convince the rest of the scholarly world that what he said about allegory, humanists, Puritans, the drab, and the golden is correct? Certainly, Lewis is still regularly cited by scholars today and is treated as something of a force to contend with, positively or negatively. His revisionary impulse may be appreciated now more than ever, in these days of revisionary scholarship. His judgments about the Puritans, for example, have pretty much been confirmed by more recent scholarship and are held by anyone who has done much study of them, though the old stereotypes remain. That there was a continuum between the Middle Ages and the Renaissance is also now widely accepted. The classical humanists are now sometimes open to criticism, though usually for their politics rather than for what Lewis labeled as their "new ignorance."

That some of Lewis's theses are now somewhat accepted is not necessarily due to Lewis's influence, however. Certainly, the drab is still preferred to the golden, in both contemporary criticism and contemporary literature (even though fantasy has come back in vogue, as opposed to the modernist insistence on literary realism). Although historical criticism has returned, it tends

115

rather to look at the past through the lens of the present, to anatomize the power relationships and social inequalities. Lewis, on the other hand, preferred to look at our own times through the lens of the past.

At the time, Lewis was reacting against certain facets of literary and critical modernism, which might be thought to ally him with today's postmodernists who are also challenging the assumptions of modernism. His revisionism, his attention to cultural paradigms, and his championing of the radical fiction that is fantasy could be said to be postmodern (though Lewis, of course, was actually trying to be *pre*-modern). And yet in other ways Lewis was himself a modernist.

When Lewis's contribution to the Oxford History of English Literature came out in 1954, he must have braced himself for the reaction. Although many academic critics found his approach to literary history exasperating, the book's reviews for the most part were quite positive. Journalists marvelled at how the book, despite its unpromising subject matter of obscure and forgotten authors, was so entertaining to read, so unboring. "Mr. Lewis is today the only major critic of English literature who makes a principle of telling us which authors he thinks we shall *enjoy*," said John Wain in *The Spectator*, "this may not sound like much, but most dons have moved a long way from any recognition that literature is something that people used to read for fun. Mr. Lewis, now as always, writes as if inviting us to a feast" (qtd. in Hooper 507).

Major scholars also paid tribute to Lewis's infectious enthusiasm and to his provocative, stimulating discussions of works that they had assumed were exhausted. Helen Gardner's pleasure in finding a work of literary history that is capable of making the reader laugh in delight has already been noted. She also praised his learning and conscientiousness. "By far the most important," she writes, "is the strength of his capacity for enjoyment. This enables him to write with astonishing freshness on subjects which might be thought to be exhausted" (508). Another distinguished scholar, Donald Davie, called it "the best piece of orthodox literary history that has appeared for many a long year," citing as its great virtue "the critic's ability to enter sympathetically into literary conventions so alien to a modern temper that one had thought them irrecoverably lost" (508).[11]

For many readers, from Tolkien—who described the volume as "a great book, the only one of his that gives me unalloyed pleasure" (Sayer 326)—to the less friendly A. N. Wilson (241–43), the book represents Lewis at his very best.

Even those who praised the book caviled at some of its judgments. Dame Gardner, for all of her delight in Lewis's approach to literary history, took him severely to task for minimizing the humanists (Green and Hooper 283). Lewis's Oxford colleague A. L. Rowse wrote an important and favorable review, but privately confronted him over his disparagement of the classicists and gaps in his coverage (Wilson 244). George Sayer reports that to this very day, Oxford dons recommend their students read the book, but with an important caveat, saying that it is "unsound but brilliantly written" (326).

The capacity of these scholars to take pleasure in a book that they disagree with points, in a way, to a quality they share with Lewis. They are appreciating the book for its aesthetic merits, even as they question some of its content. Lewis did the same in his book, assessing tract writers, contestants in theological controversies, prose speculations, and formulaic poetry in rigorously *aesthetic* terms. This is all to say that Lewis, like most of the critics of his day, was a formalist.

The so-called New Critics of the time stressed that a literary work should be studied as a self-contained aesthetic object. A work's historical background, information about the author, the truth of its moral or religious themes, all should be bracketed and set aside; the literary critic's concern should be on the "artfulness" of the work, its structure, technique, and aesthetic design. Lewis differed with the more extreme New Critics in insisting on the importance of literary history, but he used his historical research to elucidate the work's *aesthetic* qualities.

Lewis in fact sided with the New Critics in an important critical debate. In an essay "The Personal Heresy in Criticism" and in a series of exchanges with the important Milton scholar E. M. W. Tillyard (collected and published in 1939), Lewis challenged the notion that a poem is to be understood primarily as an expression of the poet's personality. What matters is not the biography of the writer or what the poem implies about the state of the author's mind; rather, the poem is the author's creation and operates on its own terms. What Lewis called "the personal heresy" is a variation of the New Critics' "intentional fallacy," the notion that the meaning of a work is to be found in its author. Both Lewis and the New Critics were taking issue with the approach to literature that emerged out of the Romantic movement, with its focus on the "self" of the artist, which often substituted biographical speculation and hero-worship for attention to the literary qualities of the work.

This side of Lewis as a critic of Renaissance literature—and his facility with the New Critical set piece of the "close reading"—can be seen in his essay "Hero and Leander" (1952). Here Lewis takes a little-read poem drawn from Greek mythology about the tragic love of a priestess of Venus, a work whose chief claim to fame is that it is the source of the line "Whoever loved, that loved not at first sight?" The poem was begun by Marlowe and finished by Chapman. Although both could be classified as "golden," the two authors are extremely different in their styles, their temperaments, and themes. Practioners of the personal heresy find it difficult to deal with a work that has two different authors; at best, the work might be divided up, so that the contributions of each author could be considered separately. Lewis, however, argues

117

that *Hero and Leander* has an artistic unity to which both authors, in their distinct ways, contributed. "Each poet has contributed what the other could not have done, and both contributions are necessary to a worthy telling of the story" ("Hero" 58).

The first part, by Marlowe, Lewis describes as "perhaps the most shameless celebration of sensuality which we can find in English literature" (59). The account of the priestess Hero's passionate love—not to mention "the gods in sundrie shapes, / Committing headdie ryots, incest, rapes"—is characteristic of Marlowe's unrestrained and often perverse imagination. But here C. S. Lewis the moralist sets aside, temporarily, the moral issues. The question that concerns him here is an aesthetic one. "The question which Marlowe's sestiads invite is not a moral one. They make us anxious to discover, if we can, how Marlowe can write over eight hundred lines of almost unrelieved sensuality without ever becoming mawkish, ridiculous, or disgusting. For I do not believe this is at all easy to do" ("Hero" 59).

Lewis shows how Marlowe pulls this off with a witty comparison to Shakespeare's similar *Venus and Adonis* and with his characteristically sweeping yet illuminating generalizations (e.g., "Licentious poetry, if it is to remain endurable, must generally be heartless: as it is in Ovid, in Byron, in Marlowe himself" ["Hero" 62]). Although Lewis emulates the formalist New Critics in bracketing moral issues, his commentary nevertheless has a strong moral resonance. But it remains essentially an aesthetic analysis. Lewis, the Christian, never confuses his theological agreements or disagreements with his aesthetic judgments about a work. Marlowe's eroticism, though he disapproves of it morally, is at least very well done, in a genre difficult to do well.

Marlowe's hot-house imagery is balanced and countered, however, by the very different sensibility of Chapman, who takes over the poem after Marlowe's death. The passionate Marlowe has written the poem's rising action, dealing with the love affair of Hero. The falling action, showing the passion's tragic consequences, is written by a new poet better suited to the job. "At the very moment when the theme begins to demand a graver voice, a graver voice succeeds" ("Hero" 62). "Chapman's sestiads are a celebration of marriage in contrast to, and condemnation of, the lawless love between Hero and Leander" (63).

In the course of the discussion, Lewis returns to the theme of the Renaissance (one might say Reformation) exaltation of marriage first developed in *Allegory*. He also offers one of his illuminating renderings of the point of view of another age. In Chapman's part of the poem, a key character is the goddess and allegorical figure Ceremonie. In not waiting to get married, Hero and Leander are portrayed as having defied "Time" and "Ceremonie." For Chapman, Lewis explains, ceremony "is what distinguishes a fully human action from an action merely necessary or natural. As he says, no praise goes to the food which 'simply kils our hunger' or the dress that 'clothes but our nakednes'. We reserve praise for 'Beautious apparell and delicious cheere'" ("Hero" 66). Hero and Leander's sexual passion was merely "ranke desire." The marriage *ceremony*, with all that it means, orders and humanizes sexuality. For Chapman and his time, ceremony is "our defence against utter ruin and brutality."

> It is tempting to say that Ceremonie is simply Chapman's name for civilization. But that word has long been prostituted, and if we are to use it we must do so with a continual reminder that we mean not town-planning, and plumbing, and ready-cooked foods but etiquette, ball-rooms, dinner-parties, judges' robes and wigs, Covent Garden, and coronations in Westminster Abbey. In a word, we must realize that what we should regard as the externals of civilization are, for Chapman, essential and vital. (67)

For all of his formalism, Lewis, in this example and elsewhere, brings to bear on the text philological scholarship and empathy for the perspective of the past. While still being something of a modernist, he carries on a running critique of modernity.

Lewis demonstrates that in *Hero and Leander*, the whole is greater than the sum of its two authors. "Marlowe's part, with all its limitations, is a very splendid and wonderful expression of accepted sensuality: Chapman's, a very grave and moving reply—an antithesis, yet arising naturally, almost inevitably, out of the thesis" ("Hero" 73). The aesthetic impact of the work comes precisely from the interplay and conflict between its two very different writers. New Critics were always demonstrating a work's "unity," where postmodernists are at pains to uncover its disunity. At their best, New Critical readings, with their close interaction with the text, remain perhaps the most illuminating introductions to a piece of literary art.

If Lewis's essay amounts to a New Critical explication of a text, it is one which manages not to neglect either the work's historical context or its continuing human context. It shows, above all, Lewis's ability to make an obscure piece of literature more interesting and more pleasurable to read than it would ever have been without his mediation. He unveils the poem's aesthetic achievements, which are not at all obvious, while still noting its faults. "But heaven forbid that we should never read—and praise—any poems less than perfect" ("Hero" 73).

Literature of Transcendence

In showing how medieval and Renaissance literature were closely related, Lewis had to contend with multiple misunderstandings. Today, our under-

119

standing of both periods is marred by inaccurate stereotypes. In his essay "Tasso," on the Italian Renaissance author who like Spenser continued the medieval literary tradition of the romance, Lewis discusses "how ignorant these early medievalists were of the true Middle Ages, and secondly how ill provided the Middle Ages are with the sort of poetry they wanted to read" (114): "They wanted chivalry, not scholastic philosophy; enchanters, not allegory. They wanted, quite simply, knights in armour, castles, and love stories. They wanted precisely the imaginary Middle Ages which Boiardo had created, Ariosto perfected, and Tasso delivered from their satiric elements." Ironically, then, the medieval stereotypes, beloved by the Victorians and still cultivated today in popular novels and video games, were themselves creations of the Renaissance.

As for the popular stereotypes of the Renaissance, they are also incorrect. Lewis refers to other critics who "wrote under the spell of not the imagined Middle Ages but the imagined 'Renaissance'—the glorious, coloured, full-blooded Pagan phantasmagoria of poisoning cardinals and Machiavellian Popes and wicked beauties which so enchanted our fathers" ("Tasso" 115).

Although he claimed that the Renaissance did not, properly speaking, exist, in elucidating the two periods, from the inside, Lewis nevertheless uncovered some differences after all. The sublimation of courtly love into the institution of marriage—a theme Lewis returns to again and again in his Renaissance scholarship—was not, of course, due to the classical humanists, but to the Reformation with its rejection of the celibate ideal in favor of the Christian family. As Lewis points out in "Tasso," "Asceticism is far more characteristic of Catholicism than of the Puritans. Celibacy and the praise of virginity are Catholic: the honour of the marriage bed is Puritan" ("Tasso" 117).

What Lewis did find continuous in both the Middle Ages and the Renaissance was the literary form of the romance, the tales of wonder, fantasy, and supernatural adventures—and, more importantly, the imagination and world view that produced them. Whether he was writing about Tasso's romances, or allegory, or Spenser's synthesis of the two, or the "golden" style, Lewis was drawing attention to literature that conveyed some sense of transcendence. The quotations in practically all of his scholarly studies are of lines and imagery that he finds evocative and stirring for some ineffable reason. Lewis was most interested in literature that carried connotations of the infinite, poetry that was elevating to the point of the elusive, numinous taste of transcendence he termed "Joy."

In romance, its associated genres, and the ages that produced them, he found literature that testified to and evoked this transcendence. In the seventeenth century, this whole sensibility began to be lost. "Far more important," says Lewis of the decline in Tasso's popularity in the seventeenth century, "because it went down to deeper preferences and aversions, was the

120

revolt against the supernatural and the marvelous, in that sense the counter-romanticism, which we see in Davenant, Hobbes, and Rymer" ("Tasso" 113).

Lewis, in other of his writings, finds something of the medieval and Renaissance spirit in the nineteenth century, with the revival of imaginative fantasy and the golden language of Keats and Shelley, whose sources are admitted in the very name of the Romantic movement. But the twentieth century is different. "At the moment, we live in the full tide of the most violent counter-romanticism that has ever been seen" ("Tasso" 115). His literary scholarship, his fiction, and his Christian apologetics were attempts to reverse that tide.

Notes

1. Charles Huttar told me about working in the library of Magdalen College in Oxford and seeing the register of books Lewis had taken out in the late 1940s and early 1950s, while he was working on his volume for the Oxford History of English Literature. According to Professor Huttar, Lewis appears to have essentially checked out the entire sixteenth-century collection.

2. See Tolkien's "Beowulf: The Monsters and the Critics."

3. See Green and Hooper 282–84 and Sayer 323–26.

4. The poems are quoted and discussed in *Sixteenth* 325–27.

5. See Frye's *Anatomy of Criticism*. For Frye, however, the categories are not so much matters of style, as they are in Lewis, but matters of genre: epic is "high mimetic"; satire is "low mimetic."

6. As reported in Sayer 323. And yet, Lewis could write brilliantly about him. For his antipathy toward Donne and his insights into his poetry, see Lewis's essay "Donne and Love Poetry in the Seventeenth Century" in *Literary* 106–25.

7. See "Shelley, Dryden, and Mr Eliot," in *Literary* 187–208. For Lewis's often iconoclastic taste, which tended to go against the grain of modernist critics, read the whole of his *An Experiment in Criticism*.

8. See, for example, Green and Hooper 88–89.

9. Lewis told Walter Hooper that he hoped, when he arrived in heaven, to find that Spenser had finally completed the other six books so that he could read them too (Green and Hooper 292).

10. Besides the exposition here, see Doris Myers's chapter in this volume as well as her *C. S. Lewis in Context*, especially 169–75.

11. These reviews are quoted from Walter Hooper, *Companion* 507–08, which gives samples from other reviews as well.

Works Cited

Coghill, Nevill. "The Approach to English." *Light on C. S. Lewis.* Ed. Jocelyn Gibb. New York: Harcourt Brace Jovanovich, 1965.

Frye, Northrop. *Anatomy of Criticism: Four Essays.* Princeton: Princeton UP, 1966.

Green, Roger Lancelyn, and Walter Hooper. *C. S. Lewis: A Biography*. New York: Harcourt Brace Jovanovich, 1974.

Hooper, Walter. *C. S. Lewis: A Companion and Guide*. San Francisco: Harper San Francisco, 1996.

Lewis, C. S. *The Allegory of Love: A Study in Medieval Tradition*. 1936. New York: Oxford UP, 1960.

———. *The Discarded Image: An Introduction to Medieval and Renaissance Literature*. Cambridge: Cambridge UP, 1964.

———. "Edmund Spenser, 1552–99." *Medieval* 121–45.

———. *English Literature in the Sixteenth Century Excluding Drama*. Oxford: Oxford UP, 1954.

———. *An Experiment in Criticism*. Cambridge: Cambridge UP, 1961.

———. "Hero and Leander." *Selected Literary Essays*. Ed. Walter Hooper. New York: Cambridge UP, 1969.

———. *Studies in Medieval and Renaissance Literature*. Ed. Walter Hooper. Cambridge: Cambridge UP, 1966.

———. "Tasso." *Medieval* 111–20.

Myers, Doris T. *C. S. Lewis in Context*. Kent, OH: Kent State UP, 1994.

Sayer, George. *Jack: A Life of C. S. Lewis*. Wheaton, IL: Crossway, 1994.

Tolkien, J. R. R. "Beowulf: The Monsters and the Critics." *The Monsters and the Critics*. Ed. Christopher Tolkien. Boston: Houghton Mifflin, 1984. 5–48.

Wilson, A. N. *C. S. Lewis: A Biography*. New York: Norton, 1990.

7
Shakespeare

Colin Manlove

Teaching Shakespeare

While C. S. Lewis's writings are well known, his occupation as a teacher remains largely a closed book. We have several broad and sometimes conflicting accounts by ex-pupils, but none has described in detail the content of Lewis's tutorials and lectures; and now memories have faded, and few former students remain. We are left to guess at Lewis's teaching from his published work, which in the case of Shakespeare's plays amounts to just one essay on *Hamlet*. Yet throughout his time as Tutor in English at Magdalen College, Oxford, from 1925 to 1954, Lewis had to cover the whole range of English literature from *Beowulf* to 1830 over the seven terms of an undergraduate B.A. degree, and Shakespeare and the English drama were an integral part of this.[1] While there would not always have been scope to teach Shakespeare's plays individually, and it seems that sometimes they were grouped into comedies, histories, tragedies, Roman plays, and late romances,[2] they and Elizabethan and Jacobean drama occupied a whole term or more of instruction. Lewis did not lecture extensively on the plays, but he would from time to time have been called upon to do so; his essay on *Hamlet* was originally a lecture delivered at the Oxford Examination Schools in Michaelmas Term 1938 (Griffin 195–96).

Nevertheless the paucity of Lewis's publication on Shakespeare remains marked in comparison to that on such other "great" writers as Chaucer, Spenser, or Milton. The theater did not greatly attract him, nor did drama as a genre;[3] he was drawn more to Shakespeare's poems and the *Sonnets*, which "seldom present or even feign to present passionate thought growing and changing in the heat of a situation: they are not dramatic" (*Sixteenth* 508); and his essay on *Hamlet* is an attempt to turn the play from a drama to a poem. When Lewis wrote his monumental *English Literature in the Sixteenth Century* (1954), drama was excluded.

Scattered comments on Shakespeare's plays in Lewis's writings and notes give some insight into his possible standpoints in teaching them. His annotations to some of his copies of the plays, mainly from before 1934, show him setting out facts about the texts and assembling schools of critical thought to provide a foundation for teaching; and they also shed light on the cast of mind Lewis would bring to his tutorials.[4] Lewis would demand thorough knowledge and precision concerning the material, and a "social" sense of each word, phrase, book, or viewpoint as properly to be understood only in relation to others in the past. As for his views on individual plays, the flyleaf of Lewis's personal copy of *Othello* has a long note by him,[5] describing the play in terms of the hero's frightening blackness for its contemporary audiences (not the same as color- or race-prejudice), and seeing Othello as a good but dangerous ogre from the wild outside, whom the foolish white lady marries, like Beauty and the Beast. Othello "may do anything," Iago serving as a mere catalyst for a primed explosive. Othello's essence, not the situation in the play, makes him jealous and mad. Lewis moves us away from character and dramatic situation, to seeing the play in terms of fairy tale or myth. There is only one exception to this, and that is in an early note on *Hamlet*, in which Lewis sees the play as "the tragedy of weakness";[6] but he is immediately at pains to say that this weakness has nothing to do with character, and everything to do with unfortunate experience. He also says that the weakness is overcome, and that it is nothing "abnormal," because Hamlet is every reflective man, and our representative.

Lewis's published work contains a few incidental comments on the plays. In "Hamlet: The Prince or the Poem?" he describes *The Merchant of Venice* as concerned with financial versus natural and human wealth, Shylock making money breed unnaturally by usury, and Bassanio rejecting the rich caskets for the leaden one that hides Portia's heart. Here as with *Othello*, Lewis turns aside from character analysis, seeing *Hamlet* as "not so much about men as about metals," and as less a drama of "real-life" people than a fairy tale in which a princess marries a noble pauper ("Hamlet" 95–97). In his *A Preface to "Paradise Lost"* (1942), Lewis extends the "failure of degree," which he sees in Satan's and man's rebellions in Milton's poem to Shakespeare's *Lear, Macbeth, Troilus and Cressida,* and *The Taming of the Shrew*: "Hierarchy is a favorite theme with Shakespeare. . . . It seems to me beyond doubt that Shakespeare agreed with Montaigne that 'to obey is the proper office of a rational soul'" (*Preface* 75–76). It is possible that the hierarchical principle also guided some of Lewis's opinions in tutorials on the history plays and the Roman plays. As for Shakespeare's fantasy plays such as *A Midsummer Night's Dream, The Winter's Tale,* and *The Tempest*—"the only things of Shakespeare I really appreciate except the *Sonnets,*" Lewis wrote as early as 1916 (*Stand* 146)—we hear strangely little about them. In a 1931 letter describing *The Winter's Tale* as a story of resurrection, Lewis says, "I must confess that more and more the value of plays and novels becomes for me dependent on the moments when, by whatever artifice, they succeed in expressing the great *myths*" (*Stand* 420). Similarly, in his essay "William Morris" (1939), Lewis remarks, "in *The Winter's Tale* the Pygmalion myth or resurrection myth in the last act is the substance and the characters, motive, and half-hearted attempts at explanation which surround it are the shadow" ("Morris" 224).[7]

Writing on Shakespeare: Hamlet

Our main concern here must be with Lewis's published work specifically on Shakespeare. We have three pieces: "Variation in Shakespeare and Others" (1939), "Hamlet: The Prince or the Poem?" and the twelve-page section on Shakespeare's poems and the *Sonnets* in *English Literature in the Sixteenth Century.* Of these, the *Hamlet* essay, addressed by invitation to the British Academy in 1942 and separately published, is by far the best known, even (by some) celebrated, and certainly the most revealing.

In many ways, *Hamlet,* with its claustrophobia, its mother-fixation, and its tortured inwardness, would seem precisely the one play of Shakespeare's with which Lewis would *not* engage, but his actual interpretation turns out to involve the removal of all these perceived aspects of the play for a deeper and more universal vision beyond them. *Hamlet* clearly fascinated Lewis, in drawing from him his only full interpretation of a Shakespeare play. We find him writing to his friend Arthur Greeves in 1931,

125

> I have been studying Hamlet very intensely, and never enjoyed it more. I have been reading all the innumerable theories about him and don't despise that sort of thing in the least: but each time I turn back to the play itself I am more delighted than ever with the mere atmosphere of it—an atmosphere hard to describe and made up equally of the prevalent sense of death, solitude, & horror and of the extraordinary graciousness and lovableness of H. himself. Have you read it at all lately? If not, do: and just surrender yourself to the magic, regarding it as a poem or a romance.[8]

As a poem, Lewis writes, not as a drama. Already we are aware that what draws him is not an action, a relationship, or a struggle, but an atmosphere, an essence, a marvellous boy, something that is more a quality than a process. In this he is not unique; others in his day were beginning to view Shakespeare's plays as poems more than dramas, and certainly to move away from the obsessive character analysis that had long preoccupied criticism: G. Wilson Knight, E. E. Stoll, L. C. Knights, Caroline Spurgeon, and Derek Traversi. What is marked in Lewis's approach is its focus on the essence, the center of the play; in the whole of his essay on *Hamlet* scarcely any character apart from Hamlet is mentioned save the ghost.

Lewis's essay has two concerns: a conspectus of past interpretations of the play, and then his own. We perhaps forget how much and for how long interpretations of Hamlet's character had dominated critical approaches to the play. John Dover Wilson's famous work, *What Happens in Hamlet*, had appeared as recently as 1935. One of the central issues fueling "character" approaches to the play concerned the reasons for Hamlet's apparent delay in carrying out the ghost's order to revenge his father's murder. This was variously assigned to such psychological features in Hamlet as an Oedipal conflict, an over-intellectual disposition, or a sickened spirit. Some commentators, most notably T. S. Eliot, had found no adequate motive for Hamlet's delay, and viewed the play as a failure. Others still argued that Hamlet did not really delay at all, but was hindered by circumstance and simply waited for the best opportunity.

Lewis deals with the critics of *Hamlet* in these three broad groups, and sets about dismissing them all. To those who maintain that Hamlet does not delay, he answers that Hamlet himself tells us he does so: "He pronounces himself a procrastinator, an undecided man, even a coward: and the ghost in part agrees with him" ("Hamlet" 91). This deals with them: now we are left "with those who think the play bad and those who agree in thinking it good and in placing its goodness almost wholly in the character of the hero, while disagreeing as to what that character is" (91). Lewis argues that we might be inclined to agree with the former class, because

126

> Is it really credible that the greatest of dramatists, the most powerful painter of men, offering to . . . an audience [of trained critical sensibilities] his consummate portrait of a man should produce something which, if any one of them is right, all the rest have in some degree failed to recognize? . . . Does the meeting of supremely creative with supremely receptive imagination usually produce such results? (91–92)

That for Lewis deals with the "character" critics; there is no sense that the myriad differing views the play provokes could be a measure of its greatness. Last, there are those who regard the play as a failure. Lewis argues that they are wrong because most people are enchanted by it.

If this is failure, then failure is better than success. We want more of these "bad" plays. From our first childish reading of the ghost scenes down to those golden minutes which we stole from marking examination papers on *Hamlet* to read a few pages of *Hamlet* itself, have we ever known the day or the hour when its enchantment failed? That castle is part of our own world. The affection we feel for the Prince and, through him, for Horatio, is like a friendship in real life. (92)

With this last fusillade, Lewis feels that he has done with most remaining critics of *Hamlet*.

This approach, however, is less than persuasive. Lewis has made a reductive argument and a series of assertions do the job of literary criticism. Each point he makes is open to question. Though Hamlet says he delays, he also says he is impeded by circumstances ("The time is out of joint"); he cannot be certain that the ghost is not a goblin from hell sent to tempt him, and sets about proving Claudius's guilt for himself through the play "The Mousetrap"; and he may well be paralyzed by a poisonous spiritual atmosphere in Denmark itself (an idea already part-canvassed by Derek Traversi in his *Approach to Shakespeare* [1938]). It is only an extra-textual argument to say that *Hamlet* is a good play because generations of critics have thought so (and suppose the next generation changes its mind, who then is right?). The one-page argument refuting the myriad interpretations of Hamlet's character is an inappropriate deployment of logic against human sensibility. And it is questionable as an argument. Why should there not be diverse views of Hamlet's nature?

Here the argument interlocks with one of Lewis's prejudices concerning art. In Lewis's view the play can only, Platonically, have one good. It cannot spawn so many and conflicting goods; variety of interpretation is a sign of error, or at best only one step on the way to the Truth beyond mortal confusion. Therefore he argues that what these critics are finding as their goods is not within the character of Hamlet, but in some fixed good beyond it and unacknowledged by them. "If the picture which you take for a horse and I for a donkey, delights us both, it is probable that what we are both enjoying is the pure line, or the colouring, not the delineation of an animal" ("Hamlet" 93). We do not need to cite the visually ambiguous duck-rabbit of E. H. Gombrich's *Art and Illusion* (1960) to oppose this: one man's notion of what is a fine representation of a donkey may differ from another's. Lewis seems rather too ready to find reality only in what transcends the subjective.

At any rate he now sets out to find this further reality. And before he does so, he reveals his broad critical kindred here:

I confess myself a member of that school which has lately been withdrawing our attention from the characters to fix it on the plays. Dr. Stoll and Professor Wilson Knight, though in very different fashions, have led me in this direction; and

\...as long seemed to me simply right when he says that tragedy is an imi-
...of men but of action and life and happiness and misery. ("Hamlet"

...critical position involves seeing the character of the hero not as a singu-
larity but as representative of the whole fabric of the play. To Lewis, for
instance, the ghost of Hamlet's father is essential, not simply the means by
which Hamlet is informed of his father's murder. Thus, "The Hamlet formula,
so to speak, is not 'a man who has to avenge his father' but 'a man who has
been given a task by a ghost'" (97). Wonder and mystery are at the heart of the
play.

At this point mid-way through his talk, Lewis has moved from arguments
about schools of criticism to his actual interpretation of *Hamlet*. He remarks
(97–98) that, uniquely in Elizabethan drama, the ghost in *Hamlet* has doubtful reality, and this leads to painful uncertainty in Hamlet and "the other characters" (which other characters?—Claudius? Ophelia?): "the appearance of
the spectre means a breaking down of the walls of the world and the germination of thoughts that cannot really be thought" (98). Lewis then proceeds
to see the central subject of *Hamlet* as death, the prime source of uncertainty.
Questions about the nature or desirability of death litter the play, unlike others by Shakespeare, where death is simply the end of life.

> They think of dying: no one thinks, in these plays, of *being dead*. In *Hamlet* we
> are kept thinking about it all the time, whether in terms of the soul's destiny
> or of the body's. Purgatory, Hell, Heaven, the wounded name, the rights—or
> wrongs—of Ophelia's burial, and the staying-power of a tanner's corpse: and
> beyond this, beyond all Christian and all Pagan maps of the hereafter, comes
> a curious groping and tapping of thoughts, about "what dreams may come".
> It is this that gives to the whole play its quality of darkness and of misgiving.
> (99)

128

The focus of the play is not on the special character of one man, but on
humanity at its most sensitive confronted by death. Hamlet is not singular
but our representative. He speaks for all our fears and hopes and doubts.
More than this, he does it not in the mere prose of any man, but in the finest
poetry, which takes the subject to its highest bent. With him it is most truly
a case of "what oft was thought, but ne'er so well exprest." Lewis remarks, "I
would go a long way to meet Beatrice or Falstaff or Mr. Jonathan Oldbuck or
Disraeli's Lord Monmouth. I would not cross the room to meet Hamlet. It
would never be necessary. He is always where I am" (102). For Lewis the oft-
canvassed mystery of the play lies not in the character and motivation of
Hamlet but "in the darkness which enwraps Hamlet and the whole tragedy

and all who read or watch it. It is a mysterious play in the sense of being about mystery" (103).

Beyond all this, as not infrequently in Lewis's criticism, is a certain child-like and untutored excitement. The *Hamlet* he gives us is in the end not one to be circumscribed by an interpretation, but a play that breaks through every category until it is filled with immensity. It is here not really about death and loss: it is about the wonder of being able to wonder at all at death, and to do so in magnificent poetry.

> I am trying to recall attention from the things an intellectual adult notices to the things a child or a peasant notices—night, ghosts, a castle, a lobby where a man can walk four hours together, a willow-fringed brook and a sad lady drowned, a graveyard and a terrible cliff above the sea, and amidst all these a pale man in black clothes . . . a dishevelled man whose words make us at once think of lone-liness and doubt and dread, of waste and dust and emptiness, and from whose hands, or from our own, we feel the richness of heaven and earth and the com-fort of human affection slipping away. (104)

Not this, not this . . . but this: so we have gone, rejecting every past view of *Hamlet*, throwing out the character, the story, the motivation, and ending with this universal spokesman for all we ever hoped and feared, this slight Prince of Denmark who is our spiritual home and our window on the night. In so inviting the response of the naive and wondering imagination rather than the sophisticated intellect, Lewis may stir our emotions, but at the cost of ignor-ing the particular situation of the play.

This is the substance of Lewis's interpretation, which for its time was certainly up to the minute, though not, as he admitted (104), particularly original in its broad approach; G. Wilson Knight, for instance, had seen the theme of the play as death in his *The Wheel of Fire* in 1930 (34–50). Lewis also owed much here to Owen Barfield's idea of great literature as mythic rather than discursive in effect (Barfield, "The Form of *Hamlet*"). Two con-temporary reviews of the published lecture were both admiring and criti-cal. One speaks of its "arresting quality" and agrees with its interpretation of the central theme of *Hamlet*, while criticizing Lewis for ignoring the revenge-play tradition and for his rough treatment of the critics and com-mentators.[9] The other, written by W. W. Lawrence, praises Lewis's "urbane yet provocative argument," but remarks that *Hamlet* is a play before it is a poem, and that "when he [Lewis] says that the true hero of *Hamlet* is not the Danish Prince, but 'man', some of us might reply that we believe that the play was written, not to set out any abstract or philosophical concept, but to portray a moving struggle affecting certain definite human beings."[10] Nevertheless the essay became celebrated, and later an anthology piece,

129

because it succeeded in encapsulating in brief and pithy compass the new direction of *Hamlet* studies.

Taken as a whole, the essay exhibits a tendency in Lewis toward philosophy *per se*, a desire to find the particular opening out into the universal—not the least reason for his love of allegory. (Lewis was trained as a philosopher, indeed for a time tutored in the subject.) His account of *Hamlet* scarcely mentions such prominent figures as Hamlet's mother, Ophelia, Claudius, Polonius, or Laertes. Hamlet's universal character is seen by Lewis to radiate out like some star to engulf not only the characters of the play, but all its watchers and readers in itself. That character is not seen as something changing or evolving under circumstance and contact with others; it is a quintessence, even a stasis.[11] Lewis says nothing of the action of the play, or of the particular task assigned to Hamlet; the hero exists not to do but to be, and to strike philosophical attitudes. The same tendency is seen in the way Lewis corrals critics of the play in groups of general views, and in the peculiar application of logical rather than literary argument to confute them.

On Shakespeare's Style—"Variation"

Lewis wrote one other essay touching on Shakespeare's plays—"Variation in Shakespeare and Others," from the same year as the original of the *Hamlet* lecture, 1938.[12] Broadly, this is a comparison between styles of writing Lewis finds in Shakespeare and Milton respectively, though he sees it as an opposition that can be found throughout English poetry. Shakespeare's poetry, Lewis finds, makes one point and illustrates it several ways; but Milton is always giving us new matter from line to line. Lewis's observation is actually a brilliant one, and one that has never fully received its due. It has been obliterated by those who mine every word of Shakespeare and who read him in terms of metaphor rather than simile, whereby the subject is seen as altered by each trope rather than staying the same. This tendency is already present in the work of L. C. Knights[13] and Derek Traversi, whose *Approach to Shakespeare* first appeared in 1938, the same year as Lewis's talk. This mode of reading has validity, but it is not the whole truth. Lewis is finding in Shakespeare something that is not unlike one of his own rhetorical techniques: "It is as if he kept on having tries at it [the subject], and being dissatisfied. He darts image after image at you and still seems to think that he has not done enough" ("Variation" 75).[14]

For example, Lewis cites Shakespeare's Cleopatra on Antony when he is dead:

> His legs bestrid the ocean; his rear'd arm
> Crested the world; his voice was propertied

As all the tuned spheres, and that to friends;
But when he meant to quail and shake the orb,
He was as rattling thunder. For his bounty,
There was no winter in't, an autumn 'twas
That grew the more by reaping; his delights
Were dolphin-like, they show'd his back above
The element they lived in. . . .

Lewis then comments,

You have the ends of the earth all brought together. You begin with the gigantic hyperbole of a man bestriding the ocean, or an arm cresting the world; you go on to the music of the spheres, to thunder, to the seasons, to dolphins. Nor does one image grow out of another. The arm cresting the world is not a development of the legs bestriding the ocean; it is *idem in alio*, a second attempt at the very same idea, an alternative. The dolphin idea is not a continuation of the autumn idea. It is a fresh start. He begins over again in every second line. If you extract the bare logical skeleton, the prose "meaning" of each image, you will find that it is precisely the same in most of them. . . ."He was great. He was great. He was great enough to help his friends. He was great enough to hurt his enemies. He was generous. He was generous. He was great." ("Variation" 76)

Read simply as the account of a hero by Shakespeare, what Lewis says has force; and of course it is the privilege of an obituary to mute irony. These are the words of Cleopatra about Antony, the passionate queen of Egypt about her Roman love; and because of this the words are the struggle of her large nature to find what is adequate to express his; failing which, the only expression left is her suicide. Moreover the speech is necessarily full of ironies: the speaker has herself partly brought about Antony's death through her apparent deceptions, and Antony, though great and generous, so gave himself to Cleopatra and pleasure, that he rather sank than bestrid, crested, thundered, or revealed himself above the waves. Lewis misses this because he is not interested in personalities, in who is speaking about whom. His more Olympian view takes in general properties and large appearances only, just as in the essay on *Hamlet*.

In Lewis's view, variation is used in Shakespeare as an ornament, whereby a subject is lit up by a profusion of examples. But for him it has another purpose also. He tells us that Shakespeare's distinction as an artist is his ability to fuse poetic genius with brilliance in realistic character-portrayal (81): most other artists have one or the other but not both. Lewis argues that one of the means by which Shakespeare succeeds in joining these apparently contrary powers is through variation. A character who makes several attempts at saying something necessarily sounds spontaneous even while he or she is uttering the highest poetry. "He [Shakespeare] must give his poetic metaphors the

131

air of being thrown off accidentally as he gropes for expression in the very heat of dialogue" (81). It is a somewhat curious justification, and one feels that while it may work for the tragic heroes (on whom Lewis at once seizes), their minds are uniquely disturbed and fumbling: we are less inclined to feel such stammering in more deliberate contexts such as Ulysses's speech on "degree" in *Troilus and Cressida*, or the Archbishop of Canterbury's description of England in terms of a beehive in *Henry V*. It is a blanket explanation of Shakespearean realism, which once again ignores the conditioning circumstances of individual plays and characters. Nevertheless, as general truth, it has undeniable value.

On Shakespeare's Poems and Sonnets

The final piece by Lewis on Shakespeare is that on the poems and *Sonnets*, in *English Literature in the Sixteenth Century* in 1954. The Shakespeare he visits here is not so isolated but the culmination of a long poetic tradition explored throughout the book. The first poem Lewis considers, *Venus and Adonis* (1593), gives him difficulty because it portrays Venus as far more powerful and passionate than Adonis. He singles out the comic moment where Venus drags the reluctant Adonis from his horse while he is out hunting:

> Over one arm the lusty courser's rein,
> Under her other was the tender boy,
> Who blush'd and pouted in a dull disdain
> With leaden appetite, unapt to toy.

(31–34)

Lewis remarks, "Certain horrible interviews with voluminous female relatives in one's early childhood inevitably recur to the mind" (498). What Lewis dislikes is doubtless the hierarchic upset in the woman so mannishly pursuing the man, but it is also the portrayal of uncontrolled female sexuality: he singles out with amazed disgust the recurrent words conveying physical passion and exclaims, "And this flushed, panting, perspiring, suffocating, loquacious creature is supposed to be the goddess of love herself, the golden Aphrodite. It will not do" (499).[15] We in turn might exclaim in surprise that Lewis has forgotten the vulgarities of Venus/Aphrodite in classical tradition: he seems here to show a rather Edwardian and sentimental view of divine behavior. Lewis feels that "Shakespeare may . . . have failed because he was embarrassed by powers, essential for drama, which he could not suspend while writing an epyllion [in the tradition of Marlowe's *Hero and Leander*]" (499). He also says that the disgust he feels with the poem is incompatible with its moral purpose. But it is Lewis who has said the poem is an epyllion, that it disgusts and that it has a moral purpose. The poem may not be great, but it is better than Lewis allows here.

With *The Rape of Lucrece* (1594) Lewis is on more neutral ground. He quickly assigns the poem a literary context—"heroic poetry as the heroic was understood before Virgil had been sufficiently distinguished from Lucan and Ovid"— and remarks how Shakespeare avoids the monotonous "tragedy" pattern of the *Mirror for Magistrates* (499). He points out what he sees as the "prettinesses and puerilities" that mark it as Shakespeare's early work, and various infelicities such as Lucrece inviting the nightingale to use her hair as a grove. He objects to the loss of narrative drive in the poem through digression, description, and elaborate emotional rhetoric; and here he also finds often flabby ornamental use of Shakespeare's characteristic device of variation (500). But he is quick to see the strength of the poem in the depiction of the rape. His analysis here exhibits Lewis as the critic of style and technique; he spends time on Shakespeare's unusual use of a "Simpsonian" rhyme at lines 352–54 as readily as on what he sees as the unequalled power of the rape scene, which itself is analyzed in terms of the effectiveness of the poetry rather than of the psychology. Here Lewis is at the elbow of Shakespeare the craftsman, always asking "Does it work?" and bringing us close to the artist striving to hit his poetic targets.

The *Sonnets*, however, were for Lewis "the highest and purest achievement of the Golden way of writing" (502). His account of them is part of the more interpretative treatment of them that began in the early 1950s. He starts with the issue of their dating, on which he can only conclude, "We do not know when, or at what different times, they were written" (503). He points out that they differ from earlier sonnet sequences in telling a story (always an attraction for Lewis). We cannot, however, read them as a psychological novel, because "the precise mode of love which the poet declares for the Man remains obscure": it is too passionate for that of ordinary male friendship, and yet it lacks all the distinctive features of homosexuality (for example, he bids the man to marry). But this, Lewis tells us, does not affect our delight. Several of the sonnets are only lightly attached to the subject of the central relationship; they have the effect, he says, of taking the passion beyond narrow confines, making it more universal. Further, the love of the poet is not selfish but enormously generous and rich of spirit. For Lewis, it is nothing less than charity. And charity, in the sense of loving while loving too the freedom of the beloved, is what Lewis finds at the core of the *Sonnets*. The "real" story is not one of closeted relationship, but of an often painful but also joyous opening of the heart. Here we touch again on the light and joy at the center of much of Lewis's criticism and work:

133

> The love is, in the end, so simply and entirely love that our *cadres* are thrown away and we cease to ask what kind. . . . The self-abnegation, the "naughting", in the *Sonnets* never rings false. This patience, this anxiety (more like a parent's than a lover's) to find excuses for the beloved, this clear-sighted and wholly unembittered resignation, this transference of the whole self into another self without the demand for a return, have hardly a precedent in profane literature. In certain senses of the word "love" Shakespeare is not so much our best as our only love poet. (505)

The transference of attention from the personal to the universal is what we also saw in the essay on *Hamlet*.

This might be a brilliant reading, and one solution to the problem of the *Sonnets*, were it not that Lewis gives scarcely any place, except as an unfortunate contrast, to the sonnets written to the Lady. They cannot be separated from those to the Man, since she interferes in their relationship. And they are "dark"—full of anger, twisted sexual passion, jealousy, and despair—not a trace of charity here. That Lewis says nothing about them suggests the lengths to which he could go to escape talking about female sexuality. Yet had *English Literature in the Sixteenth Century* been written two or three years later, when Lewis had fallen in love with Joy Davidman, we might have had a different view.

As in much of his writing, Lewis argues to a missing term. We saw it in the *Hamlet* essay where what "really" drives Hamlet was found by a series of reductions of critical positions until only one conclusion, involving an unfathomed mystery, was possible. So too in the *Sonnets* (to paraphrase Lewis)—if not friendship, and not homosexuality, then only a passionate charity is left. Lewis supposes too that a right reading is to be reached by deduction—if not this, or this, then this. It is the procedure he also follows in his spiritual life, in which he felt from his earliest conscious years a desire, or as he calls it *Sehnsucht*, spiritual yearning, for an unknown object. Following his idealizing tendency, Lewis in his autobiography *Surprised by Joy* (1955) identified this desire with a longing for God, and thus with his conversion to Christianity; and he viewed his previous response to it as a series of earthly misidentifications from which he learnt its true source. The whole analytic process, however, is conditioned as much by flight *from* something—whether it be the vulgarities of Incarnation or the shames of secularity—as by the drive toward something.[16]

The remainder of Lewis's remarks on the *Sonnets* concerns their style. This shows how for Lewis the medium and the message are distinct, how he sees the "style" operating as an analogy to the subject rather than in fusion with it.[17] For the subject, he says, a plain and clear style was needed, nearer to "Drab" than "Golden," yet more Golden because of the proximity: "He has to avoid the stunning regularity of Drab, yet to avoid it only by a hair's breadth" (505). Lewis sensitively points out extensive use of alliteration and assonance, of words inviting emotion and sensuous imagination. He finds the rhetorical structure in the *Sonnets* to be "often that of theme and variations"—an uncomplicated, expansive idiom, both formal and flowing, a musical arrangement. Here his analysis is at its finest, bringing out the best and sweetest and most poignant in the poems. The *Sonnets* thus embody the features of Shakespearean style outlined in the "Variation" essay. This style suits, says Lewis, with the way that the *Sonnets* "very seldom present or even feign to present passionate thought growing and changing in the heat of a situation; they are not dramatic. The end of each is clearly in view from the beginning, the theme already chosen" (508). This view is not that of some later commentators, who find a good deal of emotional and rhetorical struggle in the sonnets to the Man;[18] and of course it omits the sonnets to the Lady which are certainly "passionate thought growing and changing in the heat of the situation." Here again Lewis chooses the quiddity rather than the evolving and dramatic *quid*: "it is as if he [Shakespeare] sang from above, moved and yet not moved; a Golden, Olympian poet" (508).

Lewis last turns to *The Phoenix and the Turtle*, a poem which he admires, again because of its implicitly Christian view of mutual love, its formality, and its use of an excluded and mysterious middle term. Reason, which is made the speaker of the threnody, "rationally recognizes what is beyond reason" (509). The love of the phoenix and turtle had nothing to do with the personal, nor with emotion, only with a continual self-giving that found itself in the other. The doctrine of the poem

> consummates that of the *Sonnets*. In them the "naughting" has been one-sided. The poet had lost himself in another, but that other had not lost himself in Shakespeare. Now Shakespeare celebrates the exchanged death, and life, of a fully mutual love. He is not writing metaphysical poetry in the technical sense critics give to that term, but he is writing in the true sense, a metaphysical poem. (509)

Overview

Where then does this leave us with Lewis the critic of Shakespeare? His strengths and weaknesses are alike obvious and intertwined. He has a unique power for showing the brightest, most joyous and morally most uplifting aspects of Shakespeare's work. On one hand, Lewis takes us continually beyond potentially myopic personal considerations to the large and Olympian dimension; he has a lucid energy of style and argument, and a particular facility in the deployment of analogies; he is not afraid to point out the obvious, and surprise us with it; and he is often original, as in his remarks on Shakespeare's technique of variation and on the stylistic methods of the *Sonnets*. On the other hand, Lewis's rejection of the personal and the dramatic leads to all sorts of critical blindsides; his deployment of logical argument and moral prejudice distorts what he reads; and his feeling that a work of art really has only one true meaning restricts both artistic and critical freedom. One commentator has remarked, "it is external, abstractable, theoretical issues that engage Lewis's mind; in the actual practice of criticism he is too often conventional" (Robson 67). And another writes, "His greatness lay in extraordinary powers of clarification and illumination. His weakness lay in this very strength: he could not resist oversimplification and beautifully neat conclusions" (Bayley 81).

It has been remarked that the whole of Lewis was present in whatever he wrote,[19] and this is true of the attitudes revealed in these essays. The Lewis who disliked the merely personal looked continually to self-transcendence by the critic in his *An Experiment in Criticism* (1961), and by the Christian throughout his apologetics; and all his fantasy fictions involve the characters going beyond themselves into some larger form of being. The man who believed in art as ultimately "non-evolutionary," in essences more than existences, writes stories designed to catch in their nets of successive events "something that is not successive," an elusive "bird" from another country ("On Stories" 20–21). The man who could think of style as an ornament sometimes viewed his own stories the same way, as mere images of the very real: "Myth does not essentially exist in *words* at all" (*MacDonald* 15).

In Lewis's fiction, of course, such positions are not questioned; it is only when they attempt to persuade us directly that they become open to challenge. Indeed, in his fiction, Lewis's very limitations can often become strengths, his biases turn to clarity of vision, his arguments become part of larger cosmic patterns, his refusals of "mere personality" lead to the wonders of Aslan or Tinidril or the *sorns* of Mars; and his thirst for the universal can give us the moving beauty of his Celestial Commonwealth or the multiple zones of heaven that end the Narnia books. But then fiction is a magic circle that criticism of necessity steps outside.

Notes

1. On Lewis as tutor see John Lawlor in Gibb 67–77; George Bailey in Keefe 106–22; Luke Rigby, Derek Brewer, and Peter Bayley in Como 38–40, 41–67, and 77–80; Alan Rook, Norman Bradshaw,

W. R. Fryer, E. L. Edmonds, Rosamund Cowan, Patricia Berry, Peter Philip, and others in Schofield 11–13, 17–19, 25–26, 29–30, 39–50, 61–62, 67–70, 93–96, 150, 167, 169–70, 172–73; and Sayer, *Jack* 117–22. I am also indebted to Professors John Bayley, Kenneth Fielding, Paul Piehler, and John Lawlor for commentary and for further information on Lewis as a teacher of Shakespeare. All information relates to the period 1935–49 only.

2. See Brewer in Como 48; it is only one occasion, though.

3. Griffin 195. Nevill Coghill remarks, "He tended to avoid the theatre, as a result, I suppose, of some North of Ireland Protestant scunner against it" (qtd. in Gibb 56).

4. I rely here on Lionel Adey's account of these. The Shakespeare texts to which Adey refers are in Magdelene College Library, Cambridge, to which Lewis donated them.

5. This note was brought to my attention by Tom Martin; it is available in the Marion E. Wade Collection, Wheaton College, Wheaton, IL.

6. Quoted in Adey 4; Adey, however, takes it at face-value as character-criticism and thus inconsistent with Shakespeare's later "mythic" view.

7. Lewis continues, "We may even regret that the convention in which Shakespeare worked did not allow him to make Paulina frankly a fairy or an angel and thus be rid of his 'improbable possibilities.'" In the next year he himself created such a Paulina in his poem "Hermione in the House of Paulina" (1940; rpt. in his *Collected Poems* 32), one who has changed from a human character to a golden and angelic "great spirit."

8. *Stand* 422. Lewis also initiated in May 1935 a correspondence in *The Times Literary Supplement* on the text of *Hamlet*, which drew in several leading scholars of the time—John Dover Wilson, W. W. Greg, F. W. Bateson, M. R. Ridley, and W. J. Lawrence (2 May–13 June).

9. Anonymous review in *Notes and Queries*, 184 (April 1943): 269–70, rpt. in Watson 152–55.

10. Review in *Modern Language Review*, 38 (1943): 140–42, rpt. in Watson 150–51.

11. Compare Owen Barfield, close friend of Lewis: "My abiding impression is that the very notion of *development* of any sort was somehow alien to Lewis's mind" (*Barfield on Lewis*, 76. See also 76–77 and 112–13).

12. "Variation" was first published in 1939 in *Rehabilitations*; references here are to the reprint in *Selected Literary Essays* 74–87.

13. E.g., in *How Many Children Had Lady Macbeth?* (1933), rpt. in his *Explorations* (1946).

14. This is precisely the method of what in 1929 Morris W. Croll described as the Baroque and "Anti-Ciceronian" style of literature of the period c. 1580–1630 ("The Baroque Style," esp. 209–13, 218–19, 224–26). This was brought to my attention by Michael Price.

15. Lewis earlier wrote a similarly appalled account of the poem in his *Hero and Leander* (1952), rpt. in *Literary* 59–61: "I cannot forgive Shakespeare for telling us how Venus perspired."

16. Compare W. W. Robson in "The Romanticism of C. S. Lewis": "Where . . . he is an apologist . . . all the emphasis falls on conversion *to* something. There is much less awareness of it as conversion *from* something" (59).

17. Barfield speaks of "interpenetration . . . the thing that Lewis didn't like in Williams" (*Barfield on Lewis* 149). In *Experiment* 132–36, Lewis sees a poem as having two modes: "It both *means* and *is*. It is both *Logos* (something said) and *Poiema* (something made)." Lewis finds the distinction unfortunate but "unavoidable."

18. For example J. W. Lever (1956), Hilton Landry (1963), Murray Krieger (1964), Philip Edwards (1968).

19. Barfield 122: "what he thought about everything was secretly present in what he said about anything."

Works Cited

Adey, Lionel. "C. S. Lewis's Annotations to His Shakespeare Volumes." *CSL: The Bulletin of the New York C. S. Lewis Society* 8.7 (May 1977): 1–8.

Bailey, George. "In the University." *C. S. Lewis: Speaker and Teacher.* Ed. Carolyn Keefe. London: Hodder and Stoughton, 1974. 79–92.

Barfield, Owen. "The Form of *Hamlet*." 1933. *Romanticism Comes of Age.* Middletown, CT: Wesleyan UP, 1967. 104–25.

———. *Owen Barfield on C. S. Lewis.* Ed. G. B. Tennyson. Middleton, CT: Wesleyan UP, 1989.

Bayley, Peter. "From Master to Colleague." *C. S. Lewis at the Breakfast Table and Other Reminiscences.* Ed. James Como. London: Collins, 1980.

Croll, Morris. "The Baroque Style in Prose." 1929. *Style, Rhetoric and Rhythm: Essays by Morris W. Croll.* Ed. J. Max Patrick and Robert O. Evans. Princeton: Princeton UP, 1966. 207–33.

Edwards, Philip. *Shakespeare and the Confines of Art.* London: Methuen, 1968.

Gombrich, E. H. *Art and Illusion: A Study in the Psychology of Pictorial Representation.* London: Phaidon Press, 1960.

Griffin, William. *C. S. Lewis: The Authentic Voice.* Tring, Hertfordshire: Lion, 1988.

Knight, G. Wilson. "The Embassy of Death: An Essay on Hamlet." *The Wheel of Fire: Essays in Interpretation of Shakespeare's Sombre Tragedies.* London: Oxford UP, 1930.

Knights, L. C. *How Many Children Had Lady Macbeth? An Essay in the Theory and Practice of Shakespeare Criticism.* Cambridge: Gordon Fraser, 1933.

Krieger, Murray. *A Window to Criticism: Shakespeare's Sonnets and Modern Poetics.* Princeton: Princeton UP, 1964.

Landry, Hilton. *Interpretations in Shakespeare's Sonnets.* Berkeley: U of California P, 1963.

Lawlor, John. "The Tutor and the Scholar." *Light on C. S. Lewis.* Ed. Jocelyn Gibb. London: Geoffrey Bles, 1965. 67–85.

Lever, J. W. *The Elizabethan Love Sonnet.* London: Methuen, 1956.

Lewis, C. S. *The Collected Poems of C. S. Lewis.* Ed. Walter Hooper. London: HarperCollins, 1994.

———. *English Literature in the Sixteenth Century Excluding Drama.* Oxford: Oxford UP, 1954.

———. *An Experiment in Criticism.* Cambridge: Cambridge UP, 1961.

———. "Hamlet: The Prince or the Poem?" Annual Shakespeare Lecture of the British Academy, 1942. *Literary* 88–105.

———. "Hero and Leander." 1952. *Literary* 58–73.

———. Letters on the text of *Hamlet* in *Times Literary Supplement* (May-June 1935).

———. Notes on *Othello* in the flyleaf of Lewis's copy of the play in the Marion E. Wade Collection, Wheaton College, Wheaton, IL.

———. "On Stories." 1947. *Of Other Worlds: Essays and Stories.* Ed. Walter Hooper. London: Geoffrey Bles, 1966. 3–21.

———. *A Preface to "Paradise Lost."* 1942. London: Oxford UP, 1960.

———. *Selected Literary Essays.* Ed. Walter Hooper. Cambridge: Cambridge UP, 1969.

———. *Surprised by Joy: The Shape of My Early Life.* London: Geoffrey Bles, 1955.

———. *They Stand Together: The Letters of C. S. Lewis to Arthur Greeves (1914–1963).* Ed. Walter Hooper. London: Collins, 1979.

———. "Variation in Shakespeare and Others." 1939. *Literary* 74–87.

———. "William Morris." 1939. *Literary* 219–31.

———, ed. *George MacDonald: An Anthology*. London: Geoffrey Bles, 1946.

Robson, W. W. "The Romanticism of C. S. Lewis." *Critical Essays*. London: Routledge, 1966. 56–75.

Sayer, George. *Jack: C. S. Lewis and His Times*. London: Macmillan, 1988.

Schofield, Stephen, ed. *In Search of C. S. Lewis*. South Plainfield, NJ: Bridge Publishing, 1983.

Stoll, E. E. *Art and Artifice in Shakepeare: A Study in Dramatic Contrast and Illusion*. Cambridge: Cambridge UP, 1933.

Traversi, Derek. *Approach to Shakespeare*. London: Sands, 1938.

Watson, George, ed. *Critical Thought Series 1: Critical Essays on C. S. Lewis*. London: Scolar Press, 1992.

Wilson, John Dover. *What Happens in Hamlet*. Cambridge: Cambridge UP, 1935.

8

Seventeenth Century

Michael W. Price

The vast majority of C. S. Lewis's literary criticism focuses upon either the Middle Ages and sixteenth century, or Milton, the periods immediately before and after the period in English literature known as the seventeenth century (1603–60). Indeed, bracketed on either side by such towering works as *The Allegory of Love* (1936), *A Preface to "Paradise Lost"* (1942), *English Literature in the Sixteenth Century Excluding Drama* (1954), and *The Discarded Image* (1964), to say nothing of his myriad lectures, essays, notes, and reviews, Lewis's comparatively few (and comparatively minor) writings on seventeenth-century writers often escape notice.[1] Nevertheless, Lewis's commentary on the literature of this period may surprise readers because of the important ways it illuminates C. S. Lewis as a critic and (Christian) man.

Lewis's commentary primarily consists of three essays: "Donne and Love Poetry in the Seventeenth Century" (1938), his contribution to a festschrift honoring the Donne scholar Sir Herbert Grierson; his "Epilogue: New Tendencies" to *Sixteenth*, where, in adumbrating literary trends as they passed into the seventeenth century, he comes closest to offering a survey of the period; and "The Vision of John Bunyan" (1962), an essay originally broadcast over the BBC. Additionally, references to seventeenth-century English writers pepper Lewis's writings, not only demonstrating his broad and deep familiarity with the texts of this period but also deepening the significance of his remarks upon the writers that occur in his three essays. This chapter synthesizes Lewis's commentary in his essays with that of his letters and other writings, proceeding author by author in their order of importance to Lewis: most importantly, John Donne, George Herbert, and John Bunyan; and secondarily, the major prose writers of the period, Thomas Traherne, Sir Thomas Browne, Jeremy Taylor, Robert Burton, Francis Bacon, and Richard Baxter.[2] This survey aims to grasp the essence of Lewis's commentary upon each writer and demonstrate the ways Lewis's perspective on these writers changed (or did not change) over the course of his lifetime. The conclusion meditates upon Lewis's likes and dislikes, his integration of faith and scholarship, and finally, his Johnsonian tastes and tendencies.

John Donne and the Metaphysical Manner: Lewis's Uneasy Truce

Lewis wrote more about John Donne (1572–1631) than about any other seventeenth-century writer, devoting an entire essay to him and positioning him at the center of his survey of the period in the "Epilogue" to *Sixteenth*. Furthermore, references to Donne abound in Lewis's writings. Typically, Lewis ransacks Donne for quotations and illustrations which serve, among other things, to substantiate a concept or establish a backdrop against which to evaluate a different poet or style.[3] *Discarded*, for example, cites Donne ten times to illustrate the medieval-Renaissance cosmology, far and away more than any other seventeenth-century writer. The prominence of these references is as startling as their prevalence: in addition to the examples previously mentioned, Jane Studdock, a character in *That Hideous Strength* (1945), writes her doctoral thesis on Donne; a quotation from Donne's "A Litanie" ("That our affections kill us not, nor dye") appears as the epigraph on the title page to *The Four Loves* (1960); and Lewis's poem, "The Apologist's Evening Prayer," draws heavily upon Donne (Christopher 2–4). Aside from these discrete references, Donne informs the totality of Lewis's writings: "The key to my books is Donne's maxim, 'The heresies that men leave are hated most.' The things I assert most vigorously are those that I resisted long and accepted late" (*Surprised* 213).

Although Lewis combed Donne's works and awarded to Donne privileged places in his writings, his commentary reveals profoundly mixed feelings. In fact, as Lewis's long-time associate Owen Barfield once put it, "Lewis admired Donne . . . but he didn't much like him" (qtd. in Morris 210). For now, let us concentrate upon a pivotal passage in *Surprised* which epitomizes Lewis's ambivalence. After praising George MacDonald, G. K. Chesterton, Samuel Johnson, Edmund Spenser, John Milton, and other Christian authors who coaxed him toward conversion, he pauses to mention being "intoxicated (for a time)" by Donne, contrasting this temporary "intoxication" with deep and

141

lasting "satisfaction" by another seventeenth-century writer, Sir Thomas Browne (214). Later I will consider the deeper ambivalence underlying this statement, but for now, let us simply observe that it demarcates at least two stages in Lewis's lifelong assessment of Donne: an early infatuation followed by a cooler (and less favorable) reassessment.

Lewis's period of "intoxication" can be reconstructed, at least partially, from his diary between 1922–27, *All My Road Before Me*. He records on 19 October 1922 having read "one or two poems of Donne's which I liked" (123). Evidently, Lewis must have liked those poems a great deal, for according to his diary entry for 1 January 1923, he not only asked for the two-volume set of Donne's poetry (probably Grierson's edition) for Christmas, but received them from his father that day with great excitement: "I think I shall love Donne," he exclaims. His entry continues with a question, "surely the only old poet who understands love?" that reveals both his interests and expectations (167). On 18 January he records that although *The Progress of the Soule* is "mostly bosh," *The Second Anniversary* is a "'new planet': I never imagined or hoped for anything like it" (181). This enthusiasm motivated him, on 22 January, to "attack" his own essay "on the influence of Donne on the 17th century lyric" (183). This attack included studying Samuel Johnson's commentary upon metaphysical wit in the "Life of Cowley." Johnson's opinions evidently ran counter to his own, for Lewis "found" that he "had been rather off the track," a discovery which compelled him to "work . . . hard to put it straight" (184). After mentioning Donne in the entry for 26 January, Lewis refers to Donne only twice more between 1922–27 (339, 456). Perhaps, then, January 1923 marked the temporary "intoxication" Lewis experienced.

In a 1936 essay, Lewis declared, "The excellence of Donne's pornographic elegies is a fact" (*Heresy* 67). Nevertheless, by 1938, when he wrote "Donne and Love Poetry in the Seventeenth Century," the intoxication had lifted. This essay, in addition to identifying what Lewis perceives to be the essential qualities of Donne's love poetry ("Donne *simpliciter*"), addresses three overarching questions: Why, after years of neglect, has Donne's love poetry suddenly achieved critical acclaim? Does this poetry merit such acclaim? And most broadly, does it constitute poetry that will endure for all times? In response to the first two questions, Lewis believes Donne's poetry has suddenly captivated modern critics merely because it features characteristics that correspond to moderns' own critical prejudices—put bluntly, modern critics' biases, and not the poetry's merits, largely account for Donne's vogue. Even worse, he continues, modern critics' biases cause them to commit numerous errors in judgment, such as overestimating Donne's actual achievements. For example, when modern critics read Donne's love poetry, they tend to compare Donne's realistic, conversational speaking voice with the artificial, courtly voice of Petrarchanism, concluding that he is "the innovator who substituted a realistic for a decorated kind of love poetry" ("Love Poetry" 107). Overlooking the larger poetic tradition (represented by Wyatt) from which Donne's style derives, they mistakenly believe that "Donne had invented what in fact he only brought to perfection":

> In so far as we admire Donne for being our first great practitioner in one of the many possible kinds of lyric, we are on firm ground; but the conception of him as liberator, as one who substituted "real" or "live" or "sincere" for "artificial" or "conventional" love lyric, begs all the questions and is simply a prejudice *de siecle*. (107, 108)

Similarly, modern critics err by "exaggerat[ing] the amount of learned imagery in his poems and even the amount of his learning" because Donne's knowledge "so seldom overlaps with our own" (110). After all, how many of us have information at our fingertips concerning, say, angelic consciousness? Modern criticial preferences for conversationality and difficulty thus result in Donne's love poetry being "overrated" (106).

Now to the third question: does Donne's love poetry constitute truly great poetry? Although conceding to it some merits, Lewis cautions us "to beware of giving to this highly specialized and, in truth, very limited kind of excellence, a place in our scheme of literary values which it does not deserve" (112). Significantly, Lewis does not devalue the poetry because of its subject matter, for "it would not be impossible to imagine a poet dealing with this same stuff, marginal and precarious as it is, in a way that would permanently engage our attention." Instead, he continues, "Donne's real limitation is not that he writes *about*, but that he writes *in*, a chaos of violent and transitory passions. He is perpetually excited and therefore perpetually cut off from the deeper and more permanent springs of his own excitement" (121). Furthermore, because Donne's love poetry merely corresponds to modern prejudices, it will fall out of favor as soon as critical prejudices again change: "its interest, save for a mind specially predisposed in its favour, must be short-lived and superficial, though intense. Paradoxical as it may seem, Donne's poetry is too simple to satisfy. Its complexity is all on the surface—an intellectual and fully conscious complexity that we soon come to the end of" (122).[4]

If another way of assessing poetry's greatness is to measure its influence upon contemporary and subsequent poets, then how influential was Donne's love poetry? Lewis insists that contrary to popular belief, Donne's influence upon love poetry in the seventeenth century has been overblown. True, subsequent poets incorporated aspects of his style, but those poets succeed only "by adding something else to what they have learned from Donne" (124). To illustrate, Lewis characterizes Andrew Marvell, Donne's successor, as "an

143

Olympian, ruling at ease for his own good purposes, all that intellectual and passionate mobility of which Donne was the slave" (125), sentiments he rephrases in his poem entitled, "To Andrew Marvell" (*Poems* 82). Lewis concludes his essay with a backhanded compliment to Donne's influence: "the final cause of Donne's poetry is the poetry of Herbert, Crashaw, and Marvell; for the very qualities which make Donne's kind of poetry unsatisfying poetic food make it a valuable ingredient" (125).

In order to assess the value of Lewis's essay on "Donne and Love Poetry," I think we need to situate it in two particular contexts. First, Lewis addresses here only Donne's love poetry, not the entire corpus of Donne's poetry. Indeed, this focus forces Lewis to "leave . . . out much of his best work," which includes "the dazzling sublimity of his best religious poems, the grotesque charm of *The Progress of the Soule*, and those scattered, but exquisite, patches of poetry that appear from time to time amidst the insanity of *The First and Second Anniversaries*. Even in the epistles there are good passages" (121). Despite the backhanded compliments and heavy qualifications, Lewis nevertheless consents to award Donne high marks in some regards, as we shall see further in his 1954 reassessment. For now, let us contrast Lewis's disdain for the love poetry with his esteem for the devotional poetry, whose "excellence," Lewis had first declared in 1936, "is a fact" (*Heresy* 67). In "Donne and Love Poetry," Lewis argues that this poetry is so good, in fact, that Donne's "influence at its best . . . is seen in the great devotional poetry of the period" (123). Lewis elaborates on the merits of Donne's devotional poem, "A Litanie," in a 1941 letter, where he cites the same line that he will, some twenty years later, choose as the epigraph to *Loves*. Commenting upon the line, he remarks, "One of the minor rewards of conversion is to be able to see at last the real point of all the old literature which we are brought up to read with the point left out" (*Letters* 358). "A Litanie" also seems to have influenced Lewis's poem, "The Apologist's Evening Prayer" (Christopher 2–4). What is more, the phrase, "the world's last night," which became the title of one of Lewis's essays and indeed the volume in which that essay appears (1960), comes from one of Donne's holy sonnets, "What if this present were the world's last night?" Clearly, then, we should note Lewis's esteem for Donne's devotional poetry and accordingly limit, for now, the essay's critique to Donne's love poetry specifically.

Secondly, Lewis's remarks appear in a particular critical milieu. Between the 1920s to 1950s, Donne's reputation suddenly skyrocketed, propelling him from relative obscurity to celebrity, a phenomenon which stemmed from (and caused still further) extravagant critical claims for Donne's poetry. (T. S. Eliot's essay, "The Metaphysical Poets" had appeared in 1921, for example.) Two features of this vogue especially provoked Lewis's ire. First, Lewis characteristically devoted his critical energies to controverting (or at least opposing) precisely just such (unwarranted) claims, arguing, for example, against certain trends in education in *The Abolition of Man*, against the putative influence of the Authorized Version in "The Literary Impact of the Authorised Version" (1950), against the idea of an English Renaissance in *Sixteenth*, and so on. Therefore, given his repeated references to Donne's poetry being "overrated," his attempt to deflate Donne's overinflated reputation probably represents an early instance of this predilection. Indeed, on the basis of conversations with Lewis's associates Owen Barfield and Walter Hooper, Francis Morris finds this to be the case: "the reservations which Lewis expressed in his essay towards Donne's work stemmed as much from his irritation at the extravagance of the claims made on the poet's behalf as they did from any particular insensitivity to his poems" (Morris 211).

The second feature almost naturally attends the first: once something becomes fashionable, people not only affect a love for it (regardless of their own personal tastes or the work's literary merit) but also fancy themselves to be superior to everyone else. Lewis characterized this combination of disingenuous appreciation and snobbery, when it occurs in matters of literary taste, as "priggery." Indeed, becoming a prig is so egregious that Lewis devoted a lengthy passage in *Surprised* to describing, in self-mortification, the period at Wyvern when he himself crossed the threshhold into priggery, characterizing it, in fact, as "a kind of Fall" (104). More broadly, Lewis's entire approach to reading, delineated in *An Experiment in Criticism*, is largely designed to combat priggery. And elsewhere in his writings on seventeenth-century writers, as we shall see, Lewis restates this aversion to priggery by emphasizing, instead, the virtues of its antithesis: authenticity. For now, however, let us note that in "Donne and Love Poetry in the Seventeenth Century," Lewis objects to the unnecessary difficulty of Donne's metaphysical conceits, that which he elsewhere described as "violent and knotty" poetry ("Hero" 70), precisely because this esotericism "repels some humble readers and attracts some prigs" ("Love Poetry" 110). Lewis's aversion to priggery in Donne studies specifically may, in fact, explain why Lewis directed Jane Studdock in *Hideous* to write her thesis on the fashionable but hackneyed subject of Donne's "triumphant vindication of the body," adding that "Jane was not perhaps a very original thinker" (14). As he informed a correspondent, "her thesis on Donne was all derivative bilge" (*Letters* 379).

These two contexts position us to assess the value of Lewis's essay on Donne's love poetry. To begin with its weaknesses, I would say that, in general, the polemical context in which he writes obliges him to overstate his case for the sake of controverting, apparently single-handedly, an entire critical movement. Although I do not think Donne is infallible, and although I think the extravagant claims for Donne then circulating should have been tempered, I also think that surely, in countering these sentiments, Lewis stretches the point when he claims Marvell surpasses Donne in the same way that a conquerer parades a conquered slave behind his chariot ("Love Poetry" 125). Donne is simply a far better poet than Lewis admits. I similarly think that this essay exemplifies a weakness attending one of Lewis's greatest strengths, namely, his ability to survey a vast field of knowledge, systematize it, and formulate general truths about it. In other words, Lewis's ability to comprehend the overarching system sometimes entails a tendency to over-look or, at worst, ride roughshod over details and exceptions to the rule. Joan Bennett's rejoinder, "The Love Poetry of John Donne: A Reply to Mr. C. S. Lewis," published alongside Lewis's essay in the festschrift to Grierson, con-vincingly critiques this tendency, demonstrating, for example, that Lewis oversimplified Donne's treatment of sex and love (85–104). Most broadly, critical history has proven Lewis wrong about Donne's stature and the poetry's endurance.

Despite the essay's weaknesses, it has many strengths, not the least of them Lewis's ability to capture "Donne *simpliciter*," the essential Donne. Indeed, the essay articulates insights so trenchant that they have since become com-monplace. He grasps, for example, the characteristic way Donne's poems engage readers in an "extremely exacting way":

> poem after poem consists of extravagant conceits woven into the preposterous semblance of an argument. The preposterousness is the point. Donne intends to take your breath away by the combined subtlety and impudence of the steps that lead to his conclusion. . . . if we do not hold our breaths as we read, won-dering in the middle of each complication how he will resolve it, and exclaim-ing at the end "How ever did you think of *that*?" . . . we are not enjoying Donne. ("Love Poetry" 111, 112)

I could list many other specific observations. Most broadly, the essay is valu-able because it contextualizes Donne's love poetry with respect to the larger tradition of love poetry, and because it contextualizes the critical tastes which motivated the modern revival of Donne. The essay's emphasis upon contex-tualization displays one of Lewis's greatest critical strengths.

Because metaphysical wit represents the main trajectory of Golden Age verse as it passed into the seventeenth century, Lewis makes it (and Donne) the centerpiece of his "Epilogue: New Tendencies" in *Sixteenth* (1954). In many ways Lewis's discussion of the metaphysical manner reprises observations he had made in the 1938 essay "Donne and Love Poetry in the Seventeenth Cen-tury." Again, he emphasizes that contrary to popular misperception, meta-physical wit did not appear spontaneously with Donne as a brand new poetic style; indeed, "no one can point to a moment at which [such] poetry came to be" (*Sixteenth* 541). Instead, because features of metaphysical wit already existed (both in English and Continental poetry), "the novelty, like most lit-erary novelties, consisted in doing more continuously or to a greater degree something that had been done before" (539). These novelties include employing recondite imagery and deliberately violating decorum (readers' expectations of appropriateness) in order to produce an aesthetically pleasing affront to readers' sensibilities. Concerning the latter, the metaphysicals differ from other poets only "in doing this sort of thing more often, and perhaps more violently, than previous poets had done, and indeed making it almost the mainstay of their poetics. For I think it is this *discors concordia* . . . far more than its learning, that gives Metaphysical poetry its essential flavour" (540). To illustrate this manner's preexistence, he illustrates its presence in Guillaume de Salluste du Bartas, Joshua Sylvester (du Bartas's translator), Robert Southwell, and John Hoskyns (541–46).

Donne, of course, remains its most brilliant practitioner, and it is in the context of the metaphysical manner that Lewis revisits three categories of Donne's poetry: those poems bearing Ovid's influence, those featuring a "violently contorted metre," and the lyrics (546–48). Lewis not only modified his views of Donne since the 1938 essay, but apparently did so in response to Joan Bennett's rejoinder. He explicitly cites his previous essay, Bennett's rebuttal, and his own change of mind when he concedes, "though I am still unable to agree with those who find a valuable 'philosophy' of love in 'The Ecstasy,' I now think that I erred equally in the past by criticizing the supposed 'philosophy'" (549). Similarly, Bennett upbraided Lewis for failing to recognize the varieties of amorous experience in *The Songs and Sonnets* (Bennett 87–104). Upon second thought, Lewis now recognizes the "great versatility of mood in the collection as a whole" and concedes that "it is remarkable that in such short space so many modes of love . . . have found such striking expression" (*Sixteenth* 549).

Lewis's observations upon the "astonishing novelty" of these poems represent perhaps his most insightful commentary upon Donne. "Donne creates a kind of poem that had never been heard before," Lewis claims, doing so "by combining two qualities which, had he not combined them, we might still regard as incompatible" (548). On one hand, his lyrics "sound like *ex tempore* speech and imply a concrete situation"; on the other hand, as we have seen, Donne "weaves into these seemingly casual utterances . . . recondite analogies and *discors concordia*" which had hitherto merely ornamented verse. Donne unites these two seemingly incompatible qualities by assuming the role of "pleader" (548). In a classic formulation, Lewis foregrounds the uniqueness of this synthesis by contrasting Donne's lyrics with Shakespeare's sonnets:

> In Shakespeare each experience of the lover becomes a window through which we look out on immense prospects—on nature, the seasons, life and death, time and eternity. In Donne it is more like a burning [i.e., magnifying] glass; angelol-

147

ogy, natural philosophy, law, institutions, are all drawn together, narrowed and focused at this one place and moment where a particular man is mocking, flattering, browbeating, laughing at, or laughing with, a particular woman. And they all have, for Donne in the poem, no value or even existence except as they articulate and render more fully self-conscious the passion of that moment. His imagination is centripetal. . . . Each of Donne's lyrics is a world in itself; or, if you prefer, is the whole world foreshortened and transformed by, and sacrificed to, some one precise shade of passion. (549)

Donne's brilliance is accentuated by the way he balances the "intense concentration" within individual poems with a "great versatility of mood" in the *Songs and Sonnets* as a collection (549). Lewis concludes by ranking Donne as an "immensely influential poet" (551). Although Lewis still maintains some reservations, his "Epilogue" marks the phase when Lewis's enthusiasm thawed.

To conclude our survey of Lewis's treatment of Donne, let us now return to his reflection in *Surprised*, published one year after *Sixteenth*, that he had been "intoxicated (for a time)" by Donne. Not only does it demonstrate that his passion had passed through periods of enthusiasm and reservation; it equipoises mighty opposites—attraction and revulsion—in an uneasy truce which indicates, at minimum, that Lewis still has profoundly mixed feelings. It is as though Lewis, writing his spiritual biography at age fifty-seven, recasts his attraction to Donne as a youthful sin that he subsequently grew out of (or repented of). The irony is that Lewis may have derived this disclaimer from Donne himself, who, after he had been ordained later in life, attributed his earlier iconoclastic defence of suicide, *Biathanatos*, to the youthful "*Jack Donne*, and not . . . [the minister,] *D. Donne*" (Donne, *Letters* 22). More ironically still, although Lewis applied Donne's maxim ("The heresies that men leave are hated most") to describe the evolution of his own theological views, it may apply just as well to the evolution of Lewis's literary views of Donne.[5]

George Herbert: "The Most Alarming of All"

On the other hand, Lewis's attitude toward George Herbert (1593–1633) was less ambiguous. Indeed, it is almost impossible to overstate the importance of George Herbert's poetry to Lewis the man and Christian. As a student and tutor, Lewis was responsible for covering English literature to 1830 (Como 43), ensuring that he read (and presumably taught) Herbert's poetry, much as he read other Christian writers; furthermore, Herbert's Christianity, like that of the other Christian writers, helped lure him into the fold (*Surprised*

191, 225; "Old Books" 203). But Herbert stood out among them. As Lewis recounts in *Surprised*, to the young atheist attempting to resist God, Herbert was "the most alarming [writer] of all": "Here was a man who seemed to me to excel all the authors I had ever read in conveying the very quality of life as we actually live it from moment to moment; but the wretched fellow, instead of doing it all directly, insisted on mediating it through what I would still have called 'the Christian mythology'" (214). The opening lines to Herbert's first poem to *The Temple*, "Perirrhanterium," seem perfect for describing the effect Herbert's poetry had in contributing to Lewis's conversion. As though addressing the worldly young Lewis by name, the poem begins:

> Thou, whose sweet youth and early hopes inhance
> Thy rate and price, and mark thee for a treasure;
> Hearken unto a Verser, who may chance
> Rhyme thee to good, and make a bait of pleasure.
>   A verse may finde him, who a sermon flies,
>   And turn delight into sacrifice. (Herbert 33)

Herbert's verse apparently "found" Lewis; perhaps in contributing to his conversion, it redirected his literary artistry from "delight" to "sacrifice." Certainly Herbert's importance to Lewis's spiritual journey is demonstrated by Lewis's five references to him in *Surprised* (more than to any other seventeenth-century writer), including Lewis's choice of a quotation from "The Collar" to serve as the epigraph to his chapter entitled, "I Broaden My Mind." Like the speaker in "The Collar," Lewis, too, experienced frustration with religion, left it temporarily, but finally succumbed to God's relentless calling.

Lewis's choice of this particular example exemplifies his passion for Herbert's authenticity: what Lewis called Herbert's ability to convey "the very quality of life as we actually live it from moment to moment," particularly in religious experience. Lewis considered Herbert's authentic portrayal of religious experience to be so important that in his handwritten index to his copy of Herbert's poetry, he devotes an entire section—indeed, by far the largest section—to those metaphysical conceits categorized as "real" (i.e., realistic), such as the one in "Providence" which likens storms to "crying children holding God's hand."[6] Perhaps Lewis valued authenticity in religious experience so highly because he lacked it so sorely in his developmental years. Significantly, in *Regress* book 1, Lewis's Steward (i.e., the local parish priest) and the Steward's religion stand out for lacking precisely this authenticity. At first the Steward engages John in a pleasant chat about "fishing tackle and bicycles," but then, donning a mask, he changes the subject to the Landlord's rules. While wearing the mask he advocates keeping the rules, but then, removing the mask, he advises John to lie to cover

149

up his *not* keeping the rules. Even the rules themselves keep changing, John learns (*Regress* 4–6). This lack of authenticity, both in the Steward and in the religion he advocates, at least partially contributes to John's early alienation from the religion of his fathers.

Herbert fascinated Lewis for another (and related) reason, one that will become clearer when we reach Lewis's commentary upon John Bunyan: both men portrayed spiritual experience not only in authentic detail but also in terms of spiritual allegory. In this regard, critics have rightly noted Bunyan's influence upon *Regress*,[7] yet few (if any) have remarked Herbert's. Beyond the consideration that Herbert's poetry played a role in Lewis's spiritual pilgrimage, "The Pilgrimage" suggests itself as a possible influence for at least three reasons: it, too, is a spiritual allegory, portraying spiritual experience as a journey through various temptations ("Phansies medow," "Cares cops," "the wilde of Passion"); it achieves authenticity by refusing to sanitize the underside of the Christian experience, which Herbert characterizes as "so foul a journey"; and, perhaps most importantly, its title and argument feature details which resemble many in *Regress*. For example, Herbert's "long" and "weary" journey in a rocky setting (stanza one) resembles John's pilgrimage through the "Grand Canyon," complete with rocks and caves. Herbert's "wilde of Passion" (stanza three), too, corresponds to various episodes (such as in book 2) where John also realizes these "sometimes rich" places are ultimately "wasted" (Herbert 151–52). Readers can undoubtedly identify more. The possibility of Herbert's influence is enhanced by the fact that Mother Kirk's story of the great catastrophe (*Regress* book 5, chapter 2) allegorizes God's relationship to man in terms of a landlord-tenant relationship, much as Herbert allegorizes it in "Redemption" (Lindskoog 46–47).

At this point, I will pause to mention Henry Vaughan (1621–95), who is principally known for his collection of religious verse, *Silex scintillans* (1650, 1655), over which Herbert's poetry exercised a deep and pervasive influence. Lewis cites Vaughan as another one of those great writers whose Christianity, particularly his "mild, frightening, Paradisial flavour," coaxed him toward conversion ("Old Books" 203). Like Herbert's "The Pilgrimage," Vaughan's poem "Regeneration" is a spiritual allegory, and its details, too, might have found their way into *Regress*. For example, Vaughan's persona, like Lewis's, characterizes his journey as "a monstrous, mountain'd thing / Rough-cast with Rocks, and snow" (Fogle lines 11–12). Vaughan similarly portrays the soul's post-conversion state as repose in a lush natural setting (lines 27–69), much as Lewis characterizes "the land beyond the canyon" (*Regress* 169–70). Perhaps most importantly, after tasting the delights of conversion, Vaughan's pilgrim hears a rushing wind whispering "*Where I please*," beckoning him to follow. However, in order to follow, the pilgrim must pray, "Lord, . . . *On me one breath, / And let me dye before my death!*" (Fogle lines 80–82), indicating the necessity of dying to self in order to live. Similarly, in *Regress*, Death confronts John and informs him, "The cure of death is dying" (164), characterizing it as crossing through water from one side of the canyon to the other. Both this verbal echo and this characterization recur at an analogous point in *Till We Have Faces* (1956) when Orual hears a mysterious voice which not only commands her not to drown herself but also instructs her, "Die before you die. There is no chance after" (279).

Aside from any role Herbert's poetry may have played in Lewis's conversion, it remained for Lewis an important resource throughout his life. Indeed, when asked to list those works which "did most to shape" his "vocational attitude" and "philosophy of life," Lewis ranks Herbert among those precious few (Hooper 752). This ranking explains why Lewis recommended Herbert as a must-read to a correspondent petitioning Lewis for a reading list (*Letters* 345). It also correlates with his few instances of explicit critical commentary upon Herbert. To one correspondent he asks, "Do you read poetry? George Herbert at his best is extremely nutritious" (*Letters* 497). To another he recommends Herbert's poetry as "the sweetest of religious writings" (*Letters* 415). Elsewhere he relishes Herbert's "delicious home-spun, earthy flavour," his "sharp homeliness," and his "prose-like, yet never prosaic, sobriety," praise which corroborates his passion for Herbert's authenticity (*Stand* 313; *Sixteenth* 545).

John Bunyan: Lewis's Model Pilgrim

Lewis originally read aloud (from his own armchair, no less) his essay about "The Vision of John Bunyan" (1628–88) for broadcast on the BBC on 16 October 1962 (*Stand* 562 and 562 n. 2). The word "vision" adumbrates the two directions of the essay, designating the allegorical dream "vision" which constitutes the content of the story, and the author's "vision," or artistic sensibility. Although this essay appeared at the end of his life, references throughout Lewis's writings demonstrate that Bunyan—particularly *The Pilgrim's Progress*—served as a touchstone for his thinking since his childhood. Evidently Lewis devoured *The Pilgrim's Progress* as a child because he refers to his "old nursery copy" and the many children, presumably including himself, who "read and reread" the work but were "hardly aware" of its theology ("Vision" 149, 146). In 1916 he wrote Arthur Greeves and mentioned that he had been "awfully bucked [i.e., elated]" by rereading *The Pilgrim's Progress* (*Stand* 150). Part 3 of *Abolition* features as its epigraph a quotation from Bunyan, and Lewis's introduction to St. Athanasius's *The Incarnation of the Word of God* (translated in 1944), later retitled "On the Reading of Old Books," singles out Bunyan among those "great English writers" whose Christianity lured him to conversion ("Old Books" 203). A 1949 letter, similarly, cites *The Pilgrim's Progress* as an example of a book "where the doctrine is as good on its own merits as the art" (*Letters* 390). "The Literary Impact of the Authorised Version" (1950) devotes a page and a half to Bunyan and the noninfluence of the King James Version upon *The Pilgrim's Progress* ("Literary Impact" 139–40). Viewed in context of these (and other) references, then, the 1962 essay climaxes a lifelong passion.

"The Vision of John Bunyan" also culminates at least four themes in Lewis's own assessment of Bunyan. First, although Lewis never wavered in his admiration for Bunyan's art, at times he felt discomfort with some of Bunyan's doctrine.[8] "The Vision of John Bunyan" expands on this theme, noting the "somewhat repellent" doctrine that occasionally bogs down the narrative and the "unpleasant[ness]" that stems from "the extreme narrowness and exclusiveness of Bunyan's religious outlook" ("Literary Impact" 46; "Vision" 152). Ultimately, though, Bunyan's doctrines of heaven and hell, as well as the pervasiveness of doctrine more generally, do not disqualify it as a work of art—neither for himself, nor even for modern readers who might find such material distasteful. For despite these elements, Lewis insists that "unless we are very hidebound," modern audiences can still interpret and enjoy the allegory in terms of their own life experiences:

> Many do not believe that either the trumpets "with melodious noise" or the infernal den await us where the road ends. But most, I fancy, have discovered that to be born is to be exposed to delights and miseries greater than imagination could have anticipated; that the choice of ways at any cross-road may be more important than we think; and that short cuts may lead to very nasty places. ("Vision" 153)

Secondly, "The Vision of John Bunyan" culminates Lewis's long-time pattern of depicting his own spiritual experience in terms of Bunyan's spiritual allegory. These depictions occur not only in *Regress*, but also in his *Letters*. Evidently, the "valley of humiliation," of all Bunyan's allegorical episodes, particularly resonated with Lewis, for he cites it in a 1951 letter (*Letters* 415), a letter to Greeves (*Stand* 379), and selects it for his illustration when, in "The Vision of John Bunyan," he discusses "the pernicious habit of reading allegory as if it were a cryptogram to be translated"—precisely the way *not* to interpret allegory: "We ought not to be thinking 'This green valley, where the shepherd boy is singing, represents humility'; we ought to be discovering, as we read, that humility is like that green valley. That way, moving always into the book, not out of it, from the concept to the image, enriches the concept" ("Vision" 149).

152

As this last remark suggests, "The Vision of John Bunyan," thirdly, culminates Lewis's remarks about allegory in *The Pilgrim's Progress* specifically and includes some important observations about allegory more generally.[9] In order to read allegory properly, "All depends upon respecting the rights of the vehicle, in refusing to allow the least confusion between the vehicle and its freight" ("Vision" 148). By that Lewis means readers of allegory must value the story as a story—for its own sake—apart from its allegorical interpretation—or, as Lewis put it in *Experiment*, to "receive" rather than "use" it (82–83). Writers of allegory, on the other hand, must avoid having their characters "step out of the allegorical story altogether" and launch into sermons, as Bunyan's occasionally do. When this happens, the vehicle dissolves, dissolving with it the necessity of the allegory: "allegory frustrates itself the moment the author starts doing what could equally well be done in a straight sermon or treatise. It is a valid form only so long as it is doing what could not be done at all, or done so well, in any other way" ("Vision" 146).

The last theme extends beyond Bunyan to Lewis's reading of seventeenth-century literature as a whole. Dealing with the other aspect of Bunyan's "vision," his sensibility, Lewis praises *The Pilgrim's Progress* for its "homely immediacy"—that is, its authenticity, the same quality we have seen him praise elsewhere (148). Lewis's esteem for Bunyan's authenticity reaches back to December 1929, when he wrote Arthur Greeves describing his reaction to having read Bunyan's *Grace Abounding* while crossing Britain on an uneventful train ride. "Some of the sentences in it reach right down," he gasps, citing example after example (*Stand* 319). "The Vision of John Bunyan" demonstrates the ways Bunyan incarnates his spiritual quest in terms of authentic details common to seventeenth-century England, such as the commotion caused by a dog barking on the other side of the door as you stand knocking at it (147–48). Bunyan's authenticity extends to his ability to capture the idioms and cadences of common speech, an ability that Lewis praises as "perfect naturalness in the mimesis of ordinary conversation" (146). Doubtlessly Lewis emphasized this "perfect naturalness" when he read aloud examples of Bunyan's prose for his BBC audience. Ultimately Lewis cherishes *The Pilgrim's Progress* because it is simply an enjoyable story. Illustrating his dictum that readers respect the story for its own sake, apart from its allegorical import, Lewis revels in the story's ability to capture readers through its "enthralling narrative" and "genuinely dramatic dialogue" (146). Because of this and the work's other transcendent qualities, it will remain among those books "which, while didactic in intention, are read with delight by people who do not want their teaching and may not believe that they have anything to teach" (146).

153

Major Prose Writers

At this point, it may be helpful to invoke a distinction Lewis develops in "The Literary Impact of the Authorised Version." Lewis distinguishes between a "source," which "gives us things to write about," and an "influence," which "prompts us to write a certain way" ("Literary Impact" 133). The writers we have heretofore considered served, to varying extents, not only as "sources" for but also as "influences" upon Lewis. However, the major prose writers to whom we now turn constituted "sources" more than "influences."

Known both to Lewis and modern audiences for *Centuries of Meditations*, Thomas Traherne (1637–74), like Herbert and Bunyan, stands out as one of those Christian writers whose artistic excellence initially attracted Lewis and whose Christianity eventually won and possessed him ("Old Books" 203; *Letters* 345). Lewis illustrates his esteem for Traherne by repeatedly recommending the *Centuries* to those who asked him for reading lists—both for its excellent prose and its inspiration (*Letters* 497; *Stand* 560). In a 1941 letter to Arthur Greeves, Lewis declares Traherne's *Centuries of Meditations* "almost the most beautiful book (in prose, I mean, excluding poets) in English" (*Stand* 492). Lewis's 1954 *Sixteenth* echoes this sentiment, singling out Traherne's writings as one of the "great triumphs" of English prose (536). Lewis additionally honors Traherne by choosing from him a quotation to serve as the epigraph for the chapter in *Surprised* entitled "Renaissance," which celebrates Lewis's discovery of "Northernness," and, with that discovery, the rebirth of his imagination (*Surprised* 71).

Indeed, Lewis repeatedly associates Traherne with imagination and joy, art and worship. His introduction to St. Athanasius's translation of *The Incarnation of the Word of God*, later retitled, "On the Reading of Old Books," mentions the "mild, frightening, Paradisial flavour" of essential Christianity in Traherne ("Old Books" 203–04). A related, and even more revealing, remark occurs in the preface to the paperback edition of *The Screwtape Letters* (1961). While discussing Screwtape's hellish prose style and perspective, Lewis stresses the difficulty humans have in producing the corresponding heavenly prose style and perspective.[10] In order to match Screwtape's prose style, Lewis explains, "every sentence would have to smell of heaven." Whose prose can aspire to such heights? Traherne's alone (*Screwtape* xiv).

These themes—the exquisite prose, the associations with imagination and worship, the "mild, frightening, Paradisial flavour," the "smell of heaven"—are expressed most fully in a letter to Arthur Greeves in 1930 which meditates upon crafting literature and attempting to assess its ultimate purpose:

> Remember too what [*sic*] Traherne says that our appreciation of this world—and *this* becomes fully conscious only as we express it in art—is a real link in the uni-

versal chain. Beauty descends from God into nature: but there it would perish and does except when a Man appreciates it with worship and thus as it were *sends it back* to God: so that through his consciousness what descended ascends again and the perfect circle is made. (*Stand* 386)

In other words, art not only signifies our appreciation of the Creator's handiwork; as such, it both constitutes and facilitates further worship. This worship, in turn, conveys the original creation, now modified by man's artistic sensibility, back to the Creator, forming the "perfect circle"—a creative fellowship between man and God. One wonders about the extent to which this concept of the "perfect circle" of creative fellowship characterizes Lewis's relationships with, among others, the Inklings. In addition, to the extent this fellowship approaches prelapsarian fellowship between God and man, art becomes a means not only of worshiping the Creator but also of overcoming the Fall.

Lewis ranks the writings of Sir Thomas Browne (1605–82) among the "great triumphs" of English prose (*Sixteenth* 536). As with Donne and the writers yet to follow, Lewis ransacked Browne's writings for illustrations and quotations; additionally, he included Browne in his list of must-reads for those who petitioned him for reading lists (*Letters* 345; Como 44–45). Most all of Lewis's commentary upon Browne occurs in his *Letters*, where he and Warnie, over a period of months and years, conducted an intensive exploration of Browne's writings (293, 307). A 1931 letter features Lewis's most detailed commentary. Warnie, who was at that time reading through Browne, had recently asked Jack, "Was there anything he [Browne] didn't love?" Warnie's question "hits the nail on the head," Lewis exclaims, and prompts the following observations upon Browne's "peculiar strength":

> It seems to me that his peculiar strength lies in liking everything *both* in the serious sense (Christian charity and so forth) *and* in the Lambian sense of natural gusto: he is thus at once sane and whimsical, and sweet and pungent in the same sentence—as indeed Lamb is. I imagine that I get a sort of double pleasure out of Thomas Browne, one from the author himself and one reflected from Lamb. (*Letters* 290)

Perhaps Lewis's highest praise for Browne occurs in *Surprised*, where Lewis, in citing Browne as one of the most influential Christian writers to him, recounts that he was "deeply and lastingly satisfied" (214) by Browne, a statement which elaborates upon what he had earlier described as his "double pleasure."

Lewis lists Jeremy Taylor (1613–67) as another one of those "great English writers" whose artistic excellence primed him for Christianity ("Old Books" 203). In his "Epilogue" to *Sixteenth*, Lewis cites Taylor's work as one of the "great triumphs" of English prose (536). He observes to Greeves that although Taylor is "severe and has little of the joyous side of religion in him" and that "some of his incentives . . . seem to me unspiritual or at least highly dangerous," nevertheless, his "painstaking, practical attitude has the charm of an old family doctor: beautifully homely and sincere"—precisely the same authenticity he found in Herbert and Bunyan (*Stand* 419). One of Taylor's sermons provided him with "about all" he "knew" concerning the "*refrigerium*"—the period of rest from suffering granted to tormented souls in hell—an idea central to *The Great Divorce* (*Letters* 505; Hooper 279–81).

Lewis familiarized himself with *The Anatomy of Melancholy* (first edition 1621) by Robert Burton (1577–1640) while at Great Bookham. He often selected it for tea-time reading because as a "gossipy, formless book which can be opened anywhere," it lends itself to casual reading (*Surprised* 142–43). In 1918, while convalescing in a hospital, he asked his father to acquire and send to him an edition of *The Anatomy*, mentioning that "it used to be a fancy of mine" (*Letters* 74). Although Lewis occasionally got bogged down in *The Anatomy*, it remained an important source of ideas, quotations, and illustrations. His *Sixteenth* and *Discarded* (among other works) repeatedly mine it. He even derived from *The Anatomy* the idea of coloring Adam and Eve green in *Perelandra* (1943) (Hooper 221–22).

Although Lewis ransacked the writings of Francis Bacon (1561–1626) for ideas and illustrations (much as he did Browne's and Burton's), he "thought Bacon (to speak frankly) a solemn, pretentious ass" (*Surprised* 214). This disparagement is elaborated in his critique of the *Essays* in the "Epilogue" to *Sixteenth*. Although conceding limited praise to Bacon's style in his *Essays*, Lewis considers this collection a "book whose reputation curiously outweighs any real pleasure or profit that most people have found in it. . . . The truth is, it is a book for adolescents" (537). Even worse, Bacon's *Essays* resemble Montaigne's "about as much as a metallic-looking cactus raised on the edge of a desert resembles a whole country-side of forest, filled with light and shade, well stocked with game, and hard to get out of." This cactus, Lewis continues, is "interesting, striking, worth going to see once, but sterile, inedible, cold and hard to touch" (538).

Richard Baxter (1615–91), who wrote *The Saint's Everlasting Rest* (1651), provided for Lewis in that work the phrase "mere Christianity," which Lewis appropriated to entitle his perhaps most famous work of apologetics. Arguing that there is "a pervasive coincidence of idea and emphasis" between Lewis's writings and Baxter's, N. H. Keeble suggests that Baxter's works provided for Lewis not only a phrase but an entire nonsectarian approach to Christianity (27).

Conclusion: A Twentieth-Century Samuel Johnson?

At least three conclusions can be derived from our survey. The first concerns Lewis's likes and dislikes. As Lewis surveyed seventeenth-century English literature, he prized authenticity and eschewed its antithesis, priggery. He savored the rhythm and music of the language, both in poetry and prose, illustrating his dictum, "Good reading is always aural as well as visual" (*Experiment* 90). Although he gravitated toward Donne, Herbert, Bunyan, Traherne, and the major prose writers, he virtually ignored others. Lewis's writings contain almost no mention of the Jacobean Drama, despite his evident knowledge of the material (Como 50).[11] Although Lewis knew the material well enough to cite it for illustrations, it apparently lacked appeal for any further use. The dearth of references to the Cavalier Poets and the period's prose fiction (other than, of course, *The Pilgrim's Progress*) suggest the same conclusion.

References to seventeenth-century writers appear across the full spectrum of Lewis's writings, illustrating not only his familiarity with them but also the extent to which he had internalized them. These references, furthermore, tend to fall into two broad patterns, and studying these patterns can lead us to a second conclusion. References to devotional writings appear primarily in his post-conversion writings which we might classify as "personal" and not ostensibly works of literary criticism (e.g., *Letters, Surprised, Regress, Dock*, etc.). References to non-devotional (or less ostensibly devotional) writings tend to appear primarily in his literary criticism, which we might classify as "professional" (e.g., the essays, *Sixteenth, Discarded*, etc.). Although there is some overlap, this distribution of sacred material to personal writings and secular material to professional writings suggests a dichotomy between personal and professional. Indeed, this dichotomy may underlie his treatment of Donne and Bunyan: Lewis's two essays address Donne's love poetry, while his more personal poems, letters, and other materials incorporate Donne's devotional writings. Similarly, Lewis's essays on Bunyan tend to address the non-religious aspects of *The Pilgrim's Progress*, such as its style, while his *Letters* concentrate on its spiritual dimensions and applications. Most notable of all, references to the devotional writer who had the most impact of all upon him, George Herbert, appear almost exclusively in Lewis's personal writings.

Finally, as a critic of seventeenth-century English literature, Lewis displays some general resemblances to his predecessor, Samuel Johnson, especially as Johnson articulates his tastes in "The Life of Cowley." First, Lewis and Johnson share a number of tastes: both disliked ostentatious displays of erudition and eschewed the unnecessary difficulty of metaphysical wit (along with the priggery that attended it); instead, they liked imagery that is accessible to gen-

157

eral audiences, appeals to common sense, and corresponds to nature—in short, decorum, not *discordia concors*. Both rejected the novel for the timeless, the specific for the general. Both upheld traditional values. Lewis and Johnson similarly share a number of critical tendencies: both could survey vast fields of information, systematize them, and formulate generalizations; both could simplify the complex and elucidate the opaque; both resisted fads, advocating moderation and curbing excess. Although Lewis's tastes and tendencies, like Johnson's, have certain weaknesses, his literary criticism, I predict, will remain valued for precisely its Johnsonian strengths: its sheer lucidity, breadth, and common sense.

Notes

1. Many of those essays, reviews, and notes are anthologized in such works as *Studies in Medieval and Renaissance Literature* (1966) and *Selected Literary Essays* (1969). For a summary and discussion of Lewis's lectures on medieval and Renaissance literature throughout his career at Oxford and Cambridge, see Walter S. Hooper, *C. S. Lewis: A Companion and Guide* 524–26.

2. Although many authors surveyed in this chapter fall slightly later than the traditional endpoint (1660) for this period, they are included in discussions of seventeenth-century English literature because their sensibility corresponds more with it than with that of the Restoration and eighteenth century.

3. For comparisons between Donne and Spenser, see "Spenser" 142–43; between Donne and Dante, see "Similes" 72–73; between Donne and Chapman ("Hero and Leander" specifically), see "Hero" 69–70; between Donne and Elizabethan satirists, see *Sixteenth* 469–71. Certain Donne poems seem to have become favorites. *The Second Anniversary* provided one of his favorite examples of metaphysical wit: the image of Elizabeth Drury's liberated soul (it "baits not at the moon"), which he cites in at least three different works (*Discarded* 95; "Hero" 69; *Sixteenth* 541). Similarly, Lewis refers to "The Ecstasy" three times in *Discarded* to illustrate the medieval-Renaissance cosmology, directs two characters in *The Pilgrim's Regress* to quote it (book 2, chapter 6), and even wrote a poem by the same title.

4. Lewis beautifully rephrases these views when comparing Donne's imagery with Dante's and with Spenser's ("Similes" 72–73; "Spenser" 143).

5. Lewis's handling of "The Ecstasy" epitomizes his mixed feelings. Although in the context of literary criticism, Lewis referred to it (for illustrations) more often than almost any other Donne poem, one wonders why, in *Regress*, he causes John to befriend (prior to repenting of that association) two unsympathetic characters who epitomize their lifestyle by quoting "The Ecstasy." Indeed, Lewis later characterized this poem as "much nastier" than even Elegy 19 ("Love Poetry" 118).

6. Lewis's copy of Herbert's poetry is preserved in the Marion E. Wade Collection, Wheaton College, Wheaton, IL.

7. See, for example, Lindskoog.

8. See *Road* 327; *Stand* 319; *Letters* 497.

9. Lewis had earlier broached this topic in a 1958 letter to a Mrs. Hook, where he finds himself in the position of having not only to explain the concept of allegory to a layperson, but also to dis-

tinguish allegory from supposition, the former appearing in *The Pilgrim's Progress*, and the latter in the Chronicles of Narnia:

> If Aslan represented the immaterial Deity in the same way in which [Bunyan's] Giant Despair represents Despair, he would be an allegorical figure. In reality, however, he is an invention giving an imaginary answer to the question, "What might Christ become like if there really were a world like Narnia and He chose to be incarnate and die and rise again in *that* world as He actually has done in ours?" This is not allegory at all. . . . This . . . works out a *supposition*. . . . Allegory and supposals differ because they mix the real and unreal in different ways. Bunyan's picture of Giant Despair does not start from supposal at all. It is not a supposition but a *fact* that despair can capture and imprison a human soul. What is unreal (fictional) is the giant, castle, and the dungeon. (*Letters* 475–76)

10. Lewis elaborates this point in *Preface* 100–01.
11. According to *Road*, Lewis liked Beaumont and Fletcher (172, 153) but detested Jacobean tragedy (456, 169, 155).

Works Cited

Bennett, Joan. "The Love Poetry of John Donne: A Reply to Mr. C. S. Lewis." *Seventeenth Century Studies Presented to Sir Herbert Grierson*. Oxford: Clarendon, 1938. 85–104.

Christopher, Joe R. "An Analysis of 'The Apologist's Evening Prayer.'" *CSL: The Bulletin of the New York C. S. Lewis Society* 5 (Oct. 1974): 2–4.

Como, James T., ed. *C. S. Lewis at the Breakfast Table and Other Reminiscences*. New York: Macmillan, 1979.

Donne, John. *The Complete English Poems*. Ed. A. J. Smith. Harmondsworth: Penguin, 1986.

———. *Letters to Severall Persons of Honour (1651)*. Ed. M. Thomas Hester. Delmar, NY: Scholar, 1977.

Eliot, T. S. "The Metaphysical Poets." *Selected Essays*. New ed. New York: Harcourt, 1978. 241–50.

Herbert, George. *The English Poems of George Herbert*. Ed. C. A. Patrides. London: Dent, 1988.

Hooper, Walter. *C. S. Lewis: A Companion and Guide*. San Francisco: Harper San Francisco, 1996.

Johnson, Samuel. "The Life of Cowley." *Lives of the Poets*. Ed. S. C. Roberts. London: Collins, 1967. 19–74.

Keeble, N. H. "C. S. Lewis, Richard Baxter, and 'Mere Christianity'." *Christianity and Literature* 30.3 (1981): 27–44.

Lewis, C. S. *The Abolition of Man*. 1943. New York: Macmillan, 1957.

———. *All My Road Before Me: The Diary of C. S. Lewis 1922–1927*. Ed. Walter Hooper. New York: Harcourt Brace Jovanovich, 1991.

———. "Dante's Similies." *Medieval* 64–77.

———. *The Discarded Image: An Introduction to Medieval and Renaissance Literature*. 1964. Cambridge: Cambridge UP, 1994.

———. "Donne and Love Poetry in the Seventeenth Century." *Literary* 106–25.

———. "Edmund Spenser, 1552–99." *Medieval* 121–45.

———. *English Literature in the Sixteenth Century Excluding Drama*. Oxford: Oxford UP, 1954.

––––––. *An Experiment in Criticism.* 1961. Cambridge: Cambridge UP, 1992.

––––––. *The Four Loves.* 1960. New York: Harcourt, 1988.

––––––. "Hero and Leander." *Literary* 58–73.

––––––. *Letters of C. S. Lewis.* Ed. W. H. Lewis. 1966. Rev. ed. Ed. Walter Hooper. New York: Harcourt, 1993.

––––––. "The Literary Impact of the Authorised Version." *Literary* 126–45.

––––––. "On the Reading of Old Books." *God in the Dock: Essays on Theology and Ethics.* Ed. Walter Hooper. Grand Rapids: Eerdmans, 1970. 200–07.

––––––. *Perelandra.* 1943. New York: Macmillan, 1965.

––––––. *The Pilgrim's Regress: An Allegorical Apology for Christianity, Reason and Romanticism.* 1933. Grand Rapids: Eerdmans, 1995.

––––––. *Poems.* Ed. Walter Hooper. London: Geoffey Bles, 1964.

––––––. *A Preface to "Paradise Lost."* 1942. New York: Oxford UP, 1961.

––––––. *The Screwtape Letters.* 1961. New York: Macmillan, 1977.

––––––. *Selected Literary Essays.* Ed. Walter Hooper. Cambridge: Cambridge UP, 1969.

––––––. *Studies in Medieval and Renaissance Literature.* Ed. Walter Hooper. Cambridge: Cambridge UP, 1966.

––––––. *Surprised by Joy: The Shape of My Early Life.* New York: Harcourt, 1955.

––––––. *That Hideous Strength: A Modern Fairy-Tale for Grown-Ups.* 1945. New York: Macmillan, 1965.

––––––. *They Stand Together: The Letters of C. S. Lewis to Arthur Greeves (1914–1963).* Ed. Walter Hooper. New York: Macmillan, 1979.

––––––. *Till We Have Faces: A Myth Retold.* New York: Harcourt, 1956.

––––––. "The Vision of John Bunyan." *Literary* 146–53.

––––––, and E. M. W. Tillyard. *The Personal Heresy: A Controversy.* London: Oxford UP, 1939.

Lindskoog, Kathryn. *Finding the Landlord: A Guidebook to C. S. Lewis's* Pilgrim's Regress. Chicago: Cornerstone, 1995.

Morris, Francis J. "Metaphor and Myth: Shaping Forces in C. S. Lewis's Critical Assessment of Renaissance Literaure." Diss., U of Pennsylvania, 1977.

Vaughan, Henry. *The Complete Poetry of Henry Vaughan.* Ed. French Fogle. New York: Norton, 1964.

9
Milton

Charles A. Huttar

In 1930 the young C. S. Lewis lectured in Oxford on the text of the young John Milton's Ludlow masque (Hooper, *Companion* 459), whose several contemporary versions, manuscript and printed, show stages of its composition. Two years later appeared Lewis's first scholarly publication, "A Note on *Comus*."[1] Writing on *Comus* must have pleased him; it had long been favorite reading. Its tale of ethical idealism, perilous woods, and supernatural enchantments combined the qualities he enjoyed in medieval romance, and he memorized and mulled over large portions of it (*Stand* 130–31, 198, 347). In August 1932 a phrase borrowed from it, "clad in complete steel," described the militant virgin Reason in *The Pilgrim's Regress* (*Comus* line 420; *Regress* 63–64).[2]

Lewis's "Note" studied nine passages where Milton altered his stage version of 1634 for publication in 1637. He found a pattern: Milton "subdued" his work to achieve a more unified tone ("Note on *Comus*" 181). He exchanged striking for more ordinary diction, evoked reflection rather than excitement, and made the printed version less dramatic and more gnomic. The "poetic chastity" ("Note on *Comus*" 181) of his movement toward classical decorum and "gravity" (180) should be appreciated, though modern taste might prefer the Metaphysicals.[3] This early publication exhibits characteristic qualities, Lewis's critical awareness of contemporary fashions in reading and his readiness to offer meticulously researched and vigorously argued corrections. Thus, any study of Lewis as a guide to reading Milton will also be, inextricably, an account of his engagements with other leading critics. Furthermore, it will provide glimpses of Lewis's constant habit in his critical writing of attending to broader contemporary concerns in life and society. And incidentally (therefore without special indication), portions of the following account will also reveal a maturing process in Lewis's opinions.

Critical Warfare and Informed Explanation in A Preface to "Paradise Lost"

Even above *Comus* Lewis valued *Paradise Lost* (*Stand* 198), which he first encountered at age nine (Hooper, *Companion* 459). He bought a copy at seventeen, read it at least twice within a few months (*Stand* 123, 127, 159, 165, 176), and called it, in a celebratory poem, a "joyous tale" (*Collected Poems* 190). As an undergraduate he addressed the Martlets on tragic elements in book 10 (Hooper, "Preface" viii). Over the years his love of *Paradise Lost*, undeterred by antipathy toward the author (Hannay, *Lewis* 172–73)[4] nor even by Milton's Christianity (*Surprised* 213), outgrew his early enthusiasm for its romantic aspects.[5] Already in 1927, before his conversion, he was developing cogent arguments against the romantic idea that Satan was Milton's hero (*Road* 433). In a time of growing denigration of Milton,[6] Lewis believed many cultural factors prevented a proper appreciation of *Paradise Lost*. One, which he dubbed "The Personal Heresy," confused a literary work with the author's personality, judging the first in terms of the second or even studying the first mainly for knowledge of the second. E. M. W. Tillyard, for example, had written that *Paradise Lost* is "really about" the "state of Milton's mind when he wrote it" (qtd. by Lewis, *Heresy* 2). That idea (along with several non-Miltonic examples) Lewis considered dangerous; and he wrote what was to be the first of six essays, Lewis alternating with Tillyard, to debate the issue, clarify their positions, find points of agreement, and define more sharply their differences. Without attempting here to summarize their essentially theoretical discussion, we may note Lewis's view (implicitly rebutting an earlier critic, Samuel Johnson) that knowing whether or not Milton "really grieved" for Edward King does not matter when we read *Lycidas* (*Heresy* 9).[7] Poetry is "an art or skill"; its essence is making things, not expressing oneself; everyone knew that, once; it was a "platitude," but is now "obscured" by the Romantics' focus on the poet's personality (103).

Lewis thought there were other stumbling blocks, too, keeping us from Milton, and by the late 1930s he was at work on a book to help readers overcome these obstacles.[8] He was not so much dueling with particular antagonists as trying to correct more widespread errors, which in his mind leading critics represented and were partially responsible for. Some of the errors sprang from sheer ignorance, some from new attitudes. With Sir Thomas Browne he wonders "how so many learned heads should so far forget . . ." (*Preface* viii). The success of Charles Williams's 1940 lectures at Oxford and his introduction to a new edition of Milton later that year[9] encouraged Lewis to believe that, despite the intellectual climate, the job could be done.

Lewis devoted roughly half of his *Preface* to questions of form and half to content: form first, because he believed interpretation depends on first grasping the purposes implicit in the genre of a work. He addressed various charges that Milton's use of the English language was defective, and the current disparagement of any poetry that relies on evoking a reader's "stock responses."[10] He laid his groundwork slowly. He observed that many readers approach epic wrongly; they read for excellences proper to other *kinds* of poetry (Lewis preferred the English term over the French *genre*), experience disappointment, and misprize the very qualities that, "rightly enjoyed" (2), would give most delight. Disarmingly, Lewis admits that he once read that way (2). Modern authors often first decide what their message is, then ask what form can best convey it. But *Paradise Lost* began with Milton's choice of genre. He considered both biblical and classical models in various genres. This effort to integrate pagan culture with Christian was typical; Milton combined "in a live and sensitive tension" (7) polarities such as rebelliousness and discipline, voluptuousness and chastity. His greatness exemplifies not the modern ideal of intensifying some one quality, but a more classical ideal. Within the epic form, Milton's choice of the classical over the romantic subgenre, entailing a distinct structure (unified plot) and "sacrifice" (7) of the Arthurian themes that interested him, exhibits authorial self-discipline like that discernible in the *Comus* revisions.[11]

Now Lewis is ready to address the objections to Miltonic language voiced by T. S. Eliot ("artificial" and "conventional" language ["Milton I" 158], "syntax . . . determined by the musical significance" [161]) and F. R. Leavis ("heavy rhythmic pattern," "hieratic stylization," "magniloquence," lacking "concrete realization," "remote" from the colloquial [45, 46, 50, 51]). The epic form exemplified in Homer and *Beowulf* is oral court poetry of a certain sort, lofty, grave, festive, "ceremonial"—in a word, *solemn* in the older sense (*Preface* 15, 18). "The element of ritual which some dislike in Milton's poetry" is an essential quality he inherited from Homer, and it functions to "pattern" the "flux of our feelings" according to "wise custom" (21). By this technique Homer creates a world possessing splendor, pathos, an "unusual degree" of credibility (22), and unsurpassed "objectivity" (24).[12] Also at Milton's disposal as part of the epic genre was what Virgil added, a sense of vastness, of past and future, of epochal events or turning points (33–35; cf. P. Andrew Montgomery's chapter on classical literature in this volume).

Milton finally takes center stage in chapter 7, an investigation of the style appropriate to his chosen genre. He had to maintain "solemnity" befitting the grandeur of subject, and do it without the public, festive occasion assisting. Style alone must compensate for "the privacy and informality of silent reading." Thus "to blame it for being ritualistic or incantatory, for lacking intimacy or the speaking voice," is to take as a blemish precisely what is the poet's achievement and glory (*Preface* 39). Milton uses "slightly unfamiliar" diction and syntax, evocative proper names (more for connotation than mere sonority), and sensory images, "all . . . with an air of magnanimous austerity" (39–40). He works on two levels simultaneously, surface statement and underlying suggestion. "Like . . . some moderns," Milton "throws ideas together because of those emotional relations which they have in the very recesses of our consciousness," but by providing also a "façade of logical connections" he promotes an immediacy of effect that modern verse often lacks (41).[13] He uses contemporary science evocatively—it is not "pedantry" as some think; "Heaven and Earth are ransacked for simile and allusion, . . . not . . . for display"—inverting Samuel Johnson's criticism of the Metaphysical poets whom Eliot and his school favored[14]—but "to guide our imaginations with unobtrusive pressure . . . where the poet wishes them to flow" (43). Here Lewis remarkably anticipates a major emphasis in Milton criticism of the half-century succeeding him. Even the Latinate syntax, "that feature . . . most severely criticized" (43),[15] contributes to this effect: its complex constructions yield also a compensating "simplicity of the broad imaginative effects . . . and the perfect rightness of their sequence" (44), and its un-English connectives and inversions enable greater fluidity—a mimesis of the "flowing quality of immediate experience" without loss of epic "dignity" (46). Lewis examines the description of Eden in *Paradise Lost* 4.131–286, arguing the particular aptness of this style for the Miltonic subject and addressing a charge the critics had stressed, that Milton fails in "visual imagination" (Eliot, "Milton I" 158 [see also 161–62]) and has no "interest in sensuous particularity" (Leavis 50). Precisely so, says Lewis:[16] Milton "arouses" archetypal images in our minds (*Preface* 46–47) rather than realistic pictures of Paradise because no "original" (48) picture a poet might invent could do justice to the reality.[17] "The garden is found" at "humanity's centre, not some private centre of the poet's" (49).

Lewis proceeds to defend this style on three fronts. First, some readers were doubtless offended to be told that Milton manipulates us (40); they associate that with the worst aspects of "rhetoric." To this modern prejudice Lewis replies that rhetoric is not inherently vile but noble, though liable to abuse. Further, while rhetoric aims at arousing emotion to produce action or practical resolve, poetry aims at a "vision of concrete reality," including emotional response (53).[18]

Second is the issue of stock responses. Lewis names I. A. Richards as the attacker, but his quarrel is really with Richards's less discriminating followers, "his school" (*Preface* 54). Richards wanted poetry to challenge readers' habitual attitudes, absorbed casually in childhood and shaped often through prejudice and popular stereotypes, by exposing them freshly to "the free direct play of experience" (*Principles* 202).[19] Lewis, who hasn't enough faith in raw human nature to trust the mere "play of experience" undirected, answers that "most people's responses are not 'stock' enough" (*Preface* 54). Society has the task of teaching every new generation the "delicate balance of trained habits, laboriously acquired and easily lost," that are needed for sheer survival (55). Schools bear a large responsibility in this, Lewis would argue a year later in *The Abolition of Man.* So, traditionally, he says now, has poetry, but "since poetry has abandoned that office" (*Preface* 56) we can no longer (with Milton) count on morally right responses to such elemental realities as pride, treachery, death, pain, and pleasure. Hence, poetry like Milton's is now "more than ever necessary" (56).

On the third front of defense, Milton's "calculated grandiosity" (57) does not, as some think, prove insincerity. Although present fashions may value spontaneity, epic calls for ceremony; where we expect the poet's self-revelation, the poem gives us instead a persona, the archetypal Blind Bard; where we want to look hard at the poem itself and study its operations, Milton invites us rather to participate, and the poem becomes a window through which to see the world more truly.

In the second division of his book Lewis turns, as I have said, to the content of *Paradise Lost.* His formidable erudition well equips him—as will be evident in the paragraphs that follow—to explain the concepts needed in order to understand the poem, many of them belonging to an unfamiliar world view. But is such explanation necessary? Does not the poem's value to us lie in the perennial, in what remains after stripping away the "superficial" bits (61), the outmoded theology, science, and so on? No, says Lewis: the "human heart"— the whole complex of attitudes and assumptions by which people live—has undergone changes from one era to another; thus by an "effort of historical imagination" (70) we must read the poem Milton wrote, not one remade after today's outlook and prejudices. Serious reading requires suspending disbelief.[20] Lewis, in reading, tried to enter the world of a book not only to understand it fairly—the purpose he here enjoins on the reader of Milton—but beyond that, to enjoy it for itself even if it conflicted with his own beliefs.[21] Thus he writes on rereading *Paradise Lost* in 1917, when Milton's theology was still alien to him, "So may she ["the weird spirit of unexplained delight"] come to me, teaching me well / To savor all those sweets that lie ... / In ... this pleasant land / Though it be not the land where I would dwell" (*Collected Poems* 190).

Milton inherited and "substantially" followed certain traditional doctrines in framing his account of the Fall; modern readers, uninformed about these, are, Lewis noticed, vulnerable to "various false emphases" (*Preface* 65). Lewis summarizes the theological traditions in eleven propositions, with sources in Augustine's *City of God* and parallels in Milton's epic (65–69). If readers find some of these propositions surprising, well, popular versions of doctrines are not necessarily accurate ones. Lewis hopes that knowing (as fact, not opinion) that these were indeed the received doctrines in Milton's time will forestall several common misunderstandings. But why, he asks, do even "great modern scholars" persist in thinking Milton believed otherwise? Because they find the real teaching "so uninteresting or so intensely disagreeable" that "psychological necessity" drives them to other readings (70). This is one of several places in the book where Lewis oversteps the strict boundaries of criticism to comment—some might think, gratuitously—on contemporary culture. It is not a flattering picture of human motivation. Yet it is credible.

The doctrine Lewis calls "Hierarchy" is a more philosophical than theological one: Aristotle, not Augustine, is Lewis's source text. Readers who wonder how Milton could endorse rebellion against Charles I but condemn Satan's rebellion against God fail to understand that in his world view and that of his age (contrary to twentieth-century assumptions), not all beings are equal. Between God and all creatures there is a gulf; among the creatures there are lesser hierarchical scales. Rebellion against one's natural superior is wrong (Abdiel's confutation of Satan in book 5 echoes Aristotle). Equally wrong is arrogating rule over one's natural equals, as in book 12 the sin of Nimrod, founder of monarchy. To insist, despite these logical distinctions, that the republican Milton had to be emotionally on Satan's side is to project on him a sympathy springing from "preconceptions" alien to him (77). Though the man Milton may have failed always to behave according to his ideals, "the Hierarchical idea" commanded from him a commitment not merely intellectual but deeply emotional. In fact, its appeal to his "imagination" (78) was likely the prior claim. It informs even his antiprelatical and revolutionary tracts (79) and appears constantly in the poem: beatitude must include order, the "ceremonious interchange of unequal courtesies," an "intricate dance" (78), elaborate and precise, full of vitality, a "heavenly frolic" (80), a "discipline" paradoxically "exist[ing] for the sake of . . . freedom, almost for extravagance" (79). Hierarchy even extends into Milton's prosody, playing off "licences and variations" against the "decasyllabic norm" (80).

But is the catholicity of *Paradise Lost*—what Lewis elsewhere called "mere" Christianity without denominational particularity—marred, as many think, by heresy? Lewis acknowledged Arianism in *De Doctrina Christiana*[22] but rejected Denis Saurat's ascription of numerous heresies to *Paradise Lost*. Though appreciative of Saurat for daring to value Milton as a thinker (*Preface* 91), Lewis argued that some of the views Saurat thought heretical were orthodox theology, others were heretical but not in Milton, and one (the Arianism) Milton had excluded from *Paradise Lost*. A fourth category Lewis headed

"Those which are possibly heretical and do really occur in *Paradise Lost*" (85); but after discussing the relevant texts of both poem and treatise and the nuances of their interpretation, he concluded that neither the heretical nature of these views nor their presence in *Paradise Lost* is certain.[23] Thus his statement that "heretical elements exist in [the poem]" concedes more than would have been necessary, but at any rate his main contention stands, that the "catholic" quality is "predominant" and only "by search" (if then) could heterodoxy be found (81). Though Milton might have had heretical beliefs outside the poem, we as readers should avoid the Personal Heresy; besides, the "decorum" of epic required a discipline that excluded "private theological whimsies," and Milton obeyed (90).

Paradise Lost is "overwhelmingly Christian" in its theology, Lewis concludes, "not even specifically Protestant or Puritan . . . except for a few isolated passages" (*Preface* 91). One might respond that the theology of predestination, free will, and the nature of divine grace—on which there existed no statement universally approved by the church(es) of Milton's day, no "catholic" agreement—looms larger in the poem than the term "isolated passages" would imply. Perhaps Lewis avoided discussing this doctrine to keep the book short, not just to avoid complicating his neat formula of a poem with studied catholicity. Yet I think that formula would not have been greatly impaired by some attention to these important matters on which Milton labored. They were not ones on which he could remain discreetly silent in his poem, as he could on the finer points of Christology.

Next Lewis examines specific theological topics. Concerning Milton's Satan, he faced not recent influential critics but 150 years of romanticizing. The theological tradition on which Milton drew considered Lucifer's rebellion not admirable but sinful and foolish, grounded in false conceptions and "entangled in contradictions" (*Preface* 94). Folly deserves ridicule, but epic cannot be merely comic; Milton must depict Satan as not merely petulant (93) but as capable of inflicting immense misery.[24] Yet he could not ignore Satan's absurdity: heavy ironies enter when the Father of Lies is deceived by his own posturings, and in Heaven there is laughter—here, says Lewis, Milton risks alienating even sympathetic readers (93). Satan's degradation intellectually to "Nonsense" (95, 96) is matched on the moral level—goodness is beyond his imagining (96)—and the physical (97). Milton's conception is too unified to support a theory that he inadvertently made Satan too attractive and then tried to repair the damage. Milton counted on readers theologically acute enough not to trust naively in the Deceiver's rhetoric (98). His portrait of Satan has undeniable energy, only because artists, as humans, necessarily have through experience a surer grasp of evil character than of good (98–99).[25] The analytical power of Milton's understanding of evil appears in the four ways Satan's subordinates respond to their hopeless situation

(book 2). Moloch's futile rage, Belial's calculated indolence, Mammon's incapacity to distinguish counterfeit bliss from real, Beelzebub's petty spite vented
on helpless innocents—each reveals "further recesses of misery and evil" and
imparts "fuller understanding of the Satanic predicament" (104).

A common mistake about Milton's angels goes back at least to Johnson,
who considered their materiality an inept fiction. Lewis explains that Scholasticism had indeed believed angels to be spirit (a concept Donne exploited),
but Milton adopted the newer view of Renaissance Platonism: that angelic
bodies are made of matter, exceedingly light and rarefied. Milton, therefore,
is not indulging in whimsical invention but employing up-to-date science
when he depicts Satan contracting into a toad and then dilating, being protected by armor and healing quickly after a wound, or Raphael eating lunch
in Eden and discoursing on angelic sexuality.

A common mistake about Adam and Eve equates innocence with childishness. "They were created full-grown and perfect" (*Preface* 112), Lewis
explains; so the Church Fathers taught, and Milton, with Dante, adopts this
view. Adam's commanding intellect and "kingly manner" (115) should evoke
awe, not condescension; Eve, though ranking below him, possesses grandeur,
majesty, and poise. She "compels deference" (116). Her intellect is quick and
wide-ranging (117). Her humility toward Adam is "often misunderstood"; it
belongs to that "minuet" of mutual "courtesy" which marks their relationship
(115). On the sexual aspect of that relation, Milton for once departs from
Augustine: though they agree hypothetically on the nature of sinless sex, Milton risks including it in his mythos as an actuality.[26]

In Lewis's analysis of the Fall in *Paradise Lost*, Eve recapitulates Satan's sin of
pride (65, 121), with two quick results: first "Nonsense"—hoping to evade God—
and "false sentiment," contemplating tyranny and murder and calling it love
(123, 121). Milton's remarkable achievement here is to show successively Eve's
sinful choices as they are made. Second, her pride is humbled: from aspiring to
godhead, she descends to "worship[ing] a vegetable" (122). Adam sins "by uxo-
riousness," Lewis's term for elevating conjugal attachment above obedience to
God. Despite a "half-nobility," this is still, on Milton's "premises," a sin. Adam
fails to imagine that God *might* have had a way of redeeming the situation—
though neither Adam nor we can know (122–23). Adam's personality changes in
a way "opposite" to Eve's: he becomes a cavalier. Both Adam and Eve then discover a "new" sexuality that has "perversely" a "tang of evil" and alters their relationship so that Eve willingly assumes the role of a sex object (124).

Lewis here breaks off his account of the results of the Fall. On its ecologi-
cal consequences and on the great drama of book 10 he is silent, presumably
because these topics, not being currently subject to controversy or misunderstanding, lay outside his purpose. It seems odd, however, that he did not
mention the theory of the "fortunate Fall" then being promulgated by Arthur

Lovejoy and others (and more recently exploded), since it relates closely to points four and five in his list of Augustinian doctrines (*Preface* 66–67). Perhaps he saved that critique for *Perelandra*.[27]

Finally, Lewis turns from dismantling "hindrances" to evaluating the poem as a whole. First, he says, it has a "grave structural flaw." Milton attempted to be like Virgil in projecting a future far beyond the actual narrative, but did it unadvisedly in one great "lump" in the last two books, where he also fell into bad writing, though ending with "a great recovery" (*Preface* 125). Stanley Fish suggests, however, that Lewis's emphatic expression may be a "politically astute" rhetorical ploy: he "sacrificed" books 11 and 12 so as to "defend the rest of the poem in the face of its influential detractors" and by their own criterion of structural artistry ("Transmuting" 254–55).[28] Second, Milton's "presentation of God the Father" is "unsatisfactory"—but not for the reasons sometimes given. The poet's "religious defects" or a conception of God as "cold, merciless, or tyrannical," Lewis attributes, in some cases at least, to religious or antireligious feelings the critic has brought to the poem.[29] Still, he deems Milton imprudent to risk (perhaps misled by Homeric precedent) such an anthropomorphic picture of God (*Preface* 126–27; see also 93). Third, Milton's handling of the Son is also frequently criticized, but here Lewis disagrees, though acknowledging that "only lately," with guidance from Williams's "Introduction," has he "come to appreciate the War in Heaven at its true worth." Given a fixed mythos, Milton still manages surprise, by having the war end not with Michael's victory but by God's intervention—otherwise it would be endless—and then having the Son with "appalling majesty" overthrow the rebels by his mere presence (127). To a fourth criticism, that the poet's failure in presenting God "destroys" the epic "as a religious poem," Lewis replies that it is not intended as a religious poem[30] but rather as a depiction of the "objective . . . complex pattern" of cosmic reality. Having contemplated that picture, readers may (or may not) go on to apply it individually in a religious manner. The success of the poem, however, does not hang on a wholly "adequate symbol" for God (127–28). Overall, Milton tells a "great story," greater than any other because with "truth and passion" he "records a real, irreversible, unrepeatable process" in universal history (129).

Lewis believes that adverse criticism from Blake on, distorted by "hatred or ignorance" of the "central theme," has, though offered as literary analysis, sprung more from political and ethical attitudes (*Preface* 129). Attacks on Milton's style are included in this judgment. Without naming T. S. Eliot, Lewis quotes (130) from his 1936 "Note" phrases that, in effect, blame the epic for not being a lyric.[31] He does, however, name F. R. Leavis as an example of critics driven by a nonliterary antagonism to Milton's beliefs and values[32] and desiring an end to the structures of civility necessary to maintain those values. Lewis offers a classification of anti-Miltonians: those (who used to be called philistines) having no use for the old world of humane values that Milton represents; those misled by a spurious realism into rejecting the supposed artifice of Milton's kind of poetry; and those (like Eliot) who seek a spirituality above such mere civility, failing to realize that strategically the civility needs defending lest the great majority fall below it.

Lewis holds that *Paradise Lost,* even to a sympathetic reader knowing the background, is not faultless. Besides his criticisms already mentioned, he considers Milton's portrayal of Edenic sexuality a "failure" (124). Before the Fall it is presented too familiarly for its innocence to be credible—it should have been more "mysterious" (120)—and for that reason postlapsarian love-making differs insufficiently from that before. These pronouncements have been rebutted by any number of critics.[33] Other critiques appear in passing in other books by Lewis: of Milton's handling of the problem of foreknowledge (*Discarded* 88); of the "great harm" done by the "grandeur and high poetry" in his portrayal of devils (*Screwtape* ix);[34] and of the military discipline of Heaven, "silly" since Heaven is ruled by love, not law (*Malcolm* 148). The last, however, is the comment of a Lewis persona; had he spoken in his own voice he might have observed how that judgment is complicated by the degree to which Heaven "surmounts the reach / Of human sense" (*PL* 5:571–72). Certainly in 1942 he did not appear to find Milton's disciplined heaven silly (*Preface* 79; cf. *Planet* 158). To return to the general point, however, he regularly placed Dante's poetic achievement above Milton's—sometimes with respect to what he considered Milton's faults (*Preface* 120, 128; "Shelley" 204 [cf. 208, and the earlier, briefer statement in *Stand* 369]; *Malcolm* 148).

Lewis's *Preface* was accurately titled; it aimed to prepare readers to join Milton's "fit audience"—not to be a complete commentary. Moreover, he wrote within the time constraints of a lecture series. Lewis was well equipped to have dealt with other issues such as forbidden knowledge, the likeness of earth to heaven, and the status of work before and after the Fall. The last problem did occupy his thoughts while he was working on Milton (*Letters* 187–88), but he left it out of the book. It is curious that the word *myth* appears not once in the *Preface,*[35] when Lewis had so much to say on the subject elsewhere. Commenting years later on Shumaker's essay on *Paradise Lost* as myth, he praised Milton's "success" in preserving "the *quality* of myth" alongside a more sophisticated "credal affirmation" (*Letters* 303; original emphasis).

Lewis's Preface in a Half-Century Perspective

What has been the *Preface*'s impact? No other book on Milton that old has remained continuously in print to the present day. The Milton Society of America in 1954 named Lewis as one of its "honored scholars." Together with Charles Williams, he revitalized Milton scholarship, especially but not solely concerning the figure of Satan. He provoked vigorous opposition as well as agreement, but many of his insights have become commonplaces of Milton criticism, and a lengthy catalogue could be made of those who have taken some idea in Lewis's book and built upon it further structures of understanding. A few examples will have to suffice. It is now taken for granted that distinctions of genre, as contemporaneously understood, are crucial to interpretation and evaluation; in his insistence on form, Lewis was a pioneer. His defense of Milton's style has been more than vindicated by later studies (see Fowler's brief summary in Milton 430). Another major theme developing in post-Lewis Milton scholarship has been the unreliability of language, signaled, for example, in the differing quality of human speech before and after the Fall. Lewis's observations on the corruption of Eve's and Adam's rhetoric (*Preface* 122–24) pointed scholars in this direction. I wish not to exaggerate; I realize that fresh insights emerge from a complex of ingredients beyond tracing and cannot be attributed to any one predecessor. Still, the ghost of Lewis's *Preface* is constantly showing on the battlements.[36]

Perhaps the most fruitful of Lewis's judgments, invertedly, has been his low valuation of books 11–12. This has led, directly or indirectly, to extensive scholarship demonstrating these books—stylistic flattening and all—to be integral to Milton's plan and evidence of his artistry. For example, Stanley Fish in 1967 reviewed the abundant work on this topic since Lewis and proceeded to add his analysis, citing Lewis as the source not only of misjudgments to be corrected but also of authority for his own reader-oriented procedure (Fish, *Surprised* 286–331, esp. 300–03). Milton is an "organist" who plays upon the reader (*Preface* 40); "we are his organ" (47). Fish gave the latter statement a different twist, emphasizing what he believed was the poet's purpose in thus tapping "sources of energy existing in his reader's mind" (*Surprised* 303), to complete readers' education regarding their own participation in Adam's errors and, it may be hoped, his restoration.

Lewis's adumbration of reader-response theory,[37] though independent of the continental writings that prevailed in the seventies, is but one example of his pervasive interest in literary and critical theory. With some present-day enthusiasms we find him at odds, or at least offering cautionary observations worth pondering. Thus in a paper contemporaneous with his *Preface* he uses an example from *Paradise Lost* 4 to show that Freudian criticism can be reductive; the garden is of interest inherently, according to Lewis, not merely as concealed eroticism ("Psycho-Analysis" 293–96). In the book where he goes farthest toward a reader-oriented approach, he also warns, "We must not let loose our own subjectivity upon [artworks] and make them its vehicles. . . . The first demand [a work of art] makes upon us is surrender" (*Experiment* 18–19).

171

But with some directions of contemporary theory Lewis is refreshingly in tune. He realizes that in the literary realm, as well as in the laboratory, pure objectivity is a will-o'-the-wisp, for an object of study is altered by being studied (*Preface* 132). His up-front identification of allegiance ("In order to take no unfair advantage I should warn the reader that I myself am a Christian" 64) is a move well in advance of the critical practice of his time, though more familiar today.[38] Further, Lewis's suggestion that being a Christian gives him an edge as an interpreter of Milton must, understood in its lecture context, be at least half playful. For the primary attitudes undergirding the *Preface* are a commitment to rigorous historical scholarship and a suspicion of modernism (which naturally produces certain resemblances in Lewis to postmodernism, though its roots are quite different), and both these already characterized Lewis's outlook before his Christian conversion. By a decade later, to be sure, when he wrote the *Preface*, they had doubtless been strengthened and perhaps further shaped by his Christianity.[39] Possibly a Christian sense of vocation helped bring the book into being (cf. *Preface* 55, "one of the reasons") and propelled him beyond strictly literary criticism to comment on cultural matters he thought transcended literature (thus irritating some readers). Yet it is significant that when Lewis defines his essentially extraliterary differences from Leavis, he does not enunciate a uniquely Christian position (130).

Lewis's refusal to confine literary criticism within disciplinary boundaries when larger social and individual issues are at stake, while it drew fire from some of his contemporaries, anticipated a major critical trend. He crusaded against cultural elitism; his talk "High and Low Brows," though never using the word *canon*, was directed against the demonstrably groundless snobbishness of the educational establishment in denying the label *literature* to whole classes of books read mainly by ordinary people. Part of his objection to the Leavis crowd, indeed, was to their unshakable assurance in the sole rightness of their taste—not defended, simply asserted—and in their duty to elevate others to their level. He did not in later life share Eliot's antipathy toward Milton as a person—even if he had, he would have remembered his principle (discussed above) of enjoying for its own sake even what one dislikes—but was troubled by what seemed Milton's aristocratic contempt for the "ordinary mass of humanity" (*Letters* 64). He thought this attitude marred the characterization of Christ in *Paradise Regained*[40] and the defense of free reading in *Areopagitica* ("Culture" 17–18). Milton's republicanism, though it made Samuel Johnson ("the old die-hard Tory") "so unfair" to him (*Stand* 373), Lewis found hard to reconcile with the man's "almost archducal" attitude (*Letters* 64). It was for him an ethical matter: "the Christian . . . knows that the vulgar since they include most of the poor probably include most of his superiors" ("Literature" 10). Good taste has nothing to do with the kingdom of heaven and is therefore not the overriding virtue that the priests of the religion of art would make it.⁴¹ "A schoolboy who reads a page of Milton by chance, for the first time, and [discovers that it has] transformed his world, is nearer to the truth than they," Lewis writes in *Preface* (60).

Still, judged by current standards that privilege a critic's direct engagement with issues of power and oppression, the *Preface* may seem lacking. The question of Milton's politics enters into Lewis's chapter on hierarchy, but the design of the book, to address matters then at issue, precluded further attention, a fact which tends to blunt attacks like those of Freedman (32–35) made from a vantage point fifty years along. On a related issue, however, one equally in the foreground of criticism today—Milton's ideas about women—Lewis comments extensively. He thinks an Augustinian characterization of Eve as "less intelligent and more credulous" than Adam (*Preface* 67) underlies the temptation sequence in book 9. Milton inherited doctrines of husbandly authority (74–75), but Lewis reminds us that ideal, prelapsarian hierarchy included, for him, mutual "interchange" and "freedom" (78, 80). Lewis emphasizes mutuality through dance imagery (115), and when he calls Eve "Adam's inferior, in her double capacity of wife and subject" (116) he points to a juridical, not an inherent, difference. The fullest statement of marital inequality in book 4 proceeds from Eve's own courteous humility ("often misunderstood"), and it is not clear that Lewis supposes her view to be Milton's own (116); it takes her "greatness" and Adam's "deference" toward her (115, 116) to complete the picture.⁴² Shortly before the *Preface*, Lewis interpreted 1 Corinthians 11 in terms of the metaphor of headship, seen as a straightforward hierarchical image though qualified by being only one "aspect" of the whole "truth" ("Literature" 4–5). Twenty years later, however, he gave a reading of Ephesians 5 that stands hierarchy on its head and reveals his changed attitude toward Milton's view. He writes that "Christian writers (notably Milton) have sometimes spoken of the husband's headship with a complacency to make the blood run cold. We must go back to our Bibles." Headship is not a matter of command and obedience, but "most fully embodied . . . in [the husband] whose marriage is most like a crucifixion" (*Loves* 121).

173

Notices of Milton Elsewhere in Lewis

Such was Lewis's familiarity with Milton's works that observations about them are scattered throughout his writings. He finds in Milton not only survivals of medieval ideas and attitudes—on the torments of the damned and the brightness of space⁴³—but also the loss of the medieval harmony between pagan and Christian (*Spenser's* 90), and the earliest known use of *space* in the modern sense (*Discarded* 100). In his image of the hanging cosmos Milton "ingenious[ly]" combined the "modern feeling" of immensity and the "old glories of the . . . finite Universe."[44] Milton's interest in geographical exploration, according to Lewis, was greater than Shakespeare's or Drayton's (*Sixteenth* 16). On Milton's style, Lewis speaks of the humanistic ideal he successfully followed, one of few who could (25); of the invective power of his prose (*Road* 428); of the "gigantic loftiness" of his epic style ("Spenser" 142); and of the qualities of the Miltonic sublime ("Shelley" 204). Lewis relished the auditory effects of poetry (cf. *Surprised* 111) and gave them close attention. Taking a cue from Milton's calling for metrical variety within pattern for the sake of the sense (Milton 457), Lewis scanned selected irregular lines and commented on their mimetic or emotive effect.[45] Milton shared with Donne this technique of "wide departures from the norm" (*Sixteenth* 505). For lines from Milton's classical tragedy, Lewis illustrated scansion using "classical" feet ("Metre" 284 [Milton 115, 124]).

Next to *Paradise Lost*, Lewis had more to say about *Comus* than any other poem of Milton. It was the author's "least Puritan poem" ("Tasso" 117), merging pagan thought with Christian (*Allegory* 355; "Hero" 65; *Spenser's* 47); in it he worked with emblematic images (*Spenser's* 11, 24; "Variation" 78; "Cupid" 166), and at the end Milton included his paradisal vision (*Spenser's* 60n), expressed perhaps in the terms of a Platonic cosmology ("Above" [1]). Other hints of Platonism he saw in *Il Penseroso* and *Paradise Lost* ("Above" [2]). The *Nativity Ode*—very different in spirit from Dunbar's lyrical poem on the same subject (*Sixteenth* 96)—places a welcome emphasis on the heroism of the infant Christ (*Psalms* 125). Its stanza form may owe something to Sidney (*Sixteenth* 327) (I find Lewis unconvincing on this point). Lewis finds, in "the young Milton, the quality of joyful seriousness" (342). He comments on a line in the sonnet "How soon hath time" (Brewer 67), on the Christ of *Paradise Regained* in relation to Stoicism (*Sixteenth* 54 [see also note 40 above]), on the Latin elegies *L'Allegro* and *Il Penseroso*, and on *Samson Agonistes* (Hart 3–4, 70; *Experiment* 31; on *Samson*, line 303, see also *Pain* 41), and on Milton as a historiographer (*Discarded* 179–81, 183). He places Milton in an English tradition of rural poetry (*Sixteenth* 59), in the rear guard of taste as regards the epic ("Tasso" 112), in the camp of Sidney's admirers (*Sixteenth* 338), and in an Aristotelian tradition as regards the purposes of education ("Syllabus" 81). He glosses words, phrases, and occasionally longer passages to suggest textual emendation, to query an apparent inconsistency, and to note possible relics of dramatic composition in *Paradise Lost*. Over the whole range of Milton's works he explains the cosmological background or connections to ideas and tastes of the period, points out parallels in earlier literature, comments on style, identifies a reference, and offers semantic and grammatical explanations, on occasion calling attention to perhaps deliberate ambiguities.[46] Lewis could quote long passages of *Paradise Lost* from memory (Hooper, "Preface" 17), and would casually embed phrases from Milton in his own writing on a wholly different topic.[47] It was perhaps a habit picked up from his father.[48]

Presence of Milton in Lewis's Fiction and Poetry

Finally, since creative borrowing and reworking are forms of critical comment, we consider traces of Milton in Lewis's fiction and poetry. Some resemblances, of course, indicate only that they each drew from older material available to both. The treatment of space and the hierarchical social structure in *Out of the Silent Planet* (1938) display Lewis's long fascination with the Medieval Model. So does the dance imagery; Lewis's description of the intricate, frolicsome Great Dance of Perelandra weaves together echoes of Dante and many other remembered ideas. Yet these must have included the heavenly dance or "game" he only months earlier described in the *Preface* (79–80), building on *Paradise Lost* 5.620–24.[49] Such echoing from *Paradise Lost* continues in the intricate Narnian Snow Dance in chapter 15 of *The Silver Chair* (1953). Both passages well illustrate Lewis's method of creative adaptation. Similar reservations hold regarding possible Miltonic influence on his narrative technique. Several times in his fiction Lewis used a device he had praised in Milton (*Preface* 47–50), that of describing a slow, expectant approach to a goal; but perhaps he noticed it in *Paradise Lost* because other reading had already alerted him to it (see Christopher 99; Haigh 197).

The Pilgrim's Regress, published a year after the *Comus* article, echoes Milton in various ways. Epigraphs from *Paradise Regained* precede books 5 and 6, Vertue's despairing speech (*Regress* 139) quotes Adam's,[50] and Vertue's song contains Miltonic diction ("the shadowy vast"; "potent rod" [197]). More complicated is the alteration of Milton's line, "Freely they stood who stood, and fell who fell" (*PL* 3.102) into "Nearly they stood who fall" to begin the Guide's song (*Regress* 181). Also from Milton are the ideas that by the original covenant ("lease"), Adam and Eve "could leave [the garden] when they chose" and "go up to live" with God and angels (79; cf. *Preface* 66–67); the canyon Peccatum Adae (Adam's Sin) formed by an earthquake "at the moment" of eating the fruit (80), an echo of *Paradise Lost* 9.781–82 ("plucked") and 1000; and the reference to angelic sexuality "with no bar" (198; cf. *PL* 8.624–25). The phrase from *Comus* that Lewis called "marvellous" ("Variation" 78), "dragon watch with unenchanted eye," may have been the imaginative origin of the dragon's song (*Regress* 192–93).

In Lewis's other early poems Milton's presence is evident not only in the frequent use of rhythms reminiscent of *Il Penseroso* but also in verbal echoes of that poem (oppositionally), of a favorite *Comus* passage, and of portions of *Paradise Lost* that fed his adolescent rebellion and *Weltschmerz*.[51] The title

175

Spirits in Bondage: A Cycle of Lyrics (1919) alludes to *Paradise Lost* (1.658), but that title was not Lewis's first choice. A line in *Dymer*, "If Balder had led back the blameless spring" (9.35; *Narrative* 91), faintly echoes Milton's "led on the eternal spring" (*PL* 4.268).

Four books written near the time Lewis was working intensively on Milton are *The Screwtape Letters* (1941), *Perelandra* (1943), *The Great Divorce* (1945), and *That Hideous Strength* (1945). I will not, however, discuss these works in this order. Surprisingly little in the first is specifically Miltonic. The most prominent debts are Screwtape's involuntary metamorphosis into a centipede at the end of Letter 22, where the debt to *Paradise Lost* 10.511–17 is explicit in the devil's insistence that Milton misrepresented the phenomenon; the idea of damned human souls as devils' food, echoing *Paradise Lost* 4.375–81 and 10.399–402, 490;[52] and the devils' general inability to conceive of such motives as love (cf. *Preface* 96). *Divorce* contains embedded quotations from *Comus* adapted to quite different situations (*Divorce* 6 [line 816] and 107 [454]) and two verbal echoes of *Lycidas* 78–84 (83 ["perfect judgment"; cf. line 82], 107). Lewis's portraits of the damned sometimes reflect *Paradise Lost*: there are theological debates in hell but with no "finality" (45, 43; cf. *PL* 2.555–65); the Intelligent Man is a Mammon figure who aims to improve hell by economic means (21; cf. 77–78 and *Preface* 100); other ghosts, Moloch-like, incite violence in terms reminiscent of the initial rebellion and war in heaven (77); and some are willing "to plunge [someone] they say they love in endless misery" sooner than lose possession (105; cf. *Preface* 121). That hell finally proves infinitesimal (122–23) is related to Lewis's Augustinian point about the nonentity of evil (*Preface* 65). And Milton is cited to define damnation: "The choice of every lost soul can be expressed in the words 'Better to reign in Hell than serve in Heaven' " (69; *PL* 1.263). In *Hideous* the destruction of Bragdon Wood by an earthquake may parallel the despoiling of Eden to forestall any sacralizing of place (*PL* 11.829–37; cf. Piehler 208), and the idea that Ransom will return to Venus for healing may conflate memories from the closing song in *Comus* (976–80, 997–1001; see *Hideous* 322, 440–41).

In Narnia, the creation of the animals owes some details to *Paradise Lost* 7.453–92—in the general idea of the ground swelling and bursting open to release new forms, in some of the particular animals that are mentioned, lion, stag, elephant, mole, bee, and in phrases like "crumbled earth"—but it is much more detailed in Lewis's narrative and written in the lighter tone suitable to his genre. The use of music may have grown out of Lewis's reflections on *PL* 7.253–59, 558–64, and 594–601, as well as *Nativity Ode* 119–24, which in turn developed out of Job 38:7; Lewis, however, makes the music an instrument of creation and not just celebration. A more likely influence, if influence must be sought, might be conversations with his friend J. R. R. Tolkien (whose "Ainulindalë," however, had not yet been made public).[53] The walled hilltop paradise in the newly created Narnia is Miltonic, with its sweetly scented approach, its eastern gate, its tempter who enters over the wall, and the tree of life in its center (*Nephew* 153–58). Similar gardens in other volumes of the Chronicles reflect both Milton and Dante's *Purgatorio* (see Christopher 119). The various temptations in the Chronicles have some elements in common with those in *Comus* and, especially, *Paradise Lost*: the quarreling couple in Charn; Digory's driving curiosity there and Lucy's in the Magician's room, more pointedly for *forbidden* knowledge; the witch Jadis's use of an apple and of specious rhetoric, employed also by the underground witch along with an enchanted immobilizing chair.[54] Aslan's "Well done" (*Nephew* 164) exactly imitates *Paradise Lost* 6.29, but also Matthew 25:21. The god Tash's appearance as a "demon" (*Battle* 87) echoes Milton's account of the fallen angels (*PL* 1.367–73; Gibson 212)—which drew on yet older traditions. Lewis's imagining of precious metals and gems "alive and growing" in the intense heat of Bism (*Chair* 185) may owe something to *Paradise Lost* 3.591–612.

In Lewis's later poetry, "blind mouths" (*Collected Poems* 47) is borrowed from *Lycidas* 119, and "After Aristotle" (94–95) imitates Milton in theme and syntax, as well as borrowing outright.[55] "The Turn of the Tide" (63–65) is Lewis's Nativity Ode; with but few overt allusions—the dumb oracle (line 12), the stilled sea (15–16), the emperor's arrested movement (17–20), the heavenly bodies that await, "gaz[ing]" (31–36), the music (especially lines 61–62), and the closing manger scene—Lewis firmly links his poem to Milton's on the same theme. In "Lines Written in a Copy of Milton's Works" (*Collected Poems* 97) the speaker laments his loneliness, contrasting it, like Adam before Eve's creation (*PL* 8.364–66, 392–97), with the gregariousness of animals. The stanzas get progressively shorter and more melancholy, moving from language evoking *L'Allegro* in stanza 2 to that of *Il Penseroso* at the end. But the similarities are not insistent; perhaps we see them only because the (editor's?) title reveals the provenance. Lewis translated one of Milton's Latin poems that he enjoyed (an "exquisite grotesque").[56]

I come to *Perelandra* last because it is connected most closely to Lewis's study of Milton.[57] Lewis poses a question of the kind he repeatedly says (e.g., in *Preface* 123) should not be asked with reference to real history because one cannot know: *What if Eve had resisted the temptation?* Speculation, however, is allowed, so Lewis provides a parallel Eden on a different planet and reenacts the Satanic temptation of the first woman. This scheme let Lewis follow what seemed to him Milton's successful moves while avoiding his mistakes (Hannay, "Preface").[58] It also enabled him to probe the essential meaning of the Fall (*Preface* 67) by replacing the apple with a different prohibition.

Implicit in the scheme were some innovations. On encountering initial resistance (as he did not in Milton) the tempter would continue, and bringing temptation to an end would require a new act of mythmaking; Lewis uses a Christ figure (*Perelandra* 148, "My name also is Ransom"; see *Letters* 283) who conquers the enemy in a symbolic death and resurrection. His Adam figure is not uxorious like Milton's but, taught by the earthly Adam's example (through a device resembling the visions of Milton's eleventh book), would risk everything to obey (*Perelandra* 210; cf. *Preface* 123). His plan also made it possible, by having unfallen humanity grow in knowledge, to address the persistent confusion between knowledge in general, viewed in a Promethean way, and the particular kind of moral knowledge—knowing evil only by tasting it—brought by the Fall. "We have learned of evil," says the King, "though not as the Evil One wished us to learn"; to know it experientially would have been "a darker ignorance" (*Perelandra* 209).

With the advantage of hindsight—observing what elements in *Paradise Lost* had proved especially liable to modern misunderstanding—Lewis makes his tempter much less grand (and more comic, though retaining for the vehicle, Weston, a certain pathos), while keeping the "sense of injured merit" and the sophistry (and illusions of self-existence).[59] He avoids the problems of an anthropomorphic presentation of God and angels—an artistic, not theological, difference—and of portraying sexual behavior in Eden, though still attributing to his human pair an intense sexuality (*Perelandra* 207). His device for showing angels—eldils who are "almost invisible lights" (221)—may take a cue from *Paradise Lost* 11.211–12. He also follows Milton in emphasizing the majestic appearance of the primal pair and the hierarchical position of the King, who, like Adam, is given special knowledge in private. (The intellectual function of naming, however, is shared mutually [206, 211], not as in Milton, distributed [*PL* 8.272–73, 352–54; 11.277]. But the Lady's relationship with the animals is a Miltonic touch.) Like Milton, Lewis makes free choice central to standing or falling and has the tempter, who encounters the Lady "separated from the King" (115)—a detail found in Milton but not in Genesis—try to corrupt her imagination even while her will remains firm. He questions hierarchy, employs storytelling—a device parallel to Eve's dream—and uses a mirror, which echoes Eve's experience at the pool (with the additional purpose of teaching false pretense).[60] He avoids the appeal to appetite that is prominent in Milton's temptation scene[61] but does take a hint from *Paradise Lost* 9.693–97, where Satan argues that God really wishes Eve to disobey, and builds upon that for the Un-man's most persuasive arguments.[62] Finally, his unfallen pair assume the destiny—to rule the planet (*Perelandra* 206), surrounded by their descendants (211–12), and then to become angel-like (211)—that Milton projects for Adam and Eve had they been found obedient.[63]

Basic in all Lewis's response to myths was the search for their essential meaning. The myth of the dying god and that of Cupid and Psyche may serve as examples. In Eden, the apple was not intrinsically dangerous, nor need we allegorize it—the forbidding *per se* is the main thing—but Lewis had seen how easily readers of *Paradise Lost* could misunderstand.[64] So he substitutes for that prohibition a command against staying overnight on the Fixed Land. This also is not itself dangerous. Both commands merely test obedience. Lewis's device of the Fixed Land, however, has two advantages. It is less vulnerable than the fruit (Milton's given, admittedly, from Genesis) to a false cause-effect interpretation, and, offering predictability and thus an illusion of security, it clearly symbolizes the core temptation in both stories, to reject creaturely dependence and—the word appears in *Perelandra* (208)—"trust."

In his readings of Milton, Lewis exemplified a range of ways to engage with an author. These include giving close attention to the text and the significance of its variants, exercising one's historical imagination (aided by scholarship) in order to read with sympathy and understanding, savoring the work for its "very quiddity," carrying whatever truth it tells across the boundary line between the armchair and the rest of one's living, and letting it through reflection or sheer wordplay beget new creations.

Notes

1. Although the title *A Mask* is now preferred, I will refer to Milton's dramatic poem by the title Lewis used.

2. Lewis, *Stand* 444. In a 1958 letter, lines 21–23 of *Comus* came to mind when he wanted to describe Ireland (quoted by Hannay, *Lewis* 4).

3. Cf. his characterization in 1952 of Milton's style as "harder and severer" than that of Marlowe ("Hero" 70). Lewis attributes the difference to changes in taste, and E. M. W. Tillyard (138) makes a similar suggestion in commenting on Lewis's "Note on *Comus*."

4. Hannay quotes a 1921 letter but misprints the date as 1941.

5. A 1922 diary entry hints at such maturing of his appreciation (*Road* 114). See also his 1941 account of his changing perception of *Paradise Lost* 4.449–91 in "Religion" 39. He continued, however, to value the romantic element: in 1962, he recalled that "the idea of perilous adventures in enchanted forests . . . moved Milton" ("Anthropological" 305–06).

6. Influenced no doubt by Ezra Pound and T. S. Eliot and confirmed by F. R. Leavis, who remarked in 1933 that Milton's "dislodgment" had apparently been easily "effected" (*Revaluation* 42). Morris summarizes these attacks and lists others from the period 1922–34 (217–19, 233).

7. In a similar vein is the comment cited from a Lewis lecture by Evans (37).

8. Lewis began lecturing on *Paradise Lost* in 1937 (Hooper, *Companion* 221). Hart analyzes *Preface* as pedagogy (103, 109–20).

9. Williams lectured on *Comus* on 5 February 1940 (Carpenter 119) and "delight[ed]" his audience with "something so strange and new . . . as the praise of chastity" (Lewis, "Dedication," *Preface* v; see also Lewis, *Letters* 177). In addition to his "Introduction," see Williams, "The New Milton."

10. On Milton's language, see Eliot, "Milton I," and Leavis; on stock responses, Richards, *Principles* 199–206, and *Practical Criticism* 235–54. Lewis also challenged the notion (Eliot, "Milton I" 157) that only "the ablest" poets could pass judgment on such matters, thus disbarring academics. He had previously addressed this issue in *Heresy* 116–18. His rebuttal of it in *Preface* need not concern us, as it relates only tangentially to Milton. But Eliot's subsequent retraction is a tacit tribute to Lewis's chapter. Eliot continued to maintain only that the best poets should decide whether

Milton is a good model for poets; he still believed poets of the 1920s had been harmed by Milton's influence, but now (1947) he felt poets could profit from studying the artistry of "the greatest master in our language of freedom within form" ("Milton II" 169–72, 181–83).

11. Lewis grants that form is not the critic's *only* legitimate concern—just "now most neglected." Every poem "has two parents . . . the mass of experience, thought, and the like inside the poet, and . . . the pre-existing Form" found "in the public world" (*Preface* 2). In other words, Tillyard was partly right. Still, Lewis has no interest, here or elsewhere, in exploring Milton's biography or his psyche. Thus the *Preface* bypasses some approaches that interest many of today's critics.

12. See P. Andrew Montgomery's discussion of Homeric poetic diction and verbal formulae in chapter 3.

13. In *Heresy* 113–14, Lewis had distinguished between "what the poet 'says'" and the "apparent . . . propositions" on the surface. He cited approvingly the labors of I. A. Richards in combating the common confusion between them.

14. Some years before, Lewis had shown that he viewed the rise of Donne and the decline of Milton in current critical esteem as correlate "phenomena" ("Love Poetry" 106).

15. See, e.g., Leavis 52–55.

16. But elsewhere, he adopts a different strategy and insists on the strength of Milton's visual imagination in his portraits of Adam and Beelzebub ("Variation" 74–76) and in his cosmological descriptions (*Words* 254–55). On the whole, however, he is willing to grant that Milton's "images [are] vague" *Sixteenth* 387.

17. The art of *Paradise Lost* is concerned not with imaging the concrete but with "making us believe we have imagined the unimaginable," Lewis said (*Discarded* 207n).

18. Lewis develops this point in "The Language of Religion" 134 (written after 1953). Note that in *Preface* he a) finds common ground with I. A. Richards, though he immediately proceeds to sharper distinctions that define his opposition to Richards (see also *Experiment* 134–35); and b) anticipates recent criticism in believing the effect of poetry on its audience to be paramount; to privilege the poet and make the audience's role mere eavesdropping "is a foolish novelty in criticism" (53).

19. Lewis, in quoting Richards (*Preface* 53), inadvertently transposes the words "free" and "direct." Lewis's views on stock responses and their relation to poetic language are discussed more fully in Huttar, "Lifelong" 97–103.

20. Coleridge's phrase had come to enjoy a new currency and approbation in the time when Lewis was writing.

21. Cf. *Heresy* 63. This is related to Lewis's zest for the "essence" of things that he encountered. See Daniel 10–16.

22. Lewis commended (with reservations) Sewell's study (*Preface* 81n); Kelley's evidently came too late to use (he had finished writing the *Preface* in the spring of 1941).

23. On one issue, "Milton is perhaps following the *Zohar* where the *Zohar* is perhaps heretical" (*Preface* 87); on another, the word "essentially" in the treatise "probably means something heretical (though I do not clearly understand what)," and *Paradise Lost* 5.403ff. "presumably" reflects this although without clues from *De Doctrina* it would be read as orthodox (88). The heresies within the poem turn out to be "very small and rather ambiguous" (89).

24. Lewis hints elsewhere that not only the choice of genre but the spirit of the age influenced this characterization. In discussing the Elizabethan Machiavel he observes that devils in medieval drama were comic, but "Marlowe's and Milton's are new" (*Sixteenth* 51).

25. Lewis drew a distinction between Milton and Spenser in this respect. See *Spenser's* 65–66, 91n.

26. Not utterly without precedent: see Lewis's citation of Albertus Magnus and others (*Allegory* 15–16) and of David Lyndsay (*Sixteenth* 104).

27. So Gunnar Urang proposed as early as 1971. *Felix culpa* is one of the tempter's arguments and is refuted by Ransom (*Perelandra* 121; Urang 16, 19). For later refutations see Danielson, chapter 7, "*Paradise Lost* and the Unfortunate Fall" (202–27), and other scholars cited in his n. 4 (263).

28. Lewis appears to have previously believed books 11–12 deserve more appreciation (see *Road* 442), and twenty years after the *Preface* he confines himself to reporting that "for me" those books lose the mythic quality that characterizes the earlier books (*Letters* 303).

29. Lewis seems here to anticipate the complaints of William Empson.

30. Not, at least, in the sense of "religious" implied in the criticism. Already in *Allegory* 355 he had characterized *The Faerie Queene* as a "much more religious" poem than *Paradise Lost*. Ulreich develops this insight.

31. "Solemn game" ("Milton I" 163), "making a speech" (161).

32. Leavis's description of Milton's style is not questioned, but "he sees and hates the very same that I see and love" (130). Carl Freedman sees in this sentence a "subtext" evoking Abdiel vs. Satan in their attitudes toward God and thus suggesting that "the very same" includes deeper matters than mere style (44 n. 11). This is an astute observation, but it overemphasizes the religious realm; Lewis sees the "question at issue" as a question still valid in a pluralistic society: whether societal structures that affirm human nobility should continue despite the present evidences of human "infamy" (130).

33. See, for example, the cogent critiques of it by Gardner (84–87) and Danielson (184–88).

34. See also "Variation" 77, where he asserts the "romantic" effect of the "dim vastness" and "ruined splendour" of Milton's Beelzebub.

35. *Mythical* is used twice (56, 129).

36. McBride gives a partial survey of the most direct responses to *Preface*. See also Fish, "Transmuting"; Christopher and Ostling 201–13, 247–49. Denis Saurat in his review of *Preface* praised Lewis's "great feat" of "caus[ing] . . . to arise" many topics for criticism (quoted in Como 5).

37. This direction in Lewis's critical thought may be seen in *Heresy* where he argues for a "poetless" text and notes the implication, "in such cases it is we who make the poetry" (16). At this point he backs away from the idea, but later, in *Experiment* (1961), he would use the notion of different kinds of reading as the starting point for an entire book.

38. Unfortunately this handed some unfriendly reviewers an instrument whereby to evade serious confrontation with his arguments—e.g., the reviewer quoted by Fish, "Transmuting" 255. But Fish here misreads Lewis's declaration; being a Christian is not "assert[ed]" to be "his chief qualification as commentator."

39. Cf. a) *Heresy* 51: "the uneasy Theophobia of . . . our contemporaries"; b) his aversion to viewing poetry or art as a surrogate religion (Owen Barfield, cited in Morris 225; cf. *Heresy* 65).

40. *Discarded* 80; cf. "Addison" 155, where Lewis calls Milton's Christ a man of "surly contemptuous virtue."

41. "Christianity and Culture" 12–13; cf. "Christianity and Literature," "the greatest poems have been made by men who valued something else much more than poetry" (10).

42. See also Lewis's interpretation of that "most profound" scene in which Eve first meets Adam ("Religion: Reality or Substitute" 39–40) and his 1943 essay "Equality" (*Concerns* 19).

43. "The Genesis of a Medieval Book" 35, with reference possibly to *PL* 2.580–95; "Imagination and Thought in the Middle Ages" 53, quoting *Comus* 976–78—the same lines that he had Ransom quote "to himself lovingly" upon discovering what Space really was like (*Planet* 32).

44. *Discarded* 100, referring also to other passages in *Paradise Lost* and to *Il Penseroso* 70. See also "*De Audiendis Poetis*" 7.

45. "Metre" 283 (on *PL* 6.866); *Sixteenth* 551–52 (on *PL* 1.24–26, 3.1ff., 7.411, with conjectures on the possible influence of Thomas Campion). In the *Preface* (80) Lewis cites this play of pattern and variation as a type of dance.

46. Emendation: *Preface* 135 (*PL* 9.506). Inconsistency: *Preface* 134–35. Dramatic elements: *Preface* 134–35 (4.36, 9.157, 9.482). Cosmology: *Preface* 134–36 (*PL* 2.1106, 3.74, 5.257–61, 10.329); *Discarded* 40 (*PL* 3.461), 63 (7.237ff.), 72 (*PR* 1.447–48), 94–95 (*PL* 2.898–900), 110–11 (on the word *influence*), 112 (*PL* 3.556–57 and *Comus* 978), 118 (*PR* 1.46), 123–24 and 127–30 (*fairies* in *Comus*, *PL*, and *PR*), 134 (*PR* 4.201), 161 (on *reason*), 167 (*PL* 4.805–06); letter to Frank Goodridge 22 Sep-

tember 1952 (Marion E. Wade Collection, Wheaton College, Wheaton, IL.; analyzing the ontological status of the Attendant Spirit in *Comus*). Contemporary ideas and taste: *Preface* 135 (*PL* 5.349; 9.442); *Sixteenth* 542 (on taste in gardens and landscape); *Words* 283 (*PL* 11.553); *Discarded* 173 (*Doctrine and Discipline of Divorce*). Parallels in prior literature: *Preface* 134–35 (*PL* 4.241, 6.236); "Tasso" 118–19 (*PL* 3.56–59, 6.68–71, 103–04; *PR* 3.337–43); *Sixteenth* 52 (*PL* 11.494–99), 53 (8.571–72), 132 (*Lycidas* 132), 522 (*Lycidas* 142, *Nativity Ode* 132ff.), 544 (*PL* 5.396, 7.224ff., 453ff.), 552n (3.1); *Words* 87 (*PL* 8.75–84), 210n (8.82 and *Divorce*); *Discarded* 14 (*PL* 8.82), 27 (5.171), 81 (*Samson* 667ff.), 83 (*PL* 1.690–92), 86 (*Divorce*), 146 (*Comus* 20–78); *Spenser's* 126n (*PL* 3.600–05). Style: *Preface* 134 (*PL* 3.1–7); *Sixteenth* 543 (*Nativity Ode* 229). Reference: "Genius and Genius" 171n (*On Education*). Semantic/grammatical: *Preface* 134–35 (*PL* 1.467, 3.299, 6.268, 8.228, 8.415–19, 8.512, 9.442, 9.686); *Words* 20 (*Reason of Church Government*), 40 (*PL* 2.911), 47 (4.242), 48 (5.451), 76 (11.585), 141 (*PR* 4.264), 144 (*Samson* 1685), 158 (*Samson* 913), 174 (trans. of Horace), 186 (*PL* 6.521), 189 (8.502), 197 (3.195), 205–06 (4.23 and 10.842), 248 (4.272 and *Samson* 1707), 258 (*PL* 9.11); *Surprised* 16 (*PL* 5.297). Ambiguity: *Words* 158 (*PL* 2.278), 179 (12.365), 200 (title "New Forcers of Conscience"). Unpublished marginalia in Lewis's copy (Marion E. Wade Collection, Wheaton College, Wheaton, IL.) of the Bohn edition of Milton's *Prose Works*, vol. 2, reflect his careful reading of these works in 1927.

47. Hannay, *Lewis* 4; *Stand* 102, 268; Sayer 209 ("Blest pair of sirens"); Lewis, letter to Ruth Pitter 22 September 1949 (Bodleian Library; Marion E. Wade Collection transcript 34-T/042. Slightly misquoting *PL* 5.297 and citing the sonnet to Lawrence); "The 'Morte D'Arthur'" 108; *Surprised* 3 (*PL* 4.370); 5 and 187 (quoting *PL* 4.397); *Experiment* 128 (*Comus* 394); *Preface* 133 (*PL* 2.933); *Hideous* 376 (*Samson* 1675–78, slightly misquoted); *Concerns* 18 (*PL* 4.740). See also *Perelandra* 49, where quoting *Comus* 262 helps characterize the literary scholar Ransom.

48. See the quotation from a letter of Albert Lewis, given by Hooper in his introduction to *Collected Poems* (xiii).

49. See *Perelandra* 214 ("Great Game"), 218; Hannay, "Preface" 217 n. 11.

50. "All that I eat or drink, or shall beget, / Is propagated curse" (*PL* 10.728–29).

51. "The Philosopher" (*Collected Poems* 186), 15–32 (*Il Penseroso* 65–68, 76, 85–92, 122–25). "Song" (206), 13–16, and "Hesperus" (217), 27–28 (*Comus* 981–82). "Sonnet" (237), 13–14 (*PL* 1.26). "Victory" (170), 13 (*PL* 1.94). "Against Potpourri" (231), 7–10 (*PL* 4.269–71). *Dymer* 7.19 (*Narrative* 70; *PL* 4.765).

52. I owe this connection in part to Werblowsky, 15.

53. Lewis, *Nephew* 110–12 for the animals; 97–98, 102, 104 for the music; discussed more fully in Huttar, "Narnia" 123–26. Tolkien, *Silmarillion* 15–22. Milton's account of animal creation was not the only precedent available for Lewis; see *Allegory* 92–93, on Bernardus Sylvestris.

54. *Nephew* 51–54, 158–61; *Voyage* 141–44; *Chair* 148–49, 152, 157–63. For a fuller analysis of parallels, see Huttar, "Narnia" 130–31, and, on the chair, Cox 221 n. 4.

55. Syntax: see especially the last eight lines. Borrowings: "live laborious days" (*Lycidas* 72), "twin-born progeny" (*Sonnet XII* 6).

56. "From the Latin." I owe this reference to the assiduous labors of Don W. King. "The Adam Unparadised" (*Collected Poems* 57–58) and "The Adam at Night" (59–60) speculate about aspects of the story that Milton left out entirely.

57. Not that the Miltonic connection exhausts *Perelandra*. Lewis himself insists on the importance of Wagner, Dante, and Augustine (quoted with commentary in Hooper, *Companion* 222–23). On the Dante connections, see Christopher 96–98. A case for the influence of Charles Maturin is made by Manlove 119, 281–83.

58. Hannay's detailed study enables me in the next two paragraphs to summarize, adding my further comments in parentheses and in note 62. Downing (130) offers two parallels besides those mentioned here. Tanner, whose excellent study appeared after this essay had been completed, concentrates on three aspects of Lewis's novel in a way that largely complements my briefer summary in the next three paragraphs.

59. See *Preface* 93–95; *PL* 1.98; 5.860. The last point I owe to Gibson (54). Milton himself in *Paradise Regained* had made Satan less grand, the logical result of millennia of continuing "progressive degradation" (*Preface* 97) since Eden (see *PL* 1.591–92; Carey in Milton, 1064). The devil in *Perelandra* is two thousand years farther along in the same process.

60. Even though he did not make room for the topic in his *Preface*, Lewis surely was sensitive to the question, much debated among Miltonists, of how to interpret the steps by which Eve becomes more receptive to the serpent's assault yet remains innocent (a point on which both writers are explicit: *PL* 9.659; *Perelandra* 134).

61. Myers points out (68) that the enjoyment of fruit does enter into the temptation, but abstractly as part of the argument (*Perelandra* 105).

62. At the close of chapter 16 he echoes Milton's locating Paradise "within" (*PL* 12.587) and having his primordial couple walk "hand in hand" (4.689; 12.648). He addresses the question of theodicy (*Perelandra* 213–18) but without foregrounding it as Milton did (*PL* 1.25–26).

63. Cf. *PL* 5.497–501; 7.155–59, 530–31; 11.342–46; *Preface* 66–67. Carpenter (181–82) suggests that a scene Lewis imaginatively described in *Preface* (113–14) may be the germ of these elements of *Perelandra*. Hamm (283) traces the Meldilorn scene in *Planet* to the same passage in *PL* 11.

64. See *Preface* 67. A mistake that dies hard: see Hannay, "Preface" 86.

Works Cited

Brewer, Derek. "The Tutor: A Portrait." *C. S. Lewis at the Breakfast Table and Other Reminiscences.* Ed. James T. Como. New York: Macmillan, 1979. 41–67.

Carpenter, Humphrey. *The Inklings.* Boston: Houghton Mifflin, 1979.

Christopher, Joe R. *C. S. Lewis.* Boston: Twayne, 1987.

———, and Joan K. Ostling. *C. S. Lewis: An Annotated Checklist of Writings about Him and His Works.* Serif Series 30. Kent, OH: Kent State UP, 1973.

Como, James. "C. S. Lewis in Milton Criticism." *Bulletin of the New York C. S. Lewis Society.* 3.12 (1972): 5–6.

Cox, John D. "Epistemological Release in *The Silver Chair*." *The Longing for a Form: Essays on the Fiction of C. S. Lewis.* Ed. Peter J. Schakel. Kent, OH: Kent State UP, 1977. 159–68, 221–22.

Daniel, Jerry L. "The Taste of the Pineapple: A Basis for Literary Criticism." *The Taste of the Pineapple: Essays on C. S. Lewis as Reader, Critic, and Imaginative Writer.* Ed. Bruce L. Edwards. Bowling Green, OH: Bowling Green State University Popular Press, 1988. 9–27.

Danielson, Dennis R. *Milton's Good God: A Study in Literary Theodicy.* Cambridge: Cambridge UP, 1982.

Downing, David C. *Planets in Peril: A Critical Study of C. S. Lewis's Ransom Trilogy.* Amherst: U of Massachusetts P, 1992.

Eliot, T. S. "Milton I." *On Poetry and Poets.* New York: Noonday, 1961. 156–64. Originally published as "A Note on the Verse of John Milton." *Essays and Studies* 21 (1936): 32–40.

———. "Milton II." *On Poetry and Poets.* New York: Noonday, 1961. 165–83. Revised from his *Milton.* Oxford: Oxford UP, 1947.

Empson, William. *Milton's God.* London: Chatto & Windus, 1961.

Evans, J. Martin. "Lycidas." *The Cambridge Companion to Milton.* Ed. Dennis Danielson. Cambridge: Cambridge UP, 1989. 35–50.

183

Fish, Stanley. *Surprised by Sin: The Reader in Paradise Lost.* London: Macmillan / New York: St. Martin's, 1967.

———. "Transmuting the Lump: Paradise Lost, 1942–1979." *Doing What Comes Naturally: Change, Rhetoric, and the Practice of Theory in Literary and Legal Studies.* Durham and London: Duke UP, 1989. 247–93.

Freedman, Carl. "How to Do Things with Milton: A Study in the Politics of Literary Criticism." *Critical Essays on John Milton.* Ed. Christopher Kendrick. New York: G. K. Hall, 1995. 19–44.

Gardner, Helen. *A Reading of Paradise Lost.* Oxford: Clarendon, 1965.

Gibson, Evan K. *C. S. Lewis, Spinner of Tales: A Guide to His Fiction.* Grand Rapids and Washington: Christian University Press, 1980.

Haigh, John D. "C. S. Lewis and the Tradition of Visionary Romance." *Word and Story in C. S. Lewis.* Ed. Peter J. Schakel and Charles A. Huttar. Columbia and London: U of Missouri P, 1991. 182–98.

Hamm, Victor M. "Mr. Lewis in Perelandra." *Thought* 20 (1945): 271–90.

Hannay, Margaret. *C. S. Lewis.* New York: Ungar, 1981.

———. "A Preface to *Perelandra.*" *The Longing for a Form: Essays on the Fiction of C. S. Lewis.* Ed. Peter J. Schakel. Kent, OH: Kent State UP, 1977. 73–90, 216–18.

Hart, Dabney Adams. *Through the Open Door: A New Look at C. S. Lewis.* Tuscaloosa: U of Alabama P, 1984.

Hooper, Walter. *C. S. Lewis: A Companion and Guide.* San Francisco: Harper San Francisco, 1996.

———. "Preface." *Literary* vii–xx.

Huttar, Charles A. "C. S. Lewis's Narnia and the 'Grand Design.'" *The Longing for a Form: Essays on the Fiction of C. S. Lewis.* Ed. Peter J. Schakel. Kent, OH: Kent State UP, 1977. 119–35, 219–20.

———. "A Lifelong Love Affair with Language: C. S. Lewis's Poetry." *Word and Story in C. S. Lewis.* Ed. Peter J. Schakel and Charles A. Huttar. Columbia and London: U Missouri Press, 1991. 86–108.

Kelley, Maurice. *This Great Argument: A Study of Milton's De doctrina christiana as a Gloss upon Paradise Lost.* Oxford: Oxford UP, 1941.

Leavis, F. R. "Milton's Verse." *Scrutiny* 2 (1933): 123–36. Rpt. as chap. 2 of *Revaluation: Tradition and Development in English Poetry.* London: Chatto and Windus, 1936. New York: George W. Stewart, 1947. 42–61.

Lewis, C. S. *The Abolition of Man.* 2nd ed. London: Geoffrey Bles, 1946.

———. "'Above the Smoke and Stir.'" Letters. *Times Literary Supplement.* 14 July 1945, 331. 29 September 1945, 463.

———. "Addison." *Literary* 154–68.

———. *The Allegory of Love: A Study in Medieval Tradition.* 1936. New York: Oxford UP, 1958.

———. *All My Road Before Me: The Diary of C. S. Lewis 1922–1967.* Ed. Walter Hooper. New York: Harcourt Brace Jovanovich, 1991.

———. "The Anthropological Approach." *Literary* 301–11.

———. "Christianity and Culture." *Reflections* 12–36.

———. "Christianity and Literature." *Reflections* 1–17.

———. *Christian Reflections.* Ed. Walter Hooper. London: Geoffrey Bles, 1967.

———. *Collected Poems.* Ed. Walter Hooper. London: HarperCollins, 1994.

———. "De Audiendis Poetis." *Medieval* 1–17.

———. *The Discarded Image: An Introduction to Medieval and Renaissance Literature.* Cambridge: Cambridge UP, 1964.

———. "Donne and Love Poetry in the Seventeenth Century." 1938. *Literary* 106–25.

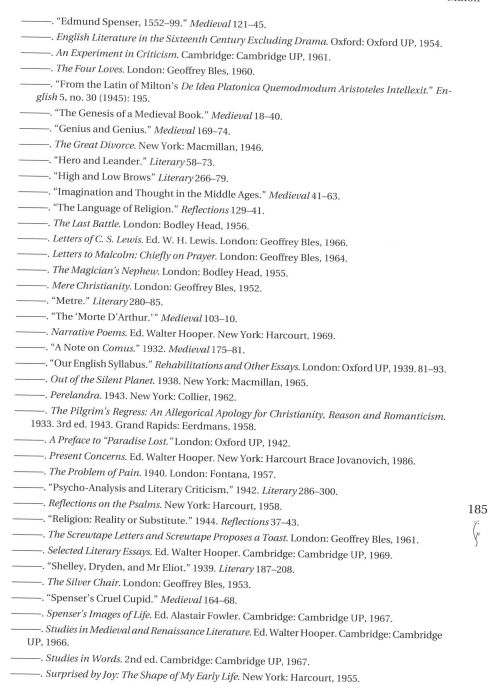

———. "Edmund Spenser, 1552–99." *Medieval* 121–45.

———. *English Literature in the Sixteenth Century Excluding Drama.* Oxford: Oxford UP, 1954.

———. *An Experiment in Criticism.* Cambridge: Cambridge UP, 1961.

———. *The Four Loves.* London: Geoffrey Bles, 1960.

———. "From the Latin of Milton's *De Idea Platonica Quemodmodum Aristoteles Intellexit.*" *English* 5, no. 30 (1945): 195.

———. "The Genesis of a Medieval Book." *Medieval* 18–40.

———. "Genius and Genius." *Medieval* 169–74.

———. *The Great Divorce.* New York: Macmillan, 1946.

———. "Hero and Leander." *Literary* 58–73.

———. "High and Low Brows" *Literary* 266–79.

———. "Imagination and Thought in the Middle Ages." *Medieval* 41–63.

———. "The Language of Religion." *Reflections* 129–41.

———. *The Last Battle.* London: Bodley Head, 1956.

———. *Letters of C. S. Lewis.* Ed. W. H. Lewis. London: Geoffrey Bles, 1966.

———. *Letters to Malcolm: Chiefly on Prayer.* London: Geoffrey Bles, 1964.

———. *The Magician's Nephew.* London: Bodley Head, 1955.

———. *Mere Christianity.* London: Geoffrey Bles, 1952.

———. "Metre." *Literary* 280–85.

———. "The 'Morte D'Arthur.'" *Medieval* 103–10.

———. *Narrative Poems.* Ed. Walter Hooper. New York: Harcourt, 1969.

———. "A Note on *Comus.*" 1932. *Medieval* 175–81.

———. "Our English Syllabus." *Rehabilitations and Other Essays.* London: Oxford UP, 1939. 81–93.

———. *Out of the Silent Planet.* 1938. New York: Macmillan, 1965.

———. *Perelandra.* 1943. New York: Collier, 1962.

———. *The Pilgrim's Regress: An Allegorical Apology for Christianity, Reason and Romanticism.* 1933. 3rd ed. 1943. Grand Rapids: Eerdmans, 1958.

———. *A Preface to "Paradise Lost."* London: Oxford UP, 1942.

———. *Present Concerns.* Ed. Walter Hooper. New York: Harcourt Brace Jovanovich, 1986.

———. *The Problem of Pain.* 1940. London: Fontana, 1957.

———. "Psycho-Analysis and Literary Criticism." 1942. *Literary* 286–300.

———. *Reflections on the Psalms.* New York: Harcourt, 1958.

———. "Religion: Reality or Substitute." 1944. *Reflections* 37–43.

———. *The Screwtape Letters and Screwtape Proposes a Toast.* London: Geoffrey Bles, 1961.

———. *Selected Literary Essays.* Ed. Walter Hooper. Cambridge: Cambridge UP, 1969.

———. "Shelley, Dryden, and Mr Eliot." 1939. *Literary* 187–208.

———. *The Silver Chair.* London: Geoffrey Bles, 1953.

———. "Spenser's Cruel Cupid." *Medieval* 164–68.

———. *Spenser's Images of Life.* Ed. Alastair Fowler. Cambridge: Cambridge UP, 1967.

———. *Studies in Medieval and Renaissance Literature.* Ed. Walter Hooper. Cambridge: Cambridge UP, 1966.

———. *Studies in Words.* 2nd ed. Cambridge: Cambridge UP, 1967.

———. *Surprised by Joy: The Shape of My Early Life.* New York: Harcourt, 1955.

———. "Tasso." *Medieval* 111–20.

———. *That Hideous Strength: A Modern Fairy-Tale for Grown-Ups.* New York: Macmillan, 1946.

———. *They Stand Together: The Letters of C. S. Lewis to Arthur Greeves (1914–1963).* Ed. Walter Hooper. New York: Macmillan, 1979.

———. "Variation in Shakespeare and Others." 1939. *Literary* 74–87.

———. *The Voyage of the Dawn Treader.* London: Geoffrey Bles, 1952.

———, and E. M. W. Tillyard. *The Personal Heresy: A Controversy.* 1939. London: Oxford UP, 1965.

Lovejoy, A. O. "Milton and the Paradox of the Fortunate Fall." *ELH* 4 (1937): 163–81.

Manlove, C. N. *Modern Fantasy.* Cambridge: Cambridge UP, 1975.

McBride, Sam. "C. S. Lewis's *A Preface to 'Paradise Lost,'* the Milton Controversy, and Lewis Scholarship." *Bulletin of Bibliography* 52 (1995): 317–31.

Milton, John. *Poems.* Ed. John Carey and Alastair Fowler. New York: Norton, 1972.

Montgomery, P. Andrew. "Classical Literature." See above.

Morris, Francis Joseph. "Metaphor and Myth: Shaping Forces in C. S. Lewis's Critical Assessment of Medieval and Renaissance Literature." Ph.D. diss., U of Pennsylvania, 1977.

Myers, Doris T. *C. S. Lewis in Context.* Kent, OH: Kent State UP, 1994.

Piehler, Paul. "Myth or Allegory? Archetype and Transcendence in the Fiction of C. S. Lewis." *Word and Story in C. S. Lewis.* Ed. Peter J. Schakel and Charles A. Huttar. Columbia and London: U of Missouri Press, 1991. 199–212.

Richards, I. A. *Practical Criticism.* 1929. New York: Harcourt, Brace, 1952.

———. *Principles of Literary Criticism.* 1924. New York: Harcourt, Brace, 1950.

Saurat, Denis. *Milton, Man and Thinker.* New York: Dial, 1925.

Sayer, George. "Jack on Holiday." *C. S. Lewis at the Breakfast Table and Other Reminiscences.* Ed. James T. Como. New York: Macmillan, 1979. 202–09.

Sewell, Arthur. *A Study in Milton's Christian Doctrine.* London: Oxford UP, 1939.

Shumaker, Wayne. "*Paradise Lost*: The Mythological Dimension." *Bucknell Review* 10 (1961): 75–86. Rpt. and rev. as chapter 1 in *Unpremeditated Verse: Feeling and Perception in* Paradise Lost. Princeton: Princeton UP, 1967. 3–25.

Tanner, John S. "The Psychology of Temptation in *Perelandra* and *Paradise Lost*: What Lewis Learned from Milton." *Renascene* 52 (2000): 131–41.

Tillyard, E. M. W. *The Miltonic Setting, Past and Present.* 1938. London: Chatto & Windus, 1949.

Tolkien, J. R. R. *The Silmarillion.* Boston: Houghton Mifflin, 1977.

Ulreich, John C. "Prophets, Priests, and Poets: Toward a Definition of Religious Fiction." *Cithara* 22.2 (1983): 3–31.

Urang, Gunnar. *Shadows of Heaven: Religion and Fantasy in the Writings of C. S. Lewis, Charles Williams, and J. R. R. Tolkien.* Philadelphia: Pilgrim Press, 1971.

Werblowsky, R. J. Zwi. *Lucifer and Prometheus: A Study of Milton's Satan.* London: Routledge and Kegan Paul, 1952.

Williams, Charles. "Introduction." *The English Poems of John Milton.* London: Oxford UP, 1940. vii–xx. Rpt. as "John Milton" in *The Image of the City and Other Essays* [by Charles Williams]. Ed. Anne Ridler. London: Oxford UP, 1958. 26–36.

———. "The New Milton." 1937. *The Image of the City and Other Essays.* Ed. Anne Ridler. London: Oxford UP, 1958. 19–25.

10

Restoration
and Eighteenth Century

Peter J. Schakel

Writing to Arthur Greeves in 1917, C. S. Lewis asked, "Tell me more about [Laurence Sterne's *Tristram Shandy*] in your next letter and try to shew me its merits: one often learns to appreciate a book through one's friends in this way" (*Stand* 197). Lewis has provided countless readers just such help in appreciating books, through comments and examples in letters, essays, and his own fictional works. He turns out, later, to be helpful in appreciating Sterne himself, and Sterne's era, English literature 1660–1800, though it was not an area in which he considered himself an expert.

"Classicism" and Humanism

That he is helpful for the Restoration period and the eighteenth century could be considered surprising, since the literature of this period is not best known for the qualities Lewis valued most. Lewis loved romance and myth; apart from the myth in *Robinson Crusoe*[1] and the romance in Austen's novels, this period produced little of either. Lewis loved long narrative poems; this period does not. Much of the literature of this period is considered "classical," of a sort of classicism Lewis did not endorse. Lewis did, however, find its empiricism, emphasis on morality, satiric bent, and didactic purpose appealing (Lobdell 213–31). References in biographical and critical writings reveal that he read most (if not all) of the major authors and works—as he seems to have done for virtually every period. He alludes to and comments on many of them, though the comments fall into a fairly restricted range.

Lewis can serve as a guide not only in our reading of specific texts, but in the way we approach reading itself. Many of the writers and works from this period which he enjoyed most are ones which lend themselves to what he called mealtime reading: "Eating and reading are two pleasures that combine admirably. Of course not all books are suitable for mealtime reading. It would be a kind of blasphemy to read poetry at table. What one wants is a gossipy, formless book which can be opened anywhere" (*Surprised* 142). *Tristram Shandy* is that sort of book; so are Pepys's *Diary* and Boswell's *Life of Samuel Johnson*. Often, for this era, Lewis guides us toward works he enjoyed, rather than conveying discoveries about works he studied closely and in depth as a literary scholar.

In approaching English literature 1660–1800, Lewis can first help us, as readers, in dismissing a stereotype, that of treating this era as the "classical," or "neoclassical," period of English literature. Such labels (as well as "Augustan") were dropped long ago by scholars within the field, partly for reasons Lewis suggests. As Lewis put it, "It would be hard to find any excellence in writing less classical than wit; yet it is in wit that these poets admittedly excel. The very forms in which the greatest and most characteristic of classical poetry is cast—the epic and the tragedy—are the forms which they attempt with least success. Their favourite form is Satire, a form not invented by the Greeks, and even in Roman hands not very like *MacFleknoe* or the *Dunciad*" ("Shelley" 188). What we have instead, according to Lewis, are works defined as "classical" by the humanist tradition, of which they are the offspring. Humanism's type of classicism was created by imitating external qualities of Latin literature, its obvious gestures and accents, its desire for order, discipline, weight, decorum, and correctness, not its inner spirit.

188

Lewis in his *English Literature in the Sixteenth Century Excluding Drama* regrets the influence of humanism, and for the same reason is unenthusiastic about much literature traditionally viewed as characterizing the 1660–1800 period. In particular he regrets its constrictive and obscurantist tendencies. Humanism is a movement against, not toward, freedom and expansion; it opposes the Romantic drive toward the primitive and spontaneous, which Lewis appreciated more (*Sixteenth* 23).

> Pope and Swift are true inheritors of the Humanist tradition. It is easy, of course, to say that Laputa is an attack not on science but on the aberrations of science. I am not convinced. The learning of the Brobdingnagians and the Horses is ruthlessly limited. . . . Bentley is not forgiven for knowing more Greek than Temple,

nor Theobald for knowing more English than Pope. . . . The terror expressed at the end of the *Dunciad* is not wholly terror at the approach of ignorance: it is also terror lest the compact little fortress of Humanism should be destroyed, and new knowledge is one of the enemies. ("Addison" 163–64)

It is not surprising, then, as one surveys his comments on the genres and authors of this period, that although he alludes to and quotes widely from "classical" writers of this era, his enjoyment and enthusiasm come through particularly for authors and works outside that tradition.

The Restoration Period

For the Restoration period, 1660–1700, Lewis had little to say that will prove helpful in appreciating its best-known genre, Restoration comedy. Lewis wrote in *Surprised by Joy* that he "yawned [his] way through Restoration Comedy" (214), probably because of its superficiality and triviality;[2] thus, references and allusions to Restoration drama occur infrequently in his works and letters. It is worth noting, however, that the ribaldry and bawdiness which infuses them and other works of the Restoration and eighteenth century did not lead him to think that the comedies should be avoided: "I have no quarrel with Wycherley, I admire Congreve," he notes in "Shelley, Dryden, and Mr Eliot" (193).

His opinion regarding references to sex in literature comes out in regard to one of his favorite works from the Restoration period, the *Diary* of Samuel Pepys. In 1960 Magdalene College, which owns the original text of the diary, was considering whether to publish an unexpurgated version of the work.[3] Lewis was told that his opinion on the issue might be sought, and he gave it in a letter. After dismissing prudential concerns about whether the college might be prosecuted or ridiculed, Lewis turned to moral concerns:

The moral problem comes down to the question "Is it probable that the inclusion of these passages will lead anyone to commit an immoral act which he would not have committed if we had suppressed them?" Now of course this question is strictly unanswerable. No one can foresee the odd results that any words may have on this or that individual. We ourselves, in youth, have been both corrupted and edified by books in which our elders could have foreseen neither edification nor corruption. But to suggest that in a society where the most potent aphrodisiacs are daily put forward by the advertisers, the newspapers, and the films, any perceptible increment of lechery will be caused by printing a few obscure and widely separated passages in a very long and expensive book, seems to me ridiculous, or even hypocritical. (*Letters* 490)

Quotations from and references to Pepys are sprinkled throughout Lewis's prose and letters, usually just in passing. This suggests that the way to appreciate Pepys is as a source of intimate historical background details and as a source of anecdotes and quips.

Important works by two authors of this era who influenced Lewis strongly, John Milton and John Bunyan, were published during the Restoration period but are treated elsewhere in this volume. That should alert us to the issue of canon, another area of literary study in which Lewis can be instructive. The traditional literary canon of "Restoration literature" includes mainly the work of men, of course; Lewis does not comment on, and probably did not read, the many interesting women writers of the period who have gained recognition in the past couple of decades. And it includes mainly the work of the Court and courtiers, that of a fairly thin slice of the upper echelons of society. The "Restoration period" is stereotyped as a period of loose morals. That in fact describes most accurately only a part of the population and of published works. The majority of the population were decent, sober, hard-working folk who were appalled by the lifestyle of the Court and courtiers.

Restoration comedy, for example, is a vital part of the traditional canon, but it should be pointed out that the vast majority of the population of England lived outside of London and never had access to the theater; and even the majority of Londoners avoided the theater. The name John Dryden was probably unknown to Englishmen of his day except for the educated minority and literary elite. Citizenry of all levels, however, read sermons, devotional literature, and *The Pilgrim's Progress*. That *Paradise Lost* and *Paradise Regained* were written and published during the Restoration period serves as a reminder that academic methods of periodization can frequently lead to rather misleading results.

Lewis provided a balanced and incisive critique of John Dryden, poet, playwright, critic, and the leading literary figure of the later seventeenth century. He recognizes Dryden's greatness, "a greatness to which the name of *genius* is peculiarly applicable" ("Shelley" 188). Dryden has genuine strength as a writer, "exuberant power," as well as a transforming power that enables him to make the prosaic poetical and the obscure and complicated clear and simple—as illustrated by the way *Absalom and Achitophel* clarifies and elevates the political situation of 1681 by transforming it into the political situation of Davidic Israel. Within the poem are passages of splendid poetry. Lewis praises "the masculine vigour of his English, the fine breezy, sunshiny weather of the man's mind at its best—his poetical health; the sweetness (unsurpassed in its own way) of nearly all his versification" ("Shelley" 194; see also *Sixteenth* 97–98).

Countering these traits, however, according to Lewis, is Dryden's inability to sustain such power throughout an entire poem. "He excels in beginnings," Lewis says ("Shelley" 188), pointing to the openings of *Absalom and Achitophel* and *The Hind and the Panther*. He lacked, however, the ability to construct and develop the plan for a poem as a whole. *Absalom and Achitophel* builds toward a powerful climax, but ends anticlimactically. The plan of *The Hind and the Panther*, "conducting in verse a theological controversy allegorized as a beast fable," suggests in the author "a state of mind bordering on aesthetic insanity" (191). Dryden also lacks good judgment, falling frequently into an inappropriate humor which undermines the serious or noble effect he had chosen to pursue. In the end, he admires Dryden greatly, but as a writer who "can produce good poetry but not good poems" (190).

The Early Eighteenth Century

For the early eighteenth century, Lewis provides helpful suggestions for appreciating three leading figures, Jonathan Swift, Alexander Pope, and Joseph Addison. Of the three, Swift appealed to and influenced Lewis most. Swift and Pope, unlike Addison, were imprisoned by the humanist tradition, and lacked the curiosity and openness to possibility Addison always exhibited. But Swift, Lewis says, reached depths which Addison never could reach, had a more brilliant wit than Addison, and at his height had far more strength and splendor, though Swift can slip into depths of hatred, bigotry, and even silliness ("Addison" 167–68).

Of the wide range of Swift's prose—*A Tale of a Tub*, *The Battle of the Books*, and "A Modest Proposal"—Lewis enjoyed *Gulliver's Travels* most, from his early years: "*Gulliver* in an unexpurgated and lavishly illustrated edition was one of my favorites" (*Surprised* 14). Lewis liked *Gulliver's Travels* as a comic work. As Derek Brewer points out, "He enormously enjoyed Swift's humour and thought his work fuller of real laughs than almost any other" (49). It also appealed to him for the same reason science fiction—and fantasy and myth generally—did, that it fulfills "an imaginative impulse as old as the human race . . . to visit strange regions in search of such beauty, awe, or terror as the actual world does not supply" ("On Science Fiction" 63). This provides a valuable starting point for introducing *Gulliver*, especially to readers who like fantasy. The *Travels* in the first place is a good story, full of realistic detail in order to make its other world seem believable and to enable us to live imaginatively in that other world for a short time. Lewis points out that effects which in the twentieth century can be achieved only by voyages to outer space could in the eighteenth century still be achieved by voyages to remote seas (*Stories* 64).

Lewis also proves helpful when he points out that "the first two books of *Gulliver* depend much more on the 'idea' of big and little men than on any great novelty or profundity in Swift's 'ideas' about politics and ethics" (*Six-*

191

teenth 385). Concentrating on that imaginative idea, especially as it manipulates the way readers identify with characters, carries one a long way into the book's strategies, which can be brought out by asking why we identify with Gulliver initially, why not with the Lilliputians; why Swift started with little people rather than giants; why it is difficult to continue to identify with Gulliver in Brobdingnag; how the problem of identifying creates a tension for the reader; and how the structure and the tensions carry over from parts 1 and 2 to part 4 as well.

Lewis also calls our attention to a central theme throughout the *Travels*, the theme of pride. The theme appears in part 1 in Gulliver's pride at his relative size and strength, and in the hubris of the tiny people who regard themselves as the center of the universe; it continues in Gulliver's attempts to achieve esteem and self-esteem despite his minute size in part 2, in his pride in abstract reason found in part 3, and in the Houyhnhnms' self-satisfaction and Gulliver's arrogance in part 4. Lewis's comment on the significance of this steadily intensifying theme can help bring out deeper levels of meaning and give focus to the consideration of it: "The ferocity of the later *Gulliver* all works up to that devastating attack on Pride which is more specifically Christian than any other piece of ethical writing in the century, if we except William Law" ("Addison" 159).

Lewis's fiction may be even more helpful than his criticism in getting at Swift's themes and methods. *Gulliver's Travels* served as a primary model for Lewis's *Out of the Silent Planet*. Thus, to grasp what Swift is up to in the *Travels* (or to bring it out more clearly, for those who know Lewis's fiction), one can compare approaches and ideas in the two works. Lewis follows Swift in using an imaginary voyage as a means of social criticism. Each takes his main character out of usual surroundings and plunges him into a place with new and unfamiliar customs. Each thus imposes on the character, and on the reader, a fresh perspective on our culture, one which reveals competitiveness, greed, pride, and selfishness in humankind which we prefer not to recognize. As Swift has the Brobdingnagian king ask Gulliver probing questions about the English political and social system, so Lewis has the *hrossa* and *sorns* question Ransom and provide an outsider's assessment of our world. As Gulliver in the land of the Houyhnhnms suddenly realizes that the disagreeable Yahoos are (or appear to be) human, so Ransom suddenly recognizes that the odd-shaped, unattractive creatures approaching him are humans, are in fact Weston and Devine. And as Gulliver in Houyhnhnmland has difficulty finding words to describe human attitudes and activities, so Ransom struggles to translate Weston's unreasonable, inhumane philosophy into Old Solar. The simplifications and reductions both writers employ in explaining human affairs to nonhumans become a key part of the satire against human folly and evil (see Schakel 134–38 and Keefer 210–15).

Lewis wrote to his brother in 1929, "satire tends always to bore me" (*Letters* 271). Perhaps that is true for Renaissance satire, like that of Rabelais in this letter or the attempts by Donne and Marston to imitate the *Satira* of the Romans (*Sixteenth* 468–77). However, his comments on satire, especially his distinction in *English Literature in the Sixteenth Century Excluding Drama* between *satire* as a form and *the satiric* as a mode (that is, a use of humor, wit, and irony to hold up vices, follies, and abuses to ridicule and contempt), can be very helpful in clarifying what satire is. Lewis seems to have enjoyed works from the great age of satire in England. Among works generally called "satires" he includes mostly examples from this period, "*Gulliver*, the *Dunciad*, the *Rape*, *Absalom*, and *Hudibras*" (*Sixteenth* 468). These he describes as "all fantastic or mock heroic narratives" whose ancestors are Rabelais, Cervantes, Lucian, and the *Frogs and Mice*, not the Roman *Satira* (*Sixteenth* 468). Lewis's relish for satire is further indicated by the fact that satire forms an important ingredient in many of his own works, as he jabs at contemporary vices and evils in *The Pilgrim's Regress*, *The Screwtape Letters*, *That Hideous Strength*, *The Great Divorce*, and many of his poems (Schakel 129–48).

If *Out of the Silent Planet* is indebted to Swift, *Perelandra* may be indebted to Swift's contemporary, Daniel Defoe. So Jared Lobdell contends: "*Out of the Silent Planet* is classical; in *Perelandra* the romance pushes against the classical bounds, but the bounds are still there. It is not, I believe, accidental that when Ransom is on his first floating island, the simile Lewis uses is 'looking down like Robinson Crusoe on field and forest to the shores in every direction' (*Per*, 45). Certainly Lewis must have had Crusoe in mind as he was writing" (Lobdell 225).

In regard to the poetry of the early eighteenth century, among Lewis's most helpful suggestions is for readers to focus on its universal themes and to recognize that the form and style were of temporary appeal. He makes the point in an essay on period criticism. On one hand, he says, a writer "may be of his period in the negative sense. That is to say he may deal with things which are of no permanent interest but only seemed to be of interest because of some temporary fashion." On the other hand, a writer "may be 'dated' in the sense that the forms, the set-up, the paraphernalia, whereby he expresses matter of permanent interest, are those of a particular age." He then applies the point to Pope and *The Rape of the Lock* which, he says, "is a perfect (and never obsolete) period piece" ("Period Criticism" 115). If readers, then, can be directed toward the universal motifs and themes—the perpetual war between the sexes and the enduring tendency to favor appearance above reality, the present above the future, the superficial above the lasting—they may come to see the significance of a work which was, as Lewis stated, at least "ostensibly corrective" (*Sixteenth* 137).

Readers should also come to value the imaginative achievement of the poem's artistry. The detail bringing to life the universe of the sprites which surrounds ours and recreating the frivolous world of Belinda and the Baron is creativity and craft of the highest order. Lewis calls it a work of love, and in doing so he points the way toward appreciating the work and raising questions about how to engage with it: "He loved, if not Belinda, yet her toilet, and the tea-cups, and the 'shining altars of Japan,' and would have been very little pleased with any 'reform of manners' which interfered with them" (*Sixteenth* 137). If love for the things he mocks was one element in Pope's attitude, is the same true for the reader? Does Pope lead us partly to love that which we also must reject? How do we deal with both the frivolity and the seriousness of the rape and the *Rape*?[4]

Lewis discusses Joseph Addison not only as a contrast to Swift and Pope, but also as a pivotal figure who exemplifies the new directions thought and literature will take later in the eighteenth century. Lewis was drawn to Addison in part because Addison avoided the humanist heritage that, Lewis holds, very much influenced Swift and Pope. At the heart of the essay on "Addison" is a discussion of Addison's *Spectator* paper on "Chevy Chase," in which Addison calls "the neo-classical bluff" by showing that the ballad is not Gothic, as classical critics would have it, but is actually more classical in spirit than the imitations the critics call "classical." Addison shows that "if the *nominal* standards of Augustan criticism are ever taken seriously they must work out in favour of the ballads (and much medieval literature) and against most of the poetry the Augustans themselves produced" ("Addison" 162). In rejecting the closed, nostalgic attitudes of humanism, Addison lives in a bigger world than Swift or Pope, one of horizons and possibilities they never touched (164). He has broader curiosity and a more inclusive attitude.

Addison, says Lewis, stands exactly at the turning point between the older attitude toward nature, which feared or disliked the strange and unruly, and the newer attitude of the Gothic writers and the Romantics, who sought out such aspects:

> Almost everything which my own generation ignorantly called Victorian seems to have been expressed by Addison. It is all there in the *Spectator*—the vague religious sensibility, the insistence on what came later to be called Good Form, the playful condescension towards women, the untroubled belief in the beneficence of commerce, the comfortable sense of security which, far from excluding, perhaps renders possible the romantic relish for wildness and solitude. (167)

It is easy to identify some of the reasons Lewis was attracted to Addison. Yet, some of the ways Addison contrasts with Swift and Pope, politically and economically, would seem to provide reasons for Lewis to react against Addison. Addison, unlike Swift and Pope, supported the merchant and trading classes over landed wealth, and the Court party and Parliament over the opposition Country party. Addison thus represents a forward-looking, "progress"-oriented outlook contrary to what Swift and Pope endorsed and to what Lewis himself favored. His critique of "progress" opening the fifth chapter of *Mere Christianity* (echoed in the fourth chapter of *The Voyage of the "Dawn Treader"*) is much more in the spirit of Swift and Pope than of Addison. A part of Lewis, however, seems to have been drawn toward Addison, toward his good sense, pleasing melancholies, and gentle humor; he writes that "Addison is, above all else, comfortable. He is not on that account to be condemned" ("Addison" 168). That side of Lewis also wrote the poem "In Praise of Solid People" (no. 24 in *Spirits in Bondage*). It is fortunate that this side of Lewis did not dominate his life.

The Mid-Eighteenth Century

In literature of the mid-eighteenth century, Lewis read widely in the novel. He liked Fielding, mentioning him as a writer whose works originally were considered lowbrow, but now are considered highbrow ("High" 272). He says that "Sophia [in *Tom Jones*] is good. She comes during that lucid interval when good heroines were possible in novels written by men, when the restoration tradition by which a heroine must be a whore was dead,[5] and the Victorian tradition by which she must be a fool had not been born" (*Letters* 229).

The most interesting example from this period of Lewis's own development as a reader and the way he can help other readers appreciate works involves *Tristram Shandy*. Initially he could not respond favorably to it. In a letter to Arthur Greeves in 1916 he wrote, "I have read to day . . . some 10 pages of 'Tristam [*sic*] Shandy' and am wondering whether I like it. It is certainly the maddest book ever written. . . . It gives you the impression of an escaped lunatic's conversation while chasing his hat on a windy May morning. Yet there are beautiful serious parts in it though of a sentimental kind, as I know from my father. Have you ever come across it?" (*Stand* 141–42). That comment seems to have spurred Greeves to try it and like it, though Lewis, nine months later, still did not: "I was interested to hear that you liked Tristram Shandy. . . . I have tried in vain to see the good points of it. The absolute disconnection or scrappiness, the abundant coarseness of an utterly vulgar, non-voluptuous sort and the general smoking-room atmosphere of the book were too much for me. In all these points it is the direct opposite of our quiet, balanced & delicately humourous Jane Austen" (*Stand* 197).

Later, however, perhaps as a result of the answers Greeves supplied in response to the request with which I opened this essay, Lewis came to enjoy it greatly, and offers comments that can help other readers see what to appreciate in it. In 1931 he wrote to Arthur, "Glad to hear you are at *Tristram Shandy*. What good company! Isn't Uncle Toby [eccentric but loveable central character], seriously and morally, one of the loveliest characters ever created" (*Stand* 402). A week later he remarked on the inappropriate conjunction of minds Sterne delights in bringing together. "Don't you think the great beauty of that book is its picture of affection existing across unbridgeable gulfs of intellect? My Father & Uncle Toby never understand one another at all, and always love one another. It is the true picture of home life: far better than the modern nonsense in wh. affection (friendship is a different thing) is made to depend on mental affinities" (*Stand* 405; see also *Loves* 55, 69–70). He goes on to mention "the over-flowing goodness at the heart of the book" (*Stand* 405–06).

The Later Eighteenth Century

Among authors of the later eighteenth century, Lewis's favorites are Samuel Johnson and Jane Austen. His affinity for Johnson clearly ran deep, both the Johnson of Boswell's *Life*, which he quotes frequently, and the Johnson of the *Rambler* essays and the *Lives of the Poets*. He includes Boswell's *Life* as the kind of book that is "suitable for mealtime reading" (*Surprised* 142), and mentions it when discussing the reading of the unliterary, those who read books only once: "There is hope for a man who has never read Malory or Boswell or *Tristram Shandy* or Shakespeare's *Sonnets*: but what can you do with a man who says he 'has read' them, meaning he has read them once, and thinks that this settles the matter?" ("On Stories" 16). A great deal about how he viewed Boswell is revealed by his comment in a letter to his brother about how remarkable it was that "a dead man out of a book [Johnson] can be almost a member of one's family circle" (*Letters* 331).

In indicating what a reader should appreciate in Johnson, Lewis points first to Johnson's ability to pierce to the heart of an issue and to state ideas concisely, exemplified most fully in the *Rambler* essays. "Isn't it a magnificent style—the very essence of manliness and condensation. I find Johnson very *bracing* when I am in my slack, self pitying mood. The amazing thing is his power of stating platitudes—or what in anyone else wd. be platitudes—so that we really believe them at last and realise their importance. Doesn't it remind you a bit of Handel?" (*Stand* 364). Johnson's essays have "iron in them"; they "stir the depths" ("Addison" 167). "I personally get more pleasure from the *Rambler* than from anything else of his & at one time I used to read a Rambler every evening as a nightcap. They are so *quieting* in their brave, sensible dignity" (*Stand* 364).

Lewis recognized the importance of Johnson's style, and the importance of paying attention to it, but he says very little specifically about it. The reason probably, as he says in a letter to his brother, is that so much has already been said: "There is no subject on which more nonsense has been talked than the style of Johnson." Rather than technical analysis, he attempts to talk sense through metaphors: "For me his best sentences in writing have the same feeling as his best conversation—'pop! it was so sudden.' I don't know anyone who can settle a thing so well in half a dozen words" (*Letters* 257). He also enjoyed, and frequently quoted from, Johnson's *Lives of the Poets*. To his brother, serving in the Far East, he wrote, "I can imagine that the atmosphere, the Englishness, is specially delightful to you in 'furrin parts'" (258).

That same quality of Englishness surely was part of the appeal of Jane Austen. Although her works were published in the nineteenth century, many of them were written earlier and her thought and attitudes were sufficiently of the eighteenth century to justify including her in this essay. So Lewis thought of her, anyway, as he writes, "She is the daughter of Dr Johnson: she inherits his commonsense, his morality, even much of his style" ("Austen" 186). In commenting on *Persuasion*, he refers to "the Johnsonian cadence of a sentence which expresses a view that Johnson in one of his countless moods might have supported" (179).

Austen was definitely a favorite Lewis author. He credited Arthur Greeves for leading him to see her merits: "Under Arthur's influence I read at this time [1914–16] all the best Waverleys, all the Brontës, and all the Jane Austens" (*Surprised* 151). In 1914 he told Greeves "I am now engaged in reading 'Sense and Sensibility'" and mentions rereading it in 1916 (*Stand* 49, 129). Often, however, he seems to be encouraging Arthur, urging him in 1915 to buy a Temple Classics edition of *Mansfield Park* ("I should almost say it was her best"— *Stand* 76) and in 1916 asking "Have you finished 'Persuasion' and . . . what do you think of [it]?" (99).

The first guidance Lewis would offer on appreciating Austen would be that these are novels to be read for pleasure, as, for example, when one has a minor illness or is recovering from the flu. Lewis mentioned such an approach to reading in a letter to his father in 1926: "Will you think me affected if I number a small illness among the minor pleasures of life? . . . Work is impossible and one can read all day for mere pleasure with a clear conscience" (*Letters* 218; see also *Surprised* 189). He read *Sense and Sensibility* yet again while ill in 1929 and in 1937 wrote, "I've had a grand week in bed" and included

197

Northanger Abbey among half a dozen books he read (*Letters* 313). "Jane Austen, Scott, and Trollope are my favourite authors when ill," he wrote to a former pupil in 1943 (371).

His pleasure in reading her novels derives from the way they enable him to enter and imaginatively experience their world. When he tries to convey what he likes about Malory, he uses a comparison to Austen: "To me it is a world of its own, like Jane Austen. . . . It is very fully realized, and all the characters are old friends . . . whom you get to know better & better as you go on" (*Stand* 145). Thus, "we hold our breath with anxiety . . . while we wonder how . . . the disgrace of the Bennet family will affect Darcy's love for Elizabeth [in *Pride and Prejudice*]" (*Experiment* 38). Lewis's remark about getting to know characters as old friends helps explain why he alludes so often to characters from Austen novels, or uses them as bases for comparisons, as if they were actual acquaintances: "We always are like the ladies in Jane Austin [*sic*]" (*Stand* 173); "Or like our brother in law Mr Suckling" (347); "Don't tell her I repeated this to you, because, as Miss Bates says 'It would be so very'" (491); "I never had a handsomer present (both in a bibliophile's and in Mr Woodhouse's sense of the word *handsome*)" (*Letters* 442).

But Lewis would also direct us to read Austen novels for their "seriousness." Early on he explained to Greeves that he could not stand too steady a diet of such authors as Austen because "I don't think myself I could stand such a dose of stolidity" (*Stand* 95). Later he came to value such stolidness: "I am glad you think J. Austen a sound moralist. I agree. And not platitudinous, but subtle as well as firm" (*Letters* 423). In his short "Note" on Jane Austen, he discusses a common pattern of "undeception" or "awakening," of heroines discovering in pivotal situations that they have been making mistakes about themselves and about the world, in four of her most characteristic novels, *Northanger Abbey, Sense and Sensibility, Pride and Prejudice*, and *Emma*. Lewis celebrates in Austen a "hardness" or at least "firmness" of thought:

The great abstract nouns of the classical English moralists are unblushingly and uncompromisingly used [in Austen]: *good sense, courage, contentment, fortitude,* "some duty neglected, some failing indulged," *impropriety, indelicacy, generous candour, blameable distrust, just humiliation, vanity, folly, ignorance, reason.* These are the concepts by which Jane Austen grasps the world. In her we still breathe the air of the *Rambler* and *Idler*. All is hard, clear, definable; by some modern standards, even naïvely so. ("Austen" 178)

Later he adds, "'*Principles*' or '*seriousness*' are essential to Jane Austen's art" as a comic writer. "Where there is no norm, nothing can be ridiculous. . . . Unless there is something about which the author is never ironical, there can be no true irony in the work" (185).

The essay points out qualities to appreciate not just in Austen, but also in other key figures of the Restoration and the eighteenth century. One finds such "hardness" or "seriousness" in authors like Dryden, Milton, Bunyan, Swift, Pope, and Johnson, but missing from more sentimental authors like Addison, Richardson, Fielding, Sterne, and Boswell. One of the central motifs of his essay on Addison is the way Addison's essays mark a turn from the "uncompromising creeds" of the past, to the "Rational Piety" of the future, which shaped much of the religious thought of our own century:

> The essays do not invite criticism in terms of any very definite theology. They are everywhere "pious." Rational Piety, together with Polite Letters and Simplicity, is one of the hall-marks of the age which Addison was partly interpreting but partly also bringing into existence. And Rational Piety is by its very nature not very doctrinal. This is one of the many ways in which Addison is historically momentous. He ushers in that period—it is just now drawing to a close—in which it is possible to talk of "piety" or (later) "religion" almost in the abstract; in which the contrast is no longer between Christian and Pagan, the elect and the world, orthodox and heretic, but between "religious" and "irreligious." . . . Perhaps the most illuminating passage is the essay on "Sir Roger at Church," and specially the quotation from Pythagoras prefixed to it—"Honour first the immortal gods according to the established mode." That is the very note of Rational Piety. A sensible man goes with his society, according to local and ancestral usage. And he does so with complete sincerity. Clean clothes and the sound of bells on Sunday morning do really throw him into a mood of sober benevolence, not "clouded by enthusiasm" but inviting his thoughts to approach the mystery of things. ("Addison" 157–58)

In that light he remarks that "Christianity is in constant danger of relapsing into theological hedonism. It had so relapsed in the eighteenth century when Boswell could say (without contradiction from Johnson) that the doctrine of future rewards and punishments was its very essence" (*Sixteenth* 189). It is not surprising that, except for Addison, most of Lewis's enthusiasm for and allusions to eighteenth-century writers come from writers in the "hard" tradition, like Swift, Pope, Johnson, and Austen, rather than in the softer, sentimental tradition which, though it anticipates the Romanticism of the next century, still lacked the sense of the marvelous and the *Sehnsucht* that Lewis found so appealing in many writers of the nineteenth century.

Because Lewis was not engaged in scholarly work on literature of the Restoration and eighteenth century, but was commenting on works he enjoyed, he does not guide us toward or provide help on some works from this period which deal with Christianity and which can be helpful to someone tracing the development of Christian thought in England and of the Church of England as an institution. I can find no mention, for example, of

Dryden's *Religio Laici*, which provides an excellent summary of the Anglican position of the "middle way." He does not refer to the splendid sermons of Tillotson, or to the work and writings of George Whitefield and John Wesley, or to the deeply Christian, and influential, strains in *Joseph Andrews* and *Tom Jones*. Given his dislike of hymns,[6] it is not surprising that Lewis pays scant attention to the great tradition of eighteenth-century hymn writers, which includes Nahum Tate, Joseph Addison, Issac Watts, William Cowper, Charles Wesley, and John Newton.

He does recognize, however, what was missed until Maynard Mack's ground-breaking scholarship of the 1940s, that Pope's Roman Catholicism was not as superficial as scholars earlier in the century had claimed and that *An Essay on Man* is thoroughly Christian ("Addison" 158). He offers a balanced, judicious assessment of Swift's Christian commitment, praising specifically the depth from which he attacked the English for practicing only nominal Christianity, "the other [Real Christianity] having been for some time wholly laid aside by general consent, as utterly inconsistent with our present schemes of wealth and power."[7] And he reminds us that recognition of the spiritual dimensions of the Christian writers throughout this era is crucial to a full understanding and appreciation of them. He puts it well in a letter to his brother in 1939, in appropriately Johnsonian style: "How on earth did we manage to enjoy all these books so much as we did in the days when we had really no conception of what was at the centre of them? Sir, he who embraces the Christian revelation rejoins the main tide of human existence!" (*Letters* 331).

In his assessments of eighteenth-century literature, then, Lewis offers, for the most part, not the judgments of a literary scholar working in his specialty, but the appreciative observations of a skilled and sensitive reader commenting on authors and works he has enjoyed. As he does, he achieves himself what he praises Johnson for as a critic, that "he always makes me want to read the people he talks of" (*Letters* 258).

Notes

1. See Lewis's letter on "*Robinson Crusoe* as a Myth," *Essays in Criticism* 1 (1951): 313.
2. J. R. Christopher, "C. S. Lewis vs. Restoration Comedy," *CSL Bulletin* 4 (November 1972): 4–5.
3. Presumably *The Diary of Samuel Pepys*, ed. Robert Latham and William Matthews, 11 volumes, published 1970–83 by G. Bell and Sons (later Bell and Hyman) in Britain and the University of California Press in the United States.
4. Because of his dislike of works that try to be "classical" by imitating external characteristics of Roman literature, Lewis rarely mentions and only occasionally quotes from Pope's verse satires

and epistles, works that best typify the poetry of this period. His attitude is revealed in the following comment: "The days are, or ought to be, long past in which any well-informed critic could take the couplet poets of our 'Augustan' school at their own valuation as 'classical' writers. . . . They are neither bad poets nor classical poets. Their merits are great, but neither their merits nor their limitations are those of ancient literature or of that modern literature which is truly classical" ("Shelley" 188).

5. This is a witty line, but such well-known heroines of Restoration comedies as Alithea in *The Country Wife* and Millamant in *The Way of the World* force one to question its accuracy.

6. See "On Church Music," *English Church Music* 19 (April 1949), rpt. *Christian Reflections*, ed. Walter Hooper (Grand Rapids: Eerdmans, 1967), 94–99.

7. "An Argument against Abolishing Christianity" (see *The Prose Works of Jonathan Swift*, ed. Herbert Davis, vol. 2 [Oxford: Blackwell, 1940], 28), quoted in "Addison" 159.

Works Cited

Brewer, Derek. "The Tutor: A Portrait." *C. S. Lewis at the Breakfast Table and Other Reminiscences.* Ed. James T. Como. New York: Macmillan, 1979. 41–47.

Christopher, J. R. "C. S. Lewis vs. Restoration Comedy." *CSL Bulletin* 4 (November 1972): 4–5.

Keefer, Sarah Larratt. "Houyhnhnms on Malacandra: C. S. Lewis and Jonathan Swift." *American Notes and Queries* 7.4 (1994): 210–15.

Lewis, C. S. "Addison." *Literary* 154–68.

———. *English Literature in the Sixteenth Century Excluding Drama.* Oxford: Oxford UP, 1954.

———. *An Experiment in Criticism.* Cambridge: Cambridge UP, 1961.

———. *The Four Loves.* New York: Harcourt, 1960.

———. "High and Low Brows." *Literary* 266–79.

———. *Letters of C. S. Lewis.* Ed. W. H. Lewis. 1966. Rev. ed. Ed. Walter Hooper. London: HarperCollins, 1988.

———. "A Note on Jane Austen." *Literary* 175–86.

———. "On Church Music." *Christian Reflections.* Ed. Walter Hooper. Grand Rapids: Eerdmans, 1967. 94–99.

———. "On Science Fiction." *Stories* 55–68.

———. "On Stories." *Stories* 3–20.

———. *"On Stories" and Other Essays on Literature.* Ed. Walter Hooper. New York: Harcourt Brace Jovanovich, 1982.

———. "Period Criticism." *Stories* 113–17.

———. *"Robinson Crusoe* as Myth." *Essays in Criticism* 1 (1951): 313.

———. *Selected Literary Essays.* Ed. Walter Hooper. Cambridge: Cambridge UP, 1969.

———. "Shelley, Dryden, and Mr Eliot." *Literary* 187–208.

———. *Spirits in Bondage: A Cycle of Lyrics.* 1919. Ed. Walter Hooper. San Diego: Harcourt Brace Jovanovich, 1984.

———. *Surprised by Joy: The Shape of My Early Life.* 1955. New York: Harcourt, Brace and World, 1956.

⸻. *They Stand Together: The Letters of C. S. Lewis to Arthur Greeves (1914–1963)*. Ed. Walter Hooper. New York: Macmillan, 1979.

⸻. *The Voyage of the Dawn Treader*. London: Geoffrey Bles, 1952.

Lobdell, Jared C. "C. S. Lewis's Ransom Stories and Their Eighteenth-Century Ancestry." *Word and Story in C. S. Lewis*. Ed. Peter J. Schakel and Charles A. Huttar. Columbia: University of Missouri Press, 1991. 213–31.

Schakel, Peter J. "The Satiric Imagination of C. S. Lewis." *Studies in the Literary Imagination* 22 (1989): 129–48.

11
Romantics

Wayne Martindale

After a good soak in Italian culture, with the words "Classicism is health, Romanticism sickness," Goethe criticized vast portions of his own work and the spirit of his age. In many ways, Lewis came to the same conclusion about himself and about the spirit and literature of the early British nineteenth century. In his spiritual autobiography, *Surprised by Joy*, he calls his "earliest aesthetic experiences . . . incurably romantic" (7) and laments that before his conversion to Christianity "my feelings for nature had been too narrowly romantic. I attended almost entirely to what I thought awe-inspiring, or wild, or eerie, and above all to distance" (152).[1] Yet he approvingly refers to "my Romanticism" as the thing which divided him from the cynical and debunking "orthodox Intellectuals" he read (173). And in a late letter to poet and close friend Ruth Pitter, he could say, "I . . . admire the XIXth century more than almost any other period" (Letter to Pitter #54). Furthermore, against the attacks of T. S. Eliot he wrote a ringing defense of that most radical of Romantics, Percy Shelley. In finding the resolution to this paradox, we gain valuable insight not only into Lewis's sensibility but also into the spirit and the writers we designate as Romantic. Reading Romantic literature with Lewis yields insight in five areas: 1) the definition of "Romanticism," a notoriously slippery term, 2) Lewis's attraction to the period, 3) the works of individual writers, 4) Romantic critical theory, and 5) Lewis's critique of Romanticism.[2]

"Romanticism" as a Term

Lewis is uniquely positioned to help us read the British Romantics, having slipped on Romanticism both as an outlook and as a term, then recovering from both falls. Let's start with the term. It is no small problem saying just what Romanticism is. In the first half of the twentieth century alone, over five hundred books and articles attempted to capture its elusive meaning. The number has grown exponentially in the half century since, and the debate goes on apace.[3] Lewis had to come to grips with the term early in his writing career. In his first book after his 1931 conversion, *The Pilgrim's Regress*, he employed the subtitle *An Allegorical Apology for Christianity, Reason, and Romanticism* (1933). When the third edition came out a decade later, Lewis felt obliged to write a preface apologizing for his obscurity. Most of the preface attempts to explain what he meant by "Romanticism." We may be grateful for his mistake. The correction is a masterpiece of clarity in an arena where obscurity still often prevails.

In his preface, Lewis delineates seven common uses of the word "Romanticism." They are: 1) adventure stories featuring great danger; 2) fantasy or the "marvellous" when it is not a part of religious belief; 3) characters or emotions presented on a grand scale; 4) interest in the abnormal, as in an obsession with death; 5) "subjectivism" or individualism, focusing on the self; 6) anti-institutionalism or a revolutionary spirit; and 7) responsiveness to nature. To this array of customary uses, Lewis adds the definition (number eight in this essay) he originally intended: what he calls "Sweet Desire" in the preface and "Joy" in *Surprised by Joy*. Romanticism in this specialized sense is an "intense longing" for something never possessed, a desire never satisfied in this life. Helping us come to grips with this longing, much misunderstood but supremely important, is among Lewis's major contributions. It will figure largely in this chapter. To these eight usages, I will add a ninth—the simplest and perhaps most common of all: "Romanticism" designates the forty-year period of British literature from the French Revolution (1789) to the passage of the First Reform Bill (1832).[4] In this essay, we will be most concerned with definitions eight and nine, that is, with Joy and the works falling into this historical period.

Despite Lewis's attraction to this period, he wrote very little about it. Lewis wrote no books and only two articles that deal with Romantic writers at any length (three if we count Jane Austen), and both of these are occasional. This lack of attention in print, however, does not result from Lewis's neglect in reading or understanding the Romantics or thinking them unimportant. Rather, it grows out of Lewis's opinion on what should and should not be taught in a formal educational setting.[5] The practical result for those of us interested in the Romantics and in Lewis is that we must smelt a vast quantity of ore (all rich enough in various minerals) to get a small quantity of this particular metal. So much must come from the illustrative remark and by inference, but the little that exists more than repays the effort to recover it.

Longing

What attracted Lewis to the literature of the Romantics was its intensity and preoccupation with longing. It continues to attract many readers because we all feel intensely about many of the same things: nature, love, literature, imagination, apocalyptic social and political change. Even common things and common people evoke those same feelings: Blake's children, Wordworth's leech-gatherer and idiot boy, Shelley's passion for the commoners of Ireland. On the other hand, the Romantics felt intensely what they called the sublime (anything characterized by grandeur or inspiring awe). Yet, neither they nor we are satisfied by any of these things, which are often the very things evoking the stab of desire Lewis calls Joy.

A distinctive of the Romantic spirit is the search for both a moral guide *in* nature and a sense of belonging *to* nature.[6] Wordsworth, like Lewis after him, observed that a stab of desire came unbidden at moments throughout life. It came through any number of objects—nature, people, events of his youth— but he could not tell when it would come nor could he make it come at will. In his masterpiece, *The Prelude*, Wordsworth called such moments "spots of time" (book 12). The day he saw the field of daffodils dancing in the breeze was such a spot of time, recorded in the poem "I Wandered Lonely as a Cloud." At the outset of the poem he is "lonely," but by the end he can affirm, "Then my heart with pleasure fills / And dances *with* the daffodils" (emphasis mine). The middle part of the poem recounts his process of imaginative identification, finding harmony in nature, then joining in the harmony he finds there. The significance of the experience is the healing of the old wound, as Lewis calls it, which opened between us and nature in the Fall. Many of Wordsworth's poems record the same kind of experience, and book 1 of *The Prelude* recounts numerous such episodes.[7]

However, this sense of healing and belonging is an illusion, says Lewis. In "Intimations of Immortality" Wordsworth laments that "there hath past away a glory from the earth"; our very "birth is but a sleep and a forgetting" (lines 17, 58). Though the poem ends in recovering a childlike sense of unity, we know with poignancy that the inevitable follows. In "The Weight of Glory" Lewis quotes Keats, who says we make "the journey homeward to habitual self." "For a few minutes," Lewis continues, "we have had the illusion of belonging to that world" ("Glory" 35). Then we discover that we have been "mere spectators." It is this illusion of belonging that drove all the Romantics to seek, above all else, wholeness and unity. Geoffrey Hartman, following Carlyle, calls it the search for "antiselfconsciousness" (passim). Typically, the attempt is to merge with the object of beauty through which the stab of desire comes. For example, in "Ode to a Nightingale," Keats (or his speaker) yearns to merge with the bird's song, which symbolizes immortality and freedom from humanity's painful lot.

When Lewis labeled himself a Romantic, he did so in reference to the same experience that consumed all the Romantics: the intensity of his desire for something beyond himself that would give his solitary life significance in the wider universe. Lewis, like Shelley, was an avowed atheist until he was nearly thirty. He spent most of his early adult life pursuing the source of this desire he came to call "Joy." The term, adopted from Coleridge and Wordsworth, can be a confusing one. In *Surprised by Joy*—Lewis's spiritual autobiography, which borrows its title from a Wordsworth sonnet—he defines Joy as "an unsatisfied desire which is itself more desirable than any other satisfaction" (17–18). He explains further, "Joy is distinct not only from pleasure in general but even from aesthetic pleasure. It must have the stab, the pang, the inconsolable longing" (72). Lewis says we commonly call this secret desire by many names—like "Nostalgia, Romanticism, and Adolescence"—and thereby think we have understood it ("Glory" 28). The Romantics usually confounded this desire with a longing for beauty. They made the thing through which the longing comes the object of their desire. Keats made of it a literal religion.[8]

In "The Weight of Glory," Lewis confesses to a certain shyness about this desire. He says: "I am trying to rip open the inconsolable secret in each of you. . . . The secret we cannot hide and cannot tell, though we desire to do both. We cannot tell it because it is a desire for something that has never actually appeared in our experience. We cannot hide it because our experience is constantly suggesting it" (28). This desire is "only the scent of a flower we have not found, the echo of a tune we have not heard, news from a country we have never yet visited" (29). Though difficult to explain, this desire, he says, is more desirable than any earthly fulfillment. "We cannot tell each other about it. It is the secret signature of each soul, the incommunicable and unappeasable want, the thing we desired before we met our wives or made our friends or chose our work, and which we shall still desire on our deathbeds, when the mind no longer knows wife or friend or work. While we are, this is. If we lose this, we lose all" (*Pain* 146–47). Lewis complained, along with the Romantics, that he could never recapture Joy when he pursued it. Only when he pursued something else (books, music, nature) did the desire return. But it "vanished" at the "very moment when I could first say *It is*" (*Surprised* 73). When the feeling came to him unexpectedly after a long absence, Lewis remembers, "at once I knew (with fatal knowledge) that to 'have it again' was the supreme and only important object of desire."

In *Till We Have Faces*, the book Lewis judged his best, Joy is the very thing for which Psyche is willing to die, a thing opaque to the rationalistic Orual. Psyche confides in her: "I have always—at least, ever since I can remember—had a kind of longing for death." When Orual misunderstands the desire as unhappiness and sees herself as the cause, Psyche explains:

> Not that kind of longing. It was when I was happiest that I longed most. It was on happy days when we were up there on the hills. . . . Do you remember? The colour and the smell, and looking across at the Grey Mountain in the distance? And because it was so beautiful, it set me longing, always longing. Somewhere else there must be more of it. Everything seemed to be saying, Psyche come! But I couldn't (not yet) come and I didn't know where I was to come to. It almost hurt me. I felt like a bird in a cage when the other birds of its kind are flying home. . . .
> The sweetest thing in all my life has been the longing—to reach the Mountain, to find the place where all the beauty came from— (74–75)

Psyche says it is "not like going, but like going back" to our true home (76). For Wordsworth, Coleridge, and Lewis, the desire pointed ultimately in the direction of heaven as the only possible hope of fulfillment. Even for the other Romantics, who never found that hope, the desire "teased out of thought" and stirred with "intimations of immortality."

Individual Romantic Writers

Blake

In only one place does Lewis speak of William Blake (1757–1827) at any length, his preface to *The Great Divorce*, and that is to refute him. Lewis's very title is intended as a corrective parody of Blake's *The Marriage of Heaven and Hell*, in which Blake maintained, among other outrageous claims, "Sooner murder an infant in its cradle than nurse unacted desires" (Plate 10). In Blake's view, good and evil are opposites that attract and complete; Lewis took the classical view of Augustine that evil is a parasite on good, a perversion of it. Blake postulates that only by a "marriage" of "contraries" can we "progress" toward the reintegrated and prefallen state, claiming in his "prophecy," *Milton*, that the path to hell can also be a road to paradise, "a place where Contraries are equally True" (518). The archetypically evil Weston, in my view, echoes these Blakean sentiments: "*Your* Devil and *your* God . . . are both pictures of the same Force" (*Perelandra* 93).[9] Lewis paraphrases Blake's "belief that reality never presents us with an absolutely unavoidable 'either-or' "

207

(*Divorce* 5), countering that "evil can be undone, but it cannot 'develop' into good. . . . If we insist on keeping Hell (or even earth) we shall not see Heaven: if we accept Heaven we shall not be able to retain even the smallest and most intimate souvenirs of Hell" (6).

As is the case with all of the Romantics, Lewis also finds things to praise in Blake. The most substantial statements are the following two. In *The Personal Heresy*, his protracted debate with E. M. W. Tillyard, Lewis finds "abundantly in Blake" (and others, pre-eminently MacDonald) "a new and nameless sensation, or even a new sense, to enrich me with the experience which nothing in my previous life had prepared me for" (102–03). In other words, Blake aroused in him a rich sense of the "other." Secondly, in the last book Lewis wrote, the posthumously published *Letters to Malcolm: Chiefly on Prayer*, speaking of the importance of not falsifying our prayers by limiting our mental images or metaphors, Lewis suggests that we "must do as Blake would do with a joy; kiss it as it flies" (86). Readers for two centuries have joined Lewis in relishing the spontaneous joy represented in poems like Blake's *Songs of Innocence*.

Wordsworth

Though he wrote no essay specifically on him, Lewis mentions William Wordsworth (1770–1850) in his writing at large more often than any other Romantic writer. That Wordsworth's works were among those of greater importance to Lewis is easy to demonstrate. He wrote to his brother Warnie in 1928 that he did not expect to discover any other long poems in English that would become a part of his "permanent stock." Here he puts *The Prelude* on his short list of long poems, including *The Faerie Queene, Paradise Lost, The Ring and the Book, Earthly Paradise*, and "a few others" (*Letters* 129). Warnie took the hint and followed Lewis's lead, writing in his diary toward the end of his life, "Today I finished *The Prelude* for the fifth time since I first read it twenty eight years ago at J's [Jack's] instigation. . . . Certainly the most unequalled of any of the first rank poets we have produced" (296).

Perhaps Lewis's closest female friend before meeting Joy Gresham was the poet Ruth Pitter, to whom he writes, "I'm re-reading the *Prelude*. Always just a little better than one remembers from the last reading, I think" (Letter to Pitter #22). He later mentions a volume of her poems written after her conversion, exclaiming his praise that she has, unlike Wordsworth, written even better after the event. "I had feared that you might be one of those who, like poor Wordsworth, leave their talent behind at conversion: and now—oh glory—you come up shining out of the frost far better than you were before" (#60).

On the other hand, Lewis calls Wordsworth "the romantic who made a good end," that is, he became a Christian: something far more important in Lewis's view than writing well ("Literature" 9).

The year before Lewis died, *The Christian Century* (6 June 1962) asked him what ten books "did most to shape your vocational attitude and your philosophy of life?" The first five books on his list are all imaginative works: MacDonald's *Phantastes*, Chesterton's *The Everlasting Man*, Virgil's *The Aeneid*, Herbert's *The Temple*, and Wordsworth's *The Prelude*. It is hard to imagine Lewis giving *The Prelude* higher praise.

Because of Lewis's appreciation for Wordsworth and other Romantics, some have made Lewis a Romantic pure and simple. A. N. Wilson, the most controversial of Lewis's biographers,[10] labels him "a Romantic egoist in the tradition of Wordsworth and Yeats," all of whom "make themselves and their own sensations the subject of their work" (291). He adds, condescendingly,

> A taste for Lewis is, in large part, a taste for reading about him. Though it was denied him to become a great poet, he shares with 'the last Romantics' a vivid awareness of his own consciousness, a sense that the chief end of writing is to communicate sensation and experience. A high proportion of Lewis's *oeuvre* when properly considered can be found to be of the same kind as Wordsworth's *Prelude*, a book which was always very dear to him. (290)

The statement that Lewis wrote "to communicate sensation and experience" contains a kernel of truth. As we shall see in the section devoted to "Romantic Critical Theory," Lewis did write about his experiences as a reader in an effort to help us, with him, "taste" literature sensitively and fully. What he attempts is no idiosyncratically personal reading, however, but a genuine approximation of a text's broad and resonant meaning. We may all taste pineapples with subtle differences, but we can agree in distinguishing their peculiarities from other fruits.

Most importantly, Lewis, while often sublime (as Wilson allows), is not of the "egotistical sublime" that Keats distinguishes; i.e., Lewis is not the "subject of [his] work." According to Wilson, a "failure" to understand Lewis as the "subject of [his] work" results in "two of the grosser extremes": seeing Lewis as a "*poseur*" or a "holy" man. Wilson's characterizations do little justice to the man himself (291–92). A more accurate view is expressed by Scott Oury, who claims that Lewis the reader was consistently focused outside of himself on "the object itself" (2). "To C. S. Lewis, the very idea of 'the thing itself' assumed as its starting point something real *out there* with qualities that belong to it or inhere. . . . It excludes only those qualities that one encountering 'the object' *adds* to it—in short, the projections of one's own makeup upon 'the object'" (3). Speaking of novels and narrative poems, Lewis says, "[t]hey are

209

complex and carefully made objects. Attention to the very objects they are is our first step. To value them chiefly for reflections which they may suggest to us or morals we may draw from them, is a flagrant instance of 'using' instead of 'receiving'" (*Experiment* 82–83). This self-effacing attitude to the world and to works of art is far from Wordsworthian.

Ruby Dunlap believes that a person who spent a lifetime studying Lewis for the purpose of finding him in his work would not find Lewis at all but discover "in the end that what mattered to Lewis was that Lewis didn't matter, that Lewis consistently, determinedly, directly or indirectly, points us to his Source, his Love, the Ground of his being, He whom Lewis worshipped, He to Whom all glory and credit must be given that such a man as Lewis should exist in the first place." Lewis complained that no one who had tried to guess a biographical source for any of his fictional incidents ever got it right and advised that "it is never safe to attribute a man's imaginations too directly to his experience" (*Sixteenth* 58).

Comparing Wordsworth and Lewis, Daniel Kuhn specifies the differences. While both "knew similar romantic conceptions of the nature of being," they took "rather opposite approaches. Wordsworth's genius awakened to the immanent immediacy of essential being in the universe while Lewis, over a much more circuitous route, realized first the utter transcendence and only later the immanent nature of unconditioned being. They share the experience of being 'surprised by Joy' in their initial awakening to the transcendental mode" (Kuhn 189–90). Lewis began *Surprised* as a verse autobiography, and he shares with Wordsworth the "parallel" theme of what Kuhn calls "an urge for man in his personal being to partake of the divine quality of life" (193). But Wordsworth "sees everything, nature and Spirit, in its bearing upon man and his experience" (203). The result is "a mind" that can "build up greatest things / From least suggestions" that is "made more prompt / To hold fit converse with the spiritual world" (*The Prelude* XIV 101–02, 107–08). This is humanity reaching to God.

210

By contrast, Lewis's books (except two of poetry) were all written after the hints of Joy had led him to a belief in a transcendent God who reaches down to humanity, who reveals himself in both general (natural) and special (scriptural) revelation. In his nonfiction books, Lewis approached the physical universe from above, having begun with God; Wordsworth, beginning from nature, approached God from below. But readers of Lewis's fictional books will begin as he and Wordsworth did, from below, taking the inductive hints from human experience and using them as signposts to God. Doris Myers illustrates this idea. In Narnia, the children are "surprised by Joy" in the same way Wordsworth and Lewis were; in that place where their hearts' desires are met, and they commune with Nature without obstruction, as symbolized by their talk with the animals (129). Myers sees the whole series as unfolding around the theme of Joy. The first three Chronicles deal with the "nature of Joy and the search for it." *The Lion, the Witch and the Wardrobe* elicits the "early emotional response toward mythical beings" that parallels Lewis's own early experience of Joy. *The Voyage of the Dawn Treader* moves from Joy to hungering for the realm Joy hints at (Meyers 126–27). Unlike the Wordsworthian experience, which can be maddeningly vague and inconclusive, one feels with Lewis that the journey is leading somewhere definite. His theology gives his fiction both coherence and point.

Corbin Carnell says Lewis is far from being *like* Wordsworth, the quintessential Romantic. In fact, he sees Lewis's treatment of "romantic longing" as the "death-blow to Romanticism, . . . for once the Romantic Way is viewed as one of the roads to Byzantium (and often a long way round), the traveler must inevitably ask himself: why not take the direct route of Christian mysticism?" (*Bright* 10, 147). Having found the pursuit of Joy to be fruitless, since it stands as only a "signpost" on the way to heaven, Lewis came to seek the destination itself. Does this move result in a devaluing of nature and art? Not at all, explains Carnell. It is a central paradox of Christianity that in loving God most, secondary things can be loved more because they are loved truly and suffused by the greater love of God and can be valued as works of God. We don't cease to love a painting because we have come to love the painter. Carnell notes well the paradox, "One cannot simply *use* Creation; we are too much a part of it. This is the difficult task: to know that Romantic art is often a reflection of man's longing for God and yet still to respect and cherish it as art" (146–47). As Lewis rightly observes, it is those who love heaven who love earth most.

In writing of his own mistakes about Joy, Lewis implicates Wordsworth, too. He admits to thinking that the experience points to a possible possession, thinking that Joy could dwell "in the temple I had built him; not knowing that he cares only for temples building and not at all for temples built. Wordsworth, I believe, made this mistake all his life" (*Surprised* 167). There are both possible benefits and dangers in following Wordsworth. Speaking of the transition from pantheism to theism, Lewis says:

> For some souls I believe, for my own I remember, Wordsworthian contemplation can be the first and lowest form of recognition that there is something outside ourselves which demands reverence. To return to Pantheistic errors about the nature of this something would, for a Christian, be very bad. But once again, for 'the man coming up from below' the Wordsworthian experience is an advance. Even if he goes no further he has escaped the worst arrogance of materialism: if he goes on he will be converted. ("Culture" 22)

Going on is the key. Yet Lewis is not so sanguine about unaided human nature as is Wordsworth. Lewis's views on the perpetually evil bent of human nature are so clear that his critique of Wordsworth on this point is obvious. For Lewis, the only hope was the abandonment of self to the all-consuming love of God in Christ. Radical the malady; radical the cure.

Coleridge

Carnell maintains that Lewis was trying to achieve in his fiction what Samuel Taylor Coleridge (1772–1834) attempted in *Lyrical Ballads*: making the "supernatural seem real" (*Bright* 11). Coleridge attempted to articulate his sense of "the other," the thing that led him and Lewis from naturalism to pantheism to theism and thence to Christianity. Coleridge's poetic output was not large. His reputation rests chiefly on three poems: *The Rime of the Ancient Mariner* and two fragments, "Kubla Khan" and "Christabel."[11] Each has in common an attempt to evoke the spiritual world by using elements in myth as literary symbolism. Lewis contributes to the understanding of Coleridge by showing how and under what conditions mythic elements will work in suggesting "otherness."

In *The Allegory of Love*, Lewis uses the term "Romantic" to describe the sense of "the remote and the mysterious" in Gower's *Confessio Amantis* (Lawlor 122). The work's effectiveness lies in the sense we gain of "the other" or "the numinous" and depends no longer upon our believing in the thing described. If we believed in it, the story would be useless in evoking the unspeakable. Witches may evoke dread if really believed in, but they cannot then evoke something beyond and bigger than themselves, that *nameless* dread we all feel. Such feelings cannot, by definition, attach to images of the known.[12]

This is a key element accounting for the nearly universal appeal of Coleridge's *The Rime of the Ancient Mariner*. Since his fiends are symbolic, works of "the pure imagination," as Coleridge said, they can effectively conjure the unknown spiritual world. The reader experiences what Coleridge calls a "willing suspension of disbelief." The "romantic" can work in the positive direction, too, producing an attraction rather than dread. Keats's poems also work by borrowing heavily on a "dead belief." In his poetry, resurrected Greek mythology soars afresh in the imagination. In "Ode to Psyche" Keats pointedly adopts a goddess too late in the pantheon to be believed. Lewis followed suit in his creative retelling of the Psyche myth in *Till We Have Faces*.

Elsewhere in Coleridge's poems, it is possible to identify expressions of Joy like those Lewis was drawn to in Wordsworth. Both poets were keenly interested in the product of the imaginative interaction with nature that yielded

212

the intuition of both the divine and the harmonious wholeness of creation. Not surprisingly, Wordsworth and Coleridge held corresponding views on the power of the imagination to perform this function.[13] In "Dejection: An Ode," Coleridge refers to Joy as "strong music in the soul" which exists in mystery, though he confidently calls it "This light, this glory, this fair luminous mist, / This beautiful and beauty-making power," which, if captured, could bring about an apocalypse: "Joy, Lady! Is the spirit and the power, / Which wedding Nature to us give in dower / A new Earth and new Heaven." Of course, it cannot be captured, and the resultant *angst* gives Romantic poetry its peculiar poignancy.

Keats

Lewis says less in print about John Keats (1795–1821) than any of the other Romantics. Nevertheless, as with the other Romantics, Lewis finds things to both praise and criticize in his poetry. In a letter to his lifelong friend Arthur Greeves, Lewis criticizes Keats's *Endymion* (1817) for its confusion and shallowness. Lewis cites Keats's age and suspects that the root problem is his "lack of spiritual experience." In referring to Joy or longing, Lewis says that though he sees Keats "hunting for 'it' and longing and wandering," he believes Keats "has, as yet, no real idea of what it wd. be if [he] found it" (*Stand* 429). That he liked Keats's work (remembering that *Endymion* is a very early poem) is clear. After criticizing Keats's failure to successfully depict romantic love, he says: "It is horrible to use such words of Keats, but I think he would be the first to agree." We find in Keats, pre-eminently among the Romantics, an exuberance in the world of the senses. As in Keats's poems, so with Lewis's prose works, we not only see, but hear, feel, and taste them.

Shelley

A notable curiosity is that The Kilns, Lewis's Oxford home for thirty years, has a connection with Percy Bysshe Shelley (1792–1822). Lewis's brother Warnie writes in his diary for 2 November 1930: "I hear this week end that our lake has quite distinguished literary associations, being known locally as 'Shelley's pool' and there is a tradition that Shelley used to meditate there" (W. H. Lewis 72). The Lewis brothers loved it and swam there often. And Warnie thinks of Shelley when he has his own experience of Joy, probably because Jack taught him to. While waiting for a communion service at St. Cross, he "had one of those blinding flashes of exquisite happiness which come and go like lightening [*sic*]. Always a mysterious thing, and must I think be a direct individual intimation of heavenly bliss—and a strong hint to strive for it. I suppose this was Shelley's 'spirit of delight'" (223–24). The desire to "strive for it" is a common thread in Lewis's writing and in the writing of the Romantics.

Shelley responded to Joy with the same intensity. His term "Intellectual Beauty" approximates Lewis's Joy. When it goes, as it always does, he feels the same compulsion to have it back that both Lewis brothers had. Shelley said, "I vowed that I would dedicate my powers / To thee" ("Hymn to Intellectual Beauty" 61–62). And when the momentary "shadow of some unseen Power" leaves him, he asks, "where art thou gone? / Why dost thou pass away and leave our state, / This dim vast vale of tears, vacant and desolate?" (15–17). Like Lewis, Wordsworth, and Coleridge, Shelley also associates the experience with the eternal and immortal: the transient intimations

> like clouds depart
> And come, for some uncertain moments lent.
> Man were immortal, and omnipotent,
> Didst thou, unknown and awful as thou art,
> Keep with thy glorious train firm state within his heart. (37–41)

Lewis's 1924 poem "Joy" is surprisingly close to many points in Shelley's "Hymn to Intellectual Beauty." First, there is the sense that if the state Lewis calls Joy and Shelley calls "Intellectual Beauty" could last, the one receiving this visitation would be immortal: "I boasted that this mood could never die, / ... Rapture will not stay / Longer than this, lest mortals grow divine" (11, 50); that a personal regeneration would take place—"Here the new life begins . . ." (12); and, finally, that the source of the visitation (at the time the pieces were written) is unknowable—"She has no answer to our questioning, / And ease to pain and truth to one who seeks / I know she never brought and cannot bring" (31, *Collected Poems* 243–44). Like Lewis, Shelley had his first experience of Joy when a boy. He sought to reclaim it through religious experience, both traditional and occult, but he too found her a coy mistress.

This connection with Joy is Lewis's closest point of affinity with the Romantics and the reason he identified with them by so designating himself. However, we have a greater scope of opinion from Lewis in the case of Shelley, one that allows us to move from inference to explicit views on Shelley's literary work. Those views come from an essay entitled "Shelley, Dryden, and Mr Eliot," in which Lewis assesses Shelley's faults and strengths, which poems he likes and dislikes and why, and characterizes Shelley's uniqueness.

Lewis faults Shelley for metrical lapses from "ignoble fluidity" to "jingle," his political thought, and his idealism about the perfectibility of human nature ("Shelley" 187). He sees almost nothing redeeming in the *Revolt of Islam*, *Letter to Maria Gisborne*, and his satire on Wordsworth, *Peter Bell the Third* (202).

Epipsychidion he rates "rather low" because it is philosophically and theo-logically flawed in commending a kind of Platonic love that "does not exist," but he praises its "great energy and sensibility" (203).

Countering many of the prejudices against Shelley, Lewis praises him (by comparison with Dryden, greatest of the Restoration poets) generally for "the greatness of his subjects," "moral elevation," the "unity of his actions," "archi-tectonic power," decorum (fitness of subject to style and genre), and disci-plined composition (194). Lewis also traces Shelley's connections to the clas-sical authors like Plato, Aristotle, Aeschylus, and Dante in defending him from charges of "Godwinian" silliness. And some of his themes, like that of the apoc-alyptic regeneration of all creation in *Prometheus Unbound*, owe a great deal to biblical sources.

On one point, Lewis gives Shelley credit for his insight, matching that of the apostle Paul, into the natural and universal depravity of humanity. The crucial difference is that Paul knew what to do about it, Shelley did not—a fact that explains in great part the despair that dogged the end of his short life. On the notion of humanity's *potential* for goodness (as opposed to our actual record of evil), the rejection of God and revelation regarding humanity and human history, and the resultant idea that the human race will progress, Lewis finds Shelley too simplistic: Where did evil come from? What of history? In another essay Lewis warns against putting our faith in this excessive Roman-tic trust of human nature:

> One of the most dangerous errors instilled into us by nineteenth-century pro-gressive optimism is the idea that civilization is automatically found to increase and spread. The lesson of history is the opposite; civilization is a rarity, attained with difficulty and easily lost. The normal state of humanity is barbarism, just as the normal surface of our planet is salt water. Land looms large in our imagina-tion of the planet and civilization in our history books, only because sea and sav-agery are, to us, less interesting. ("Syllabus" 82–83)

As a maker of myth and as a craftsman, however, Shelley receives highest praise. Lewis says of *Alastor* that it is "a poem perfectly true to itself" ("Shel-ley" 199). Further, it has "the energy of imagination, which supports so lofty, remote, and lonely an emotion almost without a false note for seven hundred lines." It "deserves to be admired" (200). In *The Witch of Atlas*, "the lightness and liquidity of this piece, the sensation which we feel in reading it of seeing things distinctly, yet at a vast distance, cannot be paralleled in any poem that I know. We must go to another art, namely to music, to find anything at all similar; and there we shall hardly find it outside Mozart." In *Adonais*, Shel-ley's pastoral elegy on Keats, Lewis acknowledges his "artistry, the discipline and power of obedience which makes genius universal" (201). The *Triumph of Life*, which was unfinished at Shelley's death, Lewis extols for having the

215

"air and fire" of Dante that makes us "imagine while we are reading him that we have somehow left our bodies behind" (204).

The highest praise of all of Shelley's work Lewis reserves for *Prometheus Unbound*, calling it "the greatest long poem in the nineteenth century, and the only long poem of the highest kind in that century which approaches to perfection" (205). He praises the great theme of "rebirth" and the mythic quality in its penetration of human nature, especially humanity's depravity and need of redemption; he also admires its structuring, which presents dramatically the rejuvenation of the soul. He praises, in this regard, Shelley's choice to embody love in the character of Asia, who must make the classic "descent into hell" before joining the suffering Prometheus to bring him freedom from the self-imprisonment of hatred. In this, Shelley feels more keenly than any other poet "the necessity for a complete unmaking and remaking of man" (207).

Of the fourth act, Lewis says, "It is an intoxication, a riot, a complicated and uncontrollable splendour, long, and yet not too long, sustained on the note of ecstasy such as no other English poet, perhaps no other poet, has given us. It can be achieved by more than one artist in music; to do it in words has been, I think, beyond the reach of nearly all" (208). Joe Christopher draws a parallel between what Shelley attempts here and Lewis in *Perelandra*:

> No one would argue that the liturgical praises of Maleldil that pass into the vision of the Great Dance in the last chapter of *Perelandra* are at Shelley's level as Lewis perceives it; but surely Lewis is attempting something of the same type in his prose. The plot does not call for the vision, but the vision illumines that type of mystical knowledge that resistance to sin has allowed. (96)

Lewis will not allow that Shelley is greater than either Milton or Dante. No small part of the preference is that "there is one Way, and only one," which Milton and Dante testify to and which Shelley, as an avowed atheist, eschewed. Like Samuel Johnson, a favorite to whom he is often compared in his evaluation of literature, Lewis never disallows the moral question. He will acknowledge artistic achievement whatever the theme, but is also ready to point out that something may be more dangerous by being more effective.[14] If Lewis's high praise for several of Shelley's poems is surprising, his opinion of Shelley's life is not. In discussing heroes in *The Personal Heresy*, Lewis remarks:

216

> If there lives any man so destitute of all traditions human and divine and so unfortunate in his acquaintance that he can find no better example among the living or the dead than Shelley or Baudelaire, I no more blame him for following them than we blame a castaway on an island for making shift to use a pen-knife as a saw. But my pity will not induce me to say that pen-knives are made for sawing. (98–99)

Byron

Lewis has almost as little to say about George Gordon, Lord Byron (1788–1824), as Keats, but as with the others, we find him speaking his mind and, like a compass needle seeking north, finding hints of Joy. Lewis did not like *Childe Harold's Pilgrimage*, the work which made Byron famous overnight. In a letter to Ruth Pitter, Lewis mentions a book she and Barfield had recommended to him, but Lewis finds himself "to be no more able to read it than I can read *Childe Harold*" (#54). He would not have liked its absorption in self, especially its self-pitying hero. But he liked *Don Juan* ("Shelley" 193), the work our age has judged Byron's masterpiece. It is a rollicking satire, sometimes bawdy, but Lewis was not squeamish about how he took his humor—only let it have gusto, and in Byron there is no want of it.

In addition to the humor, Lewis—who loved playing Scrabble in all known languages simultaneously—would have relished the sheer inventiveness of Byron's wordplay. What is often called Byron's urbanity, Lewis would condemn as worldliness and cynicism. On the other hand, I think he would have allowed some of Byron's claim for *Don Juan* as a moral book, though not perhaps as Byron intended. Behind every joke is a solemn truth; behind every satire a standard. Beneath all the human frailty and perversity of his characters is an awareness of the good and true. The morality which inheres in creation Byron could not escape. In life, having denied himself no pleasure, he found nothing that pleased. Screwtape's scheme had worked on him to a tee: "ever increasing craving for an ever diminishing pleasure is the formula" (54). Lewis recalls: "As Byron had said, there is no sterner moralist than pleasure"; the enjoyment passes away, engendering a longing for its source and for its permanence ("Morris" 225).

Byron's *angst* or melancholy may be the darker expression of the kind of longing for unity and contact with the transcendent and real that engendered optimism in Wordsworth. Differences in personality and experience could account for the differences in response. Byron had a powerful sense of the ideal but distrusted human nature too much to expect our ever achieving it. When there is a gap between the real and the ideal, as Leslie Marchand observes, one way Byron copes is to satirize the real for not living up to the ideal (6–7). Byron's poetry is yet another kind of response to the visitation of Joy.

217

Sir Walter Scott

Lewis originally gave his essay "Sir Walter Scott" to the Sir Walter Scott Club of Edinburgh, a city which raised a conspicuous monument in Princes Park to honor Scott. Lewis takes the occasion to talk about what constitutes "serious literature," observing that, as with Cervantes, Chaucer, and Dickens, art is sometimes best when it is "play" to its author. Scott was not a "serious" artist in the modern sense, because, as Lewis notes, "there is little sign, even in his best days, of a serious and costly determination to make each novel as good in its own kind as he could make it." He quotes Scott himself as saying, "I think it is the publick [*sic*] that are mad for passing these two volumes [*Castle Dangerous* and *Count Robert of Paris*]. But I will not be the first to cry them down" ("Scott" 214). Lewis acknowledges the artistic faults, but sees Scott's desire to write what will sell in order to pay off his debts as being more honest and having a higher claim than "artistic integrity." Art, in other words, is not the highest good. Here, too, Lewis sides with Samuel Johnson on morality in art. Art is what Lewis calls "a second thing," and second things put first always go bad.

Among Scott's faults, Lewis cites a "flaccid" narrative and descriptive style, a penchant for the polysyllabic, minor historical flaws, and notes that his journal has a more sensitive style than his novels. Lewis praises Scott for his "sense" and "proportion." Unlike writers in our own age, Scott is given neither to exaggeration nor to creating overblown characters or events. His other strengths include his gift for concrete dialogue and "jauntiness," but his unique contribution is historical thinking, a thing absent in Shakespeare and Chaucer. With great wit and aphoristic power Scott's novels "almost created that historical sense which we now all take for granted, and by which we often condemn Scott himself" (216). He created our sense of historical period, Lewis adds, "for good or ill." Ever iconoclastic on historical matters, Lewis acknowledges that finite human minds need categories and generalizations like historical periods, but also laments the oversimplifications which inevitably result.

Romantic Critical Theory

In light of this undying quest for Joy and stress on the imagination, should we consider Lewis a Romantic literary critic? Others have noticed his assertion that reason is the organ of understanding and imagination the organ of meaning, and that Lewis's thought squares with Coleridge's on the role of humans as (to borrow Tolkien's term) subcreators imitating God.[15] In these he is at one with the Romantics. Adding to these observations, I wish to trace a connection I have not seen discussed elsewhere, and that is the link between Lewis and the Romantic prose writer, William Hazlitt, and Keats, whom Hazlitt greatly influenced. Lewis's view, radically expressed for its day in *An Experiment in Criticism*, is that we should judge literature, not by artificial canons of taste, but by what it does to and for us, what kind of readers it makes of us.[16] By exploring this connection, I will try to show how Lewis's approach is both similar to and distinct from Romantic literary criticism.

At one time or another, all the Romantic poets both wallowed in and longed for an escape from self. For Lewis, literature provided not only an escape from self, but also a return. This paradoxical result of finding oneself by losing oneself comes when we approach literature as a means of seeing with eyes other than our own. To do this, we must "receive" literature, take it on the terms it establishes, not on our own preconceived terms. As a consequence, we discover in a good book something unique, which may be relished for its blessed otherness. Jerry Daniel calls it "Lewis's love of the essence. . . . Just as he immersed himself in the quality of the world around him, he immersed himself in the quality of a story or a poem he was reading" (10). The movement outside the self and immersion into others leads finally to an "enlargement," and not a diminishment, of the self (*Experiment* 138–41).

One of Lewis's most common metaphors for the uniqueness experienced in a good book is the physical sense of taste. Using Charles Williams as an example, Lewis says that "*Taliessin* is like the pineapple. You may like or dislike that taste; but once you have tasted it, you know you can get it from no other book in the whole world" ("Review" 250). In his comments on books, then, he so often attempts to give a taste, sending us to the original for ourselves, if we like the appetizer.

This is precisely what Hazlitt does. First, he chooses a work for comment because it has, in his term, "gusto," which he defines as a "power or passion" in art (641). He continues, "There is hardly any object entirely devoid of expression, without some character of power belonging to it, some precise association with pleasure or pain. And it is in giving this truth of character from the truth of feeling, whether in the highest or the lowest degree (but always in the highest degree of which the subject is capable), that gusto consists" (641). Hazlitt then gives several examples from art and literature. Of the painter Titian, for instance, he claims that his flesh is "as different from that of other painters, as the skin is from a piece of white or red drapery thrown over it. The blood circulates here and there, the blue veins just appear, the rest is distinguished throughout only by that sort of tingling sensation to the eye, which the body feels within itself. This is gusto" (641).

From attending Hazlitt's London lectures, Keats adopted a similar method of responding to both nature and art. His idea of "negative capability," or going out of oneself to enter into the essence of something else, is owing to Hazlitt (Abrams 831). In a famous example, Keats says, "if a Sparrow came before my Window I take part in its existence [*sic*] and pick about the Gravel" (830). In a letter to his friend Richard Woodhouse, Keats contrasts himself with Wordsworth and uses Hazlitt's very term, "gusto":

> As to the poetical Character itself, (I mean that sort of which, if I am any thing, I am a Member; that sort distinguished from the wordsworthian [*sic*] or egotistical sublime; which is a thing per se and stands alone) it is not itself—it has no self—it is every thing and nothing—It has no character—it enjoys light and shade; it lives in gusto, be it foul or fair, high or low, rich or poor, mean or elevated—It has as much delight in conceiving an Iago as an Imogen. (836)

Lewis himself uses Hazlitt's term "gusto" to describe the exuberance of Sir Walter Scott, calling it his "greatest permanent attraction" ("Scott" 212). One soon discovers in Lewis this same catholicity of taste, a zest for life in its fullness, and a love of each thing for its distinctness, from all kinds of weather to all kinds of books. His criticism, like Hazlitt's and Keats's, reflects his sense of gusto in the original. The idea is so foundational to Lewis's thinking about reading that he introduces it in the first chapter of *Experiment*. In playing games as in reading, Lewis says that a person must have "genuine gust." To do the one for exercise and good health or the other for "self-improvement" or culture is, in both cases, to make self the center. That is, "both treat as a means something which must, while you play or read it, be accepted for it own sake" (*Experiment* 9). He elaborates that "the true reader reads every work seriously in the sense that he reads it whole-heartedly, makes himself as receptive as he can. But for that very reason he cannot possibly read every work solemnly or gravely. . . . What is meant lightly he will take lightly; what is meant gravely, gravely" (11). Reading with "gust" is an act of humility, of submission to the work, for the sake of its quiddity. So, in a sense, Lewis *is* a Romantic literary critic.

In many respects, however, Lewis's literary criticism is at the far pole from the Romantics. Although he acknowledged with Coleridge and others the mysterious origins of poetic inspiration and with Blake would say "didactic poetry is my abhorrence," he had none of Blake's hubris ("I must make my own system or be enslaved by another's"). Lewis eschewed Wordsworth's self-referential bent and his notion of poetry as common language. Neither would he admit Keats's dictum, "I am certain of nothing but of the holiness of the Heart's affections and the truth of the Imagination," nor abide Shelley's hollow vaunt that "Poets are the unacknowledged legislators of the world." Lewis would not have liked the prophetic overtones in Keats's "axiom" that "if poetry comes not as naturally as the Leaves to a tree it had better not come at all" (Abrams 1266) or Keats's claim to Shelley, "my Imagination is a Monastry [*sic*] and I am its Monk." In his thinking about poetic composition, he was closer to Pope and Johnson and the eighteenth-century notion of the poet as craftsman. Lewis writes, "Poetry is an art or skill—a trained habit of using certain instruments to certain ends. This platitude is no longer unnecessary; it has been becoming obscured ever since the great romantic critics diverted our attention from the fruitful question, 'What kind of composition is a poem?' to the barren question, 'What kind of man is a poet?'" (*Heresy* 103).

More than any other element, Lewis is averse to the egoism that taints the Romantic view of literature. For example, Wordsworth, in his egalitarianism, distinguishes a poet from "other men" by claiming superiority in "tenderness," "enthusiasm," and "sensibility" (preface to *Lyrical Ballads*, Abrams 147). Lewis shows that even among contemporary poets, many lack these and other laudable human qualities. He wants nothing to do with "romantic critics" who see poets as "a separate race of great souls or *mahatmas*" (*Heresy* 104). No, a poet is "a man who can invent stories . . . with a taste for words" and has undertaken the necessary discipline to perfect his craft. He wants none of the religious aura that came from the romantic view of poets as "spiritual supermen." Lewis admonishes us to "praise the art and show charity to the men." Poets "are not great souls. Wash their feet, and I will praise your humility: sit at their feet, and you will be a fool" (106). In this sense, Lewis is clearly *not* a Romantic literary critic.

Lewis's Critique of Romanticism

We conclude with the most useful aspect of Lewis's writing for our subject. Though Lewis writes little on the Romantics, he writes much on Romanticism as Joy, both the turn of mind that distinguishes the Romantic engagement of reality and the values that emerge as a result. It may be useful to think again of our opening paradox, Lewis's apparent love-hate attitude toward Romanticism. As he sees it, in pursuing Romanticism, glories and advantages exist side by side with dangers and delusions. Coming as he did from atheistic, philosophical materialism to belief in a transcendent God, Lewis found the Romantics to be important in weaning him from mere nature to that which was behind it. Lewis reflects in *Surprised by Joy* on the time when he was struggling to reject God and discovered that "the only non-Christians who seem to me really to know anything were the Romantics; and a good many of them were dangerously tinged with something like religion, even at times with Christianity" (214).

Lewis shared with the Romantics, in part learned from them, a conviction that the rationalistic, scientific approach to life, unaided by the imaginative and spiritual, would result in incalculable evil. In Lewis we find a full prose

221

treatment of this idea in *The Abolition of Man*, the character Weston in *Perelandra*, and the lengthy fictional portrayals in the members of the N.I.C.E. in *That Hideous Strength*. In these worlds, the philosophers and scientists bring civilization to the brink of collapse. In *Till We Have Faces*, we see it in the rationalistic Greek tutor, the Fox, and in an internalized struggle as Orual battles the positive pull of the spiritual, represented by Psyche. Of course, it was not science as such to which Lewis and the Romantics objected. Blake, Wordsworth, and especially Coleridge and Shelley were all steeped in formal philosophy, while Wordsworth, Coleridge, and Shelley were all keenly interested in natural science (Shelley nearly blew himself up once with an experiment). Rather, they objected to the encroachment of the scientific method into realms belonging rightly to the metaphysical, whose truths are grasped only by means of the metaphoric and imaginative.

Blake castigates legalistic thought in his poem "London" as "mind-forg'd manacles" that produce the "dark, Satanic Mills" of the Industrial Revolution in his poem *Milton*. Wordsworth, clearly more to Lewis's taste, also decries "Our meddling intellect," warning, "We murder to dissect," by which he means to analyze or take apart, rather than seeing the meaning of the whole (Abrams 136). The Romantics were no more anti-scientific than they were anti-intellectual, but they all knew that the most important issues of life were inaccessible to the scientific method. Shelley says in his *Defence of Poetry*, "Poetry is indeed something divine. It is at once the centre and circumference of knowledge; it is that which comprehends all science, and that to which all science must be referred" (Abrams 1763). Shelley's stress on imagination and metaphor ("poetry") is not a bad reminder for an age as enamored of technology as ours.

Lewis agrees with the Romantics that the highest truths, the spiritual, can be expressed only imaginatively, through metaphor. "The very essence of our life as conscious beings, all day and every day, consists of something which cannot be communicated except by hints, similes, metaphors, and the use of those emotions (themselves not very important) which are pointers to it" ("Language" 140). In discussing the value and necessity of poetic language for expressing what is beyond our experience, Lewis turns naturally to the Romantics. Regarding Wordsworth and Shelley he says, "This is the most remarkable of the powers of Poetic language: to convey to us the quality of experiences which we have not had, or perhaps can never have, to use factors within our experience so that they become pointers to something outside our experience" ("Language" 133). Far from being "an optional thing which poets" use as "decoration," metaphor is our only way of talking "about things which are not perceived by the senses" (*Miracles* 72). Christian doctrines of the supernatural "not only cannot be asserted—they cannot even be presented for discussion—without metaphor. We can make our speech duller; we cannot make it more literal" (79).

But one can err in the opposite direction, too, and the Romantics did. They were all, especially in their youth, radical in virtually every area: politics, religion, morals, and literature. These excesses explain why Goethe concluded, "Classicism is health, Romanticism sickness." Lewis walked the same path of Joy or longing as the Romantics and even shared their religious extremes (including years of atheism). He knew the allure, danger, and benefit of the thing variously called Romanticism, Joy, and longing—but, for Lewis, it was a necessary part of, a divine earnest toward, the path to truth.

Notes

1. In illustration of the Romantic appeal of distance, Lewis says of the Castlereagh Hills of Belfast, "they taught me longing—*Sehnsucht*; made me for good or ill, and before I was six years old, a votary of the Blue Flower" (*Surprised* 7). Calling himself a "votary of the Blue Flower" is another way of saying he is a Romantic. The Blue Flower image became a symbol of Romanticism from Novalis's use of it in his unfinished novel, *Heinrich von Ofterdingen*, where it is the flower of miracle and fortune. (This was brought to my attention by Jerry Root.)

2. A longer study or one that emphasized Joy less would also include a systematic study of Lewis's views on nature and imagination compared to the Romantics. These topics may be easily surveyed in *The Quotable Lewis* or referenced in *The C. S. Lewis Index*.

3. See, for example, the recent discussion on the definition, contribution, and dangers of Romanticism by Netland and Lundin in "Christianity and Romanticism," *Christian Scholar's Review*, 25:3, March 1996.

4. Though these dates are among the commonly chosen, there are other possibilities, like the publication of *Lyrical Ballads* by Wordsworth and Coleridge in 1798 for the opening, and the death of Coleridge in 1834 for the close. When referring to the Romantics in this chapter, I have in mind chiefly the six major poets of the period: William Blake, William Wordsworth, Samuel Taylor Coleridge, John Keats, Percy Shelley, George Gordon Lord Byron; the novelists Mary Shelley and Sir Walter Scott; and their contemporaries. Jane Austen is often included among the novelists of the period, but is treated in this book with eighteenth-century writers. The term "Romantics" in this chapter generally refers to this group and their circles.

5. In "Our English Syllabus," Lewis expresses his belief that teachers should not be needed for reading contemporary writers; anyone should know the thought of one's own time well enough. The purpose of a tutor was to supply what had been lost to modern thinking from the past but recovered by the scholar's habitual reading in the period in question.

> We naturally wish to help the students in studying those parts of the subject where we have the most help to give and they need help most. On recent and contemporary literature their need is least and our help least. They ought to understand it better than us. . . . There is an intrinsic absurdity in making current literature a subject of academic study, and the student who wants a tutor's assistance in reading the works of his own contemporaries might as well ask for a nurse's assistance in blowing his own nose. ("Syllabus" 91)

223

In determining where to draw the line on what gets excluded as "contemporary," Lewis, himself born in the nineteenth century, argues for a very large slice off the recent past: "We begin then by cutting off a hundred, or two hundred, or any reasonable number of years from this end, and still we have too much left." So for Lewis, the English syllabus (that which should be studied in school) ended with the eighteenth century. His reason for cutting so deeply into this side of the historical loaf is that "things are understood by what precedes them rather than by what follows them" (91). We don't need the later periods to understand the earlier.

6. See Wasserman.

7. For a reading of Wordsworth's best-known poems as attempts to solve the alienation problem, see Durrant.

8. For more information, see Sharp.

9. For an interpretation of Blake as a Christian poet (a minority view), see Malcom Muggeridge's video commentary *The Third Testament*, Time Life Films, 1976. Interpretations of Blake are diverse, to say the least, and Lewis himself demurs in his preface to *The Great Divorce*.

10. For more, see my review of Wilson's book (see Works Cited).

11. However, with others, Walter Jackson Bate argues in *Coleridge* that "Kubla Khan" is not a fragment and that Coleridge's story of the poem's genesis is a fiction.

12. In "Christianity and Culture," Lewis suggests that such an evocation of otherness is one of the essences of Romanticism, which he sums up as "either the enjoyment of nature (ranging from pantheistic mysticism at one end of the scale to mere innocent sensuousness at the other) or else the indulgence of *Sehnsucht* awakened by the past, the distant, and the imagined, but not believed, supernatural" (16).

13. We know that the two poets had a symbiotic relationship for several years during their most creative periods. For example, Coleridge's "Dejection: An Ode" was composed after hearing Wordsworth read the opening stanzas of "Ode: Intimations of Immortality" and was intentionally published on Wordsworth's wedding day (and the seventh anniversary of Coleridge's own failed marriage to Sara Fricker). He addressed an early version to Wordsworth, though the final version is directed to Sara Hutchinson.

14. So in his essay on "William Morris" (whom he also termed "romantic"), Lewis praises Morris for knowing that the "great use of the idyllic in literature" is "to find and illustrate the good" (227).

15. See Coleridge's famous treatment of this idea in his *Biographia Literaria*, chapter 13, and Tolkien's "On Fairy Stories."

16. See also Lewis's essay "On Stories" (*Stories* 3–20).

224

Works Cited

Abrams, M. H., et al., eds. *The Norton Anthology of English Literature: The Major Authors*. 6th ed. New York: Norton, 1996.

Bate, Walter Jackson. *Coleridge*. New York: Macmillan, 1968.

Blake, William. *Blake: Complete Writings*. Ed. Geoffrey Keynes. London: Oxford UP, 1969.

Carnell, Corbin Scott. *Bright Shadow of Reality: C. S. Lewis and the Feeling Intellect*. Grand Rapids: Eerdmans, 1974.

———. "The Dialectic of Desire: C. S. Lewis's Interpretation of *Sehnsucht*." Diss. U of Florida, 1960.

Christopher, Joe R. *C. S. Lewis*. Boston: Twayne, 1987.

Daniel, Jerry L. "The Taste of the Pineapple: A Basis for Literary Criticism." *The Taste of the Pineapple: Essays on C. S. Lewis as Reader, Critic, and Imaginative Writer.* Ed. Bruce L. Edwards. Bowling Green, OH: Bowling Green State U Popular Press, 1988. 9–27.

Dunlap, Ruby. "Literary Criticism." Cited 2 Aug 1997. MereLewis list on listserv@listserv.aol.com.

Durrant, Geoffrey. *William Wordsworth.* Cambridge: Cambridge UP, 1969.

Gleckner, Robert F., and Gerald E. Enscoe, eds. *Romanticism: Points of View.* 2nd ed. Englewood Cliffs, NJ: Prentice-Hall, 1970.

Goffar, Janine. *The C. S. Lewis Index: A Comprehensive Guide to Lewis's Writings and Ideas.* Wheaton: Crossway, 1998.

Hartman, Geoffrey H. "Romanticism and Antiself-consciousness." Gleckner and Enscoe 286–97.

Hazlitt, William. "On Gusto." *Romanticism: An Anthology.* Ed. Duncan Wu. Oxford: Blackwell, 1994. 641–43.

Kuhn, Daniel K. "The Joy of the Absolute: A Comparative Study of the Romantic Visions of William Wordsworth and C. S. Lewis." *Imagination and the Spirit: Essays in Literature and the Christian Faith Presented to Clyde S. Kilby.* Ed. Charles A. Huttar. Grand Rapids: Eerdmans, 1971. 189–214.

Lawlor, John. "On Romanticism in the 'Confessio Amantis.'" *Patterns of Love and Courtesy: Essays in Memory of C. S. Lewis.* Ed. John Lawlor. Evanston: Northwestern UP, 1966. 122–40.

Lewis, C. S. "Christianity and Culture." *Reflections* 12–36 .

———. "Christianity and Literature." *Reflections* 1–11.

———. *Christian Reflections.* Ed. Walter Hooper. 1967. Grand Rapids: Eerdmans, 1980.

———. *The Collected Poems of C. S. Lewis.* Ed. Walter Hooper. London: HarperCollins, 1994.

———. *English Literature in the Sixteenth Century Excluding Drama.* 1954. Oxford: Oxford UP. 1973.

———. *An Experiment in Criticism.* Cambridge: Cambridge UP, 1961.

———. *The Great Divorce.* New York: Macmillan, 1946.

———. "The Language of Religion." *Reflections* 129–41.

———. *Letters of C. S. Lewis.* Ed. W. H. Lewis. 1966. New York: Harcourt, 1975.

———. *Letters to Malcom: Chiefly on Prayer.* New York: Harcourt, 1963.

———. Letter to Ruth Pitter. Feb. 12, 1947, #22; Dec. 29, 1951, #54; and May 12, 1953, #60.

———. *Miracles: A Preliminary Study.* 1947. New York: Macmillan, 1960.

———. *"On Stories" and Other Essays on Literature.* Ed. Walter Hooper. New York: Harcourt Brace Jovanovich, 1982.

———. "Our English Syllabus." *Rehabilitations and Other Essays.* New York: Oxford UP, 1939. 81–93.

———. *Perelandra.* New York: Macmillan, 1943.

———. *The Pilgrim's Regress: An Allegorical Apology for Christianity, Reason and Romanticism.* 1933. 3rd ed. Grand Rapids: Eerdmans, 1943.

———. *The Problem of Pain.* 1940. New York: Macmillan, 1962.

———. "Review of *Taliessin Through Logres.*" *Oxford Magazine* 64 (14 March 1946): 248–50.

———. *The Screwtape Letters.* Grand Rapids: Revell, 1976.

———. *Selected Literary Essays.* 1969. Ed. Walter Hooper. Cambridge: Cambridge UP, 1980.

———. "Shelley, Dryden, and Mr Eliot." *Literary* 187–208.

———. "Sir Walter Scott." *Literary* 209–18.

———. *Surprised by Joy: The Shape of My Early Life.* New York: Harcourt, 1955.

———. *They Stand Together: The Letters of C. S. Lewis to Arthur Greeves (1914–1963)*. Ed. Walter Hooper. New York: Macmillan, 1979.

———. *Till We Have Faces: A Myth Retold*. 1956. New York: Harcourt, Brace, 1984.

———. "The Weight of Glory." *The Weight of Glory and Other Addresses*. Ed. Walter Hooper. New York: Simon and Schuster, 1996. 25–40.

———. "William Morris." *Literary* 219–31.

———, and E. M. W. Tillyard. *The Personal Heresy: A Controversy*. 1939. London: Oxford UP, 1965.

Lewis, Warren H. *Brothers and Friends: The Diaries of Major Warren Hamilton Lewis*. Ed. Clyde S. Kilby and Marjorie Lamp Mead. New York: Harper, 1982.

Marchand, Leslie A. *Byron's Poetry: A Critical Introduction*. Cambridge, MA: Harvard UP, 1968.

Martindale, Wayne. Review of *C. S. Lewis: A Biography*, by A. N. Wilson. *Touchstone* 4.1 (1990): 39–42.

———, and Jerry Root, eds. *The Quotable Lewis*. Wheaton: Tyndale, 1989.

Mason, Michael, ed. *William Blake*. Oxford: Oxford UP, 1988.

Myers, Doris. *C. S. Lewis in Context*. Kent, OH: Kent State UP, 1994.

Oury, Scott. " 'The Thing Itself': C. S. Lewis and the Value of Something Other." *The Longing for a Form: Essays on the Fiction of C. S. Lewis*. Ed. Peter J. Schakel. Kent, OH: Kent State UP, 1977. 1–19.

Sharp, Ronald S. *Keats, Skepticism, and the Religion of Beauty*. Athens: U of Georgia P, 1979.

Tolkein, J. R. R. "On Fairy Stories." *Essays Presented to Charles Williams*. Ed. C. S. Lewis. 1947. Grand Rapids: Eerdmans, 1966. 38–39.

Wasserman, Earl. "The English Romantics: The Grounds of Knowledge." Gleckner and Enscoe 331–46.

Wilson, A. N. *C. S. Lewis: A Biography*. New York: Norton, 1990.

12
Victorians

Kate Durie

Introduction: The Problems

There are two problems in surveying Lewis's treatment of Victorian writers. The first lies in the nature of the sources available. Lewis was not a Victorian specialist, and wrote only two essays dealing with Victorian writers, both of whom are to some extent peripheral to the main area of study. Most of the references to the field are scattered; some are used as examples or quotations in essays and books on other literary subjects. They are usually fairly brief, although they offer a fleeting glimpse of the way Lewis's mind traversed the terrain. Other references are diffused through his letters to his father, his brother, assorted friends, and especially his best friend, Arthur Greeves. These comments are lively, opinionated, quirky and—perhaps an advantage to those whose cultural background is not as extensive as Lewis's own—do not always assume prior knowledge of the texts. Often they have an introductory or explanatory edge.

Extracts from the letters, however, need to be treated with caution; an example will indicate the reason. Lewis comments to Arthur Greeves on *The Tenant of Wildfell Hall* in the following terms: "In spite of some excellent passages it is a bad book. People who have been brought up as gentlemen don't even when drunk, fight and beat their wives in their hostesse's drawing room. It is all very melodramatic & gives you the impression of being written by a lady's maid" (*Stand* 172). These are the reactions of a very young Lewis, indeed little more than an adolescent, with small experience of the world;

the precocity of his literary taste and the confidence of his judgments are often deceptive insofar as they carry a kind of assurance that outruns the experience which might validate it. The snobbery and class-consciousness here compound the problem; but comments in a personal letter often and pleasurably deviate from the norms of measured evaluation which published criticism would demand. It is unlikely that Lewis's high praise for Hawthorne would conclude in the academic arena as it does in the letter: "What a pity such a genius should be a beastly American" (153). There is in effect a trade; the letters have an immediate, spontaneous, highly individual quality of response, but they are neither developed nor defended as an academic article would be. Additionally, the bulk of the Greeves letters date from Lewis's early life; although he clearly reread many of the books he discusses in them, only rarely are second thoughts and later judgments given. Sometimes he changed his mind; sometimes he did not. Almost the first of the letters to Greeves reports on reading the romances of William Morris, and *Shirley* by Charlotte Brontë. Lewis was, in different ways, enthusiastic about each, but whereas the substance of his judgment of Morris remained a constant throughout his life, elaborated only in sophistication and depth, his view of *Shirley* had altered by 1945. It is consistent with earlier thoughts only in his liking for the character of the eponymous heroine; by the later date he was harshly critical of the absurd and unsatisfactory devices of dialogue, rhetoric, and narrative technique.

The second problem is located in Lewis's assessment of the period. Its dominant form was the realist novel—a form for which Lewis had only a limited sympathy and liking; George Watson has said that Lewis read the great realists with a more than tolerant affection, and this is true. Real enthusiasm, however, lay elsewhere; although he read with appreciation all the great names, what he enjoyed most was a diet of Morris, Kipling, MacDonald, Rider Haggard, Beatrix Potter, E. Nesbit, and Kenneth Grahame. Simply to list these appetites suggests that Lewis lacked some relish for the age. Here we encounter a paradox. John Wain has claimed that Lewis was quintessentially an Edwardian, whose tastes were those of that period (and for that reason I have included authors like Kipling who produced a substantial body of work before the outbreak of war in 1914). Yet Lewis, as a don in the English school at Oxford, was instrumental in removing from the compulsory syllabus texts written after 1830; he thought any educated human being would read by choice extensively in the period, but that no serious student of English should study it. Why not? He believed that students did not and should not need help with these texts in the way in which they did medieval or Renaissance ones. More than that, as his inaugural lecture at Cambridge showed, he felt a deep disquiet about the nineteenth century. The lecture argues that there is a great gulf fixed—of consciousness and sensibility—between the age when Scott and Austen wrote

228

and the modern age. This gulf reflects changes consequent on the birth of the machine, and the loss of a superstructure of belief. There is little real sense of where the Victorians figure in this account, except that they are obviously on the wrong side of the divide. Lewis's medieval training made him a systematist; the Victorian period is not tidy. The very qualities that excite many Victorian enthusiasts—the period's stretching of norms, the shaking of the foundations of both religious belief and personal morality, the fertility of experiment, the extremes of post-Romantic exuberance and despair, appall Lewis. A self-proclaimed dinosaur, he took pleasure in asserting pugnaciously that his allegiances lay elsewhere, although he drew from the period and was nourished by it. So an overview of the Victorian literary scene must be constructed warily. Lewis's comments on fiction will be surveyed first, next those on poetry, and then a brief view of other works. After that, an appendix must be added on the nature of the gaps.

Fiction: Overview

Lewis liked long books, and the Victorian novel is particularly rich in this field; what then did he assume students and book lovers should read? Dickens is an obvious choice, although in making it at that time Lewis was to some extent going against the grain of Leavisite criticism. Although he was negative about the faults of style, he felt Dickens's novels belonged in the category of momentous books; Lewis always liked best the Dickens he had read most recently, but confessed that overall he would put *Bleak House* at the top of the list for sheer prodigality of invention, a judgment with which many contemporary critics would concur. He also recommended *Little Dorrit, The Old Curiosity Shop*, which was "homely and friendly" (*Stand* 480), and *The Pickwick Papers*, but with reservations, disliking the jokes but liking the "festive and friendly" world with its "charm of goodness—the goodness of Pickwick himself, and Wardle and both Wellers" (*Stand* 446). As a young man Lewis liked George Eliot; he enjoyed *Adam Bede*, but later criticized the happy ending, found *The Mill on the Floss* better, and responded seriously and thoughtfully to her best novel, *Middlemarch* (although he was repelled somewhat—a fairly common reaction—by Dorothea's eventual marriage to Ladislaw). He praised Eliot for her understanding of so many different kinds of life, and for her humor. *Romola*, Eliot's historical novel, was the kind of leisurely, old-fashioned read he found soothing, and he was struck by its insights into the ease with which a human being (Tito) can slide into corruption and moral decay; but the history, he said, was over-researched, and the morality unduly ponderous.

Lewis often bracketed together Trollope and Thackeray for the purposes of comparison. He argued that Thackeray was the greater genius and had a more extensive range, but that his personal preference lay with Trollope, who wrote the better books. Of Trollope he had certainly read *The Warden, Barchester Towers, Dr. Thorne,* and *The Last Chronicles of Barset,* as well as *The Belton Estate* and *The Small House at Allington.* Thackeray seemed to compel his reluctant attention and even admiration in a different way; he commented particularly on *Pendennis,* tiring of its episodic nature and the hero's cycles of misbehaviour and repentance, and *The History of Henry Esmond.* A fuller consideration of these will be offered in due course. Other major authors highlighted, albeit often briefly, are all the Brontës, where greatest praise is reserved for *Wuthering Heights* (which, however, he misnames) because of the "excellent stroke of art to tell it all through the mouth of a very homely, prosaic old servant, whose sanity and mother-wit thus provides a cooling medium through which the wild, horrible story becomes tolerable" (*Stand* 436). Lewis also read Wilkie Collins with pleasure, and with antagonism *The Egoist* by George Meredith, which he nevertheless pronounced to be "a rare instance of the conception being so good that even the fantastic faults can't kill it" (*Letters* 313). He always had a soft spot for Stevenson, both the adventure stories and *Dr Jekyll and Mr Hyde,* which he saw as having mythical qualities.

Poetry: Overview

It appears the poetry of the Victorian period offered relatively little deep and lasting satisfaction to Lewis. References to Browning are few and disparaging; Tennyson he knew well and occasionally quoted, but expressed little enthusiasm for him. While he thought *In Memoriam* very good, he found it unsatisfactory because of "a sorrow neither being transmuted, nor ending in tragedy, but just petering out" (*Letters* 364). Swinburne was attractive to the youthful reader, but these feelings seem not to have stood the test of time. Three poets are consistently highly rated by Lewis: Arnold, Patmore, and Kipling. All of them are associated in his mind with some notion of what the "real thing" in poetry is. The story that Lewis once challenged an Australian student of his to a duel (with a pair of broadswords left conveniently around) for his refusal to admire *Sohrab and Rustum* is well known; whether it is true or not, Lewis certainly loved the poem for its irony and pathos, "seen with a double vision at once Homeric and Victorian, blended with his own sad lucidity, filled with the charm of strange, remote places; it is a very complex poem" (*"Audiendis"* 10). He saw it as a poem that envelopes you "till you tremble and grow hot and cold like a lover" ("Different Tastes" 156). A passionate response is also elicited by Patmore, at least partly for his subject matter, which treats of divine and human love, but also for the brilliance of individual lines. Kipling, whose reputation was already secure for his stories, is esteemed as much for his poems: "I know hardly any other poet who can deliver such a *hammer-stroke*" (*Letters* 332). Lewis tells of an evening in Balliol College when one of the dons read a Swinburne ballad followed by Kipling's "Heriot's Ford," a pastiche medieval ballad with cracking dialogue, powerful narrative concerned with justice, revenge, death, and intense emotion. Only Lewis among the listeners recognized it as Kipling, but all agreed that it killed Swinburne "as a real thing kills a sham" (*Letters* 331). Lewis then proposed that the company should be treated to "Iron, Cold Iron" and "McAndrew's Hymn"; the reader today who wants to follow Lewis's tastes in Victorian poetry, and to see what he saw in it, might well choose to start here.

Other Works

There are of course many works in the period that fit into neither of these categories. Lewis read Newman, Pater, and Carlyle—the heavyweight sages—and just as readily Carroll, Nesbit, Grahame, and Potter. One's sense of the period is stretched by the breadth of his interests. Morris's prose romances scarcely seem to fit with the realist novel, but they absorbed so much of Lewis's mental and emotional energy that they will require their own treatment elsewhere in this chapter. Yet whereas Lewis spends time in commenting on a writer like Kinglake, whose *Eothen* is an early and delightful example of a travel book, he entirely omits to deal with many authors who would seem to be crucial to the period. This does not mean that he had not read them, but again emphasizes the difficulty in using him as a guide. He applauds Gaskell for *The Life of Charlotte Bronte*, and he likes *Cranford*, but her substantial novels are not mentioned. Hardy, according to A. J. P. Taylor, was disapproved of by Lewis, though he seems to have made an exception of the realistic treatment of the rustics, and neither that novelist nor Henry James, "that phantasmal man," really figure. One is left perplexed and empty-handed when one seeks Lewis's evaluation of Hopkins or Christina Rossetti or Barrett Browning.

231

Lessons in Discriminating Reading

By now it should be clear that Lewis's underlinings in the period follow his own rather eccentric tastes and interests, but in general veer away from some aspects of realism, and from many of the names one might expect to find in poetry. Nevertheless, there are several skills in which he is expert and which he can readily communicate to those who take him as a mentor. First, he teaches—and this is never wasted—how to read with discrimination, and how to read attentively, actively distinguishing between weak and strong features of a text. Throughout his life Lewis possessed an exceptional eye for a telling, startling scene, and an acute ear for a line that suddenly quivers into life. For instance, he uses a scene from *Little Dorrit* when he is explaining that the novel differs from romance because it must account for an image naturalistically:

> ... the final horror of the whole nightmare in which Affery has been living comes when she creeps downstairs to see what her terrible husband Flintwinch is doing—and sees two Flintwinches, a waking Flintwinch and a sleeping Flintwinch, exactly alike. Since the story is a novel, this terrific image has of course to be explained away by some nonsense about a long-lost twin brother. (*Spenser's* 118)

This both renders the reader alert to a moment of great intensity, and encourages a wider perspective, in which we begin to question the ways in which the novel—unlike Spenserian allegory where duplication is possible—has to work hard and uneasily to explain something which is psychologically apt. In a similar way, Lewis is quick to diagnose flaws, to locate the point at which the novelist fails the reader by breaking the contract; puzzling over why, despite liking the Wellers and the trial, he feels *The Pickwick Papers* will not pass muster, Lewis senses that his own discomfort centers on Jingle in prison. He argues that a comic rogue should not suffer the consequences that in real life would follow his actions, but that the forgiveness of comedy rather than the strict veracity of realism should apply. "To invite us to treat Jingle as a comic character and then spring the tragic side on us, is a mere act of bad faith" (*Letters* 264). Lewis claims that this punishes the reader unjustly; our expectations of the genre have led us to categorize and respond to a comic character as just that. Suddenly we are left struggling with both a tragic and a real-life dimension for which we are unprepared. In fact Lewis is always good when suggesting what kind of novels Dickens wrote; here he instructs his brother on how to read *Martin Chuzzlewit*:

> ... get rid of all idea of realism—as much as in approaching William Morris or the music hall. In fact I should say he is the good thing of which the grand Xmas panto. is the degeneration and abuse: broadly typical sentiment, only rarely intolerable if taken in a jolly after dinner pantomime mood, and broadly effective "comics": only all done by a genius, so that they become mythological.... (*Letters* 245–46)

While this is no more adequate as a summary of Dickens's style than any other five-line comment, the reader who is ignorant of Dickens will instantly get a clue as to how to read the novels; the reader who knows them already is challenged and extended by the notion of pantomime-becoming-mythology. Lewis also suggests how to compose a general picture of the unpleasant young men in Dickens and Thackeray; he concludes that we often experience a sense of decline as the novel progresses, and attributes this both to the excellence with which many authors, writing in the first person, write about childhood, and to Victorian scruples about the depiction of sexuality. Therefore, failures in chastity are represented by substitutes, "less probable and (to me) more repellent sins" (*Letters* 370). Always we find the same blend of engagement and distance; Lewis surveys his own pleasure in a character, and uses this response to distinguish between character and point of view in *Barchester Towers*: "When I read about Mrs Proudie I am not in the least interested in seeing the world from her point of view, for her point of view is not interesting; what does interest me is precisely the sort of person she was" ("Hamlet" 101). He constantly reminds us that we are not to be so drawn into a novel that we forfeit our objectivity, for it is that which enables us to go beyond sympathy and form mature moral judgments.

While there are far fewer insights into poetry, those comments on *The Angel in the House* by Patmore, "really great within his own limited sphere," are illuminating in terms of showing exactly what moved Lewis so much about the poem:

> Do you remember the comparison of the naturally virtuous person who receives grace at conversion to a man walking along and suddenly hearing a band playing, and then "His step unchanged, he steps in time". Or on the poignancy of spring, "With it the blackbird breaks the young day's heart". Or the lightening [*sic*] during a storm at sea which reveals "The deeps / *Standing* about in stony heaps". That is sheer genius. (*Letters* 320)

This makes it easy for the reader to understand something about how a sharp, apt image works, or the way in which a single word can carry poetic and emotional freight, or how the lyrical impulse works. Although Lewis says little more than—in effect—"Just listen," it could be seen as a valuable part of the building of a discerning response, and perhaps a corrective to the kind of teaching of literature which endows students with a sophisticated technical vocabulary, without teaching them to see details or hear a cadence.

Reading for Pleasure

Another emphasis to be found in Lewis's writings is how to read for pleasure and from pleasure; in an essay, "High and Low Brows," he insists on a the-

233

ory of literature that will include *The Tale of Peter Rabbit*. The division of books into categories like good and bad, momentous and trivial, aesthetic and entertaining will not do. Rider Haggard's *She* cannot simply be described as a good "bad" book; it must instead be seen as a book which is both good and bad. The novels of Rider Haggard were among Lewis's favorite leisure reading; he had an absolute relish for them, and praises the opening of the narrative, "What story in the world opens better than *She*?" ("Gift" 128), with its approach across vast tracts of time and space, the quest motifs, and its morally convincing goodness and badness. Even so, he censures the novel for its banal and imprecise style, and for the unconvincing philosophizing of the eponymous heroine; "If she was really Wisdom's daughter, she did not take after her parent" (130). It is liberating to discover that the canon is subverted; Lewis gives us permission to read where we find enjoyment, as long as we bring the same critical principles to bear. That said, Lewis does indulge in special pleading and overstatement; the reader may well wish to rejoin that many stories in the world open better than *She*. The friends of Lewis knew that he often talked for victory; there is a kind of mischievous determination to see how far an argument can be pushed, and sometimes that note can be detected in his criticism. The proper reaction is to follow one's own genuine and whole-hearted responses to a work with the qualities Lewis teaches—enthusiasm, scholarship, and acumen—rather than slavishly ape his taste.

Another advantage of examples taken from Rider Haggard and Kenneth Grahame is that such works are accessible and widely known; Lewis demystifies the study of literature, insisting that any theory which operates only in relation to elitist texts is inadequate. Here he is expounding what might broadly be termed atmosphere, but which more accurately is that special place in which the physical landscape of a book and its unique emotional quality come together; he says *King Solomon's Mines* is not important for excitement:

... but for a sense of the quality of the danger; and this quality is something indefinable. To speak of the tons of rock between the *treasure* chamber and the outside world, of the Hall of the Dead with its petrified corpses all round you, and of the huge door of rock that nips and crushes Gagool, is only to make vague verbal gestures in its direction. Similarly, we can say that we go back to *The Wind in the Willows* for a sense of the sinister mounting unfriendliness of the Wild Wood, and of its sheer contrast with the homeliness of Badger's House. But to say that is to fail to communicate something in itself quite precise and definite. (*Spenser's* 114)

It is refreshing to meet this refusal to be abashed, to play the academic game of one-upmanship, in a book on Spenser. Lewis only read Grahame for the first time when he was in his twenties, which might be a part of his lack of embarrassment in championing it; but a part of his creed, in all his writings, is trying to find common ground with the reader, so that he can start off from something the reader already knows. Not that he oversimplifies Grahame; he has read Jung, and knows that the fairy tale liberates *Archetypes*. He also recognizes how characters function as an index to English social history and the class system, as well as being a "hieroglyphic which conveys psychology" ("On Three Ways" 62). Mr. Toad fuses a real animal's face with a particular kind of foolish and vain human face, and from that accidental resemblance, Grahame forges a character, the literary antecedent of which is a Jonsonian humor. This is typical of the way in which Lewis fizzes with ideas, establishes connections, and manages to amuse and educate at the same time; through it all the enjoyment he feels, and which he expects the reader to echo, is the lure that leads us to understand the wider picture.

Pleasure and the Unfashionable: Morris and Kipling

The two essays Lewis wrote on Victorian writers, Morris and Kipling, illustrate the same kind of thinking. The Morris essay shows Lewis demonstrating how to read the romances evocatively and against the grain of literary fashion. Morris was not in vogue when Lewis wrote, and despite the Morris centenary recently, he is still relatively neglected as a writer (his contributions to the Arts and Crafts movement, design, and socialist thought have perhaps received more attention). To be unfashionable is of course a recommendation as far as Lewis is concerned; but in his attempts to rehabilitate Morris, he perhaps goes too far. In 1919 he gave a paper on Morris to the Martlets, an Oxford literary society, in which he claimed him as a storyteller second only to Homer, and as a writer of lyrics which were the most original contribution to the period's poetry. The Martlets were unconvinced. The essay is more moderate; it is weakest when defending Morris against the charge of artificial language. Lewis claims that all language in longer works is artificial, and that Morris's style is characterized by matter-of-factness, generalities (like Johnson), deliberate plainness, and a few archaic words. A reading of such romances as *The Glittering Plain*, though, might suggest that this is an overstatement, another example of Lewisian special pleading; one sample of Morris's style can be taken from the opening of *The Wood beyond the World*:

> Now ye may well deem that such a youngling as this was looked upon by all as a lucky man without a lack; but there was this flaw in his lot, whereas he had fallen

235

into the toils of love of a woman exceeding fair, and had taken her to wife, she
nought unwilling as it seemed. . . . (1)

While it is not obscure, it is convoluted and the archaism more pronounced
than Lewis allows; but then, he tends to overplay his hand when one of his
heart's-core writers is at stake. Yet at the same time, Lewis evokes very well
some of the oppositions in Morris: with a subtlety of analysis he couples
together the idyllic aspects and the need for these to be rooted in and to return
to community. He is always interested in complexity, even in conflicting tendencies, and carefully draws together—without false reconciliation—the poet
and the socialist, the anti-romantic and the eroticist, and the pagan and the
prophet. If the essay as a whole does not always carry conviction, it suggests
distinctions and directions in a very few pages, which go a long way in unfolding Morris to the reader.

A variation on this technique, introductory and seeking the large view
of the subject, is found in the essay on Kipling; above all, Lewis shows how
to read with clarifying simplicity. The difference is that here Lewis does not
have the same impassioned involvement, lifelong and formative of personality, that he has with Morris. He sees Kipling as both intensely loved
and hated, and speaks of his own ambivalence and fluctuations between
delight and revulsion. The major stylistic flaw is excessive compression;
Kipling polishes and prunes until he has left no spaciousness, but instead
"we are bombarded with felicities till they deafen us. There is no elbow
room, no leisureliness" ("Kipling's" 233). But where Lewis offers the reader
one single, strong guideline into Kipling is in his discernment of Kipling as
the poet of work, a subject largely omitted from eighteenth- and nineteenth-
century literatures, and one which restores a whole range of emotions that
occupy humanity. If the essential needs of the species—clothing, food, shel-
ter—are to be met, says Lewis, then Kipling alone realizes that there must
be a "vast legion of hard-bitten, technically efficient, not-over-sympathetic
men" (235). To acknowledge this is not to defend the system, least of all the
machinery of imperialism itself, because Kipling is wise enough to know
the frustrations of bureaucracy and has a deep concern and admiration for
other ranks. Lewis thus gives the reader a central idea, clear, accessible, and
sympathetic, as a way of approaching Kipling; while the essay is concen-
trated and tightly written, it still finds the time to hint at other aspects of
the author who had an "almost quivering tenderness—he himself had been
badly hurt—when he writes of children or for them" (249). It also maintains
a sharp critical focus on Kipling the moralist. Lewis is suspicious of the lack
of ends in Kipling's gospel of work; the job is to be done, but to what purpose? An emptiness at the core of Kipling's writing—whether due to frivolity or skepticism—is set before us; characteristically, Lewis straightfor-

wardly answers the question he assumes any intending reader would want to ask: why read this author? Both this essay and the one on Morris act to whet the appetite, to introduce without patronizing, and to offer a perspective within which further exploration can take place; they seek to determine the essence of a writer, and in identifying the yearning of one, and the work ethic of the other, they also say something significant about the age from which they are drawn.

Moral, Ethical, and Theological Concerns

No one who has read much of Lewis will be surprised at the close relationship between his literary criticism and his moral, ethical, and theological concerns; he had no time for literature as an end in itself. Like Samuel Johnson, whom he so much admired, he believed that the purpose of writing was to enable the reader better to enjoy life or to endure it. Many ideas which are developed at length elsewhere first germinate in perceptions of literature. For example, the Kipling essay observes: "What he loves better than anything in the world is the intimacy within a closed circle—even if it be only a circle of shared misery" (245). The discussion which arises from this is also found in a fuller and more universally applicable form in the essay entitled "The Inner Ring," in which the desire to belong to a group and to leave others out in the cold is anatomized. This essay in turn looks back to Victorian literature for raw material: "Victorian fiction is full of characters who are hag-ridden by the desire to get inside that particular Ring which is, or was, called Society" (*Screwtape Proposes a Toast* 32). Lewis's primary aim is to identify how the desperation to be accepted within a closed circle, with its air of exclusivity and secret intimacy, can sap moral integrity and independent habits of thought; what the literary essay and the ethical one have in common is a preoccupation with worldliness.

Worldliness is worth pursuing, although other forms of evil are occasionally also targeted by Lewis as a result of his Victorian reading. Lewis uses Becky Sharp in *Vanity Fair* as an example of the evil in the inner self; and he reports, on glancing through Housman's *A Shropshire Lad* for the hundredth time, in 1929: "What a terrible little book it is—perfect and deadly, the beauty of the gorgon" (*Stand* 312). As he does not expand on this deadliness, it is impossible to be sure what is meant; the comment is clearly strongly felt, and could indicate the book's homoerotic content, or its pessimism and morbidity. However, the Flesh and the Devil never occupy Lewis to the same extent as the World. All his liking for Trollope does not counterweigh the moral flaw he scrutinizes in *The Belton Estate*: "this bit of uncharitableness

237

and that bit of unconscious cynicism, and throughout, the bottomless world-liness (not knowing itself for such)" (*Stand* 398). Worldliness not only does not know itself; Thackeray, who most enrages and engages Lewis's moral imagination, unwittingly reveals another area of shortfall: "He is the voice of 'the World'. And his supposedly 'good' women are revolting: jealous *phar-isiennes*. The publicans and sinners will go in before Mrs Pendennis and La. Castlewood" (*Letters* 437).

The real failure brought about by worldliness, it seems, is its incapacity to distinguish between the humility of true goodness and manipulative hypocrisy. These female characters, deprived of inner life and self-awareness, stand as models of sanctity, but we see them as self-righteous and self-seeking. We learn more about Thackeray, and about how Lewis perceives goodness, as he explores the theme further:

> ... all his "good" people are not only simple but simpletons. That is a subtle poison wh. comes in with the Renaissance: the Machiavellian (intelligent) villain presently producing the idiot hero. The Middle Ages didn't make Herod clever and their devil was an ass. There is really an un-faith about Thackeray's ethics: as if goodness were somehow charming & ... infantile. No conception that the purification of the will ... leads to the enlightenment of the intelligence. (*Letters* 437)

Goodness, then, depends on the systematic and intelligent application of the will; it is not an instinctive response or natural impulse, but is something to be worked at obediently and thoughtfully. As such it is a tough and a maturing discipline.

Unsurprisingly, the Victorian novelist who would probably come closest to embodying this definition (although Lewis had reservations, as noted before) was George Eliot. Lewis agreed with Dom Bede Griffiths in calling Dorothea Brooke a saint *manquée*, adding "nothing is more pathetic than the potential holiness in [the] quality of the devotion which actually wrecks itself on Casaubon" (*Letters* 336). Eliot's emphasis on the duty which transforms emotion, and Lewis's on the practice of virtue through obedience, which is not unduly concerned with feelings because right feelings will follow right action, clearly have a certain commonality. The nature of the realist novel tends to preclude unmixed descriptions of good or evil in human personality; however, one scene in Thackeray makes Lewis's antennae for evil quiver, and is well worth brief consideration as a way of concluding the theme of good and evil: "There is one v. subordinate scene in *Pendennis* where you meet the Marquis of Steyne and a few of his led captains and pimps in a box at a theatre. It only lasts a page or so—but the sort of rank, salt, urinous stench from the nether pit nearly knocks you down ..." (*Letters* 307). This scene, which is to be found in the fourteenth chapter of the novel, is remarkable, and once more compels us to admire the sensitivity of Lewis's reading. It makes apparent—and the indirectness of treatment only increases the impact and our disquiet—that a rich, powerful man attends the theater in order to prey sexually on young female flesh. His power, and the vulnerability of the dancers, is suggested by their semi-nakedness and by their complicity in their own corruption; they keep their eyes fixed on his box, watching for the applause of his pair of white gloves. Lewis knows that evil lies in the ability to control another human being so completely that the victim acquiesces in her own downfall with little sense of what she has lost; the violator loses as well, of course.

The Nature of Love

Thackeray also provides material for another outworking of Lewis's moral universe; Lewis is very concerned with the nature of love, and it is Thackeray who permits him to identify what happens when love becomes an idol. Reflecting on *The History of Henry Esmond*, he remarks,

> What a detestable woman is Lady Castlewood: and yet I believe Thackeray means us to like her on the ground that all her actions spring from "love". This love is, in his language "pure" i.e. it is not promiscuous or sensual. It is none the less a wholly uncorrected natural passion, idolatrous and insatiable. Was that the great 19th century heresy—that "pure" or "noble" passions didn't need to be crucified and re-born but wd of themselves lead to happiness? Yet one sees it makes Lady C. disastrous both as a wife & a mother and is a source of misery to herself and all whom she meets. (*Letters* 373)

The point being made here is one that we can easily see translated, as a keystone of Lewis's moral philosophy, into examples like several of the characters in *The Great Divorce*, who under the guise of love seek only to control the objects of their devotion. In much the same way, *The Four Loves* is frank about the way in which natural affections can become rivals for the love of God. Perhaps a rather mellower and more pastoral attitude holds sway in that book, for Lewis is at least prepared to acknowledge that natural loves do not merely compete with the love of God, but may in some cases prepare the way for it, acting as a kind of training for the spiritual life.

Inevitably, then, the polar opposite of love as idol is to be found in a mystical image of love as the approach to divine love; this Lewis discovered in Patmore's *The Angel in the House*. The tightness of the poem's form and meter in itself reveals to him a fanatical love of incarnation—presumably because it shows how something infinitely greater chooses the path of con-

239

straint and limitation. The poem tells a story of love leading through courtship to marriage; Lewis finds in it insights into male and female desire, and a championing of romantic love as the route toward God, in preference to asceticism. In 1930, Lewis was imaginatively gripped by all this, but rather puzzled about the problems it raised both in relation to the church's traditional attitude to asceticism and in the implications for single people. Later Charles Williams, another great advocate of romantic love as a part of spiritual ascent, convinced him of the validity of this view; but even at the earlier date Lewis was very moved by what he found "sublime," a delight in the Love which is God. Such glimpses of divine glory are for Lewis the spur to self-knowledge and moral and spiritual improvement; he reports that this poem, along with Morris's *Love Is Enough*, has shown him his own shortcomings, his failures against a real and open generosity of spirit: "I have aimed at too much austerity and even dishonoured love altogether. I have become a dry prig" (*Stand* 366). Lewis believed in the capacity of novels and poems to change us for the best of reasons; they changed him. The growing sense of vulnerability and flexibility learnt from writers like Patmore ultimately led Lewis to defend "the dangers and perturbations of love" (*Loves* 112), even in its most morally disordered forms, against a "self-invited and self-protective lovelessness." Eros has been rehabilitated and is reconciled with Agape.

Desire

Eros is only one part of the wider theme of desire, which dominates so much of Lewis's thinking and which is crucial to his theology; *Surprised by Joy* shows how much of his life revolved around yearning, craving, wanting—experiences which in their very resistance to gratification point to a reality beyond the senses. *Mere Christianity* makes the point in a nutshell: "If I find in myself a desire which no experience in this world can satisfy, the most probable explanation is that I was made for another world" (118). The part played in this process by the works—especially the fantasies—of George MacDonald is well known; but the works of Morris were also formative. Lewis's descriptions of the desire created by and through Morris function both as a diagnosis of how desire works and, for the responsive reader, an evocation of this desire. "No full-grown mind wants optimism or pessimism—philosophies of the nursery where they are not philosophies of the clinic; but to have presented in one vision the ravishing sweetness and the heart-breaking melancholy of our experience, to have shown how the one continually passes over into the other, and to have combined all this with a stirring practical creed" ("Morris" 231). This sentence sets out what almost amounts to a manifesto of the core of Lewis's own artistic and theological creed; we have the emphasis on maturity and flexibility, the insistence that longing is both delightful and agonizing, the need to hold on to both extremes and the exchanges between them, and the grounding of all this in an everyday sense of how to live. Lewis—whose imagination is also much haunted by death—argues that Morris focuses on mortality as a part of a passion for immortality, "as wild, as piercing, as orgiastic and heartbreaking as his presentations of sexual love are simple, sensuous and unimpassioned" ("Morris" 224–25). The mischievous pleasure in inversion and surprise is entirely characteristic of Lewis; however, the difference between Morris's treatment of desire and Lewis's is that the former only very rarely gives any indication of where this desire is pointing. That indication is to be found in *Love Is Enough*, where Lewis discovers the transfiguration of Morris's pagan worth into eternal values, through the power of holiness: "For the first (and last?) time the light of *holiness* shines through Morris's romanticism, not destroying it but perfecting it" (*Stand* 365).

For Lewis himself, there is never any doubt where desire is leading; what he wants is not immortality as an escape from death, nor a deathless world, but the good death that is the entry to bliss where desire is finally and eternally satisfied. This theme runs through the Narnia stories, especially the last, *The Screwtape Letters*, and *Out of the Silent Planet*, where Ransom is taught by his friend, Hyoi, that the numinous is revealed through the proximity of death: "There I drank life because death was in the pool. That was the best of all drinks save one . . . Death itself in the day I drink it and go to Maleldil" (*Planet* 87). The concept of death Lewis had found in Pauline theology and in MacDonald's fantasies finds both emotional harbor and a kind of amplification in Morris. It provides a good example of how Lewis uses literature; it creates responses, which in turn are worked through into fundamental tenets of belief, and which often later express themselves in the creative works. Literature is far more than a vehicle for other concerns; it is a part of the truth, even though the writer may have been unconscious of this, as was Morris: "He is an unwilling witness to the truth. He shows you *just how far* you can go without knowing God, and that is far enough to force you . . . to go further. . . . All he has done is to rouse the desire: but so strongly that you *must* find the real satisfaction. And then you realise that *death* is at the root of the whole matter . . ." (*Stand* 422). The root of the whole matter—death, and with it desire, love, the nature of good and evil—grows in the rich soil of many works of the Victorian period; the flowering for Lewis is prolific, but is found less in his literary criticism than in the apologetic, ethical, and narrative works.

Conclusion

In conclusion, it is necessary to ask why, when Victorian criticism has become a major industry, a reader would choose to browse in Lewis's writings, which are the largely dispersed and fragmentary comments of a nonspecialist in the field, who makes no secret of his lack of sympathy with the era. It is, after all, noticeable that Lewis praises Scott for proportion, "the air of sense" ("Scott" 218), in order to dispraise Dickens and Moore for their want of these qualities; that he distrusts as selfish both the passion for story and the tendency to identify with characters; that he thinks an absolute of literary value is the capacity to express the great myths. If these principles are taken to logical conclusions, the great age of the English novel disappears at a stroke; but then, what is satisfying about Lewis is that his own instinctive and wide-ranging enjoyment so often triumphs over a principle. Good is still good, even if it is of a kind that is not his particular favorite.

For most readers, Lewis's greatest appeal is that he has all the strengths of a first-rate teacher. He has extensive knowledge, worn lightly and transmitted without being patronizing, and he is lucid, especially about the obscure. He is opinionated, but charitable, and often challenges the reader to disagree, or to test whether the thesis will hold water. For instance, although he is right about the nauseating mother worship of Mrs. Pendennis in Thackeray, some readers may feel Lewis could have recognized that Thackeray himself shows a sharp sense of irony about both her ignorance and her harshness to other women. Lewis enjoys revaluation and surprise. One learns not to make easy assumptions about the position he will take up. Although in the main he has no time for feminism, he is capable of a sharp comment that in a Victorian novel written by a man, the heroine must be a fool. Or, long before political correctness, he expresses his discomfort with the racial contempt that Thackeray shows for Costigan, an ignorant Irish character; the source of his comment is Christian respect which must be extended to every individual; but it makes us aware that we often read in ways that are slack, or mindlessly partisan.

In much the same way, he liberates the reader by insisting that it is perfectly respectable—indeed a mark of intellectual integrity—to ignore the literary orthodoxies of the day. With robust common sense, he tells us to read what we like and to trust our own responses; a friend relates that Lewis could relish a single sentence, like the opening of *The Trial* by Charlotte M. Yonge, a novelist whom he liked precisely for her old-fashioned, solid, settled, Christian family sagas. Anything less obviously "clever" or pretentious is hard to imagine. In fact, Lewis loved what he described as "homeliness" in novels, a kind of ordered simplicity and decency. He also fought hard for the value of atmosphere—Blind Pugh tapping with his stick in *Treasure Island,* or the petrified hall of chieftains in *King Solomon's Mines.* He claimed the right for the reader to read excitedly; there is, he says, nothing wrong in reading for excitement, as we read to find out the secret of the mysterious benefactor in *Great Expectations,* as long as we do not read merely for excitement. All of these emphases defend the right of the reader to experience as valid literary responses a whole range of imaginative, emotional, and enthusiastic reactions to books. They encourage readers to trust the real impact a piece has on them, rather than follow the tastes of current fashion; it is a valuable lesson.

Lewis is also preeminent in demonstrating how to perceive telling moments, and how to couple that eye for detail with an overarching sense of a general picture. He is pithy, belligerent, and quite unexpectedly tender in revealing just how much a work has moved him. Literature is read in the pulses as well as with acuity of mind. In all of this he demands that any work offers truth to life, at some level, because literature has a moral and educative function. Good literature leads to good reading, which leads to the good (mature, sensitive, and balanced) person. Lewis offers us his lifetime of experience of good reading to encourage and to stimulate.

These qualities are offered without jargon or excessive doses of literary theory; they seem to arise from a kind of friendship with books which widens to embrace the reader. But does Lewis, then, in this field have a contribution to make to contemporary literary theory? In one sense what is noticeable is that Lewis professes a profound skepticism about the value of literary criticism; he once suggested a ten- or twenty-years abstinence from the reading and writing of evaluative criticism. He did not see criticism as a worthwhile product in itself, and as a scholar, no doubt, he would have been chary about anyone who attempted to measure his contribution to a field in which he operated as an enthusiastic amateur. Yet some critical ideas that can be extrapolated from his work—his keen sense of the limitations of originality, the absence of the author, the valuing of nonsense and myth as opposed to realism—are actively pursued in literary criticism today. His insistence on reading genre was ahead of its time; anyone seeking to encounter the Victorian novel today would have to incorporate that level of thinking. Perhaps most of all Lewis anticipated the redefinition of the canon. His starting point, once more, was the deep distrust of literary fashion: "Tell me the date of your birth and I can make a shrewd guess whether you prefer Hopkins or Housman, Hardy or Lawrence" (*Experiment* 105). Few critics have the honesty to admit the influence of changing tastes; Lewis's near eccentricity in relation to the Victorian period saved him from going out of date, and established a subversion of the canon. He rehabilitates children's literature and popular literature in ways that broaden the canon long before other attempts were made. Readers of the Victorian period who follow Lewis will find their sense

243

of the age extended, their knowledge increased, and their sensitivity enhanced; the faculties of surprise and delight, and quite possibly exasperation, are awakened. In all of this, Lewis simply offers himself as an example; this, he says, is what works for him. The challenge by implication to the reader is: Now go away, and read, enjoy, develop your own eye, enrich your mind and heart, and reach your own conclusions.

Works Cited

Lewis, C. S. "*De Audiendis Poetis*." *Studies in Medieval and Renaissance Literature*. Cambridge: Cambridge UP, 1966. 1–17.

———. "Different Tastes in Literature." *Of This and Other Worlds* 153–61.

———. *An Experiment in Criticism*. Cambridge: Cambridge UP, 1961.

———. *The Four Loves*. London: Geoffry Bles, 1960.

———. *The Great Divorce*. London: Geoffry Bles, 1945.

———. "Hamlet: The Prince or the Poem?" *Literary* 88–105.

———. "Kipling's World." *Literary* 232–50.

———. *Letters of C. S. Lewis*. Ed. W. H. Lewis. 1966. Rev. ed. Ed. Walter Hooper. London: Harper-Collins, 1988.

———. *Mere Christianity*. London: Geoffrey Bles, 1952.

———. "The Mythopoeic Gift of Rider Haggard." *Of This and Other Worlds* 128–32.

———. *Of This and Other Worlds*. Ed. Walter Hooper. London: Fount, 1984.

———. "On Three Ways of Writing for Children." *Of This and Other Worlds* 56–70.

———. *Out of the Silent Planet*. 1938. London: Pan Books, 1952.

———. *Screwtape Proposes a Toast*. Glasgow: Fontana, 1965.

———. *Selected Literary Essays*. Cambridge: Cambridge UP, 1969.

———. "Sir Walter Scott." *Literary* 209–18.

———. *Spenser's Images of Life*. Ed. Alastair Fowler. Cambridge: Cambridge UP, 1967.

———. *They Stand Together: The Letters of C. S. Lewis to Arthur Greeves (1914–1963)*. Ed. Walter Hooper. London: Collins, 1979.

———. "William Morris." *Literary* 219–31.

Morris, William. *The Wood beyond the World*. London: Longmans, 1913.

13

Modern Literature

Joe R. Christopher

An easy statement of C. S. Lewis's relationship to modern literature would be to exclaim that he was conservative and disliked it. There is a element of truth to this—but, when his actual comments are examined, it is an overstatement. Many works he admired.

A clearer way to indicate Lewis's combination of attitudes is to suggest that three processes were going on at the same time: (1) In his young adulthood, when he was planning primarily to be an author—a poet—himself, Lewis read widely in the contemporary literature, although he approved mainly the type of narrative works he wished to write.[1] In later times, involved in his scholarly work, he may not have kept up as much, although what he read sometimes is surprising. (2) Across these contemporary interests runs a strand of moralism, found early and continuing late. This is complicated, however, by a partial separation of artistry from content. Lewis's approach in *An Experiment in Criticism*, for example, means that a reader first considers the art, and only later (if at all) considers the work's philosophical and moral implications (82–86). (3) Typical of many bookish youths, Lewis took his literary standards from his reading of past works; his intelligence also led him to read far beyond the average youth. The materials available to him seem to have been mainly his parents' many books and the volumes in school libraries, none of which were *avant-garde* in taste. Environmental influence should not be pushed too far, of course—Lewis commented that his taste for romantic verse was not shared by his parents (*Surprised* 12–13)—but a conservative literary taste and theory is typical of Lewis.

Also based on his environment as he grew up was a love of nature. This and his conservative attitude explain his comment about English nature poetry beginning in the sixteenth century: ". . . there arose that rural poetry which, descending from the Elizabethans into Milton, Vaughan, and Herrick and then, through poets like Thomson and Cowper, into the Romantics, was never quenched till the nineteen-thirties" (*Sixteenth* 59). This statement seems objective, but implicit is a dislike of the urban imagery of W. H. Auden and his circle. ("Quenched" suggests putting out a pleasant fire.) We see the same view in *The Pilgrim's Regress*, where Lewis's satire of modern poetry includes one character celebrating a motorcycle as a poem (46–47).

With this sensibility, then, Lewis read modern literature. The following survey is divided into three sections: Irish, English, and American writers. Most of the major names are here: Yeats, Shaw, Joyce, Conrad, Woolf, Lawrence, Orwell, James, and Eliot. The Irish names also include James Stephens, usually considered a minor writer but one whose use of Irish myth attracted Lewis; the English names also include Chesterton, and some of Lewis's friends, such as Sayers and Williams—as well as William Golding, whose appearance shows Lewis did not stop reading in the 1930s.

As a scholar of the Middle Ages and Renaissance, Lewis was under no academic obligation to comment on modern literature. Thus what follows here is more a matter of occasional statement, in most cases, than full presentation. No doubt Lewis had read many works that never occasioned any statements. These are simply *some* of the things he would have said about modern literature if he had been discussing it in a tutorial or in a lecture.

Irish Writers

Lewis, being born and raised in Ireland (now Northern Ireland), thought at one time of sending a book of poems to a Dublin press and thus declaring his allegiance with "the Irish school" (*Stand* 195); about the same time, he was planning to read a "nationalist poet," meaning patriotic Irish (185). This does not mean that he commented at length on Irish literature, but certainly he read a number of Ireland's writers. However, he does not mention at all such writers as Elizabeth Bowen, Frank O'Connor, and Flann O'Brien. (Edmund Spenser, an Irish writer of a kind, receives a whole chapter in this book.)

His most interesting comments on William Butler Yeats (1865–1939) occur in a letter to his brother, describing his two meetings with the poet in 1921—but those are personal descriptions, not literary criticism (*Letters* 122–26). A few years later Lewis combined some details of Yeats with some of his foster mother's brother to produce the Master in cantos 6 and 7 of *Dymer* (1926), but the portrait does not involve Yeats's poetry—rather, his occult beliefs.

Lewis had purchased an edition of Yeats's works in 1918 (*Letters* 82–83), and he offers a critical comment, in a letter in 1944, that the early works are "worth twenty of the reconditioned 1920 model" (375); he also praises "the early mythical plays" of Yeats as cleansing the imagination from reading modern journalism (469). The "modernizing" of Yeats's style is usually attributed in part to his friendship with Ezra Pound and is often said to start about 1910–12 (Henn 106), but the publication of the books would be somewhat delayed—and Lewis's 1920 is satisfactory for a round number. In terms of specific works, Lewis reconsiders *The Wanderings of Oisin* (1889)—reconsiders it in 1926—and says he wonders "how I could ever have thought it anything more than mildly pleasant: it is far below [William] Morris" (*Road* 420). He praises *The Countess Cathleen* (1892) for the eeriness of its opening (*Stand* 205); he refers to the "wonderful beauty" of *The Land of Heart's Desire* (1894) (*Road* 15); he comments about "The Two Kings" (in *Responsibilities: Poems and a Play* 1914), only to say that Yeats used "a story I wanted to write on myself," while he considers the poems in that volume "too obscure" (161); he shows knowledge of *Per Amica Silentia Lunae* (1918) (*Stand* 287); and had read "Rosa Alchemica," an early short story (*Surprised* 165). These indications of having read Yeats are not of great critical value in themselves, but they certainly indicate that Lewis liked the earlier works more than the later. What critical comments there are tend to support Lewis's romantic appreciation, with their emphasis on beauty and eeriness. The complaint about the obscurity of some poems may be a foreshadowing of Lewis's later famed clarity—in prose.

Another Irish writer that Lewis read is George Bernard Shaw (1856–1950). In his autobiography, he mentions his early reading of Shaw's works:

> I was . . . a great reader of Shaw about the time I went to Wyvern [Malvern College, c. 1913]. . . . Shaw was an author on my father's shelves like any other author. I began reading him because his *Dramatic Opinions* contained a good deal about Wagner and Wagner's very name was then a lure to me. Thence I went on to read most of the other Shaws we had. . . . My father told me that Shaw was "a mountebank" but that there were some laughs in *John's Bull's Other Island.* (*Surprised* 102)

The reading of Shaw gave the youthful Lewis "vaguely socialistic" political opinions (164). But, by the time Lewis was finishing his academic work at Oxford (c. 1922–23), he was finding Shaw's (and H. G. Wells's) works "a little thin; what as boys we called 'tinny'"; they, and some like earlier writers, were entertaining but "too simple" in their treatment of life (202). Lewis later gave

247

to Weston, the scientist in *Out of the Silent Planet*, the statement, "... it is enough for me that there is a Beyond" (149). This is based on Lilith's last words, the closing words of the play, in Shaw's *Back to Methuselah* (1921): "It is enough that there is a beyond." Lewis's rejection of what he had once accepted implies, if not a literary rejection, at least philosophical disagreement, as becomes clear in the parodic treatment of Weston's humanistic ideas. Another reference to *Back to Methuselah* appears in an essay "The Funeral of a Great Myth," in which Lewis discusses the nineteenth and early twentieth centuries' belief in progress, in development or emergence—in short, in popular evolution—and ties its first literary expressions to John Keats's *Hyperion* (written 1818) and Wagner's *Nibelung's Ring* (1853–74). Then he writes:

> If Shaw's *Back to Methuselah* were really, as he supposed, the work of a prophet or a pioneer ushering in the reign of a new Myth, its predominantly comic tone and its generally low emotional temperature would be inexplicable. It is admirable fun: but not thus are new epochs brought to birth. The ease with which he plays with the Myth shows that the Myth is fully digested and already senile. Shaw is the Lucian or the Snorri of this mythology: to find its Aeschylus or its Elder Edda you must go back to Keats and Wagner. ("Funeral" 84)

But Lewis's most famous rejection of Shaw's ideas is in *The Screwtape Letters*, in which the demonic Screwtape has unintentionally changed into a centipede form: he rejects the Miltonic explanation that such changes are the devil's punishment and states: "A more modern writer—someone with a name like Pshaw—has ... grasped the truth. Transformation proceeds from within and is a glorious manifestation of that Life Force which Our Father [Satan] would worship if he worshipped anything but himself" (115).

The third major Irish author of the first of the century, James Joyce (1882–1941), receives less mention. A passing reference in an essay in 1939, "High and Low Brows," does not prove Lewis has read Joyce, but certainly he knows of him: "... those who dislike Pound or Joyce are told 'so you would have disliked Wordsworth and Shelley if you had lived then'" (107). A more specific reference occurs in the last chapter of *A Preface to "Paradise Lost"* when Lewis speaks of those modern critics who believe the stream of consciousness is "the reality, and it is the special function of poetry to remove the elaborations of civility and get at 'life' in the raw. Hence (in part) the popularity of such a work as *Ulysses*" (131). Lewis's subsequent argument against these critics' position does not involve Joyce's book. A different critic wrote, rather snidely, "With a sure scent for the real peril, Mr. Lewis saw a supreme danger to Milton's literary reputation in the public response to Joyce" (Hughes 32). He is right insofar as the analysis belongs to the moralistic side of Lewis.

248

The fourth modern Irish writer that Lewis discusses is James Stephens (1882–1950). In his autobiography, Lewis mentions reading one of Stephens's books in his schooldays when he was studying the *Bacchae*: "Euripides' picture of Dionysus was closely linked in my mind with the whole mood of Mr. Stephens's *Crock of Gold* [1912], which I had lately read for the first time with great excitement. . . . A new quality entered my imagination: something Mediterranean and volcanic, the orgiastic drum-beat" (*Surprised* 111). But Lewis's fullest treatment of Stephens is in an essay titled "Period Criticism" (1946). Lewis mentions four books by Stephens: *The Crock of Gold* again, *The Demi-Gods* (1914), *Here Are the Ladies* (1913), and *Deirdre* (1923), reserving his highest praise for the last. He says that the paragraphs of "dead wood"— the theosophy or other transcendental materials—in the first three "are bad [literarily], sometimes even nonsensical"; but the comic effects—Lewis gives some examples—are excellent. *Deirdre*, on the other hand, has no dead wood (148–49). It is "the one unmistakably great and almost perfect book among the author's many good books" (151); it has "some of the finest heroic narrative, some of the most disciplined pathos, and some of the cleanest prose which our century has seen" (152). *Deirdre*, it should be emphasized in the present connection, is a retelling of an Irish myth.

English Writers

Until all of Lewis's letters are published (and a good index is supplied), any discussion of his views of modern literature will be inevitably incomplete. For example, among English authors, the poet Ruth Pitter was a close friend, and she and Lewis exchanged copies of their poems with comments on each other's work—but these are not yet published. (Lewis calls her an "exquisite" poet in "Period Criticism" [150].)

Although the Irish writers were not treated chronologically by birth, perhaps in this longer catalogue it is best to organize that way. Joseph Conrad (1857–1924), although certainly born during the Victorian Period (in Poland, however), did not publish his first novel until 1895, so he fits in this modern period. In 1923 Lewis bought a copy of *Typhoon* (1903) (*Road* 226); in 1925 Lewis read *Chance* (1913), commenting soon after beginning that it was "one of the very best novels I have read" (372); and after finishing the novel, comments that "[i]t is a good book; even great. Whether the denouement has any justification I don't know. He seems to kill Anthony for no reason except the whimsical one of avoiding a happy ending, and then to marry Flora to Powell in a moment of sentimental repentance. Perhaps I have misunderstood it" (374). Lewis was also enthusiastic about *Lord Jim* (1900): "a great novel, espe-

249

cially Marlow's conversation with Stein, and the whole picture of Stein, where the incredible is made convincing" (415). Years later Lewis commented about *Nostromo* (1904): "A fault . . . is that we have to read so much pseudo-history before we get to the central matter, for which alone this history exists" (*Experiment* 84). Robert F. Haugh, commenting that *Nostromo* is often ranked as Conrad's greatest novel, adds, "Yet the ordinary reader finds it heavy going: the historical prelude is intolerably slow, the issues unengaged for many pages and not made to flow through compelling situations until quite late in the book" (147). Lewis's point, therefore, seems to be well founded. Lewis's casual use of "great" in his diary may be misleading, but certainly he raises a plot question about *Chance*. He sees the thematic importance of the Marlow and Stein conversation in *Lord Jim* and reacts to the "story" element in *Nostromo*.

The most important of Lewis's comments on Walter de la Mare (1873–1956) appear in his letters to Arthur Greeves. His second comment about the poet, in 1927, seems extravagant: "De la Mare's poems I have had for a long time and I read them more often than any other book. I put him above Yeats and all the other moderns, and in spite of his fantasy find him nearer than any one else to the essential truth of life" (*Stand* 297). Lewis does not say what this "essential truth" is; presumably de la Mare's emphasis on estrangement and a sinister other world appealed to Lewis in his pre-Christian days. (Since this comment was written after Yeats's shift in style, probably Lewis's previously high estimate of Yeats had dropped.)

Lewis's other comments are more closely tied to individual books by de la Mare. In 1918 he decides to keep a copy of *Peacock Pie: A Book of Rhymes* (1913) which Greeves had sent (226–27); in 1930 he is looking forward to reading *Desert Islands* (of that year) (372), but reacts to Greeves's first negative comments with:

250

> My idea is that he really bade good bye to the best part of himself in the lovely poem 'Be not too wildly amorous of the far' [from "The Imagination's Pride" in *The Veil and Other Poems* (1921)]. The peculiar kind of vision he had was of a strangely piercing quality and probably almost unbearable to the possessor: only a man of great solidity, of real character, sound at the bases of his mind & braced with philosophy, could have carried it safely. But De La Mare was not such a man. . . . Hardly knowing what he did, and yet just knowing, he *sent* it away. (374)

In 1924, before the above theory was advanced, talking with a friend, Lewis agreed that de la Mare was "the only great Georgian" and that "the common view of de la Mare as the poet of faery and fantasy leaves out all one side and that the most important one"; in 1926 Lewis met de la Mare at a dinner arranged by Nevill Coghill (*Road* 291, 379)—but neither of these events needs to temper Lewis's 1930 judgment that there was a falling off in the quality of de la Mare's poetry. Lewis's fondness for de la Mare is no doubt due to de la Mare's romanticism, to his use of the images inherited from the early Romantics, to his feeling for an innocent world (captured at times in childhood), and to his suggestion (with a type of unresolved irony) that there is something beyond this world.

Lewis's indebtedness to G. K. Chesterton (1874–1936) as an influence on his return to Christianity is well known, since Lewis mentions it in *Surprised by Joy.* ". . . I read Chesterton's *Everlasting Man* and for the first time saw the whole Christian outline of history set out in a form that seemed to me to make sense. Somehow I contrived not to be too badly shaken" (210). But this is religious writing, not literary. Earlier in his autobiography, Lewis describes his first reading of Chesterton's essays, and analyzes their appeal:

> His humour was of the kind which I like best—not "jokes" imbedded in the page like currants in a cake, still less (what I cannot endure), a general tone of flippancy and jocularity, but the humour which is not in any way separable from the argument but is rather (as Aristotle would say) the "bloom" on dialectic itself. . . . For the critics who think Chesterton frivolous or "paradoxical" I have to work hard to feel even pity; sympathy is out of the question. Moreover, strange as it may seem, I liked him for his goodness. I can attribute this taste to myself freely (even at that age) because it was a liking for goodness which had nothing to do with any attempt to be good myself. (180)

There are a number of references to Chesterton in the letters, but the main discussion of his works as literature appears in "Period Criticism," the essay mentioned above in connection with James Stephens. Lewis says that Chesterton's books of essays deal with "ephemeral" topics and so are now mainly of historical interest,[2] but that the imaginative works are quite different. Lewis mentions three examples: *The Ballad of the White Horse* (1911), a narrative poem, and two prose romances, *The Flying Inn* (1914) and *The Man Who Was Thursday* (1908). Lewis dismisses the anti-Germanicism of the poem as "silly" but goes on to praise its central theme: "Does not the central theme of the *Ballad*—the highly paradoxical message which Alfred receives from the Virgin—embody the feeling, and the only possible feeling, with which in any age almost defeated men take up such arms as are left them and win?" (150). Basic to Lewis's argument is the attempt to say that these works are not dated, despite their ties to the period in which they were written: their basic messages are eternal (or at least long lasting). In the case of *The Flying Inn*, Lewis refers to two characters as perennial types. His argument for *The Man Who Was Thursday* involves a comparison:

251

> Compare [the book] with another good writer, Kafka. Is the difference simply that the one is "dated" and the other contemporary? Or is it rather that while both give a powerful picture of the loneliness and bewilderment which each one of us encounters in his (apparently) single-handed struggle with the universe, Chesterton, attributing to the universe a more complicated disguise, and admitting the exhilaration as well as the terror to the struggle, has got in rather more; is more balanced; in that sense, more classical, more permanent? (151)

Lewis of course knew that Kafka's reputation in the twentieth century was immense and Chesterton's was limited; but his argument at least would put the onus on the Kafka enthusiasts to defend the complexity of Kafka's world view. Lewis's argument about this larger world view is an interesting one: it may be, at root, a moralistic argument—Chesterton sees something besides terror—but it is phrased in critical terms, terms which give merit to the comprehensive work. Lewis had made a parallel point in *The Allegory of Love* when he said that the second part of *The Romance of the Rose* "attempted vast designs with inadequate resources" (141–42); he contrasts it to *The Divine Comedy* where "the resources were adequate," the Dantean results being "a unity of the highest order, because it embraces the greatest diversity of subordinated detail" (142). Here he suggests that Kafka's design is not vast enough.

Lewis's comments on John Masefield (1878–1967) come mostly from his 1922–27 diary, when Lewis was writing narrative verse. Perhaps that interest influenced his interest in Masefield's poems. (Lewis does not mention Masefield's most famous book of lyrics, *Salt-Water Ballads* [1902], which may support this supposition.) Lewis praised Masefield's *The Tragedy of Pompey the Great* (1910): "it has the merit of forcing you to ACT each speech as you go along[;] it is finely realistic and moving"; he says the play is only behind *Dauber* (1913) and "parts of" *Reynard the Fox* (1919) in merit (*Road* 19). That was in 1922; four years later, he mentions rereading *Dauber*: "Read *Dauber* in the evening. It's as great as ever but Lord!, how incredibly bad in single lines and stanzas. . . . Read *Dauber* again in the evening and got some vivid impressions, giving me a good realistic shock to counterbalance my growing idealism in metaphysics. All the part about the wind from the Pole drives home the sense of 'an other' . . ." (419). A reader may suspect that Lewis's reaction to Masefield's style is the beginning of a reconsideration of the poet's merits—but one which Lewis, intent on belief in narrative verse, does not yet accept.

A greater, more experimental writer receives less praise from Lewis. In a letter, he admits, about Virginia Woolf (1882–1941), the skillful style of *Orlando* (1928) while dismissing its content—an early version of Lewis's aestheticism *vs.* moralism (*Stand* 348). Lewis refers to Woolf's works elsewhere, but seemingly without critical intent, to the structure of *The Waves* (1931) in "*De Descrip-*

tione Temporum," and to her use of the word *life* in "Modern Fiction" from *The Common Reader* (1925) in *Studies in Words* (293). Possibly it was the sexual shifts in *Orlando* that bothered Lewis; but most critics take its content as a *jeu d'esprit*, so they are not far from Lewis's dismissal.

D. H. Lawrence (1885–1930) arouses a stronger negative reaction in Lewis. Lewis's early comments seem to be moral judgments, not literary ones. Later, Lewis phrases his discussions in literary terms. In 1930, Lewis writes to Greeves of one of Lewis's friends that "He was all mucked up with naturalism. D. H. Lawrence, and so on, but has come right . . ." (*Stand* 342). In the preface to *The Pilgrim's Regress*, Lewis mentions Lawrence three times, but the significant reference is when he is speaking of his allegorical use of directions. In Lewis's book, to the South lies "the sub-Romantics" (11), where "[e]very feeling is justified by the mere fact that it is felt" (12). Of this area, Lewis writes, ". . . when our age is 'Southern' at all, it is excessively so. D. H. Lawrence and the Surrealists have perhaps reached a point further 'South' than humanity ever reached before" (12). These are the early references. Lewis seems to be reacting to Lawrence's content, so perhaps these should be balanced with one passage (of 1961) in which Lewis indicates that at least in descriptions of nature Lawrence writes well: "Good writing may offend [the unliterary reader] by being either too spare for his purpose or too full. A woodland scene by D. H. Lawrence . . . gives him far more than he knows what to do with . . ." (*Experiment* 33). Thus, Lewis can say that some things in Lawrence are well written, implicitly (in the context of the above quotation) memorable, and fresh recreations of experience, even though he may feel the overall import of the work is morally suspect.

But not everything is well written in Lawrence. Just after the British court case over the English publication of *Lady Chatterley's Lover* (1929) in 1961, Lewis wrote an essay "Four-Letter Words,"[3] in which he surveys the use of traditionally obscene words in Middle English, Latin, and Greek, and finds that they are always used for farce or vituperation. He reaches two conclusions: (1) Lawrence's book does not present a moral danger through its vocabulary, and (2) Lawrence's usage will be unsuccessful in introducing reverence or in overcoming inhibitions about sex, for "[i]t is a rebellion against language." He concludes that "*Lady Chatterley* has made short work of a prosecution by the Crown. It still has to face more formidable judges. Nine of them, and all goddesses" (174). This reference to the muses is a literary judgment, of a sort, on Lawrence's style, based on his use (or misuse) of language.

Lewis also discusses Lawrence in his revised *Studies in Words*, in the essay on "Life." In two of his sections, Lewis uses Lawrence's praise of "life" to show, for example, *life* used to mean "emotion in general, as against intellect" (285–86). But sometimes it seems to mean, approvingly, "the sort of life that Lawrence values": "[w]hat that is we are to find out from our general knowledge of his books and behaviour" (287–88). Lewis's comment is neutrally phrased, but loaded. Finally, Lewis uses a passage from *Sons and Lovers* (1913) in which a couple in the woods are "carried by life." Although he goes on to make his linguistic analysis of *life* being used "as a real supra-personality entity," Lewis has fun with this, writing, "Since the young people in *Sons and Lovers* never appear either to hope or fear fertility, we may assume that they have prudently taken measures to be 'carried by life' just so far as is convenient and no further" (298–99).[4] These passages show Lewis the moralist again, but in his later, gentler manner.

A friend of Lewis, Charles Williams (1886–1945) is considered here only for his Arthurian poems, his late ones, in *Taliessin through Logres* (1938) and *The Region of the Summer Stars* (1944). After Williams's death, Lewis gave a course of lectures on the poems at Oxford in the autumn of 1945 (Williams and Lewis 1), which was published as "Williams and the Arthuriad." Lewis basically does two things in his discussion. He arranges the poems from both books into one sequence, based on the Arthurian chronology, and he provides a running commentary on the poems, with emphasis on explaining their obscurities—the latter takes far longer than the first. (More recent critics see differences between the two books that Williams published, not so much in myth as in poetic intention, and no longer organize as Lewis did.) In a survey of this sort, a full treatment of "Williams and the Arthuriad" is impossible; but Lewis's approach is very much in the tradition of a lecturer moving from crux to crux. For example, in his discussion of the first poem, "The Calling of Taliessin," he reaches the Wood of Broceliande and states, "We must here make our first halt, to contemplate the nature of Broceliande" (99). Three pages later, Lewis continues with his paraphrase of and comments on the poem. It is also notable that Lewis does not, like many commentators, quietly skip the highly obscure; for example, of the lyric "Taliessin's Return to Logres," he writes, "There are things in this piece (notably the 'golden sickle') which I do not understand" (110).

254

If this suggests Lewis's approach (at least with such an obscure series of lyrics as Williams's), nonetheless at the end of the discussion comes a valuable evaluative statement: "So far I have been trying to explain rather than to judge" (187). Lewis sets up the chief problem of Williams's poems as their obscurity, due mainly to an unshared background with most readers (although he gives also an example of poor syntax); then he discusses three virtues of the cycle: its "Wisdom," its beauty ("Deliciousness"), and its creation of an imagined world ("Strength of Incantation"). The first two of these points are Horace's principle that a poem teach and delight, with a slightly sophisticated emphasis. When Lewis discusses the third, he emphasizes not the geography of Williams's world, which Lewis discussed earlier, in connection with "The Vision of the Empire" (104–09), but its flavor: "The world of the poem is a strong, strange, and consistent world." This is created partly by the use of "'romantic' images in the 'metaphysical' way"; it is a world without snugness (198), a world with gaiety (a gaiety of high courtesy and defeated irony), with splendor, and with balances (as of eroticism and austerity) (199). Although Lewis does not use the example, an instance of a simpler "world" in a cycle of lyrics is A. E. Housman's Shropshire. Williams's Logres and the other areas of his world—stretching to Byzantium and beyond—are likewise unified by their mode of presentation.

Dorothy L. Sayers (1893–1957) was another friend, exchanging with Lewis a number of letters, not yet fully published. In 1941, Lewis wrote Arthur Greeves, "Dorothy Sayers['s] *The Mind of the Maker* I thought good on the whole: good enough to induce me to try one of her novels—*Gaudy Night*—wh. I didn't like at all. But then, as you know, detective stories aren't my taste, so that proves nothing" (*Stand* 492–93). Actually, Lewis reviewed *The Mind of the Maker*, but that is more a religious topic than literary—although Sayers's book is an attempt to set up a Christian approach to literature. The point for this discussion is that Lewis, as he said a number of times, had no taste for detective novels; thus, he offers no firsthand analysis of Sayers's novels. Lewis also writes to Greeves, in 1943, "One thing I *have* read recently is D. Sayers' *The Man Born to be King* wh. I thought excellent, indeed most moving. The objections to it [the use of Cockney for Matthew, *etc.*, in the radio plays] seem to me as silly as the similar ones to *Green Pastures* . . ." (497). Sayers's radio-play sequence is a life of Christ, but this is an aesthetic comment about it. In "A Panegyric for Dorothy L. Sayers," Lewis writes of the play: "The architectonic qualities of this dramatic sequence will hardly be questioned" (93).

Perhaps Lewis's most famous comment in his published letters to Sayers is, "Although you have so little time to write letters you are one of the great English letter writers. (Awful vision for you—'It is often forgotten that Miss Sayers was known in her own day as an Author. We who have been familiar from childhood with the Letters can hardly realise! . . . [')]" (*Letters* 380). In "A Panegyric," written for her funeral, Lewis emphasized Sayers's craftsmanship, and her emphasis on it, whether in detective novels, plays, or translations. "She aspired to be, and was, at once a popular entertainer and a conscientious craftsman: like (in her degree) Chaucer, Cervantes, Shakespeare, or Molière" (123). He also discussed Sayers's translations, finding her *Song of Roland* "too violently colloquial" for his taste, and commenting on the aspects of Dante's *Divine Comedy* which she captured in her translation of the "Inferno" and which she lost (125–26). Thus, his points about Sayers are rather scattered among her works, but he points to some legitimate results of her craftsmanship.

George Orwell (1903–50) and Lewis were basically contemporary authors, both writing very clear prose, but very different in their social orientations.

255

Orwell was negative in his review of *That Hideous Strength*, regarding it as a crime story marred by the supernatural. Lewis disliked *1984*, but the concern here is with *Animal Farm*.[5] In *English Literature in the Sixteenth Century*, while discussing the verse satire descended from Roman models, Lewis writes:

> The great works in the modern vernaculars which we usually call "satires" do not descend from the *Satira* of the Romans. *Animal Farm, Erewhon*, [and others, of the seventeenth and eighteenth centuries,] belong to a different family. They are all fantastic or mock heroic narratives, and their true ancestors are Rabelais, Cervantes, the *Apocolocyntosis*, Lucian, and the *Frogs and Mice*. (468)

This generic classification is important both because Lewis thought in terms of genres and because he applied the term "great" to *Animal Farm*. In his essay "George Orwell," Lewis generalizes about *Animal Farm*, but the generalizations are entirely praise:

> Wit and humour . . . are employed with devasting effect. The great sentence "All animals are equal but some are more equal than others" bites [deep]. . . . The greed and cunning of the pigs is tragic . . . because we are made to care about all the honest, well-meaning, or even heroic beasts whom they exploit. The death of Boxer the horse moves us. . . . And not only moves, but convinces. Here, despite the animal disguise, we feel we are in a real world. . . . *Animal Farm* is formally almost perfect; light, strong, balanced. There is not a sentence that does not contribute to the whole. The myth says all the author wants it to say and (equally important) it doesn't say anything else. ("Orwell" 103–04)

By *myth* Lewis seems to mean a universal statement. Orwell has distanced himself artistically from his disappointments with communism, and created, in the animal fable, a truth: ". . . the whole thing [the Stalin era in Russia] is projected and distanced. It becomes a myth and is allowed to speak for itself" (103). This is not the only basis on which Lewis praises books, but it certainly serves here. His reference to the reader being "in a real world" ties this statement to Lewis's discussion of Chesterton and Kafka (the complexity of the fictional universe) and to Williams ("a strong, strange, and consistent world"); Lewis may not mean quite the same thing in these statements, but generally he is attempting to create a basis for the literary evaluation of a world view as it is projected in non-realistic works.

The last of these English authors, William Golding (1911–93), is significant because he shows that Lewis continued to read contemporary authors, for *Lord of the Flies*, Golding's first novel, was published in 1954. The knowledge of Golding shows up in a taped conversation Lewis had with Kingsley Amis and Brian Aldiss (published as "Unreal Estates"). Lewis says of *Lord of the Flies*, "It was a very terrestrial island; the best island, almost, in fiction. Its sensuous effect on you is terrific" (*Stories* 148). He also describes another Golding novel, *The Inheritors* (1955), in similar terms: ". . . the detail of every sensuous impression, the light on the leaves and so on, was so good that you couldn't find out what was happening. I'd say it was almost too well done. All these little details you only notice in real life if you've got a high fever" (148–49). Thus a casual conversation, recorded, shows Lewis's reading of post-World War II works.

If there were space, comments on other English writers could be added,[6] but the above survey indicates Lewis read, outside of his romantic tradition, the major English authors of the twentieth century—with varied responses.

American Writers

Lewis also read other modern authors—Kafka (as indicated above), Sartre (*Letters* 495), Roy Campbell (writing "To the Author of *Flowering Rifle*" before meeting him).[7] And Lewis read a number of American authors—perhaps one should even include his wife, Joy Davidman, for, before their marriage, he comments on her poems in his preface to her *Smoke on the Mountain* (1955). But the two major American authors are Henry James and T. S. Eliot.

He read several books by James (1843–1916), commenting on *The Turn of the Screw* (1898), "The style certainly is wonderfully unnatural, but it gets there" (*Road* 62). He debated with one friend about what happened in the story (63) and agreed with another "that the boy is 'saved' in the last scene" (66). After reading the first volume of James's letters, Lewis commented in a letter: "An interesting man, tho' a dreadful prig: but he did appreciate Stevenson. A *phantasmal* man, who had never known God, or earth, or war, never done a day's compelled work, never had to earn a living, had no home & no duties . . ." (*Letters* 427). This view is echoed in a comment about James's characters in *Experiment*: "In some of his books the protagonists live a life as impossible for most of us as that of fairies or butterflies; free from religion, from work, from economic cares, from the demands of family and settled neighbourhood" (91). This is hardly an exhaustive treatment of James's fiction, but Lewis's concern in the passage is about the attraction of some works for daydreams by readers—he says that no one who just wants fiction for that purpose will continue long with James. These comments are hardly critical in a standard sense, but the general comment about the protagonists in some of the novels may be taken as a comment about the "world" that James creates: like Kafka's world but in a different way, it may be limited.

T. S. Eliot (1888–1965), Lewis's *bête noire*, first appears in Lewis's writings in his 1926 diary, obviously not too long after *Prufrock and Other Observations* (1917) and *The Waste Land* (1922) had appeared. Eliot had founded the quarterly *Criterion* in 1922 and joined the Faber and Gwyer publishing firm in 1925, so he must have seemed to Lewis to be the center of the modernist movement—come from America in 1915 and now redirecting British poetry.

In 1926 Lewis gathered three others into a plan to write mock Eliotic verses, submit them to *The Criterion*, and then to reveal them as parodies if they were published. Lewis wrote a poem titled "Cross-Channel Boat": "very nonsensical, but with a flavour of dirt all through" (*Road* 409; title on 411); a later parody by Lewis was titled "Nidhogg" (413). Lewis makes an interesting comment that he did not keep clearly in mind: "If he [Eliot] does not [accept the first poem for *The Criterion*,] I shall have proved that there is something more than I suspected in this kind of stuff" (410). Lewis, his tutee Henry Yorke (later known as the novelist Henry Green), William F. R. Hardie, and Nevill Coghill sent some poems in, but none was accepted (410–11, 413–14, 417–18). Lewis says he is in this plan because of "burning indignation" (414). Presumably there were two factors involved for him. First, part of the modernist movement in poetry involved the "associational flow of [the] unconscious" and an influence from "the collage in painting" (Perkins 450)—both of these tendencies being against the type of narrative poetry that Lewis, influenced by the whole tradition of narratives from the classics on down through the Victorian period to those of his own period, wanted to write (cf. Coghill 53, 58–60); second, Lewis mentions "dirt" in connection with his understanding of Eliot-like poetry. Lewis was in reaction against the physical during the First World War (*Stand* 214); later, after he became a Christian, his attitude no doubt had a biblical basis. In referring to "dirt," perhaps Lewis had in mind such passages as the seduction of the typist in section 3 of *The Waste Land*. Lewis's basic statement about the period is found in *The Personal Heresy* (1939):

> The 'Dirty Twenties' of our own century produced poems which succeeded in communicating moods of boredom and nausea that have only an infinitesimal place in the life of a corrected and full-grown man. That they were poems, the fact of communication and the means by which it was effected, are, I take it, sufficient proof.... [I]f it [the experience communicated] truly reflected the personality of the poets, then the poets differed from the mass, if at all, only by defect. (106)

Lewis's satire of the poets of the time—"the Silly Twenties" reads a headline—is found in *The Pilgrim's Regress*.[8] None of the three satiric portraits reflects Eliot, but at a meeting of the Inklings in 1947, the association between Eliot and attitudes of "boredom and nausea" is suggested:

Some enjoyable talk arising out of T. S. Eliot [writes W. H. Lewis in his diary], one of whose poems J[ack—that is, C. S.—Lewis] read superbly, but broke off in the middle, declaring it to be bilge: Hugo [Dyson] defended it, J[ack] and [George] Sayer attacked. I thought that though unintelligible, it did convey a feeling of frustration and despair. J[ack] thought he had nothing to say worth saying in any case. (209)

The title of the poem would be interesting to know.

Lewis retained his dislike of Eliot's poetry for years—and of many of Eliot's critical positions. In 1936 in *The Allegory of Love*, Lewis commented that the vision in Deguileville's *Pelerinage de la Vie Humaine* of ultimate evil—"something almost omnipotent yet wholly mean; an ultimate deformity"—reminds a reader of some of Eliot's poetry (271); this, by itself, might be taken as a neutral comment. In another passage, referring to Ariosto's *Orlando Furioso*, he quotes a "modern American critic" to the effect that the British critical tradition relies too heavily in evaluation of literature on a sublimity influenced by Shakespeare and Milton (the source is not given, but it is drawn from the fifth paragraph of Eliot's "John Dryden"); Lewis then lines up Greece and England *vs.* Rome and America, saying that, if one accepts the latter, Ariosto's poem is as great as the *Iliad* and *The Divine Comedy* (303). This is a clever argument; but, since Eliot appreciated the realistic detail (among other things) in Dante and did not celebrate Ariosto, it does not really do what it should; Lewis is arguing against some phrasing out of context. (Calling Eliot an "American critic" nine years after he became a British citizen is also loaded.)

In *Rehabilitations* (1939), the first essay is "Shelley, Dryden, and Mr Eliot." Eliot had written in praise of Dryden and, in the course of the essay, depreciated Shelley (the essay, not named, is again "John Dryden," this time the second paragraph, which Lewis may have found in Eliot's *Selected Essays* of 1932). By this time, Lewis knows that Eliot had announced himself "a classicist in literature" in the preface to *For Lancelot Andrews* (1928), and so Lewis uses that term throughout, to argue that Dryden did not write tonally unified poems and was not able to rise to the heroic themes of some of his poems. Lewis then argues that Shelley, on the other hand, is classically great: he chooses great topics and unifies them. Since Eliot probably only meant a "traditionalist in literature"—his tradition being Dante, the Jacobean dramatists, the Metaphysicals, and the French *symbolistes*—Lewis might seem to be off the topic again; but in this case a reader may suspect that Lewis was deliberately using Eliot's term to suggest that Eliot himself was no kind of classicist. Lewis also has several asides to Eliot, usually loaded; this is the strongest: "*Swellfoot* is almost an attempt to revive the Old Comedy—an attempt which should interest Mr. Eliot since Shelley in it faces the cardinal problem of much of Mr. Eliot's poetry: namely, whether it is possible to distinguish poetry about squalor and chaos from squalid and chaotic poetry. I do not think it a great success" (21). (There may be an ambiguity to the *it* in the last sentence.)

In the series of arguments between Lewis and E. M. W. Tillyard published as *The Personal Heresy* (collected in the same year as *Rehabilitations* was published), Lewis quotes a passage from Eliot in which Eliot indicates that Shakespeare's cynicism and Dante's use of rage in their works are workings out of their personal problems (*Heresy* 3); Tillyard replies, quite correctly, that the main direction of Eliot's critical theory is away from the personal (31–32). The two go on to argue about the application of their topic to a passage from Eliot's *The Rock*, but it is more theory than discussion of Eliot (36–37; 63–65). Lewis mentions at one point that Eliot's poetry can open him to new experience— the passage is not very clear, but it seems to refer to a mythic or archetypal quality, for (besides de la Mare and Edith Sitwell) Lewis mentions George Mac-Donald's prose "works" (probably the romances) as having this quality— despite literary defects (102–03). Presumably in Eliot's poetry Lewis found a type of negative new experience.

Lewis's most famous disagreement with Eliot was over Milton. Eliot's "A Note on the Verse of John Milton" (1936)—reprinted as "Milton I" in *On Poetry and Poets* (1957)—had attacked Milton as a bad influence (and a bad man). In *A Preface to "Paradise Lost"* (1942), Lewis challenges Eliot, however, on a statement that the only "jury of judgment" he will accept on Milton is the best contemporary practicing poets. Lewis argues elaborately that this position, taken at its fullest, does not allow anyone to criticize poetry at all, since a person must assume he is a poet—that is, beg the question—before he can be a critic (*Preface* 9–11). (Eliot, in "Milton II" [1947], reversed some of his positions on Milton, and rather neutrally referred to Lewis's "skilfully arguing that Milton . . . can be acquitted of heresy.") After the publication of Lewis's *Preface*, Charles Williams brought Lewis and Eliot together; the meeting did not go well, but, according to a biography, Eliot asked Lewis not to write any more about his criticism, and Lewis agreed (Green and Hooper 223–24).

While it is true that Lewis and Eliot got along well late in life when they were asked to collaborate (with others) in a revision of the Psalter for *The Book of Common Prayer*, there is no real suggestion that Lewis ever came to enjoy Eliot's early poetry. In 1954—nine years before Lewis died—he published a poem "*Spartan Nactus*" (reprinted as "A Confession"), which began with a parody of (or reply to) the opening of "The Love Song of J. Alfred Prufrock":

> I am so coarse, the things the poets see
> Are obstinately invisible to me.
> For twenty years I've stared my level best

> To see if evening—any evening—would suggest
> A patient etherized upon a table;
> In vain. I simply wasn't able.[9]

Lewis, in his poem, goes on to celebrate stock responses, rather than Eliot's (or, more precisely, Prufrock's) private sensibility. Lewis, in *Preface*, argued that people need more stock responses (53–57); in the same place he refers to "Prufrock" as "a striking picture of sensibility in decay" (55). On the other hand, Lewis *does* refer to "the penitential qualities of his [Eliot's] own best work" (133), presumably thinking of *Ash Wednesday* (1930) and probably the first three of the *Four Quartets* (1943), for he quotes in passing from "The Dry Salvages" (59), and seems to make a distinction between Eliot's early poems and later ones—although how good Lewis thought Eliot's "best work" is not certain.

Conclusion

What can be said about Lewis's criticism of modern authors and about his reading in the field? This survey started from his love of the narrative, his moralism (*vs.* his aestheticism), and his conservatism. He reacted against some writers on moral grounds (Lawrence, Eliot, and other 1920s writers), and against others on what seems to be largely aesthetic grounds (the later Yeats) or on a conservative basis (Auden and the 1930s poets). Certainly, his temperament did not include what David Perkins has called the High Modernist Mode (which is fragmented and not narrative); but when a friend, Charles Williams, wrote in an at least semi-modern style, Lewis accepted it, although still complaining about aspects. Lewis's one published passage of free verse in a poem ("The Queen of Drum," Canto 5, ll. 229–48) is meant to show a moment of psychic dissolution—perhaps the only topic for which he thought free verse useful.

In prose fiction (a form of narrative), he has one criticism of one of the experimenters; Lewis dismisses the content of Woolf's *Orlando* while commending the skillful style. He highly praises, however, such conservative (and equally imaginative) prose fiction as Chesterton's *The Man Who Was Thursday*, Stephens's *Deirdre*, and Orwell's *Animal Farm*—all fiction which was something like his own, in the Ransom Trilogy, the Chronicles of Narnia, and *Till We Have Faces*. It should be noted that only one of the three authors he praises is Christian, so it is not so much religious faith which causes his praise as a conservative form and, perhaps, traditional content.

Other narratives interested him. His response to Conrad is varied—high, youthful praise, and a soberer, later comment on structure. He thinks Golding displays a beautiful style to the point of distraction. He gives mixed reviews to such writers as Henry James, de la Mare, and Masefield—as well as to friends like Sayers. But with de la Mare one has moved away from the narrative, and with Sayers Lewis praises most her radio-play sequence.

In short, for a medieval and Renaissance scholar, Lewis is aware of modern literature, interested, and surprisingly well read in it; and for a Christian conservative, Lewis is very open to reading works before he judges them. He does tend to see the meanings of works in terms of morality (the universal Tao of his *The Abolition of Man*), but at least in theory—and often in practice—he separates the art from the content. As three of the discussions above indicate, literary works create imaginative worlds; Lewis was a lifelong explorer of these worlds, the newly created ones as well as the older. He did not approve of everything he found, but that did not keep him from exploring.

Notes

1. The narrative emphasis comes out in various ways, including his essay "On Stories" (1947).

2. Lewis elsewhere cites an essay "On Man: Heir of All the Ages" from *Avowals and Denials* (1934), calling it "wholly admirable," so evidently not all Chesterton's essays were "ephemeral" (*Preface* 63).

3. "Four-Letter Words" is collected in *Selected Literary Essays*, but Walter Hooper, the editor, seems to have not understood its application because he put it in the eighteenth century in his chronological arrangement.

4. Lewis is clearer in his judgment on the scene in *Experiment* (126).

5. See comments on *Animal Farm* and *1984* in chapter 15 in this volume.

6. For example, Robert Bridges (1844–1930) (e.g., *Road* 442–43), P. G. Wodehouse (1881–1975) (*Letters* 324), Edith Sitwell (1887–1964) (satirized as Victoriana in *Regress* 50–51 [bk. 3, ch. 1]; cf. Lewis's unpublished letter to Robert Edward Palmer, 8 [?] November 1945), Robert Graves (1895–1985) (*Road* 394, 399; *Stand* 492), Owen Barfield (1898–1997) ("Note"), Martyn Skinner (1906–c.1993/94) (*Letters* 366, 384), and Kingsley Amis (1922–95) ("Unreal Estates" 150).

7. The poem was originally published in 1939 as "To Mr. Roy Campbell"; Lewis and Campbell met in 1944. For details, see Christopher 39.

8. Bk. 3, ch. 1–3, with the sexual material in ch. 2; the headline appears in the 3rd ed. at the start of ch. 1.

9. This poem is collected as "A Confession" in *Poems* (1); Kathryn Lindskoog has argued that the revisions to the poem weaken it and only the original version should be considered Lewis's ("Would C. S. Lewis Have Made These Changes?" *The Lewis Legacy* No. 68 [Spring 1996]: 16). The opening lines, quoted above, do not include any of the revisions in question.

Works Cited

Barfield, Owen. *Orpheus: A Poetic Drama*. West Stockbridge, MA: Lindisfarne, 1983.

Christopher, Joe R. "Roy Campbell and the Inklings." *Mythlore* 22:1/83 (Autumn 1997): 33–46.

Coghill, Nevill. "The Approach to English." *Light on C. S. Lewis*. Ed. Jocelyn Gibb. London: Geoffrey Bles, 1965. 51–66.

Green, Roger Lancelyn, and Walter Hooper. *C. S. Lewis: A Biography*. New York: Harcourt Brace Jovanovich, 1974.

Haugh, Robert F. *Joseph Conrad: Discovery in Design*. Norman: U of Oklahoma P, 1957.

Henn, T. R. *The Lonely Tower: Studies in the Poetry of W. B. Yeats*. 1950. London: Methuen—University Paperbacks, 1965.

Hughes, Merritt Y. *Ten Perspectives on Milton*. New Haven: Yale UP, 1965.

Lewis, C. S. *The Allegory of Love: A Study in Medieval Tradition*. 1936. New York: Oxford UP, 1958.

———. *All My Road Before Me: The Diary of C. S. Lewis 1922–1927*. Ed. Walter Hooper. New York: Harcourt Brace Jovanovich, 1991.

———. *English Literature in the Sixteenth Century Excluding Drama*. Oxford: Oxford UP, 1954.

———. *An Experiment in Criticism*. Cambridge: Cambridge UP, 1961.

———. "Foreword." *Smoke on the Mountain: The Ten Commandments in Terms of Today*. By Joy Davidman. 1955. London: Hodder and Stoughton, 1963. 7–11.

———. "Four-Letter Words." *Selected Literary Essays*. Ed. Walter Hooper. Cambridge: Cambridge UP, 1969. 169–74.

———. "The Funeral of a Great Myth." *Christian Reflections*. Ed. Walter Hooper. Grand Rapids: Eerdmans, 1967. 82–93.

———. "George Orwell." *Stories* 101–04.

———. "High and Low Brows." *Rehabilitations* 97–116.

———. *Letters of C. S. Lewis*. Ed. W. H. Lewis. 1966. Rev. ed. Ed. Walter Hooper. London: HarperCollins, 1988.

———. *Narrative Poems*. Ed. Walter Hooper. London: Geoffrey Bles, 1969.

———. "Note by C. S. Lewis." Barfield, *Orpheus* (printed on the back cover).

———. *Of This and Other Worlds*. Ed. Walter Hooper. 1982. London: Collins, 1984.

———. "*On Stories and Other Essays on Literature*." Ed. Walter Hooper. New York: Harcourt Brace Jovanovich, 1982.

———. *Out of the Silent Planet*. 1938. New York: Macmillan, 1943.

———. "A Panegyric for Dorothy L. Sayers." *Stories* 91–95.

———. "Period Criticism." Orig. pub. as "Notes on the Way." *Time and Tide* 9 Nov. 1946. Rpt. in *Of This and Other Worlds* 147–52.

———. *The Pilgrim's Regress: An Allegorical Apology for Christianity, Reason and Romanticism*. 3rd ed. London: Geoffrey Bles, 1943.

———. *Poems*. Ed. Walter Hooper. London: Geoffrey Bles, 1964.

———. *A Preface to "Paradise Lost."* London: Oxford UP, 1942.

———. *Rehabilitations and Other Essays*. London: Oxford UP, 1939.

———. *The Screwtape Letters*. New York: Macmillan, 1943.

———. "Shelley, Dryden, and Mr Eliot." *Rehabilitations* 1–34.

———. *Studies in Words*. 2nd ed. Cambridge: Cambridge UP, 1967.

———. *Surprised by Joy: The Shape of My Early Life*. London: Geoffrey Bles, 1955.

———. *They Stand Together: The Letters of C. S. Lewis to Arthur Greeves (1914–1963)*. Ed. Walter Hooper. New York: Macmillan, 1979.

———. "Unreal Estates." *Stories* 143–53.

———. "Williams and the Arthuriad." *Arthurian Torso*. London: Oxford UP, 1948. 91–200.

————, and E. M. W. Tillyard. *The Personal Heresy: A Controvery.* London: Oxford UP, 1939.

Orwell, George. Review of *That Hideous Strength.* "The Scientist Takes Over." *Manchester Evening News*, 16 August 1945, p. 2.

Perkins, David. *A History of Modern Poetry: From the 1890s to the High Modernist Mode.* Cambridge, MA: Harvard UP, 1976.

14
Myth

Maria Kuteeva

What is *myth*? The definitions given in the *OED*, however prestigious that work is among scholars of English, are not entirely exhaustive. The dictionary suggests two main definitions. Under the first it is classified as: "a. A purely fictitious narrative usually involving supernatural persons, actions or events, and embodying some popular idea concerning natural or historical phenomena. Properly distinguished from *allegory* and from *legend*." And in generalized use: "b. an untrue or popular tale, a rumor." The second meaning of myth is identified as concerned with "a fictitious or imaginary person or object." Whether regarding a tale or an object, one quality seems to be particularly underlined in these definitions of myth, that of falsehood. One is inclined to agree that the understanding of myth as fictitious prevails among the general public.[1] How then does the matter stand with a more learned audience?

The attention of this essay is centered on C. S. Lewis. By now Lewis studies have become a large interdisciplinary area, and fragmentary discussions of his ideas about myth have been conducted by scholars of literature, theology, and philosophy.[2] Yet there are still blank spaces to fill. The present survey endeavors to examine the evolution of Lewis's thought in order to gain a fuller appreciation of his understanding of myth. Two major aspects of Lewis's work with myth will be examined: his reading and scholarship.

Childhood and Adolescence: Lewis's Reading of Myth

The most useful information concerning Lewis's childhood reading of mythologies and mythopoeic literature can be found in his autobiography. To anyone reading *Surprised by Joy* it becomes obvious that from the age of nine Lewis lived almost entirely in the world of books and the imagination. One of the reasons for this was the grievous loss of his mother. However, the young boy's spiritual life was soon enriched by a genuine interest in Norse and other ancient mythologies. It is noteworthy that Lewis's first encounter with Norse mythology (before his mother's death) coincides with the first manifestations of what he calls "Joy"—a peculiar state of mind and spirit, different from Happiness and Pleasure and associated with unhappiness and grief—"an unsatisfied desire which is itself more desirable than any other satisfaction" (*Surprised* 23–24). Turning the pages of Longfellow's *Saga of King Olaf*, Lewis accidentally came across the unrhymed translation of *Tegner's Drapa*:

> I heard the voice that cried,
> Balder the beautiful
> Is dead, is dead—

And he suddenly found himself "uplifted into huge regions of northern sky" (23).

New glimpses of Joy came around 1911 (at age 13), after a long period of inert imagination which followed Lewis's early childhood. What Lewis later called "personal Renaissance" or "Northernness" was directly connected with his reading. Fascinated by Arthur Rackham's illustrations to *Siegfried and the Twilight of the Gods* and Wagner's music, he started his acquaintance with the Eddaic Universe. This was undertaken through the reading of Guerber's *Myths of the Norsemen*, Mackenzie's *Teutonic Myth and Legends*, and Mallet's *Northern Antiquities*, which included an appendix containing most of *The Prose Edda*. The impression made upon him by Norse mythology was so deep that it led Lewis to confess that "[my] imaginative life began to be so important and so distinct from my outer life that I almost have to tell two separate stories" (*Surprised* 78).

Northernness stimulated Lewis's interest in other mythologies. He found classical mythology, as retold by Ovid, Virgil, and Euripides, to be different from Norse: "Pan and Dionysus lacked the cold piercing appeal of Odin and Frey. A new quality entered my imagination: something Mediterranean and volcanic, the orgiastic drum-beat" (113). As a result of the interest in both mythologies, in 1914 Lewis even attempted to write his own tragedy entitled "Loki Bound," "Norse in subject and Greek in form" (113).

The next significant episode in Lewis's biography before he went to Oxford is connected with his tutor, William Kirkpatrick. During his studies with "Kirk," Lewis was introduced into the reading of Homer in ancient Greek, along with many other authors and texts drawing on mythological material: Milton, Spenser, Malory, *The High History of the Holy Grail*, *Beowulf* and *Sir Gawain and the Green Knight*, Apuleius, the *Kalevala*, Sir John Mandeville, Sidney's *Arcadia*, and nearly all of William Morris. By 1916 he had become a true expert on the Eddaic cosmos, and his interest in Valhalla and Valkyries "began to turn itself imperceptibly into a scholar's interest in them" (157).

As Lewis admits in his autobiography, his "Atheism and Pessimism were fully formed" before his studies with Kirk, another atheist of "the anthropological and pessimistic kind" (133). Lewis's beliefs of that period are well expounded in the letters to Arthur Greeves, at that time his best friend. Arthur was a Christian, and Lewis argued against his beliefs on anthropological grounds, quoting statements about "dying gods" and "fertility rites" from Andrew Lang's *Myth, Ritual and Religion* and Frazer's *The Golden Bough*.[3] Apparently, Kirk's tutelage fostered his own understanding of myth. Thus in 1916 (at age 18) he wrote:

> All religions, that is, all mythologies to give them a proper name are merely man's own invention—Christ as much as Loki. Primitive man surrounded himself by all sorts of terrible things he didn't understand. . . . Gradually from being mere nature-spirits these supposed being[s] were elevated into more elaborate ideas, such as old gods: and when man became more refined he pretended that these spirits were good as well as powerful.
>
> Thus religion, that is to say mythology grew up . . . and so Christianity came into being—one mythology among many, but the one that we happen to have been brought up in. (*Stand* 135)

Later in this letter Lewis admits that these comments are not his original thoughts, but firmly based upon "the recognized scientific account of the growth of religions." One can see that his understanding of myth was deeply rooted in the explanation given by Darwin's evolution theory adopted by the anthropological school, as originated by Tylor. In spite of this "unoriginality," we should note that the matter of myth was already of such particular importance for the adolescent Lewis.

This brief biographical account has been necessary to demonstrate the part played by reading in Lewis's early life. The survey suggests that it was closely associated with, and became part of, his religious experience. During the period of "Northernness," the stories about ancient gods came to replace his fading Christian faith and helped to develop a taste for other mythologies. Although intimately connected with the study of great mythopoeic authors, this interest was largely "scientific." Yet it did play its part in providing the young Lewis with food for thought. As he later confessed to Greeves, the stories about dying and reviving gods prepared him to "feel the myths as profound and suggestive of meaning beyond my grasp even tho' I could not say in cold prose 'what they meant'" (*Stand* 427). Many things changed after his arrival at Oxford.

Oxford: The Dramatic Change of Beliefs

Lewis's friendship with Owen Barfield started in 1919 on the basis of their shared dislike of modernism in poetry. However, after 1922 their relations were also determined by an intense intellectual debate known as "The Great War."[4] There was no winner in this prolonged dispute, and yet one of its outcomes was Lewis's reconsideration of his positive attitude to contemporary culture. Barfield delivered him from what Lewis himself called "chronological snobbery," "the uncritical acceptance of the intellectual climate common to our age and the assumption that whatever has gone out of date is on that account discredited" (*Surprised* 196). After this change Lewis adopted a different attitude toward the outlook and literature of the Middle Ages. The study of medieval literature, in turn, caused him to reconsider his attitude to religion and Christian beliefs.

Barfield's ideas also became crucial for the change of Lewis's understanding of myth. In his first two published works, *History in English Words* (1926) and *Poetic Diction* (1928), Barfield argues that myth has a central place in the study of language and literature. Examining the history of words, he concludes that myth is closely associated with language and its origins.[5] In brief, Barfield's theory can be presented as follows. Once myth, language, and human perception of the world were inseparable. Thus one can trace the plurality of meanings of a word back to the stage when the word had all its present meanings in one. All diction was literal, and there was no distinction between concrete and abstract meanings. Humans perceived the cosmos as a whole, and themselves as part of it. In our age, on the contrary, humanity distinguishes itself from the rest of nature, and words and myths are looked at from the point of view of abstraction.

Barfield's theory was appreciated by one of Lewis's other close and influential friends, Professor J. R. R. Tolkien.[6] Developing Barfield's argument, Tolkien declared that languages, especially modern European languages, can be regarded as the product of "a disease of mythology" ("On Fairy-Stories" 122).[7] Lewis was also fascinated by Barfield's ideas and became interested in the nature of myth. In 1928 he wrote to Barfield:

By the bye, we now need a new word for the "science of the nature of myths" since "mythology" has been appropriated to the myths themselves. Would "mythonomy" do? I am quite serious. If your views are not a complete error this subject will become more important and it's worth while trying to get a good word before they invent a beastly one. (*Letters* 255)

No, "they" still have not invented the word, and Lewis's original linguistic proposal has been memorialized in the *OED* under the entry on *mythonomy*. In this letter he came out with a few other suggestions: *mytho-logic* (noun), *mythopoeics,* and *mythologics*, or, otherwise, the invention of a new word like *gas*. The solution was never found, but Lewis's search for a fuller understanding of myth continued.

By 1929 Lewis came to what in *Surprised* he calls the "New Look," a kind of theism. Lewis's final conversion to Christianity coincides with a long debate about the veracity of myths, in which Tolkien argued against Lewis's account of myths being "lies and therefore worthless, even though they breathed through silver" (Carpenter, *Inklings* 43).[8] He explained that the first people, the ones who gave names to things, saw reality in a way which was different from the perception adopted by contemporary humanity. The world of the earlier people was inhabited by mythological beings. Since all humankind comes from God, not only abstract thought but also their imaginative invention originates in God, and reflects something of eternal truth. When naming things, people (both earlier and later) invent their terms about them. So as speech is invention about objects and ideas, so myth is invention about truth. In practicing mythopoeia a storyteller or "sub-creator" fulfills the Creator's purpose, and catches fragments of the true light. Therefore, even pagan myths cannot be totally "lies" since they always capture something of the truth.[9]

Such a concept of myth totally contradicts the prevailing opinion about myth being synonymous with "lie." In fact, Tolkien entirely reverses the juxtaposition. The story of Christ appears to him as the culminating point of human history and the summit of Fairy-story. This belief also laid the foundations for Lewis's Christianity: "Now the story of Christ is simply a true myth: a myth working on us in the same way as the others, but with this tremendous difference that *it really happened*: and one must be content to accept it in the same way, remembering that it is God's myth where the others are men's myths . . ." (*Stand* 427).[10] The myth of Christ came to be perceived by Lewis not as a symbolic expression of ultimate reality, but rather as an expression of the absolute meaning of life in actual historical context.

Thus the change of religious beliefs altered Lewis's attitude to, and perception of, myth. The anthropological beliefs of his adolescence were totally transformed into the belief in the truth of the Christian story and partial truth of the greater ancient myths. Moreover, one can claim that it was his redis-covery of Christianity that caused Lewis to become a "sub-creator" of imagi-nary worlds, where he tried to express his understanding of the veracity of Christian myth. At the moment, however, this question should remain out-side the scope of the present discussion, since we shall now consider Lewis's view of myth from a different angle. The largest part of his life was dedicated to the academic study of literature. How, then, does Lewis account for the phenomenon of myth in his scholarly works?

Myth and Literature: Lewis's Criticism

On 5 September 1931, just two weeks before his conversion to Christian-ity, Lewis wrote to Arthur Greeves, "I must confess that more and more the value of plays and novels becomes for me dependent on the moments when, by whatever artifice, they succeed in expressing the great myths" (*Stand* 420). As mentioned earlier, Lewis intensely disliked modernism. Lord David Cecil, his Oxford colleague and a member of the Inklings, recollects:

> Lewis's taste in *light* literature was that of an imaginative Victorian schoolboy.
> . . . His *serious* literary taste was also nineteenth century; but that of a mid-nine-
> teenth century scholar and man of letters. He liked the grand, the noble, or the
> Romantic: Homer, Virgil, Milton, also Spenser, Malory, etc.—though he did get
> a great pleasure from writers as different as Lamb and Jane Austen. But his taste
> did stop about 1890. (qtd. in Carpenter, *Inklings* 219n)

Likewise Lewis's dislike of modernism extended to his scholarship. In his academic works he argues against some approaches to the study of myth, fashionable at the time, and especially their application to the study of liter-ature: "Jung's theory of myth is as exciting as a good myth and in the same way. . . . But I have an idea that the true analysis of a thing ought not to be so like the thing itself. I should not expect a true theory of the comic to be funny. Of such theories one feels, for the first moments, 'This is just what we wanted'" ("*Audiendis*" 16–17). In this case, what was Lewis's own approach to the subject?

The role of myth in literature is considered in a number of Lewis's major academic works. The discussion of the part played by various mythologies in the evolution of medieval literature is already present in *The Allegory of Love*, a book widely recognized as Lewis's most important scholarly work.[11] In the chapter on "Allegory" he describes a fascinating process of transformation of the ancient gods of classical mythology into personifications of certain virtues in medieval allegory. Allegory, Lewis claims, is not merely a medieval phenomenon; it generally belongs to the human mind. But what is its relation to myth?

Lewis distinguishes symbolism, a mode of thought, from allegory, a mode of expression. The first drift toward allegory can be found in the poetry of the Roman Empire, for example, *Thebaid* of Statius. In this poem gods lose their supernatural power and become more and more like personifications of one particular quality or phenomenon: Mars of War or Bacchus of Drunkenness. Lewis calls the twilight of gods "the mid-morning of the personifications" (*Allegory* 52). Yet the causes of this twilight must not be seen to be a result of Christianity. Lewis asserts that monotheism should be regarded not as a rival but as the maturity of polytheism. In the case of Western thought, the idea of One single power moving the world appears in the philosophy of the Stoics: "The gods are to be aspects, manifestations, temporary or partial embodiments of the single power . . . personifications of the abstracted attributes of the One" (57–58). The change in the treatment of pagan gods in late classical and medieval poetry became crucial for the history of imagination:

> It is difficult for the modern man of letters to value this quiet revolution as it deserves. We are apt to take it for granted that a poet has at his command, besides the actual world and the world of his own religion, a third world of myth and fancy. The probable, the marvellous-taken-as-fact, the marvellous-known-to-be-fiction—such is the triple equipment of the post-Renaissance poet. . . . Go back to the beginnings of any literature and you will not find it. (82)

Thus, unlike the modern poet, the ancient poet only had two worlds at hand. In the course of time, it was the use of the old gods in allegory which preserved them and provided Europe with the "'third world' of romantic imagining" (82). In the first place, classical poetry treats gods as objects of worship, of fear, of hatred. As long as they are believed in, gods cannot be looked at from the point of view of aesthetics. As Lewis claims:

> The gods must be, as it were, disinfected of belief. . . . For poetry to spread its wings fully, there must be, besides the believed religion, a marvellous that knows itself as myth. For this to come about, the old marvellous, which once was taken as fact, must be stored somewhere, not wholly dead, but in a winter sleep, waiting its time. . . . Such a sleeping place was provided for the gods by allegory. Allegory may seem, at first, to have killed them; but it killed only as the sower kills, for gods, like other creatures, must die to live. (83)

It is interesting to note that in this passage Lewis uses the metaphor of Resurrection with regard to literature. Drawing on his own experience, he also claims that for the post-Renaissance author mythology becomes the source of imagery. But, if the gods are dead images, what is the purpose of using mythology in creative writing? The answer is partly given by Lewis in his other renowned work, *A Preface to "Paradise Lost."*

In the course of the discussion of Milton's poem, Lewis raises the question of originality in mythopoeic works. He urges that there should not be any attempt at novelty regarding the "ingredients" of such poetry. Whatever its author does with the ingredients can be as original as the author wishes,

> But giants, dragons, paradises, gods, and the like are themselves the expression of certain basic elements in man's spiritual experience. In that sense they are more like words—the words of a language which speaks the else unspeakable—than they are like the people and places in a novel. To give them radically new characters is not so much original as ungrammatical. (56)

In order to handle the mythical material properly, a storyteller must possess what Lewis calls "the good unoriginality." The whole point in this case is not in producing the effect of the unexpected upon the reader, but in "evoking with a perfection and accuracy beyond expectation the very image that has haunted us all our lives" (57). This task appears to Lewis to be much more challenging than creating "the short-lived pleasure of any novelty." At this point the question arises: why was Lewis so concerned about keeping mythological images unchanged?

To a certain extent, the answer comes from his attitude to myths as splinters of truth, the idea bestowed upon him by Barfield and Tolkien. In chapter 15 of *Miracles* he talks about myth as "not a misunderstood history (as Euhemerus thought) nor diabolical illusion (as some Fathers thought) nor priestly lying (as the philosophers of the Enlightenment thought) but, at its best, a real though unfocused gleam of divine truth falling on human imagination" (138n). It appears that, in Lewis's opinion, changes of mythological imagery by an individual author will inevitably cause a distortion of meaning. A similar caution is expressed by Lewis with regard to the "anatomizing" of myth by its "scientists."

The "scientists' " practice of applying the methods of depth psychology to the study of literature (including folk-tales and myths) is attacked by Lewis in his paper "Psycho-Analysis and Literary Criticism," originally published in *Essays and Studies* (1942). He examines Freud's notion that all works of art can be causally traced to the fantasies—"that is the day-dreams or waking wish-fulfilments—of the artist" (286). Lewis does not deny that day-dreaming may become the source of literature, but he emphasizes that the Freudian notion of "fantasy" is deeply rooted in such phenomena of our life as honor, power, riches, or the love of women. The doctrine of symbols is not disputed by Lewis as regards the matter of fact. He confesses that his special knowledge is not sufficient for the argument against this theory. One of the points he maintains is that not every author or reader necessarily goes through the psychological experiences in the manner described by Freud. In other words: "In order to explain the symbols which they themselves insist on we must admit that humanity is interested in many other things besides sex, and that admission is the thin end of the wedge" (296). In the Freudian view, many different stories appear simply as different versions of the same story. Lewis expresses strong objections to this idea: ". . . a story about a golden dragon plucking the apple of immortality in a garden at the world's end, and a dream about one's pen going through the paper while one scribbles a note are, in Freudian terms, the same story. But they are not the same as literature" (296). The last statement is "the most uncompromising form" of Lewis's defense against the psychoanalytic theory of literature. Having discussed Freud, Lewis looks at a different interpretation of myth and imagery, the doctrine of Primordial Images or Archetypal Patterns advanced by Jung.

According to this theory, there exists a collective unconscious that is common to humanity and, to a certain extent, the animal world. This collective unconscious contains the reactions of mind to the most universal situations, and these "primitive" reactions, in turn, are expressed in images. What we call today "myths" are the images recovered from the collective unconscious: tragic myths (about the sorrow or pain of the world) and joyous myths (about the joy of the world). What does Lewis have to say about this explanation? Interestingly enough, the generally anti-scientist Lewis (as far as the matter of myth is concerned) questions the *scientific* validity of Jung's doctrine. He says that some people, quite understandably, prefer to stay "outside the magic circle, to stick to modern, self-conscious, self-explanatory aesthetics" (297). In his opinion, the fascination of this theory rests upon the strength of the emotional reaction of its readers; some immediately revolt, others are equally enchanted. Renouncing his judgments of the scientific values, Lewis assigns himself to the latter group: "I perceive at once that even if it turns out to be bad science it is excellent poetry" (297).

Later in this essay Lewis analyzes one of the passages from Jung's "Mind and the Earth," which deals with "the beginnings and *foundations* of the mind, with *things that from immemorial time have lain buried in the depths* . . ." (298, Lewis's italics). His own reader's reaction is expressed by the exclamation: "Isn't this grand?" Lewis imagines himself together with Schliemann, Collingwood, Wordsworth, "with British Israelites and Baconians and historians of Atlantis, with Renaissance magicians and seekers for the sources of the Nile. In a word I am enjoying myself immensely" (298).

The point Lewis wishes to make here is that Jung's discussion of "primordial images" itself awakes a primordial image. This is exactly the explanation of its power to excite the human mind. He claims that Jung has not actually explained the pleasure of entertaining primordial images and concludes with a typical Lewisian analogy: "The *idea* that our sorrow is part of the world's sorrow is, in certain moods, moving enough: the mere *fact* that lots of other people have had toothache does not make toothache less painful" (300). Yet the essay does not offer any solution to the question raised by Jung. Lewis thinks that the mystery of primordial images is far deeper than one may think. Thus, humanity has been, and will be, searching for explanations—"why should I not be allowed to write in this vein as well as everyone else?" (300) This rhetorical question reminds us of his earlier proposal of *mythonomy*, the science of the nature of myths, which Lewis made in 1928.

However, Lewis does not actually write about the origins or nature of myth. The reason why he reconsiders his attitude to the study of myth can be well explained by the dramatic change which took place in Lewis's beliefs in 1931. After his rediscovery of Christianity, instead of proposing a new "science" of myth, Lewis begins to realize the limitations of any scientific or rational analysis in striving to explain the phenomenon of myth and its power. By the time of the publication of *An Experiment in Criticism* (1961), he must have been well confirmed in this opinion. In this book Lewis confines himself to looking at myth in terms of its literary value, rather than falling into the trap of trying to account for the unexplainable. In the chapter entitled "On Myth," Lewis provides the reader with his most comprehensive description of this phenomenon. He notes that there exists a particular kind of story which has a value independent of its embodiment in any literary work. The name of *myth* given to this kind of story is somehow unfortunate. First, originally the word *muthos* was used to describe any kind of story; second, not all stories that would be classified as such by an anthropologist are myths. Lewis explains:

274

> Most of them [primitive stories], whatever they may have meant to ancient and savage man, are to us meaningless and shocking not only by their cruelty and obscenity but by their apparent silliness—almost what seems insanity. Out of this rank and squalid undergrowth the great myths—Orpheus, Demeter and Persephone, the Hesperides, Balder, Ragnarok, or Ilmarinen's forging of the Sampo—rise like elms. Conversely, certain stories which are not myths in the anthropological sense, having been invented by individuals in fully civilised periods, have what I should call the "mythical quality". (*Experiment* 42)

Thus Lewis is not even content with the name given to what he means by *myth*, and most of ancient pagan myths appear to him as an expression of the childhood of humanity. The following characteristics are ascribed by Lewis to this kind of story: 1) it is "extra-literary" (one story occurs in different authors); 2) its pleasure does not depend on suspense or surprise; 3) the readers do not project themselves into the characters, who are "like shapes moving in a different world"; 4) it deals with impossibles and prenaturals; 5) the experience of myth is always grave (comic myth is impossible); and 6) the experience is also awe-inspiring, numinous (*Experiment* 44). It is noteworthy that what we are granted here is merely a *description* of the qualities of myth. Lewis does not actually conduct any *analysis* of a particular myth, for any kind of "anatomizing" in this case may be damaging for the wholeness of its meaning.[12] As Tolkien remarked in his famous lecture "*Beowulf:* The Monsters and the Critics": "The significance of myth is not easily to be pinned on paper by analytical reasoning. . . . [M]yth is alive at once and in all its parts, and dies before it can be dissected" (15).

As was the case with "Psycho-Analysis and Literary Criticism," the question of whether myths are primitive science, the remains of rituals, or revelations from the unconscious, is taken by Lewis to be outside the scope of discussion. His primary concern is with "the effect of myths as they act on the conscious imagination of minds more or less like our own, not with their hypothetical effect on pre-logical minds or their pre-history in the unconscious" (*Experiment* 45). As early as in *Allegory* Lewis points out that in order to acquire the quality that affects human imagination, myth must cease to be believed in. In that work he also asserts that today the realm of myth provides the author with vivid imagery. In *Experiment* the reader is told that the literary presentation of myth is not particularly important for its appreciation: "The value of myth is not a specifically literary value, nor the appreciation of myth a specifically literary experience. . . . [T]he behaviour of the myth-lover is extra-literary. . . . He gets out of myths what myths have to give" (46–48). This suggests a crucial distinction Lewis made between mythological imagery and plot. The story-maker or poet is free to rearrange mythological images in a story to any extent, as long as the images themselves remain unchanged. For instance, Bacchus and Pan, fauns and centaurs, naiads and dryads, or any other mythical creatures can be used in any imaginative story in many ways. The plots of the greater myths, on the other hand, have some extra-literary quality and cannot be changed: the meaning of Orpheus's story changes if any innovation is brought in the plot. This is how far Lewis goes in describing myth and its qualities.

Returning to the question of the scholarly study of myth, in *Experiment* Lewis claims that the desire to investigate the iceberg of myth below the surface "has genuinely scientific justification" (45), and remarks that for him this matter is of no personal interest or concern. Lewis was, nevertheless, concerned about the application of scientific methods to the study of literature, as the case with depth psychology has shown. Another scientific approach to literary study is attacked by him in the essay "The Anthropological Approach" (1962). Literary texts can surely be useful for the anthropologist. Lewis objects that this, however, does not mean that the reverse is true, that is, "anthropological study can make in return any valuable contribution to literary criticism. The attention now paid by medievalists to the mythical and ritual origins (real or supposed) of the romances suggests a widespread belief that it can" (301). For example, Lewis's opponent, R. S. Loomis, reduces the complexity of romances to a number of pagan myths. Still, this explains neither how nor why these romances delighted medieval readers and still delight many today. Therefore, Lewis argues against the applicability of the anthropological approach to the study of literary texts. In his opinion, it creates a great danger of substituting the real object of study for something hypothetical: "Already there are students who describe as 'enjoyment of medieval literature' what is really the enjoyment of brooding upon things (mostly hypothetical) in the dark past with which that literature is . . . connected in their minds" ("Anthropological" 310). Such a conclusion is reminiscent of that of "Psycho-Analysis and Literary Criticism." In both papers Lewis disputes the relevance of scientific explanations of literature, especially with regard to myth. Likewise in "The Anthropological Approach" he does not come out with any alternative solution, but simply insists on leaving the "mystery" of mythopoeic literature untouched by the sharp knife of scientific analysis. In fact, Lewis did not believe that there was such a thing as "modern science." If there had been any myth that he was rather dubious about, that was the myth of "Evolutionism" and "Development," promoted in the nineteenth and twentieth century. His thoughts concerning this matter are expounded in the essay "The Funeral of a Great Myth," which can be found in *Christian Reflections.*

Concluding Remarks

What then can be concluded from the survey of Lewis's reading and criticism of myth? His last essay with regard to myth and literary criticism, "The Anthropological Approach," is intended to be an objection against the validity of that way of looking at myth. Paradoxically, anthropology was the very first scientific lens through which the adolescent Lewis looked at mythology. By the end of the 1920s, partly under the influence of Barfield and Tolkien, he was gradually losing his atheism and recovering from the "chronological snobbery" toward the pre-Enlightenment period. This enabled Lewis to gain a fuller grasp of medieval and Renaissance literature, and in *Allegory* one finds a fascinating account of the evolution of the classical myth from the religious cult to the poetic imagery of Romantic poetry. In his later critical works, Lewis developed the ideas of the unchangeability of mythical images and plots, and "the good unoriginality" of mythopoeic literature.

By the year 1931, Lewis came from the idea of myth as a mere falsehood to the belief that Christianity is a "true myth" verified by a historical "fact," whereas Pagan myths chiefly remain products of human imagination. Their origins are vague and mixed: "in the huge mass of mythology which has come down to us a good many different sources are mixed—true history, allegory, ritual, the human delight in story-telling, etc. But among these sources I include the supernatural, both diabolical and divine" ("Religion" 101). Thus Lewis comes to believe that "at its best" myth is "a real though unfocused gleam of divine truth falling on human imagination" (*Miracles* 138n).

This view of myth could not but affect Lewis's attitude to the study of the origin and nature of myths. That is why his enthusiasm for "mythonomy," expressed in 1928, did not actually advance into any coherent theory or even laconic proposition. What one sees instead is his severe attack on the validity of Freudian, Jungian, and anthropological theories of myth and their use in literary criticism. Lewis's objections to the above theories must have been grounded in his reservations against the rational analysis of myth, for no scientific explanation will ever be able to account for the power of myth to produce a "numinous" experience. Thus Lewis himself also abandoned the idea of trying to find a logical explanation of "the iceberg" below the surface and confined his study of myth to literature.

And yet Lewis's chivalrous attempt to protect myth from the sharp knife of scientific analysis was doomed to be largely a failure even in the area of literary studies. It is possible that the reason for the comparative lack of success of Lewis's criticism of myth lies precisely in the lack of "scientific" methodology. In this regard, Lewis is very different from some of his contemporaries, such as Northrop Frye, whose approach to myth is based on the principles of structuralism and the theory of archetypes. Lewis's main emphasis was always on the enjoyment of reading and placing a text in its historical context so as to properly experience the "numinous" or see the imagined world. But such an approach, as well as Lewis's criticism of myth, has not received much appreciation by the succeeding generations of literary scholars.

Finally, we should remark that the understanding of myth by scholars, as well as their approach to the subject, is varied.[13] Returning to the *OED*, this diversity can be illustrated by some of the examples adduced in the entries on *myth* and its derivatives. The name of C. S. Lewis appears among the authors quoted there. In fact, one of these selected citations serves to "back up" the widely acknowledged 1.b. definition.[14] The *OED* quotation reads: "**1940** C. S.

277

Lewis *Problem of Pain* v. 64, I offer the following picture—a 'myth' in the Socratic sense, a not unlikely tale." This sentence is taken from the chapter "The Fall of Man," in which Lewis considers the Christian doctrine of the Fall and justifies his own account of it. In fact, the explanation of what he means by the "Socratic sense" is given as a footnote on the same page: "*I.e.*, an account of what *may have been* the historical fact. Not to be confused with 'myth' in Dr. Niebuhr's sense (*i.e.*, a symbolical representation of non-historical truth)" (*Pain* 64). Such a comment brings to mind Lewis's idea of myth as an expression of the absolute meaning of life in actual human history, which was discussed in connection with his conversion to Christianity. Yet, taken out of context, this sentence arouses confusion equally regarding Lewis's understanding of myth and the use of his words in the *OED*. Although Lewis emphasizes the quality of likelihood in this sentence, his words are quoted under the 1.b. definition of myth, in which the phrase "an untrue tale" inevitably creates the connotation of falsehood. Such a disagreement demonstrates the danger of confining oneself to concise dictionary definitions, and contributes to the misunderstanding of Lewis's view of myth among a general audience.

Epilogue: From Mythonomy to Mythopoeia

In the final analysis, it is not for his scholarly study of myth that C. S. Lewis is so popular today. His preoccupation with myth reached its summit in his imaginative writing. There must be certain reasons for the fact that the distinguished medieval and Renaissance scholar is known chiefly as a fantasy writer. One of them is the freedom that imagination offers to the author. As becomes clear from his inaugural lecture in Cambridge, Lewis felt out of his element in modern academia and considered himself to be "a spokesman of Old Western Culture" ("*Temporum*" 10–11). Was he capable of defending this old order? He was, though not so much in the academic world, as in his own stories. To some literary critics, even as a myth-maker, Lewis looks a bit of a "dinosaur" in the context of "post-Christian culture."

In his renowned work on myth, *The Hero with a Thousand Faces* (1949), Joseph Campbell claims: "the democratic ideal of the self-determining individual, the invention of the power-driven machine, and the development of the scientific method of research, have so transformed human life that the long inherited, timeless universe of symbols has collapsed" (387). Unlike in the times of those great mythologies (which are regarded by us as fictions), today meaning is centered on the self-expressive individual rather than the whole universe. That is why Campbell later characterized our age as the age of "creative mythology," in which great works can no longer "combine in a unified tradition to which followers then can adhere, but are individual and various" (*Masks* 40). On the other hand, the literary scholar Colin Manlove admits that, although in the post-Darwinian era much of Christian mythology was indeed open to question, the literary tradition of Christian fantasy did not die: "In the first place it ceases to be written by the dominant literary figures: it is now the product of minor, often eccentric writers" (*Christian Fantasy* 158). Lewis is mentioned by Manlove as one of this latter group.

On the one hand, Lewis's imaginative stories can indeed be considered as a form of his own "creative mythology." On the other hand, the way in which Lewis creates his mythology appears to be out of tune with our age. To start with, its major source is not the self-expressive individual spoken of by Campbell.[15] The study of classical and medieval literature had a profound effect on Lewis as a myth-maker. As a result, both metaphysical and cosmological aspects of his imaginary world seem to be deeply rooted in the beliefs of those periods.[16] Since Lewis did not regard writing as mere expression of personality, he adopted what he called the "bookish culture" of the Middle Ages.[17] A medieval author did not see any harm in rewriting what had been written by his predecessors, including those who lived in the pre-Christian world. According to Lewis, the medieval author tells us about certain images not "because his own poetic imagination invented them . . . but because he has read about them in a book" ("Imagination" 42).

In practicing mythopoeia Lewis shows a similar kind of "good unoriginality." For example, in spite of the prevalence of the Christian message in the Chronicles of Narnia, one sees an interesting mixture of motifs and characters originating in pre-Christian mythologies, as well as later mythopoeic literature.[18] Thus, in the account of Narnian creation Lewis draws simultaneously on Genesis, Ovid, Lucretius, and Milton; the scene of Aslan's sacrifice has a setting of pagan mysteries: the stone knife and the Stone Table, similar to Celtic *cromlechs*; in *The Horse and His Boy* we find a peculiar admixture of characters and motifs deriving from Arabian, Babylonian, Greek, Roman, Celtic, and Norse tales; the finale of *Prince Caspian* is marked by the arrival of Bacchus with Maenads and Silenus, and ecstatic dance reminding of Greek *Dionisias* (*Bacchanalias* in Rome); the search for the Narnian Paradise beyond the sea in *The Voyage of the Dawn Treader* can be traced to the tradition of the Irish *immram*;[19] *The Silver Chair* represents a popular motif of underworld journey into the realm of the Green Witch, a Narnian Persephone; and the Narnian apocalypse in *The Last Battle* incorporates the images of Revelation and *Ragnarök*. These are only the major and most obvious parallels one can find in the Chronicles to illustrate Lewis's rewriting of the mythological tradition.

As far as the nature and power of myth is concerned, Lewis's most mature and impressive attempt to express his views is his last novel, *Till We Have*

Faces. His own retelling of the pagan myth of Cupid and Psyche incorporates Lewis's ideas of myth as both a product of human imagination and "gleam of divine truth," of vague and mixed origins of ancient myths and of the power of myth to offer a "numinous" experience. The author also brings into his version a Christian connotation, portraying Psyche as "*anima naturaliter Christiana* making the best of the Pagan religion she is brought up in and thus being guided . . . toward the true understanding of God" (*Letters* 462). In the course of Lewis's narrative, the reader witnesses the story of Psyche through the eyes of Orual, hears the myth of Istra as told by a priest in her temple, and finally sees the story of Psyche and Orual as told by pictures in the world where everything is "true" (331). The difference between the three versions of the same story is significant with regard to the understanding of Lewis's views of the nature of myth. Thus the first version appears to be incomplete and subjective, for Orual is blinded by her love for Psyche. Since the reader is familiar with the story as seen and told by Orual, the priest's tale appears as the mixture of truth, allegory, ritual, and human invention. It is only the last "true" version that offers the "numinous" experience which makes it possible to change Orual from within and reunite her with Psyche.[20] Lewis suggests that in order to learn the truth, one must penetrate the veil of the present reality. In fact, the name *Maia* which Psyche uses to call Orual is reminiscent of the Hindu concept of "maya," the illusion into which humans are brought by living in the material world. This illusion disables Orual to see the Palace on the Mountain.

With regard to mythological imagery, *Faces* draws largely on various traditions of the Hellenistic world. The range and diversity of the material used by Lewis is by far wider than in Apuleius's version. Moreover, the way in which Lewis changes and mixes mythical "ingredients" can suggest further interpretations of the story. The city of Glome stands on the banks of the river Shennit, and the area is flooded in the spring. This immediately reminds the reader of the ancient civilizations, in particular Babylon and Egypt. The main temple of the city is the House of Ungit, the goddess signifying the earth, "the womb and the mother of all living things" (281). Lewis's description of the House of Ungit could be based on the sanctuaries of Astarte, Cybele, and Isis, whose cults were characterized by terrible and cruel sacrifices. There is also the god of the Mountain, Ungit's son and husband, who represents the air and the sky. The main yearly celebration in the temple of Ungit is the rite of the Year's birth, "when the Priest is shut up in the house of Ungit from the sunset, and on the following noon fights his way out and is said to be born" (279). All this is strongly reminiscent of "dying gods" and "fertility rites" which fascinated Lewis in adolescence. Indeed, the rites of death and revival are more widely and solemnly celebrated in the lands bordering the Eastern Mediterranean, where people annually celebrated the decay and revival of life, personified in a deity who dies every year and comes to life again. In Western Asia and Egypt this god was known under the names of Tammuz, Adonis, Osiris, and Attis, and his mother/spouse as Ishtar, Astarte, and Cybele. Their yearly rites varied in detail from land to land but were the same in substance.[21] The similarities between Oriental Mother Goddesses and Ungit are evident, but it is also striking that the name *Ishtar* (otherwise spelt "Istar") strongly resembles Psyche's native name, *Istra*. Besides, for a while Orual comes to identify herself with Ungit, so the parallels between the stories of Psyche and the myths of Mother Goddess explain the prophecy given to Orual by the god of the Mountain: "You also shall be Psyche" (182). By means of rewriting and combining the elements of various mythical images, Lewis creates his own version of myth.

Lewis's mythopoeic work illustrates his belief that myth in one world might be fact in another. In other words, what we consider a myth may be reality in a different dimension: "What flows into you from myth is not truth but reality. . . . Myth is the mountain whence all the different streams arise which become truths down here in the valley; *in hac valle abstractionis*" ("Myth Became Fact" 66).[22] Most of the ancient myths have today become meaningless or even absurd, and a similar destiny has almost overwhelmed the Christian story. For Lewis, the rediscovery of Christianity became one of the main sources of inspiration. As he guides Orual through myth "toward a true understanding of God," he leads the reader of his fictions down that same path. Trying to represent Christian values in a new light, Lewis inevitably brings into his imaginary worlds the ideas derived from the two major areas of his life: his reading and scholarship.

Notes

1. The reason for this phenomenon in European languages is explained in Eliade 1–2.

2. Recent publications on this subject include essays by Kath Filmer and David H. Stewart in Edwards; and by Colin Manlove, Stephen Medcalf, Paul Piehler, and Gregory Wolfe in Schakel and Huttar, *Word*.

3. Although originally both Lang and Frazer were followers of Sir E. B. Tylor, their own explanations of mythology differed. Lang criticized Frazer in his *Magic and Religion*, especially chapters 5 and 11.

4. An excellent study of the "Great War" has been undertaken by Adey. Among the questions argued about by Lewis and Barfield was the role of imagination and its relation to fact.

5. A good account of Barfield's work is presented in Reilly 13–97. The question of the origins of, and the relationship between, myth and language is addressed in particular detail in my doctoral thesis: "Scholarship and Mythopoeia: Myth and Language in the Works of Barfield, Lewis and Tolkien" (U of Manchester, 1999).

6. The similarities between the ideas of Barfield and Tolkien are discussed in detail by Flieger (especially chapters 3 and 4).

7. This remark was ironically made by Tolkien in the objection to the theory of the nineteenth-century philologist Max Müller.

8. The famous evening of 19 September 1931 is fully described in Carpenter, *Inklings* 42–45; Carpenter, *Tolkien* 146–48; Green and Hooper 116–18; and Lewis's *Stand* 241, 425–28.

9. A more detailed account of Tolkien's view on myth is given in his essay "On Fairy-Stories." See particularly the section on "Origins."

10. For a full account of Lewis's views on the truth of the Christian story see his article "Myth Became Fact" reprinted in *Dock* 39–46. On a similar proposition adopted by Barfield and the Anthroposophists, G. K. Chesterton, and Austin Farrer, see Carpenter, *Inklings* 47n.

11. The question of how this book is regarded by medievalists today is discussed in the chapter on Lewis and medieval literature in this volume. Paul Piehler shows some deficiencies in Lewis's account of allegory in his paper "Myth or Allegory?"

12. In this regard, Lewis appears to be very different from his contemporary Northrop Frye, whose *Anatomy of Criticism* (1957) has become a classic for the study of myth in literature.

13. An interesting collection of essays by Lewis's contemporaries was published in Sebeok (ed.). For a more recent study of major twentieth-century theories of myth, see Strenski.

14. See the first page of the present essay.

15. At the beginning of his academic career, Lewis attacked the notion that poetry represents an "expression of personality." See his essay "The Personal Heresy in Criticism" (1934), reprinted in *Rehabilitations* and *The Personal Heresy*.

16. Especially Plato and Neo-Platonism. See, for example, Johnson and Houtman.

17. As Lewis claims in *The Discarded Image*: ". . . the book-author unit, basic for modern criticism, must be abandoned when we are dealing with medieval literature" (210).

18. That is Dante, Ariosto, Malory, Spenser, or Milton. The origins of Narnian images are well presented in Huttar, "C. S. Lewis's Narnia and 'Grand Design'" in Schakel, *Longing* 119–35; Ford, *Companion to Narnia*; and Schakel, *Reading with the Heart*. The present author has also undertaken research in this area—see Kuteeva.

19. A voyage tale. The word *immram* literally means 'rowing-about.'

20. It is notable that Lewis makes the "true" version of myth appear in pictures, since he believed that "Myth does not essentially exist in *words* at all . . . in myth the imagined events are the body and something inexpressible is the soul: the words, or mime, or pictorial series are not even clothes—they are not much more than a telephone" (*George MacDonald* xxvii–xxviii).

21. The cults of the Mother Goddess and her son/lover are described in detail by James Fraser in his *Golden Bough*. I discuss the influence of Frazer upon C. S. Lewis in my article, "Lewis's Istra and Frazer's Ishtar: Cults and Rituals in C. S. Lewis's *Till We Have Faces* (1956)" in *ANTROPOlógicas* 3 (2000).

22. "In the valley of separation."

Works Cited

Adey, Lionel. *C. S. Lewis's "Great War" with Owen Barfield*. Victoria, B.C.: U of Victoria, 1978.

Campbell, Joseph. *The Hero with a Thousand Faces*. 1949. London: Fontana, 1993.

———. *The Masks of God: Creative Mythology*. 1968. New York: Arkana, 1991.

Carpenter, Humphrey. *The Inklings*. London: Allen & Unwin, 1978.

———. *J. R. R. Tolkien: A Biography*. London: Allen & Unwin, 1979.

Edwards, Bruce L., ed. *The Taste of the Pineapple: Essays on C. S. Lewis as Reader, Critic and Imaginative Writer*. Bowling Green, OH: Bowling Green State UP, 1988.

Eliade, Mircea. *Myth and Reality*. Trans. by William R. Task. New York: Harper, 1963.

Filmer, Kath. "The Polemic Image: The Role of Metaphor and Symbol in the Fiction of C. S. Lewis." Edwards 149–65.

Flieger, Verlyn. *Splintered Light: Logos and Language in Tolkien's World*. Grand Rapids: Eerdmans, 1983.

Ford, Paul F. *Companion to Narnia*. San Francisco: Harper and Row, 1980.

Frye, Northrop. *Anatomy of Criticism: Four Essays*. Princeton: Princeton UP, 1957.

Green, R. L., and Walter Hooper. *C. S. Lewis: A Biography*. London: Collins, 1974.

Huttar, Charles. "C. S. Lewis's Narnia and the 'Grand Design.'" Schakel 119–35.

Johnson, William G., and Marcia K. Houtman. "Platonic Shadows in C. S. Lewis's Narnia *Chronicles*." *Modern Fiction Studies* 32 (1986): 75–89.

Jung, Carl. "Mind and the Earth." *Contributions to Analytical Psychology*. Trans. H. G. and C. F. Baynes. New York: Harcourt, Brace, 1928. 99–140.

Kuteeva, Maria B. "C. S. Lewis's *Chronicles of Narnia*: Their Origins in Mythology, Literature and Scholarship." M. Phil. thesis, U of Manchester, 1995.

Lang, Andrew. *Magic and Religion*. London: Longmans, 1901.

Lewis, C. S. *The Allegory of Love: A Study in Medieval Tradition*. 1936. Oxford: Clarendon, 1979.

———. "The Anthropological Approach." *Literary* 301–11.

———. "*De Audiendis Poetis*." *Medieval* 1–17.

———. "*De Descriptione Temporum*." *Literary* 1–14.

———. *The Discarded Image: An Introduction to Medieval and Renaissance Literature*. Cambridge: Cambridge UP, 1964.

———. *An Experiment in Criticism*. Cambridge: Cambridge UP, 1961.

———. "The Funeral of a Great Myth." *Christian Reflections*. Ed. Walter Hooper. London: Geoffrey Bles, 1967. 82–93.

———. "Imagination and Thought in the Middle Ages." *Medieval* 41–63.

———. *Letters of C. S. Lewis*. Ed. W. H. Lewis. 1966. Rev. ed. Ed. Walter Hooper. London: HarperCollins, 1988.

———. *Miracles: A Preliminary Study*. 1947. London: Collins, 1966.

———. "Myth Became Fact." *God in the Dock: Essays on Theology*. Ed. Walter Hooper. 1970. London: Collins, 1979. 63–57.

———. *A Preface to "Paradise Lost."* London: Oxford UP, 1942.

———. *The Problem of Pain*. London: Geoffrey Bles, 1940.

———. "Psycho-Analysis and Literary Criticism." *Literary* 286–300.

———. *Rehabilitations and Other Essays*. London: Oxford UP, 1939.

———. "Religion without Dogma?" *Undeceptions: Essays on Theology and Ethics*. London: Geoffrey Bles, 1971. 99–114.

———. *Selected Literary Essays*. Ed. Walter Hooper. Cambridge: Cambridge UP, 1969.

———. *Studies in Medieval and Renaissance Literature*. Ed. Walter Hooper. Cambridge: Cambridge UP, 1966.

———. *Surprised by Joy: The Shape of My Early Life*. London: Geoffrey Bles, 1955.

———. *They Stand Together: The Letters of C. S. Lewis to Arthur Greeves (1914–1963)*. Ed. Walter Hooper. London: Collins, 1979.

———. *Till We Have Faces: A Myth Retold*. 1956. London: HarperCollins, 1978.

———. "William Morris." *Literary* 219–31.

———, and E. M. W. Tillyard. *The Personal Heresy: A Controversy*. London: Oxford UP, 1939.

———, ed. *George MacDonald: An Anthology*. London: Geoffrey Bles, 1946.

Manlove, Colin. " 'Caught Up into the Larger Pattern': Images and Narrative Structures in C. S. Lewis's Fiction." Schakel and Huttar 256–76.

———. *Christian Fantasy: From 1200 to the Present*. London: Macmillan, 1992.

Medcalf, Stephen. "Language and Self-Consciousness: The Making and Breaking of C. S. Lewis's Personae." Schakel and Huttar 109–44.

Piehler, Paul. "Myth or Allegory? Archetype and Transcendence in the Fiction of C. S. Lewis." Schakel and Huttar 199–212.

Reilly, R. J. *Romantic Religion: A Study of Barfield, Lewis, Williams, and Tolkien*. Athens: U of Georgia P, 1971.

Schakel, Peter J., ed. *The Longing for a Form*. Kent, OH: Kent State UP, 1977.

———, and Charles A. Huttar. *Word and Story in C. S. Lewis*. Columbia: U of Missouri P, 1991.

Sebeok, Thomas A., ed. *Myth: A Symposium*. Bloomington: Indiana UP, 1958.

Stewart, David H. "Style and Substance in the Prose of C. S. Lewis." Edwards 92–109.

Strenski, Ivan. *Four Theories of Myth in Twentieth-Century History: Cassirer, Eliade, Lévi-Strauss and Malinowski*. London: Macmillan, 1987.

Tolkien, J. R. R. "On Fairy-Stories." *The Monsters and the Critics and Other Essays*. Ed. Christopher Tolkien. London: Allen & Unwin, 1983. 109–61.

Wolfe, Gregory. "Essential Speech: Language and Myth in the Ransom Trilogy." Schakel and Huttar 58–75.

15
Fantasy

Kath Filmer-Davies

Lewis and the Baptized Imagination

The fantasy fiction of C. S. Lewis demonstrates that its author is one of the twentieth century's best writers of fantasy, especially for children, and that he was also one of the best theorists of fantasy literature. The first point I substantiate by anecdote: during a recent spell in the hospital, mention of C. S. Lewis on my part stimulated a common response among the nursing and other staff: "Oh, *he* wrote the Narnian stories!" This point, as well as the second, I shall demonstrate in the course of this chapter, as I examine Lewis's fantasy works in the light of his own theoretical concepts. This chapter will concentrate on Lewis's fantasy novels, rather than on the short stories.

Those works are *The Pilgrim's Regress* (1933), *Out of the Silent Planet* (1938), *Perelandra* (1943), *That Hideous Strength* (1945), and *Till We Have Faces* (1956); plus the seven titles which comprise the Narnian Chronicles (1950–56): *The Lion, the Witch and the Wardrobe; Prince Caspian; The Voyage of the Dawn Treader; The Silver Chair; The Horse and His Boy; The Magician's Nephew;* and *The Last Battle.* One quality is common to them all; in each of them Lewis "baptizes" the imagination, and "redeems" the older myths from which he draws. In other words, Lewis brings the sacred into the mundane world, and sets it in its rightful pre-eminent place, enriching our understanding of pre-Christian myth, or as Tolkien calls it "pre-evangelium."

Lewis himself, upon reading George MacDonald's mythopoeic work *Phantastes,* wrote that "the whole book had about it . . . quite unmistakably, a certain quality of Death, good death. What it actually did to me was to convert, even to baptize my imagination . . ." (Preface to *George MacDonald* xxxiii). But "baptizing the imagination" is not an end in itself: it is a step on the way to further development, further growth. Lewis wrote "fairy tales" for adults and children because he believed that "fairy tales liberate archetypes which dwell in the collective unconscious, and when we read a good fairy tale, we are obeying the old precept, 'Know Thyself'" ("On Three Ways" 27).[1] He further suggests that the psychological awakening achieved by the power of archetypal images and patterns in literature may also be provoked by the use in such stories of non-human characters, such as dwarfs, giants, and talking beasts: "I believe these to be at least (for they may have many other sources of power and beauty) an admirable hieroglyphic which conveys psychology, types of character, more briefly than novelistic presentation and to readers whom novelistic presentation could not yet reach" (27). Lewis uses this approach in his criticism of George Orwell's two polemic works, *Nineteen Eighty-Four* and *Animal Farm*. Expressing a marked preference for the latter, Lewis observes that "when Orwell turns all his characters into animals he makes them more fully human" ("Orwell" 103), and "this congeries of guzzling pigs, snapping dogs, and heroic horses—this is what humanity is like; very good, very bad, very pitiable, very honourable" (104).

Certainly in Lewis's own fantasy fiction, the portrayals of the beastliness of humanity and the humanity of the Narnian beasts present the reader with psychological and spiritual truths—not merely about the human race in general, but about the universal qualities shared by individual humans as well. The fiction of fantasy, Lewis argues, stirs up within the reader a longing for what is quite definitely "Other" and transcendent, which is quite unlikely to confuse or disturb the reader in the way realistic fiction might—for example, the school story which has the effect that the heroic deeds of the protagonists encourage readers to daydream about emulating them in real life. Failure to do so might well result, Lewis says, in the reader's becoming disenchanted with the real self in the real world. Fairy tales and fantasies have the opposite effect, because fantasy fiction

286

> arouses a longing for he [the reader] knows not what. It stirs and troubles him (to his life-long enrichment) with the dim sense of something beyond his reach and, far from dulling or emptying the actual world, gives it a new dimension of depth. He does not despise real woods because he has read of enchanted woods: the reading makes all real woods a little enchanted. ("On Three Ways" 29–30)

In the same way reading about enchanted woods confers a sense of enchantment and wonder on real woods, so too does reading about "enchanted religion" deepen the sense of awe and wonder, and indeed the significance and meaning, of religion in this world. Lewis believed that Christianity is the poorer for its lack of a sense of wonder, and responses to it can be paralyzed by the demands it makes for suitably reverential attitudes and emotions. He writes of his experience in childhood, "The whole subject was associated with lowered voices; almost as if it were something medical. But supposing that by casting all these things into an imaginary world, stripping them of their stained-glass and Sunday School associations, one could make them for the first time appear in their real potency?" ("Fairy Stories" 37). The sustained response to the Narnian Chronicles has proven that Lewis's theory was correct. Additionally, it is clear that the genre of fantasy offered Lewis the greatest opportunities for creating literary works of enduring power. His recognition of the power of fantasy can be seen in the following, often-quoted passage from his essay "Sometimes Fairy Stories May Say Best What's to Be Said":

> The Fantastic or Mythical is a Mode available at all ages for some readers; for others, at none. At all ages, if it is well used by the author and meets the right reader, it has the same power: to generalise while remaining concrete, to present in palpable form, not concepts or even experiences but whole classes of experience, and to throw off irrelevancies. But at its best it can do more: it can give us experiences we have never had, and thus, instead of "commenting on life" can add to it. (38)

"Adding to life" is precisely the secret of the Narnian Chronicles, which admit readers to a world of wonder and delight. The world of the reader encountering the Narnian stories is itself a kind of "Narnia." The Ransom trilogy explores human psychological and spiritual issues by taking the reader into space—*inner* space, the place of the human spirit. *The Great Divorce* uses analogy and metaphor to mirror the faces of human selfishness and desire for "control," and Lewis's final novel, and perhaps his greatest, *Till We Have Faces*, is about the relationship of the human soul to its God, and the demand for submission and obedience—first made by the soul of God, then later relinquished in submission to God. Lewis's chosen genre for his fiction was that of fantasy; he appreciated its potency and power.

287

Lewis and Later Fantasy Critics

A number of fantasy critics emphasize the spiritual and psychological value of fantasy literature, and in so doing anticipate or echo the points Lewis himself has made. Tolkien suggests that the reader is profoundly changed by the experience of reading. Fantasy provides escape—escape from mundanity, escape into something real and compelling, escape into psychological discovery and individuation; it provides recovery—the ability to take back into the mundane world the sense of enchantment achieved in the fantasy world; and it provides consolation—the expectation of resolution of conflict, of the promise of hope, the promise in Christian theology of the ultimate happy ending, the resurrection from death into eternal life.[2]

Ursula Le Guin, whose own *Earthsea Quartet* accords with her anti-Christian, Taoist philosophy, warns that fantasy literature is similar to "psychoanalysis," and that "*it will change you*" (italics hers) (*Language* 137). Elsewhere she explains why "Americans"—and indeed any resident of a similar Westernized society—fear the imagination, the metaphorical "dragons" to which she refers:

> . . . fantasy is true, of course. It isn't factual, but it is true. Children know that. Adults know it, too, and that is precisely why many of them are afraid of fantasy. They know that its truth challenges, even threatens, all that is false, all that is phoney, unnecessary, and even trivial in the life they have let themselves be forced into leading. (*Language* 44)

Lewis, too, believes that fantasy and myth are "not merely misunderstood history (as Euhemerus thought) nor diabolical illusion (as some of the fathers thought) nor priestly lying (as the philosophers of the Enlightenment thought) but, at [their] best, a real though unfocused gleam of divine truth falling on human imagination" (*Miracles* 134n). If Le Guin and Lewis emphasize spiritual and psychological growth in fantasy, and its inherent truth, Lloyd Alexander suggests that fantasy is "a dream we have made up ourselves," and therefore a dream which can come true:

> . . . There's no law in the fantasy world or in the real world that says some wishes can't come true. If fantasy is a kind of hopeful dream it's nevertheless one that we made up ourselves.
> And after all, how can we be less than our own dreams? (174)

Lewis's *The Great Divorce* is a dream romance, after the style of Dante; and dreams feature also in *That Hideous Strength*, as Jane Studdock is won to the cause of good at St. Anne's through her dreams and visions. In fact, her dreams and visions are the reason she is eagerly sought by both the "good" group at St. Anne's and the evil and corrupt "inner ring" at the National Institute for Co-ordinated Experiments, the incredibly nasty N.I.C.E. In both theory and practice, then, C. S. Lewis is a major contributor to twentieth-century fantasy literature. What sets his work apart, of course, is Lewis's unashamed confession of his Christian faith. Lives have indeed been changed by Lewis's fiction.

There, the human imagination is truly baptized and old myths, redeemed and reborn; and there, as much as in his nonfictional works on prayer, on the nature of love, and on human pain, Lewis stands out as an apologist not only for Christianity but also for the people who find the best explanations of things of the Spirit in his fiction.

Lewis's Worlds of the Spirit

Lewis is capable of telling a story that is both autotelic and powerful on its own behalf. Occasionally, especially in the space trilogy, he allows the didactic to intervene and to spoil the effect of the narrative. Such didacticism forces the reader out of the world of the story, and involves a violent resuscitation for the reader who has, in Tolkien's words, "entered the secondary world" of the story.

Of course, there are moments of sublime writing in the space trilogy, too. As when Lewis describes the song of the Malacandrian creatures: "A sense of great masses moving at visionary speeds, of giants dancing, of eternal sorrows eternally consoled, of he knew not what he had always known, awoke in him with the very first bars of the deep-mouthed dirge, and bowed his spirit as if the gate of heaven had opened before him" (*Planet* 148). Lewis's descriptions of new "planets" stir the imagination and the spirit. Nevertheless, in his mythic fantasy novel *Till We Have Faces*, Lewis does more; he produces a world and a character in which a reader's experience of identification with the protagonist can be intense because of the universality of her experience—that is, the enslavement to self which all humans must confront and renounce in order to be redeemed. The effect of this novel on many readers is profound; it certainly compels the receptive reader to "know thyself." If the confrontation with the need for self-knowledge is spiritually demanding, the experience is compensated for by the hope which lies in the subsequent processes of rebirth and regeneration. The text at the end of the novel trails off, so that the reader slips as easily back into mundane reality as the character slips from diary-writing into death. This novel, of all Lewis's fantasies, with its use of the first-person narration, is the most disturbing. The world he creates and into which readers find themselves drawn is that of the human mind and spirit, and the struggle into which the reader is drawn is precisely that of the five-times iterated scriptural warning that "whosoever finds his life shall lose it, whosoever loses his life shall find it" (see, for example, John 12:20–26). Indeed the character Orual herself is told: "Die before you die: there is no chance after" (291); and this book, which has undeniably been influenced by George Mac-

289

Donald's two novels *Phantastes* and *Lilith*, is also about good death; not merely about but in fact inviting death to the Self, a spiritual and psychological regeneration and rebirth, on the part of the reader. In doing this, Lewis also "redeems" the ancient myth of Cupid and Psyche, seeing in the old story the symbolism of the human soul's relationship to its God.

In this novel, the purpose of death to the ego, the consuming and self-aggrandizing Self, is to become the Psyche, the true soul; this, I think it might safely be said, was Lewis's own life-goal, the center of his Christian belief. As I have argued elsewhere, this, and not *Surprised by Joy*, is his spiritual autobiography. The novel can be interpreted on one level as showing how the human imagination and spirit must be "born again." Orual is not an evil woman; in fact she is a highly intellectual, highly skilled woman, who in her role as Queen of Glome rules quite wisely and effectively. She reforms many of the old barbaric practices, and her treatment of her subjects is generally compassionate and just. Nevertheless, her fallen nature is seen clearly in her dealings with those she loves: the suffocatingly possessive affection she has for her youngest sister Psyche, demanding to come first in her sister's life; her total rejection of the middle sister, Redival, who also is a young woman in need of love and guidance; and her demanding domination of the warrior Bardia, whose personal life with his wife and children she encroaches on with her whims and fancies, prevailing on him to offer her more than his position requires. Through her encounter with the God of the Grey Mountain, however, Orual gradually begins to change and to grow, to become aware of herself as the "bloated spider" who "bleeds" the life from those close to her, and to give up the claims she has exerted on others. Finally, Orual is reborn as Psyche, the true soul, and now beautiful, now individuated and spiritually whole (239). The "true soul," of course, is the reborn, redeemed, individuated spirit, the baptized imagination, the new Self.

The Narnian Chronicles also "baptize" the imagination. They are tales that have attracted young readers for more than forty years, and in that time have never failed in their imaginative power. Of course, there have been critics of Lewis's use of violent battles, and of other elements of his narratives, suggesting they owe more to Lewis's disturbed psyche than to parable and allegory. There may be problems with some elements of the narrative: what, for heaven's sake, has happened to the realm of Narnia when its rulers suddenly disappear? The Pevensie children leave mundane reality to dwell in Narnia, taking on new identities and living new lives, growing to adulthood and ruling as kings and queens. Their sudden departure from Narnia must leave Narnians bereaved and abandoned, but this issue is never treated. However, if we overlook such issues, we can see that every entrance to Narnia is redemptive; each character who enters Narnia is given the chance (figuratively) to "repent and be baptized." Some, like Susan, reject the opportunity. The baptismal element of the Narnian stories is sometimes made explicit, as when Eustace enters the Narnian world through the watery picture of a ship at sea and when he is "undragoned" and bathed afterwards; sometimes it is less explicit, as when Eustace and Jill Pole escape from the bullies at their school. These little "deaths" are preparatory to the final, conclusive death, in which the children find they have not only died through the work of their imaginations and their spirits, but also physically. They enter the eternal Narnia, the Form of which all that has gone before is the mere copy. Lewis's description of the "new heavens and the new earth" in the redeemed Narnia is a masterpiece of restraint, and yet perhaps provides one of the most moving and sublime passages in any of his fictional writings:

> ... Aslan turned to them and said:
>
> "You do not yet look so happy as I mean you to be."
>
> Lucy said, "We're so afraid of being sent away, Aslan. And you have sent us back into our own world so often."
>
> "No fear of that," said Aslan. "Have you not guessed?"
>
> Their hearts leaped and a wild hope rose within them.
>
> "There *was* a real railway accident," said Aslan softly. "Your father and mother and all of you are—as you used to call it in the Shadow-Lands—dead. The term is over: the holidays have begun. The dream is ended: this is the morning."
>
> And as He spoke He no longer looked to them like a lion, but the things that began to happen to them after that were so great and beautiful that I cannot write them. And for us this is the end of all the stories, and we can most truly say that they all lived happily ever after. But for them, it was only the beginning of the real story. All their life in this world and all their adventures in Narnia had only been the cover and the title page: now at last they were beginning Chapter One of the Great Story, which no one on earth has read: which goes on forever: in which every chapter is better than the one before. (*Battle* 183–84)

This scene from the final Narnian Chronicle tells readers why the imagination is to be baptized: it must be prepared for the apprehension of things too marvelous for the unredeemed mind to take in.

Lewis and the Celtic Otherworld

It is evident that Lewis was influenced by "Northernness" and by Norse myth. Nevertheless, Celtic scholars have pointed out that Lewis also draws from Celtic traditions in his depiction of "the Otherworld," the world a dimension away from this, a world accessible to fictional characters by crossing a threshold—not a standing stone or stone circle, but a spaceship, a railway train, a door in a wall—and accessible to readers in the process of reading, that is, through the imagination. By providing glimpses of the Otherworld, Lewis offers opportunities for the imagination to be "baptized" so that having seen enchanted worlds, we might also see this world as a place of enchantment, and behold the works of God's creation with a fresh sense of awe and wonder.

Lewis's depiction of the Otherworld is a little less skillful in his early work than in his later. The world of *The Pilgrim's Regress* is too obviously allegorical to be entered in any but the remotest, intellectual sense—a fact which Lewis himself noted in his 1943 preface to the work. But the Malacandra of *Out of the Silent Planet* has more to offer and to attract. It is a world of wonder, but not a wonderland; it is a spiritual Otherworld, whose fate is bound up with our own, and whose ruling spirits have great interest in the fate of humanity. Lewis uses symbols—of color, of a woman's breast, of rich jewelry, of a cathedral—to depict a heavenly, though flawed planet, and provides experiences through which the protagonist and the reader may touch the world of the spirit. Indeed, as Lewis observes in his essay "On Stories," he learned from David Lindsay the important and life-imparting truth about fiction that other worlds are best used as analogues of the human spirit, which is, after all, where all the real battles, struggles, and victories in human lives take part ("Stories" 11–12).

The motherly, womb-like world of Venus in *Perelandra* is also an Otherworld of enormous charm, although more attractive to the male reader than to the female, with its insistence on maternal breast-feeding in the mystical fruit, and the gentle rocking motion of the water foundations on which the islands float. Here, the motherless Lewis seems to have compensated almost suffocatingly for the abandonment he felt at his mother's death. On this planet, death is the death of the womb, a figure at the beginning of life and the grave at its end. Ransom returns to the womb, and is "reborn," and like the King and Queen of Perelandra, he too experiences redemption. After this adventure the reborn Ransom returns as the Pendragon, the modern-day King Arthur, in *That Hideous Strength*.

This latter novel loses some of the mythic touch of its predecessors. It is too political, too didactic to invite readerly participation in the same way. The mythic elements, when they appear, are marred by undergraduate humor; the spiritual-thriller aspect seems to owe rather too much to Charles Williams. The author intrudes into the story too much, and the reader cannot really enter the world Lewis offers. It is, for a start, too much like the mundane world, despite the uncomfortable insertion of fantasy and supernatural elements into it. There is no real Otherworld into which we might enter, into which we can be reborn and return regenerated.

Nevertheless, though this criticism of *That Hideous Strength* seems harsh, this novel was more influential than some of Lewis's other books. Reviewed by George Orwell (*The Manchester Evening News* 15 August 1945, 2), the book clearly influenced Orwell's own *Nineteen Eighty-Four*. Many of the themes and motifs, especially that of the perverted *logos*, correspond—and Orwell's dislike of the supernatural elements in Lewis's novel ("they make the ending a foregone conclusion," Orwell says) can be seen in the omission of anything supernatural in Orwell's pessimistic vision. In Orwell's novel, the imagination is suppressed and eradicated; in Lewis's, it triumphs and aids in the process of repentance and redemption.[3]

The Great Divorce does not use the Celtic notion of the Otherworld; it is a dream romance, and necessarily belongs to a separate genre even from the other Lewisian fantasies. *The Pilgrim's Regress* is also a work of allegory, after the style of Bunyan's *The Pilgrim's Progress*, and that too is a different genre of fantastic writing.

The Narnian Chronicles, while drawing extensively from classical myth, also offer an Otherworld that is almost completely Celtic. The tests the children face in Narnia are comparable with the test facing the *Mabinogion* hero Pwyll, prince of Dyfed, when he exchanges places with Arawn, the ruler of Annwfn, the Otherworldly kingdom. Pwyll, through self-discipline and loyalty, wins the respect and friendship of the Otherworldly ruler, and he even rules in Annwfn during Arawn's absence, killing the threatening evil giant on Arawn's behalf and according to his instructions. Similarly, the children in the Narnian stories earn the respect of the Narnians in battle and in moral tests. Eustace, who is undragoned, undergoes death and regeneration; Edward, who betrays Lucy and the Faun, must be redeemed from the thrall of the White Witch, a figure of spiritual death. Lewis, however, does not wish the reader to be held in thrall to spiritual death or to moral slavery; rather he leads readers through the series to the reality of physical death and the possibility of rebirth in the spiritual world beyond. He does this by appealing to the imagination, by filling the Otherworld with new life and energy, with visual and sensual delights, by allowing the reader to share the sense of awe and the marvelous which makes Narnia truly "fantastic" in the colloquial sense of the word.

I am grateful to Celtic scholar Rollan McCleary (author of the radio play *The Daughter of the Sea King*, a retelling of the story of Branwen, daughter of Llyr), for the information that Narnia is almost completely a Celtic Otherworld. McCleary cites the distortion of time, the entry by means of a threshold, the series of tests, and the imaginative growth and development of visitors to Narnia as parallels with the Celtic Otherworld.[4] Micra Eliade draws no explicit parallel with Narnia, but makes essentially the same points: "Space and time

293

[in the Otherworld] are different from ours. As in dreams, movement from one location to another, even the most distant one, can take a moment . . . the shaman can go through centuries [in the Otherworld] in a matter of earthly moments . . ." (qtd. in Rutherford 43). Eliade's point about the movement of time is well illustrated by Lucy's first venture into Narnia in *The Lion, the Witch and the Wardrobe*; Lucy considers she has been away for some considerable time; but in this world her absence has been only a matter of moments and has not been noticed by her siblings.

But apart from mechanical issues of this kind, what seems very clear is that the Celtic Otherworld is a realm of the imagination, a world in which spiritual awareness is heightened. It is similar to the world Tolkien refers to as "faery," but even in the ancient Celtic tales, the Otherworld is a moral sphere and the tests that are imposed there are those of loyalty, faith, trust, and honor. What Lewis does in the Narnian Chronicles is to baptize this world of the imagination, so that the imagination can lead readers through awe, wonder, and delight to the truth of God's redemption through Jesus Christ.

Conclusion

What we find in the fantasies of C. S. Lewis is a true sense that the ancient myths and the truths they contain really do foreshadow the "myth become fact" in Jesus Christ. Accepting as fact that in the redemption of Christ the old myths have also been redeemed, Lewis offers readers the opportunity to experience "good death"—a death to all that has been finished by the work of Christ on the Cross—and a rebirth and baptism of the human imagination and spirit. Lewis's fantasies take us inward, to the deep places of our own spirit, where we can encounter Aslan, the God of the Grey Mountain, or the Voice—our God in many guises—just as He appears in many guises—the sick, the poor, the needy—in our own world. The stories take us into battle with the dragons and dangers that beset the pilgrim—battles which can be psychological and emotional as well as spiritual. The stories emphasize the truth that we humans need help, that our own strength is nothing in such conflicts. And help comes from the Voice, the vision, the Word; our protection is very surely the Lion of Judah. We see the matter of heaven in all its stern and solemn beauty; we see it in the glory of the singing stars of *The Magician's Nephew* and in the glorious reflections of Psyche and the redeemed Orual. Lewis's "redeemed myths" point unequivocally to Jesus Christ and to the redemption he has won for humankind; and the entire body of Lewis's fantasy fiction speaks from his spirit to our spirits. His invitation to us is to experience the good death, to join him in the realms of vision and majesty, where all myth is actualized in the

fact of Christ's redemption, and where Aslan no longer seems like a lion . . .
for that is where we shall all, one day, "see Him as He is."

Notes

1. According to the *Brewer's Dictionary of Phrase and Fable*, "Nosce Teipsum"—"Know Thyself"—was inscribed on the Oracle of Apollo at Delphi, but has been attributed to other Greek sources such as Solon, Socrates, Plato, and Pythagoras.

2. See Lewis's essay "Sometimes Fairy Stories May Say Best What's to Be Said" in *Of Other Worlds*.

3. See my article "That Hideous Strength 1984" and also the chapter on Lewis's politics in my book, *The Fiction of C. S. Lewis*.

4. In an interview with the author 23 November 1994.

Works Cited

Alexander, Lloyd. "Truth about Fantasy." *Top of the News* (January 1968): 168–74.

Brewer, Ebenezer Cobham. *Brewer's Dictionary of Phrase and Fable*. Ed. Ivor H. Evans. 14th ed. New York: Harper, 1989.

Filmer, Kath. *The Fiction of C. S. Lewis: Mask and Mirror*. Basingstoke: Macmillan/New York: St. Martin's Press, 1993.

———. "That Hideous Strength 1984: The Influence of C. S. Lewis's 1984." *Extrapolation* (Summer 1985): 160–69.

Le Guin, Ursula. *Language of the Night: Essays in Fantasy and Science Fiction*. Ed. Susan Wood. New York: Berkley, 1982.

Lewis, C. S. "George Orwell." *Stories* 101–04.

———. *The Great Divorce: A Dream*. London: Geoffrey Bles, 1946.

———. *The Horse and His Boy*. 1954. Glasgow: Lion, 1980.

———. *The Last Battle*. 1956. Glasgow: Lion, 1980.

———. *The Lion, the Witch and the Wardrobe*. 1950. Glasgow: Lion, 1980.

———. *The Magician's Nephew*. 1955. Glasgow: Lion, 1980.

———. *Miracles: A Preliminary Study*. 1947. Glasgow: Fount, 1980.

———. *Of Other Worlds: Essays and Stories*. Ed. Walter Hooper. New York: Harcourt, 1966.

———. "On Stories." *Stories* 3–20.

———. *"On Stories" and Other Essays on Literature*. Ed. Walter Hooper. New York: Harcourt Brace Jovanovich, 1982.

———. "On Three Ways of Writing for Children." *Of Other Worlds* 35–38.

———. *Out of the Silent Planet*. London: Bodley, 1938.

————. *Perelandra*. London: Bodley, 1943.

————. *The Pilgrim's Regress: An Allegorical Apology for Christianity, Reason and Romanticism*. 1933. Grand Rapids: Eerdmans, 1981.

————. *Prince Caspian*. 1951. Glasgow: Lion, 1980.

————. *The Silver Chair*. 1953. Glasgow: Lion, 1980.

————. "Sometimes Fairy Stories May Say Best What's to Be Said." *Of Other Worlds* 35–38.

————. *That Hideous Strength: A Modern Fairy-Tale for Grown-Ups*. London: Bodley,1945.

————. *Till We Have Faces: A Myth Retold*. London: Geoffrey Bles, 1956.

————. *The Voyage of the Dawn Treader*. 1952. Glasgow: Lion, 1980.

————, ed. *George MacDonald: An Anthology*. 1946. Grand Rapids: Eerdmans, 1981.

Rutherford, Ward. *Celtic Lord*. London: Element, 1987.

16
Science Fiction

David C. Downing

In a volume containing the names of so many classic British authors, it may come as a surprise to find a chapter as well on science fiction. For many readers this is a sub-literary genre, the stuff of comic books and mass-market movies, not a vehicle for serious literary expression. One of Lewis's enduring contributions, both as a critic and as a creative writer, was to reveal new possibilities for this popular genre, and to suggest new criteria by which it should be judged.

Lewis's most fully developed commentaries on fantasy and science fiction were gathered by Walter Hooper into a volume of essays and stories called *Of Other Worlds* (1966). The collection is aptly named, for Lewis's discussions on these popular genres focus consistently not upon epic heroes or extraordinary adventures, but rather upon the exotic regions where these adventures are enacted. Lewis also offered some of the earliest commentary on how such tales of adventure could achieve genuine literary significance.

Defining Science Fiction and Fantasy

In discussing literature of the fantastic, one inevitably encounters a problem in defining terms. Nowadays critics tend to distinguish between science fiction and fantasy, thinking of works by Jules Verne, H. G. Wells, and Isaac Asimov in one category and works by Lewis Carroll, J. R. R. Tolkien, and Madeleine L'Engle in another. The general sense is that in science fiction extraordinary events are brought about by imagined but plausible technologies, whereas in fantasy the extraordinary is brought about by magic or enchantment. Thus, science fiction writers are obliged to explain time travel or the means of surviving in space, while fantasy writers may people their stories with wizards or talking animals, without troubling themselves about how such things might come to be.

This distinction may have heuristic value, but it soon breaks down when applied to actual texts. E. R. Eddison's *The Worm Ouroboros* (1922) begins as a voyage to the planet Mercury, but soon evolves into a latter-day chivalric romance. Ray Bradbury's *Martian Chronicles* (1950) are presented as ghostly fantasies from the martian point of view; but the terrestrial chapters provide a technical explanation for "unearthly" occurrences on Mars. And to which category shall we assign Ursula Le Guin's *The Left Hand of Darkness* or Margaret Atwood's *The Handmaid's Tale*?

Such questions of genre go nearly as far back as storytelling itself. In "The Sophist," Plato distinguished between two types of imitation, the *icastic*, representing things that are truly found to exist, and the *fantastic*, which exists only in the imagination of its creator. Aristotle stated his preference for the "probable impossible," fantasy which obeyed its own inner laws, over the "improbable possible," stories based on the real world which defy our sense of plausibility. It was Aristotle's famous dictum that "not to know that a hind has no horns is a less serious matter than to paint it inartistically" (*Poetics* 25).

In trying to mark the boundaries between fantasy and science fiction, one discovers that it is really a continuum rather than a pair of opposites. All fiction presents an admixture of reality and imagination. Closest to Plato's "icastic" fiction is a rigorously realistic novel like Truman Capote's *In Cold Blood*, which strictly adheres to the details of an actual murder case. But even Capote must invent thoughts and conversations to flesh out the bare facts of the story. And as Lewis himself noted, creators of the "fantastic" are not nearly so original as might be supposed: "'Creation' as applied to human authorship . . . seems to me an entirely misleading term. . . . There is not a vestige of real creativity *de novo* in us. Try to imagine a new primary color, a third sex, a fourth dimension, or even a monster which does not consist of bits of existing animals stuck together. Nothing happens" (*Letters* 371).

The more critics have tried to explain the difference between fantasy and science fiction, the more it seems a matter of emphasis rather than a clearly definable boundary. One might be able to conclude only that science fiction writers expend more effort to make their imaginative worlds seem plausible according the laws of nature as presently understood, whereas fantasy writers make less effort.

Lewis's Trilogy: Science Fiction or Fantasy?

Nowhere is the problem of determining genre boundaries more evident than in discussions of Lewis's "space trilogy." In his preface, Walter Hooper refers to the Ransom books as "science fiction" with reference to space travel and to "scientific" accounts of eldils (*Of Other Worlds* v). James Merritt concurs, citing Lewis as "certainly one of the most literate men who ever turned his hand to science fiction" (37). And Brian Murphy calls Lewis one of "the true giants of science fiction," who can take his place among classic writers such as H. G. Wells and Olaf Stapledon (15).

Other scholars, however, do not seem comfortable applying this term to Lewis's fiction, offering labels such as "interstellar fantasies" (Brady 41), "cosmic romances" (Hume 505), or "space fables" (Phelan 405). Robert A. Heinlein, creator of well-known science fiction novels such as *Starship Troopers* (1959) and *Stranger in a Strange Land* (1961), insists that the Ransom stories should not be categorized as science fiction, but rather as fantasies. He praises them in generous terms, placing them on his short list of classics of that type including *Alice's Adventures in Wonderland* and *The Wind in the Willows*. But he goes on to describe science fiction as "imaginary but possible," while fantasy is "imaginary but impossible," concluding that *Out of the Silent Planet* belongs in the second category because it violates established scientific facts about the surface conditions on Mars (6–7, 22).

Both in his creative writing and in his criticism, Lewis seemed unwilling to recognize such lines of demarcation. He thought it significant—and prudent— that what he called "the best of the American magazines" publishing stories of this type called itself *Fantasy and Science Fiction* without trying to put too fine a point on it ("Science Fiction" 67). For him what counted was emotional evocativeness, not factual accuracy: "Nor need the strange worlds, when we get there, be at all tied to scientific probablities. It is their wonder, or beauty, or suggestiveness that matter. When I put canals on Mars [in *Out of the Silent Planet*] I believe I already knew that better telescopes had dissipated that old optical delusion. The point was that they were part of the Martian myth as it already existed in the common mind" (69).

Lewis referred to his trilogy both as "theologised science fiction" (*Letters* 444) and as "planetary romances" (*Surprised* 36). He seemed to view the Ransom books as a deliberate fusion of two genres, a narrative strategy he had encountered in the novels of David Lindsay. As Lewis explained to one inquirer, "The real father of my planet book is David Lindsay's *Voyage to Arcturus*. . . . I had grown up on Wells's stories of that kind: It was Lindsay who first gave me the idea that the 'scientifiction' appeal could be combined with the 'supernatural' appeal—suggested the 'cross' (in a biological sense)" (*Let-*

ters 375). To his friend Ruth Pitter, Lewis commented more fully on his fascination for *Voyage*: "From Lindsay I first learned what other planets in fiction are really good for; for *spiritual* adventures. Only they can satisfy the craving which sends our imaginations off the earth. Or putting it another way, in him I first saw the terrific results produced by the union of two kinds of fiction hitherto kept apart; the Novalis, G. MacDonald, James Stephens sort and the H. G. Wells, Jules Verne sort. My debt to him is very great" (qtd. in Sayer 153).

Lewis on the Different Types of Science Fiction

Lewis again held up Lindsay's *Voyage* as a prototype for speculative fiction in his address "On Science Fiction" originally given to the Cambridge University English Club in 1955. In the same talk Lewis defended science fiction as an emerging genre that could achieve genuine literary merit, and he offered some guidelines for assessing this new kind of story.

Lewis began this commentary on science fiction by noting that one cannot distinguish good from bad science fiction if one dismisses the entire genre out of hand:

> Of the articles I have read on the subject . . . many were by people who clearly hated the kind [of story] they wrote about. It is a very dangerous thing to write about a kind you hate. Hatred obscures all distinctions. . . . Many reviews are useless because, while purporting to condemn the book, they only reveal the reviewer's dislike of the kind to which it belongs. Let bad tragedies be censured by those who love tragedy, and bad detective stories by those who love the detective story. Then we shall learn their real faults. Otherwise we shall find epics blamed for not being novels, farces for not being high comedies, novels by James for lacking the swift action of Smollett. Who wants to hear a particular claret abused by a fanatical teetotaller, or a particular woman by a confirmed misogynist? ("Science Fiction" 59–60)

This plea for considering a work of fiction on its own merits seems like mere common sense today, but it was bold declaration in its time. Throughout most of Lewis's scholarly career, the academic world was dominated by literary Modernism, a movement which sharply distinguished between High Art as a vehicle of "Culture" and popular art, mere entertainment for the masses. From his early essays collected in *Rehabilitations* (1939) to his late book, *An Experiment in Criticism* (1961), Lewis critiqued the Modernist sensibility, suggesting it was becoming almost a Religion of Art, with its canonical works, its priestly elite, and its own aesthetic orthodoxies.

One of the most unquestioned of these orthodoxies, and one which continues to make many readers dismiss science fiction altogether, is the idea that serious fiction must portray complex and multi-faceted characters. When E. M. Forster coined the terms *round* and *flat character* in *Aspects of the Novel* (1927), he and most of his contemporaries took it for granted that the greatest works of fiction are those which offer the richest psychological studies. Lewis felt that might well be true for one kind of story, but it should not be expected in every kind of story. After discussing the eerie evocativeness of H. G. Wells's lunar landscapes in *First Men in the Moon*, Lewis expresses his surprise that many readers fail to recognize any imaginative power in this kind of writing:

> How anyone can think this form illegitimate or contemptible passes my understanding. It may very well be convenient not to call such things novels. If you prefer, call them a special form of novels. Either way, the conclusion will be much the same: they are to be tried by their own rules. It is absurd to condemn them because they do not often display any deep or sensitive characterization. They oughtn't to. It's a fault if they do. Wells' Cavor and Bedford [the protagonists in *First Men in the Moon*] have rather too much than too little character. Every good writer knows that the more unusual the scenes and events of his story are, the slighter, the more ordinary, the more typical his persons should be. Hence Gulliver is a commonplace little man and Alice a commonplace little girl. If they had been more remarkable they would have wrecked their books. . . . Of course, we must not confuse slight or typical characterization with impossible or unconvincing characterization. Falsification of character will always spoil a story. But character can apparently be reduced, simplified, to almost any extent with satisfactory results. ("Science Fiction" 64–65)

Lewis goes on to argue that those who insist on judging every story by the depth of its characterizations are engaging in a kind of literary imperialism:

> Of course, a given reader may be (some readers seem to be) interested in nothing else in the world except detailed studies of complex human personalities. If so, he has good reason for not reading those kinds of work which neither demand nor admit it. He has no reason for condemning them, and indeed no qualification for speaking of them at all. We must not allow the novel of manners to give laws to all literature: let it rule its own domain. We must not listen to Pope's maxim about the proper study of mankind. The proper study of man is everything. The proper study of man as artist is everything which gives a foothold to the imagination and the passions. (65)

It might be charged that Lewis is engaged in special pleading here, setting up a different standard of evaluation for a particular form of popular fiction he happens to enjoy. But it should be recalled that he made a similar argument about the mistake of trying to assess Spenser's *Faerie Queene* according to contemporary genre expectations: "The novel calls for characters with insides; but there are other kinds of narrative that do not. In literature, the narrative forms that do without character are quite numerous. They include, for example, the ballad, the Märchen, the adventure story, the myth, and . . . the chivalric romance" (*Spenser's* 113). In discussing Spenser, as in discussing science fiction, Lewis comments on the futility of judging one genre by the standards of another: "It is always a great mistake to value a work of one kind for its occasional slight approximations to some other kind which happens to be preferred. If we can't learn to like a work of art for what it is, we had best give it up" (*Spenser's* 113).

Having established that those who critique science fiction should be able to read, as Pope advised, "in the same spirit that the author writ," Lewis goes on to survey the principal "sub-species" of science fiction writing. The first kind, which he finds virtually unreadable, is what he calls the "fiction of Displaced Persons," writers who have no real interest in creating other worlds, but who seem to be trying to capitalize on a literary fad. This kind of writer sketches in some exotic setting far out in space and then never makes any good use of it. Lewis is particularly blunt in condemning this kind of narrative:

> The author leaps forward into an imagined future when planetary, sidereal, or even galactic travel has become common. Against this huge backcloth he proceeds to develop an ordinary love-story, spy-story, wreck-story, or crime-story. This seems to me tasteless. Whatever in a work of art is not used, is doing harm. The faintly imagined and sometimes strictly unimaginable, scene and properties only blur the real theme and distract us from any interest it might have had. ("Science Fiction" 61)

Apart from the work of "Displaced Persons," authors who probably should not be writing science fiction at all, Lewis admits that he also takes little interest in a second category of science fiction, what he calls "the fiction of Engineers" (62). The appeal of these stories, such as Jules Verne's *Twenty Thousand Leagues under the Sea*, H. G. Wells's *Land Ironclads*, or Arthur C. Clark's *Prelude to Space*, resides largely in the marvels of real or imagined technology. Unlike the fiction of Displaced Persons, which Lewis calls "radically bad," he confesses that his dislike of these "gadget stories" is more a matter of personal taste and values: "I am too uneducated scientifically to criticize such stories on the mechanical side; and I am so completely out of sympathy with the projects they anticipate that I am incapable of criticizing them as stories. I am as blind to their appeal as a pacifist is to *Maldon*" ("Science Fiction" 63).

The Ransom Trilogy as "Anti-Science Fiction"

Lewis was not only "out of sympathy" with the advanced technology so often celebrated in these tales, but also by the world view which often accompanied it. *Out of the Silent Planet* presents a voyage into space similar to Wells's *First Men in the Moon* in plot, but very nearly opposite in its themes. And the narrative structure of *Perelandra* echoes that of Wells's *The Time Machine* (even in minor details such as the protagonist returning to his own world with exotic blossoms and with a wounded heel). However, where Wells diagnoses society's problems as political, Lewis sees them as moral. Where Wells sees class conflict and a need to forge new truths, Lewis sees spiritual conflict and a need to recover old truths.

Lewis began the trilogy as a conscious critique of what he called "Wellsianity" ("Funeral" 82), a philosophy that applies Darwinism to the metaphysical sphere, believing that humans may evolve into a new species of gods, spreading from world to world and galaxy to galaxy. Though one finds this quasi-religious belief sometimes called "Evolutionism" in Olaf Stapledon, G. B. Shaw, and C. H. Waddington, Lewis found it most fully embodied in Wells's novels, and he set out to produce a Wellsian fantasy with an anti-Wellsian theme. Lewis's Ransom books contrast so sharply from other stories of space voyages that Robert Scholes and Eric S. Rabkin credit him with inventing a new genre: "anti-science fiction" (43).

I believe Lewis would have accepted the label as a compliment. Throughout the trilogy, Lewis turns the most common conventions of science fiction on their heads. Part of the delight of reading deeply in Lewis's books is to note how often Lewis the creative writer responds imaginatively to the very same concerns he has raised in his role as a critic of literature and culture. For example, in "*De Futilitate*" he worries that many of his contemporaries have gotten their sense of objective values almost completely backwards:

> It is widely believed that scientific thought puts us in touch with reality, whereas moral or metaphysical thought does not. . . . That is why in modern stories of what Americans call the "scientifictional" type—stories about unknown species who inhabit other planets or the depth of the sea—these creatures are usually pictured as being wholly devoid of our moral standards but as accepting our scientific standards. The implication is, of course, that scientific thought, being objective, will be the same for all creatures that can reason at all, whereas moral thought, being merely a subjective thing like one's taste in food, might be expected to vary from species to species. (61)

Having noted the problem, Lewis intends to display no such confusion in his own "scientifiction." When his protagonist, Elwin Ransom, travels into space, he first discovers how misleading modern scientific notions of the heavens are, then he learns of a cosmic moral order which everyone in the universe knows about and honors except for us, the bewildered inhabitants of "the silent planet."

Early in the first book of the trilogy, Lewis serves notice that he intends to flout the usual conventions used in describing cosmic voyages. While his reading of Wells and others as a boy had impressed upon him the "vastness and cold of space" (*Surprised* 65), his own interplanetary traveler discovers just the opposite. Ransom awakens in the spaceship to an invigorating "tyranny of heat and light" (*Planet* 29), and he comes to recognize that the very term *space* is a misnomer:

> But Ransom, as time wore on, became aware of another and more spiritual cause for his progressive lightening and exultation of heart. A nightmare, long engendered in the modern mind by the mythology that follows in the wake of science, was falling off him. He had read of "Space": at the back of his thinking for years had lurked the dismal fancy of the black, cold vacuity, the utter deadness, which was supposed to separate the worlds. He had not known how much it affected him till now—now the very name "Space" seemed a blasphemous label for this empyrean ocean of radiance in which they swam. He could not call it "dead"; he felt life pouring into him from it every moment. . . . No: Space was the wrong name. Older thinkers had been wiser when they named it simply the heavens—the heavens which declared the glory. (*Planet* 65)

Here we find Lewis employing a familiar science fiction motif—the interplanetary traveler gazing out at the stars—to undermine "the mythology which follows in the wake of science" and to suggest that we reconsider a more ancient view—that of a psalmist for whom the heavens declare the glory of their Maker (Ps. 19:1).

This is almost the exact opposite of the "gadget fiction" which Lewis took little interest in—and with which he often associated a world view antithetical to his own. We are not invited to spend time looking *at* the machine in the story, but rather to look *out* of it. Unlike Wells, who spends most of a chapter in *First Men in the Moon* speculating about substances "opaque to gravity," Lewis offers almost no information about how his spaceship works, apart from an offhand comment by its inventor about "exploiting the less observed properties of solar radiation" (*Planet* 26). Lewis confessed later that such an explanation was "pure mumbo jumbo," and that he inserted it into the story perhaps mostly to help himself suspend disbelief ("Unreal" 87). His explanation of his means and ends in speculative fiction was almost the opposite of those who are fascinated by technology for its own sake: "In this kind of story the pseudo-scientific apparatus is to be taken simply as a 'machine.' . . . The most superficial appearance of plausibility—the merest sop to our critical intellect—will do. I am inclined to think that frankly supernatural methods are best. I once took a hero to Mars in a spaceship, but when I knew better I had angels convey him to Venus" ("Science Fiction" 68–69).

Having dismissed the fiction of Displaced Persons outright and expressed his distaste for the "fiction of Engineers," Lewis goes on in "On Science Fiction" to discuss the kinds of story that are better able to command his sympathy. He does not see these as new genres at all, but traces them back to the ancient yearning to hear of travels into realms unknown. "Is any man such a dull clod," Lewis asks, "that he can look at the moon through a good telescope without asking himself what it would be like to walk among those mountains under that black, crowded sky?" (63). Lewis says that much the same sense of wonder about unreachable places animated Homer's description of Odysseus visiting the Underworld and Dante's imaginative journey to the center of the earth in *The Inferno*.

Related to speculative stories about unknown places are those about the unknown future, which Lewis calls Eschatological fiction. Aldous Huxley in *Brave New World*, Olaf Stapledon in *First and Last Men*, and Arthur C. Clarke in *Childhood's End* all present their imaginative projections about the eventual destiny of humans. Lewis notes that this kind of story has provoked some of the greatest hostility among reviewers, because stories about the future so often comment on the political realities of the present, or may be inferred as doing so.

Otherworlds of the Spirit

In discussing stories about unknown places and times, Lewis reiterates that in the kind of speculative fiction he finds most compelling, it is impossible to clearly distinguish between science fiction and fantasy. These tales are simply modern versions of the age-old itch to explore regions of "beauty, awe, or terror as the actual world does not supply" ("Science Fiction" 68). As the geographical knowledge has increased through the centuries, areas on the map marked "Terra Incognita" have shrunk, so that it seems to Lewis a natural development that imaginative writers would eventually leave our world behind in order to envision exotic otherworlds.

Lewis lists the speculative works, ancient and modern, whose excellence derives not from their characters, their technology, or from external adventure, but from an elusive quality of spiritual suggestiveness. He includes parts of the *Odyssey* and the *Kalevala*, Spenser's *Faerie Queene*, Coleridge's *The*

Ancient Mariner, Keats's *Christabel*, William Morris's *Jason*, as well as George MacDonald's *Phantastes*, *Lilith*, and *The Golden Key*. Among twentieth-century writers, he includes E. R. Eddison's *The Worm Ouroboros*, J. R. R. Tolkien's *The Lord of the Rings*, and David Lindsay's "shattering, intolerable, and irresistible work," *Voyage to Arcturus* ("Science Fiction" 71). Lewis concludes in his address "On Science Fiction" that it is the new genre's spiritual possibilities, not its technical possibilities, which provide an opportunity for genuine literary expression.

This theme is reiterated elsewhere in Lewis's critical essays. Whenever he asks his readers to consider the evocative power of setting or "atmosphere" in a story, one can be certain that Lindsay's name is soon to appear. Though Lewis was not attracted by the themes of *Voyage*, he was captivated by Lindsay's method of using features of the landscape to suggest psychological and spiritual themes. As Lewis explains in an essay titled simply "On Stories":

> His Tormance [the fictional world of *Voyage to Arcturus*] is a region of the spirit. He is the first writer to discover what "other planets" are really good for in fiction. No merely physical strangeness or merely spatial distance will realize the idea of otherness which is what we are always trying to grasp in a story about voyaging through space: you must go into another dimension. To construct plausible and moving "other worlds" you must draw on the only real "other world" we know, that of the spirit. (12)

This single remark, more than any other, explains Lewis's lifelong fascination for science fiction—and also reveals why the settings of his own Ransom trilogy are so unforgettable. For many readers of *Out of the Silent Planet* and *Perelandra*, especially, details of character and plot may begin to fade with time, but there will remain distinct and vivid mental images of the healing radiance of "the Heavens" as Ransom experienced them, of the rosy, perpendicular landscapes of Malacandra and the warm, golden seas of Perelandra. This is not merely a tribute to Lewis's descriptive powers, but also a clue to his intensely personal narrative method. From Lindsay he discovered the secret of creating imagined worlds which were objective correlatives of the spirit, employing a kind of literary expressionism to project his own inner world onto a fictional canvas.

The Otherworld of Lewis's spirit was a rich one, and he retained throughout his life vivid and evocative memories of his earliest years. Though his boyhood was not particularly happy after the death of his mother when he was nine, he did have a good many moments of exultation, usually from his love of nature or from his beloved books, including many works of fantasy and science fiction. The most intense and significant imaginative experiences of Lewis's early years were the recurrences of "Joy," his word for *Sehn-*

sucht, the longing for some lost paradise that is itself a kind of paradise to feel.

Lewis's experiences of Joy came to be associated with three constellations of images which he labeled Northernness, the island garden, and Homeliness. The first of these, "Northernness," was a nameless longing associated with pale winter skies, heroic Norse sagas, and Wagnerian opera. In his autobiography, he vividly recalls the first time he read Longfellow's translations of Icelandic myth, reading the simple words, "Balder the beautiful is dead, is dead," and feeling overwhelmed by "unsatisfied desire which is itself more desirable than any other satisfaction" (*Surprised* 17–18).

"Northernness" in Out of the Silent Planet

Throughout his life Lewis possessed an intense attraction to "Northernness," which he describes as a stern and ecstatic vision of things "cold, spacious, severe, pale, and remote" (*Surprised* 17). Sometimes the experience came to him not from art or music, but directly from nature, as we can see in this letter to his childhood friend Arthur Greeves:

> My second delightful moment was of a different kind, and takes a little arrangement to describe. Imagine first a pure rosy pink sunset: in the extreme distance a sky covered with thin "mackerel" as delicate as the veins in a shell, & all pink: in the foreground, blackly outlined against this, huge crags and castles and Valkyrie-shapes of cloud. Got that? Now;—imagine that all this existed only for a fraction of [a] second, the pink light being in fact no sunset but a vast flood of summer lightning: so that all those beetling cliffs and tottering cities of the gods, together with the rosy flush behind which made them visible, had leaped out of pure star-set darkness an instant before, and vanished into it instantaneously again—and so times without number. (*Stand* 389)

This visionary cloudscape Lewis described in 1930 looks remarkably like the terrain of Malacandra, which Lewis would begin to write about only a few years later. Note how much the mountains of that planet resemble Lewis's delightful vision of the stormclouds at sunset: "Beyond . . . was a rose-colored cloud-like mass. It might really be a cloud, but it was very solid-looking and did not seem to have moved since he first set eyes on it. It looked like the top of a gigantic red cauliflower—or like a huge bowl of red soapsuds—and it was exquisitely beautiful in tint and shape" (*Planet* 43).

Whether or not Lewis had one particular sunset in mind when he began creating the landscape of Malacandra, one senses a strong correlation between external decriptions and inner states of exultation, wonder, or anxiety. As a

307

matter of fact, the whole novel *Out of the Silent Planet* is suffused with "Northernness." The frosty blue skies and tonic atmosphere of Malacandra remind us that Lewis's favorite season was winter. The Malacandrian words *hross, handramit,* and *harandra* are taken from Old Norse, meaning horse, lowlands, and highlands. And that comic creature called a *pfifltriggi* takes its name from two Old Icelandic words combined by Lewis to give the meaning "safe monster" (Flieger 52). Even minor allusions in *Out of the Silent Planet* to Rackham (113) and Chaliapin, the Russian operatic singer (55), evoke "Northernness," calling to mind Norse mythology as seen in the illustrations of Rackham or heard in the dramas of Wagner.

Hesperides in Perelandra

If Malacandra is a delightful world of Northernness, Ransom's next planetary pilgrimage takes him to another planet of joy. Perelandra's evocations of Sweet Desire take a form more southern than northern—the image of a lush, paradisal garden. This makes us think of Eden, of course, but Lewis often associated his paradise with island gardens: Hesperides in classic myth; Tirnanog, the land of youth in Irish legends, and Avalon, the island where King Arthur was taken to heal from his wounds.

Just as Ransom's first sight of Malacandra evoked the Joy of Northernness, his first sight of Perelandra evokes the Joy of an island Paradise: "At Ransom's waking something happened to him which perhaps never happens to a man until he is out of his own world: he saw reality, and thought it was a dream. He opened his eyes and saw a strange heraldically coloured tree loaded with yellow fruits and silver leaves. Round the base of the indigo stem was coiled a small dragon covered with scales of red gold. He recognized the garden of the Hesperides at once" (*Perelandra* 45).

In general, the world of Perelandra contains pleasures in abundance. From the time Ransom first splashes down in the tropical seas of the planet until he witnesses the ceremony of the Great Dance, his time spent in this world includes a good many Edenic delights: the bubble-trees, the ambrosial gourds, rides on the backs of exotic creatures. But Perelandra also evokes a whole other species of pleasure. When Ransom, riding on a dolphin's back at night, approaches one of the floating islands, his piercing delight has an element of déjà vu:

> But he said "Hush" to his mind at this stage, for the mere pleasure of breathing in the fragrance which now began to steal towards him from the blackness ahead. Warm and sweet, and every moment sweeter and purer, and every moment stronger and more filled with all delights, it came to him. He knew

well what it was, . . . the night-breath of a floating island in the star Venus. It was strange to be filled with homesickness for places where his sojourn had been so brief and which were, by any objective standard, so alien to all our race. Or were they? The cord of longing which drew him to the invisible isle seemed to him at that moment to have been fastened long, long before his coming to Perelandra, long before the earliest times that memory could recover in his childhood, before birth, before the birth of man himself, before the origins of time. It was sharp, sweet, wild, and holy, all in one. (*Perelandra* 102–03)

In this passage we see Perelandra, not only as a garden of unearthly delights, but as an image of Joy itself. The exotic garden—whether Eden, Hesperides, or Tirnanog—is one of the pictures that Lewis associated with Joy from early childhood on.

Homeliness in That Hideous Strength

In the last book of the trilogy, *That Hideous Strength*, Ransom stays at home on planet earth, but in this world, too, Joy may be found. The Joy of this book revolves around the community at St. Anne's, around what Lewis would call the pleasures of Homeliness. In *Surprised by Joy* Lewis explains that he experienced Joy not only in the severe beauties of Northernness and the lushness of Edenic gardens, but also in the glory of simple things. He reports that Beatrix Potter's *Squirrel Nutkin*, no less than more exalted stories, was a catalyst for Sweet Desire. He said it conveyed to him the "Idea of Autumn," of quiet country lanes, snug fireplaces, and furry animals.

In *That Hideous Strength*, we sense the quiet glory of Homeliness just about every time we visit the St. Anne's community, of which Ransom is the head. Again, the Joy of the scene is most powerfully felt upon a first encounter. This time the spell is woven not upon Ransom himself, but upon Jane Studdock, an anchorless and unhappy woman who has come to consult with him. As she is led toward the house, Jane passes by a vegetable garden and a line of rosebushes that fill her with wistful thoughts: "It was a very large garden . . . like the garden in *Peter Rabbit*. Or was it like the garden in the *Romance of the Rose*. . . . Or like Klingsor's garden? Or the garden in *Alice*? Or like the garden on top of some Mesopotamian ziggurat which had given rise to the legend of Paradise? Or simply like all walled gardens?" (*Hideous* 61–62).

In this passage, the homey and wholesome grounds of St. Anne's evoke in Jane powerful associations from the classic children's stories, medieval romance, and Wagnerian opera (Klingsor is a magician in Wagner's *Parsi-*

fal)—all catalysts for Sweet Desire in Lewis. The unpretentious scene even causes her to wonder if all human myths of paradise are rooted in just such a garden.

We see then that all the worlds of the Ransom trilogy are suffused with Joy—Malacandra especially with Northernness, Perelandra with images of a garden isle, and even troubled earth has quiet refuges of Homeliness. In all three stories, Lewis hopes to evoke in the reader the same longing for paradise that stabbed his heart so often in his early years. What is more, his purpose is not just to delight, but to instruct.

Even when he first experienced Joy as a young child, Lewis recognized that the feeling evoked by the memory was not mere nostalgia or love of nature. But then what was it he desired? Trying to resolve that question became Jack's own grail-like quest, one that would cause him to follow many false objects of desire—the erotic, the occult, the acclaim of others—until he finally discovered an abiding place in the true object of Joy, or "Sweet Desire."

For Lewis, the search for the source of Joy, what he called his "dialectic of desire," ended in his early thirties when he re-embraced the faith of his childhood. Largely through the influence of his good friend J. R. R. Tolkien, Lewis came to believe that romance, fairy tales, and myths revealed their own kinds of truth not available to the unaided intellect, that they represented a "real though unfocused gleam of divine truth falling on human imagination" (*Miracles* 139n). Tolkien explained that the pivotal point in human history was the Incarnation, when myth became history. For Lewis, Christ was the reality seen dimly in so many legends and sagas; he was the master key to the world's great myths.

Lewis's Legacy in Science Fiction

Perhaps Lewis's greatest contribution as a writer of speculative fiction is his ability to recast the motifs of the cosmic voyage into those of spiritual pilgrimage. Even more powerfully than his mentor David Lindsay, Lewis was able to "show what other worlds are good for," to express the otherworld of his own spirit in terms which regale readers' imaginations and encourage them to undertake their own spiritual journeys.

Mark R. Hillegas exclaimed in 1960 that "in C. S. Lewis's trilogy, science fiction has up to now reached its highest level as literature" (27). But two years later, in a conversation with Kingsley Amis and Brian Aldiss, Lewis remarked that "probably the great work in science fiction is yet to come" ("Unreal" 93). Since that time, there have indeed been a good many novels of speculative fiction which have been acknowledged and studied as important works of literature—novels by writers of the first order including Margaret Atwood, Anthony Burgess, Doris Lessing, Walter M. Miller, Jr., Ursula Le Guin, and Jorge Luis Borges. Yet Lewis's contribution to the field rests secure, both as a pioneering critic who helped establish the criteria for assessing this new genre, and as an imaginative writer who produced classic works of their kind.

Works Cited

Brady, Charles A. *Best Sellers* 4 (May 1944): 40–41.

Flieger, Verlyn. "The Sound of Silence: Language and Experience in *Out of the Silent Planet.*" *Word and Story in C. S. Lewis.* Ed. Peter J. Schakel and Charles A. Huttar. Columbia, MO: U of Missouri P, 1991. 42–57.

Heinlein, Robert A. "Science Fiction: Its Nature, Faults, and Virtues." *Turning Points: Essays on the Art of Science Fiction.* Ed. Damon Knight. New York: Harper and Row, 1977. 3–28.

Hillegas, Mark R. "Science Fiction and the Idea of Progress." *Extrapolation* 1 (May 1960): 25–28.

Hume, Kathryn. "C. S. Lewis's Trilogy: A Cosmic Romance." *Modern Fiction Studies* 20 (1974–75): 505–17.

Lewis, C. S. *Christian Reflections.* Ed. Walter Hooper. Grand Rapids: Eerdmans, 1967.

———. "*De Futilitate.*" *Reflections* 57–71.

———. "The Funeral of a Great Myth." *Reflections* 82–93.

———. *Letters of C. S. Lewis.* Ed. W. H. Lewis. 1966. Rev. ed. Ed. Walter Hooper. London: HarperCollins, 1988.

———. *Miracles: A Preliminary Study.* 1947. New York: Macmillan, 1968.

———. *Of Other Worlds: Essays and Stories.* Ed. Walter Hooper. New York: Harcourt, 1966.

———. "On Science Fiction." *Of Other Worlds* 59–73.

———. "On Stories." *Of Other Worlds* 3–21.

———. *Out of the Silent Planet.* 1938. New York: Macmillan, 1968.

———. *Perelandra.* 1943. New York: Macmillan, 1968.

———. *Spenser's Images of Life.* Ed. Alastair Fowler. Cambridge: Cambridge UP, 1967.

———. *Surprised by Joy: The Shape of My Early Life.* New York: Harcourt, 1955.

———. *That Hideous Strength: A Modern Fairy-Tale for Grown-Ups.* 1945. New York: Macmillan, 1968.

———. *They Stand Together: The Letters of C. S. Lewis to Arthur Greeves (1914–1963).* Ed. by Walter Hooper. New York: Macmillan, 1979.

———. "Unreal Estates." *Of Other Worlds* 86–96.

Merritt, James D. "'She Pluck'd, She Did Eat.'" *Future Females: A Critical Anthology.* Ed. Marleen S. Barr. Bowling Green: Bowling Green State U Popular Press, 1981. 37–41.

Murphy, Brian. *C. S. Lewis.* Mercer Island, WA: Starmont House, 1983.

Phelan, John M. "Men and Morals in Space." *America* 113 (9 October 1965): 405–07.

311

Sayer, George. *Jack: C. S. Lewis and His Times.* San Francisco: Harper and Row, 1988.

Scholes, Robert, and Eric S. Rabkin. *Science Fiction: History, Science, Vision.* New York: Oxford UP, 1977.

17
Children's Literature

David Barratt

From time to time I used to organize day conferences on children's literature. The usual format was to invite two keynote speakers, one of whom would be a children's writer, the other a classroom practitioner or educationist. We would sandwich a series of seminars between these speakers, and then round off the day with a discussion panel or question time.

Had C. S. Lewis still been alive and had we invited him, I am sure it would have been in the "children's writer" slot. Perhaps we may also have persuaded him to lead a seminar on "children as readers" or on fairy stories, but undoubtedly his star performance would have been at question time, where his dialectic gifts would have been just the right finale for a stimulating but exhausting day.

Such a never-to-be day highlights several apparent contradictions about Lewis. Although his whole career was as a teacher, a "classroom practitioner," he never lectured on children's literature; and apart from one or two essays, he never wrote specifically on it. Indeed, he rarely referred to the genre as "Children's Literature" at all. Yet his name and fame are immediately associated with the genre by nearly everyone who has ever heard of him through the enormous popularity of the Chronicles of Narnia.

These contradictions can be partly accounted for by the low status of children's literature, together with science fiction, westerns, and other forms of "popular fiction," so that such genres were never prescribed for academic study. As genre theory has changed since Lewis's death, so such genres have achieved some marginal respectability, particularly in "Cultural Studies," as some English courses have been renamed. Lewis's own theoretical writing in *An Experiment in Criticism* may well have helped start such a change. The very term "children's literature" has only recently emerged as *the* term to use for the genre, rather than "children's books," "juvenile fiction," "young people's reading," and the like.

Nevertheless, the central contradiction remains that while Lewis was totally committed to children's literature, he left no record of taking a children's text or writer, and developing a lecture or chapter on it, her, or him. Rarely does a children's book or author receive more than a page in Lewis's academic writing, usually in a discussion on what really seemed to call out his expository powers: *the process of production* as a writer, or *the process of reception* as a reader.

Therefore, in order to fulfill the wider purpose of this book, I intend to look at his overall commitment to the genre, to gather together his theories of production and reception, and then seek to reconstitute what might have been the shape of his textual analysis and criticism of children's literature. I then want to look at his own practice of writing to see if it bears out his theory; and lastly, I want to look at objections to this practice to place it in a wider debate.

Lewis's Commitment

Lewis's commitment to children's literature was total and lifelong. For a university professor of English at the two most prestigious British universities, this is quite remarkable, only to be paralleled by his great friend J. R. R. Tolkien. The two men clearly found support for their commitment in their friendship and through the Inklings. Lewis refers again and again to Tolkien's essay "On Fairy-Stories," first given as the Andrew Lang lecture at St. Andrews University, Scotland, in 1938.[1] Tolkien's *The Hobbit* was first seen in draft form by Lewis in 1932, and it excited him immensely, seeing in it a continuation of the children's literature he delighted to read.

The theoretical strands that ran through this lifelong commitment we shall look at in a moment. The experiential strands are attached to his understanding of the "primary imagination" and to his recall of those moments of joy and desire that permeated his earlier life, and which are so graphically depicted in *Surprised by Joy*. In the first chapter, "Shape of My Early Life," he describes three moments of "enormous bliss," the second of which

came through *Squirrel Nutkin*; through it only, though I loved all the Beatrix Potter books. . . . It troubled me with what I can only describe as the Idea of Autumn. . . . [T]he experience was one of intense desire. . . . It was something quite different from ordinary life and even from ordinary pleasure; something as they would now say, "in another dimension." (16)

The Wordsworthian echo of "troubled me" and the Platonic reference to "Idea" are not coincidental, as we shall see in a moment. Clearly, it would not be surprising to learn that an imaginative child like Jack Lewis would receive pleasure from reading animal fantasy. It is the transcendent experience that came, by chance it would seem, through one particular children's book, that for him rooted his conviction that children's literature is as genuine a source of the spiritual life as any other literature. In fact, it turned his particular quest for that life toward Romance, fantasy, and myth.

His description of his own childhood reading is reminiscent of other writers, such as Jane Austen or the Brontës, whose fathers allowed their children free access to every book in their extensive libraries. One result was that the formal distinction between children's and adult literature never occurred to the children. Jack's own first literary attempts in *Animal Land* and *Boxen* were a strange mixture of the fantasy forms of children's literature and the much more realistic journalistic forms of the adult world.

Such childhood commitment may spring out of an experience, be it conversion or epiphany, but it needs to be carried through into adulthood to prove itself; otherwise we are merely studying childhood reading. Such a carryover is easy to establish with Lewis. References to young Jack's literary preferences, such as E. Nesbit's *The Amulet* or the science fiction of H. G. Wells (both writing at the same time as Lewis was reading), can be followed by similar references to the older Jack still reading the same stories. In the preface to *The Lion, the Witch and the Wardrobe* he is obviously writing personally to his goddaughter, Lucy Barfield, when he claims children get too old for fairy tales, but then as adults, they begin reading them again. Elsewhere he writes: "When I was ten, I read Fairy Tales in secret . . . now that I am fifty, I read them openly" ("On Three Ways" 25). Humphrey Carpenter notes, in a discussion of Lewis's "boyishness," his love of rereading Beatrix Potter, Rider Haggard, and *The Wind in the Willows* (219–20). Carpenter's thesis is that the Narnia stories, as well as *Screwtape* and the science fiction trilogy, were so successful because Lewis was still in touch with his boyishness and exploits it. Lewis himself wrote, "Parts of me are still twelve, and I think other parts were already fifty when I was twelve."[2]

Certainly, we need to understand Lewis's view of childhood to understand his attitude to children's literature. It was a view that was basically Platonic, mediated through Wordsworth and *The Prelude*, the title *Surprised by Joy* being taken from a sonnet by Wordsworth. In the autobiography, Lewis makes sharp distinctions between his childhood, boyhood, and adolescence. Boyhood (in contradiction to Carpenter) he saw as a "barren waste," a "dark ages," remarking "many of the books that pleased me as a child please me still; nothing but necessity would make me re-read most of the books I read at Oldie's or at Campbell" (61). Only in adolescence did he regain the transcendent experiences of childhood, particularly through the Norse myths and their "Northernness." He writes: ". . . ever since one golden summer in adolescence when I first heard the 'Ride of the Valkyries' on a gramophone and saw Arthur Rackham's illustrations to *The Ring*. Even now the very smell of those volumes can come over me with the poignancy of remembered calf-love" ("First and Second Things" 19). The same experience is recounted in *Surprised by Joy* (72–73).

But the best evidence of this lifelong commitment is to be found in his letters, especially those to children (mainly resulting from the publication of the Narnia stories) and to his fellow spirit and lifelong friend, Arthur Greeves, collected in *They Stand Together*. Of the two, the latter is better evidence, since it reflects Lewis's everyday life more spontaneously, and since the former could be suspected of an invested authorial interest. While references to children's literature do not abound in the Greeves volume (in 25 out of 296 letters), they are consistent and evenly spread. Thus in 1916 he recommends Kipling's *Rewards and Fairies* to Arthur (137); in 1920 he is reading Maureen Moore's copy of *Kim* while ill (together with Trollope and Virgil!) (276). In 1930, *The Water Babies* is a new book to him, and he envies Arthur his shelf of MacDonalds (357). Talking of *The Princess and the Goblins* [sic], he writes, "In fact I read the former for about the third time when I was ill this Spring" (360). He discusses *Alice* twice in 1917 (162, 166), is reminded of *Alice* by *The Importance of Being Ernest* in 1919 (248), and casually quotes the White Knight in 1943 (495). In 1933 he writes of reading the manuscript of *The Hobbit* "so exactly like what we would both have longed to write (and read) in 1916; so that one feels he is not making it up but merely describing the same world into which all three of us have entry" (448).

Notice "have entry"—present tense. There is nothing nostalgic here, no attempt to capture a lost childhood through rereading. A little later, he grieves for a five-year-old staying with them, denied fairy tales and nursery rhymes: "his poor imagination has been left without any natural food at all" (474). Elsewhere he writes of reading (not rereading) T. H. White's *Mistress Masham's Repose*, *The Borrowers*, *Giant Land* (while invigilating an exam), and Grimm's *Märchen* (in German).[3] Surprisingly, he admits that he never met *The Wind in the Willows* or the Bastable books till he was in his late twenties ("On Three Ways" 24). We must deduce from such references that there was an ongoing exploration of this genre (as there was of all his interests), not because it was his academic duty to do so, but out of a deep and personal commitment.

Theoretical Aspects: Production

I want now to examine the more theoretical aspects of Lewis's views on children's literature, not that the theory is ever very far from the practice. Indeed, his theory of production is grounded in his creative practice and is to be found in the series of papers variously collected as *Of This and Other Worlds* or *Of Other Worlds*, depending on which side of the Atlantic you live; or as *"On Stories" and Other Essays on Literature*. Some of the theory is more slanted toward fantasy, as that was his own modal preference, certain aspects of which have already been covered in chapter 15. Of the fantasy mode, his favorite sub-genre is animal fantasy, on which there is a good discussion in "On Stories," particularly focused on *The Wind in the Willows* (3–20, particularly 13–14).

The more obvious papers to examine, however, are "On Three Ways of Writing for Children," "Sometimes Fairy Stories May Say Best What's to Be Said," and "On Juvenile Tastes." The three ways of writing for children divide into one wrong way and two right ways. The wrong way is to write by formula—giving the children what children are supposed to like, or alternatively, producing books to fit a supposed "reading age," or to give a certain (politically correct) message. The recent debate in the U.K. over young children reading "real books" rather than reading scheme primers is an example of this sort of discussion.

The first of the right ways is the way many children's writers begin, if not continue: there is a specific child demanding a story. Thus Lewis Carroll with his young girl protégées; thus Charles Kingsley with his youngest son; and thus even Tolkien, with his growing family, for whom *The Hobbit* was produced. This audience, for Lewis, creates a community, a concept that anticipates more recent studies in reading communities.[4]

However, Lewis claims he did not have such a child centered-community, though it could well be argued that the Inklings were a good substitute. Lewis claims on a number of occasions to be very shy with children and to know very few. Writing to Arthur, he says, "I theoretically hold that one ought to like children, but am shy of them in practice" (*Stand* 474). However, Hooper notes, "During the course of this war, a number of evacuated girls were billeted at The Kilns. Lewis very much enjoyed their company as can be seen from his letter to his brother . . ." (484n). Of this limited opportunity to produce, Lewis clearly did not avail himself. This leaves the third way of production: to see children's literature as an art form, and to realize what you want to write about is best expressed in this particular art form.

This would appear to generate a more aesthetic theory, but Lewis never actually produces one, staying within a more generalized genre approach.

317

What are the advantages of writing in this particular art form? He names a number: it can create the reality of childhood; it can create types of characters without the complexities of the adult (realistic) novel; by so simplifying, it can focus on "what was said and done," so forcing restraint on "the expository demon" in himself. In "Sometimes Fairy Stories" he adds to the list of helpful omissions and constraints that of a love interest. In this essay he suggests writing for children "only means excluding what they would not like or understand" (37). This is rather a negative criterion; in "On Three Ways" he puts it positively as "a story that children can and do read" (23).

This is all a little vague. A list of advantages cannot really be a definition, let alone a theory. But he is much more specific on other aspects of production. The autobiographical account of how he produced describes a process out of mental images. Some of these images were spontaneous inventions; some formed out of his own reading. Thus, in creating *The Lion*, spontaneous images include a faun carrying parcels, and a huge lion (this occurring in a series of nightmares); and those from his reading include the white witch, from Andersen's "The Snow Queen." The story is then produced by joining these images together in a plot.

This mode of production leads him to protest against didactic modes, since they must tend toward the allegorical, a mode which he regards somewhat ambivalently, or the formulaic, which leads to superficiality. As we shall see later, he made no attempt to make the Narnia stories Christian as such. Rather, Christianity "pushed its way in." Generalizing, he claims, "Let the pictures tell you their own moral. For the moral inherent in them will rise from whatever spiritual roots you have succeeded in striking during the whole course of your life" ("On Three Ways" 33).[5] The other difficulty with didacticism is the "watchful dragons," explained in "Sometimes Fairy Stories" and enlarged upon by Walter Hooper in his *Past Watchful Dragons*. Like John Keats, children are suspicious of poetry that "has designs on us," whether it be Christianity or morality. Fantasy, particularly, slips past such vigilance. You try to teach by not trying.

318

Thus, producing a children's story comes primarily from an imaginative place rather than a rational or moral one. It is no less spiritual for that. Here Coleridge's distinction between fancy and the imagination seems to be the subtext. It is only out of imaginative truth that the desire, the "longing for he knows not what," arises in the reader. Such a reference takes us straight back to the joy/desire of the autobiography. That is the birthright of every child reader, and a good children's text may produce this; a bad one never will.

Production, however, is not all the writer's. Practically, production involves publishers, and Lewis had a certain amount to say about them, especially in "On Juvenile Tastes," where he talks of fashions in reading. In his own day, fantasy was very much out of fashion, and it is very much to Lewis's and

Tolkien's credit that it is no longer so. The only sort of fantasy "allowable" at the time was children's fantasy and science fiction. This means practically, he states, that if you want to get certain sorts of stories published, you need to write for children.[6] Thus "for children" is more a market label than an audience directive. Lewis, quoting Tolkien's "On Fairy Stories," is clearly impatient with such reductionism, not because his own creativity was inhibited by it, but because of the marginalizing it produces for the genre. It is an altruistic impatience.[7]

Theoretical Aspects: Reception

The other side of Lewis's theoretical model is reception. By this I mean the consideration of the reader, both adult and child, and the reading process. The latter is, for Lewis, an evaluative literary one rather than a psychological or educational one. The concern is both to evaluate a text in terms of the good readings it produces, and also to evaluate the good reader. While Lewis does not go into the complexities of this reader/reading web, he certainly anticipates something of reception theory in his *Experiment*.[8] I will confine my remarks on this book to those which concern children's literature, after considering statements made elsewhere.

Writing on *The Hobbit*, Lewis states: "It is a children's book only in the sense that the first of many readings can be undertaken in the nursery" ("Hobbit" 82). The construct of "the nursery" sounds a little quaint to our ears, but it admirably conveys a childhood state where the reader is probably a grown-up, mediating an oral performance to the child, whose "reading" is thus pleasurable, protected, and warmly emotional. Whether children's first reading is actually like this is neatly sidestepped by the phrase "can be undertaken," though the assumption is there. *The Hobbit* is thus a good book because it can bear many rereadings at different stages of maturity. It is universal, therefore, and many-layered.

Part of "On Juvenile Tastes" deals with the child reader, noting that while children have as many different tastes as adults, the one constant is that they always read for enjoyment. Unlike adults, they do not read because a certain book or author is fashionable. Compared to later educational research on children's tastes and reading habits, such remarks may seem simplistic.[9] But that is not quite the point: Lewis is laying groundwork. To raise the status of children's literature, he needs to raise the status of the child reader, and this returns us to my earlier remark that, for Lewis, to understand children's reading, we must understand childhood, especially those qualities of childhood that need to be taken into adulthood.

In his paper "On Stories," he suggests those qualities which make a good child reader and which need to be retained. One is the ability to be surprised over and over again, even though the plot is known. Another is the delight in story which then leads to the awakening of the imaginative life, which in turn enables the reception of profound experiences of reality. However, a careful reading of this essay will show just how easily Lewis slips from a reader to a book which generates a good reading. Thus "the story . . . may not be 'like real life' in the superficial sense; but it sets before us an image of what reality may well be like at some more central region" ("On Stories" 16). The text is to be praised for the way we can receive it, rather than for the qualities inherent in the reader.

In the following paragraph he posits the idea of the "inarticulate" reader. While this is not meant to be defined as "the child reader," it would seem that the child is a subset within the class of inarticulate readers. However, inarticulateness does not mean a poor reader. There can still be an equality and an aesthetic interchange of reader and text, good readers being of equal imaginative powers as the text. It is the imaginative power that is to be evaluated, not the ability to utter. There is a certain democratic feel here, even if tempered by a tone of patronage in the usage of "the masses."

Remarks elsewhere are in line with this. In his essay "Hamlet: The Prince or the Poem?" he remarks right at the end that "only those adults who have retained, with whatever additions and enrichments, their first childish responses to poetry unimpaired, can be said to have grown up at all" (105). In *That Hideous Strength*, Mark's regeneration is signaled by his ability to read a children's story he had begun and then was ashamed to read at the age of ten.

All this returns us to the status of the (inarticulate) child reader in *Experiment*, which works well for children's literature in that it disallows a hierarchy of genres. Academically, as we have said, children's literature (I have even heard it called disparagingly "kiddilit") is usually classified very low. So by abolishing hierarchy, there is a necessary raising of status. But as concerns the child reader, the essay is problematic and reveals some of the ambiguities noted earlier. In fact, it seems at first glance to disallow some of the redeeming features in his earlier essays. Even about his own childhood reading he is disparaging, stating how indiscriminately he read Beatrix Potter. By the definitions he gives in *Experiment*, he was a poor child reader since he read her as a substitute, to fill a gap or void. For a good reading, he would need to have read out of his fullness. He talks of "unliterary twelve-year-olds," somewhat grudgingly admitting in parenthesis that "not all twelve-year-olds are unliterary" (29).

What seems to emerge is a concept of a child reader who can either be a potentially good reader or an actual bad one. He cannot, however, be an actual good reader, in that his responses are without discipline or experience (*Experiment* 12–13). If the child is both inarticulate and potential, how can we know he will ever be a good reader or give a good reading to a (good) children's text? In fact, what sensible evaluations can we make about him? Lewis is in danger of making any worthwhile discussion about the child disappear. Yet without a reader, how can we know what a good text is? We would have to return to the adult articulate reader, perhaps recalling his own childhood reading through some process of Wordsworthian remembering.

In practice, this is not such a problem. We do return in our discussions of children's literature to the adult reader (usually ourselves). And we do evaluate a text as a good one if we can (re)read it well out of our fullness, still finding an original enjoyment, but also imaginative depths that may not have been struck as a child, or only inarticulately. We note children's enjoyment of a text, of course, but we do not make that an evaluative criterion. In other words, Lewis does not really need the concept of the child reader; what he needs is the *quality* of childhood reading. Thus he writes: "But who in his senses would not keep, if he could, that tireless curiosity (of childhood), that intensity of imagination, that facility of suspending belief, that unspoiled appetite, that readiness to wonder, to pity, and to admire?" (*Experiment* 72).

The rest of childhood can be safely abandoned!

Reconstructing a Lewis Reading

As I have remarked, we never see Lewis in the traditional teaching role of analyzing children's texts or authors. He creates, he writes of his creative process. He writes of his own enjoyment and tastes, of memories that were significant. It is from these that we must reconstruct, as best we can, how he might read a specific text or author. I would suggest the following features.

First, any analysis would be evaluative rather than descriptive. The whole emphasis of *Experiment* is to discriminate between good and bad readings, an emphasis also found in the Cambridge school of response criticism founded by I. A. Richards and built on by F. R. Leavis. Though *Experiment* is ostensibly a reaction to Leavisite close reading, Lewis shares more with Leavis than he realizes, since both look to Richards for their concepts of discrimination and evaluation as being both literary and moral. Both examine the quality of aesthetic response from a text. Both shun the "personal heresy" and the "intentionalist fallacy."

Lewis would evaluate a text in terms of the reading experience it allowed to the adult as well as to the child reader. The experience would be different for both, but a good text would have to allow good readings to both, hence his

321

praise for *The Hobbit* and *The Wind in the Willows*. Such a reading experience would be measured specifically in terms of a total imaginative world, and whether the experience was integrally a part of this. This imaginative world would have a spiritual dimension to it, though the reader would not necessarily have to agree with its spirituality. Lewis's praise of Lindsay's *Voyage to Arcturus* makes this clear. He calls it "that shattering, intolerable and irresistible work" ("Science Fiction" 94). Such an experience would also have to be enjoyable, since no child will read a book well that he or she is not enjoying. The elements of such enjoyment are discussed in a moment.

The assumption behind such an evaluation would be that the text is an art form, amenable to literary criticism. He would refuse an evaluation in pedagogical terms, e.g., in terms of the age range, difficulty of vocabulary, or potential for psychological development. His reading would also resist all attempts to moralize or teach from the text (i.e., use it to do something non-literary), and would evaluate as a poor text any one that sought explicitly to teach or preach—on the "past watchful dragons" principle. In "On Three Ways" he remarks: "The moral you put in is likely to be a platitude, or even a falsehood, skimmed from the surface of your consciousness . . . in the moral sphere (children) are probably at least as wise as we. Anyone who *can* write a children's story without a moral, had better do so . . ." (33). This would condemn much Victorian children's literature, of course, and explains why he had difficulties with Kingsley's *The Water Babies*. He did not seem to have had such difficulties with MacDonald, though we might think of him as moralistic as Kingsley. I would suggest his "conversion" experience on first reading *Phantastes* might explain his ability to read through such moralism.

Second, as markers in his literary criticism of a children's text, Lewis looks for a strong story line with simple but well-defined characterization, and a clearly defined mood or atmosphere. Even more importantly he would be aware of voice and tonalities which would have to embody a sense of equality between reader and writer. That is to say, childhood would need full respect, with no attempt to talk down to the child reader, no "winking" at an adult reader over the child's head, no shared adult jokes.

He states, "We must meet children as equals in that area of our nature where we are their equals" and that is not childishness; and "The child as reader is neither to be patronized or idolized: we talk to him as man to man" ("On Three Ways" 34). This is Lewis's democratic (if somewhat masculine) urge, which in his own life extended to chauffeurs and truck drivers, and which hated all ceremony where hierarchy was emphasized. Such an attitude must express itself primarily in a voice which suggests respect for the reader, and therefore the high seriousness of reading, however comic the subject matter. Any tone that suggests to the reader "you ought to like this because . . ." is the mark of a bad text, since it suggests superiority.

Finally, Lewis posits the test of rereadability and memorability. He writes, "The nearest we can come to a test is by asking whether he often *re-reads* the same story" ("On Stories" 16)—the whole passage in "On Stories" repays the closest attention. Any text that grasps "excitement for its own sake, that relies entirely on the 'what happens next' suspense of adventure" will be a poor text, since once the plot is known, there is nothing to hold a reader in rereading. Only if atmosphere, characters, the magic of another world are intensely created, will the rereading be pleasurable. The knowledge now gained of what happens next will become the pleasure of anticipation, mingling with the pleasure of discovering new features, new depths in the text.

Reading Lewis's Writing

Does Lewis's own children's writing match up to these criteria? Some people have not thought so, including the one person whose opinion mattered most for him—J. R. R. Tolkien. As discussed in chapters 14 and 19, Tolkien's main tenet was the writer as sub-creator, and as such, embodies the *imago Dei*. It is on this point that Tolkien criticized the Chronicles. He thought that Lewis's sub-creation was careless, lacking depth and unity. He objected, for example, to the mixing of Father Christmas with fauns (from Greek mythology) or talking animals.

In contrast to Tolkien's decades-long gestation of Middle Earth, with its elaborate history, geography, mythology, languages, and lore, Lewis's Narnia is an impromptu affair, being made up as he went along. Lewis was deeply upset by Tolkien's objections when he read parts of *The Lion* to the Inklings, especially after the unbounded enthusiasm he had shown for *The Hobbit* nearly twenty years earlier. He would have given up the writing, had it not been for the belief shown in it by Roger Lancelyn Green and one or two others. While Lewis did go ahead, Tolkien's hostility helped open a breach in their friendship that was never closed again.[10]

In Lewis's own criteria, meticulous attention to inventing a sub-created world was not included. Such detail, he clearly felt, was not necessary to creating a mood; nor was the mixing of mythological sources any hindrance, any more than it was for Kenneth Grahame. This latter point has already been explored by Maria Kuteeva in an earlier chapter. The fantasy mode depends on imaginative depth and originality of combination rather than detail, which is perhaps the scholar's penchant. Most readers are convinced of the concreteness of Narnia through the strength of characterization and range of Lewis's talking animals, from the majesty of Aslan to the heroics of Reepicheep and the homeliness of the badgers. As an animal fantasy, it has uniqueness and memorability; it is not interchangeable with any other land created for any other animal fantasy.

As an author, he enters that world through his child protagonists with wonderment. Even in *The Horse and His Boy*, Narnia is entered wonderingly through a child, with the talking horses having as much character as the humans. The sense of the marvelous is reestablished in every book through one Romance device or another, with the Romance quest/task device remaining a constant. This "calling" or sense of destiny is necessary for the fantasy to be heroic. The quest is the adventure, not told just for its excitement, but to test morally and spiritually. The one book where the children are not tested as moral heroes and heroines is the first, where Aslan becomes the hero, and the children's moral worthiness is established through sympathy, bravery, and repentance.

I want to look at three of the other criteria: tone, lack of didacticism, and rereadability. The first two interlink, of course; for the tonalities to be right, any talking at or down has to be avoided. Here Lewis plays a dangerous game, that of the intrusive author, addressing his readers as "you," an apostrophizing that in much children's writing becomes patronizing at the least. Consider the opening pages of *The Silver Chair*. The "I" voice is avuncular—the sympathetic adult sharing with the child reader his horror of boarding schools.[11] Although Lewis is attacking a certain sort of boarding school, what conveys itself is the tone of shared dislike of the worst features of school life: its bullying in-groups ("the bloodery"), its confinement, and the institutionalized hypocrisies of the adults in charge.

The "you" apostrophe is not the preached-at "you," but part of the author's search to find corresponding experiences in his readers. He does not judge Jill's tears, for example, but takes it for granted that crying is a normative but difficult experience. It is restrained sympathy. The opening of chapter 2 is another good example of sensitivity to tone. Lewis censors Eustace when the latter's tone is false—"he meant well, but he *did* talk rather like someone beginning a lecture." The wry humor is just right. What the I/you nexus is doing is linking Lewis's concern for the child reader outside the text to his portrayal of the child protagonist within the text. Both are his equals. It is a difficult task and some critics, such as Colin Manlove, suggest some faltering through creating fictive children as both children and child-adults (Manlove 122–23). My own feeling is that Romance allows a flexibility here which realistic fiction does not, and Lewis exploits this soundly enough.

It is not only in tonalities that didacticism is avoided but also in his refusal to allegorize. There is a theology of Narnia which Lewis openly shared with his child correspondents. He lists seven points where there are parallels between biblical and Narnian theology, but he prefaces this by saying: "Suppose there were a world like Narnia and it needed rescuing, and the Son of

God went to redeem, as He came to redeem us. What might it, in that world, all have been like?" (*Children* 8/6/60). The "let's suppose" is a much more exploratory approach leading away from "this means that" toward "I imagine it could be like this" and then to "I image these episodes and characters." At the end of *The Voyage of the Dawn Treader*, Lewis voices similar concepts through Aslan, having used biblical symbolism immediately beforehand (the lamb), and biblical episode (the post-resurrection breakfast with his disciples). We feel that all this came spontaneously out of Lewis's imaginative wellsprings rather than out of some allegorical set piece.

Finally, what of Narnian rereadability? Is there a good adult reading? Clearly there is: many adults read the Chronicles, sometimes not having read them as children at all. The Chronicles have been analyzed and commented upon sensitively and subtly by many writers—they clearly generate many varied readings out of the fullness of amateur and professional readers alike. To return to *The Silver Chair*, the comments about progressive schools will have a fuller meaning for adults, forcing them to look at such institutions from a child's point of view, as well as reminding them of their own playground experience of bullying and in-groups. The testing of Jill by Aslan, in its simplicity, can be read as the testing of all of us as we seek to come to faith. We are desperate for "the waters of life," yet terrified of its own true spiritual source, are we not? Lewis's own conversion experience lies right behind the imaginative thrust of the episode, giving it its concreteness.

Is not *The Last Battle* an emblem of the (re)reading experience of the Chronicles? The door of the book leads to a world larger on the inside than on the outside. And is not such fantasy best at relating a symbolic geography of transcendence? How else could the littleness and triviality of evil that we experience in daily life be seen as having cosmic significance? How else could the glories of heaven and the end of time be portrayed? Lewis's writing here engenders in us a confidence that just the right art form has been chosen.

325

Criticisms

C. S. Lewis's practice, I would therefore suggest, does live up to his own critical criteria. Both his theory and practice were consciously placed within "The Nesbit Tradition," one strand of what is often referred to as "The Golden Age of Children's Literature." Lewis's Chronicles can be seen as part of the renaissance of that age that occurred after World War II, and which lasted for the next four decades. As I have said, Lewis's particular contribution was to revive and renew the fantasy mode within that renaissance.

The continuing massive sales of the Narnia stories and their continuing acceptance by most writers, parents, and teachers together with many testimonies of the joys of rereading them, all point to the genius of Lewis's imagination, and give the lie to Tolkien's criticism. The growth of academic criticism and theory in the field of fantasy, some of which concerns itself with children's fantasy, also points to the rising status of children's literature, again helped in no small part by Lewis and Tolkien.

However, we need to be aware that, inevitably, there have been other criticisms of Lewis's practice that have stemmed from more than personal dislike. Children's literature has become quite politicized in recent years and inevitably well-known texts and authors have been drawn into the ensuing debates. In this context, I want to refer specifically to one attack on Lewis, and more generally, to look at a wider debate over the political nature of fantasy with reference to the Chronicles.

The name of David Holbrook was well known in British educational circles between 1960 and 1980; his progressive ideas on the teaching of English certainly influenced many young teachers—for the good, I believe. His own baseline was Leavisite, agnostic, and psychologized, quasi-Freudian in tone. His attack on the Chronicles[12] was in fact a highly psychologized one, taking the attack back to Lewis's personality, an approach adopted by a recent biographer, A. N. Wilson, though generating a rather different reading of Lewis. Holbrook complains of Lewis's "continual aggressive stance," his "aggressive posture of hate," his "paranoically conceived menaces," and his "intense self-righteousness" (117). He sees a deep ambivalence in Lewis's Christianity, containing "a fear of love," only to be overcome by "paranoid self-strengthening" (123). The terms "aggressive" and "aggression" are frequently repeated—Lewis conveys to his readers "that . . . aggression is glorious, exciting and fully justified . . . conveyed with undertones of a sadistic-sexual kind" (124).

In fact, we might suggest that such strong language is in itself highly ambiguous, slipping in and out of moral, political, and psychological discourse, and its own lack of systematic evidence could be deconstructed in terms of Holbrook's own paranoid obsessions. Alternatively, we could deconstruct this argument in terms of Holbrook's progressivist brand of liberal humanism which reacts violently and automatically to any religious or conservative commitment. Holbrook certainly fudges on the nature of the "unconscious" message—for whom is it unconscious? He also misunderstands Romance. He accuses Lewis of being reactionary in terms of disallowing the children any real choice in their own destiny. But the quest-task feature is central to all Romance: the children still have to make moral choices and are capable of failing the quest (Jill and Eustace forget three of the four instructions given them by Aslan). Holbrook's criticism that Lewis encourages greed in a "new super-hedonism" (i.e., the real Narnia of *The Last Battle*) is merely a jaded materialist rejection of Platonic idealism and no serious criticism of Lewis's actual writing. In fact, the piece tells us more about Holbrook than Lewis, and represents a philosophic failure by the liberal left to critique Lewis's practice or get to grips with his theory.

This leads to a more general discussion as to whether the fantasy mode is inherently conservative, or subversive and therefore radical; but this is far too wide to enter at this point.[13] I will take just one typical left-wing criticism of Lewis which argues that fantasy is by nature conservative. Bob Dixon argues, in fact, that Lewis's own religious fantasy is doubly conservative, since Lewis abandons "personal responsibility with religion as an excuse." For evidence in the Narnia books he cites Lewis's stress on royalty and hierarchy, that regal and aristocratic terms run throughout, reinforced by being fixed in a medieval period (vol. 2, 155–61).

In fact, if we look systematically at the Chronicles, we could say that Lewis's royalist urges are held in balance by his democratic ones. In *The Magician's Nephew*, two very ordinary citizens become the first king and queen of Narnia; the exercise of Narnian authority is very low-key, and when it is not, Aslan makes sure it is overthrown. The talking animals suggest an equality for all— literally a voice of the people—and a lack of discrimination. And in *The Last Battle*, this political voice of talking animals is contrasted to the totalitarianism and exploitation of the Calormenes. The naiveté of an entropic Narnian society is surely Lewis's argument against political quietism and withdrawal, and for the need for proactive political vigilance. Royalist structures are marginalized; it is the moral structures that signify. Thus the political revelation given by Lewis can be read as democratic at least, if not radical.

I would like to argue in closing that Lewis's true subversion is not political at all, but the traditional Christian one: the subversion of material appearances, of all political power structures, and of death itself—a point argued fully in chapter 15. The theological subverts the political; death is swallowed up in victory; the inside is greater than the outside. To have expressed such subversion so completely in the form of children's fantasy is an amazing achievement. The Carnegie Medal that Lewis received for *The Last Battle* in 1956 is the merest token of recognition of such an achievement.

Notes

1. Tolkien's views on sub-creation can, in fact, be traced back to George MacDonald's crucial essay "The Fantastic Imagination."

2. Quoted by Sibley. Sibley's account is the fullest one of Lewis's reading of children's literature. The illustrations by Pauline Baynes are a bonus.

3. References are to *Children* 26/1/53; the essay "On Juvenile Tastes" in *Of This and Other Worlds*; and *Stand* 498. The point being made is that these books had only recently been published. Lewis was thus keeping up with his reading of children's fantasy, not merely rereading childhood favorites.

4. On reading communities see Marshall.

5. Cf. "The life of which it [a story] comes will be impregnated with all the wisdom, knowledge and experience the author has; and even more by something which I can only vaguely describe as the flavour or 'feel' that actual life has for him" (*Experiment* 81–82).

6. Cf. Jill Paton Walsh's essay "The Rainbow Surface." She writes, "Some writers are choosing Children's Literature, who prefer its constraints," adding they are "making a full serious *adult* statement . . . and making it utterly simple and transparent" (213).

7. "On Three Ways" 27, "Fairy Stories" 37, "Juvenile" 40. Tolkien's point is that in an oral tradition fairy stories received an undifferentiated audience. Lewis's echoing of this is, perhaps, somewhat nostalgic.

8. The major critical texts here are Iser, *The Act of Reading* and *The Implied Reader* (especially chapter 12, "The Reading Process: A Phenomenological Approach"); Fish; and Freund, who revisits the older and more recent debates, from I. A. Richards to Fish.

9. For example, Tucker, "How Children Respond to Fiction." Note that Tucker is a child psychologist, whose approach to production is exactly what Lewis sees as the wrong one.

10. Carpenter discusses the affair in *The Inklings* 223–26.

11. In a letter to a child, Lewis once wrote, "I never hated anything so much (as my three boarding schools), not even the frontline trenches in World War I" (*Children* 24/3/62).

12. David Holbrook, "The Problem of C. S. Lewis." He enlarges his views in *The Skeleton in the Wardrobe*.

13. At a general level, see Jackson, *Fantasy: The Literature of Subversion*; as opposed to Lynette Hunter, *Modern Allegory and Fantasy*, who argues, against Lewis, that serious readings of fantasy become allegorical. For specific references to children's literature, see Zipes, *Fairy Tales and the Art of Subversion*; Inglis, "Reading Children's Literature: Notes on the Politics of Literature" and his *The Promise of Happiness: Value and Meaning in Children's Fiction*.

Works Cited

Carpenter, Humphrey. *The Inklings*. London: Allen & Unwin, 1978.

Dixon, Bob. *Catching Them Young*. 2 vols. London: Pluto, 1978.

Fish, Stanley. *Is There a Text in This Class?* Cambridge, MA: Harvard UP, 1980.

Fox, Geoffrey, et al., eds. *Writers, Critics and Children: Articles from "Children's Literature in Education."* London: Heineman, 1978.

Freund, Elizabeth. *The Return of the Reader: Reader-Response Criticism*. London: Methuen, 1987.

Holbrook, David. "The Problem of C. S. Lewis." *Children's Literature in Education*. Vol. 10. Rpt. in Fox et. al., eds. 116–24.

———. *The Skeleton in the Wardrobe: C. S. Lewis's Fantasies—A Phenomenological Study*. Lewisburg: Associated UP, 1991.

Hooper, Walter. *Past Watchful Dragons*. London: Collins Fount, 1980.

Hunter, Lynette. *Modern Allegory and Fantasy: Rhetorical Stance in Contemporary Writing.* Basingbroke: Macmillan, 1989.

Inglis, Fred. "Reading Children's Literature: Notes on the Politics of Literature." *Children's Literature in Education.* July 1971. Rpt. in Fox. 170–79.

——. *The Promise of Happiness: Value and Meaning in Children's Fiction.* Cambridge: Cambridge UP, 1981.

Iser, Wolfgang. *The Act of Reading: A Theory of Aesthetic Response.* Baltimore: Johns Hopkins UP, 1978.

——. *The Implied Reader: Patterns of Communication in Prose Fiction from Bunyan to Beckett.* Baltimore: Johns Hopkins UP, 1974.

Jackson, Rosemary. *Fantasy: The Literature of Subversion.* London: Methuen, 1981.

Lewis, C. S. *Boxen: The Imaginary World of the Young C. S. Lewis.* Ed. Walter Hooper. London: Collins, 1985.

——. *An Experiment in Criticism.* Cambridge: Cambridge UP, 1961.

——. "First and Second Things." *First and Second Things: Essays on Theology and Ethics.* Ed. Walter Hooper. Glasgow: Fount, 1985.

——. "Hamlet: The Prince or the Poem?" *Selected Literary Essays.* Ed. Walter Hooper. Cambridge: Cambridge UP, 1969. 88–105.

——. "The Hobbit." *Stories* 81–82.

——. *Letters to Children.* Ed. Lyle W. Dorsett and Marjorie L. Mead. London: Collins, 1985.

——. *Of Other Worlds: Essays and Stories.* Ed. Walter Hooper. 1966. New York: Harcourt Brace Jovanovich, 1975.

——. "On Juvenile Tastes." *Of Other Worlds* 39–41.

——. "On Science Fiction." *Of Other Worlds* 59–73.

——. "On Stories." *"On Stories" and Other Essays on Literature.* Ed. Walter Hooper. New York: Harcourt Brace Jovanovich, 1982. 3–20.

——. "On Three Ways of Writing for Children." *Of This and Other Worlds* 22–34.

——. "Sometimes Fairy Stories May Say Best What's to Be Said." *Of Other Worlds* 35–38.

——. *Surprised by Joy: The Shape of My Early Life.* New York: Harcourt, 1955.

——. *They Stand Together: The Letters of C. S. Lewis to Arthur Greeves (1914–1963).* Ed. Walter Hooper. London: Collins, 1979.

MacDonald, George. "The Fantastic Imagination." *A Dish of Orts.* London: Edwin Dalton, 1908. Rpt. *A Peculiar Gift.* Ed. Lance Salway. Harmondsworth: Kestrel, 1976. 162–67.

Manlove, Colin. *C. S. Lewis: His Literary Achievement.* Basingstoke: Macmillan, 1987.

Marshall, Donald. "Reading and Interpretative Communities." *The Discerning Reader.* Eds. David Barratt, Roger Pooley, and Leland Ryken. Grand Rapids: Baker, 1995. 69–84.

Sibley, Brian. *The Land of Narnia.* London: Collins, 1989/New York: Harper and Row, 1990.

Tolkien, J. R. R. "On Fairy Stories." *Tree and Leaf.* London: Allen & Unwin, 1964. 11–70.

——. *The Hobbit.* London: Allen & Unwin, 1937.

Tucker, Nicholas. "How Children Respond to Fiction." Fox 177–88.

Walsh, Jill Paton. "The Rainbow Surface." *Suitable for Children.* Ed. Nicholas Tucker. Brighton, England: U of Sussex, 1976. 212–15.

Zipes, Jack. *Fairy Tales and the Art of Subversion.* London: Heinemann, 1983.

329

18
Literary Criticism

Bruce L. Edwards

> "The truth is not that we need the critics in order to enjoy the authors, but that we need the authors in order to enjoy the critics. . . . If we have to choose, it is always better to read Chaucer again than to read a new criticism of him." (*Experiment* 123–24)

Few practicing literary critics in his time were as contemptuous of their common trade as C. S. Lewis.[1] In fact, speaking of Lewis as a *literary critic* inevitably draws attention to aspects of his profession at which Lewis himself would likely demur. According to poet Kathleen Raine, a Blake scholar and one of his colleagues at Cambridge in the 1950s, Lewis took "a poor view of 'literary criticism,'" once asking her "if I did not think it entirely useless? I said that I did: scholarship can help towards the better understanding of a poem whose difficulty arises from our lack of certain knowledge; but criticism is a kind of mould or cancer" (103). They, in fact, shared the conviction, eminently on display in my epigraph from Lewis, that criticism at its best impedes the reader's encounter with the primary text. Lewis's pessimistic stance toward literary criticism is further evident in his remarks on the difficulty modern readers face in approaching the work of Edmund Spenser filtered through such academic vantage points:

> *The Faerie Queene* suffers even more than most great works from being approached through the medium of commentaries and "literary history." These all demand from us a sophisticated, self-conscious frame of mind. But then, when

we have used all these aids we discover that the poem itself demands exactly the opposite response. Its primary appeal is to the most naive and innocent tastes: to that level of our consciousness which is divided only by the thinnest veil from the immemorial lights and glooms of the collective Unconscious itself. ("Spenser" 132)

Making a work captive to the conventional wisdom of the critic's own era or subject to its dubious criteria of approval was the bane of modern criticism, and, for Lewis, its most disturbing feature.

Literary historian George Watson, characterizing Lewis's achievements as a critic, suggests, "The chief purpose of his critical writings, in a negative sense, was the discrediting of sixteenth-century Humanism and twentieth-century modernism, both of which he saw as dry, starved, and stultifying," and that "explaining, justifying, and consolidating ancient truths was what he did best" (3; 5). However, Raine attributes Lewis's strong anti-critical posture not so much to his aversion to modernity, which was profound, but rather to his quite palpable love of reading itself, observing that it stood in vivid contrast to the attitudes of "bored superiority or active hatred" toward literature displayed by many other academic figures of their times. Given "his love of the material itself [which] was life-giving as a spring in a desert. . . . I went to some of his lectures on the 'matter' of Rome, France, and Britain," she explains, "and remember how he made the dullest Latin text seem enthralling . . ." (103). Echoing Raine's sentiments, Helen Gardner, the medieval and Renaissance scholar who turned down the Cambridge position Lewis eventually obtained, categorizes Lewis's *The Allegory of Love* as a work "written by a man who loved literature and had an extraordinary power of stimulating his readers to curiosity and enthusiasm" (16). Lewis's quite principled approach to criticism was expressed in a letter to Raine only two weeks before his death. One should offer his readers, he wrote, "Plenty of fact, reasoning as brief and clear as English sunshine, and no personal comment at all" (103–04).

The Reader as Reluctant Critic

The kind of reader Lewis proved himself to be, and the sort of reluctant "critic" he would eventually become, was dramatically influenced by one of his Oxford professors, A. K. Hamilton Jenkin, who is immortalized in *Surprised by Joy* as a man who "seemed to be able to enjoy everything; even ugliness"; "I learned from him that we should attempt a total surrender to whatever atmosphere was offering itself at the moment. . . . There was no Betjemannic irony about it; only a serious, yet gleeful, determination to rub one's nose in the very quiddity of each thing, to rejoice in its being (so magnificently) what it was" (199). Yes, as a reader, Lewis is always and everywhere determined to promote the experience of what he calls here a text's *quiddity*—what it essentially "is," "says," and "does," understood within its own historical and cultural milieu. Consequently, he is hardly ever concerned with judging a text's ultimate worth or debating the credibility of its ideas when measured according to the vagaries of contemporary tastes and standards. While Lewis certainly believed in the value of *textual* criticism, especially for assuring accuracy in historical, cultural, and philological reconstruction, its sole purpose was to preserve the text itself so the "real past" may emerge: "We want to know—therefore, as far as may be, we want to live through for ourselves—the experience of men long dead. What a poem may 'mean' to moderns and to them only, however delightful, is from this point of view merely a stain on the lens. We must clean the lens and remove the stain so that the real past can be seen better" ("*Audiendis*" 2). It should be observed then that Lewis as critic was determined mainly to offer his readers an earnest travelogue to prepare them for their own adventures and discoveries inside the text. Along the way, this effort might indeed require explaining an obscure term, illustrating a genre with multiple, judiciously chosen examples, historicizing a text's original readership and its expectations, or pointing out potential misconstruals from the contemporary reader's vantage point. But these efforts are all in the name of allowing the reader *entrée* into a textual world made more "visible" by the critic's quick exit from the line of sight: when we "read Plato," Lewis avers in "On the Reading of Old Books," we do so to "know 'what Plato actually said'— something which the commentator cannot deliver. The intervening modern may be more a threat to clarity than a help to understanding" (200).

For Lewis, modern criticism substituted a jaded twentieth-century sensibility that prizes obtrusive secondary sources and morbid speculation above encounter with the primary text, therein supplanting real reading with tendentious interpretation: "if we are not careful criticism may become a mere excuse for taking revenge on books whose smell we dislike by erecting our temperamental antipathies into pseudo-moral judgments" ("Culture" 31). Another way of saying all this is that, long before our late twentieth-century obsessions with such matters came to vogue within the realm of "literary theory," Lewis was anachronistically concerned with *what happens* when people read—and sought to equip willing readers with effective strategies to escape the "chronological snobbery" of their times. Thus, the label "literary critic," though superficially applicable given the scholarly company he kept, is somewhat misleading when used of Lewis; it is, perhaps, more illuminating to describe Lewis's academic vocation primarily as that of the literary *phenomenologist*.

I use the term "phenomenologist" advisedly, attempting to underscore Lewis's own preoccupations as a reader, and the role he enjoined other readers to adopt. It might be stated this way: become a willing inhabitant within the text's imagined universe, submitting to its narrative or poetic "map," traversing its landscapes, and listening to its myriad voices with the motive of leaving behind one's own predilections, dogmas, and biases. The "criticism" that results from such exploits is the genuine, disinterested report of the earnest explorer who has experienced what it is to look through others' eyes, to think as they have thought, to behave as they behaved within their cultural period. As he puts it in the grand climax of *An Experiment in Criticism*, his only sustained work of critical theory, "in reading great literature I become a thousand men and yet remain myself. Like the night sky in the Greek poem, I see with a myriad eyes, but it is still I who see. Here, as in worship, in love, in moral action, and in knowing, I transcend myself; and am never more myself than when I do" (141).

To read well is to "transcend the self"; to engage the text on its own terms, to make oneself vulnerable and available to its form, themes, images, points of view, etc., while yet remaining "oneself": this is the privilege and the challenge of readership. Criticism worthy of such unencumbered rendezvous will err on the side of minimalism in the process. Just this sort of critical practice may be observed in a thorough examination of Lewis's scholarly work over his whole career—from his first publication on Milton's *Comus* (1932) to his last full-blooded treatment of the literary enterprise in *An Experiment in Criticism* (1961); here is revealed a mind consistently fixed on the enjoyments and adventures of reading itself, and a writer voluntarily sublimating his own tastes, expectations, and desires to the affective choreography of the text before him.

For Lewis, anything less than this self-effacing effort means inevitably to impose upon the text the prejudices, even the errors, of one's contemporary milieu, resulting in the loss of both the "original text" and the reader's potential enrichment:

> I am sometimes told that there are people who want a study of literature wholly free from philology, that is, from the love and knowledge of words. Perhaps no such people exist. If they do, they are either crying for the moon or else revolving on a lifetime of persistent and carefully guarded delusion. If we read an old poem with insufficient regard for change in the overtones, and even the dictionary meanings, of words since its date—if, in fact, we are content with whatever effect the words accidentally produce in our modern minds—then of course we do not read the poem the old writer intended. What we get may still be, in our opinion, a poem; but it will be our poem, not his. (*Words* 3)

333

It is not too much to say that one can classify the great majority of Lewis's published critical works in one of two ways: (1) informed, enthusiastic reports of his own perspicacious and powerful readings of texts, texts great and not-so-great, those well-known and those obscure, texts accessible and others profoundly elusive; or, (2) polemical works designed to defend, rescue, or rehabilitate authors, themes, texts, or whole eras that have been misconstrued or unfairly marginalized through intentional scholarly embargo or simple ignorance.

Lewis's critical canon is replete with both kinds of influential studies; his truly magnum opus, which will be considered in more detail below, *The Allegory of Love* (1936), radically altered critical perceptions of Edmund Spenser's *The Faerie Queene* and reinvigorated discussion and debate about the role and meaning of both courtly love and the genre of allegory in the medieval tradition. His *Preface to "Paradise Lost"* (1942) nearly single-handedly rehabilitated Milton's reputation in an era in which his epic poem was either undervalued or valued for the wrong reasons; while his massive *English Literature in the Sixteenth Century Excluding Drama* (1954), volume 3 in the Oxford History of English Literature, offered lucid summaries of and challenging observations about scores of texts, authors, and movements with incisive grace. Lewis was equally adept at terse, well-targeted rebuttals of critical judgments of works or authors he felt arrogantly deprived readers of joy and instruction, praising Jane Austen for her ethical "hardness," rescuing *Hamlet* from damnation as a "failed play," or defending Shelley as a "great, flawed poet"—as such collections as *Rehabilitations* (1939), *Studies in Medieval and Renaissance Literature* (1966), and *Selected Literary Essays* (1969) well exemplify.

In our quest to understand the nature and achievement of Lewis's criticism, I would like to first examine, albeit briefly, the Christian foundations of his scholarly work, and then focus on four readerly principles that informed his critical stance: (1) readers should always start with the "text itself"; (2) critics' main duty is to provide an informed, unobtrusive "map" for works particularly dense or linguistically or culturally distant; (3) while authors may "intend," it is text which "means," and the locus of our critical judgments should be derived from our actual experience of the text and not the psyche of the author or the social constructs which may explain or explain away the origins of the text; and (4) the ultimate goal of all reading should be to "receive" rather than "use" the literary text, and, consequently, to seek "an enlargement of our being" through truly encountering the "other."

334

The "Quiddity" and "Cartography" of the Text Itself

The Christian premises of Lewis's professional career may be seen in nascent but credible form in his essay entitled "Christianity and Literature," first published in 1939. Here Lewis takes up the question of whether there is or can be a distinctively "Christian" form of literary experience and, therefore, whether there is any symbiosis between fidelity to religious dogma and literary achievement. To have answered "yes," that there is a set of skills and effects unique to the artistry in which Christians engage, would have painted Lewis into an aesthetic corner, for it would have forced him to define a Christian poetics in such a way as to exclude his own experiences as a reader and writer. But Lewis refuses here to confine literariness to a special kind of introspection or contemplation available only to the pious few, or to couch it within an occultic code or narrowly conceived ideology, thus confirming the unbeliever's worst epistemological suspicions. Rather, taking the terms at face value, Lewis's answer to both questions is *no*: "Christian Literature . . . could succeed or fail only by the same excellences and the same faults as all literature; and its literary success or failure would never be the same thing as its obedience or disobedience to Christian principles" ("Literature" 1–2). Except in the most trivial sense, there is no more a "Christian literature" than there is a "Christian cookery," Lewis says. However, there may still be crucial questions to be raised about Christian principles of literary criticism and theory—specifically, how one recognizes and assesses literary accomplishment in light of Christian conviction.

There is a crucial difference, Lewis posits, between the modern critic's obsession with *creativity, spontaneity,* and *freedom*—typically juxtaposed approvingly with the more pejorative terms, *derivation, convention,* and *rule-keeping*—and the Christian critic who takes seriously the model of Christ. The Son of God's incarnation teaches us not to despise but rather to honor imitation, order, and reflected glory; the New Testament, Lewis wryly testifies, is not interested in genius, but in goodness. Thus, the epitome of the Christian critic is not therefore his or her preoccupation with originality or novelty, but with the "artifact" itself and how it does or does not embody, imitate, or reflect that which is eternal.

There is, concealed within this premise, Lewis's penchant for "quiddity"— the world as it is and not as we wish it to be, the world (or text) as it is to be found and not accompanied by false (even sinful) hopes for something "new" or "fresh" or "innovative" *under the sun*. A fallen world entails not only creatures but also "words and things" which require redemption—as well as demanding a concept of authorship that it inevitably, for good or ill, bears creaturely witness to its origins outside the Garden. As a result, the Christian critic's starting point is always to be on guard against that which announces itself as different, unique, or un- or anti-traditional, for these will usually be tell-tale indicators of their opposite qualities. (Nothing is more mundane or futile—serpentine, if you will—for Lewis than to strive for "originality.") Nevertheless, such a principled critic will always first seek "encounter"—resisting the imposition of interpretive schemes or personal agendas, lest the provincial, temporal measures of truth and of craftsmanship will compromise

335

what he or she "sees." A resisting critic, like Lewis, will never "make literature a self-existent thing to be valued for its own sake," but rather will see this as an idolatry that must give way to the recognition that "the salvation of a single soul is more important than the production or preservation of all the epics and tragedies in the world" ("Literature" 10). Here Lewis can be seen affirming both a confessional poetics that exhibits a nonpartisan commitment to public truth seeking and a set of redemptive criteria for humane and principled readership, platforms that put literature and literary criticism in their places *sub specie aeternitatis.*

Lewis's essay on William Morris well illustrates this dynamic posture in a thorough analysis of the thematic concerns and narrative style of the nineteenth-century British fantasist. Lewis suggests at the start that he is writing with a twofold purpose: first, to defend Morris's work against certain recurrent criticisms (for example, that his works were primarily escapist or that he offers a "false medievalism"); and, secondly, to commend Morris as a worthy writer whose vision is poignant and relevant to the aspirations of both believer and unbeliever.

Illustrating his propensity for finding value in even that which is contrary to his own convictions, Lewis praises Morris as a modern Pagan poet who offers something invaluable to the Christian reader, namely, the depiction of "a true skepticism," a "chemically pure" statement of Pagan experience without "a bias to the negative." As such, in Lewis's estimation, Morris is "one of the greatest Pagan witnesses," a prophet as reliable as "Balaam's ass" to speak the truth about what life without God sadly must entail (230). Lewis's perhaps unusual appreciation of Morris is in character with his statement in *The Personal Heresy* about the essential value of reading anything literary: "The only two questions to ask about a poem, in the long run, are, firstly, whether it is interesting, enjoyable, attractive, and, secondly, whether this enjoyment wears well and helps or hinders you towards all the other things you would like to enjoy, or do, or be" (119–20). Lewis regarded Morris as a salutary influence on his own fiction, and it is easy to trace in Morris's fantasies the Lewisian concept of *Sehnsucht*, that bittersweet longing for the transcendent in a temporal world that points one either in hope to the reality of eternity or in despair to the emptiness of materialism. For Lewis, no author the caliber of Morris, who imbues his characters with such a futile "thirst for immortality," can fail to be instructive to the Christian. The quiddity of Morris, like the quiddity of any text when respected, can empower readers to learn more about the cosmos, i.e., created order, in which they live, and therefore more about themselves and their relationship to God.

One can see then that one of Lewis's signal attributes as a literary critic is his ability to enable a reader to better understand with more immediacy the conceptual framework and commitments which undergird a particular work or, indeed, an entire period. In explaining his reasons for writing *The Discarded Image*, Lewis conceded that "frequent researches *ad hoc*" in the midst of confronting a poem "sadly impair receptive reading"; as a result, "sensitive people may even come to regard scholarship as a baleful thing which is always taking you *out of* the literature itself" (vii). Lewis proposed that a solution may be found if the reader could "acquire beforehand" a "tolerable (though very incomplete) outfit" which, "taken along" in the reading, might "lead in" instead of out of the text: "To be always looking at the map when there is a fine prospect before you shatters the 'wise passiveness' in which landscape ought to be enjoyed. But to consult a map before we set out has no such ill effect. Indeed it will lead us to many prospects; including some we might never have found by following our noses" (vii). A critical method that refuses to see the place of such a temporary map, will yield, in Lewis's words, "the worst method of all," which he describes in his essay, "*De Audiendis Poetis*":

> . . . to accept the first impression that the old text happens to make on a modern sensibility and then apply to this the detailed methods of "practical criticism" . . . is to make the worst of both worlds. If you are content that the Heraclitus epigram should mean to you what it meant to Cory, if you are content with Hopkins, to find sprung rhythm in *Piers Plowman*, best enjoy these phantoms lightly, spontaneously, even lazily. To use the microscope, yet not to focus or clean it, is folly. You will only find more mares' nests. You are passing from uncorrected illusions to positively invited illusions. The critic who said (of medieval poetry, as it happens), "one cannot find what is not there" was unduly optimistic. Here, as elsewhere, untrained eyes or a bad instrument produce both errors; they create phantasmal objects as well as miss real ones. (4)

This essay, begun as a book about medieval poetics he never brought to completion, starts characteristically with Lewis challenging a contemporary critic who disdains the critic who seeks to receive the original poem in context. He quotes a "Mr. Speirs" who "announces as 'discouraging' the notion 'that before the modern reader can properly appreciate a medieval poem he must first have somehow put himself back into the age when it was composed.' For thus he will be seeking not 'what the poem *means*,' but 'what it once meant' and will become 'concerned less with reading and responding to a poem than with reading and researching outside it'" (1). On the surface, Speirs seems to concur with Lewis's notion that the quiddity of the text above all should be the center of attention. Lewis, however, suggests that the issue is not quite so simple: "That anything which takes us outside the poem and leaves us there is regrettable, I fully agree. But we may have to go outside it in order that we may presently come inside it again, better equipped" (1). This "going outside the

337

text," according to Lewis, is necessary but only temporarily because "a man who read the literature of the past with no allowance at all for the fact that manners, thought, and sentiments have changed since it was written, would make the maddest work of it" (1). Critics should encourage the reader to be "led by it to newer and fresher enjoyments," "things I could never have met in my own period, modes of feeling, flavours, atmospheres, nowhere accessible but by mental journey into the real past. I have lived nearly sixty years with myself and my own century and am not so enamoured of either as to desire no glimpse of the world beyond them" ("*Audiendis*" 3–4). Lewis's teaching career was certainly predicated on this kind of literary "cartography," and a vast majority of his lectures and tutorial conversations were attempts to assist the naive reader of medieval and other literatures to consider his "map" only long enough to find one's way. Here the critic may prevent modern readers from reading into the text their present experiences and assist them in preserving the "poem itself" without displacing it, thus enabling them to "glimpse the world beyond them."

Authorship, Intention(s), and Readers

One of the specific challenges Lewis faced in his times within the precincts of literary criticism was rescuing the "poem itself" from a host of practitioners determined to waylay it. The biographical critic strove to divine the meaning of the text primarily by way of the author's personal experience and "psychology"; the historical critic probed the socio-economic conditions of the era in which the work was produced and read, sometimes losing the text in its own milieu; the philological critic patiently traced the history of single words and phrases, denotatively and connotatively, at an extreme reducing the text to its particles; the source critic labored to uncover influences and origins of particular plots, themes, or characters in the work at hand, scouring it for originality or its lack thereof, and forgetting to attend to the work in its own time. Each of these traditional critical postures problematized the question of criticism's true center; where in all of this *data* is the "poem," where is the "meaning" or experience of the text? In such essays as "What Chaucer Really Did to *Il Filostrato*" (1932), "High Brows and Low Brows" (1939), "Psycho-Analysis and Literary Criticism" (1942), "The Anthropological Approach" (1962), and, most compellingly, "*De Descriptione Temporum*," his 1954 inaugural address as Professor of Medieval and Renaissance Literature at Cambridge, Lewis was combating critical excesses on all fronts that would rob readers of the "poem itself," while failing to discern the proper relationship of authorship and intention within and the text as a guide to reader response.

338

The Anglo-American movement which came to be known in the 1930s and 40s as New Criticism rebelled against the assumptions that animated traditional critical practices and, at first blush, may seemed to have articulated notions with which Lewis might agree. Their platform offered *explication de texte*, or close reading, as an antidote to preoccupations with peripheral matters that led readers "outside the text"—a strategy intended to reveal a text's "organic unity," sifting its diction, internal rhetoric, and symbol system to provide readers all the information needed to experience and "understand" the work. Rejecting the notion of authorial intention, which is either unavailable or unreliable, the New Critics declared, "a poem should not mean, but be," suggesting that the text is best encountered as an autonomous artifact whose "meaning" is not a paraphrase of its "message," but the total immersion of the reader in its evoked world. Such formidable proponents as William Empson, Monroe Beardsley, William Wimsatt, and T. S. Eliot endeavored to keep criticism from "confusing the poem with its effects," and thus losing the "poem itself" in a morass of subjective responses peripheral to the text.

While understanding the motives of the New Critics, and sympathetic to some of their notions of textual unity, Lewis was never at heart a New Critic. He solved the dilemma of what to do about the "text itself" in its relationship to the author, the reader, and the world at large not by isolating the text but by refusing to locate "meaning" exclusively within it. Instead, Lewis chose to reckon the text as the essential "meeting place" for the encounter between author and reader, reminding in "On Criticism," "It is the author who *intends*; the book *means*," and defining the "meaning" of a work as "the series of emotions, reflections, and attitudes produced by reading it" (56–57). Such a heady move establishes a creative tension among the roles of author, reader, and text that conscientious readers and critics cannot ignore, and tries to insure that the product of criticism will not merely be an arbitrary examination of one or more isolated components of the text. The result is a brand of criticism that could help produce "the ideally true or right 'meaning,'" namely one that is "shared (in some measure) by the largest number of readers after repeated and careful readings over several generations, different periods, nationalities, moods, degrees of alertness, private preoccupations, states of health, spirits, and the like canceling one another out when (this is an important reservation) they can be fused so as to enrich one another" ("On Criticism" 56–57). To assist the reader in appropriating this experiential meaning of a work, the critic may need to contextualize the work's original form, survey both its first and the present reader's likely expectations, and explicate any and all aspects of the author's narrative craft and intention as may be recovered. However, the latter territory should never devolve into a spelunking of the author's psyche between the lines of the work nor into a deconstruction of the text's inten-

339

tion as concealed biography—a point Lewis makes stridently in his published debate with E. M. W. Tillyard, *The Personal Heresy* (1939).

Therein Lewis opposed the notion that "all poetry is about the poet's state of mind" (2), writing, "To see things as the poet sees them, the reader must share his consciousness and not attend to it" (12). Here, as elsewhere, Lewis opposes notions of reading or theory that equate knowing an author's psychology with knowing his or her poem. Lewis proposed instead that the successful poet's achievement is to create an object that is universal not local, public not private, impersonal not personal, since thereby the poet allows the reader to see what the poet sees—and not the poet "himself" in some crude psychoanalytical fashion: "The poet is not a man who asks me to look at *him*; he is a man who says 'look at that' and points; the more I follow the pointing of his finger the less I can possibly see of *him*" (11). The reader earnestly interested in encounter needs no degree in psychology to achieve his goal. As Lewis sardonically observes near the end of the debate, "Whether we regard it as fortunate or unfortunate, the fact is there is no essential qualification for criticism more definite than general wisdom and health of mind" (116).

As a would-be "theorist," Lewis chose his battles wisely, waiting for provocations from critics who happened to attack works or genres counted among his enthusiasms. Neither a New Critic nor a strict intentionalist, it is proper to say that Lewis's eclectic notion of the critical task is one informed by authorial and contextually derived intentions and one whose consistent aim is to invite readers to consider "the poem the author really wrote" instead of one of their own making, and to avoid the equally egregious error of aggrandizing the self at the expense of the author. Such themes are at work in Lewis's *An Experiment in Criticism*, which offers a kind of *Summa* of Lewis's mature critical views about the role of the reader, delivered within the framework of an impassioned defense of the ordinary reader as an active participant in "meaning-making." The "experiment" signified in Lewis's title consists of reversing the normal procedures of evaluative criticism, whose main purpose is to judge the "quality" of works by their compliance with a series of abstractions ordained by professional critics. Instead of judging readers' literary tastes by the things they read, Lewis objects, why should we not instead judge literature by the way they read it? In other words, let us define what constitutes "good reading" rather than what criteria make for "good books."

Lewis thus begins his experiment with a clever depiction of two kinds of readers: the "Literary" and the "Unliterary," the "Few" and the "Many." The literary, because they are schooled in literary technique and appreciative of aesthetic achievement, reread "the great works" throughout their lives, feel impoverished when denied the "leisure and silence" which sanctifies their reading experience, find first readings so momentous they can only be compared to love, religion, or bereavement, and talk to each other about books "often and at length" (*Experiment* 1–3). The unliterary, by contrast, rarely reread a work, use reading only for "odd moments of enforced solitude" or pure diversion, finish a work without perceptible change to their world view, and rarely think or talk about their reading with others. Identifying himself with the literary, Lewis concludes, "We treat as a main ingredient in our well-being something which to them [the unliterary] is marginal" (3). Lewis's aim is to inspire a legion of impassioned and informed readers, yet not at the cost of valorizing the "literary," who in their sophistication and inordinate concern for "taste" can surreptitiously grant literature a cultic status that displaces true piety.

Indeed some critics, whom Lewis labels "the Vigilants," have sought high-handedly to fulfill the prophecy of Victorian critic, Matthew Arnold, that "poetry would replace religion" in the popular mind. The literary, Lewis points out, tend to "confuse art with life," something the unliterary rarely do, and thereby make of literature a solemn creed that will reinforce a "tragic 'view' or 'sense' or 'philosophy' of life" (*Experiment* 77). Having described what one might call the motives of reading, Lewis then articulates a tool for distinguishing "good" reading from "bad": "A work of (whatever) art can be either 'received' or 'used.' When we 'receive' it we exert our senses and imagination and various others according to a pattern invented by the artist" (88). "Receptive reading" invites in the reader the reflective awareness of difference, of something new, challenging, or ineffable and thus the possibility of change or "enlargement of being." By contrast, readers who "use" a text treat it as an appliance to reinforce their pre-existing set of values or to push them along in familiar and established ways of thinking and behaving.

It is Lewis's point that both literary and unliterary readers may be "users" rather than "receivers" of art, and that, in fact, literary readers may be the worst offenders. The latter may inculcate in their comrades and pupils a process of reading that devalues primary experience of a work and elevates a stylized "critical reading" that demands evaluation of the work before it is fully "received." Consequently, the "necessary condition of all good reading is 'to get ourselves out of the way,'" and thus to encounter fully what an author has provided, untethered to the motive of evaluation. The works of great writers resist "use" and demand "reception," and thus stand the test of time. By contrast, modern critics have succeeded only in discouraging "primary experience" in readers, and such are doubly disadvantaged by critics who, on the one hand, condition readers to become mere "users" of texts, and, on the other, create a market for literature that demands such "use."

Lewis has in mind here modernist poetry and fiction that exalt obscurity and ambiguity, solicit idiosyncratic or pluralistic readings, and deliberately frustrate the "common" reader's quest for accessible meaning. In the book's last two chapters, Lewis offers a grand resolution of his "experiment," first challenging the popular formalist slogan discussed in the previous section, "poems should not *mean* but *be*." Not so, Lewis counters, for a literary work both *means* and *is*: it is both "Logos" (something said) and "Poiema" (something made). The pleasure of an aesthetic experience cannot be reduced to its form or Poiema, and the content of a text or Logos cannot be divorced from its experienced beauty. Readers respond to both, and both are crucial to primary experience of a text. A mark of the *receptive* reading Lewis is at pains to articulate is that "we need not believe or approve the Logos" of a text in order to enjoy it. Likewise, we may find compelling the message of or deeper myth behind a text whose form is significantly flawed or negligible.

In the end, good reading actualizes what is typically only a potential aesthetic experience: readers are enabled to inhabit another's selfhood in a foreign landscape, yet remain themselves—a marriage of vicarious experience and objective reflection on that experience:

> The man who is contented to be only himself, and therefore less a self, is in prison. My own eyes are not enough for me, I will see through the eyes of others. Reality, even seen through the eyes of many is not enough. I will see what others have invented. Even the eyes of all humanity are not enough. I regret that the brutes cannot write books. Very gladly would I learn what face things present to a mouse or a bee; more gladly still would I perceive the olfactory world charged with all the information and emotion it carries for a dog. (*Experiment* 140)

Experiment is at once a winsome apology for Lewis's own reading habits and preferences, and a cogent critique of all forms of critical snobbery that rob readers of literary pleasure in the dubious name of "good taste" or as part of a nefarious brand of social engineering.

Codifying: Understanding Lewis's Critical Method

As we recount Lewis's approach to the critical enterprise, a synthesis might look something like this:

> An *author* creates a *text* out of the language and cultural context of her historical period, influenced in good measure by such factors as politics, station in life, linguistic background, race, gender, and so on. Her text reflects, when successful, her *intention*, that is, her conscious plan or purpose in constructing the text. Her targeted audience must be enabled to discern some semblance of purpose or focus of her original conception in order to respond meaningfully to it— even if the author intentionally undermines the conventions of textuality which would permit such a determination. Once a text leaves the author it may inad-

vertently *mean* more (or less) than she intended. This is to say that her text may come to have greater or lesser significance in the times in which it is read than she could have originally imagined.

The *reader* brings to the text his own set of expectations and viewpoints which may be confirmed or questioned or undermined in the course of reading, experiencing the text as a purposeful, non-arbitrary expression or communication from an author's mind. The reader's task is first to read and respond to the text which the author actually wrote and not one he simply makes of his own ingenuity. The text is both a *Logos* (something said) and a *Poiema* (something made). A reader may respond favorably to a text's shape or form without necessarily accepting its implicit world view or admire a text's perceived message or vantage point without believing it is a well-made artifact.

The text exists as an objective entity apart from the author's or reader's consciousness; as such it may delight, teach, or move the recipient. But the reader's ultimate strategies for understanding and responding to a text are dictated by the text itself, made possible by engagement with authorial intention or other contextual cues or clues, and not by a single, monolithic interpretive strategy. The text's significance ("use") may change from age to age or culture to culture, but the text's original meaning ("reception") remains stable and is recoverable by historical and philological study.

While one can never fully escape the imprint of his language, times, gender, and cultural heritage upon perception, such literate inquiry assists him in stripping away falsehoods and pointing him in the direction of truth and knowledge. The unspoken premise behind this stance is that through reading a reader may travel out of his own time and culture, and, indeed, himself, enabling an understanding of his own meaning and place in society, and in history.

To best see how these principles are at work in Lewis's criticism, it is most instructive now to move to a closer look at one of his extended critical works, and I have chosen to discuss here his first, and most famous and influential scholarly work, *The Allegory of Love*. Warmly dedicated to Owen Barfield, whom he calls "the wisest and best of my unofficial teachers," Lewis accentuates in his preface that the work at hand exemplifies the wisdom he attributes to Barfield's interaction: "not to patronize the past . . . and to see the present as itself a 'period'" (i); thus *Allegory* is designed to be the epitome of what we have seen that Lewis prizes in all other critical works: "an effort of the historical imagination," that is, a reconstruction of "that long-lost state of mind for which the allegorical love poem was a natural mode of expression" (1).

Such a motive for scholarship was a wake-up call to the community of literary historians Lewis had now exuberantly joined, one settled in its familiar judgments about medieval literature in general and allegory in particular. Lewis's tactics in *Allegory* represent his signature approach not only to literary scholarship in his field of expertise, medieval and Renaissance literature, but to other eras and genres as well. Originally submitted to Oxford's Clarendon Press under the title *The Allegorical Love Poem*, the work was given for review to none other than Charles Williams, who would shortly become a close associate of Lewis, and, indeed, an "Inkling" with a profound effect on Lewis's theology and writing. Williams suggested that the title be changed to *The Allegory of Love*, and wrote Lewis an ebullient letter of praise, prefiguring the adulation the work would receive when published in May 1936. Extraordinarily impressed with its original thesis and its sweeping command of such a vast array of texts and historical eras, a critic none other than William Empson, who later offered repudiations of much of Lewis's critical practice, reviewed *Allegory* as "learned, witty, and sensible, and makes one ashamed of not having read its material; in the first flush of renewed admiration for the Romaunt of the Rose I tried to read the Chaucerian version. But it is intolerable. Far better to read Mr. Lewis and his admirable quotations, and recognise that these works were developing a method which is still normal and living, and frankly admit that there are great pleasures not our own" (Watson 79). E. H. W. Meyerstein, writing in "English Poetry and Allegory" for the *London Mercury* (1936), exclaimed:

> His book is full of sound scholarly paradox, such as "The coming of Christianity did not result in any deepening or idealizing of the conception of love," and luminous expressions such as "plashing fluidity," in reference to the French ease of Gower. Provocative, it keeps to its times and their business, without losing touch with the modern scene. (90)

In *Review of English Studies* (1937), Kathleen Tillotson wrote of *Allegory*: "It is rarely that we meet with a work of literary criticism of such manifest and general importance as this. No one could read it without seeing all literature a little differently for ever after" (96). Lewis, who had been little known outside academic circles in Oxford before its publication, found himself now established as a premier scholar with uncommon scope and depth.

344

In his characteristic frankness, Lewis confesses in the first lines of the work, "The allegorical love poetry of the Middle Ages is apt to repel the modern reader both by its form and its matter," and then proceeds by his winsome style and prodigious knowledge of his subject matter to engage the attentive reader, against all odds making interesting and clear what is almost by definition dense, obscure, and elusive. *The Allegory of Love* might be best read as an ingenious detective story in which Lewis, clue by clue, explicates the nature of allegorical form and its relationship to the paradoxical medieval love tradition—or as Lewis described its main themes when he submitted the manuscript for publication in 1935, "the birth of allegory and its growth from what it is in Prudentius to what it is in Spenser . . ." and "the birth of the romantic conception of love and the long struggle between its earlier form (the romance of adultery) and its later form (the romance of marriage)."

Chapter 1 of *The Allegory of Love* surveys the phenomenon of "courtly love," which depicts the love between a man and a woman in terms of the kind of fealty relationship a feudal vassal owes his lord. He must obey his Lady implicitly, promise feats of great courage in her honor, and lavish her with inordinate praise; most importantly, his beloved must not be his wife, for arranged marriages made personal attraction between spouses unlikely and unwarranted. The medieval age, Lewis generalizes, finds room for "innocent sexuality," but not "passion"; pleasure in sex even for one's spouse is a sin, akin to adultery and just as damning as any lust. As a result, the tradition of courtly love succeeds in inventing (and exulting in) "romantic love," volitional, dynamic love between a man and woman, something rare or unknown in the literature of classical or biblical times, or even the early medieval age, but universal in our modern era.

In chapter 2 Lewis suggests that allegory is less a literary form than a state of mind, for "it is the very nature of thought and language to represent what is immaterial in picturable terms" (44). How then, he asks, does something "latent" in human speech suddenly become explicit in the structure of poems and predominant as a genre in the Middle Ages? To answer his question, Lewis exhaustively surveys the development of allegory from classical times forward. In reaching the Middle Ages, Lewis calls allegory "the subjectivism of an objective age," by which he means its poets frequently used allegory to present inner conflict or spiritual reality in picture form. Allegory in one way or another involves an equivalence of the material and immaterial; medievals started with immaterial fact—a passion or a sin—and sought a visible item to represent it; moderns, by contrast, prefer *symbols*, which work in the other direction, directing the reader away from the "copy" to a world that is "more real." Thus, the allegorist takes the given and invents something, a fiction, that is less real, to convey its meaning; the symbolist employs the given as a means to point to and discover what is transcendent beyond the local and time-bound. It is Lewis's contention that to understand the Middle Ages aright, we must attune ourselves to the fact that its poets are allegorists, not symbolists, at work.

Lewis follows with five chapters of rigorous, direct application, beginning with *The Romance of the Rose*, and then moving on to Chaucer, Gower, and Thomas Usk. After this painstaking reconstruction of the history of allegory and romantic love, Lewis offers the work's greatest contribution, his exposition of the volume's theme in Spenser's *The Faerie Queene*. By the time allegory has reached Spenser's time, Lewis argues, it is dominant, and a monotonous sameness pervades it, unnoticed by the age in which it has evolved. In Spenser, however, both allegory and courtly love are transformed, the intertwining of the form and the sentiment yielding "the final defeat of courtly love and its displacement by the romantic conception of marriage." Ultimately, Spenser's work is to be seen as having had enormous influence on "all our love literature from Shakespeare to Meredith," and Spenser himself as the "great mediator between the Middle Ages and the modern poets, the man who saved us from the catastrophe of too thorough a renaissance" (360).

The Allegory of Love well illustrates most of the features of Lewis's criticism we have been discussing in this essay, but three elements particularly characteristic of Lewis's critical practice throughout his career stand out. First, *Allegory* demonstrates Lewis's supreme command of language and literature across time, genre, culture, and thus his uncanny ability to multiply relevant and convincing example after example in service of his main thesis. Any critic attempting to refute Lewis is obliged to commandeer as much or more terrain in fashioning a response of any merit. Secondly, in *Allegory* Lewis performs his most distinctive mode of criticism, that of "rehabilitation," defending and/or reconceptualizing a period (the Middle Ages), a genre (allegory), or an author (Spenser) for which appreciation or critical understanding had been lacking. Finally, *Allegory* is filled with what Spenser and Lewis scholar Margaret Hannay has called "provocative generalizations," which categorize, summarize, and evaluate whole genres and eras with such intuitive force that one finds them difficult to counter. Simply put, *Allegory* illustrates that Lewis had few rivals as a scholar who could skillfully extrapolate from its texts the operating world view of a civilization or period, thereby creating in his readers the sensation of truly leaving behind one's own age to inhabit another. The good critic, he steps aside so that his readers may experience the quiddity of an experience he himself has so richly imbibed.

In conclusion, as a literary historiographer, Lewis is uncommonly prescient in noting the logical ends to which seemingly innocent premises lead. His epilogue to *The Discarded Image* clearly anticipates philosopher of science Thomas Kuhn's 1962 work, *Structure of Scientific Revolutions*, in describing the power of models—"paradigms"—to rule the consciousness of an era. As a literary historian, his estimable analytical prowess and chronological breadth and depth mark him as the most astute chronicler of words, images, ideas, and meanings and their impact over time.

But in all this, as a literary critic, Lewis is ever *reluctant*.

In reading him, one encounters an uncommon enthusiasm for reading itself rather than an allegiance to a particular school of criticism or set of theories *about* reading. Here one finds a contagious pleasure in residing in the poetic landscapes of other authors, times, and cultures. (Often one discovers that he wants to find in these texts the same fulfillment and delight Lewis has, though learning that once one arrives, the "native culture" is not as enticing or as exotic as it was when looking through his eyes.)

Here, first and foremost, as in his apologetics and his fiction, what one most treasures is the generous and earnest spirit that enlists readers in a partnership of joyful discovery, the chief benefit being the companionship of Lewis himself.

Notes

1. The author appreciates the permission to adapt several of his entries from Jeffrey Schultz, ed., *C. S. Lewis: A Reader's Encyclopedia* (Zondervan, 1998) for use in this essay.

Works Cited

Empson, William. "Love and the Middle Ages." Watson 79–81. First publication: *The Spectator* 4 (September 1936): 241–43.

Gardner, Helen. "British Academy Obituary." Watson 417–28.

Lewis, C. S. *The Allegory of Love: A Study in Medieval Tradition.* Oxford: Oxford UP, 1936.

———. "The Anthropological Approach." *Literary* 301–11.

———. "Christianity and Culture." *Reflections* 12–36.

———. *Christian Reflections.* Ed. Walter Hooper. Grand Rapids: Eerdmans, 1967.

———. "*De Audiendis Poetis.*" *Medieval* 1–17.

———. "*De Descriptione Temporum.*" *Literary* 1–14.

———. *The Discarded Image: An Introduction to Medieval and Renaissance Literature.* Cambridge: Cambridge UP, 1964.

———. "Edmund Spenser, 1552–99." *Medieval* 121–45.

———. *English Literature in the Sixteenth Century Excluding Drama.* Oxford: Oxford UP, 1954.

———. *An Experiment in Criticism.* Cambridge: Cambridge UP, 1961.

———. "High Brows and Low Brows." *Literary* 266–79.

———. "On Criticism." *Of Other Worlds: Essays and Stories.* Ed. Walter Hooper. New York: Harcourt, 1966. 43–58.

———. "On the Reading of Old Books." *God in the Dock: Essays on Theology and Ethics.* Ed. Walter Hooper. Grand Rapids: Eerdmans, 1970. 200–07.

———. *A Preface to "Paradise Lost."* London: Oxford UP, 1942.

———. "Psycho-Analysis and Literary Criticism." *Literary* 286–300.

———. *Selected Literary Essays.* Ed. Walter Hooper. Cambridge: Cambridge UP, 1969.

———. *Studies in Medieval and Renaissance Literature.* Ed. Walter Hooper. Cambridge: Cambridge UP, 1966.

———. *Studies in Words.* Cambridge: Cambridge UP, 1960.

347

————. *Surprised by Joy: The Shape of My Early Life.* New York: Harcourt, 1955.

————. "What Chaucer Really Did to *Il Filostrato*." *Literary* 27–44.

————. "William Morris." *Literary* 219–31.

————, and E. M. W. Tillyard. *The Personal Heresy: A Controversy.* London: Oxford UP, 1939.

Meyerstein, E. H. "English Poetry and Allegory." Watson 89–90. First publication: *London Mercury* 34 (1936): 270–71.

Raine, Kathleen. "From a Poet." *Light on C. S. Lewis.* Ed. Joycelyn Gibb. New York: Harcourt, 1965. 102–05.

Tillotson, Kathleen. "Rev. of *The Allegory of Love: A Study in Medieval Tradition*." Watson 96–98. First publication: *Review of English Studies* 13 (1937): 477.

Watson, George, ed. *Critical Essays on C. S. Lewis.* Hants, England: Scolar Press, 1992.

19

In the Library:
Composition and Context

Colin Duriez

My purpose is not to set out the contours of Lewis's critical thought, which Bruce Edwards has already done in the previous chapter.[1] Rather, I examine how Lewis composed his literary criticism and in what major critical contexts. Because of limited space, I focus particularly upon Lewis's formative years, roughly the 1920s and 1930s, leading up to the publication of *A Preface to "Paradise Lost"* in 1942.

My interest lies in the insights we might draw from the biographical context and intellectual currents surrounding his scholarship. Lewis's uniqueness as a literary critic might suggest that he concocted his ideas with the minimum of help from others. In fact, I hope to suggest that he benefited from several key contemporaries, from the wider scholarly community, and from long hours in Oxford's Bodleian library. While his colleagues and friends provided a stimulating forum where ideas could be put to the test, the library gave him access to a wide variety of sources and authorities stretching back centuries or millennia. The library, the lecture hall, and the college rooms where tutorials and informal discussions took place, as well as his favorite pubs (where theology was washed down with beer), all figured prominently in Lewis's formation as a literary critic.

Besides considering the issues of composition, I glance at how Lewis's literary criticism was perceived and received in the scholarly world. This involves acknowledging the impact and relevance of his criticism during the formative years of his life and how it has stood up over time. It is clear that Lewis's enterprise has much larger ramifications than his immediate Oxford (and later Cambridge) world. According to the eminent literary critic William Empson, Lewis was "the best read man of his generation, one who read everything and remembered everything he read" (qtd. in D. Russell 138). The fruit of Lewis's close, firsthand reading was many literary essays over the years, most collected together posthumously,[2] and four major studies: *The Allegory of Love: A Study in Medieval Tradition* (1936), on the growth of allegory and the developments of romantic love; *A Preface to "Paradise Lost"* (1942), reassessing Milton's epic poem; *English Literature in the Sixteenth Century Excluding Drama* (1954), Lewis's contribution to the Oxford History of English Literature; and *The Discarded Image: An Introduction to Medieval and Renaissance Literature* (1964), based on lectures presenting the dominant world view of that period. Also of importance is Lewis's work on Spenser, scattered throughout his essays. David L. Russell perceptively comments that "most literary criticism is dated within its generation, but Lewis' remains highly readable, provocative, and, perhaps more significantly, in print more than three decades after his death, a forceful testimonial to his powers as a scholar" (138). Few works of literary criticism are so enduring.

What emerges from Lewis's bookish background, connections to scholarly community, and long, silent hours in the library, is a richness of thought, imagination, and writing that has influenced literary criticism, science fiction, children's literature, literary approaches to the Bible, and Christian apologetics throughout the West.[3]

The Oxford Context in the Twenties

In the 1920s, particularly in Oxford, idealism predominated in philosophy, while realism offered such resistance as it could. The philosopher John Mabbott, a colleague of Lewis during that period, describes the intellectual isolation of Oxford at this time in his *Oxford Memories*.[4] He writes:

> Oxford philosophy, as we found it, was completely inbred. It had practically no contacts with Cambridge, or the Continent, or America. The traditional doctrine was Hegelian idealism, filtered through the great Scottish prophets, [Edward] Caird, [Andrew Seth] Pringle-Pattison, [Andrew] Seth, [David George] Ritchie and [William] Wallace, and our own T. H. Green, [Bernard] Bosanquet and [F. H.] Bradley. The basic issue was between the idealists and their view that reality is spiritual and therefore that the world around us is akin to or determined by mind, and our realists, [John] Cook Wilson, [Sir W. David] Ross, [Harold Arthur] Prichard, holding that the objects of knowledge and perception are independent of mind. (73)[5]

Idealism was linked in many minds with Christianity, or with spiritual views which opposed a rapidly spreading secularism and what Lewis in *Miracles* called naturalism. Idealism in England was especially associated with T. H. Green (1836–82), F. H. Bradley (1846–1924), and J. M. E. McTaggart (1866–1925). The idealists typically held that physical objects can have no existence apart from a mind conscious of them. For idealists, the divine mind and the human share fundamental similarities. As a young atheist in Oxford, Lewis was at first staunchly opposed to idealism. He was an out-and-out realist and naturalist. He believed, for instance, that the resemblance between human languages was due to the similarities of human throats rather than the result of an innate structure in humans.[6] Naturalism was defined by Lewis as the view that "every finite thing or event must be (in principle) explicable in terms of the Total System" (*Miracles* 12), which is Nature; and Nature is the whole show.[7] His later rejection of naturalism was embedded in everything he wrote after his early poetry, *Spirits in Bondage* (1919) and *Dymer* (1926).

Lewis taught philosophy for the year 1924–25 in University College before getting his teaching post at Magdalen College in English Literature. Because of a distinguished literary career, his ability as a philosopher is easily overlooked. In fact, his "Great War" with his friend Owen Barfield (see below) was often carried on at a sophisticated philosophical level, and his philosophical interests were well known to others. Indeed, he continued teaching some philosophy after taking up his lecturing in English. Mabbott describes the formation of a philosophical discussion club for the young lecturers in which Lewis actively participated (the "Wee Teas") at the period of his teaching in philosophy.[8] Mabbott's description gives insight into the kind of discussion club in which Lewis thrived and which he always had to have. Even at this stage of his life, Lewis made his mark on his peers:

> Our seniors had an institution called "The Philosophers' Teas". They met on Thursdays at 4 o'clock. Anyone present could raise a point for discussion. We juniors were invited to join and we found the occasions friendly and unstuffy (again the genuine democracy of the faculty could be clearly felt). But, as a forum for discussion, they were not a success. . . . Tea-time is not a philosophic hour: and, by the time the crumpets had gone round, it would be 4.15 or 4.30. We juniors were under such tutorial pressure that we had to teach daily from 5 to 7 o'clock, so we had to leave at 4.50 to get back to our Colleges. . . . We juniors established a group built on our experience of the "Teas". We agreed that evening is the time for thought. . . . Membership should be limited to the number ideal for a discussion, which we agreed to be six. To avoid competitive luxury, dinners were to be three-course, and with beer not wine. (This rigour was not pedantically maintained.) Our original membership was: Gilbert Ryle, Henry Price, Frank Hardie, C. S. Lewis, T. D. Weldon and myself. C. S. Lewis soon seceded from phi-

losophy to English Literature, popular theology and science fiction; but not before he had assisted in a happy contribution to our proceedings. . . .

It was understood that opening remarks need not be finished papers but rather flying kites (even in note form if desired). We knew each other so well that our basic methods and interests could be taken for granted, and our growing points exposed straightaway to lively, frank and friendly scrutiny. . . . I am sure that everything any of us published would have been considerably less well-argued but for running this gauntlet. . . . Quite apart from its value to our philosophy, I count my membership as, apart from my marriage, the happiest and most refreshing experience of my life. (77–78)

It was not only in philosophy that Oxford in the twenties had an affinity with the nineteenth century but also in language and literature, a subject still gripped by the paradigm of philology, with its historical emphasis and zest for source hunting. The philologist at his best was embodied in J. R. R. Tolkien, who left Leeds University in 1925 to take the Chair of Anglo-Saxon at Oxford. Lewis and he met in 1926 and soon became good friends. It was this friendship, along with those with Hugo Dyson and Owen Barfield, that became the basis of the Inklings. Lewis took on many of Tolkien's concerns, such as the serious writing of fantasy, and shared his passionate love of language, evidenced in his *Studies in Words* (1960). At one time Lewis and Tolkien planned to collaborate on a book about language.[9] Lewis affectionately was to fictionalize his philologist friend in the figure of Elwin ("Elf-friend") Ransom in *Out of the Silent Planet* (1938).[10]

Perhaps the most radical current crossing the twenties was what Lewis and his colleagues tended to dub "the new psychology," stemming particularly from the insights of Sigmund Freud (satirized as Sigismund Enlightenment in Lewis's *The Pilgrim's Regress* [1933]). This trend had a devastating impact which exists in various forms to this day.[11] One Cambridge literary critic responsible for disseminating such psychological insights was the influential I. A. Richards (1893–1979). He radically reformulated the criteria and techniques for evaluating literature, particularly in *Principles of Literary Criticism* (1924) and *Practical Criticism: A Study of Literary Judgment* (1929).[12] Like Freud, Richards is ultimately a naturalist. He reduces values (such as beauty) to what was empirically (i.e., measurably) available to the reader. Values in literature are merely a capacity to satisfy the feelings and desires of readers. The language of literature is emotive, rather than descriptive of an objective state of affairs in the real world.[13]

Regarding this trend, Lewis looks back in his preface to the 1950 edition of *Dymer* (1926) and explains the context of writing his poem: "In those days the new psychology was just beginning to make itself felt in the circles I most frequented at Oxford. This joined forces with the fact that we felt ourselves (as young men always do) to be escaping from the illusions of adolescence, and as a result we were much exercised about the problem of fantasy or wishful thinking" (4). The "new psychology," exemplified in Richards's approach, created a distrust of the romanticism which had so marked the nineteenth century, reinforced by bitter memories of the First World War. Lewis was, as he says, affected by this distrust, forcing him to rethink the whole basis of romanticism and literary fantasy, a process which eventually led to his move from atheism, via a modified idealism, to theistic belief in 1929 and to his Christian conversion in 1931.

Controversy

The new criticism, much of it coming out of Cambridge, tended to re-evaluate the traditional literary canon, and some of Lewis's favorites, such as Milton and Shelley, were casualties. Lewis had already attacked T. S. Eliot's downgrading of Shelley in an essay reproduced in *Rehabilitations and Other Essays* (1939), but he was also troubled by a wider tendency to see poetry as the expression of the poet's personality. He called this tendency "the personal heresy." This led him into a courteous dispute with E. M. W. Tillyard, which began with an essay citing Tillyard's book on Milton as an example. Tillyard responded, leading to a reply from Lewis and eventually a jointly authored book (1939). Lewis argues against the view that poetry provides biographical information about the poet and that it is necessary to know about the poet to understand the poem. He focuses on the intrinsic character of a work of literature, rather than on extrinsic factors. In reading a poem we look *through* the poet, rather than *at* him or her. We see with his or her eyes. The poet's consciousness is a condition of our knowledge, not the knowledge itself. Lewis's analysis is remarkable in anticipating new schools of literary criticism that would focus upon the intrinsic character of literature.[14]

Several years later, he comes more fully to Milton's defense with *A Preface to "Paradise Lost"* (1942). What Lewis sees as misreadings of Milton, or, more seriously, downgradings of him (as in the work of Cambridge critic F. R. Leavis [1895–1978]), are for him symptomatic of a modern trend he finds alarming. Lewis argues that most recent Milton scholarship hinders rather than helps a proper reading of the poem. Consciously following the lead given by Charles Williams's short preface to an edition of Milton's poetical works, Lewis attempts "mainly 'to hinder hindrances' to the appreciation of *Paradise Lost.*" He defends the epic form of literature that Milton chose to use, arguing that it had a right to exist, as does ritual, splendor, and joy itself.

353

The new, re-evaluative criticism also disturbed Lewis because of its "high-brow" emphasis. From his wide experience of reading, he instinctively rejects a distinction between high-brow and low-brow literature, serious and popular, and even between so-called good and bad books. A far more important and fundamental distinction for him is that between good and bad readers. Literature, he later argues in *An Experiment in Criticism*, exists for the enjoyment of readers, and books therefore should be judged by the kind of reading they evoke. Instead of judging whether a book is good or bad, it is better to reverse the process and consider good and bad readers. "The good reader," he explains, "reads every work seriously in the sense that he reads it wholeheartedly, makes himself as receptive as he can"(11). This is how Lewis can write in appreciation of Rider Haggard, Tolkien, Sir Walter Scott, and science fiction, as well as of Chaucer, Spenser, Shakespeare, Bunyan, and Milton.[15]

During his years of painstaking research into the genre of allegory, and the Christianization of romantic love in the Middle Ages, Lewis also wrote a number of short works, published in 1939 in *Rehabilitations*. Many of these short pieces originated in essays for F. P. Wilson when studying as an undergraduate in the Oxford English School, 1922–23, when he earned the third of his First Class degrees. Others began as ideas in George Gordon's discussion classes in the same period, or as papers to the Martlets,[16] an undergraduate literary club. Some were read to literary societies. In his preface to *Rehabilitations*, Lewis explains that he wrote many of the essays in defense of the things he loved that were under attack. The first two essays defend great romantic poets like Shelley and William Morris against the "popular hatred or neglect of Romanticism." The third and fourth defend the "present" Oxford English syllabus of 1939. The fifth supports the reading of many popular books which have, he believes, greatly increased his power of enjoying more serious literature as well as what is called "real life." The sixth essay champions Anglo-Saxon poetry. The next, "Bluspels and Flalansferes: A Semantic Nightmare," is a seminal essay on the relationship between thinking and imagining, and the centrality of metaphor. Then follows an essay on Shakespeare's poetic method. "Christianity and Literature," the last piece, is an important early attempt by Lewis to relate his faith to literature.

Books and Friends

The Books

From childhood onwards, Lewis read voraciously and eclectically. He typically defended the value of "low-brow" authors such as Rider Haggard and John Buchan. This bookishness and eclecticism remains an important characteristic of Lewis throughout his life, and is consistently reflected in his diaries and letters.[17] The "house full of books" Lewis was indebted to is, he writes in *Surprised by Joy* (1955), "almost a major character in my story." He was, he says, a product of "endless books":

> My father bought all the books he read and never got rid of any of them. There were books in the study, books in the drawing-room, books in the cloak-room, books (two deep) in the great bookcase on the landing, books in a bed-room, books piled as high as my shoulder in the cistern attic, books of all kinds reflecting every transient shade of my parents' interests, books readable and unreadable, books suitable for a child and books most emphatically not. Nothing was forbidden me. In the seemingly endless rainy afternoons I took volume after volume from the shelves. I had always the same certainty of finding a book that was new to me as a man who walks in a field has of finding a new blade of grass. (17)

Lewis's capacity for endless reading made him a natural library dweller from his undergraduate studies onwards. Oxford's Bodleian Library has a central place in Lewis's life, work, and affection, as this extract from a letter to his father on March 31, 1928, shows:

> I spend all my mornings in the Bodleian. . . . If only one could smoke, and if only there were upholstered chairs, this would be one of the most delightful places in the world. I sit in "Duke Humphrey's Library", the oldest part, a Fifteenth-Century building with a very beautiful wooden painted ceiling above me and a little mullioned window on my left hand through which I look down on the garden of Exeter where, these mornings, I see the sudden squalls of wind and rain driving the first blossoms off the fruit trees and snowing the lawn with them. . . . The library itself—I mean the books—is mostly in a labyrinth of cellars under the neighbouring squares. This room however is full of books . . . which stand in little cases at right angles to the wall, so that between each pair there is a kind of little "box"—in the public house sense of the word—and in these boxes one sits and reads. By a merciful provision, however many books you send for, they will all be left on your chosen table at night for you to resume work next morning: so that one gradually accumulates a pile as comfortably as in one's own room. There is not, as in modern libraries, a forbidding framed notice to shriek "Silence": on the contrary a more moderate request "Talk little and treat lightly". There is indeed always a faint murmur going on of semi-whispered conversations in the neighbouring boxes. It disturbs no one. I rather like to hear the hum of the hive. . . . (*Letters* 252–53)

The literary critic Helen Gardner noticed his reading habits in the Bodleian in later years with admiration: "One sometimes feels that the word 'unreadable' had no meaning for him. To sit opposite him in Duke Humphrey when he was moving steadily through some huge double-columned folio in his reading for his Oxford history was to have an object lesson in what concentration meant. He seemed to create a wall of stillness around him" (419).

As well as using the Bodleian, Lewis accumulated over the years a considerable personal library, over two thousand volumes, which are now housed in the Marion E. Wade Collection at Wheaton College in Wheaton, Illinois. He frequently moved house until becoming established at The Kilns in 1930, and thereafter his books were divided between his home and his college rooms. Even then, shelf space was always insufficient.[18]

Lewis's interest from the beginning, and increasingly so, was in the books of an older era, even larger than but including the medieval and Renaissance periods. The Bodleian was ideal for following this interest, housing as it does millions of books in the English language, as well as classical texts. For Lewis, all books before the period of modernism, spanning the millennia at least since the ancient Greeks, share important values, and thus interrelate in a constantly stimulating way. It was reading, even more so than intellectual debate and friendship (though he hungered for the latter), that fed his mind and imagination and kept him mentally alive. He saw the world through texts, as part of a symbolic perception of reality.[19] Thus, while experiencing the horrors of wartime trench warfare, he reflected: "This is War. This is what Homer wrote about" (*Surprised* 196).

What were some of the texts which helped to provide an intellectual framework for the young scholar? Near the end of his life, Lewis responded to the question from *The Christian Century*, "What books did most to shape your vocational attitude and your philosophy of life?" The list of ten is striking as no book is more recent than Lewis's formative years of the twenties and thirties. The list therefore gives a good intellectual picture of the books that particularly may have influenced Lewis at this time:[20]

Phantastes, by George MacDonald

The Everlasting Man, by G. K. Chesterton

The Aeneid, by Virgil

The Temple, by George Herbert

The Prelude, by William Wordsworth

The Idea of the Holy, by Rudolf Otto

The Consolation of Philosophy, by Boethius

Life of Samuel Johnson, by James Boswell

Descent into Hell, by Charles Williams

Theism and Humanism, by Arthur James Balfour

This group of books reflects Lewis's wide interests. There are two works of prose fantasy, three of poetry (two of them in narrative), one biography, and the remaining four books philosophical theology. Lewis described MacDonald's *Phantastes* as "baptizing his imagination" long before his Christian conversion, in its account of Anodos's journeys in Fairyland. Charles Williams's horror fantasy *Descent into Hell* traces a process of damnation to which Lewis felt professional scholars are particularly prone, which he seems to have taken as a moral warning to himself. Virgil's *The Aeneid* is an epic poem about the founding of Rome by its Trojan hero, Aeneas, and is one of the greatest Latin literary works. It is also one of the principal classical works adopted by Christian Europe during the Middle Ages. *The Temple, Sacred Poems and Private Ejaculations* is a collection of some 160 of Herbert's devotional poems, published shortly after his death. Lewis remarked, in *Surprised*, "Here was a man who seemed to me to excel all the authors I had ever read in conveying the very quality of life as we actually live it from moment to moment" (202–03). *The Prelude, or, Growth of a Poet's Mind* is a confessional quasi-religious narrative poem in praise of the poetic imagination by Wordsworth, and his greatest work. From another poem Lewis took Wordworth's phrase "surprised by joy" for his own autobiography, which he started composing in verse, perhaps modeled on *The Prelude*. Lewis was a great admirer of Dr. Johnson, and resembled him in the sharpness of his wit. He comes alive in James Boswell's *Life*. Warren Lewis, looking over his uneven diary, laments that he did not "Boswellise" his brother.[21] The earliest theology listed by Lewis Christianized the wisdom of classical paganism, and provided a model for philosophy for a thousand years, Boethius's *The Consolation of Philosophy*. No other book in the medieval period was more widely read ("Boethius" 52, 53). One-time British Prime Minister Arthur James Balfour based *Theism and Humanism* upon the first of his two Gifford Lecture series for the University of Glasgow. He was concerned with the way naturalistic humanism impoverished reality, in contrast to theism. Rudolf Otto's *The Idea of the Holy* is a phenomenological study of the sacred which deeply influenced Lewis's understanding of the numinous, and similar experiences of otherness such as "Joy."[22] G. K. Chesterton was a formative influence on Lewis. The book he chooses for his Top Ten, *The Everlasting Man*, is typical of Chesterton's apologetics and characteristically highlights the persuasive power of the Gospels. It was the nature of the Gospels in combining history with the quality of great story that was pivotal in Lewis's conversion from naturalism to Christianity. Lewis remarks in *Surprised* that in reading *The Everlasting Man* he saw for the first time "the whole Christian outline of history set out in a form that seemed to me to make sense" (*Surprised* 223).

His Friends

In the Preface to *The Allegory of Love* (1936), references are made to three members of the Inklings:[23] Tolkien, Hugo Dyson, and Owen Barfield—to whom the book is dedicated, and to whom Lewis acknowledges the greatest debt, after his father:

> There seems to be hardly any one among my acquaintance from whom I have not learned. The greatest of these debts—that which I owe to my father for the inestimable benefit of a childhood passed mostly alone in a house full of books—is now beyond repayment; and among the rest I can only select. . . . Above all, the friend to whom I have dedicated the book, has taught me not to patronise the past, and has trained me to see the present as itself a "period". I desire for myself no higher function than to be one of the instruments whereby his theory and practice in such matters may become more widely effective. (vii–viii)

Lewis pays tribute to Owen Barfield particularly for demolishing what he calls elsewhere his "chronological snobbery." This change in thinking is the watershed event which helped Lewis break away from modernism, exemplified in his earlier naturalistic realism. Hereafter, Lewis is characteristically anti-modernist. Lewis believed that the relentlessness of progress is one of the strongest of the modernist myths, in which change is considered to have a value in itself. The dangerous consequence of this attitude is that we become increasingly cut off from our past (and hence a proper perspective on the strengths and weaknesses of our own age). Lewis expresses his concern with the myth of progress in his inaugural lecture at Cambridge University, "*De Descriptione Temporum.*" And he explains the logic of chronological snobbery in the following passage from *Surprised*:

> Barfield . . . made short work of what I have called my "chronological snobbery," the uncritical acceptance of the intellectual climate common to our age and the assumption that whatever has gone out of date is on that account discredited. You must find out why it went out of date; was it ever refuted (and if so by whom, where and how conclusively) or did it merely die away as fashions do? If the latter, this tells us nothing about its truth or falsehood. From seeing this one passes to the realization that our age is also "a period," and certainly has, like all periods, its own characteristic illusions. They are likeliest to lurk in those wide-spread assumptions which are so ingrained in the age that no one dares to attack or feels it necessary to defend them. (196)

Along with this intoxicating freedom from the invisible presuppositions of one's age, Lewis also inherited some of Barfield's highly original insights into the nature of poetic language. These were embodied in his book *Poetic Dic-*

tion (1928), dedicated to Lewis, which also influenced Tolkien. This book is a highly significant part of Lewis's intellectual context, embodying as it does themes he and Barfield endlessly discussed. It must be noted, however, that Barfield was also influenced by ideas of Lewis in composing the book—their "Great War" wages behind it.[24]

In *Poetic Diction* Barfield develops a theory of knowledge as well as a theory of poetry. At its heart is a philosophy of language for which "the individual imagination is the medium of all knowledge from perception upward" (22). The alternative, argues Barfield, is to see knowledge as power, to "mistake efficiency for meaning," leading to a relish for compulsion. He speaks of those who "reduce the specifically human to a mechanical or animal regularity":

> Language is the storehouse of imagination; it cannot continue to be itself without performing its function. But its function is, to mediate transition from the unindividualized, dreaming spirit that carried the infancy of the world to the individualized human spirit, which has the future in its charge. If therefore they [the mechanists] succeed in expunging from language all the substance of its past, in which it is naturally so rich, and finally converting it into the species of algebra that is best adapted to the uses of indoctrination and empirical science, a long and important step . . . will have been taken in the . . . liquidation of the human spirit. (23)

This fighting talk anticipates much of Lewis, as in his *Abolition*. Indeed many of Lewis's preoccupations, and those of the Inklings, are anticipated in Barfield's book, which is not surprising when one considers it was written in the context of their "Great War."

Barfield had gone up to Oxford in October 1919 and studied at Wadham College, reading English, and attempting some of his own writing. At that time he formed his lifelong friendship with Lewis, and also in the early twenties became an anthroposophist, an advocate of the religious school of thought developed by Rudolf Steiner.[25] After graduation Barfield began a B.Litt., the thesis of which became *Poetic Diction*. In 1925 he published a children's book, *The Silver Trumpet*, and in 1926, *History in English Words*. As undergraduates, Lewis and Barfield had often walked together or asked each other to lunch; but it was not until after graduation that the "Great War" started between them. The battle was carried on primarily through extensive correspondence between graduation and Barfield's move back to London in 1929, when he began to train in his father's firm of solicitors. Barfield was only able to attend Inklings meetings a dozen or more times after that, although he saw Lewis much more frequently, and remained his solicitor.[26]

About 1930 Barfield had finished his "metaphysical argument" with Lewis, which roughly coincided with the process of Lewis's conversion to Christianity. After the "War" Barfield jokingly said to his friend that while Lewis had taught him to think, he had taught Lewis what to think. Lewis undoubtedly forced Barfield to think systematically and accurately, passing on hard-won skills he acquired from his tutelage under W. T. Kirkpatrick. Barfield in his turn helped Lewis to integrate better his imagination with his formidable intellect.

Lewis's other friends who shaped his thinking and approach to literature in this period were Dyson and Tolkien, particularly in the 1930s and 1940s. Dyson was a friend from undergraduate days who played a key role in helping Tolkien to persuade Lewis of the truth of Christianity. He was a member of the Inklings from the very beginning, retaining his contact with the club even during the period he lectured at Reading University (approximately twenty-five miles from Oxford, and easily accessible by train).[27] Dyson was very much part of the emotional support that Lewis needed from the Inklings, but was not a significant literary influence like Barfield and Tolkien, and later Charles Williams.[28]

Tolkien was of colossal importance to Lewis—indeed, their friendship is comparable to that between Wordsworth and Coleridge. While in the formative years of the 1920s Barfield's influence was much greater, Tolkien's influence increased in the 1930s as Barfield's declined. The first important area of Tolkien's influence on Lewis was his Christianity. When they first met, Lewis was not a Christian and had previously been a naturalist (as recorded in *Surprised*). Tolkien's Christian faith is a complex matter, and Lewis inherited some of its cast.

The essence of Tolkien's Christianity is captured in lines he wrote to Lewis at the time of their early acquaintance:

> The heart of man is not compound of lies,
> but draws some wisdom from the only Wise,
> and still recalls Him. Though now long estranged,
> Man is not wholly lost nor wholly changed.
> Dis-graced he may be, yet is not de-throned,
> and keeps the rags of lordship once he owned. . . .
> (Carpenter, *Tolkien* 190)

He quoted these lines in an Andrew Lang lecture, "On Fairy Stories," given at St. Andrews University in 1939,[29] about eight years after Lewis's conversion.

Essential to Tolkien's Christianity is his view of the relationship between myth and fact and how myth can become fact. Tolkien had worked out a complex view of the relationship of story and myth to reality, involving the way language itself relates to reality. For Tolkien, story and language were "integrally related" and a part of one human inventive process. The view can be seen as a theology of story and is encapsulated in the poem "Mythopoeia," written for Lewis, and quoted above. Tolkien's view of story was a sacramental one. The gospel story of Christ's incarnation, death, and resurrection—a story told by God himself in the real events of history—has broken into the "seamless web of story." Story—preceding and subsequent to the gospel—is joyfully alive with God's presence.

Related to Tolkien's view of myth become fact is his distinctive doctrine of sub-creation, the view that the highest function of art is the creation of convincing secondary or other worlds. Without the impact of Tolkien's view of sub-creation, I doubt that we would have Malacandra, Perelandra, or Glome, particularly Perelandra, one of Lewis's most successful creations. The concept of secondary worlds is very versatile and will continue to be fruitful in many varieties, I believe, far beyond the mode of fantasy.

Along with their mutual friend Owen Barfield, Tolkien was responsible for helping along the process which led Lewis to become aware of a dramatic shift from the Old to the Modernist West, a shift which made the change from medieval to Renaissance culture insignificant by comparison. Barfield, as we have seen, was responsible for ridding Lewis of his earlier chronological snobbery, an abiding vice of the modern world. Tolkien, in turn, was responsible for pointing out to Lewis that the values of pre-Christian paganism were not merely of aesthetic interest, but were life-and-death matters reflecting an objective state of affairs. As a result of Tolkien's arguments, reinforced by Dyson, Lewis came to the conclusion that similarities between Christian teaching and ancient myths can argue for the truth of Christianity as well as against it. At the heart of Christianity, Lewis came to believe, is a myth that is also a fact—making the claims of Christianity unique. But by becoming fact, it did not cease to be myth, or lose the quality of myth. In "On Fairy Stories," Tolkien spoke of the "seamless web of story," in which human stories were interrelated, and, by God's grace, carried insights into the true nature of things. It is the gospel, however, that has broken into this web of story from the real world. Tolkien's belief that God in his grace had prefigured the gospel *evangelium* in human stories, a view shared by Lewis, was a kind of natural theology.

In the later 1920s, Tolkien began sharing with the Inklings his early versions of *The Silmarillion*. Tolkien's tales in their own manner embody antimodernist themes as powerfully as any stories written by Lewis, disclosing Old Western values. Antimodernism can be seen clearly, for instance, in Tolkien's treatment of the related themes of possession and power, themes central to his work.[30]

The Context of The Allegory of Love (1936)

In the young scholar's mental geography, as we have seen, Barfield's *Poetic Diction* retains a vital place. Lewis's first scholarly book, *The Allegory of Love: A Study in Medieval Tradition* (1936), is among the outstanding works of literary criticism of the century. "To mediaeval studies in this country Lewis's logical and philosophical cast of mind gave a wholly new dimension," commented Professor J. A. W. Bennett, his successor at Cambridge.

Lewis was working on *Allegory* back in 1928, and so it spanned the period of his conversion to theism and then Christianity. Around this same time he also wrote *The Pilgrim's Regress* (1933), influenced both by his discoveries about the allegorical tradition and his conversion. Material he gathered while writing the study eventually led to his Oxford Prolegomena lectures. In a letter written in 1934, as *Allegory* neared completion, he suggested that the secret to understanding the Middle Ages, including its concern with allegory and courtly love, was to get to know thoroughly Dante's *The Divine Comedy*, *The Romance of the Rose*, the classics, and the Bible, including the apocryphal New Testament (*Letters* 309–11).

While in search of a publisher, he summarized the book to Oxford University Press, which accepted it for publication: "The book as a whole has two themes: 1. The birth of allegory and its growth from what it is in Prudentius to what it is in Spenser. 2. The birth of the romantic conception of love and the long struggle between its earlier form (the romance of adultery) and its later form (the romance of marriage)."

Allegory demonstrates Lewis's concern to help the reader enter as fully as possible into an author's intentions. He concentrates on textual criticism, which he valued above other types of critical activity, as a later comment makes clear: "Find out what the author actually wrote and what the hard words meant and what the allusions were to, and you have done far more for me than a hundred new interpretations or assessments could ever do" (*Experiment* 121). Lewis was committed to the *authority* of the author. *Allegory* also expresses his characteristic interest in the Christianization of paganism (in this case, romantic love), an interest deeply shared by Tolkien.[31]

Harry Blamires points out that Lewis "revived the genre of historical criticism by his work on Medieval and Renaissance literature in *The Allegory of Love* (1936) and *English Literature in the Sixteenth Century* (1954)" (*History* 15). His revival of this genre is perhaps even more significant than these works themselves.[32] Notably, while Lewis's conclusions in the books are by no means always accepted, yet as books of historical scholarship, they are universally admired.[33]

362

A New Context: A Minor Christian Literary Renaissance

The 1930s and 1940s saw a minor renaissance in Christian literature, a movement not reflected in theology, which then was in the grip of modernist liberal theology. Lewis's own popular theological writings ran against the stream of this liberalism, but as a writer of literary criticism and Christian fiction he represents a wider countermovement. He was not as isolated and disconnected with contemporary culture as he thought. Even then, modernism was not everything.

This point is summed up admirably by Lewis's former pupil, the literary historian Harry Blamires:

> Lewis began writing just at the point when this minor Christian Renaissance in literature was taking off. His *Pilgrim's Regress* came out in 1933. And the 1930's were a remarkable decade in this respect. Eliot's *Ash Wednesday* came out in 1930, *The Rock* in 1934, *Murder in the Cathedral* in 1935 and *Burnt Norton* in 1936. Charles Williams's *War In Heaven* was published in 1930, *The Place of the Lion* in 1931, *The Greater Trumps* in 1932, and his play *Thomas Cranmer of Canterbury* in 1936. Helen Waddell's *Peter Abelard* came out in 1933. Meanwhile on the stage James Bridie had great popular successes with his biblical plays *Tobias and the Angel* (1930) and *Jonah and the Whale* (1932). Then by 1937 Christopher Fry was launched with *The Boy with a Cart*. That same year saw Dorothy Sayers's *The Zeal of Thy House* performed, and David Jones's *In Parenthesis* and Tolkien's *The Hobbit* published. Lewis's *Out of the Silent Planet* followed in 1938 along with Williams's *Taliessin through Logres* and Greene's *Brighton Rock*, Eliot's *Family Reunion* followed in 1939, Greene's *The Power and The Glory* in 1940. During the same decade Evelyn Waugh was getting known and Rose Macauley was in spate. Edwin Muir, Andrew Young and Francis Berry appeared in print. ("Against the Stream" 15)

So when the literary historian looks back at the English literary scene in the 1930s and 1940s, he or she will see C. S. Lewis and Charles Williams, not as freakish throwbacks, but as initial contributors to a Christian literary renaissance, even if a minor one.[34]

Learning from Lewis

We are now in a position to consolidate some of the insights from Lewis's response in the composition of his early literary work to his intellectual and biographical context. What lessons are there implicitly in his formative reading habits and approach to literature for us?

He advocates and demonstrates the close reading of texts, where readers and critics have a firsthand experience of an author's work. Lewis argues that "we invariably judge a critic by the extent to which he illuminates reading we have already done" (*Experiment* 122). Such close reading ought to be in the original languages, if possible. It is important therefore, believes Lewis, for a student and reader of English Literature to be acquainted with Anglo-Saxon. As well as classical languages, Lewis himself was able to read German, French, and Italian, and these language skills enriched his critical work. Complementary to his textual concern is an historical engagement. He is always interested in the intellectual and cultural currents of a period, as attested by his most ambitious works of criticism, *Allegory*, *Sixteenth*, and *Discarded*.

Lewis feels that the extrinsic features of the literary work are essential to consider, such as its world view, including the model of reality and the universe it embodied, and authorial intention. For him this does not mean that the text is a personal, cultural, or moralistic expression, or simply a quarry for anthropologists, theologians, psychologists, and sociologists. The work is *poiema* as well as *logos*, something made as well as something said. Therefore as a unique entity it should be taken on its own terms.

He emphasizes the interrelationship of literary works, particularly in what he perceives as a unified period before the rise of modernism, a period he sees as stretching from ancient pagan times to sometime in the nineteenth century.[35] Literary works illuminate each other, contributing to a symbolic language and iconography. Lewis is not a narrow specialist but rather something of a polymath. He bears comparison with Michael Polanyi in the sciences. He is at ease in a number of disciplines, such as philosophy, classics, and history, but usually humble about the extent of his knowledge when he steps out of his professional field, as when he writes popular theology.

Related to this wideness of view is his preoccupation with Christianizing paganism and with a rehabilitation of premodernist literature and values. The vast ancient continuity he sees gives him a strong polemical purpose: he would not simply rehabilitate the medieval period but the entire premodernist period. Lewis paints the inner world using allegory, symbol, or myth—just like the medievals and (if Barfield is correct) the earlier ancient Western world. His fiction and literary work are therefore of a piece. He believes that, with skill, contemporary literature can take us into the literature of the Old West, by our recognizing likeness, going from the more familiar to the less. A child, for example, may read *The Voyage of the Dawn Treader* and later discover Homer's *The Odyssey* is familiar.[36]

In his literary criticism he maintains both continuity and discontinuity with the present (he is a premodernist who has a postmodern appeal). He is thus valuable in giving a transcendent perspective on our times. His early rejection of "chronological snobbery" allowed this freedom. His preoccupation with story and metaphor as a condition of all good thinking was fought out in opposition to modernism and its characteristic naturalism. These interests are highly palatable in our postmodern era. Yet at the same time Lewis's work refuses to be reduced to a postmodernist position; he is unashamedly premodernist in his chosen beliefs and tastes. Another (and related) feature of his work that appeals to a postmodern climate is his hallmark emphasis upon particularity—the distinctiveness that exists in people, places, and books. A perhaps related feature is his emphasis on the symbolic and the imaginative as playing a central role in thought. In Lewis's case they were significant factors in the move from atheism to Christianity, as well as in his professional life thereafter. He advocates what might be called a symbolic perception of reality.[37]

The flair of his criticism is notable: it is elegantly written and bears a timeless element. Furthermore, his literary and related criticism fuels his imaginative writing. There are often parallels, for instance, between his works of criticism and his particular fictions. The pattern is established in the inspiration that *Allegory* gives to the writing of *The Pilgrim's Regress* (1933): his *A Preface to "Paradise Lost"* (1942) naturally leads to *Perelandra* (1943); *The Abolition of Man* (1943) theoretically treats the themes of *That Hideous Strength* (1945); his many explorations of myth and pre-Christian paganism results in *Till We Have Faces* (1956); and it could perhaps be argued that his consideration of Spenser's *The Faerie Queene* over many years provides a pattern for the imaginative eclecticism yet coherent unity of the Narnian Chronicles (1950–56).[38]

Lewis's uniqueness and particularity are not easy to capture. It is easier to show him (as this essay has tried to do) as a child of his times—an upper middle-class Ulsterman, a reluctant product of the British public school system, and a brilliant scholar of the type best nurtured by a traditional university setting like Oxford, which encouraged cross-disciplinary exploration. There are contemporaries similar to him, like Barfield and Tolkien, and many other Christian writers who belong to Blamires's "minor Christian literary renaissance." However, like Tolkien and Barfield, his great friends and mentors, he is remarkably relevant to the context that confronts us at the cusp of the millennium. Postmodernity has proved a haven for the unique antimodernism of Lewis and his closer mentors. Alas, to fully demonstrate his relevance to this whole new context would take at least another chapter.

365

Notes

1. The author acknowledges permission to use portions of earlier materials, substantially reworked and enlarged here, from his *C. S. Lewis Encyclopedia* (Wheaton, IL: Crossway, 2000).

2. Most of Lewis's essays have been compiled and edited by Walter Hooper.

3. Not least, Lewis has profoundly shaped the evangelical movement, not only in the United States, but also in the United Kingdom, the rest of Europe, including the new post-Soviet democracies, and elsewhere. See Duriez, "C. S. Lewis and the Evangelicals."

4. See chapter 13 of Mabbott's book.

5. Some of the key writings are as follows. Idealism: Green's *Prolegomena to Ethics*; Bradley's *Appearance and Reality*; Bosanquet's *Knowledge and Reality* and *A History of Aesthetic*; and McTaggart's *The Nature of Existence*. Realism: Wilson's *Statement and Inference*; Ross's *The Right and the Good*; Prichard's *Kant's Theory of Knowledge*; Russell's *The Problems of Philosophy*; Moore's *Philosophical Studies*; and Broad's, *Perception, Physics and Reality*.

6. Owen Barfield (discussed below) persuaded Lewis eventually to accept some tenets of idealism. Lewis did not stay long here, however, but moved from idealism to theism, and eventually to Christian belief. After his conversion, Lewis's philosophical position was a modified realism. Significantly, he was influenced by the great realist metaphysician, Samuel Alexander (1859–1938). Lewis rejected the grand impersonality of idealist systems, and even the goal of a total system of thought. He preferred the individuality of places and people, seasons and times, moods and tones of feeling. God himself was the most concrete of existences. Realism can take many forms, theistic and naturalistic; Lewis was not inconsistent in retaining important elements of realism. For more on Lewis's philosophical ideas (beyond the scope of this chapter), see Patrick, *The Magdalen Metaphysicals*, and Walker and Patrick, *A Christian for All Christians*.

7. *Miracles*, chapter 3 (first ed.). A vivid picture of his naturalistic thinking at this time is revealed in a letter to Arthur Greeves (*Stand* 223–24).

8. The origin of the phrase the "Wee Teas" is from Wee Free Church (of Scotland)—the Free Church of Scotland broke away from the Church of Scotland in the last century. The original membership listed by Mabbott includes Gilbert Ryle (1900–76), author of the influential *The Concept of Mind* (1949), Henry Habberley Price, whose major work *Perception* was published in 1932, and Thomas Dewar Weldon (1896–1958), Fellow and Tutor in Philosophy at Magdalen College (1923–58). See also Martin Moynihan, "C. S. Lewis and T. D. Weldon."

9. According to Tolkien (Letter 92, 18 December 1944), the book was to be called "'Language' (Nature, Origins, Function)"; according to Lewis, it was to be "Language and Human Nature." The idea was still active in 1948, for Lewis told Chad Walsh that the book was due to be published the next year by Student Christian Movement Press (*Letters of J. R. R. Tolkien* 440 n. 92; cf. *Letters of C. S. Lewis* 399).

10. The characterization of Ransom is not consistent throughout the cosmic trilogy and the unfinished *The Dark Tower*, the resemblance to Tolkien only really applying to the first two volumes. Interestingly, Moseley shows how Tolkien as Ransom anticipates the later linguistic theory of Noam Chomsky when he speculates that he might uncover the "very form of language itself, the principle behind all possible languages" (Moseley 18; *Out of the Silent Planet* 55).

11. In, for example, A. N. Wilson's biography of Lewis (1990), which favors psychoanalytical interpretations of motivation, e.g., seeing a birth experience behind the passage through the coat-lined wardrobe in Lewis's *The Lion, the Witch and the Wardrobe*.

12. Many years later, when Lewis moved from Oxford to Cambridge University, he ruefully discovered (what he had always no doubt suspected) "that there is something at Cambridge which fills the same place philosophy filled at Oxford: a discipline which overflows the faculty of its birth and percolates through all the others and about which the freshman must pick up something if he means to be anybody. This is Literary Criticism (with the largest possible capitals for both words). You were never safe from the philosopher at Oxford; here, never from the Critic" (*The Cambridge Review* 77 [21 April 1956]; qtd. in Hooper, *Companion* 73).

13. See Doris Myers, *C. S. Lewis in Context* (e.g., 30–36, 72–77). Myers's book usefully shows that the ideas of the "Green Book" discussed in *The Abolition of Man* were heavily influenced by

I. A. Richards. Thus, when challenging them, Lewis is also expressing disquiet at Richards's basic ideas.

14. Lewis was against the *re-evaluation* of the literary canon by Leavis and others, and not against evaluation as such. Lewis heartily applauded healthy or wholesome literature in *Preface* (his terms are "general wisdom and health of mind"), seeing the meaning of wholesome literature being universally agreed in the millenia before the rise of modernism. One of the best pieces of his sustained thinking, *The Abolition of Man* (1943), defends such premodernist values.

15. See Lewis's *An Experiment in Criticism* for an extensive case for his position.

16. See Walter Hooper, "To the Martlets."

17. It is in striking contrast to his friend Tolkien, whose reading at that time was focused upon northern European early medieval literature, and whose approach and thinking, relatedly, were not at all eclectic.

18. See Hooper, *Companion* 770.

19. I explore Lewis's contribution to a symbolic perception of reality in "The Theology of Fantasy in Lewis and Tolkien."

20. The list was published in *The Christian Century* (6 June 1962), and reprinted in *The Canadian C. S. Lewis Journal*, No. 58 (Spring 1987): 27.

21. See W. H. Lewis, *Brothers and Friends: The Diaries of Major Warren Hamilton Lewis.*

22. This is Lewis's name for a central human experience which he explored in many writings, including *Surprised, The Problem of Pain* (particularly chapter 10), and *Regress.*

23. The exact date of the beginning of the Inklings is a matter of speculation, but it is clear that it grew out of the friendships of Lewis with Dyson, Tolkien, and Barfield, with Lewis as the natural center of the group. It was in existence in the early 1930s when Lewis's and Tolkien's doctor, "Humphrey" Havard, was invited to attend. The name was transferred from an undergraduate club which folded, according to Tolkien (Letter 298, in *Letters of J. R. R. Tolkien*). Regarding the reference to his father, there is not space in this chapter to take proper account of Lewis's whole Ulster background. This Irish context is easily overlooked because of English stereotyping, as in Wilson's *Biography*—see the review by Gillespie, "The Red Faced Ulsterman." All Lewis's Inklings friends were male. The absence of women was very much part of Lewis's Oxford context at that period. This context is clearly brought out by Mabbott, particularly in his chapter, "Co-ed." In contrast, in his Ulster context, Lewis did have female friends, like Jane McNeill.

24. Lewis acknowledges the importance of *Poetic Diction* in *Surprised* (189), and in the chapter "Horrid Red Things" in *Miracles.*

25. Barfield drew inspiration from Steiner for his many writings, and his adherence to anthroposophism formed the basis for that "Great War" between Lewis and himself. Steiner's ideas can be seen as part of a contemporary quest for a new consciousness which tries to transcend the rational scientific model of reality imposed by the Enlightenment, despite his claim to be following a "scientific method." This quest seeks to find an alternative to modernism, what had become Lewis's great enemy. Barfield's *Poetic Diction* was concerned with the nature of poetic language and a theory of an ancient semantic unity, which require no commitment to anthroposophical interpretations of Christianity. The "Great War" of ideas helped to prepare Lewis for accepting orthodox Christianity, rather than any anthroposophist ideas. Significant differences remained between Lewis and Barfield until the end of Lewis's life.

26. For more on the Barfield-Lewis friendship see Owen Barfield, *Owen Barfield on C. S. Lewis.*

27. For further information see Humphrey Carpenter's *The Inklings* and the forthcoming *The Inklings Handbook*, by Colin Duriez and David Porter.

28. See David Bratman, "Hugo Dyson: Inkling, Teacher, *Bon Vivant.*"

29. In *Essays Presented to Charles Williams*, the date of the Andrew Lang lecture is reported as being 1938 (38). Carpenter, however, reports that the correct date is 8 March 1939, and that other published records are incorrect (*Tolkien* 191).

30. Colin Duriez, "Tolkien and the Old West."

31. See Colin Duriez, "Sub-creation and Tolkien's Theology of Story."

32. See Blamires *A History*, chapter 11, section 1.

33. For instance, Gardner draws attention to Lewis's controversial dismissal of humanism in his *Sixteenth.*

34. Harry Blamires, "Against the Stream." Further insight into the presence of Christian belief in Oxford circles in particular at this period is given in "Is There an Oxford 'School' of Writing?"

35. Lewis identified modernism (expressed, for example, in a machine mentality) as a social and cultural embodiment, not simply as a set of theoretical ideas. In this he reflected Owen Barfield's analysis of "idolatry," for instance in Barfield's *History, Guilt and Habit* 70.

36. This point is made by Maria Kuteeva in her study, "C. S. Lewis's Chronicles of Narnia: Their Origins in Mythology, Literature and Scholarship."

37. I am currently exploring this important dimension to Lewis and the Inklings. There is something about it in the forthcoming *The Inklings Handbook.* My understanding of the implications of Lewis's position is that archetypes are transmitted by story. As archetypes shape perception, story has a vital role in perception. The Bible, as the supreme source of archetypes in Western literature, validates, verifies, clarifies, and undistorts the key archetypes that shape perception. There are also other symbolic elements besides archetypes in story affecting perception, e.g., myth. For publications alert to the implications of the Bible's symbolic dimension, see Jeffrey, *Dictionary of Biblical Tradition in Western Literature*, and Ryken, *Dictionary of Biblical Imagery.*

38. See chapter 5 in this volume for an exploration of this thesis.

Works Cited

Barfield, Owen. *History, Guilt and Habit.* Middletown, CT: Wesleyan UP, 1979.

———. *History in English Words.* London: Faber, 1954.

———. *Owen Barfield on C. S. Lewis.* Middletown, CT: Wesleyan UP, 1989.

———. *Poetic Diction: A Study in Meaning.* London: Faber, 1952.

———. *Silver Trumpet.* Longmont, CO: Bookmaker's Guild, 1986.

Blamires, Harry. "Against the Stream: C. S. Lewis and the Literary Scene." *Journal of the Irish Christian Study Centre* 1 (1983): 11–22.

———. *A History of Literary Criticism.* New York: St. Martins, 1991.

"Boethius." *The Concise Encyclopedia of Western Philosophy and Philosophers.* Ed. J. O. Urmson. London: Hutchinson, 1975.

Bosanquet, B. *A History of Aesthetic.* London: Allen & Unwin, 1904.

———. *Knowledge and Reality.* London: Kegan Paul, 1885.

Bradley, F. H. *Appearance and Reality.* Rev. ed. Oxford: Oxford UP, 1930.

Bratman, David. "Hugo Dyson: Inkling, Teacher, *Bon Vivant.*" *Mythlore* 82 (1997): 19–34.

Broad, C. D. *Perception, Physics and Reality.* Cambridge: Cambridge UP, 1914.

Carpenter, Humphrey. *The Inklings: C. S. Lewis, J. R. R. Tolkien, Charles Williams, and Their Friends.* London: Allen & Unwin, 1978.

———. *J. R. R. Tolkien: A Biography.* London: Allen & Unwin, 1977.

Duriez, Colin. "C. S. Lewis and the Evangelicals." *Christian Librarian* 22 (1998): 11–31.

———. "Sub-creation and Tolkien's Theology of Story." *Scholarship and Fantasy.* Ed. K. J. Battar-bee. Turku, Finland: University of Turku, 1993. 133–50.

———. "The Theology of Fantasy in Lewis and Tolkien." *Themelios: An International Journal for Theological and Religious Studies Students* 23.2 (1998): 35–51.

———. "Tolkien and the Old West." *Digging Potatoes, Growing Trees: 25 Years of Speeches at the Tolkien Society's Annual Dinners.* Vol. 2. Ed. Helen Armstrong. Telford: The Tolkien Society, 1998. 51–60.

Gardner, Helen. "Clive Staples Lewis 1898–1963." *The Proceedings of The British Academy,* Vol. 51. London: Oxford UP, 1965. 417–28.

Gillespie, John. "The Red Faced Ulsterman." *Journal of the Irish Christian Study Centre* 5 (Feb. 1994): 45–52.

Green, T. H. *Prolegomena to Ethics.* Oxford: Oxford UP, 1883.

Hooper, Walter. *C. S. Lewis: A Companion and Guide.* London: HarperCollins, 1996.

———. "To the Martlets." *C. S. Lewis: Speaker and Teacher.* Ed. Carolyn Keefe. Grand Rapids: Zon-dervan, 1971. 37–62.

"Is There an Oxford 'School' of Writing?: A Discussion between Rachel Trickett and David Cecil." *The Twentieth Century* (June 1955): 559–70.

Jeffrey, David, ed. *Dictionary of Biblical Tradition in Western Literature.* Grand Rapids: Eerdmans, 1992.

Kuteeva, Maria. "C. S. Lewis's Chronicles of Narnia: Their Origins in Mythology, Literature and Scholarship." M.Phil. thesis, U of Manchester, 1995.

Lewis, C. S. *The Allegory of Love: A Study in Medieval Tradition.* 1936. London: Oxford UP, 1958.

———. *"The Dark Tower" and Other Stories.* Ed. Walter Hooper. New York: Harvest, 1977.

———. *The Discarded Image: An Introduction to Medieval and Renaissance Literature.* Cambridge: Cambridge UP, 1964.

———. *English Literature in the Sixteenth Century Excluding Drama.* Oxford: Oxford UP, 1954.

———. *An Experiment in Criticism.* Cambridge, Cambridge UP, 1961.

———. *Letters of C. S. Lewis.* Ed. W. H. Lewis. 1966. Rev. ed. Ed. Walter Hooper, London: Harper-Collins, 1988.

———. *Miracles: A Preliminary Study.* 1947. New York: Macmillan, 1960.

———. *Out of the Silent Planet.* 1938. New York: Macmillan, 1968.

———. *The Pilgrim's Regress: An Allegorical Apology for Christianity, Reason and Romanticism.* 1933. Grand Rapids: Eerdmans, 1943.

———. Preface to *Dymer.* 1950. Rpt. in *Narrative Poems.* Ed. Walter Hooper. New York: Harcourt, 1969. 3–6.

———. *A Preface to "Paradise Lost."* London: Oxford UP, 1942.

———. *The Problem of Pain.* 1940. New York: Macmillan, 1962.

———. *Rehabilitations and Other Essays.* London: Oxford UP, 1939.

———. *Studies in Words.* 2nd ed. Cambridge: Cambridge UP, 1967.

———. *Surprised by Joy: The Shape of My Early Life.* New York: Harcourt, 1955.

———. *They Stand Together: The Letters of C. S. Lewis to Arthur Greeves (1914–1963).* Ed. Walter Hooper. New York: Macmillan, 1979.

———, ed. *Essays Presented to Charles Williams.* 1947. Grand Rapids: Eerdmans, 1966.

Lewis, W. H. *Brothers and Friends: The Diaries of Major Warren Hamilton Lewis.* Ed. Clyde S. Kilby and Marjorie L. Mead. San Francisco: Harper and Row, 1982.

369

Mabbott, John. *Oxford Memories*. Oxford: Thornton's of Oxford, 1986.

McTaggart, J. *The Nature of Existence*. Cambridge: Cambridge UP, 1927.

Moore, G. E. *Philosophical Studies*. London: Routledge, 1922.

Moseley, Charles. *J. R. R. Tolkien*. Plymouth: Northcote House, 1997.

Moynihan, Martin. "C. S. Lewis and T. D. Weldon." *Seven* 5 (1984): 101–05.

Myers, Doris. *C. S. Lewis in Context*. Kent, OH: Kent State UP, 1994.

Patrick, James. *The Magdalen Metaphysicals*. Macon, GA: Mercer UP, 1985.

Price, Henry Habberley. *Perception*. London: Meuthen, 1932.

Prichard, H. *Kant's Theory of Knowledge*. Oxford: Oxford UP, 1909.

Richards, I. A. *Practical Criticism: A Study of Literary Judgment*. London: Paul, Trench, Trubner, 1929.

———. *Principles of Literary Criticism*. London: Paul, Trench, Trubner, 1924.

Ross, Sir W. *The Right and the Good*. Oxford: Oxford UP, 1930.

Russell, B. A. *The Problems of Philosophy*. London: Williams & Norgate, 1912.

Russell, David L. "C. S. Lewis." *British Children's Writers*. Vol. 160. *Dictionary of Literary Biography*. Detroit: Bruccoli Clark Layman, 1996. 134–49.

Ryken, Leland, et al., eds. *Dictionary of Biblical Imagery*. Downers Grove: InterVarsity, 1998.

Ryle, Gilbert. *The Concept of Mind*. London: Hutchinson's University Library, 1949.

Tolkien, J. R. R. *The Letters of J. R. R. Tolkien*. Ed. Humphrey Carpenter. London: George Allen & Unwin, 1981.

Walker, Andrew, and James Patrick, eds. *A Christian for All Christians: Essays in Honour of C. S. Lewis*. London: Hodder & Stoughton, 1990.

Wilson, A. N. *C. S. Lewis: A Biography*. New York: W. W. Norton, 1990.

Wilson, John Cook. *Statement and Inference*. Oxford: Clarendon Press, 1926.

20

Lewis:
A Critical Prospective

Thomas L. Martin

What can Lewis teach us about criticism in an age of poststructuralism and postmodernism, a time when criticism has propelled us beyond literature, beyond the humanities, and even beyond philosophic inquiry? In a sense, *Reading the Classics with C. S. Lewis* stands as an alternative to such criticism. Still, one wonders what Lewis would have said about literary criticism at the turn of the century. As we enjoy literature with Lewis, let us not underestimate the important role of criticism in this era: enlightened critique sustains us after the demise of aesthetics and the "death of the author," after Foucault's declaration that "man is in the process of perishing as the being of language continues to shine ever brighter upon our horizon," and after Rorty's solemn descriptions of the end of philosophy.[1] Such criticism considers literature a thing to be opposed, for appreciating a text may make us unwitting slaves of its ideological subtext. In this brave new world where everything is reducible to discourse or power struggles, reading becomes a means of resistance, rupture, and reinscription. Reading and literature are thus set at odds. Duke University's Fredric Jameson is not the only English professor to admit he derives his highest satisfaction from breaking his students' fascination with literature.[2]

Lewis obviously never addressed postmodern critical theory, so why force him into such a strange arena? Throughout this essay, I will show that Lewis was well in touch with the germination of postmodern thought.[3] Glancing ahead in 1962, he comments on an emerging realignment in literary studies, something never witnessed before in its history, where fanciful practitioners can be found wresting from literary texts "the most profound ambiguities and social criticisms" ("Unreal" 93). He calls it "the discovery of the mare's nest by the pursuit of the red herring." Less metaphorically he comments in an essay four years prior, "The literary world of today is little interested in the narrative art as such; it is preoccupied with technical novelties and with 'ideas', by which it means not literary, but social or psychological, ideas" ("Juvenile" 41). As to the outcome of this ill-conceived and misdirected criticism, he remarks to his colleagues: "This is going to go on long after my lifetime; you may be able to see the end of it, I shan't" ("Unreal" 93).

To a pronounced degree, Lewis witnessed the new approach in undergraduate critics, those with more "excuse" than the vanguard professors they imitated, but who nonetheless would fill future teaching positions. In a Cambridge University *Broadsheet* in 1960, Lewis diagnoses four problems of this "Undergraduate Criticism": 1) its adverse criticism bears a tone of resentment, even abuse, where the writer seems "more anxious to wound the author than to inform the reader"; 2) it too quickly accepts radical reinterpretations of long-standing works, heedless of their *prima facie* improbability; 3) it lacks the necessary background in the classics and the Bible which form the context for most traditional literature, but, what is worse, it remains unaware that such intertextual illiteracy is a limitation; and 4) it takes literary *divertissements* as serious statements of philosophy, psychotherapy, or religion, in what amounts to a strong misreading of genre. Even from these few comments, we can already sense that what Lewis saw in bud we who come after him witness in full flower.

In this essay, I profile what has transpired in critical theory after Lewis's lifetime. While we, too, have not seen the end of critical excesses in these decades, we have seen a bit more than Lewis did. I survey critical practice during this time, looking briefly at formalist, structuralist, historicist, and ideological criticisms. Although Lewis writes when these critical schools have scarce begun, he responds to their nascent principles with characteristic perspicacity and wit. After rehearsing definitions and quotations from representatives of each school (and updating them as appropriate), I bring Lewis's critical thought to bear on them. From there, I turn to the more constructive task of investigating what Lewis said about the nature of literature. Noting both the advantages and disadvantages of his statements, I end by considering what Lewis saw as reading's moral dimension. Hazarding a glance toward the future, I suggest that his statements on reading and love will be Lewis's most important contribution as a critic.

Reductio ad Absurdum

Lewis's consistent strategy for dealing with revolutionary critical approaches is to show that most often they treat literature not *as* literature, but as an instance of something else. Whatever the preoccupations of these approaches, "The text before them comes to exist not in its own right but simply as raw material; clay out of which they can complete their tale of bricks" (*Experiment* 7). In short, the text becomes a pretext: claims the text makes about the way things are, whether real or imagined, are subsumed to the critic's own view of the way the world is (or perhaps should be). Reductionism therefore is the view for which a literary text presents not a reality of its own, but is reinscribed into some other system. This, of course, assumes that the critic is predominantly correct and the literary text incorrect, that works of imagination have no value in and of themselves, that such works may be tainted by the power structures "authorizing" them, and that the role of the critic is to "see through" the smoke and mirrors to the stern realities underneath. (Presumably, the critic is in a unique position to tell us what those realities are.) Whereas earlier critics distinguish between the "outside" and "inside" of a text, postmodern critics tend to problematize the distinction, substituting for it most often the distinction between "surface" and "depth." Readers now are encouraged to "read between the lines," "read against the grain," and "interrogate texts" in order to come to terms with the "depth" meaning of literary works. Whatever the full rationale, the reductive mode of inquiry remains fundamental to modern and postmodern critical theory. And Lewis, who championed the fight against reductionism in his day, leaves us a few instructive lessons.

While it might seem that Lewis battles reductionism every time he picks up a pen, his *locus classicus* on the subject is *The Abolition of Man*. From it and *An Experiment in Criticism*, two general arguments emerge: first, reductionism is not interested in *reading* literary texts but *using* them for other purposes, and, second, that in so doing it can never expect to escape its insularity from, indeed its relative ignorance about, the world at large. Now, I should make clear that I don't think Lewis would begrudge political scientists and sociologists from bringing within the ken of their studies works of literature, but yet for their one slice of reality they should not think they have the whole pie. More dangerous still is when reductionism is introduced into the classroom. Students who naturally see the world from a limited perspective and often have little sense of how much educated people disagree need to learn from a variety of sources and from differing viewpoints. A reductive pedagogy, of course, runs counter to their needs. Reductionism's operative formula "only" reinforces a narrowness of outlook, maintains Lewis. Perhaps this is

373

the inevitable paradox of reductive criticism. Although students may quickly become as adept as their teachers at swinging a reductive scythe, Lewis finds the scenario anomalous: "The task of the modern educator is not to cut down jungles but to irrigate deserts" (*Abolition* 24).

Aestheticism

Those who set up "'the aesthetic' as a mode of experience irreducibly distinct both from the logical and the practical" may be of many types (*Experiment* 130). While Lewis refers specifically to Croce, we also might mention certain New Critics, the resuscitated Russian formalists, and especially the miscellany of nineteenth- and twentieth-century aesthetes whose credo is "art for art's sake."[4] Undeniably, literary art bears a formal aspect, which should be subject to careful study. But insofar as these critics identify literature primarily with its formal features, apart from its meaning and pragmatic context, theirs is a reductive understanding. Lewis observes that aestheticism in this sense is a relatively recent phenomenon:

> Until quite modern times—I think, until the time of the Romantics—nobody ever suggested that literature and the arts were an end in themselves. . . .
>
> It was only in the nineteenth century that we became aware of the full dignity of art. We began to "take it seriously" as the Nazis take mythology seriously. But the result seems to have been a dislocation of the aesthetic life in which little is left for us but high-minded works which fewer and fewer people want to read or hear or see, and "popular" works of which both those who make them and those who enjoy them are half ashamed. Just like the Nazis, by valuing too highly a real, but subordinate good, we have come near to losing that good itself. ("First" 279–80)

Aesthetic reductionism's dislocation of art runs the risk of excessively limiting what counts as art, treating many beloved "names in . . . literature— except for the half dozen protected by the momentary critical 'establishment'—. . . as so many lamp-posts for a dog" (*Experiment* 112). And when it runs low on literary works to disdain, aesthetic reductionism may ultimately work against itself. In practical terms, as we shall see below, this kind of reductionism may be attended by pedantry, priggery, and scornful elitism.

An informal typology of aesthetic reductionism can be sketched from Lewis's works. He writes of "Style-mongers," "Culture-mongers," and "Clevers." The first he describes in *Experiment*:

> On taking up a book, these people concentrate on what they call its "style" or its "English". They judge this neither by its sound nor by its power to communicate

but by its conformity to certain arbitrary rules. Their reading is a perpetual witch hunt for Americanisms, Gallicisms, split infinitives, and sentences that end with a preposition. (35)

Of course, we may widely vary the stylistic details these readers pursue. The point is that in seeking lesser matters they miss the greater. In his well-known formulation, Lewis argues that literary art is much more than its style or language—*poiema*, "something shaped" (82). He finds it significant, for example, that "[t]he story of Orpheus strikes and strikes deep, of itself; the fact that Virgil and others have told it in good poetry is irrelevant" (41). That such a story comes to us in words is "logically accidental." Besides language, literary art is also meaning—*logos*, "something said" (82). And its meaning may even come to us in a form other than language: "If some perfected art of mime or silent film or serial pictures could make it clear with no words at all, it would still affect us in the same way" (41). How difficult it is to maintain a view of art that does not, at least at times, take us outside of art: "The first word of the *Iliad* directs our minds to anger; something we are acquainted with outside the poem and outside literature altogether" (27–28).

Lewis also describes "Culture-mongers," those who "hypostatize" culture, "set [it] up on its own, [make it] a faith, a cause, a banner, a 'platform'" ("Lilies" 38). They may be mere dabblers, those who participate in culture only as a means to improve their social status. Lewis depicts a scenario, a sherry party, where talk about culture is abundant, but where the discussion seems to turn on its subject as a matter of fashion. "[C]ataracts of *culture*," he explains, "but never one word or one glance that suggested a real enjoyment of any art, any person, or any natural object . . ." (39). These trend-conscious poseurs appear more concerned with which author is "in" and which is "out" than with the natural merits of the art itself. Lewis says his heart warms rather to the boy on the school bus reading *Fantasy and Science Fiction*: "For here also I should feel that I had met something real and live and unfabricated; genuine literary experience. . . ." On the other hand, devotees of culture may be very serious about their pursuit, so serious that they, like Matthew Arnold, set it up as a kind of substitute religion.

That is where we encounter "The Clevers." They appear in *The Pilgrim's Regress* as a group wholly given to the mutual enjoyment of culture. A problem with such an undertaking is that their art is so reactionary and so unconventional that access to it through common sense or experience is barred. Even when John asks for help to appreciate it, they bully rather than instruct him. Their art seems purposely cut off from anything familiar, isolated and turned in on itself. Consequently, when their *pursuit* of aesthetic pleasure combines with their *judgment* of the same, a cruel social game ensues. Pretense and pettiness appear the only rules: "'They are not angry,' said Gus; 'they are talking about Art'" (50). Without basis for agreement, they continue their critical bantering. Victoriana sings to them, and they hold "their noses in the air," looking "very stiff." When she is finished they praise her to her face, but when she leaves they malign her. They subordinate all matters of wisdom or morality entirely to their art. These nonconformist aesthetes eventually chase John out of Eschropolis for his nonconformity. In a spirit of intolerance, they hurl at him both ordure and insults: "Puritanian! Bourgeois! Prurient!" (55). The Clevers represent for Lewis the final outworking of the doctrine "art for art's sake."

Less extreme is Mr. Halfways, who shows us not only the road into pure aestheticism, but also, by extrapolation, the road out. In a chapter entitled "Leah for Rachel" in *The Pilgrim's Regress*, Mr. Halfways sings his song to John, and John becomes transfixed by it. The singer's voice is not like his speaking voice, but "strong and noble and full of strange over-tones" (43). As he listens intently, John sees a clear vision of the beautiful island which his imagination has until now only glimpsed. And more than just seeing a picture in his head, he genuinely *seems to be there*: "in the water, only a few yards from the sand of the Island. He could see more than he had ever seen before." Shortly, the vision fades, and John requests that the song be sung again and again. By the third time, however, he notices more about the music and less about the Island. He sees "how several of the [song's] effects were produced and that some parts were better than others" (44). The vision of the Island has become "a little shadowy," the song more prominent. In the end he dwells on the message only until tedium sets in; he wonders when the messenger will cease. John has grasped the figure and lost the ground: he has learned that Romanticism can turn to aestheticism and then to formalism and finally to boredom. As Lewis says elsewhere, "if we do overvalue art, then art itself will be the greatest sufferer; when second things are put first, they are corrupted" ("Scott" 215).[5] To pure aestheticism Lewis offers an alternative, as we shall see below.

Scientism

The next reductive "-ism" we consider is scientism. An aspect of the modern world that especially concerns Lewis, scientism is "causally connected with the popularisation of the sciences. It is, in a word, the belief that the supreme moral end is the perpetuation of our own species, and that this is to be pursued even if . . . our species has to be stripped of all those things for which we value it" ("Reply" 71–72). Distinct from science, scient*ism* generally proceeds from the conviction that the scientific method is the only sure means of establishing genuine knowledge and that before its tribunal all matters must pass. But it is not certain that everything in heaven and earth is amenable to scientific inquiry. As Lewis quips, "Waves at sea are not less beautiful because you cannot represent them in a contour map" ("Neoplatonism" 161). And even Einstein—accosted by a starry-eyed journalist asking whether we might explain *everything* by the theory of relativity—exclaims, "My good man, that would be like putting Beethoven's Ninth Symphony on a *sound pressure curve.*" Like many of us, Lewis valued science, but in its proper place. He once remarked, "though I could have never been a scientist [without the mathematical talents], I had scientific as well as imaginative impulses . . ." (*Surprised* 137). Moreover, he understood that a mathematical description of physical reality, where an object is "stripped of its qualitative properties and reduced to mere quantity," is not altogether real (*Abolition* 82). He reminds us that the greatest scientists, too, recognize the abstractness and artificiality inherent in their operations—something the popularizers of science tend to overlook as they promote science as the answer to the full range of humanity's problems.

Throughout the twentieth century the unwarranted optimism in science has also influenced the study of literature. During this time, theorists have produced scientific accounts of literary language as well as of the behavior that accompanies it. Are any of these scientists guilty of the reductive "stripping away" Lewis mentions above? Claude Lévi-Strauss, for one, maintains, "The goal of the human sciences is not to constitute man but to dissolve him."[6] Earlier, in the first two decades of the twentieth century, Swiss linguist Ferdinand de Saussure laid the foundation for the structuralist approach to language, literature, and culture that would influence not only anthropologists like Lévi-Strauss, but also literary theorists like Roland Barthes and cultural historians like Michel Foucault. Structuralism and its successor poststructuralism (both with a strong reliance on language's immanent features, those internal relations or syntactic features visible to science) would establish the reigning critical paradigm in the United States and France from the 1960s to the 1990s. Saussure asserts, "A science which studies linguistic structure is not only able to dispense with other elements of language, but is possible only if those other elements are kept separate" (14). To be excluded from this science of language is not only a world that language refers to, but also meaning itself. A little later, in the United States, the linguist Bloomfield admits the difficulty of dealing with meaning in scientific terms, and the Vienna Circle concludes outright that syntax is the only possible science of language. In these statements of method or their application, does humanity indeed become "dissolved," as Lévi-Strauss and Foucault claim, or are we simply abstracted out of an intentionally delimited inquiry? If we want to conduct a scientific investigation into, say, the boiling point of milk, we must set aside a host of realities—in much the same way that if we want to make cheese we must set aside the cow. If the principles of physics do not dissolve the realities of biology (or the principles of any science the realities that concern another), then why this strange rush to dissolve humanity especially? Furthermore, when poststructuralists in general and Derrida in particular *de*construct the scientific biases of structuralism, we may be inclined to see them as our allies. Yet their goal is not to reintroduce anything like meaning (or humanity, for that matter), but in a world already dispossessed of these to accentuate the indeterminate nature of language. Neither position is ultimately acceptable. As I have argued elsewhere, if structuralist principles are by no means necessary, then *post*structuralism is one of the great *non sequiturs* of contemporary thought.[7]

We turn from a scientific explanation of literary language to the behavior that accompanies it. Much can be said here, but I limit my comments to the psychoanalytic approach since Lewis addresses it directly. The first, and most obvious, problem Lewis sees in psychoanalytic criticism is its reductive handling of literary phenomena. Psychoanalytic hermeneutics operates upon a principle of symbolic exchange whereby literary features and fictional events are understood merely as expressions of unconscious desires, primarily sexual in nature. Freud himself explains that when a fairy tale tells us "once upon a time there were a king and queen," it "simply mean[s]" that "once upon a time there were a father and mother" (qtd. in "Psycho-Analysis" 292). The phrase "simply means" is what most bothers Lewis the literary critic. The logical force of Freud's statement is, as Lewis rightly observes, "this is all that they mean, they mean neither more, nor less, nor other, than this." We can readily see how to unite the principle with the task of interpretation, for Freud himself provides the key to understanding the symbolism: the appearance of trees, weapons, umbrellas, and other such objects are references to the male body; the appearance of doors, gardens, and ships, the female body (Freud 153–65). Accordingly, his theory translates the literary landscape into little more than a sexual tableau.

Freud's followers apply the principle with aplomb, supplying the inevitable sophistications over time. In his classic study *Hamlet and Oedipus*, Ernest Jones sees Hamlet's problem not so much his lack of resolve regarding Claudius as his desire to kill his father and marry his mother, the very things Claudius has beaten him to, indeed the *real* source of tension between him and his uncle. William Kerrigan's *On the Psychogenesis of Paradise Lost* achieves much the same result with Milton's epic, reading the poem as the product of an "oedipal child" who is blinded as a result of "poisoned nourishment from a weak-eyed mother and an embittered wife" (244). In a more recent example, Michael Schoenfeldt gives George Herbert's sacred poems a carnal reading, seeing them less an exercise in spiritual worship and more a meditation on the poet's own sexual inutility and auto-erotic fantasies.

That leads us to another of Lewis's points, that the psychoanalytic approach to literature quickly becomes pathology. Indeed, Norman Holland describes his manner of reading literary texts as though he were listening to a patient on the couch relate his or her dreams "in iambic pentameter" (136). The critic's job, explain Kaplan and Kloss, is to discern behind those dreams "the unspoken motive." Besides the limited evidence this approach necessarily relies on and the tenuous conclusions it inevitably yields, a larger problem is to determine where the inquiry will end and what its outcome will be. Certainly, Lewis himself never imagined just how pathological criticism would become only three decades after his death. A quick browsing of recent conference titles gives us some idea: "Early Modern Male Sexual Anxiety," "Medieval Queer Religious Legacies," "Eighteenth-Century Genitalia," "Nineteenth-Century Female Vampyrism," and "Bending Gender in the Wild West." Insofar as theorists who participate in such conferences are interested in sexual pathology, they miss the literary value of the works they scrutinize. In the economy of symbolic substitution, argues Lewis in a memorable illustration, "a story about a golden dragon plucking the apple of immortality in a garden at the world's end, and a dream about one's pen going through the paper while one scribbles a note" are about the same thing ("Psycho-Analysis" 296). Such a violent reduction certainly makes manageable the great complexities of life, but at what cost? One is reminded of the scene in *The Pilgrim's Regress*, where prisoners of the Spirit of the Age lie trapped in a dungeon, their skin utterly transparent to each other: looking around, they are horrified at the spectacle. Instead of seeing persons, they only see "lungs panting like sponges," "saliva moving in the glands and the blood in the veins," and intestines twisting "like a coil of snakes" (60–61). Is that all humanity is? For Lewis, the problem with psychoanalytic theory is not so much the attention to sexual desire as the exclusion of everything else—"not what the wiseacre would force upon us, but what he threatens to take away" ("Psycho-Analysis" 293).

Historicist and Ideological Criticisms

The final category of reductive criticism we consider includes the historicist and the ideological schools. Marx, something of a literary critic himself who wrote on Goethe and Shakespeare, explains that art and indeed all culture is merely the effect of underlying material conditions. In his labor theory of value, economic and political realities are the sole fountainhead of all we cherish as true, right, and beautiful. So widespread is this ideological assumption in critical circles that one does not have to read too many articles or books, or attend too many classrooms or conferences, before one meets it in the oft-cited maxim "Everything is political." One way of transferring the assumption to literary criticism is to treat all language use as a kind of propaganda. Lewis was well aware of such an interpretive strategy. Believing the best of motives behind the work of these critics, however, he labels them the Vigilant School. The Vigilants find "in every turn of expression the symptom of attitudes which it is a matter of life and death to accept or resist. . . . Nothing is for them a matter of taste. They admit no . . . specifically literary good . . . " (*Experiment* 126). In this view, language is a means of political manipulation that must be laid bare of all other pretensions. Literature neither teaches nor delights; it stupefies and controls. The concepts employed by these critics are not difficult to grasp, observes Lewis, but what if they are wrong? In this case they "have prevented many happy unions of a good reader with a good book" (127). Not only the books: if these critics are wrong, readers have been diverted from all manner of important realities. And for readers who disagree with these critics' view of what constitutes the political good life, such criticism must always remain unenlightening. Lewis aptly concludes, "you can admire them as critics only if you also revere them as sages" (127).

The logic at the heart of much ideological critique, says Lewis, is the surreptitious shift of the burden of proof. This mode of argument he calls "Bulverism" and indeed considers it the foundation of twentieth-century thought:

> The modern method is to assume without discussion *that* . . . [a person] is wrong and then distract his attention from this (the only real issue) by busily explaining how he became so silly. In the course of the last fifteen years I have found this vice so common that I have had to invent a name for it. I call it Bulverism. Some day I am going to write the biography of its imaginary inventor, Ezekiel Bulver, whose destiny was determined at the age of five when he heard his mother say to his father—who had been maintaining that two sides of a triangle were together greater than the third—"Oh you say that *because you are a man.*" "At that moment," E. Bulver assures us, "there flashed across my opening mind the great truth that refutation is no necessary part of argument. Assume that your opponent is wrong, and then explain his error, and the world will be at your feet." ("Bulverism" 273)

380

Notwithstanding the fact that too many arguments in current critical discourse succeed based on innuendo and zealous denunciation alone, the most devastating argument against Bulverism is that it can be turned against itself. Lewis foists his own Christian assumptions upon the Bulverists as an example: "I . . . can, of course, play the game the other way around, by saying that 'the modern man has every reason for trying to convince himself that there are no eternal sanctions behind the morality he is rejecting'" (273). But once the game is turned around like this, it is nullified. Although we can continue trading one hermeneutical blow after another, flinging ever more mud in each other's face, the real question remains unanswered: Who is right? Of course we will have to shift the ground of discussion back to address the question.

This mention of hermeneutic struggle leads naturally to the issue of power. Lewis remarks in his *The Abolition of Man*, "When all that says 'it is good' has been debunked, what says 'I want' remains" (77–78). For many critics today, power themes are all that remain for the enlightened reader. Power is seen more *through* the work than expressed *in* it, what poets say less important than how their words reveal the surrounding social and political realities. Literary language for such critics is merely a social tool, created by and bearing the marks of social interaction. This general orientation has dominated literary criticism through the 1980s and 1990s, mainly in the schools known as "cultural studies" and "new historicism." Lewis wrote his 1950 essay "Historicism" on the then popular Hegelian and Marxist historicisms that sought to read the hidden message behind history. Unlike these "older" historicisms that rely on monolithic explanations, new historicism and cultural studies are concerned with more localized phenomena. Yet the older and newer theorists alike, rather than read a literary text, prefer to read the text of history, or what critics now call "the social text." Their work might properly be distinguished both from the literary critic and the historian.[8] Lewis's problem with historic*ism* is that the object it purports to study is absent. Instead of contenting themselves with the literary text, which comes to us in its entirety, they would read the meaning of history or a social group, which can be read only indirectly and through overwhelmingly partial evidence. We know from reading literary texts that it is impossible to make pronouncements on, say, a play that survives only in fragment form. How, then, are we to read the historical or social text? What conclusions we do derive should be held lightly and kept open to revision. We may see that we found exactly what we went looking for. As Screwtape well knows, "suspicion often creates what it suspects" (164). Because for these critics everything they study is already constructed in the conflux of social, political, and economic forces, they may discover that they end where they began: historical and political realities are the only realities, and, correspondingly, economic and social parities the highest good. Like other reductive critical approaches, the greatest problem with ideological and historicist criticisms is their narrow view of humanity, which from their own principles can never be corrected by consulting human history. *Is* all of human life confinable to the socio-economic and political realm? Can we really, in Lewis's parodic paraphrase, subscribe to the view, "Man lives by bread alone, and the ultimate source of bread is the baker's van" (*Abolition* 41n)?

Possible Worlds

As we turn our attention away from reductive interpretive strategies to consider what Lewis said about the nature of literature, we can draw at least one conclusion. Whatever else we may think about Lewis's critique of modish critical approaches in his own day, we see that today we continue to face many of the same issues. Marx, Nietzsche, and Freud are very much alive in current critical discourse, and any good accounting of them can be of value to us now.[9]

Having completed our survey of reductive reading strategies and established the ongoing relevance of Lewis's critique, it is time to come back out into the open. Here we find ourselves in much the same situation as Jill, Scrubb, and the rest of their company toward the end of *The Silver Chair*. The Queen of the Underland has seized them and begins to work her enchantments over them; not satisfied with trapping their bodies, she would also have their minds. Thrumming a mandolin-like instrument, she with enticing voice declaims, "There is no Narnia." Over and over again she utters the denial, always in the most dreamy and solemn tones, adding reason upon reason. Jill and Scrubb give way:

> "No. I suppose that other world must be all a dream."
> "Yes. It *is* all a dream," said the Witch, always thrumming.
> "Yes, all a dream," said Jill.
> "There never was such a world," said the Witch.
> "No," said Jill and Scrubb, "never was such a world."
> "There never was any world but mine," said the Witch . . . .
> "There is no Narnia, no Overworld, no sky, no sun, no Aslan. And now, to bed all. And let us begin a wiser life tomorrow. But first, to bed; . . . sleep without foolish dreams." (154, 157)

382

The company soon break out of their stupors, thanks in part to some real-world pain (which the story tells us does wonders for clearing the head), and thanks to Puddleglum's vigorous refutation of the witch's logic. The witch's charms are broken, and the company soon emerge from her prison-house free and with full faculties intact.

If Lewis likewise provides a rationale for our rejecting the suffocating confinement of modern and postmodern reductionism, then what alternative is left? Well, if a reductive treatment of literature won't do, then perhaps an *expansive* one will. I suggest that this is precisely what Lewis offers. His is a more or less informal approach I call "possible-worlds theory." Let me explain what I mean. Although Lewis the Christian holds a firm conviction about the nature of the world, he is able to appreciate differing points of view without stamping his own on them. Alternately stated, even Christian critics should not be reductive. As he remarks in *A Preface to "Paradise Lost,"* "The possible Lucretius in myself interests me more than the possible C. S. Lewis in Lucretius" (64). The important question is not whether Lucretius holds the same kind of Christian belief as I, or what he teaches me about the doctrine of depravity or atonement, or where in his work I find the hidden message of cupidity, charitas, or eucatastrophe. By the same token, the important question is not whether Lucretius really is a postmodern literary critic born out of due time—say, a very early Derridean, Lacanian, or Althusserian—a prophetic voice harbingering the high postmodern age to come. As Lewis cites Shaw in *The Pilgrim's Regress*, "The more ignorant men are, the more convinced are they that their little parish and their little chapel is an apex to which civilization and philosophy has painfully struggled up" (49). Although we would like to think so, all roads do not lead home. They lead to populous areas all over the intellectual map.

Across that map, language is a means of talking not only about the way the world is, but also about the manifold ways it might be. We encounter the great diversity of both in texts that come to us from places and times far beyond our own, and even further from the vast frontiers of the imagination. When we read these texts, unless we can (so to speak) travel outwards and sympathetically attend to what we find new and different, we will always remain trapped in a reductive understanding. We will be stuck, as it were, in our own world, confined to our own provincial outlook. Although we cannot pursue the technical aspects of the subject here, much of twentieth-century thought concedes this point from the outset, subscribing to the view that language is the inescapable medium of all thought and human interaction. In the words of the philosopher Jaakko Hintikka, this foundational issue, and whether there might be an alternative understanding of language, remains "the most important and most neglected general feature of the philosophy of language and philosophy of logic in the twentieth century" (53). Most thinkers during this period view language as the universal and unbreachable medium of human thought—that language ultimately determines both the contents and outer limits of our world. To arrive at that conclusion some thinkers replaced Kantian categories with linguistic ones, others considered language the essential mode of human being in the world, and still others saw human values constructed in socially shared and historically specific language groups. Whether we consider Anglo-American analytical philosophers like Russell and Wittgenstein, continental thinkers like Heidegger and Saussure, or critical theorists like Derrida and Foucault, we find the assumption that language is the unavoidable ether directing the language theory. Despite the variety of theoretical concerns and practical commitments these thinkers represent, they remain fundamentally committed to this view, which in its extreme form leads to a linguistic or cultural relativism where each of us is isolated in, let alone a product of, our local language community. But this view of language as inescapable medium is by no means necessary. Its best challenge has come from advances in philosophic semantics, and particularly a field that (interestingly enough) goes by the name of "possible-worlds semantics." As I say, here I can only glance in the direction of that technical material, but I think Lewis was operating upon many of its basic principles.[10]

Possible-worlds semantics argues that far from confining us within a linguistic or cultural prison-house, language operates as a calculus, that is, it can be varied like a calculus. Language, along with its logic, is freely reinterpretable so that, among other things, it can express language-world relations and otherwise talk meaningfully about itself. Most importantly, for the view of language as calculus, language can apply to any number of possible worlds, and not just to this world only. Reductive critics see themselves trapped in their one world and approach diversity as so many masks on the same old world—the Freudian, Marxist, and so on—the world from which they would have all masks removed. Lewis, on the other hand, would have us see works of literature as other worlds, with a right to be considered on their own: "Instead of stripping the knight of his armour you can try to put his armour on yourself; instead of seeing how the courtier would look without his lace, you can try to see how you would feel *with* his lace; that is, with his honour, his wit, his royalism, and his gallantries . . ." (*Preface* 64). To read about the knight, to read Lucretius, and to read any other author is to take them on their own terms. As possible-worlds theorist Umberto Eco states, "A fictional text has an ontology of its own that must be respected" ("Small" 60). In like manner, Lewis disagrees with those who cannot "really bring themselves to believe that the poet cared about the shepherds, lovers, warriors, voyages, and battles. They must be only a disguise for something more 'adult'" (*Sixteenth* 28). Before it is anything else, the literary work is about characters, places, actions, motives—in short, the work bears the logical and ontological structure of a world, albeit a possible one. If the literary work is subject to as many interpretations as the real world, that is because the two stand in a fundamentally analogous relationship. Scholars have long noticed the connection between Lewis's understanding of literature and Tolkien's notion of the literary artist as sub-creator of secondary or alternate worlds. The fundamental view also has proponents in Aristotle, Sidney, and Breitinger as well as in recent theorists Eco, Lubomír Doležel, and Marie-Laure Ryan.[11] Lewis's notion of literature is therefore far from being the quixotic flight of fancy. The disadvantage of his approach may be that it provides the more informal account where (from our perspective) we would prefer the formal one, with the fully developed language philosophy properly positioned in contemporary hermeneutic and linguistic debate. Yet, as the work of these other theorists shows, his view turns out to be a surprisingly rigorous and theoretically sustainable critical orientation, one that offers a promising pathway for understanding literary phenomena.

Once we acknowledge that a literary work displays the structure of a possible world, then we can resume our formal analyses, content-based analyses, and pragmatic-contextual analyses. But the first step the reader must take is to let the text speak for itself without confusing or otherwise conflating his or her own outlook with that of the text. All subsequent literary judgment presumes that the reader has taken this step. Arguing for a sympathetic reading of the *Arcadia*, Lewis maintains, "To judge between one *ethos* and another, it is necessary to have got inside both, and if literary history does not help us to do so it is a great waste of labour" (*Sixteenth* 331). Our experiences as readers suggest that such movement is possible, indeed desirable: "One of the things we feel after reading a great work is 'I have got out'. Or from another point of view, 'I have got in' ..." (*Experiment* 138). We even feel like we have been there: "We visualise Lear in the storm, we share his rage, we regard his whole story with pity and terror" (136). Among the pleasures and benefits of reading, Lewis explains, is that the move outwards can "lift the student out of his [or her] provincialism" to consider something new (*Concerns* 29). To the extent that students can make that move, they will have minimized the limitations of their own perspectives.

For Lewis, reading ultimately can be carried out in one of two ways, which he illustrates in terms of two kinds of travelling:

> There are two ways of enjoying the past, as there are two ways of enjoying a foreign country. One man carries his Englishry abroad with him and brings it home unchanged. . . .
>
> But there is another sort of travelling and another sort of reading. You can eat the local food and drink the local wines, you can share the foreign life, you can begin to see the foreign country as it looks, not to the tourist, but to its inhabitants. You can come home modified, thinking and feeling as you did not think and feel before. So with the old literature. ("*Audiendis*" 2–3)

As Lewis often explains, books, like foreign countries, should be *received* and not simply *used*, which leads us to our final point.

385

Reading and Love

In discussing the nature of the critical enterprise, Lewis often compares the act of reading to the act of love. This is both a surprising and happy statement. Love is not what first comes to mind when one thinks about those who profess literature in today's English departments. Tendentious and self-promoting scholarship, theoretical factionalism, and political infighting seem to be the rule. Because the situation is so bad in some places, departments have actually gone into receivership.[12] The outrageous ethics of some of the highest profile theorists and teachers is enough to cause concern to the most jaded: Derrida's prosecuting others in court for violating his authorial rights, he the champion of deconstructing authorial ownership; Foucault's "inventing new pleasures beyond sex," which, at the end of his life, included knowingly spreading and receiving AIDS with his sexual contacts; Heidegger's and de Man's active membership in the Nazi party, including de Man's writing for the Nazi propaganda machine; Althusser's strangling his wife; and other outrageous acts we could name.[13] When Nietzsche contends that all philosophers have hidden motives driving their philosophies, he is, of course, drawing a double-edged sword. It certainly can be used against those critics who are always "seeing through" to the motives of others. But long before Nietzsche's time, Pascal told us that the heart has its reasons. Instead of playing that motive game *ad nauseam*, however, Lewis would have us analyze the issues that set the game in motion in the first place. (The *why* never cancels the *what*: pursuing motives for Lewis is a matter more suitable to narrative and hortatory treatments, not the theoretical and philosophical.) Besides his famous words about hidden motives, Pascal also said, "We not only look at things from different points of view, but with different eyes; we do not care to find them alike" (672). That hunger for something outside the self, for listening and learning from people of other times and places, is what Lewis thinks modern readers especially lack. The entire thrust of *Experiment* is directed toward reinstating this ideal. But to look out and see with the eyes of others, Lewis reminds us, will require an act of love.

With Pascal, Lewis would also have us see from as many viewpoints as we can, and so somehow escape our narrow and selfish interests: "Broaden your mind, Malcolm, broaden your mind! It takes all sorts to make a world. . . . If grace perfects nature it must expand all our natures into the full richness of the diversity which God intended when He made them, and Heaven will display far more variety than Hell" (*Malcolm* 10). To broaden one's understanding is to resist the impulse to reductionism, which in its worst form is ultimately a reduction to the self. Lewis would have us, as far as possible, move out of the confines of the self (the very condition of damnation in *The Great Divorce*), "to see with other eyes, to imagine with other imaginations, to feel with other hearts, as well as with our own" (*Experiment* 137). It turns out that the best kind of reading has something in common with the best kind of listening. And, equally, loving listening depends upon the imagination as much as imaginative reading depends upon love.

Despite our best evasions and theoretical protestations to the contrary, reading does bear this moral dimension. We have a responsibility to complete "a careful reading of what [we] criticiz[e]" ("On Criticism" 46). (If nothing else, we expect those who criticize *us* to read or listen carefully.) For that reason, I would argue that Barthes's call for "the death of the author"—which he assures us will usher in the great age of the reader—is, in fact, a call for the death of reading. In the place of reading, Barthes would establish a new kind of authorship, the authorship of the self-asserting ego: this reader cum author cheerfully fills the empty ciphers of texts with his or her own meanings. Reading, by Barthes's lights, is thus the ultimate authorial act. But if *this* author is authorized to go on living, then why not also the author who wrote the literary text? Lewis observes, we can be "so busy doing things with the work that we give it too little chance to work on us. Thus increasingly we meet only ourselves" (*Experiment* 85). If we can slow down our activities of doing things with texts, if in the midst of our own clamoring thoughts we can listen to what these texts are trying to say to us, then perhaps we might learn something—about others and even ourselves in the process. Moreover, we need not worry that a listening attitude will open us to being hoodwinked by what we read. Lewis would have us read widely not because we are more likely to repeat the errors of the past but because we will be less likely.[14]

No, we need not become Barthes's homicidal reader, nor Derrida's deconstructive reader, nor Blake's and Bloom's devouring cherub to avoid being mastered by a text. We need not take a kill-or-be-killed approach to reading. Lewis explains, "In the moral sphere, every act of justice or charity involves putting ourselves in the other person's place and thus transcending our own competitive particularity. In coming to understand anything we are rejecting the facts as they are for us . . . . The primary impulse of each is to maintain and aggrandise himself" (*Experiment* 138). Lewis's cure for self-protecting and self-preoccupied reading is love. "In love," he affirms, "we escape from our self into one other" (138). It is the basic movement in all our acts of justice and charity. It also attends our knowledge-gathering activities: "In love, in virtue, in the pursuit of knowledge, and in the reception of the arts, we are doing this [act of self-denial]. Obviously this process can be described either as an enlargement or as a temporary annihilation of the self. But that is an old paradox; 'he that loseth his life shall save it' " (138). The reference to Christ is a fitting one: for of all the criticisms of Lewis's distinction between use and reception[15] (and no matter how technical on that issue one wants to get), I cannot see how to dispose of it and at the same time retain the New Testament's distinction between listening and speaking. There we are enjoined to be slow to speak and quick to listen. This advice alone would go a long way in curing not only the cynicism of our profession, but our talk-show obsessed and conspiracy-theory haunted society. A loving and listening approach to

387

others opens our eyes to all sorts of qualities we might miss otherwise. As Lewis states, "You cannot be armed to the teeth and surrendered at the same moment" (128). So when one approaches literary texts, "one may say . . . not only (as Wordsworth says of the poet) that 'you must love it ere to you it will seem worthy of your love', but that you must at least have loved it once if you are even to warn others against it" ("Science Fiction" 60). Lewis explains, "we need not believe or approve the Logos" of the work in question, but if we want to read it, we must listen to what it says (*Experiment* 136). While "using" a text of literature may constitute an act of egoism, "reading" requires an act of love, of self-denial, and of identification with someone or something outside ourselves.

We see that reading with C. S. Lewis leads us far beyond C. S. Lewis, as we try to model his attentiveness as a reader. We see, too, that those who take up books truly stand in a "wood between the worlds": they can remain content where they are, residing among old certitudes and reassuring themselves that the small spot they inhabit is all they really need be concerned with; or they can boldly and expectantly explore new regions of experience, coming to terms with radically new ideas and different sensibilities, becoming more even as they move away from their familiar selves. Lewis's own attitude is that "[t]he man who is contented to be only himself, and therefore less of a self, is in prison. My own eyes are not enough for me, I will see through those of others" (*Experiment* 140). One sure way to open the prison doors and readmit the light of understanding is to bestow a loving hearing on what we read. In the future, when we readers and teachers of literature are tempted to start up our critical grist mills—or sidle up to our lamp-posts—we would do much for our ourselves and our profession if we recall Lewis's reminder of "a more excellent way."

Notes

1. See Eagleton, Barthes, Foucault 386, and Rorty, respectively.

2. Jameson declares that "pleasing, exciting and 'beautiful stories'" are really the means for "promoting acquiescence to, and even identification with, the relations of domination and subordination peculiar to the late-capitalist social order. . . . Nothing can be more satisfying for a Marxist teacher than to 'break' this fascination for students . . ." (qtd. in Sykes and Miner 246).

3. Anyone who doubts this appraisal after reading the present essay should consult Lewis's "The Empty Universe," originally written as the preface to D. E. Harding's *The Hierarchy of Heaven and Earth*. There one will find a lucid, if short, account of how the linguistic turn in twentieth-century philosophy leads to an anti-foundational and anti-essentialist outlook, where, in today's parlance, "there's nothing outside the text." Looking back on Lewis's piece several decades later, we see that he gives the very outline of the rise of postmodernism.

4. For a good introduction to this material see Leitch 24–59, and his bibliography. On the question of Lewis and New Criticism, see Edwards 60–78. On Lewis and the ideational value of literature, one

might also see Daigle-Williamson, who argues that Lewis subscribes to the traditional view that literature's function is to instruct and delight.

5. Of course, this is true not only of the audience, but of the artist as well: "Every poet and musician and artist, but for Grace, is drawn away from the love of the thing he tells, to the love of the telling. . . . For it doesn't stop at being interested in paint, you know. They sink lower—become interested in their own personalities and then in nothing but their own reputations" (*Divorce* 81). For a journalist's look at how literary theorists have turned from studying literature to writing their own biographies, see Begley.

6. ". . . le but dernier des sciences humaines n'est pas de constituer l'homme, mais de le dissoudre" (326).

7. A point made in passing in my article "On the Margin of God."

8. For elaboration of this thesis, see Lewis's essay, "Historicism."

9. For a different view of Lewis's ongoing relevance, see Jacobs.

10. We see, for example, a view of language as calculus at work in the following passage: "A theorist about language may approach his native tongue, as it were from outside, regarding its genius as a thing that has no claim on him and advocating wholesale alterations of its idiom and spelling in the interests of commercial convenience or scientific accuracy. A great poet . . . may also make alterations in it, but his changes of the language are made in the spirit of the language itself: he works from within" (*Abolition* 57).

11. The precise nature of these imagined worlds—and whether they are Platonic ideas, intentional objects, linguistic constructions, or something else—is beyond the scope of this chapter. One question would be what Lewis thought about the issue; the other, of course, would be the question at large. I examine the latter in my book manuscript "Poiesis and Possible Worlds," which I am working to bring to print in the near future.

For the major works of the authors mentioned, see Aristotle's *Poetics* bk. 9; Sidney's *Defence of Poesie*; for Breitinger see Doležel, *Occidental Poetics* 33–52. See also Eco's "Small Worlds" and *The Role of the Reader*, Doležel's *Heterocosmica*, Ryan's *Possible Worlds*, and also Pavel's *Fictional Worlds*.

12. See Allen.

13. On Derrida and Althusser, see Dasenbrock; on Foucault, see Herman 356–57 and his sources; on Heidegger, see Ott and Safranski; on de Man, see Brooks, Felman, and Miller, and Hamacher, Hertz, and Keenan.

14. Recall the words from his introduction to Athanasius's *The Incarnation of the Word of God*: "Every age . . . is specially good at seeing certain truths and specially liable to make certain mistakes. We all, therefore, need the books that will correct the characteristic mistakes of our own period. . . . [Old books] will not flatter us in the errors we are already committing; and their own errors, being now open and palpable, will not endanger us" ("Old Books" 202).

15. See Walhout and Lundin (216–24), who object on the basis of Gadamer's hermeneutics. For a critique of Gadamer from the perspective of language as calculus—as well as an overview of how the issue of language as universal medium develops in and through continental philosophy—see Kusch.

Works Cited

Allen, Charlotte. "As Bad as It Gets." *Lingua Franca* 8.2 (1998): 52–57.

Barthes, Roland. "The Death of the Author." *Image, Music, Text*. Trans. Stephen Heath. New York: Hill and Wang, 1977.

Begley, Adam. "The I's Have It: Duke's 'Moi' Critics Expose Themselves." *Lingua Franca* 4.3 (1994): 54–59.

Bloomfield, Leonard. *Language.* New York: Holt, 1933.

Brooks, Peter, Shoshana Felman, and J. Hillis Miller, eds. *The Lessons of Paul de Man.* New Haven: Yale UP, 1985.

Daigle-Williamson, Marsha. "Tradition and Lewis's Individual Talent." *Christian Scholars Review* 27 (1998): 490–505.

Dasenbrock, Reed Way. "Taking it Personally: Reading Derrida's Responses." *College English* 56 (1994): 261–79.

Doležel, Lubomír. *Heterocosmica: Fiction and Possible Worlds.* Baltimore: Johns Hopkins UP, 1998.

———. *Occidental Poetics: Tradition and Progress.* Lincoln: U of Nebraska P, 1990.

Eagleton, Terry. *The Ideology of the Aesthetic.* Oxford: Blackwell, 1990.

Eco, Umberto. *The Role of the Reader: Explorations in the Semiotics of Texts.* Bloomington: Indiana UP, 1979.

———. "Small Worlds." *Versus: Quaderni di Studi Semiotici* 52–53 (1989): 53–90.

Edwards, Bruce, Jr. *A Rhetoric of Reading: C. S. Lewis's Defense of Western Literacy.* Values in Literature Monographs. Number 2. Provo, UT: Center for the Study of Christian Values in Literature. 1986.

Foucault, Michel. *The Order of Things: An Archaeology of the Human Sciences.* New York: Random House, 1973.

Freud, Sigmund. *Introductory Lectures on Psychoanalysis.* Trans. and ed. James Strachey. New York: Norton, 1966.

Hamacher, Werner, Neil Hertz, and Thomas Keenan, eds. *Responses: On Paul de Man's Wartime Journalism.* Lincoln: U of Nebraska P, 1989.

Herman, Arthur. *The Idea of Decline in Western History.* New York: Free Press, 1997.

Hintikka, Jaakko. "Exploring Possible Worlds." *Possible Worlds in Humanities, Arts and Sciences: Proceedings of Nobel Symposium 65.* Ed. Sture Allén. Research in Text Theory 14. Berlin: de Gruyter, 1989. 52–73.

Holland, Norman. "The 'Unconscious' of Literature." *Contemporary Criticism.* Ed. Malcolm Bradbury and David Palmer. Stratford-Upon-Avon-Studies 12. New York: St. Martin's, 1970. 131–53.

Jacobs, Alan. "The Second Coming of C. S. Lewis." *First Things* 47 (1994): 27–30.

Jones, Ernest. *Hamlet and Oedipus.* Garden City, NY: Doubleday, 1949.

Kaplan, Morton, and Robert Kloss. *The Unspoken Motive: A Guide to Psychoanalytic Criticism.* New York: Free Press, 1973.

Kerrigan, William. *The Sacred Complex: On the Psychogenesis of Paradise Lost.* Cambridge, MA: Harvard UP, 1983.

Kusch, Martin. *Language as Calculus vs. Language as Universal Medium: A Study in Husserl, Heidegger, and Gadamer.* Dordrecht, Netherlands: Kluwer, 1989.

Leitch, Vincent B. *American Literary Criticism from the Thirties to the Eighties.* New York: Columbia UP, 1989.

Lévi-Strauss, Claude. *La Pensee Sauvage.* Paris: Plon, 1962.

Lewis, C. S. *The Abolition of Man.* New York: Macmillan, 1947.

———. "Bulverism." *Dock* 271–77.

———. "*De Audiendis Poetis.*" *Medieval* 1–17.

———. *English Literature in the Sixteenth Century Excluding Drama.* Oxford: Oxford UP, 1954.

———. *An Experiment in Criticism.* Cambridge: Cambridge UP, 1961.

———. "First and Second Things." *Dock* 278–81.

———. *God in the Dock: Essays on Theology and Ethics.* Ed. Walter Hooper. Grand Rapids: Eerdmans, 1970.

———. *The Great Divorce.* New York: Macmillan, 1946.

———. "Historicism." *Christian Reflections.* Ed. Walter Hooper. Grand Rapids: Eerdmans, 1967. 100–13.

———. *Letters to Malcolm: Chiefly on Prayer.* New York: Harvest, 1963.

———. "Lilies that Fester." *The World's Last Night and Other Essays.* New York: Harcourt, 1952. 31–50.

———. "Neoplatonism in the Poetry of Spenser." *Medieval* 149–63.

———. *Of Other Worlds: Essays and Stories.* Ed. Walter Hooper. New York: Harcourt, 1966.

———. "On Criticism." *Of Other Worlds* 43–58.

———. "On Juvenile Tastes." *Of Other Worlds* 39–41.

———. "On Science Fiction." *Of Other Worlds* 59–73.

———. *"On Stories" and Other Essays on Literature.* Ed. Walter Hooper. New York: Harcourt Brace Jovanovich, 1982.

———. "On the Reading of Old Books." *Dock* 200–07.

———. *The Pilgrim's Regress: An Allegorical Apology for Christianity, Reason and Romanticism.* Grand Rapids: Eerdmans, 1933.

———. *A Preface to "Paradise Lost."* London: Oxford UP, 1942.

———. *Present Concerns.* Ed. Walter Hooper. San Diego: Harvest, 1982.

———. "Psycho-Analysis and Literary Criticism." *Literary* 286–300.

———. "A Reply to Professor Haldane." *Stories* 69–79.

———. *The Screwtape Letters.* 1942. New York: Macmillan, 1962.

———. *Selected Literary Essays.* Ed. Walter Hooper. Cambridge: Cambridge UP, 1969.

———. *The Silver Chair.* New York: Collier, 1953.

———. "Sir Walter Scott." *Literary* 209–18.

———. *Studies in Medieval and Renaissance Literature.* Cambridge: Cambridge UP, 1966.

———. *Surprised by Joy: The Shape of My Early Life.* New York: Harcourt, 1955.

———. "Undergraduate Criticism." Cambridge University Broadsheet 8.17 (9 March 1960).

———. "Unreal Estates." *Of Other Worlds* 86–96.

Lundin, Roger. *Culture of Interpretation: Christian Faith and the Postmodern World.* Grand Rapids: Eerdmans, 1993.

Martin, Thomas L. "On the Margin of God: Deconstruction and the Language of Satan in *Paradise Lost*." *Milton Quarterly* 29 (1995): 41–47.

Ott, Hugo. *Martin Heidegger: A Political Life.* Trans. Allan Blunden. New York: Basic, 1993.

Pascal, Blaise. *Pensées.* Trans. A. J. Krailsheimer. London: Penguin, 1966.

Pavel, Thomas G. *Fictional Worlds.* Cambridge, MA: Harvard UP, 1986.

Rorty, Richard. *Philosophy and the Mirror of Nature.* Princeton: Princeton UP, 1979.

Ryan, Marie-Laure. *Possible Worlds, Artificial Intelligence, and Narrative Theory.* Bloomington: Indiana UP, 1991.

Safranski, Rüdiger. *Martin Heidegger: Between Good and Evil.* Trans. Ewald Osers. Cambridge, MA: Harvard UP, 1998.

Saussure, Ferdinand de. *A Course in General Linguistics*. Ed. Charles Bally and Albert Sechehaye. Trans. Wade Baskin. New York: McGraw, 1966.

Schoenfeldt, Michael C. "'That Ancient Heat': Sexuality and Spirituality in *The Temple*." *Soliciting Interpretation: Literary Theory and Seventeenth-Century English Poetry*. Ed. Elizabeth D. Harvey and Katherine Eisaman Maus. Chicago: U of Chicago P, 1990. 273–306.

Sykes, Charles J., and Brad Miner. *The National Review College Guide: America's Top Liberal Arts Schools*. New York: Fireside, 1991.

Walhout, Clarence. "The Problem of Moral Criticism in Christian Literary Theory." *Christian Scholar's Review* 24.1 (1994): 26–44.

List of Lewis's Major Critical Works

1936. *The Allegory of Love: A Study in Medieval Tradition.* Oxford: Oxford UP.

1939. *Rehabilitations and Other Essays.* London: Oxford UP.

1939. *The Personal Heresy: A Controversy* (with E. M. W. Tillyard). London: Oxford UP.

1942. *A Preface to "Paradise Lost."* London: Oxford UP.

1943. *The Abolition of Man: Reflections on Education with Special Reference to the Teaching of English in the Upper Forms of School.* London: Oxford UP.

1949. *Transposition and Other Addresses.* London: Geoffrey Bles.

1954. *English Literature in the Sixteenth Century Excluding Drama.* Oxford: Oxford UP.

1955. *Surprised by Joy: The Shape of My Early Life.* London: Geoffrey Bles.

1960. *Studies in Words.* Cambridge: Cambridge UP.

1961. *An Experiment in Criticism.* Cambridge: Cambridge UP.

1962. *They Asked for a Paper: Papers and Addresses.* London: Geoffrey Bles.

1964. *The Discarded Image: An Introduction to Medieval and Renaissance Literature.* Cambridge: Cambridge UP.

1966. *Studies in Medieval and Renaissance Literature.* Ed. Walter Hooper. Cambridge: Cambridge UP.

1966. *Letters of C. S. Lewis.* Ed. W. H. Lewis. London: Geoffrey Bles.

1966. *Of Other Worlds: Essays and Stories.* Ed. Walter Hooper. London: Geoffrey Bles.

1967. *Spenser's Images of Life.* Ed. Alastair Fowler. Cambridge: Cambridge UP.

1969. *Selected Literary Essays.* Ed. Walter Hooper. Cambridge: Cambridge UP.

1979. *They Stand Together: The Letters of C. S. Lewis to Arthur Greeves (1914–1963).* Ed. Walter Hooper. London: Collins.

These critical (and closely related) works are presented here as a quick resource, providing a chronological list of Lewis's major critical works at a glance—without the more familiar fictional and apologetic works, as important as they are. Certainly, any such list has its limitations. Lewis himself reminds readers not to assume that an author's books "were written in the same order in which they were published and all shortly before publication" ("On Criticism").

For a full bibliography of Lewis's works, see Joe Christopher and Joan Ostling's *C. S. Lewis: An Annotated Checklist* (Kent, OH: Kent State UP, 1973) or Walter Hooper's *C. S. Lewis: A Companion and Guide* (San Francisco: HarperSanFrancisco, 1996).

Index

395

405